Handbook Organisation and Management

Dedicated to: Anjette, Jasper, Hugo and Yannick

HANDBOOK ORGANISATION AND MANAGEMENT

A PRACTICAL APPROACH

Jos Marcus
Nick van Dam

Fourth Edition 2019

Noordhoff Uitgevers Groningen / Utrecht

Cover design: 212 Fahrenheit, Groningen
Cover illustration: Getty Images, Londen

Any comments concerning this or other publications should be addressed to Noordhoff Uitgevers bv, Afdeling Voortgezet onderwijs, Antwoordnummer 13, 9700 VB Groningen or via the contact form at www.mijnnoordhoff.nl.

The information contained in this publication is for general information purposes only. No rights or liability of the author(s), editor or publisher can be derived from this information.

0 / 19

ISBN: 978-0-367-81876-0 (hbk)
ISBN: 978-90-01-89564-8 (pbk)
ISBN: 978-1-003-02243-5 (ebk)
NUR 802

Acknowledgements

This book offers a comprehensive introduction to the field of Organisation and Management, making it a suitable choice for many higher educational studies at both the Bachelor and Master levels. Furthermore, it is a useful handbook for professionals already working in organisations.

In addition to the topics traditionally associated with Organisation and Management, the current developments and international context of the discipline feature prominently. The discussion of these topics is not restricted to the realm of theory either; instead, it is illustrated through many practical examples, thus offering the reader an insight into the application of theory to practice and practice to theory.

What is new in this fully revised edition?

In recent years, there have been substantial developments in the field of Organisation and Management – developments in terms of technology, politics, and society – that have also had an effect on the approach towards, and the development of, organisations.

Among the strengths of this book have always been its relevance, practical orientation, and innovative character. It is with these strengths in mind that there have been many adjustments and modernisations to this new edition.

The structure of the book has remained the same. New added chapters feature in all three parts of the book, expanding and deepening its theoretical framework. There have also been adjustments to the existing chapters, aimed at expanding and deepening the theoretical basis. Considering these substantial adjustments to the theoretical basis, we felt compelled to change the book's title, as well. This Handbook of Organisation and Management now offers a truly practical approach, having naturally been supplemented with many practical examples.

In addition to the modernisation of the theory, numerous practice-oriented texts and examples have been updated, thereby maintaining and safeguarding the book's high degree of relevance and practical orientation. All practice-oriented texts and examples in this edition have been rebranded 'O&M IN PRACTICE'. Chapters open with the familiar 'Start-up' texts: practical examples of young and innovative Dutch and international organisations.

The interviews at the beginning of each part of the book have also been replaced with new ones, and now feature the following managers of three well-known international enterprises:

Part A: Raymond Cloosterman, founder of Rituals;
Part B: Peter Wennink, CEO for ASML and Harry de Vos, CHRO for ASML;
Part C: Henk Jan Beltman, Chief Chocolate Officer for Tony's Chocolonely.

The following is a list of the chapters that are new to the book's component parts:

Part A: Environments and Organisations
Chapter 3: Digital Transformation
Chapter 4: Internationalisation
Chapter 5: Corporate Social Responsibility, Corporate Governance, and Ethics

Part B: People and Organisations
Chapter 6: The Future of Work
Chapter 7: Human Resource Management

Part C: Structure and Organisations
Chapter 12: Culture

Additionally, some chapters from the previous edition have been merged and/or strongly revised in terms of their contents:
- Former Chapters 2 'Strategic Management' and 3 'Collaboration' have been merged into a new Chapter 2, entitled 'Strategic Management'.
- Former Chapters 6 'Management' and 7 'Decision-making' have been merged into a new Chapter 9, entitled 'Leadership and Management'
- Former Chapter 10 has been updated and substantially expanded, and has become Chapter 13, 'Organisational Change and Development'.

A final note is that the book's interior has been significantly renewed, thus reinforcing and updating its contemporary nature, and making it an eminently useful and challenging handbook.

Website
In recent years, there has been a noticeably declining trend with respect to the use of the workbook by students. We have therefore decided to discontinue the workbook. In addition to the aforementioned trend, we are seeing students making increasing use of the website companion to the book. We have therefore decided to integrate the workbook with the existing website. For example, the website now offers up-to-date cases for each chapter of the book. Integrating these cases with the website offers the advantage of enabling us to continue to update and supplement these cases over the course of this new edition.

 Also, the QR-codes are no longer documented in this book, but on the website. The website-icon in the margins refers to these QR-codes.

With regards to the website, the exam database of test questions for students has been aligned with the expansion of the theoretical framework and the new chapter layout. In addition to the exam database, the concept trainer and PowerPoint presentations have also been updated.

Teachers can use 'Toets-op-maat' to easily create their own exams, supplemented with their own questions. These exams can be compiled using test questions unavailable to students.

Acknowledgements

For this new edition, we resumed the distribution of questionnaires among our users (teachers). We want to thank all participants, and want to assure them that the information thus obtained was naturally put to good use in developing this revised edition. Our special thanks to the following people: Judith Grimbergen for processing the many practical example text and contributing to the theoretical topics; Narda Vermeulen for writing the texts on agile and horizontal organisation; Jacqueline Brassey for contributing to Chapter 13; Edwin Huijsman, Annelie Uittenbogaard and Martin van der Sluis for their dedication to developing website materials. From publishing company Noordhoff, we want to thank our publisher Petra Prescher for her continued contributions, and to Ada Bolhuis for editing this fine handbook.

Jos Marcus, Wormer
Nick van Dam, Hilversum and Madrid

About the authors

Jos Marcus

Jos Marcus studied Economic Sciences at the Vrije Leergangen Vrije Universiteit (Bachelor's) and Business Administration at the Vrije Universiteit (Master's). He currently works at the Inholland University of Applied Sciences, Diemen / Amsterdam. Part of his work over the past years has been to establish and develop a new fulltime study programme entitled 'Business Studies'. This new programme, which became available in September of 2014, can be studied at five of Inholland's branches. Business Studies is a four-year programme whose first two years comprise a common generalist basis, in which all entrepreneurial ownership positions are addressed. Then, over the last two years, students work towards a specialisation in either Marketing, Enterprising, Policy and Management, Human Resource Management, Banking & Insurance, and Logistics. The programme was developed from the professional field's demand for a future workforce with a broad basic education as well as certain specialist knowledge.

Nick van Dam

Nick van Dam is driven by a singular passion for human development. He is a consultant, author, speaker, teacher, and researcher in the field of (corporate) learning & development, sustainable organisation, and leadership development. He is a professor at the Nyenrode Business Universiteit and the University of Pennsylvania, Philadelphia. In addition, he is a member of the Executive Board of and the Chief Learning Officer for IE University, Madrid. He is a former partner, Global Chief Learning Officer and Senior Advisor for McKinsey & Company and was a partner, advisor and Global Chief Learning Officer for Deloitte.

He has written articles and has been cited by publications including *The Financial Times*, *The Wall Street Journal*, *Harvard Business Review*, *Forbes Fortune*, *Business Week*, *Information Week*, *Indian Times*, *TD Magazine* and *CLO Magazine*. He is also the author and co-author of over 25 books and numerous articles.

In addition to his tasks with regard to development, he teaches in the disciplines of Management & Organisation, Marketing, and Business Administration. He also supervises graduation assignments and internships. He has held the chair of the central curriculum committee of the Inholland Finance study programmes since academic year 2017/2018. In addition, he is a partner in 'Accompany, Innovative Learning Solutions': an enterprise specialising in the development of educational resources.

He has been the financial director of the 'Elearning for Kids' foundation since 1 February 2014.

In 2017, he published *Ga doen wat je écht belangrijk vindt! Positieve psychologie in de Praktijk*; in 2018, *Handboek Leren & Ontwikkelen in Organisaties*. In 2012, he received the 'Lifetime Learning Leadership Award' from the MASIE Center, a thinktank focussing on corporate learning, and in 2013 the 'European Leonardo Corporate Learning Award' for his efforts in the fields of corporate learning and leadership development. He is the founder and chief executive officer for the 'e-learning for kids' foundation (www.e-learningforkids.org), which has helped over 25 million children obtain free digital education.

Nick studied Economic Sciences at the Vrije Universiteit, Organisational Sociology at the University of Amsterdam, and obtained his doctorate for his thesis on Human Capital Development at Nyenrode Business Universiteit. In addition, he took part in various executive development programmes at institutions like Harvard Business School, Wharton, and IMD. Nick lived, worked, and studied in the United States from 1995 until the end of 2006, and currently lives in Madrid.

Together with Jacqueline Brassey, he has developed assessments which can help people become the best possible version of themselves: www.reachingyourpotential.org.

Concise table of contents

Table of contents

THE EVOLUTION OF ORGANISATION AND MANAGEMENT   23

PART A   ORGANISATIONS AND THEIR ENVIRONMENT   59

1   ENVIRONMENTAL INFLUENCES   65

PART C   STRUCTURE AND ORGANISATION   459

Interview with Chief Chocolate Officer Henk Jan Beltman for
Tony's Chocolonely   460

10   PROCES AND CONTROL   465

13   ORGANISATIONAL CHANGE AND DEVELOPMENT   627

Introduction

Part of everyday life

Throughout their lives, everyone comes into contact with organisations and organising.

In the home, family life contains many instances where tasks need to be organised – whether it be parents arranging activities for their children, or simply planning the shopping for the week ahead. Although running a home and a formal organisation are not the same, the two have much in common.

Children often come into contact with organisations outside the home. From quite a young age, they may join a swimming club, go to a music school to learn piano, learn to dance at a ballet school, or join the local scout group. These are all organisations. Formally speaking, an organisation exists when two or more people choose to work together to achieve a certain goal or goals. In fact, being part of an organisation is a theme that is recurrent throughout one's entire life. Put another way, organisations are such a normal part of daily life, people hardly notice that they are so ubiquitous. Everyone interacts with, talks about, and experiences both their positive and negative aspects daily.

Organisations, companies and enterprises

Organisation

A recurrent theme in this book is the functioning of organisations – but what exactly is an organisation?

An organisation can be seen as:

Any group of people cooperating to achieve a common purpose.

Following this definition, the three elements of an organisation can be seen as:
1 people;
2 cooperation;
3 common purpose.

Society
Environment

The reason why people work together in an organisation is that some tasks cannot be completed by just one person. Organisations exist because society has a demand for the products or services they provide. An organisation, therefore, is part of human society and environment.

Within this book, the word 'organisation' is sometimes used to refer to a company or an enterprise. In this context, a company is often an organisation that produces goods or services, and an enterprise is a company that aims to make a profit. From these descriptions, it is evident that enterprises are a category of company, which in turn is a category of organisation. Figure 1 illustrates these categorisations.

FIGURE **THE RELATION BETWEEN ORGANISATIONS, COMPANIES AND ENTERPRISES**

Management

Organising involves combining and structuring tasks, people, and resources in such a way that the goals of an organisation are reached.

This is often an activity allocated to several people within an organisation, and it is common for the task of organising to be a part of management's job. With this in mind, the second term used in the title of this book takes the stage: management. Management means:

Management

The leading and steering of an organisation

Managerial responsibility is given to key people, normally being the owner(s) or most senior person(s) in an organisation, plus anyone else delegated to take the role.

Their main task is to direct the entire company. Combining the principles of 'organisation' and 'management' leads to the title of this book.

A Handbook of Organisation and Management, a practical approach, explores the leading and steering of various kinds of human cooperation towards a common purpose.

THE EVOLUTION OF ORGANISATION AND MANAGEMENT

Contents

After studying this chapter:

- you will have become familiar with several important schools of thought and personalities from the history of organisational behaviour;
- you will have gained an insight into contemporary developments in the field of organisation behaviour;
- you will be able to relate schools of thought to personalities and understand the significance of these relationships for the structuring of contemporary organisations;
- you will be able to better place subjects discussed in later chapters of the book in their proper context.

Polette aiming to be low-budget powerhouse on market for reading glasses

French entrepreneurs Pauline Cousseau and Pierre Wizman met in China, where they learned to make glasses. This was followed by the launch of their company 'Polette'. Since then, they have built up an organisation with a turnover in the tens of millions, a growing number of stores, and over 60 employees.

The founders taught themselves how to design glasses, establish a webstore, and deal with local manufacturers. Frames for glasses go for 3 to 5 Euros in China; lenses are between 3 and 20 Euros. Polette cut out the distributors and stores, and ignored the concept of licensing – which had previously been the standard in the world of spectacles. Polette is, in principle, fully in charge of their prices. Their glasses, officially available from 15 Euros but generally retailing for a couple of tenners each, are supplied without an intermediary, straight from a factory in China. The duo has since become the owners of a lens factory. Their philosophy is that lower prices mean people can afford more glasses; Polette is looking to become a 'Zara' for glasses.

Cousseau and Wizman: 'The challenges mainly take the form of cultural differences; many Chinese people will say yes to anything. But products are often different from what was expected in terms of colour or shape. In these cases, clarity is important, as is collaborating with reliable people. In 2011, when the company was founded, Polette was the first online shop for glasses in Europe. Investors are currently not yet welcomed; the company strongly emphasises its own values. Employees feel as though they are part of a larger family, with everybody given room to be an entrepreneur.' In the Netherlands, Ace & Tate is a major competitor: 'Ace & Tate's network is large, and their communication is well in order. They are a bit more expensive, more high-end. We cater to all clients, the elderly as well. Our stores are intended to function purely as showrooms for trying on and fitting glasses, and we do not keep an active inventory. Ace & Tate do, thus increasing their investment costs.'

Source: www.sprout.nl, 15-10-2018

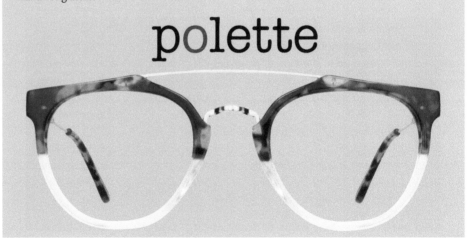

1   INTRODUCTION

The introduction to this book states that its topic is organisation and management. However, the original and more widely used name for this field is that of organisational behaviour!

Organisational behaviour
Organisational behaviour can be defined as 'an interdisciplinary science concerned with the study of the behaviour of organisations, as well as with the factors that

determine this behaviour, and the manner in which organisations can be directed with maximum effectiveness'. In this context, the concept of behaviour is given to include actions and reactions within organisations.

This definition of organisational behaviour encompasses two aspects of the subject, namely:

1 **a descriptive aspect.** This is a description of the behaviour of organisations, including motives and consequences; Descriptive aspect
2 **a prescriptive aspect.** This is advice about recommended organisational design and course of action. Prescriptive aspect

This double-sided nature can also be seen in other practical sciences, including medicine, psychology and pedagogy. Even more so than these other fields, however, organisational behaviour is oriented towards practical application and pragmatism. This means that the importance of a methodologically sound line of reasoning and sound evidence are considered to be less important than the identification of practical ramifications.

The term interdisciplinary is sometimes linked with organisational behaviour, although the term is often misused. To clarify: organisational behaviour contains many elements that have originated with other sciences. The study of organisations involves many disciplines from various scientific fields. Examples of such fields are business studies, which comprises topics likes financing, accounting and bookkeeping, marketing, technical sciences, information technology; behavioural sciences, like organisational psychology or sociology; and law. Interdisciplinary

Combining all of the contributions from these fields in order to undertake and complete a study or project does not make for an interdisciplinary approach, but for a so-called multidisciplinary approach. An interdisciplinary approach takes matters one step further. That is to say: the various contributions from the other subject areas are individually evaluated and then used to develop a new insight, one that reviews the subject in its entirety. Here, the existing disciplines cease to be recognisable in their original forms (contrastingly, this situation does not apply to a multidisciplinary approach). The interdisciplinary approach, therefore, is an ambitious one. It is an often pursued ideal, which tends to be unattainable. Often, it is impossible to move past the multidisciplinary approach, even in organisational behavioural research. Multidisciplinary

Two other aspects of the definition of organisational behaviour are direction and effectiveness. The first of these can be described as 'attempted targeted persuasion'. In a more specific organisational sense, it may be described as giving direction to the processes occurring within an organisation. This direction refers to a goal which should be determined in advance. Processes take place within the framework of a structure. Development and adjustment of this structure is an important directional aspect. Direction

The extent to which direction is successful is defined using the concept of effectiveness. The matter of who should carry out which tasks is expressly disregarded, whether they be formal organisational management, a consultant, a member of the board of consultants, or an employee who comes up with a suggestion during a staff meeting. Effectiveness

The fact that organisational behaviour is concerned with obtaining an overall picture of an organisation, an organisational problem, or a project, means that abstraction is often required, and that details are of secondary importance – otherwise, one would lose sight of the wood for the trees. This means that an organisational expert may often feel less at home in certain organisational fields than a specialist might. The organisational expert could be described as a generalist instead of a specialist. An alternative qualification could be 'a specialist of general matters'.

As a result, organisational theory is often criticised for being a fragmented whole; a little of this, and a little of that.

Additionally, organisational behaviour is a science that is still in its infancy, and undergoing full development. This is particularly evident from the fact that there is currently no established system of knowledge and theory development; rather, organisational behaviour is subject to a collection of approaches. Together, these do not comprise a coherent whole in the same way as do mathematics and medicine.

2   ORIGINS OF THE FIELD OF STUDY

The subject of organisational behaviour was born from the need for a structured frame of thought and comprehension regarding organisations and their processes. When viewed from this perspective, it is a mature subject indeed. As early as the fourth century BC, Socrates and Plato put forward theories about leadership, task allocation, and specialisation.

It was first taught as subject in the United States in the second half of the 19th century, although not yet in its current form. Following the Industrial Revolution, as businesses emerged and expanded, management became far more complicated – and therefore required new and special skills.

One of the first people to suggest that management was a science that could and should be taught and learned, rather than a position that was awarded based on innate talent or inheritance, was Henri Fayol (1841–1925), who is discussed in greater detail in Section 1.7.

In the Netherlands, organisational behaviour was introduced as a major study at technical colleges shortly after the Second World War. The subject was initially called business organisation, and was more technical in its orientation.

Organisational behaviour in its current form was introduced into the Dutch higher educational system during the 1960s and 70s. Other disciplines, such as business studies, logistics, behavioural sciences and law, were incorporated into the subject. At the same time, the concept of the interdisciplinary approach was introduced.

The underlying reason for this introduction was the ever-increasing complexity and size of organisations, particularly enterprises, caused by significant technical and general economic developments. The management of such organisations required more than mere aptitude in an appropriate field or possession of leadership skills. There arose a need for people who could examine, integrate, and draw conclusions from the contributions made by the various fields. In short: people with a holistic vision.

The initial impetus for change came from within the business world. This explains the name of the new field of study: business administration. Later on, other organisations began to see the advantages of the approach and began to apply many of the new insights to their own methods.

Degree courses in business administration exist in a number of universities and colleges today. Within various courses and studies, the topic of business administration is known alternatively as Organisational Behaviour, Business Organisation, Organisational Theory, Management and Organisation, Organisation and Management, or simply Management.

Business organisation
Organisational behaviour

Organisation and management

Businesses should learn from the lessons of the past

We find ourselves well into a new century. What will the 21st century have to offer? How will the Netherlands make itself heard among the world's superpowers? Strange though it may seem: the solution to many economic issues can be found in what has come before. Over the past 400 years, there has only been a handful of economic superpowers, and Holland was one of these. Still a diminutive economy circa 1500, the republic developed at lightning speed following its declaration of independence, and eventually became the world's leading economic nation. In 1700, income per capita in the Republic of Holland was 50% greater than that of its most important competitor, the United Kingdom. At the time, our country was at such a distinct advantage that Adam Smith, the founder of economic science, used Holland as an example for his countrymen in his *Wealth of Nations* (1776).

Studies have shown that technological superiority was a particular key factor behind Holland's economic success. Its vast competitive strength in terms of industry and trade were not founded on low wages or low taxes, as these were much higher in Holland than anywhere else. The republic is famous for its naval superiority in the 17th century. This superiority was also based on technological pre-eminence.

A famous example is the so-called 'fluyt', a revolutionary type of sailing vessel which was developed in Holland circa 1590. A fluyt could be built at half the price of other vessels of the period. Furthermore, a 200 tonne fluyt could easily be operated by just ten men, whereas a British ship from the same period easily required a crew of 30. Therefore, you might well say that, in its Golden Age, Holland was a high-tech country 'avant la lettre'. It was also a country that enjoyed great economic independence (there were few restrictions imposed on economic life) and impressive entrepreneurship.

Source: *NRC Handelsblad*, 15 June 1994

3 DEVELOPMENT OF TRADE AND EMERGENCE OF MULTINATIONAL ENTERPRISES

The foundation of (international) enterprise has always been a combination of trade among various tribes in various (cross-border) geographical regions. The earliest examples of international trade can be traced to the so-called 'trade routes'. The Silk Road, one of the oldest trade routes, was established in the 1st century BC. It connected Europe, the Middle East, and Asia, and therefore linked major large Roman and Chinese civilisations. The Silk Road ensured that commodities like silk, fur, pottery, iron, and bronze from Asia were transported to the west, and exchanged for gold, other precious metals, ivory, wool, and glass. Trade was mainly carried out by commission agents: middlemen who travelled part of the route in caravans. The Silk Road went into decline as a trade route around 1400 AD. Other important historic commercial routes include the Roman trade routes (50 BC to 500 AD), the African trade routes (1000 AD to 1500 AD), the Indian maritime routes (from 800 AD), the Spanish trade routes (15th and 16th century) and the Portuguese trade routes (16th century).

The first international trading companies (or multinationals) were established with the support and financial backing of national governments who wished to support their colonial trade policy. In 1600, the English East India Company was established with the primary goal of trading with East and South-East Asia, as well as with India. The Dutch East India Company (Dutch VOC, short for *Verenigde Oost-Indische Compagnie* – the United East Indian Company) was founded on 20 March 1602. The States General of the day granted the VOC an exclusive charter establishing their monopoly on all trade between the Republic of the Seven United Netherlands and 'India', meaning all countries east of the Cape of Good Hope. Over the course of its 200-year existence, the Dutch East India Company developed into the largest company of its time, trading in such spices as cloves, nutmeg, cinnamon and pepper, and other products like silk, tea, and porcelain. The Dutch East India Company went into decline during the second half of the 18th century, primarily because of competition from the English and the French. It was dissolved on 17 March 1798.

Other important trading companies were:
- the Danish East India Company (established in 1614);
- the Dutch West India Company (established in 1621);
- the French West-India Company (established in 1664);
- the Royal African Company (established in 1663);
- the Hudson's Bay Company (established in 1670).

Between the establishment of the first international trading companies and the beginning of the 20th century, the number and size of companies with departments in at least two countries, so-called multinationals, saw a dramatic increase; from around 3,000 multinational businesses at the start of the 20th century to approximately 89,000 by the end of 2014.

There are a number of factors that can explain this growth pattern. From a historical perspective, governments exerted the majority of influence on trade, but began to relinquish part of this influence. Technological developments also played a key role by, among other things, shortening distances (transport) and optimising communications between people at different locations (the telephone, satellites, the internet). Technology also improved the availability of greater and better know-how in various markets and consumer groups. Lastly, companies became able to quickly address global developments by providing access to financial means for investments, setting up offices in different countries, employing staff, etcetera. The term multinational enterprise is used to refer to organisations that operate internationally. Many of these enterprises have fewer than 250 employees, yet still fall withing this definition. Approximately 445 of the world's largest 500 companies are found in North American, Europe, and Japan. The Netherlands is home to 11 of these 500.

Following this brief outline of the development of trade and the emergence of multinational enterprises, the remainder of this chapter addresses schools of thought and personalities relevant to the development of organisation and management.

4   SCHOOLS OF THOUGHT AND PERSONALITIES

Figure 0.1 places the most significant contributors in the history of organisational behaviour on a time line. These individuals often represent a particular idea or school of thought within the field of organisational behaviour. The following sections discusses those schools of thought and personalities that have had (significant) impact on the development of organisational behaviour theory. But why delve into the past in this way? The reason is that these contributions still constitute part of the present theoretical framework of the current field of study. Although they often originated in a different era and are therefore considered

School of thought

FIGURE 0.1 **IMPORTANT PEOPLE AND SCHOOLS OF THOUGHT IN THE HISTORY OF ORGANISATIONAL BEHAVIOUR**

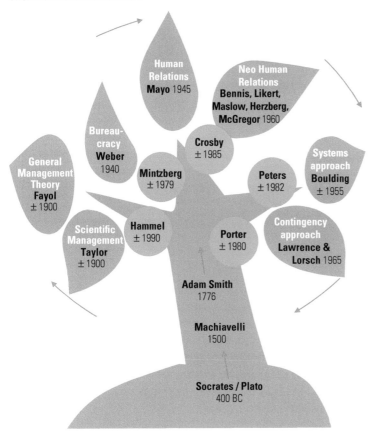

somewhat dated, they contain valuable elements whose nature is timeless. Theoretical views and personalities of more recent times are also discussed, and the reader may notice that many of the new theories have their roots in the past. The core issue has always been that of achieving goals through combined effort. Here, division and coordination of tasks, selected leadership styles, as well as communication methods play an important role.

The contributions made by the various individuals relate to different aspects of organisations. Naturally, many of the theories rely on different principles. Some theories have apparently arisen in response to earlier ones, which were subjected to critical review, called (at least partly) into question, and then countered by a different theory or approach, without completely discrediting the original ideas. As such, the theoretical framework of organisational behaviour has developed a rich and varied, albeit occasionally incoherent, character.

5   EVENTS PRIOR TO THE INDUSTRIAL REVOLUTION (400 BC–1900 AD)

As indicated in the previous section, notions about leadership, management and the design of organisations are, in fact, as old as humanity. Formal studies on these topics were, however, quite rare before the twentieth century. Nevertheless, there are some examples in the writings of ancient Greek philosophers such as Socrates and Plato, and much later in the works of Italian

Niccolò Machiavelli

Niccolò Machiavelli (1469–1527). In his book *Il Principe* (The Prince), Machiavelli provides numerous potentially useful guidelines for rulers and other leaders. These guidelines focus primarily on the preservation and expansion of power. Their nature is extremely opportunistic, based on pure self-interest and the ability to unscrupulously take advantage of a situation whenever opportunity presents itself. Il Principe represents Machiavelli's accumulated experiences as an advisor to the government and as a diplomat in Florence.

Until the second half of the 18th century, the dominant economic school of

Mercantilism

thought was that of mercantilism. A key belief of this philosophy was that one's possessions in gold and money were the only source of wealth. This changed in 1776, when Adam Smith (1723–1790) wrote his influential *An inquiry into the nature and causes of the wealth of nations*. Smith's work put forward the idea that productive labour is the source of wealth and that, by proper distribution of labour, labour productivity can vastly be improved. Adam Smith thus rejected the value of mercantilism.

From then on, management began to take a more systematic approach to operations, with greater attention being paid to efficiency.

The 18th century was an age of ground breaking technological advancement: the invention of the steam engine, the use of coal as fuel. This made it possible to maintain large factories aimed at mass production instead of product manufacture in workers' homes or small workplaces. The explosive growth of factories attracted large numbers of workers from the countryside. Western civilisation turned from agriculture to industry. In the larger cities, the growing working classes lived in poorly built workers' houses. Their pay was low and their living conditions were miserable. This development began in England. Then, after 1840, it made its way across Western Europe and the United States.

Adam Smith

By the end of the 19th century, American companies had grown dramatically in response to the ever-expanding consumer market. The existing system of checks and balances had become inadequate. The division of responsibility between supervisors and staff was unclear, production standards and wages were determined subjectively, and an air of unpredictability prevailed. Planning was almost unheard of. Managers had only one objective: to keep pushing their workers into producing as much as possible. The workers, in turn, responded by systematic and organised stalling.

The situation began to call for a more structured and systematic approach. The man who recognised the issue and was willing to address it was engineer Frederick Winslow Taylor (1856–1915), whose publications and lectures laid the foundations for what later came to be known as Scientific Management.

6   FREDERICK TAYLOR AND SCIENTIFIC MANAGEMENT (C. 1900)

Frederick Taylor

Frederick Taylor was the first to suggest a systematic, coherent approach to determining the manner in which factories should be organised. Rather than having managers fulfil the role of slave drivers, Taylor proposed they adopt a broader view of their tasks within the organisation: planning, coordinating, overseeing, and verifying results.

Henry Ford, a stubborn but brilliant businessman with eccentric tendencies

His introduction of the assembly line changed the industry, but his behaviour was that of an enlightened despot: Henry Ford was an odd character.

The implementation of the assembly line in his car factory and the notion of base salaries for his employees means Henry Ford did more than make automobiles affordable; he laid the foundations for the rise of an age in which machines and mass consumption began to determine the modern world. More than once, Ford has been referred to as the Steve Jobs of the 20th century. He had little sympathy for the world in which he lived and tended to withdraw from the society that his mechanisation had helped make faster and more impersonal. Aside from his entrepreneurship, he took on many social projects: from the construction of a hospital to the development of a number of agriculturally-oriented towns along the Tennessee River. Apart from a nature of simultaneous introversion and engagement, Ford's obsessive drive is also reminiscent of that of the twentieth century, self-absorbed CEO. Ford's views on social

development were exceptionally confusing. Ford's biography by Vincent Curcio shows that successful businesspeople who are not kept firmly in check by their surroundings will come to entertain notions that cannot bear the light of day. At the high-point of his success, Ford became America's most vocal and influential anti-Semite. He published **The International Jew**, a best-seller translated and published around the world, which was seen as an important source of inspiration by Hitler and other Nazis. In fact, Henry Ford was the first person to receive the Grand Cross of the German Eagle, the highest honour bestowed on foreigners by the Nazis. Ford later renounced his anti-Semitism, and made his apologies on multiple occasions.

But Ford did not stop at anti-Semitism; he turned from a paternalistic CEO into an enlightened despot. He grew increasingly narcissistic and blunt. Like a true Steve Jobs, Ford would fire the engineers crucial in the construction and growth of his automobile plant. His distrust of his employees grew to such proportions that he would hire company detectives to spy for him. In the 1930s, his factories increasingly came to resemble labour camps. Assembly line speeds were ramped up to stop employees being able to carry on a conversation. Many labourers contracted a case of so-called 'Forditus': a working life characterised by apathy, submissiveness, and exhaustion.

Biograph Curcio concludes that powerful CEOs benefit from a strong supervisory or governing board. History, however, shows us that no self-absorbed CEO post-Ford was hardly ever kept in check by their direct surroundings.

Source: *Het Financieele Dagblad*, 8 March 2014

Scientific management

Several key elements of the theory of management and control of organisations (Scientific Management) are:

1 Scientific analysis of the activities that should be carried out, and the time and motion studies to be used. (The results can be used to standardise and normalise the production process and machines and materials used.)
2 Extensive division of labour and workforce training, with each task and operation clearly prescribed; this results in worker routine, leading to improved production standards.
3 Close and friendly working relationships between managers and workers.
4 Managers are held responsible for seeking and analysing appropriate working methods and for creating optimum conditions for production. Formerly, this was left to the implementation phase.
5 Use of careful selection processes to obtain the best person for the job.
6 Financial rewards for adhering to prescribed methods and targets in order to reduce production costs.

Furthermore, Taylor proposed a division of front-line supervisory responsibilities within the production department into eight separate areas, with each area and its tasks to be the sole responsibility of a particular individual:

1 time and costing;
2 task instructions;
3 processes and their order;
4 work preparation and allocation;
5 maintenance;
6 quality control;

7 technical guidance;

8 personnel management.

This system has come to be known as the 'eight-bosses system'. Under Taylor's
leadership, the system worked, but it failed to become widely adopted elsewhere
due to its many coordination problems and lack of clarity for workers.
Aside from his theory of organisation mentioned above, the influence of Taylor's
ideas was enormous. Wherever his principles were applied, productivity shot
up, and his ideas began to spread rapidly. However, the increase in efficiency
was rarely matched by the increase in wages or improvement in managerial
relationships Taylor had envisaged. The impact of these consequences,
immortalised in Charlie Chaplin's 'Modern Times' and inextricably linked to Taylor
and the concept of scientific management, was the idea that workers were simply
an extension of the machinery, with monotonous labour, restriction of freedom,
and reduced job satisfaction.

Charlie Chaplin in Modern Times

Another consequence of Taylor's ideas was the improvement in management
and control of production departments across the industrial world. Administration
and sales departments took their lead from production, and were soon using
similar methods. Next was the development of various standards in production
and materials. Planning techniques were developed and applied more than ever
before, with accompanying improvements in progress control. Modern concepts
like labour studies, labour science, job descriptions and job classifications can
all be traced back directly to Taylor's ideas. He fundamentally changed working
methods in organisations and has become an important figure in the history of
organisational behaviour.

Production department at a machine plant

7 HENRI FAYOL AND GENERAL MANAGEMENT-THEORY (C. 1900)

Henri Fayol

In Europe, it was Henri Fayol (1841–1925) who first developed a coherent set of guidelines regarding the way organisations should manage their operations as a whole. His experience as the manager of a mining company led him to formulate his theory of general management, thus affecting the organisation as a whole. In this respect, Fayol took a different approach than Taylor, who looked at systems primarily from a production angle. Fayol's theory was also directed at organisations other than industrial enterprises. He thought it should be possible to formulate principles that applied wherever people worked together, and that these principles could and should form the basis for a field of study. His General Management theory was indended to be an educational model. Fayol identified six independent management activities:

General Management theory
Management activities

1 technical;
2 commercial;
3 financial;
4 security (understood to mean the safety of people and possessions);
5 accounting;
6 direction.

Direction ensures the coordination between the other activities (see Figure 0.2). Naturally, direction comprises the mainstay of the function of managers. It consists of five tasks:

1 **Planning or anticipating**: setting up of an action plan for the future.
2 **Organising**: structuring the organisation using people and resources.
3 **Commanding**: ensuring full employee participation.
4 **Coordinating**: aligning each activity to the plan.
5 **Controlling**: ensuring that the results conform to the planning.

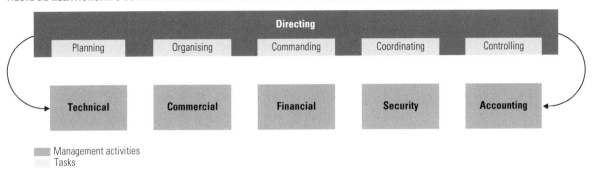

Management activities
Tasks

Unity of command was Fayol's leading principle.
Each employee should report to one immediate superior. At the time, this principle was the only structuring principle in use; it was developed in the army, where it is the supreme principle to this day. This means that Fayol's notion clashes with Taylor's view, as Taylor's functional organisation broke away from the concept of unity of command.

Unity of command

Fayol's significance lies in his belief in the universal character of management and his strong support for formally training future managers in their chosen profession. His legacy was the driving force behind the increase in attention paid to the tasks of the manager.

8 MAX WEBER AND BUREAUCRACY THEORY (C. 1920)

Whereas Taylor focussed on manufacturing companies and Fayol on management in general, Max Weber (1864–1920) studied government organisations and large businesses from a sociological perspective.

Max Weber

According to Weber, major organisations have the following characteristics:
a a clearly and definitively implemented division of tasks;
b a hierarchical command structure;
c carefully defined authorities and responsibilities;
d impersonal relationships between officials (position is placed over person);
e recruitment based on ability and knowledge instead of relying on favouritism and having the right contacts;

Max Weber

f promotion and reward based on objective criteria and procedures;
g implementation of activities according to clearly laid down procedures;
h all data is recorded in writing so that complete control of all aspects is possible;
i the power of officials, even senior ones, is bound by documented guidelines.

Weber posited that, if an organisation functions according to the characteristic listed, it is an ideal bureaucracy. In his opinion, bureaucracy was the most efficient form of organisation, since everyone in such an organisation would function coherently: like the cogs of a well-oiled machine.

The 'ideal bureaucracy' is not just a description of an organisation, but also a theoretical model helpful to the study of organisations. A number of modern-day writers in the field of organisational behaviour, writers who are discussed in greater detail elsewhere in this chapter, have also published theories in relation to such ideal types.

Ideal bureaucracy

Weber's definition should be viewed as being distinctly separate from the negative connotations that surround the word 'bureaucracy'. It is common to link the word to themes of inertia, red tape, unending successions of pointless rules, and so on. Weber's description was intended to be an objective, scientific analysis of the dominant organisational form of the time. He identified positive and effective qualities, such as the execution of rules without personal bias, and the appropriate performance of administrative tasks. He also highlighted some of the less effective, negative characteristics, such as inflexibility and the lack of initiative and creativity. He saw bureaucracy as a perfect means for reaching management targets, as well as an organisational form that functioned so perfectly in itself that its permanent continuation also became an objective. The emphasis on technical perfectionism, however, could lead to the structure being considered more important than the organisational goals which, of course, would have consequences for the continuity of the organisation.

To this day, one of the characteristics of Weber's 'ideal bureaucratic' model are recognisable in some organisations, particularly in larger ones.

9 ELTON MAYO AND THE HUMAN RELATIONS MOVEMENT (C. 1945)

Human Relations movement

The Human Relations movement arose at the time that Scientific Management, and its accompanying, highly rationalistic approach to working organisations, was the most important organisational theory. It was against this backdrop that, in 1927, research was initiated into the influence of workplace light levels on the performance of production workers in the General Electric's plant in Hawthorne, America. In one group, light levels were raised – while in a separate control group, light levels were kept as they were.

Hawthorne-plant

Hawthorne plant
Production in the experimental group did increase but, to the amazement of the researchers, so did production in the control group – by approximately the same level. Then, when the lights were dimmed to minimum levels, the results showed an additional surprise, as productivity continued to rise! The scientists were mystified, and Elton Mayo (1880–1949) of Harvard University was invited to find an explanation for the phenomenon.

Elton Mayo

Between 1927 and 1947, he carried out a series of experiments in order to examine the connection between improvements in working conditions (for example, shortening the working day, increasing the number and duration of breaks, providing free soup or coffee during morning breaks, etc.) and productivity. Each change led to an increase in production and a reduction in employee fatigue (see Figure 0.3).

FIGURE 0.3 **THE INFLUENCE OF LIGHT ON WORK PERFORMANCE**

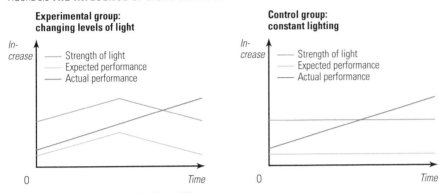

Source: De Wilde, *Stoeien met organisaties*, Kluwer 1999

In the lighting experiments, the underlying cause for the increase in productivity appeared to be simply that staff members received increased attention during the experiment. Mayo thus proved his theory that, in addition to objective factors, subjective factors – such as attention, a feeling of security, belonging to a group, and appreciation – have an effect on results. Subjective factors are, in fact, even more important. According to Mayo, group feeling was the most important factor of all. He developed his theory and explored it in his book *The Human Problems of an Industrial Civilisation* (1933), a highly influential work.

Objective factors
Subjective factors

In the wake of Mayo's work came a vast swath of new studies. A new form of management had been propagated, based on the social needs of workers in small groups; an idea vehemently opposed to the Scientific Management approach, which was strictly rational and focussed solely on individual production workers. The movement is, in fact, based on the assumption that happy, satisfied people tend to perform to the peak of their productive ability. This means that company management should cultivate good interpersonal relationships in relatively small groups, as well as give adequate attention to groups and individuals, show their appreciation, and bestow adequate personal responsibility and freedom.

Cooperation is key, which means that proper social skills are very important for managers. The movement's most significant contribution is the discovery of the link between human factors and organisational effectiveness.

Cooperation

10 RENSIS LIKERT (AND OTHERS) AND THE NEO-HUMAN RELATIONS APPROACH (C. 1950)

In the period from 1950 to 1955, criticism of the ideas of the human relations movement began to appear. Many saw it as an overly idealistic view of organisations – one that that portrayed them more as a kind of social club which would rarely, if ever, exist in practice. Moreover, the ideas were not unanimously supported by subsequent research results.

Rensis Likert

Warren G. Bennis

On the other hand, there was no desire to return to the ideas of scientific management. It was therefore time for a synthesis of the two. Warren G. Bennis described the situation like this: The Taylor approach leads to 'an organisation without men' while that of the human relations movement creates 'groups of men without organisation'. He emphasized the need for a revision of the human

Neo-Human Relations

relations approach; from this, the term neo-human relations was born. Other writers undertook to bridge the gap between the two opposing ideas, including Likert, Herzberg, McGregor, Burn and Mouton, each doing so by approaching the issue from their own individual perspective.

Rensis Likert

Rensis Likert (1903-1981) was the first to attempt to reconcile the two movements. He looked specifically at the organisational structure and internal communication,

'Linking pin' structure

and developed the so-called 'linking pin model', with the organisation consisting of a number of overlapping groups, whose leaders are also the members of a higher group (linking pin). Leaders should, naturally, lead the group, but also ensure proper communication with the higher group (see Section 11.7 for more).

Frederick Herzberg
Hierarchy of needs
Abraham Maslow

A different theory was developed by Frederick Herzberg, who based it on psychologist Abraham Maslow's hierarchy of needs. This hierarchy, presented as a pyramid (figure 0.4), consists of five levels of human needs; needs which, according to Maslo, all human beings strive to fulfil. The hierarchy of needs can therefore explain all aspects of human behaviour. Once one level has been mostly satisfied, the individual's focus turns to the satisfaction of the next level of needs up.

In ascending order, the levels of needs are:
1 physiological needs (food, drink, sleep, sex);
2 security and safety needs (protection, stability, order);
3 love or relationship needs (friendship, group membership);
4 recognition needs (prestige, success);
5 self-actualisation needs (responsibility, personal development opportunities, creativity).

Abraham Maslow

FIGURE 0.4 **MASLOW'S HIERARCHY OF NEEDS**

Although Maslow's theory has never been fully proven, many have found it to be appealing, and it has been highly influential as a result. Herzberg applied the theory to the behaviour of people in organisations.

Herzberg looked for factors that would amplify people's motivation in an organisation, as well as for factors that would lead to dissatisfaction. He concluded that there are 'satisfiers' (or 'motivators'), and 'dissatisfiers' (or 'hygiene factors'). Satisfiers are factors that lead to job satisfaction. These factors are work intrinsic, and include recognition and self-actualisation. But the absence of these stimuli does not, however, lead to dissatisfaction. Dissatisfiers lead to job dissatisfaction, and consist of work intrinsic factors such as working conditions and wages. Poor quality work intrinsic factors lead to dissatisfaction; good quality work intrinsic factors, however, will not improve staff motivation.

In 1960, Douglas McGregor (1906-1964) used his book *The human side of enterprise* to present his theories, dubbed theory X and theory Y. These theories comprise two distinct and opposite versions of people in organisations. Theory X describes how most organisations worked at the time, and is strongly reminiscent of Scientific Management. Theory Y was McGregor's own vision of how people in organisations should cooperate. It should be pointed out that the X and Y theories relate to the human, not the organisational, perspective. Section 9.5.3 covers McGregor's theories in greater detail.

Douglas McGregor

11 KENNETH BOULDING AND THE SYSTEMS APPROACH (C. 1950)

Following the Second World War, a number of neo-human relations supporters, including Kenneth Boulding (1910 –1993), developed a theory which views the organisation as a system (meaning a whole made up of coherent parts). According to this theory, all activities in an organisation are closely connected with each other. Another important element of the systems approach is that organisations interact with the outside world (the environment).

Kenneth Boulding

As figure 0.5 shows, a system (an organisation) consists of a number of subsystems (divisions), ostensibly connected with each other. When the total result of all subsystems working together is greater than the sum of their individual results, this is known as synergy. A system (organisation) is run with the help of information given (feedback) to the various subsystems (divisions).

FIGURE 0.5 **THE ORGANISATION AND SURROUNDINGS AS ONE SYSTEM**

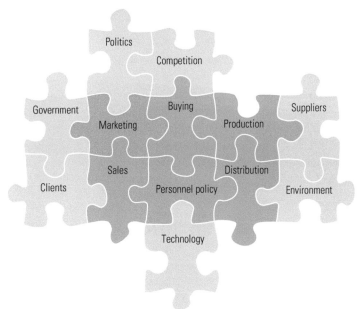

According to the systems approach, management should tackle organisational problems consistently. That is to say: if a decision needs to be made, management

Systems approach

should look not only at a single organisational component, but at the effects of the decision on the total organisation. This may seem obvious but, frequently, local management staff tries to find a perfect solution to a problem in their own area without understanding its consequences for other divisions.

For example, a reduction in retained inventory generates a saving in warehousing space but can lead to longer delivery times – which can cost an enterprise some of its customers. This example shows the importance of using the systems approach in organisations.

Jay Lorsch

12 PAUL LAWRENCE AND JAY LORSCH AND THE CONTINGENCY APPROACH (C. 1965)

At the end of the 1950s, Joan Woodward published the results of a study into a hundred English businesses. In the study, she had looked at the practical effectiveness of the organisational behaviour theories by Taylor and Fayol. Her research showed that there was no connection between the extent to which an enterprise is organised according to the rules of scientific management and whether it is economically successful. This was a sensational conclusion because, up until that time, the prevailing thought had been that there was, in fact, 'a best way of management'.

Paul Lawrence
Jay Lorsch

Americans Paul Lawrence and Jay Lorsch performed additional studies and, in 1967, concluded that, to optimise performance, different circumstances require different structures, task divisions, and working methods. The notion of 'contingency' they introduced calls for 'situationally dependent direction'.

Contingency

According to contingency theory, the choice of management technique deriving from a theory of organisational behaviour is strongly influenced by the circumstances in which an organisation finds itself. Certain management techniques can be extremely successful in some situations – while in others, they may fail completely. The art is in discovering which circumstances require the application of which techniques.

One of the most important elements of contingency theory is the relationship between an organisation and its surroundings. It is of paramount importance that organisations have a clear focus on their surroundings. The contingency approach requires management to constantly be aware of the nature of the complexity of the interrelationships within their surroundings, and to match each situation with the most appropriate strategy, organisational structure, and so on.

Over the past few decades, there have been many new studies confirming the fundamental findings of contingency theory.

13 RECENT ORGANISATIONAL THEORIES (1980+)

Recent organisational
theories

Since the 1980s, many different writers and consultants have carried out extensive studies of organisations, followed by significant contributions to the development of organisational theory. This has been of great interest to many organisations of the 1990s. Many of the newly developed theories have not yet been classified into a definitive 'school of thought'. A number of these theories and authors are briefly discussed in the following section.

Philip Crosby (1926–2001) and quality control

An important recent trend in organisational behaviour has been towards quality control in organisations. The founder of theories on this subject was American W. Deming, who first applied his ideas to companies following the Second World War. One of the best-known modern-day 'quality gurus' is American Philip Crosby (1926–2001), who developed a total quality management theory that is used extensively by companies in Japan, Europe and America. Philip Crosby was vice-president of the International Telephone and Telegraph Company, where he was responsible for world-wide quality control for fourteen years. His company, Crosby Associates, is one of the world's leading consultancies in the field of quality management.

For Crosby, working according to the concept of 'zero defects' was crucial. Zero defects means that, in organisations, one must strive to avoid mistakes in all processes. He disregarded the outdated view that quality control is only necessary in production departments and not in the board room. Crosby believed that organisations could reduce their expenses by about 20%, provided they treat quality control as the number one priority within the workplace.

Philip Crosby
Totale quality
management theory

Concept of 'zero defects'

Henry Mintzberg (b. 1939) and organisational structure and strategic planning

Canadian Henry Mintzberg continues to stand out with his remarkable contributions to the fields of organisational structure, management, and strategic planning. He is Professor of Management Studies at McGill University in Montreal and a part-time professor at INSEAD in France.

Amongst the authoritative books he has written are *The Strategy Process, Structure in 5's, The Structuring of Organisations, Mintzberg on Management* (1991) and *The Rise and Fall of Strategic Planning* (1994). He has won the McKinsey Award for the best Harvard Business Review article twice.

Henry Mintzberg

One of his most important works, *The Structuring of Organisations* (1979), can be seen as an attempt to blend the main organisational theories of how organisations ought to be structured. According to Mintzberg, the success of organisations cannot simply be explained by their choice of 'the best' organisational structure. He tells us that it is not possible to generalise about the best structure for organisations. In reality, there are many roads to success.

Henry Mintzberg

Mintzberg suggests that organisations should not view their qualities separately from each other, but that they should bring them together in a common form or configuration. A configuration can be seen as the 'ideal typical organisation'. Mintzberg identified five basic configurations that he has since extended with two new forms, namely:

a The entrepreneurial (start-up) form
b The machine bureaucracy
c The professional bureaucracy
d The diversified form
e Adhocracy (innovative)
f The missionary (ideological) form
g The political form.

Configuration
Five basic
configurations

These forms or configurations each have their strengths and weaknesses. Depending on prevailing environmental factors, the degree of turbulence or stability, and organisational goals, these strengths become clear.

Although the configuration descriptions refer to 'ideal types' which, in reality, occur rarely if ever, Mintzberg believes that the study of these configurations is certainly still worthwhile as it helps one develop an ability to understand organisations more quickly. A closer look at the strong and weak elements within one's own organisation also has obvious value. In Chapter 9, extensive attention is given to Mintzberg's theories of organisational structure.

In his book *The Rise and Fall of Strategic Planning* (1994), Mintzberg wipes the floor with the traditional views of strategic planning. He concludes that strategy cannot be planned and that strategic planning often fails in organisations. Chapter 3 takes a closer look at Mintzberg's views on strategic planning.

Tom Peters

Tom Peters (b. 1942) and management principles for excellent companies
Tom Peters is a management consultant and founder of the Tom Peters Group in California. He carried out applied scientific research to find a set of management principles for organisational development. In 1982, he published the results of a study into 43 American enterprises whose profitability had been consistent over a period of twenty years. Using these findings, he co-authored a book with Robert Waterman called *In Search of Excellence*, which went on to sell more than four million copies.

Tom Peters

To explain the success of the enterprises that were studied, which included McDonald's, Procter & Gamble, Boeing, IBM and Hewlett Packard, the researchers identified the following eight common characteristics:

1 **Strong action orientation**. Although many of the examined enterprises made decisions analytically, this did not paralyse them. The overall way of working was characterised by 'Do it, fix it, try it'.
2 **Close relationships with customers**. As an enterprise, one can learn much from one's customers, and the most innovative enterprises took the best ideas for development of new products from their customers.
3 **Creating entrepreneurship and autonomy**. One of the most significant problems for big organisations is that they are missing what originally made them grow, namely: 'innovation'. The art is in being large while, at the same time, retaining the ability to act small. For this reason, an 'entrepreneurial climate' must be created; here, highly creative employees can work on innovation. In such a culture, it is necessary to make room for the development of 'unorthodox' ideas, treating the process with a sense of freedom in which mistakes are not punished.

Innovation
Entrepreneurial climate

4 **Employees are the most important source of productivity**. Enterprises that excel see their employees as a source of quality and productivity. One of the most fundamental points here is 'respect for the individual'. It is important to get the most energy and talent from one's employees.
5 **Hands-on, value driven**. It is of great importance that an enterprise indicates its stance, its strengths, and its points of employee pride. All excelling enterprises seem to have clear values and take the creation of value seriously.
6 **Stick with what you know**. Successful enterprises do not jump into areas of which they have no understanding.
7 **Simple structure and lean supporting divisions**. All enterprises had a simple and clear organisational structure, i.e. not a matrix structure (see Chapter 9). Supporting (staff) divisions were also kept small.

8 Management is both centralised and decentralised. Many enterprises that excel are run using both centralised and decentralised aspects. These enterprises apply top-down, alsmost rigid control on core issues while, at the same time, giving divisions a large amount of freedom to use their entrepreneurial and innovative skills.

Recent history has shown that an enterprise with long-term past success is not guaranteed to repeat those results in the future.
At the end of the 1980s, IBM, for example, was forced to cut its staff numbers by nearly 50%. Of critical importance is the ability of enterprises to continually keep abreast of changes in their surroundings.
In his 1987 book *Thriving on Chaos*, Tom Peters says that chaos has become the norm. Nearly every day, managers are confronted with big changes that are linked to developments like those in IT and telecommunications. Enterprises must show absolute flexibility in order to use chaos to meet new challenges in the market. In his book, Tom Peters gives 45 recommendations to management on how to do this.
Books by Tom Peters published since 1987 include: *Liberation Management* (1992), *The Pursuit of Wow* (1994), *The Circle of Innovation* (1997), the series *The Brand You50, The Professional Services Firm50, The Project50* (1999), and *Re-Imagine* (2003) – a number 1 international bestseller.

Peter Drucker (1909-2005) and general management

Peter Drucker is thought of by many as the 'father of all management gurus'. Since 1939, he wrote 35 books, translated into 24 languages, and published worldwide. According to Drucker, following the Industrial Revolution and dramatic increases in productivity, we have now arrived at a Knowledge Revolution. Knowledge has become the critical production factor, according to Drucker. The importance of nature, labour and capital lies mainly in the limitations that they impose. Without these production factors, knowledge can produce nothing.

Peter Drucker

Knowledge Revolution

Peter Drucker

Drucker estimated that the number of people currently employed in traditional industry sectors such as agriculture and industry has fallen by 20 to 25%.
The remaining three quarters of the workforce can be divided into three approximately equal groups, namely: knowledge workers, such as high-quality specialists, professionals and technicians; highly trained service-providers, such as sales staff, instructors and civil servants; and less trained service-providers, such as cleaners, drivers and administrators, whose wages often remain below those of other groups.
Prior to 1990, management did not really direct much attention towards developments in productivity in the knowledge and services sector. But now that the productivity revolution in the agriculture and industry sectors has come full circle, there is an awareness that an increase in productivity in the knowledge and services sectors is an absolute condition for further economic growth. The key characteristic of knowledge work is that, to a large extent, knowledge workers determine the content of their job, and often without even paying much attention to productivity. Research suggests that about three quarters of employee time is frittered away due to inefficient coordination or through the performance of irrelevant tasks. Productivity can be increased significantly if employees keep in mind what they are really being paid for. Anything else needs to be rejected. Other remedies suggested by Drucker for considerably increasing productivity are: analysing and restructuring tasks; outsourcing supporting service tasks

Knowledge work

(which promotes competition); and forming teams that are particularly suited to a particular type of work. According to Drucker: 'As well as there being an economic challenge to create higher productivity, there is a hidden social challenge to the dignity of (new) people with a lower education level who are employed in the services sector.'

In his most recent work, *Management Challenges for the 21st Century* (1999), Peter Drucker offers a refreshing description of the future of management. According to Drucker, there is not one single correct organisational form. Managements should look for whichever organisational structure best matches the work that is to be performed; the organisational form is mainly of way of ensuring employee productivity. Drucker also predicts a number of other developments. Managers will increasingly have different work experience to their subordinates; a new balance will form between full-time and part-time jobs; the lifespan of the average current company will be no longer than 30 years – a number that will only shrink over time. Drucker investigated the fundamental questions of the new century, the changes in the world's economy, and the practice of management. What are the new realities, and how should companies match their strategies to stay afloat?

Michael Porter (1947) and strategy

Michael Porter

Michael Porter

Michael Porter, a Harvard professor, has had a major influence on the development of strategic thinking and behaviour within businesses. The value of his work, as is discussed in Chapter 3, has particularly been in the creation of structures for the implementation of analyses that lead to successful strategies. Porter was the first to monitor the link between the meaning of managerial work and its effect on the success of an enterprise. In an award-winning 1979 McKinsey article entitled 'How Competitive Forces Shape Strategy', Porter used his Five Forces model to demonstrate how enterprises can analyse the market and their competitors' behaviour. In his first book, Competitive Strategy (1980), Porter discusses mainly the 'what' and 'why' of strategy.

His second book, *Competitive Advantage*, focusses mainly on the 'how' of strategy. He puts forward the suggestion that companies must search for their own competitive advantage. According to Porter, examples of competitive advantage include operating at a lower cost than a competitor, or creating 'added value' so that buyers will pay more for the product or service.

Sustainable competitive advantage

In his book *Competitive Advantage of Nations* (1990), Porter says that countries or regions create the factors that determine whether enterprises are successful. He outlines a number of criteria that can be used by an enterprise to judge the attractiveness of a location. Again and again, Porter comes to the conclusion that an organisation's surroundings are the source of ongoing competitive advantage.

There's nothing new to the electric car

There is nothing new to the electric car. In fact, there was a time when there were more electric than petrol powered cars on the road. The petrol cars of the time were thought to be clunky, difficult to operate, smelly, and noisy. So what caused the about-face? Compared to the first combustion engine cars, electric ones were better, easier to use, and quieter. Even Ferdinand Porsche (yes, the racing car bloke) produced an electric car as early as 1898. Its top speed was 35 kilometres per hour, and its range was 80 kilometres. In 1899, the electric car was still ahead of the pack in terms of car development. This is illustrated very clearly by the fact that the first car to breach the 100 kilometre per hour threshold was an electric one made by Belgian Camille Jenatzy. In 1909 an Amsterdam taxi company began operating the first fleet of electric cars: 12 in total. The move was a major hit, because everybody wanted to be driven around in one of those extraordinary taxis. For the time, the taxis' top speed was an impressive 40 kilometres per hour. The main reasons for the company to opt for electric cars was the fact that they cost little to operate, and were easy to use. As a result, the company would hire cheaper, less technologically savvy drivers. At the start of the 20th century, many well-to-do ladies would choose an electric car due to its ease of use. An added bonus was the absence of unpleasant odours while driving. Mrs Clara Ford, the wife of automobile manufacturer Henry Ford, owned an electric car by Detroit Electric. Unfortunately, electric car producers were unable to adequately improve the quality of car batteries. From 1910 onwards, the combustion engine powered vehicle began to slowly overtake its electric competitor. The costs of combustion engine powered cars began to decrease following the implementation of serial manufacture. Ironically, it was the implementation of an electric starter in 1913 which sounded the death knell for the electric car. Before the arrival of the electric starter, cranking the combustion engine into life had been a difficult task – now, the press of a button was sufficient to start the engine. Petrol became more readily accessible, and was next to free. The electric car was now resigned to a life of highly localised mobility, such as for municipal parks and gardens workers, and transport around golf courses. In 1924, Amsterdam's electric cars were replaced by petrol powered versions, which were cheaper to use at the time.

Source: blog.newhippy.nl, Patrick Hogendijk, 18 March 2014

Michael Hammer (1948–2008) and business process re-engineering

Michael Hammer

Michael Hammer was one of the most authoritative management gurus of the modern age. He was a professor of computer sciences at MIT in the United States and a director at his own consultancy company. Together with James Champy, he wrote the very successful book *Re-engineering the Corporation, a Manifesto for*

Michael Hammer

Business Revolution (1993). In this book, he argued that, over the last fifty years, business has been based on three principles, namely that:
1 the basic unit of work is the 'task';
2 simple tasks should be performed by lower educated people;
3 there is a distinction between 'those that do' and 'those that manage' (hierarchy).

In a world that changes slowly, characterised by predictability and continuity, it is understandable that these principles work well. However, in the current, turbulent times of rapid technological advancement and the explosive emergence and growth of world-wide markets, organisations are having to pay more attention to flexibility, quality, service, and a reduction of overhead costs. This does not mesh with the classic 'task-based organisation' that subdivided each process into all sorts of sub-processes which are then distributed across the whole organisation. This obviously leads to unnecessary inertia, bureaucracy and inflexibility.

Hammer and Champy argue in favour of a revolution within business. At the core of this revolution is the idea that enterprises need to work in a process-orientated way. A process can be seen as a succession of activities that create value for a consumer. For example, when an organisation receives an order from a customer, dozens of departments are involved. The customer has no interest in the full range of any internal administrative and organisational processes, but only in the final outcome. The process must therefore become the organisation's starting point. In a process-orientated organisation, a significant part of administrative and management supervision disappears. Simple tasks vanish. The difference between performers and managers becomes less clear. Professionals and coaches work in new forms of organisation. The coaches concentrate mainly on inspiring and motivating the professionals, as well as on designing the work environment. According to the authors, this new organisational approach leads to major cost reductions: between 40% and 80%. Before this can become a reality, top-level management needs to be convinced of the need to make this change (see Chapter 8 for further details).

Process-oriented
Process

C.K. Prahalad (1941–2010) and competition

Coimbatore Krishnao Prahalad

Coimbatore Krishnao Prahalad (born in the town of Coimbatore, Tamil Nadu) studied physics at the University of Madras (now Chennai), followed by working as a manager in a branch of the Union Carbide battery company, gaining management experience. He continued his education in the US, earning a PhD from Harvard. He has taught both in India and America, eventually joining the faculty of the University of Michigan's Business School, where he held the Harvey C. Fruehauf chair of Business Administration.

He met Gary Hamel, then a young international business student. Their collaboration ultimately resulted in *Competing for the Future* (1994). This book described how management was in transition. According to Prahalad and Hamel, this transition was characterised by moving from the previous model of control-and-demand to a model which required managers to look for new market opportunities.

Globalisation
Collaboration with
clients/consumers

In one of his more recent works, *The Future of Competition* (2004), written in collaboration with Venkat Ramaswamy, Prahalad argued that companies had not made enough use of the opportunities provided by globalisation. The 'customer' is a more powerful and pro-active figure. Thanks to the Internet, they are better informed and more creative. Customers demand greater influence in and control over the decision-making underlying certain transactions. Prahalad predicted a greater 'hands-on'-approach with regards to business, which would require greater collaboration with customers/consumers.

Prahalad earned worldwide renowned for his book *The Fortune at the Bottom of the Pyramid* (2004), at the start of which he proposes a simple though revolutionary notion: if one stops viewing the poor (the bottom of the pyramid, or BOP) as victims or a burden, and starts seeing them as resilient and creative entrepreneurs and value-conscious consumers, a whole new world of opportunity will present itself. The new markets are not a small group of wealthy individuals or a large group with moderate incomes, but the billions of people poised to undertake their first steps onto the world's economic stage. According to Prahalad, the bottom of the pyramid consists of four billion people subsisting on less than $2 per day. This group could be the driving force behind the next round of global trade and prosperity, and a source of innovation. Providing service for customers at the bottom of the pyramid places a demand on major businesses to cooperate with social organisations and local governments. This will subsequently create millions of new entrepreneurs at a basic level. Prahalad describes this 'co-creation' between economic development and social transformation as the solution to the issue of poverty. The nine major countries which Prahalad envisions for this transformation are China, India, Brazil, Mexico, Russia, Indonesia, Turkey, South-Africa and Thailand.

To improve the purchasing power of the poor, companies could offer their goods and services in a different manner, for example through offering smaller quantities. The result is a marginalised consumer who is absorbed into the economic system, allowing them to create and improve their opportunities for achieving a required higher income. According to Prahalad, innovation is the key. The entirety of the economic structure needs to be revolutionised. Companies should first focus on the poor, and the needs and possibilities of those poor, and then translate appropriate solutions to market segments.

Coimbatore Krishnao Prahalad

Bottom of the economic pyramic

Innovation

Jim Collins (1958) and corporate culture and leadership

Jim Collins wrote the internationally best-selling *Good to Great* (2001), which is considered the most thorough, insightful, and revolutionary study of the past decades.

Born in Aurora, Colorado USA, Collins studied mathematical science, followed by an MBA at Stanford University. He then taught at Stanford University Graduate School of Business. These days, he owns his own management-research centre.

In his book *Good to Great*, Collins and a team of investigators analysed hundreds of Fortune 500-companies. But Collins' foremost interest was in those eleven companies who managed to turn a good enterprise into a magnificent, explosively growing one – and then keep their company at that level of excellence for years. Collins used his insights to formulate several principles. What differentiates these successful business from their competitors, and what might other businesses stand to learn from their practices?

According to Collins, the following factors determine company excellence:
1 **Level 5 leadership**. Leaders who combine personal modesty with a professional drive (results-oriented). They are workhorses, often originally from the company itself. They ensure good compliance and place the responsibility for success with others.

Jim Collins

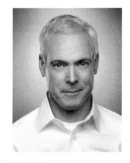
Jim Collins

Excellent companies

2 **Who before what**. The trick is to get the right people in the right places, and to get rid of the wrong people. Only then should one start determining direction and strategy.

3 **Culture of discipline**. If staff and operating methods are sufficiently disciplined, a company no longer needs bureaucracy or hierarchy. Entrepreneurship combined with a culture of discipline is the magic mix for amazing achievements.

4 **Face hard facts without losing faith**. The truth should be allowed adequate room to present itself through the creation of a climate which makes it possible for people to be heard.

5 **The Hedgehog concept**. After Greek writer Archilochus, who writes the following in one of his fables: 'The fox knows many things, but the hedgehog knows one important thing: the insight into one's potential for excellence.' According to Collins, this principle is constructed of the answers to three component questions: what activities offer a possibility for our company to be the best in the world, which activities are we the most passionate about, and which activities can earn us money?

6 **Technology**. While never being a factor that is crucial to success, the technologies that are applied should be selected carefully.

7 **The flywheel**. An excellent company does not simply happen; it is like putting into motion a great flywheel. Slow to start, it eventually starts to gain momentum. The size and scope of the transformation are only visible in hindsight.

8 **Safeguarding the core and stimulating progress**. The company's core values, what do we represent, must be safeguarded and preserved. The operational methods, on the other hand, should continually be adjusted to changes in circumstances.

Kjell Anders Nordström (b. 1958) and Jonas Ridderstråle (b. 1966) and changes in organisations

Kjell Nordström and Jonas Ridderstråle may be seen as the pioneers in a new generation of European business gurus.

Nordström and Ridderstråle met at the Institute of International Business at the Stockholm School of Economics. Their refreshing perspective on current management and their lively style of presentation make them popular speakers at conventions: Kjell and Jonas are 'rebels with a cause'. Their unorthodox combination of academic accuracy, powerful logic, and funky free-thinking spirit have led them to rewrite evolutionist rules.

Kjell Anders Nordström

Jonas Ridderstråle

Funky business

Together, they wrote the bestselling works *Funky Business: Talent Makes Capital Dance* (1999), *Karaoke Capitalism: Management for Mankind* (2004), and the sequel to *Funky Business*: *Funky Business Forever: How To Enjoy Capitalism* (2007).

In *Funky Business*, they describe how businesses (Funky Inc.) should become more fun places to be – places where people use their talents and are able to apply their creativity. Places where ideas come to life and interesting products in particular are developed more quickly. In short: funky places. First and foremost, funky business means diversity. Go for extremes, take risks, break rules, set new ones, shape the future. In order to survive, one needs to draw attention. Whatever one does, it should not be to think in terms of right or wrong. Whatever is, is. Irrelevance is a much greater problem than inefficiency. Doing business, according to the authors, is not a matter of science. It is simply one of making money. It is matter of having bits, brains, and brands. Brands are valium for our souls, and the world is the stage.

Their second book, *Karaoke Capitalism*, is more of a manifesto. It highlights their political and ideological notions. They describe how one may become successful in a world of 'karaoke capitalism'. The karaoke economy is dominated with individuals who have limitless options and possibilities available to them. For corporate life, the problem is that the karaoke club is also a breeding ground of institutionalised imitation; there are copy-cats aplenty. Nordström and Ridderstråle issue a calls to arms for greater creativity, originality, and imaginativeness, thus improving innovation. According to the authors, Karl Marx was correct: employees have no control over the production process. Instead, a 3-pound lump of grey matter, the brain, holds the key to the future. Successful enterprises distinguish themselves from their less successful competitors by recognising this fact, as a result of which they are able to more effectively put to use the intellectual and creative talents of their employees. In the New Economy, talent inspires capital to move around. The humdrum of current corporate life is no longer enough to retain employees, just like boring companies are unable to retain customers. Funky business is what is needed.

In *Funky Business Forever*, Nordströn and Ridderstråle describe how companies should have acted following the IT-boom at the end of the 2oth century. Central to their discussion are change and 'the desire to be different'. Talent is the only thing that makes one unique and think about the future.

Karaoke economy

Kjell Anders Nordström
Jonas Ridderstråle

Gary Hamel (b. 1954) and the future of management

Gary Hamel is often seen as one of the most important business thinkers, an expert in the field of business strategy.

Hamel has worked at London Business School since 1983, currently as a guest-professor of the Strategic and International Management department. Together with Prahalad, he invented the concept of 'core competences'. His book *Leading the Revolution and Competing for the Future* (1998) earned particular recognition. Hamel used this work to describe how innovations, instead of efficiency, should be the leading principle in business operations. New organisational concepts are a requirement for business success in the dotcom-era. Just like quality, innovation should be the responsibility of all employees. Key words for achieving success according to Hamel are speed, reorganising the self, tapping new markets and distribution channels.

Gary Hamel

In his most recent work, *The Future of Management*, co-written with Bill Breen in 2007, the authors argue that the current model of management has become obsolete, and that several companies have already replaced it with one of various alternatives resulting in greater innovation and a better fit with the knowledge economy.

The Future of
Management

Gary Hamel

Company management-DNA is still based on achieving improvements in productivity through systematic management under the principles of:

a standardisation;
b specialisation;
c objective outlining;
d hierarchy;
e planning;
f control and extrinsic rewards.

Key principles of new management are:

a diversity;
b enabling active experimentation;
c de-politisation of decision making;
d making use of the wisdom of masses and markets;
e de-centralisation of leadership;
f accountability from the top to the first line.

Involving all employees in the company is of crucial importance when trying to create a democracy of ideas, to reinforce human imagination, to pool collective wisdom – thus ensuring everyone has a chance to participate. In doing so, none of the employees are drained of their natural human resilience. To this end, management principles need to be revised. In the management of the future, obedience, zeal, and factual knowledge need to make room for initiative, creativity, and passion. There are companies like Google and Whole Foods Market who are already working from this vision and following certain of its principles. Their emphasis is not on the top layer, but on teams lower down the organisational ladder, and they offer employees relatively large chunks of free time to employ their creativity.

Hamel is a great advocate of management innovation: Make change into an ingrained principle.

Eckart Wintzen (1939–2008) and cell philosophy

Eckart Wintzen

'If you want to grow quickly, be sure to remain small'. Becoming big by staying small seems a contradiction in terms but, as is often the case with the entrepreneur, inspirer, and management guru Eckart Wintzen, apparent impossibilities often lead to quite fine results.

Wintzen founded his IT-company BSO in 1976. It was the first company in the world to publish an annual report for kids, compiled and written in such a way that a child could understand it. But BSO and Eckart reached their claim to fame mainly through cell philosophy. Wintzen transformed BSO from a handful of people to a company of 6,000 employees when he bade his farewell in 1996. At the time, BSO/Origin was the Netherlands' number one IT-service provider. BSO was sold to Philips – a turnover of 375 million Euros in 21 countries.

Eckart Wintzen

Though his company BSO grew like wildfire, Wintzen viewed the growth as a mixed blessing; he did not really have any interest in being the 'big boss' of a major company. So, when BSO reached its first milestone of around 50 employees, he came up with a ruse: he created a second BSO. The company was split up into two approximately equal-sized 'cells'. The manager of one cell would have no trouble remembering the names of all their staff members, and could take greater responsibility for everything that went on in a cell. Decisive individual cells ensured better results than a juggernaut controlled top-down, and soon the two cells became four cells – and this cellular division kept going at a rapid pace. BSO grew extra quickly by staying small. The various companies were able to work fully independently, and could come up with their own ideas on what to do and how to do it.

Despite Wintzen's success, his unique management and business philosophy never received a very large following. Exceptional companies do appear to depend greatly on exceptional leaders. Ten years after the individual cells had re-merged into a 'normal' company, Wintzen offered his thoughts on the matter in his book *Eckart's Notes*. That the current managers never worked in the BSO-cells is not an objection; Eckart's ideas are inspirational nevertheless. He feels that the main idea is to place one's faith in employees instead of imposing one's rules on subordinates. Which, actually, fits in very well with modern-day management philosophies, such as those of servant leadership and the flat organisational structure that many companies strive for, with a broadly supported sense of responsibility.

Long after Wintzen offered his employees greater freedom, and thus achieved success upon success, his ideas do seem to have taken the long way to become very topical. Wintzen referred to himself as a realist, not an idealist. He was a driven and busy man.

Don Tapscott (b. 1947) and Wikinomics

Don Tapscott writes influential best-sellers on digital revolutions and the necessity for innovation in a rapidly changing world. His motto: listen closely to 'the generation' and make room for massive-scale cooperation via the world wide web.

On the advice of a friend's daughter, he took up Twitter; somebody like him, involved with everything innovation-related on a daily basis, should really be taking part in the new digital world instead of analysing the situation from the side-lines, should he not? The 64-year-old Canadian best-selling author of works including *Growing up digital* and *Wikinomics* (2006) uses his personally compiled Twitter newspaper *The Don Tapscott Innovators Daily* to tweet about his specialist subject: innovation. He is inspired by the net-generation; young people like his friend's daughter, who has over 160 RSI-feeds constantly pushing new messages to her phone or computer. He is a strong believer in reversed monitoring. The younger generate should mentor the older one, not the other way around. His last book, *The Blockchain Revolution*, was published in 2016. Blockchain will be further discussed in Chapter 4.

Don Tapscott

Don Tapscott

Steve Jobs (1955-2011): visionary master of simplicity

The death of the CO-founder and former CEO of Apple in 2011 meant the loss of one of the technology sector's most important icons. Black turtleneck, white sneakers, marketing genius. But also a hippy, fruitarian, Buddhist, and Dylan afficionado. Jobs was born to an American mother and a Syrian father in 1955. He grew up in a foster home. His childhood home was where he and Steve Wozniak put together the first Apple computer in 1976. Jobs felt that other computer enthusiasts were looking for a machine they could program themselves. And thus: Apple's basis for the personal computer. Wozniak was a genius technician, Jobs a passionate, visionary salesman. Thanks to the Apple II – a machine with a keyboard – it even became possible for non-nerds to use a computer. When Apple became a listed company in 1980, 25-year-old Steve Jobs suddenly had over 200 million dollars to his name. The real growth of the computer market headed by the IBM-PC in 1981 had not yet even begun. In 1985, Jobs had to depart Apple. He was not a suitable manager. Employees from those early years offered their thoughts on the situation in their biographies, describing fierce tantrums, Jobs' lack of overview, his meddlesomeness, and his compulsive tendency towards perfection. Regarding his forced departure from Apple, Jobs later commented: 'It felt as though somebody punched me in the stomach and knocked the air from my lungs. I had just turned thirty and I wanted a chance to make things.'

Steve Jobs

Steve Jobs

With his second computer company, NeXT, Jobs was again tripped up by his perfectionism. Hardly any of the very expensive NeXT-computers were actually sold. When NeXt collapsed, Jobs was asked to become a consultant at Apple, which had hit bottom. Jobs proved that he had learned from his mistakes, and that marriage and fatherhood had had a calming effect on him. His other project, the Pixar film company, became a huge success.

Jobs saved Apple through a few simple interventions. He reconciled with arch-rival Microsoft and used NeXT-software as the basis for the new operating system, OS X. Following the self-assured iMac, designed by Jobs' protégé Jonathan Ive, came the stark-white iPod in 2001. Apple rebranded itself from a make for nerds and geeks to one for the masses. The iPod and the iTunes store changed the face of the music industry: instead of CDs, the public preferred to purchase individual songs. Later, in 2007, the iPhone was the start of a mobile internet access revolution that forced market leader Nokia to its knees. The iPad was Jobs' next trump card: a very easy to use, portable alternative to the standard desktop PC. Competitors thought it was an apparently superfluous gadget, but it proved a best-seller. The 'App-revolution' is also completely due to Steve Jobs who, after all, designed the iCloud-webservice.

Jobs was a master of simplicity, in terms of both design and use. All Apple devices and matching software had one thing in common: they were designed to make 'complicated' technology accessible. Choosing what a device should *not* be able to do was one of the most important steps of the design process, according to Jobs.

Jobs found himself at death's door more than once, a subject on which he spoke at Stanford College in Palo Alto, California, in 2005. It was an unusually personal speech. 'Stay hungry, stay foolish', he encouraged the Stanford-students. 'Listen to yourself and try to find something you truly love. Follow your heart as though it is the last day of your life.'

Daniel H. Pink

Daniel H. Pink (1964) and the changing role of work

Daniel H. Pink (1964) is the author of several provocative, bestselling books about the motivation for changes on the workplace and the changing world of work. His latest book is called *To Sell is Human: The Surprising Truth About Moving Others* (2012). But of greater importance is his best-selling *Drive: The Surprising Truth About What Motivates Us* (2009).

In *Drive*, Pink describes what motivated people. Over the past decades, various theories have been put forward with regards to peoples' drive. Pink describes three so-called Motivators. These are 'Motivator 1.0', the need to survive, which is what activates people; 'Motivator 2.0', which encompasses the management of people through punishment and reward. For most organisations, this is the basis of their policy; 'Motivator 3.0' is based on the paradigm that people are activated only when they are intrinsically motivated, by using their strengths, and by feeling useful. In his book, Pink describes the fact that Motivator 2.0 is outdated and how managers should use Motivator 3.0 to motivate people.

This new approach provides three essential elements which create drive:

Daniel H. Pink

1 **Autonomy**: the desire to direct our own (working) life after our image.
2 **Mastery**: the desire to keep improving in a relevant field, a field that motivates us.

3 **Purpose**: the desire to be part of something greater than ourselves, for example the ability to influence the life of someone less fortunate.

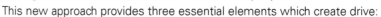

Clayton Christensen (b. 1952) and disruption

Clayton M. Christensen (1952) is the Kim B. Clark Professor of Business Administration at the Harvard Business School, where he teaches one of the most popular elective classes: 'Building and sustaining a successful enterprise.' He is regarded as one of the world's top experts in innovation and growth and his ideas have been widely used in industries and organisations throughout the world. His book *The Innovator's Dilemma* (1997) emphasises his ideas on disruptive innovation.

Clayton Christensen

Clayton Christensen

Most technologies are used to improve the performance of existing products using criteria currently applied by existing customers. Christensen calls these technologies 'sustaining'. Sustaining technologies are contrasted with so-called disruptive technologies, which create an entirely new value proposition. They improve the performance of products using new performance criteria. Products created through disruptive technologies are often smaller, cheaper, simpler, and easier to use than existing alternatives. At the moment of their introduction, however, they are not (yet) able to compete with the established, traditional products, which means there is no large market available.
Christensen performed a thorough analysis of how disruptive technologies have evolved in, for example, the computer disc industry, an industry evolving at lightning-speed.

Disruptive innovation is subject to the following set of four principles:

1 In well-managed companies, it is customers, not managers, who actually determine the patterns of resource allocation. In essence, middle-managers in companies do not tend to invest in technologies that important clients will not immediately appreciate, since these are not investments that will help them score a quick financial win.
2 Small markets cannot meet the growth needs of large companies. There are several arguments in favour of company growth. However, the fact is: the larger a company, the more difficulty it has to continue to grow. A small company (turnover of 40 million Euros) with a growth target of 20% will need to realise an 8 million increase in turnover. Applying the same growth target to a large company (turnover of 4 billion Euros) means they will have to realise an additional 800 million in turnover. Emerging markets are generally not large enough to satisfy the growth needs of big businesses; they are, however, large enough for small companies.
3 A market that does not exist cannot be analysed. The final application of a disruptive technology cannot be known beforehand. Failure is an intrinsic step along the path to success.
4 Available technology is not always equal to market demand. The speed of technological performance is often greater than that of the development of consumer needs. The performance improvement of disruptive technologies (for example the 3.5-inch disk, initially only used in the market for small laptop PCs) prepares innovations for their use in a larger market (the desktop-PC market).

In 2010, Chistensen, in a now famous speech, addressed the graduates of Harvard Business School of that year. Drawing from his extensive research, he offered them a series of guidelines for a life that is successful, happy, and meaningful in all respects. The speech went viral across social media and led to one of the most often read articles ever in the authoritative *Harvard Business Review*. Later, it resulted in the book *How Will You Measure Your Life*, in which Christensen poses the question of whether insights used in management theory can also be applied to managing personal situations. The question became more laden when Christensen found his life threatened by illness. His answer was: do not look for 'quick solutions', but think about 'how to solve problems'. Coming up with a solution on one's own turns out to offer a very effective intrinsic reward (happiness). His last book, *Competing Against Luck, The Story of Innovation and Customer Choice*, was published in 2016.

Stephen Covey

Stephen Covey

Stephen Covey (1932-2012) and the seven habits of effective leadership

Stephen Covey was a major guru in the field of living and working effectively. He wrote 12 management books in total; his best-known book *The 7 Habits of Highly Effective People* (1989) sold over 25 million copies worldwide. Born in Salt Lake City, Covey was a practicing member of The Church of Jesus Christ of Latter-day Saints; he was a missionary of the church in Ireland for 2 years. He was connected to (Mormon) Brigham Young University. Stephen Covey founded the Covey Leadership Center in 1985; over the course of ten years, the centre grew into a company of 750 employees, recording a turnover of over 100 million.

Until his death at the age of 80 years old, he travelled far and wide to promote his ideas. Among managers, Covey enjoyed 'heroic status', and he was one of the most frequently asked management speakers. He also had a number of respectable clients in the Netherlands, including AH, ABN-AMRO, Philips, and Grolsch.

The *7 Habits* in the title of Covey's best-seller are habits one should ingrain into one's personality through force of will. Covey originally formulated them as seven commandments.

According to Covey, permanent success can only be achieved through the strive for the following seven habits:

1 **Be proactive.** One's life depends on one's choices, not on one's circumstances. One should take responsibility and make conscious decisions and exert one's influence. Proactive people often have a growth mind-set (a desire for learning) and look for solutions, alternatives, and possibilities. Reactive people are quick to look for the causes of problems elsewhere than themselves. That means they also quickly stop thinking about what influence they may exert.

2 **Start by visualising a goal/objective.** Effective people look at things differently than less effective people; they see more and are able to visualise the details of their goals with greater clarity. They are able to place their day-to-day actions within a wider context of their larger ambitions. This offers them a source of focus which improves their possible effectiveness.

3 **Important matters come first.** Learn to prioritise after one's goals have been set. This habit is about dealing with the temporal factor: time management.

4 **Think in terms of win/win.** Win/win is an attitude which requires the continuous search for profit in interaction. Decisions and solutions should, therefore, be advantageous to all parties concerned; they should leave all those involved feeling satisfied and committed to the plan.

5 **First understand, then be understood.** Many people listen to others judgementally. Very effective people try simply to listen. They are able to empathise with another's thoughts and feelings very well.

6 **Strive for synergy.** Synergy is the most inspirational habit. Covey sees it as the sum of the first 5 habits. Everything seems to be going effortlessly and smoothly; a certain 'flow' is achieved.

7 **Keep fit.** Covey describes how proper maintenance and care, as well as moments of intensive reflection with regards to one's physical, mental, social-emotional, and spiritual aspects lead to improvement and renewal, and thus to growth.

His philosophy and ideas are timeless and have inspired generation after generation.

Martin Seligman and positive psychology

Martin Seligman is an American psychologist. He graduated in philosophy at the Princeton University and earned his PhD in psychology at the University of Pennsylvania in 1967. He has chaired the Positive Psychology Network since 2000. Since the beginning of the 21st century, he has mainly focussed his attention on positive psychology, a movement born from humanist psychology. Together with Mihaly Csikszentmihalyi, Seligman continued on the groundwork of this movement, resulting in positive psychology. This form of psychology mainly focusses on what makes people happy.

Martin Seligman

Martin Seligman

Formerly, psychology in the US placed emphasis on addressing problems and negative aspects of existence. Positive psychology is a movement that is based on a person's strengths under the premise that happiness is not merely the result of the right genetic make-up or simple luck, but of identifying and utilising a person's strengths and qualities. It places emphasis on one's possibilities instead of one's impossibilities. Recognising and encouraging competences and virtues earns better results than correcting weaknesses: prevail instead of bewail. Humanity as a whole and the development of humanity's strengths is the focus. These strengths are the positive, functional, and health-promoting forces (core qualities). Core qualities are positive mental mechanisms which engender a feeling of fulfilment not just in individuals, but also in the people around them.

Seligman became particularly well-known for his books *Authentic Happiness* (2004) and *Flourish* (2011).

Kim Cameron and positive leadership

Cameron is one of the co-founders of the Centre for Positive Organizational Scholarship at the University of Michigan. This research centre focusses on studying positive outlying performances, virtuousness, strengths, and organisational approaches that lead to remarkable achievements. Cameron studied at Yale University (administrative sciences). His studies in the fields of virtue, effectiveness, quality and contractionary policy, and the development of leadership skills have been published in over 120 scientific articles and 14 books. His best-known book is *Positive Leadership* (2008).

Kim Cameron

Kim Cameron

Cameron originally devoted the bulk of his career to researching the effects of forced redundancy. In most organisations, this practice led to negative effects such as distrust, conflict, and long-term performance dips. Among the organisations that experienced a happier conclusion, factors like forgiveness, compassion, and gratefulness were essential. These findings made Cameron redirect his focus to what is now known as Positive Organisational Scholarship; positive psychology for companies, prioritising positive leadership.

This leadership style is a determining factor for organisational culture. A positive approach can lead to improved performance, improved commitment, and improved organisational culture. Positive leadership focusses on work-related wellbeing, human strengths, resilience, and development. Attention, compassion, understanding, and the use of positive forces in everyday organisational practice leads to positive results. In practice, this means an active quest for positive deviations. Where and when are expectations exceeded? What is going exceptionally well? The art is in recognising and reinforcing the behaviour that is at the foundation of those achievements. Positive leadership also means working on good relationships at work, listening sincerely and investing in colleagues, taking them seriously, helping each other: in short, creating an energising culture. Leaders have a great influence on employee wellbeing and on productivity. Positive leadership revolves around personal interaction and is an exceptionally powerful force in organisation.

Chapter 9, Leadership, addresses the conceptualisation behind positive leadership.

Summary

▶ The subject of organisational behaviour was first taught in the US after 1850.
Between 1960 and 1970, organisational behaviour as it is known today developed in the Netherlands. The underlying driving force was the increasing complexity and growth of organisation.

▶ Organisational behaviour is an interdisciplinary science that focusses on the study of:
  – behaviour in organisations;
  – factors that determine this behaviour;
  – the most effective ways of directing organisations.

▶ The definition of organisational behaviour encompasses two aspects:
  – a descriptive aspect: describing the behaviour of organisations with their motives and consequences;
  – a prescriptive aspect: offering advice on the recommended approach and organisational design.

▶ The schools of thought and individuals covered in this chapter all had an influence on the development on the subject of organisational behaviour. The following is a list of key concepts per school of thought.

School of though	Key concepts
Nicollò Machiavelli (1469-1527)	Power and opportunism
Adam Smith (1723-1790)	Task division and productivity
Scientific Management (ong. 1900)	Organising production and efficiency
Henri Fayol (1841-1925)	General management theory
Max Weber (1864-1920)	Bureaucracy and organisation ideal type
Human Relations (c. 1945)	Informal organisation and subjectiveness
Neo-Human Relations (c. 1950)	Synthesis of Scientific Management and Human Relations: aligning human beings and organisations
Systems approach (c. 1950)	The organisation as a system and the interplay between organisation and environment
Contingency approach (c. 1965)	Applicability of management techniques depends on the situation
Philip Crosby (1926-2001)	Quality care in organisations
Henry Mintzberg (from c. 1979)	Configuration theory and seven configurations
Tom Peters (from c. 1982)	Management principles for good business operations
Peter Drucker (1909-2005)	Knowledge as an essential production factor
Michael Porter (from c. 1980)	Competitive advantage
Michael Hammer (1948-2008)	Restructuring operational processes
C.K. Prahalad (1941-2010)	Competition, innovation, globalisation
Jim Collins (from c. 2001)	Corporate culture and leadership
Kjell Nordstrom and Jonas Ridderstråle (from c. 1999)	Changes in organisations
Gary Hamel (from c. 1994)	Future of management
Eckart Wintzen (1939-2008)	Cell philosophy
Don Tapscott (2006)	The role of new technologies
Steve Jobs (1955-2011)	Master of simplicity
Daniel H. Pink (1964)	The changing role of work
Clayton Christensen (1952)	Disruption
Stephen Covey (1932-2012)	The 7 habits of effective leadership
Martin Seligman (1942), Kim Cameron (1946) and positive leadership	Positive leadership

This section examines the ways in which organisations interact with their surroundings. Initially, the focus is on the environmental factors that exert an influence on organisations. Then, it shifts to the ways in which organisations determine their heading in view of these factors. These strategies can sometimes lead to collaborations between various organisations.

PART A
ORGANISATIONS AND THEIR ENVIRONMENT

INTERVIEW WITH RAYMOND CLOOSTERMAN, FOUNDER OF RITUALS

Rituals' founder Cloosterman (1964) is sometimes referred to as the Dutch answer to James Bond: always trying to beat the competition, at sports, at games. His examples are Apple's Steve Jobs van Apple and Starbucks' Howard Schultz; no lack of self-confidence there. His cosmetics company Rituals is the best-growing company in the Netherlands. Rituals sells deluxe bath and care product, scented candles, tea, and leisure wear with a story. With a turnover well over 400 million Euros and an incredible circulation speed, Cloosterman has managed to work without a major marketing budget. Rituals first looks for the story of an ancient ritual. Next, the company matches the tale to natural ingredients and develops a product. This development process is supported by an anthropologist and perfumers. There is no marketing research: the shop floor is Cloosterman's lab. Turning day-to-day care into ritual, a well-thought out concept, that is the strength of Rituals.

Raymond Cloosterman started with Unilever following a study in business economics. A new job as marketing director meant a half year on tour to find inspiration for new products. Following visits to Indian temples, Turkish bath houses, and New York and Paris

boutiques, the result was a fully developed business plan which Cloosterman felt was so good that he opted to set it up outside of Unilever himself. He launched Rituals in 2000.

What, in hindsight, were key moments for the company?

Cloosterman: 'First, there was Unilever's decision to invest in Rituals for the first two years. Even though we were an autonomous company founded in part using our own savings, Unilever's support was essential. The second key moment came after some four years, working day and night and seeing little progress. We decided that it should not be the retail outlets but our own stores that should become the heart of the company. At the same time, we raised our standards: we wanted to compete only with the best products. That was a very important decision. We joined forces with the best perfumers, with providers of the finest ingredients. It also meant having to start over nearly from scratch. The third key moment was our breakthrough in Sweden and Germany circa 2014. That was the first time we found that our reputation had apparently preceded us. Business was good from the start. Germany was particularly important.'

So, those first years, Rituals was not an immediate success. Why do you think that was?

'Our passion is to make our clients enjoy the little things in life. Our dream is to build a global brand; something that required millions of Euros we did not actually have. So, we had to 'conquer' our clients one at a time, catch them by surprise, and hope they would spread the word of the quality of our product. That is a time-consuming process. Secondly, we may have been ahead of our time. Concepts like 'conscious enjoyment' and 'mindfulness' are found everywhere now, but they were not then. It was a pioneering effort, in that respect. We were the first to combine elegant stores and fine products with fair prices. That was another reason why things were so difficult at first: lower prices mean lower margins. And lower margins are only sustainable with sufficient economies of scale. The first few years were a matter of persevering. Now, things are coming together, and we can begin investing in continued innovation.'

All Rituals products have their origins in authentic and ancient Far Eastern rituals. What made you decide to use Asian rituals and habits as the foundation for the brand?

'People all over the world live their lives at high speed and do things on auto-pilot, so I looked for a way to change that. I believed then and I believe now that the way to achieve this is by realising that everyday routines should be transformed into meaningful moments. In practice, that means I wanted to reinvent and transform regular products, like shower gels and shaving foams, into something special. I had been working in this business for 15 years, and starting my own business was the only way of

changing things and taking an entirely different approach. I decided to take a step back, to look for and to find inspiration abroad. My travels made me realise that, in our western world, we are always striving for innovation and renewal without looking at the past. Ancient eastern cultures actually treasure the wisdom of the past. That was when I understood I had found my niche.'

Responsible enterprise, how important is that?

'Rituals strives to use the finest sustainable and bio-organic ingredients. We do not employ animal testing and are members of the Dierproefvrij foundation, the Dutch foundation to prevent the use of animal testing. We also try to minimise our CO_2 footprint. All materials used are recyclable. None of our products use harmful chemicals like parabens. We feel it is very important to find new ways of reducing our impact on our planet, and have made some important steps to that end. For example, we asked LCA-Center to conduct Life Cycle Assessment (LCA)-studies on our product packaging. We also offer refill products for our body and face creams and hand soaps. Our eco-chic refill system lets you cut back on CO_2 by 70%, on energy by 65%, and on water by 45%. To reduce our ecological footprint, we produce as close to home as possible. Currently, 98% of end products are made in Europe. In addition, we only use FSC-certified paper for secondary packaging and are trying our very hardest to achieve our goal of 100% recyclable packaging by 2023.'

In 2017, Rituals was the fastest growing company in the Netherlands. How did you manage that?

'Rituals started by working on brand recognition and company appeal through shop-in-shops. At the time, it was important for our chain to secure a spot in the Dutch Bijenkorf chain of department stores. There are two advantages to starting in another store: people walk past shops they do not know, but if they are already in a familiar one, they will happily take a look. And you can immediately position your brand among other well-known products; in our case, Chanel. That was a boost for our products as well. To ensure that clients who have visited our stores continue to come back, Rituals makes sure to offer 300 new products every year. New products are good for clients and staff alike: people like to work with something new. The goal is global domination: we have already expanded to the US and have set our sights on Asia. Just as long as local DNA and the Dutch mentality that is characteristic of Rituals are blended in the proper proportions. The need to de-stress is ubiquitous.'

Source: www.sprout.nl, www.deondernemer. nl, *de Volkskrant*, 28 February 2017, www. quotenet.nl

1

ENVIRONMENTAL INFLUENCES

Contents

After studying this chapter:

– you will be able to identify the various environmental factors and stakeholders that exert an influence on the organisation;
– you will have gained insight into how these influences affect individual organisations.

Catawiki, online auction house

Catawiki is one of the Netherlands' fastest growing companies. The online auction house currently employs over five hundred people. Founded in Assen, the Netherlands in 2008, Catawiki is one of the fastest growing start-ups in Europe. The company is rapidly expanding and earns money through the commission and provision from the buyers and sellers at the numerous auctions the platform provides. Catawiki is paid 12.5% on all items by sellers, as well as a percentage of commission by buyers.

Jewellery, stamps, and other products: Catawiki auctions off anything collectable. Every week, the company hosts a variety of auctions open to bidders the world over. Catawiki has offices in Germany, France, Spain, and Italy. Over the past years, Catawiki has expanded its range of auction categories. In addition to art, antiques, and true collectables, the company now also auctions off luxury goods, such as watches and jewellery.

Catawiki's rapid growth requires funding: the online auction house doubled its income to 35 million Euros in 2016, while tripling its losses to over 22 million Euros. Staff and advertising fees placed the heaviest burden on the results.

Expectations are that the company will continue its line of growth over the coming years, both in terms of staffing as well as the application of new technology, such as machine learning and artificial intelligence, with new technologies currently seen as a driving force behind the intended growth.

Source: www.catawiki.com, www.sprout.nl

1.1 INTRODUCTION

Organisations are part of society, of daily life. Human society can be seen as the

Environment environment in which organisations function.

Stakeholders An organisation's environment consists of parties or stakeholders like buyers, suppliers, competitors and financiers. All of these exert a certain influence on organisations: they inspect the products or services of an organisation, and place demands that must be met to a satisfactory level. Some examples of these demands are favourable pricing, environmentally friendly production and packaging, good quality materials and quick delivery.

Organisations can, however, also exert an influence on the aforementioned individuals and parties through such means as advertising campaigns, supplying information, providing advice, products and services, and maintaining direct contact with their stakeholders.

In addition, an organisation can be affected by environmental influences over which it does not have any significant control, but which are of high significance to the market. These aspects include economic development, technological development, climate, and demographic developments. These macro factor influences are called environmental factors.

Environmental influences

Environmental factors

Figure 1.1 shows the most important stakeholder and environmental factors that exert an influence on organisations.

FIGURE 1.1 **THE ORGANISATION WITH SURROUNDING STAKEHOLDERS AND EXTERNAL FACTORS**

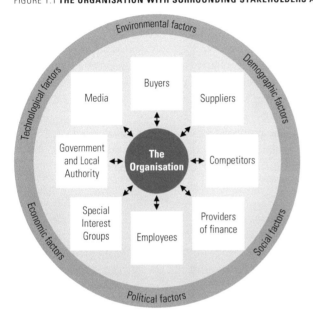

Environmental influence generates circumstances which organisations must take into careful account. Many organisations find themselves confronted by extremely unstable circumstances which have to be dealt with appropriately and effectively – possibly in the form of significant changes to the products and or services offered, or a revision of pricing strategy to change the pricing position within the market. Other examples are changes in delivery methods, production processes, organisation size and structure, the location of premises, employee relations, and so on.

Directing an organisation by taking into account the influence of its surroundings is known as harmonisation or alignment. This chapter examines the influence that stakeholders and environmental factors have on organisations.

Harmonisation

1.2   STAKEHOLDERS

As indicated in the introduction, the most significant direct influence on organisations is exerted by stakeholders and surroundings. This section discusses the influence of the following stakeholders:
– buyers;
– suppliers;
– competitors;

- capital providers;
- employees;
- special interest groups;
- government and local authority institutions;
- media.

An important aspect of these parties is the extent to which their position is dominant.

Buyers

Buyers

Known alternatively as buyers, clients, consumers or customers, this is an important group as it is the one demanding products and services. An organisation gains its right to exist by its ability to satisfy these demands. Consumer demands often change and organisations must take these changes into account when determining the composition and features of their product range.

In recent years, there have been many new products introduced onto the market as a result of changes in buyer demands, ranging from new low-fat dairy products to electrical cars, environmentally friendly washing powders, smartphones, tablets, medical equipment, cloud computing solutions, battery switching stations for cars, and new forms of mortgage and insurance.

If an organisation pays insufficient attention to changing consumer needs, the existing available products may become less popular and, as a consequence, the organisation may lose customers. Customers therefore exert a critical influence on organisations!

Suppliers

Suppliers

Every organisation uses products or services from other organisations. Thus, as a buyer, an organisation imposes demands on its suppliers, with respect to quality, price level and delivery time. An organisation's own products and services are, after all, dependent on these aspects. In recent years, supplier relationships have undergone major changes. Increased international competition has, for example, caused many changes in the choice of suppliers. In the past, there was a preference for local suppliers – but now the recurring trend is for businesses to search for suppliers across national borders. Another aspect of these business-to-business relationships that deserves attention is that buyers now want to reduce their stock held, and demand 'just-in-time' delivery from their suppliers.

Competitors

Competitors

Almost every organisation has to deal with competition. Competitors more or less determine the amount of flexibility organisations have with respect to product features, pricing, quality, distribution channels, R&D activities, advertising budgets, and so on. It is therefore of vital importance to monitor the activities of major competitors and to analyse their relative market positions.

Capital providers

Capital providers

Organisations must maintain good relationships with financiers or capital providers, such as shareholders, financial institutions, and the government.

After all, an organisation is often dependent on finance to maintain its activities, expand operations and sometimes even remain in its existing form. Providers of finance who become dissatisfied with the performance or practices of an organisation can turn off the financial supply. This can create huge problems for

What will the future hold?

2018

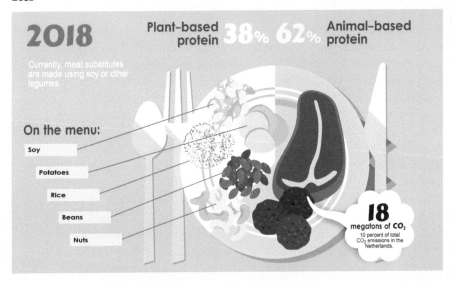

2025

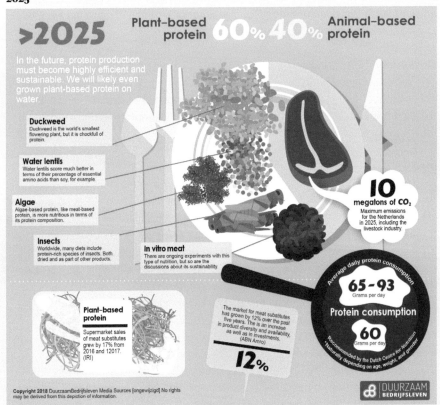

Source: *Duurzaam bedrijfsleven*, 2018

Environmental influences
CHAPTER 1

the organisation, and pose a potential threat to its survival. In large enterprises, major financiers are often represented by supervisory bodies, such as the Board of Commissioners.

Employees

Employees Cooperation and support

The employees of an organisation are its most important asset and can be seen as a critical success factor. The modern employees of the 21st century are more highly trained, liberated and individualistic than their predecessors. These employees play an even greater role in product and organisational innovations, as well as in quality improvement. Their cooperation and support influence the organisation's choice of direction, as well as its strategies in relation to social responsibility and social policy.

In other words, the employees are the players on the field who will need to gain the advantage over their competition; players that management definitely needs to take into account.

Special interest groups

Special interest groups

This group of stakeholders includes those bodies that focus on the interests of a particular group of people. Many such groups exist, and include employee and employer federations (for example, trade unions and national industry confederations), consumer organisations (homeowner's associations, car owners' associations), organisations involved in corporate social responsibility, environmental activists (Greenpeace), and other organisations targeting specific subjects (refugee relief, illness support groups).

Government authorities

Government authorities

The implementation of government policy is performed by government authorities. These authorities influence organisations through the application of legislation to the organisational field. An example is of police officers enforcing legislation with regard to opening and closing hours.

Media

Media

In the current information era, the media (including the Internet, newspapers, weekly magazines, television and radio) play a very important role. The attention of the media is directed at everything that takes place in society and has any meaning for the individuals in that society. Developments in the economy, politics and business are watched closely. International communication satellites ensure that people are informed almost instantaneously about events taking place as far away as the other side of the world – via, for example, the internet.

The role of social media, such as Instagram, Facebook, YouTube, LinkedIn, Twitter, and Snapchat, is becoming increasingly important. It is crucial fort here to be continued critical review of the sources providing information, as 'fake news' is an increasingly prevalent phenomenon.

Public opinion

The media can have a big influence on public opinion. This has led to many organisations setting up public relations departments which work closely with the media to update them on their current activities.

Dominant position of stakeholders

Dominant position

The extent to which the above-mentioned stakeholders can exercise an influence on organisations is dependent on a number of factors. Of key significance is the relative dominance that such groups have at any particular moment. Through their dominant position, they can exert tremendous pressure on an organisation in many ways, including withholding funding (financiers), halting deliveries (suppliers), boycotting (customers), other organisations in the market promoting their activities (competitors), placing the organisation in a very negative light (media), or instigating industrial action, such as a strike (employees).

It should be clear that no organisation can avoid dealing with the stakeholders in its environment, and that organisations must ensure that their relationships with these parties are maintained at the best possible level.

1.3 EXTERNAL FACTORS

While external factors exert an indirect influence on organisations, organisations can only influence external factors to a limited extent. However, external factors are crucially important in determining the success of organisations. The following sections discuss the external factors listed here in greater detail:
– environmental factors (subsection 1.3.1);
– technological factors (subsection 1.3.2);
– demographic factors (subsection 1.3.3);
– economic factors (subsection 1.3.4);
– political factors (subsection 1.3.5);
– societal factors (subsection 1.3.6).

External factors

1.3.1 Environmental factors

A clean living environment and a healthy climate are important elements of a healthy economy. Vital natural capital, after all, is an essential production factor and represents significant economic value. It has been irrefutably shown that there have been significant manmade changes to the climate, and limiting any further changes requires a strong climate policy.

Climate change is a global issue, one that is not limited to the Netherlands, but also involves its most important trade partners in and outside of Europe developing their own climate policies. Collaboration with likeminded nations can help to speed up developments and get a running start to stay ahead of the rest of the pack, which will eventually also make the transition to more climate-centric policies.

Climate change

Signatories of the 2015 Paris Climate Treaty agreed to limit global warming to less than 2 degrees Celsius compared to the pre-industrial era. The actual target is an increase of no more than 1.5 degrees. Another factor is a rapid reduction to zero of the use of fossil fuels, as this constitutes a major cause of excessive carbon emission levels. The accord requires member states to draft national climate plans (National Determined Contributions), which must be ambitious and must increase in ambition with every new plan. The accord also documents that it expects signatory nations to financially support developing countries in reducing their emissions. The accord concerns the period from 2020 onwards, and was to be implemented only following ratification by 55 countries, who contribute 55% of greenhouse gasses to total emission levels. The Treaty was ratified unusually quickly: The Netherlands ratified the accord in July of 2017. By now, 195 countries have signed the Treaty.

Paris Climate Treaty

Coal usage in Europe

Of all the fossil fuels, coal is the most harmful: it contributes most in terms of emissions, and the harmful substances released when it is incinerated, such as sulfoxides, nitrogen-oxides, or particulates, are detrimental to one's health. Over 20 countries worldwide have voiced their ambition to phase out the use of coal.

Current situation in Europe
- **United Kingdom**: wants to close all coal plants by 2025, currently 8 in use.
- **The Netherlands**: wants to close all coal plants by 2030, which is the target of the Third Rutte Cabinet.
- **Belgium**: saw its final coal plant closed in 2016, which is quite a feat for a nation in which coal saw significant use.

- **Luxembourg**: decreased the use of coal from 97.8 % in 1960 to 0% in 2015.
- **Norway**: like Sweden and Iceland, reduced dependency on coal through hydropower.
- **Germany**: is looking to announce a date for shutting down its coal plants. 4 of the 5 of Europe's most polluting coal plants are found in Germany.
- **Italy**: wants to remove coals from the energy mix by 2025.
- **France**: wants to shut down all coal plants by 2021.

Source: *Het Financieele Dagblad*, Duurzaam Bedrijfsleven, nr. 14 2018

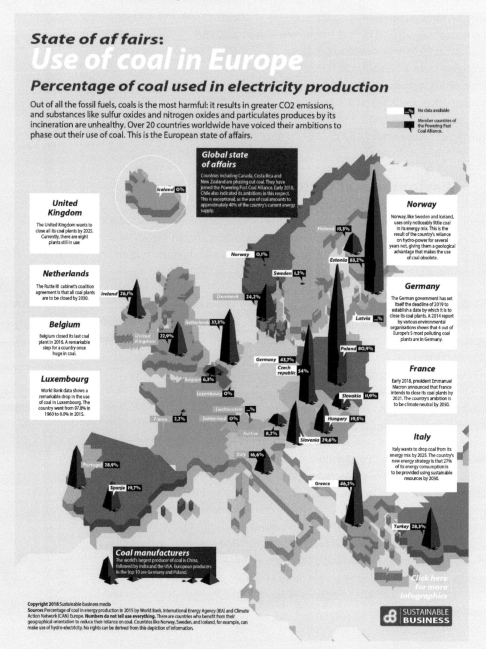

State of af fairs:

Use of coal in Europe

Percentage of coal used in electricity production

Out of all the fossil fuels, coals is the most harmful: it results in greater CO2 emissions, and substances like sulfur oxides and nitrogen oxides and particulates produces by its incineration are unhealthy. Over 20 countries worldwide have voiced their ambitions to phase out their use of coal. This is the European state of affairs.

...% No data available

Member countries of the Powering Past Coal Alliance.

Global state of affairs
Countries including Canada, Costa Rica and New Zealand are phasing out coal. They have joined the Powering Past Coal Alliance. Early 2018, Chile also indicated its ambitions in this respect. This is exceptional, as the use of coal amounts to approximately 40% of the country's current energy supply.

Iceland 0%

United Kingdom
The United Kingdom wants to close all its coal plants by 2025. Currently, there are eight plants still in use

Netherlands
The Rutte III cabinet's coalition agreement is that all coal plants are to be closed by 2030.

Belgium
Belgium closed its last coal plant in 2016. A remarkable step for a country once huge in coal.

Luxembourg
World Bank data shows a remarkable drop in the use of coal in Luxembourg. The country went from 97.8% in 1960 to 0.0% in 2015.

Norway
Norway, like Sweden and Iceland, uses only noticeably little coal in its energy mix. This is the result of the country's reliance on hydro-power for several years not, giving them a geological advantage that makes the use of coal obsolete.

Germany
The German government has set itself the deadline of 2019 to establish a date by which it is to close its coal plants. A 2014 report by various environmental organisations shows that 4 out of Europe's 5 most polluting coal plants are in Germany.

France
Early 2018, president Emmanuel Macron announced that France intends to close its coal plants by 2021. The country's ambition is to be climate neutral by 2050.

Italy
Italy wants to drop coal from its energy mix by 2025. The country's new energy strategy is that 27% of its energy consumption is to be provided using sustainable resources by 2030.

Finland 13,3%
Norway 0,1%
Estonia 83,2%
Sweden 1,2%
Denmark 24,2%
Ireland 26,1%
Netherlands 37,3%
Latvia ...%
United Kingdom 22,9%
Poland 80,9%
Germany 43,7%
Czech republic 54%
Belgium 6,3%
Luxembourg 0%
Slovakia 11,9%
Liechtenstein ...%
France 2,2%
Switzerland 0%
Hungary 19,5%
Austria 8,2%
Slovenia 29,6%
Italy 16,6%
Portugal 28,9%
Spanje 19,7%
Greece 46,2%
Turkey 28,3%

Coal manufacturers
The world's largest producer of coal is China, followed by India and the USA. European producers in the top 10 are Germany and Poland.

Click here for more infographics

Copyright 2018 Sustainable business media
Sources Percentage of coal in energy production in 2015 by World Bank, International Energy Agency (IEA) and Climate Action Network (CAN) Europe. **Numbers do not tell use everything.** There are countries who benefit from their geographical orientation to reduce their reliance on coal. Countries like Norway, Sweden, and Iceland, for example, can make use of hydro-electricity. No rights can be derived from this depiction of information.

SUSTAINABLE BUSINESS

In June of 2017, president Trump announced that the US would be withdrawing from the Accords. Formally speaking, this withdrawal cannot take effect before November of 2020. From 2023 onwards, a worldwide evaluation ("Global Stocktake") into (the reduction in) emissions will be scheduled every five years. One of the weaknesses of the Accords is that signatory nations determine their own climate objectives. Another shortcoming is the fact that no mention is made of aviation or shipping. The Accord, while binding, is not subject to any form of sanctions.

In a follow-up to the Climate Accord, seven Dutch political parties signed a national climate accord in July of 2018. The Netherlands used reports by IPCC (Intergovernmental Panel on Climate Change) as the basis for its climate policy. The most important goal is a 49% reduction in the emission of greenhouse gasses by 2030 compared to the emission levels in 1990, followed by a 95% reduction in 2050. In addition, the cabinet's European approach may lead to a further reduction, coming to 55% instead of 49% in total. Excess greenhouse gasses (particularly CO_2) cause climate change, with major repercussions for plant-life and wildlife, harvest, and water levels. This also has substantial consequences for humanity. One example is a further increase in draught levels in parts of Africa, resulting in a reduction in quality of life and forcing emigration to other countries.

Greenhouse gasses

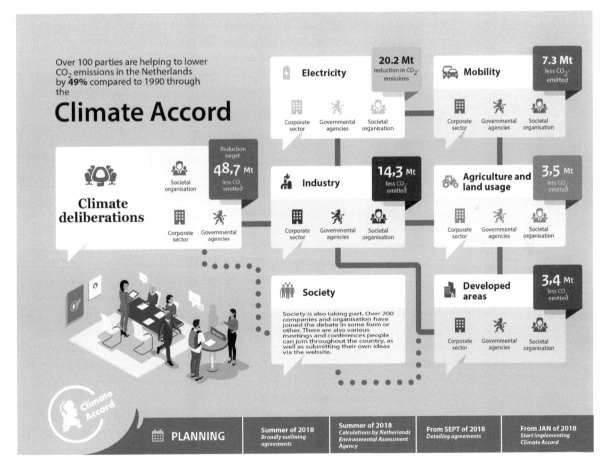

Source: Ministry of Economic Affairs and Climate Policy (Netherlands), 2018

Governments, businesses, and societal organisations have made agreements and submitted proposals for achieving the established target in five different areas. These areas and the reduction in CO_2 discussed are:

1 housing (reduce emissions by 7%);
2 electricity (reduce emissions by 41%);
3 industry (reduce emissions by 29%);
4 agriculture (reduce emissions by 7%);
5 mobility/transport (reduce emissions by 15%).

Housing. With regard to housing, proper insulation and the use of a sustainable heat source make this aspect the responsibility of all residents of the Netherlands. The Netherlands plans to shut off access to natural gas by 2050, and wants to ensure that 2 million homes are 'gas-free' by 2030. Gas taxes will gradually be raised, while taxes on electricity will gradually be lowered.

Electricity. A free electricity system is the ultimate goal. To that end, it is imperative that the switch from fossil fuels to sustainable energy is implemented quickly. Windmills are intended to provide a major contribution; there are to be additional windfarms in the sea, and windmills on land complemented with solar panels are intended to provide the remainder.

Industry. Electrification, a more efficient use of heat and warmth, and the reusing of resources are important ways of achieving the target. This aspect requires innovation and collaboration between countries.

Agriculture. Agriculture also needs to limit its emissions, for example through the reduction of methane output in the meat industry, improved use of land, restricting the use of fertiliser. An important contribution is to be made by the greenhouse and horticultural industries, for example through the use of geothermal power. In terms of food consumption, a shift from animal to plant proteins is needed.

Mobility. Electrically powered driving is a promising development in the field of mobility. Public transportation must become cleaner, and encouraging the bicycle as a mode of transport must become a priority.

Transition

The central aim of the Climate Accords, namely to reduce greenhouse gas emissions, touches on everyday life: how people live, get around, and earn a living, what they eat and buy, etcetera. Therefore, the transition is first and foremost a societal one. This transition also offers opportunities for new industry. Energy and climate ambitions will be accompanied by a strong shift in the demand for labour, and will require new skills. Government and business investments will be needed to realise the energy and climate ambitions. Civil willingness is crucial, and requires a reliable and consistent government to indicate clear directions and frameworks.

Strategic fields of interest

The environment is now seen as one of the main strategic fields of interest during the coming years. The environmental challenge for organisations has three dimensions:

1 **Cleaning up current activities**. It is vital that organisations discover and monitor the effects their activities have on the environment so that they can then begin to introduce environmental care.
2 **Utilising new opportunities**. Organisations are able to enhance offers of future products and services by repairing past environmental damage and by working to deliver new product versions developed using environmentally friendly processes.

3 **Working on a sustainable future**. Organisations must undergo radical changes to ensure a sustainable future. To put this into practice, management needs to develop a vision that utilises the new opportunities.

1.3.2 Technological factors

In the knowledge-intensive Western society, technological developments are essential for the internationally competitive position of its business life. Technological development is often called the motor of its economy. Thanks to technological development, there is continuous improvement of production methods and innovation of goods and services. As a consequence, the lifespan of existing products is continually shortened.

Technological development is pre-eminently a market-driven activity. Important stimuli for technological innovation come from competition, and the demand for more environmentally friendly goods and services of a higher quality, with a lower cost price, which can be delivered faster and more conveniently.

In the coming years, technological developments will continue at a similar pace to today. Major technological changes and successes can be expected in the areas of artificial intelligence, network speeds (5G), energy transition, biotechnology, information technology, and robotisation (automation). New technologies are expected to have a positive impact on organisational results. Chapter 3 on Digital Transformation offers greater detail and insight into the influence of new (disruptive) technologies on organisations.

Technological developments

FIGURE 1.2 **TECHNOLOGICAL TRENDS WITH A POSITIVE IMPACT ON ORGANISATION, AS PER RESEARCH RESULTS BY MCKINSEY AND GOOGLE**

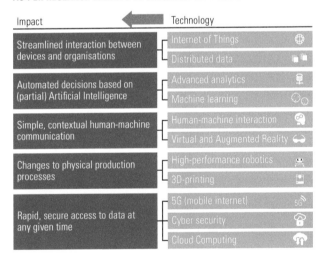

Source: *Shaping the future of work in the Netherlands.* McKinsey & Company, 2017

Biotechnology refers to living organisms. Biotechnology is an industry dedicated to the development of products for the nutritional industry (yeast extracts for bread and baked goods, beer, wine, and fruit juices), the pharmaceutical industry (medication, such as penicillin and growth hormones), agriculture (genetically enhanced livestock), cosmetics (creams, perfumes), and laundry (enzymes in detergents).

Biotechnology

Medical Aid Tattoo

Wearables have been making a steady rise over the past years. The small devices, in the form of watches, computer chips, or glasses that are worn closely to the body are becoming increasingly popular. Even though they offer benefits in the form of insight into or even improvement of behaviour, performance, or health, their main problem is that they are often cumbersome and subject to poor battery life. MIT and Harvard have now come up with a less intrusive form of wearable: the technological tattoo. Researchers have developed an ink that acts as a carrier for nanoparticles which function as sensors that change colour if their readings offer cause for alarm.

Depending on one's condition, the wearer can choose either long-term or short-term ink. Athletes who only want to keep track of their blood values over the course of a match can opt for a relatively short-lived tattoo. Diabetics and long patients may choose a more permanent tattoo that can be worn to monitor their insulin or oxygen levels for many years. Those that are uncomfortable with the idea of a visible tattoo have the option of an invisible ink that only shows up under a specific type of light. Visible results and measurements can be forwarded to a smartphone or computer, so that a doctor can keep track of a patient's medical condition at a distance.

Source: *Het Financieele Dagblad* Weekend, 2 June 2018

The MIT/Harvard tech-tattoo changes colour to inform the wearer of medical issues.

Information Technology

Information technology is concerned with the application of micro-electronics, and deals with saving and adapting information. Information can be seen as the lifeblood of the modern organisation. Some examples of products in the field of information technology are hardware (computers, tablets, smart phones, switchboards, etcetera), software (programming), communications networks, and intelligent computer chips.

The price/performance ratio of IT related activities is expected to fall by 20 percent to 30 percent every year. Consequently, investing in information technology will become progressively cheaper.

Robotisation or automation is the term for having robots perform work that is being carried out by people. Examples abound in the production industry. Nowadays, assembly-line activities are mostly performed by robots. Other applications include domestic robotics involved in vacuuming, mopping, or cutting grass; aerial reconnaissance using unmanned aircraft (drones); and performing laparoscopic surgery, with instruments entering the body under the guidance of surgeons who controls the implements remotely. Call centres now also frequently use ChatBots (intelligent robotics) that assist customers with a variety of questions and activities.

Developments in information technology will exert a big influence on all organisations in the coming years. The main consequences of this will be:
a fundamental changes in the way work is done;
b integration of functions;
c changes in economies of scale and decision-making.

Fundamental changes in the way work is done. Increasingly, communications networks are being installed within and between organisations and countries. One consequence is a reduction in 'time and distance'. As an example, financial transactions can be carried out from virtually anywhere in the world. Orders can be placed directly with producers from anywhere in the world at any time. The same goes for booking flights. Organisations can also quickly gain access to all sorts of information through electronic data banks.

Integration of functions. Through the expansion of communication networks, relevant information can be made available in the right form, at the right moment, and in the right place. There are three different identifiable categories of function integration:
1 **Within the organisation**. Within an organisation, various divisions can communicate with each other and exchange information because they are connected via a local communication network.
2 **Between organisations**. In this case, different organisational divisions are connected to each other electronically. For example, a customer's purchasing department can be electronically connected to a supplier's dispatch department.
3 **Electronic markets**. In this form of electronic integration, there is coordination between organisations that operate in an open-market situation. For example, travel agencies can electronically search for the cheapest flight to a destination and perform business transactions with any airline.

Since the end of the 1990s, the Internet has been seen as the international 'electronic superhighway' and has made all public information accessible to everyone. Many businesses have developed so-called 'self-service facilities' for their customers, and virtually any product can be purchased in a webstore. Webstore turnover has grown spectacularly over the past years, and is expected to continue to do so in future.

Changes in economies of scale and decision-making. Organisations spend much of their time on aligning activities between employees. This involves discussion and the exchange of written information. With developments in information technology (communication networks within and between organisations), coordination costs can be dramatically decreased. Smaller organisations will also be able benefit, and will therefore be able to enjoy the advangages of more flexible and less costly production processes. Information technology leads to a faster dissemination of information, which opens the door to faster decision-making.

Technological developments generally result from research carried out by universities and technical institutions, as well as R&D (Research & Development) departments in large businesses. A lot of resources (financial and otherwise) and effort are needed for these R&D activities. In this respect, because of their bigger capacity, larger businesses therefore have a clear advantage over smaller ones. Within larger businesses, R&D expenditure can be spread across a broad range of product groups. Small and medium-sized organisations simply cannot afford such expenses on their own. For this reason, it is quite common for a Ministry of Economic Affairs to support small and medium-sized businesses by offering subsidies and know-how.

Fundamental studies

However, the size of the R&D budget is not necessarily an indicator of the potential success of a business; the way in which technology is implemented and renewed within operations in comparison with competitor activity also plays a key role.
A flexible, efficient, and goal-orientated way of operating within organisations is required. Experience shows that the successful implementation of new technology is rarely easy. Problems with technological implementation are often not of a technical nature, but linked to human issues.
For technological development to be successful, it is vital that the technical experts are knowledgeable about marketing and business and that marketers and business experts understand the technical aspects.

Lastly, technologies have the potential to improve productivity at the cost of employment opportunities.

FIGURE 1.3 **THE EFFECTS OF TECHNOLOGY ON ECONOMIC GROWTH AND EMPLOYMENT OPPORTUNITIES IN THE NETHERLANDS**

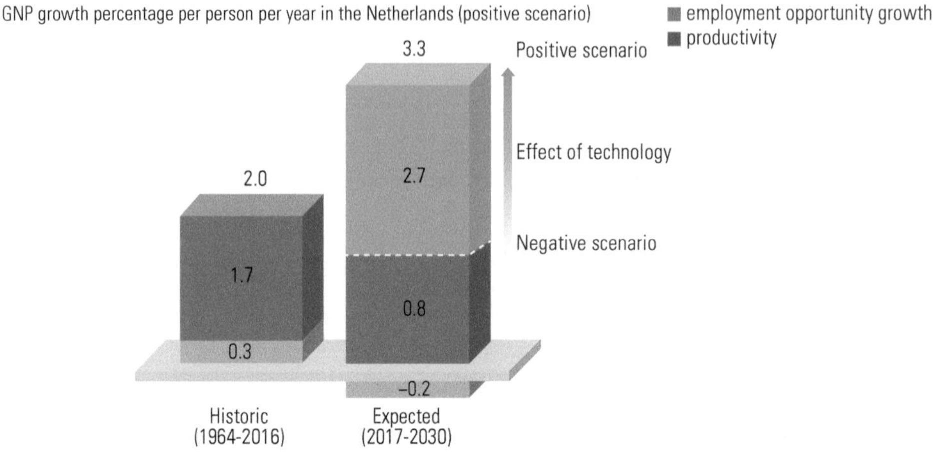

GNP growth percentage per person per year in the Netherlands (positive scenario)

■ employment opportunity growth
■ productivity

Source: *Shaping the future of work in the Netherlands.* McKinsey & Company, 2017

1.3.3 Demographic factors

Demographic factors

Demographic factors are defined as the size, growth and composition of a population. To a large extent, these factors determine which markets an organisation targets and which products and services it offers.
In 1795, at the time of the first national census, the Netherlands held slightly over two million residents. The third million was reached around fifty years later, in 1843. Just prior to the turn of the century, the country hit five million – ten million was reached only fifty years later, in 1949. It took only seven years to go from one million to the next. At the time of writing, the population of the Netherlands numbers around seventeen million inhabitants. Nowhere else in Europe has population growth been as pronounced over the past century.

The growth of the Dutch population is determined by various factors, the two most important of which are a high birth rate and a high migration balance.
The composition of the population is also set to change, due to the increase in the number of immigrants, who account for an important contribution to Dutch population growth. Whereas, in 2003, one in ten Dutch residents was a non-

No chance of a 'war for talent' for now

The decline in the percentage of Dutch professionals after 2024 is expected to be less severe than has previously been anticipated. A shortage on the labour market, or 'war for talent', is extremely unlikely.

Up till 2023, the potential professional population is expected to grow by 4.2%. This increase is largely the result of the increase in the national retirement age. The most pessimistic scenario involves a decline in the professional population, but other scenarios only expect this to happen as late as 2027 or 2032. In fact, an opposing development seems likely if the professional population continues to grow compared to 2012. Reports of a 'war for talent', resulting from a structural shortage of professionals, are premature at the very least.

In the longer term, the professional population will experience shrinkage: the retirement measure will lose its effectiveness, and the other age groups will reach maximum possible participation. In that case, shrinkage would begin to occur around 2030. Yet, a structural deficit does exist for some occupational groups; this is the result of a mismatch between supply and demand on the job market, and less the effect of the aging of the professional population.

Economic recovery (up to 2024) may result in an increased demand for workers. Depending on the rate and duration of this recovery, demand may begin to exceed supply – the sort of situation that would result in tension on the labour market, similar to the period before the financial crisis. However, speculation into these developments is highly uncertain.

Source: *Het Financieele Dagblad*, 6 January 2014

FIGURE 1 **DEVELOPMENT OF DUTCH POPULATION AND SHARE (IN %) OF POTENTIAL PROFESSIONAL POPULATION INCLUDING INCREASE IN AGE OF ENTITLED RETIREMENT, 2012-2060**

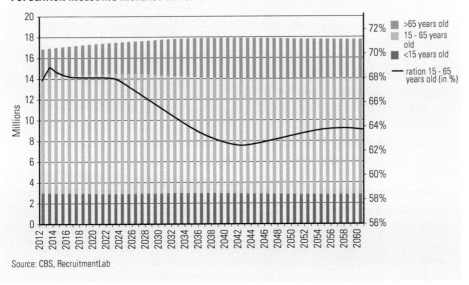

Legend:
- >65 years old
- 15 - 65 years old
- <15 years old
- ration 15 - 65 years old (in %)

Source: CBS, RecruitmentLab

Western immigrant, this figure will have doubled by 2050. The fast-growing immigrant part of the population may be able to reduce the expected structural shortage on the labour market to an important degree.

Apart from population size, age structure will also see a significant change in the future. Key changes occur in the group from middle to advanced age. The age pyramid will be slimmed down around the middle aged population, and gain size around the advanced age population as a result of aging (see Figure 1.4)

FIGURE 1.4 **AGE DISTRIBUTION IN THE NETHERLANDS BETWEEN 2019-2050**

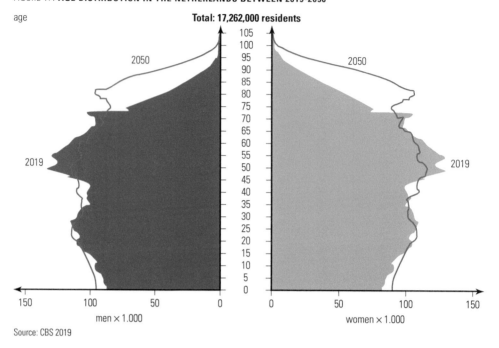

The number of births over the coming years is expected to decline as a consequence of the smaller sizes of the generations able to have children (caused by the decline in birth rates in the 1970s). This decline is virtually fully compensated for by an increase in the advanced age group. Life expectancy of both men and women, currently at 75.5 and 80.5 years old respectively, is expected to increase, due to the fact that more people are reaching an advanced age, and that people live even longer. In a number of Western countries, an expected 50% of all children born after 1997 will reach an age of well over 100 years old.
In future, the difference in life expectancy between men and women as the result of, for example, differences in smoking behaviours is expected to decline. Despite the expected increase in life expectancy, an aging population will result in a higher number of deaths over the coming decades.

An aging population comes with an increase in collective expenditure. On the other hand, there is a positive influence on government income. It is usual for there to be a positive relationship between work income and age. Studies by the Dutch CBS statistics agency show that income from direct taxation (mostly from income) is increasing, as a result of the growth and increasing average age of the population. If labour participation in the Netherlands were to rise to the level that is average among OECD countries (Organisation for Economic Collaboration and Development), it would also come with a major positive effect – the increase in the income from taxation would be nearly twice as high.

Senior citizens   The bottom age level for the classification of 'senior citizen' is set at fifty years old, at which age a number of changes occurs. Children are leaving the nest, or planning to do so soon; there is time for reflection and new activities; there is more free time; and there is a higher chance of contracting health complaints. This results in a different daily schedule and changes in time management. Modern senior citizens often (re-)enrol in school, are well-represented in the political arena, have an extensive social life, work out, and do not let others tell them what to do. The 50+ age group

FIGURE 1.5 **AGE DEVELOPMENT**

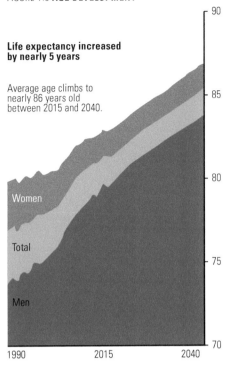

Life expectancy increased by nearly 5 years

Average age climbs to nearly 86 years old between 2015 and 2040.

Women

Total

Men

Source: RIVM, 2018

usually goes on holiday independently, is not afraid to stray further afield, is highly enterprising, and dares to be demanding in terms of price, quality, and comfort. An increasing number of organisations are discovering that seniors (those aged between 50 and 70 years old) are an attractive target group, with the highest household income. Research also indicates that seniors spend 80 percent. They also spend 40 percent more on food, 16 percent more on study and transportation, 75 percent more on domestic life and 50 percent more on personal hygiene and medical care. Demand for specific senior citizen products is expected to increase. In particular, products that provide security, that increase social contact, that promote an active and healthy life, that are part of leisure activity and hobbies, will all experience an increase in demand. It is also important to think about ways of tailoring products to this target group, for example products and services like travel (both within the country and abroad), special meals, clothing and footwear, housing, and social activities. Because senior citizens form a highly distinctive target group, they can also be viewed as a relatively complex one, one that raises a number of difficult issues for businesses of various types. How, for example, does one let senior citizens know that there is a product for them on the market without creating too much of a distinction with other groups, or projecting the image of being an 'old people brand'? What is the best tone to adopt when speaking to older people and should age determine communication strategy? The answers to these questions are essential when it comes to developing a competitive strategy for the senior market.

1.3.4   Economic factors

Economic factors play an important role in the success of organisations. Of eminent significance is the growth in national income. This growth generally leads to higher income for individuals, which then increases purchasing power. This leads to organisations that focus on the B2C (Business-to-Consumer) market ejoying

Economic factors
Growth in national income

Eastern Europe investing in robots and migrant workers

Wages in Eastern European countries are rapidly on the rise as a result of shortages in the labour market. Bad news for businesses; they are under threat of being unable to complete their workloads. The expert answer, in addition to higher wages and immigrant workers: robotisation. The market is particularly stretched in Slovakia, the Czech Republic, and Slovenia. Car industry companies are beginning to see robots as an alternative to increasingly expensive labour. Workers from the Ukraine and Serbia are especially sought after by employers. Surprisingly, wage increases have only caused greater difficulties for the labour market: higher wages mean higher consumptive spending, which means greater economic growth, which means an increased demand for personnel. Technical professions, such as engineers, welders, fitters, and IT staff, in particular, are becoming more scarce in the job market, resulting in higher wage demands. Automation and robotisation can help shrink the labour shortage.

Source: *Het Financieele Dagblad*, 30 May 2018

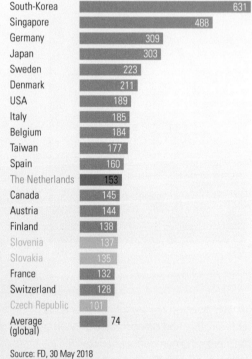

FIGURE **WHICH COUNTRY EMPLOYS THE MOST ROBOTS**

Country	Robots
South-Korea	631
Singapore	488
Germany	309
Japan	303
Sweden	223
Denmark	211
USA	189
Italy	185
Belgium	184
Taiwan	177
Spain	160
The Netherlands	153
Canada	145
Austria	144
Finland	138
Slovenia	137
Slovakia	135
France	132
Switzerland	128
Czech Republic	101
Average (global)	74

Source: FD, 30 May 2018

increased turnover. Income distribution is another important factor. Changes in income distribution can have a significant effect on the size of some markets. It is clear that, for countries like the Netherlands, where a relatively large proportion (about 30 percent) of national income is dependent on foreign trade, international economic developments will also play an important role.

Income distribution

International economic developments

Some examples of key influencing factors are:

a economic growth in other countries;
b currency fluctuations;
c developments in interest rates;
d developments in foreign wage levels.

These factors are likely to have a big influence on the competitive position of Dutch enterprises.

Between now and 2040, more Dutch workers will be leaving the labour process than new ones will be coming in, due to the effects of aging. In addition, there is a qualitative mismatch between the people looking for a job and the labour market's needs. In order to adequately address the costs of an aging population, the Netherlands will need to rely heavily on highly trained, high-income talent.

An important stimulus for improving the economic situation is the investment in knowledge and innovation. In Lisbon and Barcelona, the European Union voiced the goal of wanting to become the most competitive knowledge economy in the world. To achieve this, it will be necessary for Member States to allocate at least 3 per cent of the EU's GNP (Gross National Product) to research and development activities. The Netherlands has voiced its intentions of being among Europe's top level, but the country's current investment level is estimated by many as being insufficient to reach this goal.

From its geographical and historical background, the Netherlands has always been strongly dependent on international trade and investments. These involve not only European developments, but also those on the global stage. Predictions on long-term global economic development are rife with uncertainty.

Globalisation

Drafting prognoses for both the Dutch and global economies is one of the core activities of the Dutch Centraal Planbureau (Central Planning Bureau). Prognoses are economic analyses which use available knowledge, information, and instruments (such as economic models) to draft a substantiated expected development. The CPB distinguishes between three temporal periods: short, medium, and long term.

An example of a long-term prognosis is the study 'Four Panoramic Views of the Netherlands', which discusses four scenarios up to 2040. Dutch policy is faced with a number of strategic challenges which will have great significance for long-term economic perspectives. There is great uncertainty with regard to the coping strategies for future bottlenecks and to the expected economic backgrounds. The four scenarios offer a quantitative analysis at the national level for different industries. There are major differences between the Dutch scenarios. For example, GDP per head in 2040 will be between 30% and 120% higher than at its current level. The high-growth scenarios do present an image of extensive income inequality and poorer environmental conditions. Aging represses the growth of labour and employment, as well as the ratio between the active and the inactive across all scenarios. The distribution of employment opportunities across the industries continues to shift, particularly away from agriculture and industry towards services and care. This development has been going on for decades. Information about the scenario study can be obtained from CPB's website.

Based on centuries of experience, Dutch trade politics focus on economic systems and optimised free trade. At the same time, the Netherlands, being a relatively small country, recognises the need for international trade legislation to ensure that the global economic stage does not descend into dog-eat-dog practices, but adheres to international treaties that are respectful of the interests of all parties involved. Growing globalisation means the importance of such a legal system becomes even more important.

World Trade Organisation (WTO)

All this in mind, the Netherlands encouraged the establishment of the World Trade Organisation in 1995. A relatively young organisation with over 164 member states (2018), it has the potential to develop into the lynching pin of the multilateral trade system, in part due to its system of enforcing binding dispute settlement. Therefore, the Netherlands considers the institutional reinforcement of the WTO, in addition to the continuation of the trade liberalisation with respect to industrial products, services, and agricultural products, an important goal for the WTO for the coming years.

The WTO has been given two other fundamentally important tasks. Firstly, it has been charged with further integrating developing countries – especially the ELDCs (Economically Least Developed Countries) – in world trade and in the work of the WTO. The second task is to look at the relationship between trade and important themes like the environment, food safety and working conditions.

A study by the World Bank found that the removal of trade barriers in developing countries would raise income by about 500 billion dollars. Furthermore, research has shown that trade liberalisation since World War II has contributed to lifting billions of people out of poverty. Although the exact figure is disputed, it is accepted that the advantages of trade liberalisation are enormous.

Economic growth

The emphasis of modern economics has always been on economic growth. Increasingly, opposing forces question this ideal, because past economic growth has led to detrimental effects to the planet's environment and habitability. In her 2017 book 'Doughnut Economic', Oxford economist Kate Raworth argues in favour of discarding the idea of infinite economic growth. Instead, the focus should be on a completely circular economy. Her new economic model looks rather like a doughnut, and balances essential human needs and planetary boundaries. Instead of focussing on economic growth, economists should concern themselves with issues of access to basic needs across the world, such as adequate food, education, safety (human rights), and health. At the same time, the possibilities for future generations should not be impaired. The ecosystem must be protected. There must be a balance between the ecological upper tolerance level and the social bottom level. Raworth's model imposes strict restrictions on growth, and sends a confrontational message to policy makers and economists who see economic growth as the basis for a healthy system.

The outer circle is based on the Planetary Boundaries Framework by the Stockholm Resilience Centre, which was not developed by economists but by physicists. It represents the biosphere in which an economy exists, and includes climate change, freshwater use, and ocean acidification. The model focusses on planet over market. According to Raworth, this must become the basis for economic philosophy in the 21st century. Progressive companies should lead the transition, particularly companies in the food industry. Food influences all nine planetary boundaries (see

FIGURE 1.6 **THE DONUT: A COMPASS FOR THE TWENTY-FIRST CENTURY**

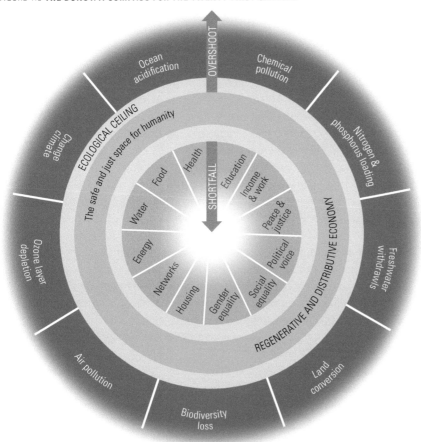

Source: *De Donuteconomie*, K. Raworth, 2017

Figure 1.6). If food could be harvested in a more sustainable manner, it would have an enormously positive impact on those boundaries, says Raworth.

Raworth sees shareholders as the biggest threat to companies looking to integrate the donut model into their business model. Companies can adapt their vision, policy, and network to improve their positive impact on the planet – but in the end, what matters is who owns the company. Listed companies depend on their shareholders, who strive for short-term financial gain. A long-term vision is of great importance when it comes to enabling a mentality shift. Politicians, in particular, find the doughnut model to be appealing: inclusive growth, sustainable growth, and resilient growth in order to enable economic progression – a new vision of the definition of wealth. The question is, however, whether these insights are shared by the population groups needed to vote for these political ideals.

1.3.5   Political factors

Governmental authorities use their political powers and responsibilities to try to steer their economy in a favourable direction. For example, governments influence price levels, the distribution of income, the job market, the balance of payments and therefore economic growth.

Political factors

In past years, there has been an increase in the level of political influence exerted on national economies from outside bodies. Within Europe, this influence has been brought about by the removal of borders between the Member States of the EU (European Union) in line with their goal of creating a single internal market. But there is also a call to limiting European power, particularly prevalent among populist parties. Brexit is a clear example of this.

The unification of Europe and a shift in political power are factors which are likely to challenge organisations in the near future. When talking about unification, it should be understood that an economic union can only be created by having the Member States merge their national economic and political institutions to a large extent.

Economic union

In general, five forms of economic integration can be identified. Arranged according to increasing levels of integration, these are the free trade zone, customs union, common market, economic union and complete political and economic union – all of which are briefly discussed below.

Free trade zone

1 **Free trade zone.** Mutual trade agreements are entered into only by those countries that wish to participate. Each country determines their own import tariffs for products that are imported from outside the free trade zone. As a result, the trade policy for members is not harmonised. Certification of origin is therefore necessary to prevent products being imported via the country with the lowest import tariffs. An example of a free trade zone is NAFTA (North American Free Trade Agreement).

Customs union

2 **Customs union.** Here, a common trade policy is adopted. The revenue from import duty is divided between Member States using an agreed formula.

Common market

3 **Common market.** Based on a customs union, it removes the barriers in the field of production factors.

Economic union

4 **Economic union.** Economic union means that the monetary policy and financial government politics are also in harmony. This step requires that central institutions, such as a single Central Bank, be implemented.

Complete political and economic union

5 **Complete political and economic union.** This is the situation where independent states or countries merge completely. An example is the formation of the United States of America.

Within the European Union, there is a common internal market. This common market is based on four economic freedoms:
1 Freedom of movement of goods;
2 Freedom of movement of services;
3 Freedom of movement of capital;
4 Freedom of movement of people.

With further development of the common internal market and the formation of an economic block, Europe can improve its competitive position in relation to the other major economic power blocks of Japan, the United States and South East Asia.

The unification of Europe will have significant consequences for many organisations. It is anticipated that increased competition will put pressure on production costs, which in turn will lead to a fall in prices. Lower prices generate increased turnover, which leads to economies of scale, and possible business expansion. Larger scale production makes innovation and R&D expenditure viable which, of course, is likely to result in the production of goods that better meet customer needs and are easier to sell. It is a chain reaction that supports the strengthening of Europe's position in relation to its competitors.

Before Europe can really become a truly open internal market, a number of obstructions needs to be removed:

Obstructions

a **Physical obstructions**. Customs controls with their associated paperwork as well as delays at borders.
b **Technical obstructions**. Country-specific differences in production regulations, commercial law, and regulations designed to protect elements within the government procurement sector.
c **Fiscal obstructions**. The differences in sales tax (VAT) rates and excise taxes that result in a demand for inspection and clearance at borders.

Well over a third of the Netherlands' national income is earned by the export sector. Compared to other countries, this is a large share.

This means the competitive position of Dutch companies requires some attention. One advantage for the Netherlands is that its historically large degree of economic accessibility can offer advantages compared to other EU-member states.

In the year 2018 AD, there are 28 EU-member states. The member states and their years of accession are:

1952 Belgium, France, Germany, Italy, Luxembourg, and the Netherlands;
1973 Denmark, Ireland, and the United Kingdom;
1981 Greece;
1986 Portugal, Spain;
1995 Finland, Austria, and Sweden;
2004 Cyprus, Estonia, Hungary, Latvia, Lithuania, Malta, Poland, Slovenia, Slovakia, the Czech Republic;
2007 Bulgaria, Romania;
2013 Croatia;
2017 On 29 March 2017, the United Kingdom formally resigned its membership in a letter to the European Union.

Following the departure of the UK, there will be 27 member states in the European Union.

FIGURE 1.7 **MEMBER STATES OF THE EU**

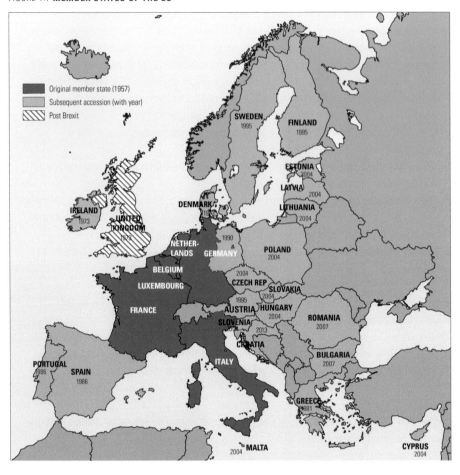

In the past, Dutch organisations have gained much in terms of experience with aspects of international competition. Past evidence shows that 71% of Dutch export occurs within the European Union. Between 2008 and 2018, export to countries outside the EU grew much more rapidly than export within the EU. A separate aspect of the unification of the European market is the position of the small to medium enterprise (SME). SMEs are a major component of the Dutch economy. SMEs are defined as private companies of fewer than a hundred employees. Having more than a hundred employees means a company is qualified as large.

An important question to ask in relation to SMEs concerns the special opportunities and threats that they face in the new Europe. Turnover from Dutch SME mainly originates from the domestic market, even though nearly two in every three SMEs are internationally active. The highest percentage of profit obtained from clients abroad is realised within the European Union.

The next and obvious question is whether small and medium businesses will benefit optimally from the removal of internal borders. National enterprises that do not plan to expand into the new European market will, in all probability, be confronted by new competitors from elsewhere in the EU – competitors who have also decided to enter the national market. The competition faced by Dutch SMEs will therefore only increase. Due to the important position of SMEs in the

Small to medium enterprise

Dutch economy, an encouraging government policy is appropriate. As stated, trade within the ranks of the European Union will mean mutual trade restrictions can be foregone.

1.3.6   Societal factors

There is a societal need to try to exert an influence on organisations because of concerns about business activities, and such issues as environmental responsibility, noise pollution, ethical business and employee participation. Criticism has been levelled by various parties, including employees and local community groups. Such bodies often use the media to gain leverage and, in some cases, campaigns may lead to the introduction of new legislation.

FIGURE 1.8 **ORGANISATIONS ARE A PART OF SOCIETY, WHICH IS PART OF THE LARGER ENVIRONMENT**

Organisations are a part of society. Society is, however, broader and deeper than the elements that make up an organisation. Friends, family, sport, hobbies and religion are often at least as important for individuals.
In turn, a society exists within the natural environment. The basic needs of society, such as air, food and water, come from nature, as do energy, raw materials, transport and some products. In the past, natural environment was, to a large extent, the factor that determined what society looked like. Now, human activities are having an increasing influence on the natural environment.

Environment

Organisations are increasingly taking into account the needs of the society, and focussing on what is called social responsibility or sustainable business.
The idea behind corporate social responsibility (CSR) is that a company is part of a larger system. An enterprise is affected by its environment; for example, global warming can lead to failed harvests, scarcity of raw materials and, therefore, increased prices. Vice versa, a company can influence its environment if, for example, its factory emits toxic substances into the air during the production process. It is therefore becoming more common for companies to act responsibly, and to take into account human, environmental, and other external factors.

CSR

What is corporate social responsibility?

CSR helps companies to consciously form a clear picture of their own social responsibility in a way that goes beyond simple legal requirements. This leads to added value for both society and company. Corporate social responsibility is also known as sustainable business, derived from the concept of sustainable development; this concept was introduced by the Brundtland Committee in 1987. Through sustainable business, companies can make an important contribution to the sustainable development of society.

Sustainable business

How to improve your company's corporate social role?

1 Insight into employee commitment
An improved focus on sustainability contributes to employee commitment. Try to ascertain what knowledge employees have of social activities and the extent to which they themselves can contribute.

2 Improve customer-orientation
High customer-centeredness is often associated with strong employee commitment. This also offers a positive impulse to the company's market price.

3 Improve corporate social responsibility
Human Resource Development (HRD) can exert an influence on a company's corporate social responsibility by organising social project. Company events can be given a societal theme which provides employees with new insights. Establishing corporate foundations with a common upheld goal is a frequently found initiative.

4 Develop talent
Talented employees can develop and display their competences through societal projects.

Outside of the regular context of fixed goals and agreements, qualities like flexibility, cooperation, stress-resistance, and creativity can be made visible.

5 Work on organisational culture
All of the aforementioned issues have an impact on the culture, norms, and values of an organisation – in particular, they have a formative effect on organisational culture. Working on organisational culture results in mutual commitment and offers handles for self-directing conduct.

6 Show your societal convictions
An organisation's societal profile is playing an increasingly important role in its employee appeal. Organisations should demonstrate what it is they stand for as much as they can.

Source: **Tijdschrift voor Ontwikkeling in Organisaties** (TvOO), nr.3 09-2017, Bas van Haastrecht: Wat niemand vertelt over ondernemen

A company that focusses on CSR no longer revolves (solely) around profit maximisation; instead, the focus becomes creating value – value for clients, employees, shareholders, the environment, the climate, and society. But what is the extent of this responsibility? What subjects should companies pay attention to? In order to establish exactly what companies are expected to do, it is important that they engage with their environment. This is known as the stakeholder approach. Stakeholders are various groups of people who represent their own, others', or environmental interests in relation to the activities of the company across the chain. The stakeholders approach offers the possibility for stakeholders to exert an influence on company policy. Through dialogue with its stakeholders, a company can learn about the effects of its operational activities on certain groups. Stakeholders can be divided into internal stakeholders (employees, managers, shareholders) and external stakeholders (clients, suppliers, NGOs, civilians, governments, financers) (see Table 1.1).

TABLE 1.1 **RELATIONAL MATRIX WITH SEVERAL EXAMPLES OF NOTABLE ASPECTS WHEN COMPARING LISTED THEMES IN RELATIONSHIP TO STAKEHOLDERS**

Stakeholder	Theme				
	Social	Cultural	Political	Ethical	Environmental
Customer			International relations	Cause-related marketing	Environmentally friendly product, recycling hallmarks
Supplier			International relations	Supplier selection (SA8000)	Supplier selection (use of raw/ sustainable materials)
Employer	Employment opportunity, part time jobs, teleworking, child care, safety, health, wellbeing	Sports facilities, art, language education	Opportunities for political activity	Personal development, opportunity for participation in societal organisation, norms and values, minorities, discrimination	Use of energy, wastage, transport
Manager	Employment opportunity, part time jobs, teleworking, child care, safety, health, wellbeing	Sports facilities, art, language education	Income ratios	Personal development, opportunity for participation in societal organisation, norms and values, minorities, discrimination	Use of energy, wastage, transport
Financer				Prospectus (flotation)	Green banking
Competitor	Social covenants		Lobbying		Industry-oriented covenants
Government	Regulation/ legislation, employment opportunity, safety		Urban policy, maintaining governmental relationships		Legislation/ regulation, permits, environmental management
Education	Knowledge transfer (internships, guest colleges)		Aligning with education to support needs	Information	Information
Media	Information	Information	Information		Information
Interest groups	Social forum information		Information	Behavioural code, cause-related marketing, ideal advertising	Information
Local residents	Neighbourhood council, safety, knowledge transfer (company visits), sponsoring	Sponsoring		Behavioural code, integration of minorities	Emissions, waste management, disturbances
(Global) citizens	Knowledge transfer (conferences, publications), sponsoring	Sponsoring		Behavioural code	

CSR is a broad term, covering various topics. Societal elements within sustainable development can be subdivided into five themes: social, cultural, political, ethical and environmental. More specifically, climate change, biodiversity, employment, economic growth, human rights, environmentally friendly business, child labour, poverty reduction, and wealth distribution are topics that have taken on great importance where the sustainable development of society is concerned.

People, planet, profit

Companies that implement sustainable business models are more affected by changes within their surroundings when they adopt the so-called 'triple bottom line' approach to these social, environmental and economic aspects. In this context, we refer to three dimensions, specifically people, planet, and profit.

People The way an organisation deals with socio-ethical issues falls into the 'people' dimension, which asks the question of how the company behaves towards its own staff and local community. Various areas are taken into account when answering this question, including respect for human rights, corruption and fraud, gender relations, diversity and discrimination, employee participation, codes of conduct, health and safety, training and development, and child labour.

Planet The 'planet' dimension looks at how a business interacts with its natural environment – from minimising damage to even benefitting the natural order. Current examples include waste chain management, eco-efficiency, cleaner production, sustainable technological development, sustainable industrialisation, reduction of energy and CO2, etcetera.

Profit The focus of the 'profit' dimension is not so much on traditional financial accounting, but more on the overall economic value generated by the business. It includes elements like employment opportunity, infrastructure investments, location policy, political commitment, outsourcing, economic effects of services and products. Sponsoring, employee participation, and profit appropriation are also issues assigned to this dimension.

Figure 1.9 demonstrates a sustainability scoring care: a 'report card' which visualises an organisation's score on various aspects of sustainability.

FIGURE 1.9 **EXAMPLE OF A PEOPLE-PROFIT-PLANET SUSTAINABILITY SCORECARD**

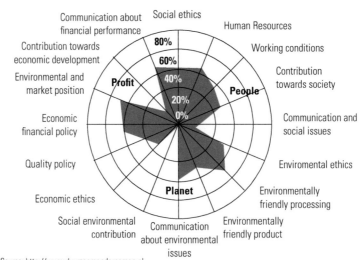

Source: http://www.duurzaamondernemen.nl

There is no single right way of being corporately socially responsible and every company has to determine which CSR activities are most appropriate for its own set of circumstances. Variables include industry size, company culture, and selected strategy. Importantly, CSR is a process and not a final destination. An organisation's goals can change over time as a consequence of various internal and external factors. As such, how can a company make the right decisions in pursuit of corporate social responsibility? One way is to incorporate a process based on the so-called plan-do-check-act-cycle. This four-stage plan helps companies to make choices about corporate social responsibility, and to set up and implement a suitable CSR policy. See Figure 1.10 for the four steps: Analyse, Policy, Implement, Evaluate.

FIGURE 1.10 **A DIAGRAMMATIC PRESENTATION OF A CONTINUOUS FOUR-STEP PLAN**

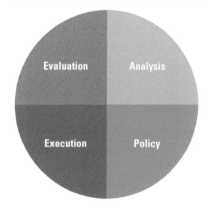

Following the analysis phase, which offers a company insight into societal developments in its environment, its image, and the expectations of relevant stakeholders, the company drafts its mission and vision statements, and aligns or integrates these with the existing mission or vision. This helps to clarify the company's position and goals with respect to CSR.

Next is the policy phase. Company policy must be in line with the general entrepreneurial policy. A number of important principles need to be detailed, including performance indicators, which can be used as the basis for setting objectives. Next comes the creation of a strategy, along with an action plan to ensure that the objectives are met. This is followed by the implementation. Specific projects should be set up to develop various key business processes. This may require additional staff training and guidance, and it is essential that clear communication and appropriate support are ensured. To ensure success, senior management needs to pay sufficient attention to the change process, and must be seen to take personal accountability for the outcome. The involvement of employees and stakeholders may also need to be expanded.

There are several ways of evaluating and improving processes; whichever of these is chosen, it represents the final stage. To determine whether or not the societal goals have been reached involves measuring, investigating, comparing, developing profiles, self-evaluating, and conducting internal group discussions. Open and transparent communication towards stakeholders is important in this regard, so channels like the company website, periodic sustainability reports, and even the annual reports should be used. During the final phase, various adjustments to the objectives and plan of action may need to be made, based on any effects of new developments linked to the company and its activities, or to changes in stakeholder expectations.

The challenge for the current generation is to continue developing the economy while also ensuring a fair distribution of wealth and the protection of the environment in such a way as to preserve the planet for future generations. As such, it is vital that the development of plans for sustainable business is carried out by multinationals and companies in the industrial sectors that have a big impact on people and the environment. These companies can then set a good example for the SMEs and companies in non-industrial sectors. Sustainable and innovative companies who are seen as industry leaders due to their size and clout can show just how much more exceptional, how much better, and how much faster their businesses can be.

Businesses may choose corporate sustainability for a number of reasons, whether for purely intrinsic reasons such as a feeling that 'this is the way it should be done', or for strategic or economic motives which may regard CSR as an interesting business model. Sometimes, companies feel compelled to adopt socially responsible procedures: for example, because of pressure from NGOs or impending legislation. It is not uncommon to be driven by a blend of different motives.

Once an enterprise has determined its operational starting point, it is wise to distinguish between image on the one hand and societal position on the other. A company's societal position is a combination of image (how a company wants to be seen) and identity (what a company really is). Company image is a vulnerable thing, and a damaged reputation can be difficult to repair. As such, it is important that a company carefully considers the position it wants to occupy in society. There are only very few enterprises that pay no attention to the needs of society at all. In reality, most companies consider both their economic interests and the interests of society.

Chapter 5 addresses Corporate Social Responsibility in greater detail.

Summary

▶ An organisation is affected by its business environment, which is comprised of parties and external factors.

▶ Parties influence and are influenced by organisations, and include:
  - customers/clients;
  - suppliers;
  - competitors;
  - capital providers/financers;
  - employees;
  - special interest groups;
  - government and local authority institutions;
  - media.

▶ For organisations, external factors are less easy to influence, and can present both restrictions and opportunities. External factors include:
  - environmental factors;
  - technological factors;
  - demographic factors;
  - economic factors;
  - political factors;
  - societal factors

▶ Environmental factors: political choices and changes in societal consensus with regard to the issue of the environment have a major influence on organisational behaviours. The 2015 Climate Accords proposed limiting global temperature increase by no more than two degrees Celsius compared to the pre-industrial age.

▶ Technological factors: technological developments allow organisations to switch to new production methods and/or new products, enabling them to establish an advantage over their competitors.

▶ Demographic factors: changes in the size, composition, and growth of the Dutch population are demographic factors which organisations will need to take strongly into account.

▶ Economic factors: economic developments determine the success of organisations to an important extent. A key economic indicator is the development in national income, which has a strong influence on spending patterns.

▶ Political factors: governments continue to offer direction to economic affairs through their political function. Increasingly, the seat of political power is shifting to elsewhere across national borders. Within the European Union, most issues of the European internal market will come to rely on mutual policy and decision-making.

▶ Societal factors: organisations are increasingly taking societal demands into account. They are continuing to shift their focus towards sustainable business (corporate social responsibility). Companies consciously and structurally define their social responsibility in a way that transcends legal obligation alone. This leads to added value for both society and companies alike.

2
STRATEGIC MANAGEMENT

Contents

After studying this chapter:

- you will have become acquainted with the main strategic management concepts;
- you will be able to differentiate between the various phases of the classical strategic management process;
- you will be able to relate strategic management to the implementation of strategies in organisations;
- you will have gained insight into recent approaches to strategic management;
- you will understand the importance of a good information system;
- you will have learned the major motives for engaging in a collaboration;
- you will have gained insight into the various types of collaborations;
- you will have gained an understanding of and insight into the participation of organisations in organisational networks;
- you will have gained an understanding of and insight into various aspects involved in mergers and take-overs.

Swapfiets: Large scale rent-a-bikes for the Netherlands

When friends and students of the Delft University of Technology Richard Burger, Martijn Obers, Dirk de Bruijn, and Steven Uitentuis saw a student cruising by on a beat-up old bicycle in 2014, they thought: there has to be a better way. They came up with an idea for a subscription model for bikes.

In January of 2015, the foursome launched *Swapfiets* – literally Swap Bike – a company where clients pay 15 Euros per month, with a reduced student rate of 12 Euros per month, to rent a bike. Damages like flat tyres are followed by a personal visit from the Swapfiets crew to fix any issues. A bike that is stolen costs the renter their 40 Euro deposit, but the cancellation term of the rental agreement is less than a month. Initially, the entrepreneurs began with 40 bicycles, which they found on Dutch online marketplace Marktplaats. In a small warehouse, they converted those into the initial versions of the Swapfiets. Nowadays, their production is a joint effort with bicycle company and PON subsidiary Union. Last week, the entrepreneurs reached their 40,000th client. The company's clientele is found across numerous Dutch cities and, as of recently, in and Germany as well. Swapfiets employs 160 people already, spread across 170 FTEs.

Brand recognition is an important factor to the success of the Swapfiets. All rental bikes are equipped with a (Delft) blue front tyre, making them instantly recognisable. The team opted for coloured tyres to help their clients find their bikes more easily. Changing two tyres on every bike was too much work, so they went with front tyres only. In a group of five people where one rides a Swapfiets, the others are quick to ask: "What is up with your tyre?" Thus giving birth to word of mouth, which accounts for 80% of new customers.

Swapfiets should be seen as a real service provider: clients pay a subscription fee to guarantee their mobility, with the company arranging maintenance. Swapfiets cleverly appeals to the millennial trend of taking out monthly renewable subscriptions. A year-long commitment is no longer a match for the continually changing lives of the young, is the idea.

A financial boost meant the entrepreneurs could certainly scale up their activities. Swapfiets expanded from Delft to Leiden to Nijmegen, Groningen, and numerous other cities. The entrepreneurs have drafted a list of one hundred potential cyclist-cities in Europe, and are now investigating the possibilities in countries from Greece to Bulgaria.

In every city, students are the primary audience, followed by the elderly – another appealing market, and one that is open to other products as well, the entrepreneurs have noticed. Swapfiets have recently begun offering a deluxe model for 19 Euros per month, and are also experimenting with e-bike subscriptions at 72.50 Euros per month. The first 100 subscribers have already signed up.

Source: www.sprout.nl, www.swapfiets.nl

Organisations and their environment
PART A

2.1   INTRODUCTION

Chapter 1 discussed how various external parties and factors affect an organisation. The survival of organisations is highly dependent on their ability to cope with these external influences.

How organisations attune to the environment is an outcome of the process of strategic management. Strategic management is the process of careful consideration of appropriate responses to the environment, as well as maintenance of standards and development of the skills required for the inclusion of possible changes to strategy.

Strategic management

As the definition shows, it is a process that involves management determining the strategy. The word 'strategy' is relatively old and is derived from Greek 'strategos', meaning 'the art (or the skills) of the military commander'. There are many definitions of strategy. It can be defined as a plan that states what an organisation needs to do to reach its goals. Planning is one of the main tasks of management.

Strategy

This chapter covers two different approaches to strategic management.
In the first approach, known as the classical school, strategic management is synonymous with strategic planning. Strategic planning is used by an enterprise to strike a balance between the resources, the strengths and the weaknesses of the enterprise on the one hand, and the opportunities and threats from the environment on the other. One of the main founders of this school is Igor Ansoff, who made a significant contribution with his 1965 book *Corporate Strategy*. Michael Porter is another important pioneer, building on this theory in the 1980s and 1990s. In his book *The Rise and fall of Strategic Planning*, Henry Mintzberg made critical comments about the classical approach to strategic management. Mintzberg's views can be recognised in the second modern approach to strategic management. Gary Hamel and C. K. Prahalad were important founders of this school. According to this new approach, strategic management is synonymous with strategic thinking. An organisation that thinks strategically is capable of putting its vision into practice. It is argued that quantitative, analytical models are no longer adequate in dealing with the present turbulent environment.

Classical school
Strategic planning

Second modern approach

Strategic decisions often deal with how an organisation wishes to achieve certain growth. This can occur through either of three possibilities: through autonomous growth, through engaging in a collaboration, or through engaging in mergers or organisational take-overs.
Collaborations and mergers and take-overs are given specific attention towards the end of the chapter.

2.2   THE CLASSICAL APPROACH TO STRATEGIC MANAGEMENT

According to the classical school of strategic management, the main issue is positioning the organisation in relation to the environment. This is done by first analysing the organisation's strong and weak points, and subsequently scanning the organisation's environment for possible opportunities and threats. Then, a particular strategy for identifying the organisation's aims must be chosen, followed by the making of plans for implementing the strategy within the organisation.

Environment

The process of strategic management consists of three phases:

1 Situational analysis (Section 2.2.1);
2 Strategy formation (Section 2.2.2);
3 Planning and implementation (Section 2.2.3).

These phases are represented in Figure 2.1. The figure shows that strategic management is a dynamic and cyclical process. It includes feedback from the planning phase and implementation in the situational analysis phase. All of the phases are discussed in the following section.

FIGURE 2.1 **THE STRATEGIC MANAGEMENT PROCESS**

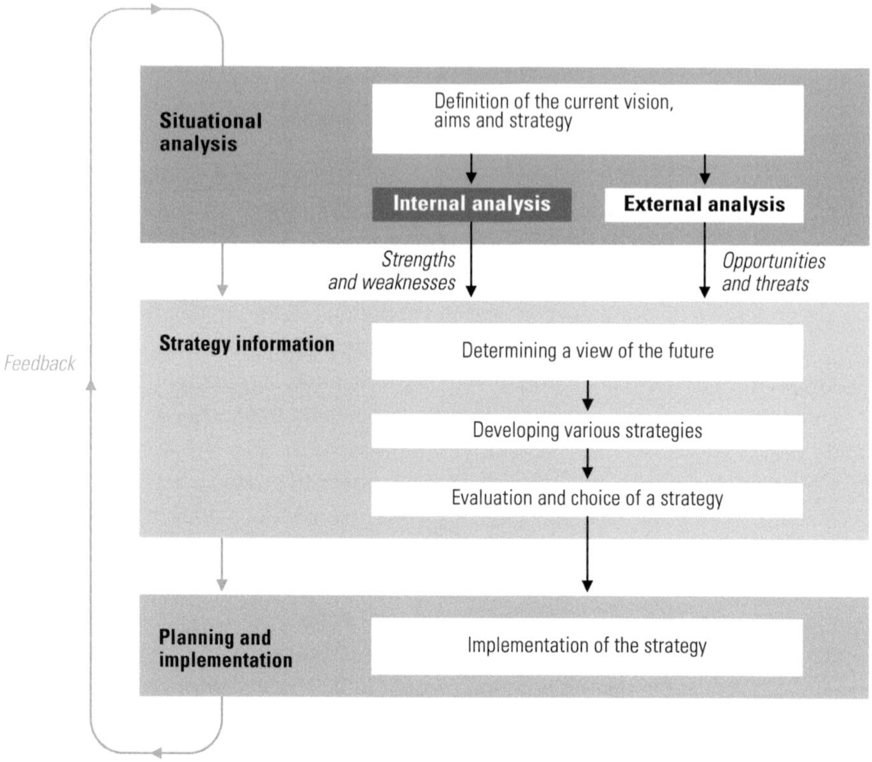

2.2.1 Situational analysis

Situational analysis

The first phase of strategic management is known as situational analysis. This is also called the strategic audit or SWOT analysis (Strengths – Weaknesses – Opportunities – Threats). The situational analysis focusses on determining the current profile of the organisation while taking into account its external environment. The situational analysis consists of:

– A definition of the current vision, aims and strategy;
– An internal analysis;
– An external analysis.

The Netherlands among Europe's leaders in innovation, headed by Philips

The Netherlands is one of Europe's most innovative countries. Dutch companies applied for 7,043 patents with the European Patent Office (EPO), a 2.7% increase compared to 2016. This places our country fourth in the list of European countries, and seventh worldwide.

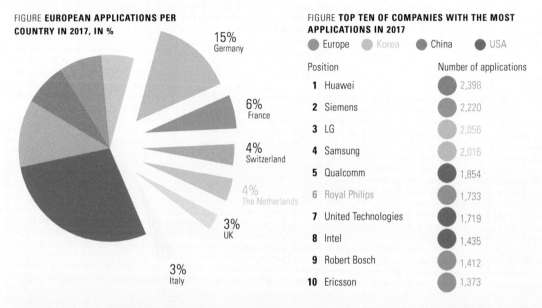

FIGURE **EUROPEAN APPLICATIONS PER COUNTRY IN 2017, IN %**

15% Germany
6% France
4% Switzerland
4% The Netherlands
3% UK
3% Italy

FIGURE **TOP TEN OF COMPANIES WITH THE MOST APPLICATIONS IN 2017**

● Europe   ● Korea   ● China   ● USA

Position		Number of applications
1	Huawei	2,398
2	Siemens	2,220
3	LG	2,056
4	Samsung	2,016
5	Qualcomm	1,854
6	Royal Philips	1,733
7	United Technologies	1,719
8	Intel	1,435
9	Robert Bosch	1,412
10	Ericsson	1,373

Source: *Het Financieele Dagblad*, 8 March 2018 https://fd.nl/economie-politiek/1244870/nederland-behoort-tot-innovatieve-kopgroep-in-europa. Consulted 7 May 2018 (translated)

Definition of the current vision, aims and strategy

The first phase of the situational analysis aims to gain insight into the organisation's existing situation, and define its current vision, aims and strategy.
In an ideal situation, these three elements have already been defined and made clear to all parties concerned. In reality, however, the definition is often insufficient – or the members of an organisation interpret the elements differently.
The first element that needs clarification is the vision held by management. A vision is a general idea or representation of the future of the organisation and usually consists of a mission statement and principles (see Figure 2.2).

Vision

FIGURE 2.2 **ELEMENTS OF AN ORGANISATION**

| Vision | = | Mission | + | Principles |

Vision as management tool

McKinsey Consultants developed their so-called 7-S model to analyse the role of vision as a management tool (see Figure 2.3).

7-S model

FIGURE 2.3 **7-S-MODEL**

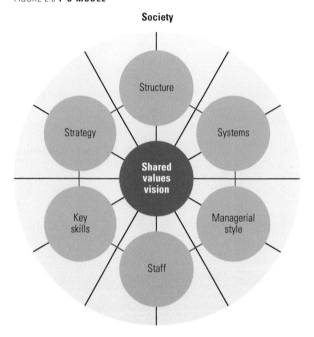

The 7-S model consists of seven management factors that are interdependent, of equal importance, and closely connected:

1 **Structure.** This refers to the way elements within the organisation relate to each other: to the organisational framework, to the distribution of tasks, and so on. According to McKinsey, the structure of an organisation can be temporarily changed (for example, by setting up project groups) without changing the basic structure of an organisation.

2 **Systems.** This refers to information and communication systems, both formal and informal, within the organisation.

3 **Managerial style.** This relates to the characteristic behavioural patterns of the top managers of the enterprise. Management style exerts a big influence on the culture of an organisation.

4 **Staff.** This focusses on the way an organisation pays attention to its human resources.

5 **Key skills.** These are the outstanding capabilities of individuals or the whole organisation; those by which the organisation can distinguish itself from its competitors.

6 **Strategies.** These are laid down in the plan that shows what the organisation needs to do in order to reach its goals.

7 **Shared values.** This is the vision.

At the core of McKinsey's model is vision. This management instrument is the link and provides the direction for the remaining factors. As an operational management tool, vision can affect operational management in the following ways:

a by motivating employees;

b by focusing the attention of employees on relevant activities;

c by creating a framework that shows employees how tasks should be done and how these tasks fit into the bigger picture.

The degree to which an organisation succeeds in utilising a more effective management strategy depends on the existing vision and how it is communicated (see Figure 3.5).

The mission statement of an organisation is a description of its product-market combinations, and can be an indication of the way the organisation makes use of its structural competitive advantage.

Principles relate to the norms and values of the organisation and can be compared to societal norms and values. The following could be aspects of an organisation's principles:

Principles

a Quality first.
b Customer first.
c Reliability and honesty.
d Employees are reliable and honest.
e Employees are the organisation's strength.
f Focussing personal self awareness.
g Contributing to society.

As each organisation uses the words 'mission' and 'principles' in its own way, the distinction between the terms may not always be clear. It is important for the process of strategic management, however, that these elements are recognisable and expressed in the vision of the organisation.

Organisational goals

The way organisational goals are defined is based on the organisation's vision. The goals show the relationship between the organisation, the environment, and the employees. Naturally, their contents are influenced by the organisation's stakeholders. Finance providers (e.g. shareholders) in particular have a very important voice in the matter.

Organisational goals

Organisational goals often relate to one or more of the following subjects:
1 **Balance of interests.** 'We are a reliable partner for our customers, shareholders, staff and suppliers.'
2 **Profitability.** 'We aim to make our products and services profitable for our customers and for ourselves.'
3 **Quality.** 'We always produce perfect products and are there when our customers need us.'
4 **Effectivity and efficiency.** 'We encourage our staff to contribute to target-setting and optimised target achievement planning.'
5 **Image.** 'We are a leading supplier of products and services.'
6 **Code of conduct.** 'We work in a disciplined manner and keep our word.'

In these times of enormous and rapid change, an awareness of organisational goals is an essential and important point of reference for those working on strategic plans. Having such an awareness prevents situations where the content of the organisational strategy is determined by ad hoc decisions. 'If you don't know where you're going, any road will take you there.'

Strategies

Once the organisational goals have been scrutinised, the chosen strategies are examined. It is important to check the degree to which these strategies can achieve the identified goals. In other words, are the current strategies successful?

Chosen strategies

Elsewhere, this chapter demonstrates how an existing strategy can be fully adapted or revised as part of the process of strategic management.

Radical innovations at Mercedes

Every industry has to deal with disruptive developments that change the face of the existing business model. More than ten years ago, Mercedes flipped the switch. Successfully.

Radical innovations at Mercedes in 3 steps:

1 **Ideation:** the innovation team selects the best ideas from those that have been submitted internally or through the company's internal crowdsourcing platform

2 **Incubation:** the idea is tested for workability and scalability, and the development team is provided expert support. Ideas are developed into prototypes and pilot-projects in sprint efforts.

3 **Commercialisation:** the idea is prepared for the market. The product or service is implemented as part of the existing business or assigned to a spin-off.

Source: *Het Financieele Dagblad* (advert), fd.nl/ mercedesnext

Internal investigation as part of the situational analysis

The next step in the situational analysis is internal investigation (see Figure 2.1). Self-awareness is a crucial personal attribute. An insight into one's own functioning leads to a better assessment of the feasibility of one's options (for example, those for training or a new job). If one acknowledges one's own strengths and weaknesses, one can correct one's weaknesses and develop one's strengths further.

Athletes continuoully measure their performance in order to check their progress and draw up further results improvements with their coach. Many people tend to blame others for causing their own problems. This also applies to organisations. Falling profits can easily be blamed on a competitor who upsets the market by introducing lower prices. It is easy to forget to question one's own performance.

Internal audit

If an organisation wants to stay healthy or solve its problems, it is vital that it regularly cast a critical eye over its own operations. An investigation that focusses on the internal organisation is called an internal audit or management audit. Its goal is to look at all internal activities and to identify the strong and weak sides of the organisation.

During this exercise, various people in the organisation need to provide a lot of information. As it is important that this information be correct, optimal commitment at every level is required.

Integral or partial approach?
An investigation into strengths and weaknesses can be carried out in either of the following ways:
1 based on functions;
2 based on results.

Internal investigation by functional area. An investigation based on functional areas identifies a number of activities of a similar nature: research and development, purchasing, sales, and so on. During an internal audit of these functional areas, performance and productivity are measured. These aspects are scored either strong, neutral or weak. Scores may be compared to the scores of important competitors. By plotting the scores, it becomes possible to create an impression of relative performance (see Figure 2.4).

Functional areas
Performance

FIGURE 2.4 **AN EXAMPLE OF A PERFORMANCE SURVEY BY FUNCTIONAL AREA**

Functional area		Performance survey		
		Strong	Neutral	Weak
Marketing	Image			
	Market share			
	Quality service			
	Distribution network			
Finance	Solvency			
	Liquid assets			
	Return			
Production	Flexibility			
	Capacity			
	Economies of scale			
	Delivery time			
Organisation	Skills staff			
	Staff motivation			
	Flexibility of the organisation			

The information necessary for the assessment can be obtained through internal research, market research, or customer research. In many organisations, account managers are regularly required to go over survey questionnaires with their customers, enabling the customer to assess a supplier's performance.
Not all aspects are equally important for the commercial success of an organisation. This is why the relative importance of each aspect is determined following the assessment. Then, the results are weighted to give a balanced overview.
The term 'partial' or 'singular' approach describes a situation where an internal audit only investigates a limited number of functional areas within an organisation. The inherent risk in this approach is that the analysed areas, combined with an incorrect or incomplete definition of the problem, may lead to an incorrect overall impression and subsequent wrong decision-making. Of course, the advantage of investigating only a limited number of areas is in saving time.

Partial approach

Integral approach
Complete picture

Using the integral approach, all functional areas are investigated, and the results subsequently related, thus providing a complete picture of the organisation. Lately, interest in the integral approach has grown as many problems cannot be approached in isolation. A good example is an organisation's logistical process, which is likely to relate to almost all functional areas.

Results

Internal audit based on results. The second approach to internal auditing is results-based. Here, the focus is on the financial attractiveness of the various business activities. Profitability (current and potential) and the strategic perspective are both important in this approach.

Organisational units

Many enterprises divide related activities into organisational units. Typically, the products or services of these organisational units focus on clearly defined markets. Almost all functions are present within the unit: sales, purchases, administration, service, and so on. Unit results are also carefully monitored. One could say that a unit is actually an autonomous enterprise within a group. These units are known as SBUs: Strategic Business Units.

The word 'strategic' in this acronym correctly suggests that SBUs determine their own strategies, though these do need to fit in with the strategies of the overall group. In big enterprises, an SBU may hold a number of product market combinations (PMCs). A PMC is an SBU at a lower organisational level. SBUs and PMCs can be defined on the basis of products, groups of buyers, distribution channels, or geographical areas.

Core activity

Many enterprises are now subdivided into a large number of SBUs. Categorically, these SBUs should be part of the core activity of the enterprise. A core activity is an activity of particular focus for the enterprise. Core activities give the enterprise its right to exist and are responsible for its success. An example is the editing of books by Prentice Hall, a British publisher. In the coming years, an increasing number of enterprises will be subdividing their structure into business units. (This is discussed comprehensively in Chapter 11 on Structuring).

Since strategic businesses units nearly always operate autonomously and in different markets, the internal audit has to focus on each unit individually.

Portfolio management

Portfolio management

Different portfolio matrices are developed, depending on the kind of enterprise and type of activity. Where management applies this technique for analysis, it is called portfolio management. The following following phases of portfolio management can be identified:

1 Reflecting the activity portfolio in the matrix.
2 Analysing the portfolio. This refers to the balanced structure of the portfolio, the vision of the future, and the question of whether it will remain possible to fund the various activities (SBUs) now and in the future.
3 Choosing an SBU strategy. As a result of the analysis, the organisation must make decisions with regard to desired development of SBUs within the portfolio (see Figure 2.5).

FIGURE 2.5 **DESIRED DEVELOPMENT OF SBU'S IN THE PORTFOLIO**

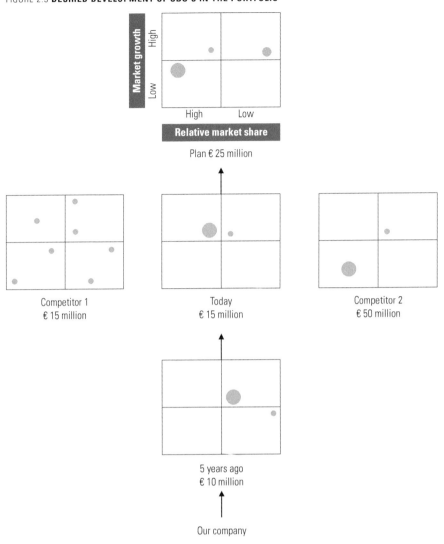

The internal audit charts all SBUs and checks whether the combination of activities is optimal. Every SBU is in a phase of the product life cycle and is thus profitable to a greater or lesser extent. It is of great importance to determine the best way of transferring funds from one SBU to another in order to foster investment in new products. Effectively tackling the allocation issue means safeguarding the future of the enterprise. It goes without saying that an enterprise should strive for a balanced activity portfolio.

Portfolio analysis

In a portfolio analysis, the various SBUs are categorised in a matrix and analysed according to a number of economic criteria. This analysis provides a coherent and total overview of the activities of an enterprise at a certain moment in time. A portfolio analysis can also serve to demonstrate how an enterprise and its activities have developed over a number of years.

The best-known and most-frequently applied approach to portfolio analysis originates with the Boston Consulting Group (BCG).

Boston Consulting Group

This approach addresses three aspects of the business unit, namely:

1 turnover (expressed as relative market share);
2 market developments (expressed in terms of market growth);
3 monetary flow (expressed as cash flow: the net profit after taxes and depreciations).

Relative market share
Market growth

With this model, the various SBUs are situated within the four-quadrant BCG matrix. Market growth is shown on the vertical axis and the relative market share (one's own market share related to the share of the largest competitor) is shown on the horizontal axis.

Within the matrix, the SBUs are represented by circles whose size corresponds to their volume of turnover within the organisation. Figure 3.9 shows data (referred to below) within such a BCG Matrix.

Assume, for example, that a brewery has identified the following strategic business units, each with their turnover and market share (see Table 2.1).

TABLE 2.1 **A BREWERY'S SBUS**

SBU	Turnover	Market growth	Market	Market share biggest competitor	Relative market share
Lager (mainstream)	110	0 – 1 %	25 %	20 %	25 : 20 = 1.25
Special beers (speciality)	50	10 – 13 %	10 %	25 %	10 : 25 = 0.4
Luxury beers (premium)	20	5 – 7 %	5 %	10 %	5 : 10 = 0.5
Seasonal beers	14	18 – 20 %	35 %	20 %	35 : 20 = 1.75
Light beers	6	3 – 6 %	5 %	7 %	5 : 7 = 0.71

Figure 2.6 shows the information from Table 2.1 in a BCG Matrix

FIGURE 2.6 **BOSTON CONSULTANCY GROUP MATRIX FOR A BREWERY**

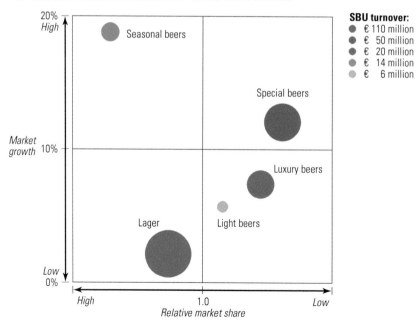

Organisations and their environment
PART A

© Noordhoff Uitgevers bv

The third aspect of the BCG Matrix is the development of the monetary flow (or cash flow) of the various SBUs. An SBU either generates money or requires money for investment, depending on the position of the SBU in the matrix. To be able to fund investments, an enterprise should strive for a balanced distribution of the various businesses in the matrix.

Cash flow

The portfolio analysis of the BCG is based on the following principles:

1 There is a positive relationship between the size of the relative market share and the amount of the cash flow. The larger the relative market share, the larger the cash flow. This can be explained in terms of the 'experience effect' and/or economies of scale. With a large relative market share, the costs per product come down to increased experience compared to competitors, resulting in more efficient deployment of staff and resources.
2 There is a negative relationship between the development of a market and the amount of cash flow. In the case of substantial market growth, an enterprise needs to invest heavily in its SBU. This diminishes the size of the cash flow. In a stable or shrinking market, hardly any money is invested in the activity. This leads to the creation of a relatively high cash flow.
3 There is a negative relationship between the development of relative market share and the volume of cash flow. In order to increase the relative market share, a large amount of money needs to be invested in the SBU.
4 Market growth decreases as a business progresses along its product lifecycle.

Based on the development of market growth, the relative market share and the cash flow, the BCG identifies four categories (as shown in Figure 2.7).

FIGURE 2.7 **SBU'S IN THE BCG-MATRIX**

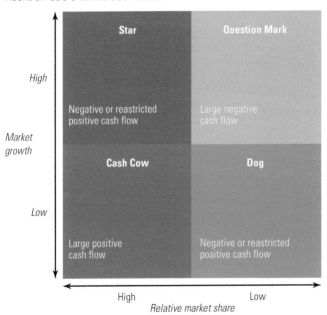

a **Question mark.** These SBUs are characterised by a high market growth and a relatively low market share. This yields a large negative cash flow. Question marks may turn out to be tomorrow's 'stars'.

Question mark

b **Star.** These SBUs have a high market growth as well as a high relative market share. They yield a negative or restricted positive cash flow. The high market growth will probably lead to an increase in competition.

Star

c **Cash cow.** This is where profit is being made. These SBUs have low market growth but a high relative market share and a large positive cash flow.

d **Dog.** These SBUs beg the question of whether these activities need to be stopped – and if so, at what point. Dogs have low growth as well as a low relative market share. They generate a negative cash flow or a restricted positive cash flow.

Investment strategies

Based on this division, we can identify the following investment strategies:

a **Dog:** *Disinvest;*

b **Star:** *Protect and increase investment;*

c **Question mark:** *Invest or disinvest;*

d **Cash cow:** *Invest to keep market share up to standard.*

In Figure 2.8, the investment strategy for the various SBUs is given by means of an arrow with a dotted line. This shows that the cash flow coming from the cash cow is invested specifically in the question mark and star SBUs. The ideal development of SBUs within the matrix is indicated by an arrow with an uninterrupted line.

FIGURE 2.8 **DEVELOPEMENT OF CASHFLOW AND SBU'S**

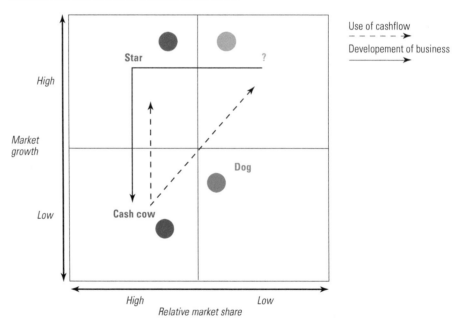

The position of an SBU in the Boston Consultancy Matrix is significant for the marketing instruments of product, price, promotion and distribution. Strategies can be determined per instrument: for example, by raising or lowering the price, or by expanding or shrinking distribution channels.

Organisation and management

Organisation and management need to meet specific requirements in order to be able to apply the portfolio technique successfully. These requirements are discussed below.

In practice, a business cannot always be compared to an organisational unit like a division or department. However, information supply and management reports are tailored to the needs of organisational units. This is why it is often difficult to obtain strategic information applicable to one particular business.

If a business belongs to more than one organisational unit, responsibility for the business is also shared. This is an important reason for placing businesses under one organisational unit whenever possible. Furthermore, financial reporting needs to be adjusted to the needs of individual SBUs. Another important issue is the (timely) availability and validity of information needed for the portfolio analysis. Often, the various information systems are not adequetely connected, so that a lot of data-input has to be repeated, increasing the potential for error.

Another portfolio management problem has to do with to the competences and the responsibilities of business unit managers. Managers of SBUs with a cash cow business are not inclined to invest their cash in businesses outside their responsibility. A manager of a question mark business needs funds badly and will urge top management to transfer the money in from other areas.

Competencies and responsibilities

In order to develop businesses successfully, it is important to have the right manager in the right place (see Figure 2.9).

Managers come in different shapes and forms. Their skills and mentality vary, and they range from genuine entrepreneurs who do not mind taking risks and looking for businesses they can build up from scratch (pioneers) to managers who avoid risks whenever possible and aim to consolidate their existing business (administrators). In general, a dog business requires a manager who takes care of reorganising and downsizing, whereas a question mark-business requires a pioneer.

FIGURE 2.9 **TYPES OF MANAGERS WITHIN THE BCG MATRIX**

	Star	Question Mark
High	**Experienced manager** — Focused on growth — Goal oriented — Enterprising — Structuring	Entrepreneur — Risk taking / experimenting — Creative / innovative — Extrovert — Dynamic — Team player
	Cash Cow	**Dog**
Low	**Administrator** — Stabilising — Integrating — Educating — Cash control	Finisher or convertor — Problem solver — Introvert — Cash control / disinvestment — Discontinuing

market growth (vertical axis, High to Low)

Relative market share (horizontal axis: High — Low)

By way of conclusion, some critical comments should be made on the BCG Matrix. Firstly, the BCG model is obviously a growth model. Market growth is considered high when it is 10% or more, meaning that the majority of businesses fall into the category of dogs. This can have a stigmatising effect and one consequence might be that profitable activities are ignored and possibly needlessly restructured.

Another issue is that investment of cash cow earnings might result in the cash cows themselves being neglected. By using the money for further investments in cash cows, various possibilities could be exploited.

Lastly, the importance of a relatively high market share is debatable. Until recently, only large organisations had the privilege of a large market share. However, they are known for their relatively high fixed costs. There are many examples of organisations that make a decent living with a relatively small market share, since they can take advantage of lower labour costs, accommodation expenses and marketing budgets.

In order to apply the BCG model correctly, it needs to be adapted to the industry as well as to the enterprise.

Europe aiming for ten battery mega-plants

Europe needs over 10 mega-factories in order to be able to meet the future demand for electric car batteries. European Commissioner Maros Sefcovic (Energy) is therefore urging all parties involved, including governments, to pick up the pace of investments.

Desert project

Europe is currently at a major disadvantage with regards to the manufacture of batteries. Companies in Asia and the USA are setting the tone. One of the most imaginative projects is the one Tesla is undertaking the US State of Nevada, where visionary

entrepreneur Elon Musk is building a factory with a capacity of 35 gigawatt hours per year in the desert.

Strategic interest

'The European market is still very fragmented. We need a much higher level of collaboration,' says European Commissioner for Energy, Maros Sefcovic.

Source: *Het Financieele Dagblad*, Tuesday 13 February 2018 https://fd.nl/economie-politiek/1241529/europa-mikt-op-tien-megafabrieken-voor-accu-s, consulted 7 May 2018

External research as part of the situational analysis

Many organisation exist in a rather turbulent environment: a reason for thorough and ongoing alertness.

External research involves developments in the external environment being mapped out and translated into possible opportunities and threats for the organisation. External research is part of the situational analysis and can be done at the same time as the internal audit (see Figure 2.1).

Like the internal audit, external research can be carried out by a combination of employees and external professionals. It should result in identification of the main opportunities and threats to the organisation.

External investigation concerns the environment of the organisation. This environment consists of a number of parties and external factors. The basic aim of external research is to discover the interconnections between the various parties and factors, which is more than simply revealing the individual influence of each element. It is also important to realise that the influence of each party and factor differ per organisation. In oder for this to be properly understood, it is necessary to structure the external components (parties and factors). There are often particular external component groupings and hierarchies within such a structure. Figure 2.10 shows the external components.

Interconnections

External components

FIGURE 2.10 **THE STRUCTURE OF THE EXTERNAL COMPONENTS**

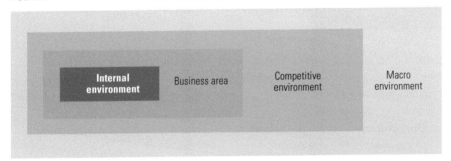

Internal environment

The internal environment relates to the organisation itself and is mostly determined by the chosen organisational structure, procedures, communication structures, and quality of the staff.

An organisation that wants to be effectively attuned to its external environment must be structured in a way that fits with the environment. In other words, the external environment dictates the design of the organisation. Important success factors are decisiveness, flexibility, and the effectiveness of the organisation. Some examples of opportunities and threats to the internal environment are:

a **opportunities – strengths**
 – availability of high-quality staff;
 – high level of automation;

b **threats – weaknesses**
 – bureaucratic organisation;
 – lack of 'entrepreneurship'.

Internal environment research (the internal audit) is discussed elsewhere.

Business areas

An organisation performs individual tasks within a broader arena, and this gives every organisation a certain function within a wider process. The specific tasks carried out by an organisation are also influenced by the tasks of the other organisations. Figure 2.11 shows the business area of various organisations within a supply chain.

FIGURE 2.11 **BUSINESS AREAS WITHIN A SUPPLY CHAIN**

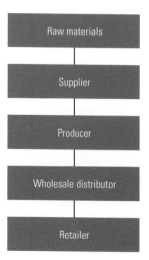

Since the activities of organisations change constantly, the tasks of the enterprise may also change. Environmental research focusses on the mapping out of the business area of an organisation. Some examples of the opportunities and threats facing hospitals are:

- **Opportunities**: hospitals will have to perform a great number of new tasks due to the aging of the population.
- **Threats**: the rising costs of health care may lead hospitals to decide to stop performing certain tasks.

Competitive environment

Competitive environment

The third part of the external research concerns the competitive environment. Organisations are influenced by competitors. To understand the opportunities and threats coming from the competitive environment, the following questions need to be answered:

A Who are the competitors?
B What information about the competitors is needed?
C How intense is the competition?
D What competitive advantages does the organisation have that allows it to make its mark on the various markets?

A Who are the competitors? The industrial sector must be defined in order to determine the competitors. An industrial sector is a group of enterprises that produce similar products, often based on a similar technology. Similar products are products that are interchangeable in the eyes of the buyers.

There are two ways of identifying competitors in an industrial sector:

1 Customer-oriented approach: competitors are determined from the perspective of the potential buyer. The buyer (or potential buyer) must make choices in their spending behaviour. They not only have a choice of similar products from various companies, but have to choose between different sorts of products. In general, organisations tend to identify their competitors at the product level. Particular Renault cars are in competition with particular Honda cars. However, possible competitors can also be found at other levels. Car manufacturers might consider their products as a means of transportation. Consequently, they have to compete not only with other car manufacturers, but also with organisations that provide other transport opportunities. A factor that also plays a role is that most consumers have a limited income and have to make choices about how to spend it. This means that car manufacturers are also competing with suppliers of other consumer goods.

2 Strategic group approach: competitors are determined according to strategic groups. A strategic group is a group of organisations that have common characteristics and use similar competitive strategies. Some strategic group criteria are the degree of specialisation, the chosen distribution structure, price strategy, product strategy and so on. An example of a strategic group in the car market is the BMW and Audi group. Both have a similar brand image, a similar price strategy and a similar distribution structure.

Strategic group

The advantage of this approach is that competitors can be analysed within a more consistent framework.

B What information about the competitors is needed? A number of additional questions must be answered to arrive at an satisfactory answer to this one:
– What are the present and the past strategies of the competitors?
– What are the strengths and weaknesses of the competitors?
– How big and profitable is each competitor?
– What is the organisational culture of each competitor like?

Based on this information, so-called reaction profiles can be created, which can be used to answer the following questions:
– What strategic decisions are the competitors mostly likely to take?
– What are the weaknesses of the competitors and how vulnerable are they?
– What reactions can be expected from the competitors?

C How intense is the competition? The attractiveness of an industry is determined mainly by long-term profitability, and this profitability depends on the intensity of competition. To a large extent, this intensity depends on two factors:

Intensity

1 Structural factors. For instance, the degree of concentration and the possibilities of entering the sector. Entrance possibilities depend on such factors as economies of scale, product differentiation, the required level of investment and the possibilities of entry into the existing distribution channels.
2 Strategic factors. For instance, the readiness to cooperate and the degree of uncertainty about the strategies of competitors.

D What competitive advantages allow the company to make its mark on the various markets? It is important to identify how strongly the organisation can profile itself against competitors. Its advantage may be based on costs, image, or unique product features. The larger the applicable competitive advantage, the less vulnerable the organisation.

Competitive advantages

Competitive analysis according to Porter

Competitive analysis

Michael Porter, a professor at the Harvard Business School, made an important contribution to the development of strategic management. He analysed the competitive environment according to the industry to which an enterprise belongs.

He identified five competitive forces within any industry. These forces determine the structure and the profitability of the industry. Figure 2.12 shows the five competitive forces:

1 new entrants;
2 buyers;
3 substitutes;
4 suppliers;
5 competitors.

FIGURE 2.12 **THE FIVE COMPETITIVE FORCES**

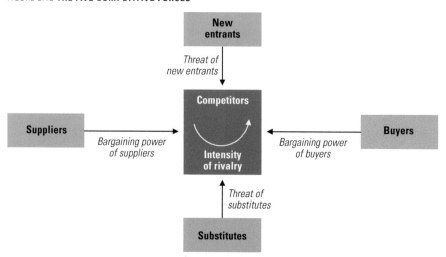

New entrants   **1 New entrants**. New entrants to the sector try to gain market share at the expense of present suppliers. Pressure could be put on prices or present supplier costs could be forced to go up (e.g. extra marketing expenses). This may decrease the average profit in the industry. The threat of new entrants depends on barriers to entry. Some examples of barriers are the need for economies of scale, brand awareness, required investment, entrance to distribution channels, and government policies. The entrance of new enterprises within an industry may cause changes to the strategies of the other enterprises in the industry.

Buyers   **2 Buyers.** Buyers set competitors against each other and, in doing so, try to reduce prices. The power of the buyers depends, amongst other factors, on the availability of information, the costs of transfer to other competitors, the number of available alternative suppliers, and the purchase volume of the buyers. If buyers have a strong position, the average profit in the industry is low, and vice versa. A possible enterprise strategy is focussing on buyers with little power.

Substitutes   **3 Substitutes.** Enterprises within an industrial sector compete with other industrial sectors if these produce substitute products. The presence of substitutes has the same effect as high entrance barriers: that is, a higher average output. As such, enterprises should be aware of the price-quality ratio of substitutes, the tendency of buyers to substitute, and the costs of changeover to substitutes. In the event of threats from substitutes, enterprises can react by changing the price-quality ratio of their own products.

Suppliers   **4 Suppliers.** Since suppliers determine the purchase price of a product, they exert a large influence on the average output. The power of suppliers depends on the presence of substitutes, the importance of the supplied product and the concentration of suppliers. There are only a few ways that enterprises can exert an influence on the power of suppliers.

5 Competitors. Within any industry, enterprises compete with each other because they want to improve their individual position. The intensity of competition depends on the number and the variety of competitors, market growth in the industry, withdrawal thresholds and cost levels.

Macro-surroundings

The last component of the environment consists of six external factors:

1 environment factors;
2 technological factors;
3 demographic factors;
4 economic factors;
5 political factors;
6 social factors.

These influencing factors are discussed in Chapter 1.

Li Shufu is Europe's new car magnate

An amount of €7.3 billion made him the largest Daimler shareholder. Li Shufu, founder and top executive at Chinese car manufacturer Geely, is expanding his empire. Twenty years ago, Li was still producing refrigerators when he made his first move into the automobile industry.

Volvo as a stepping stone

Li soon found out that the competition abroad was even fiercer. His take-over of Volvo in 2010 was therefore an extra-large one. The Swedish car maker offered the stepping stone that earned Li a great deal

of status, particularly within the People's Republic. Take-overs or participations that contributed to the ideal of 'Made in Chine 2025' turned the gates wide open. The development of the electric car is seen as a key industry. From 2019, the Swedish subsidiary will only be producing hybrid and electric cars.

Source: *Het Financieele Dagblad*, Friday 2 March 2018 https://fd.nl/ondernemen/1244153/li-shufu-is-de-nieuwe-automagnaat-van-europa, consulted 7 May 2018

2.2.2 Strategy formation

After a situation analysis, the next step is strategy formation. Strategy formation is part of the process of strategic management, and consists of three phases:

1 determining a view of the future;
2 developing various strategies;
3 evaluation and choice of a strategy.

Strategy formation

Strategy formation: determining a view of the future

The first phase of strategy formation involves sketching an impression of the organisation's future. In particular, it requires checking whether the chosen objectives can be achieved in the future by using the present strategy. This can be predicted on the basis of a situation analysis. If it seems that the objectives cannot be fully met by using the present strategy, either strategy or objectives must be adjusted to fill the gap between what is desired and what is reality.

Image of the future

This difference between desirability and reality occurs the more frequently if an organisation operates in fast-changing surroundings, or if competition is strong.

Furthermore, the objectives might be too ambitious, or the present strategy unsuitable for the desired objectives.

Strategy formation: development of different strategies

Strategy If the present strategy fails to reach the goals, other strategies should be developed: for example, developing new products, entering new markets, choosing other sales channels, increasing efficiency or collaborating with a new partner. In short, a strategy determines the options for the optimal functioning of the organisation. Strategies have the following characteristics:
- They have a medium and a long-term time span;
- They are related to the organisation as a whole;
- They create opportunities to promote new investments.

Strategic planning The type of strategic planning used depends heavily on type and size of the organisation, characteristics of the industry in question, quality of management, and knowledge of suitable methods and techniques. Organisations should select strategies in keeping with their specific circumstances. With a multitude of possible strategies available, some initial evaluation is desired when trying to make a final choice.

The following six categories are discussed:
1 strategies dependent on the organisation's market share;
2 strategies dependent on the extent of turbulence in the environment;
3 expansion strategies (the product-market matrix);
4 Michael Porter's generic competitive strategies;
5 Treacy and Wiersema's value disciplines;
6 Blue Ocean Strategy.

Ad 1 Strategies dependent on the organisation's market share

Organisations exhibit clear differences in their market share. On this basis, the following types of organisations can be identified:
a market leaders;
b challengers;
c followers;
d specialists.

Each of these types have their own specific competition strategies, which are explained below.

Market leaders **A Market leaders**. These organisations have the largest market share and function as a beacon to other organisations. Market leaders aim to:
- Increase the total market;
- Defend their own market share;
- Expand their market share.

There are various ways of achieving these objectives. The total market can be increased by increasing by the number of users, by stimulating current users to increase their consumption, or by attracting new users. To defend their market share, organisations could choose from the following competitive strategies:

Position strengthening *a* **Position strengthening.** A 'stronghold' can be built around the product through unique features, low pricing, a high distribution density, or powerful advertising.

Attacking the flanks *b* **Attacking the flanks.** There is an adage that states the best defence is a good offence, which suggests there is wisdom in attacking one's competitor. The market leader tries to discourage attacks from competitors by using directional marketing.

c **Enhancing mobility.** Positions can also be defended by increasing the mobility of the enterprise and by creating options to move activities to other markets. These competitive strategies can also be used if the market leader attempts to increase its market share.

Enhancing mobility

B Challengers. The aim of these organisations is to become market leaders. They may use the following competition strategies to do so:
–   Attack the market leader head on;
–   Attack the market leader from the side;
–   Hedge the market leader in;
–   Attack the market leader indirectly;
–   Use a guerrilla strategy.

Challengers

In head-on attacks, the challenger fights the market leader with those marketing instruments that work well for the market leader itself. The attack focusses on the strengths rather than the weaknesses of the market leader. The outcome of this fight depends mainly on the power and stamina of the competitors.

Head-on attacks

An attack from the flanks means the challenger uses the marketing instruments or other strong points of its own organisation that are less developed in the market leader's organisation.

Attack from the flanks

If the challenger chooses to hedge the market leader in, it attacks the market leader on a lot of fronts using various marketing instruments. These may include attacks in the form of better products, lower prices, greater numbers of distribution points, and more advertising activity.

Hedge the market

The challenger can also attack the market leader indiractly: entering markets in which the market leader does not operate. The final goal is to build new strongholds via new markets and or new products.

A guerrilla strategy aims at destroying the balance of the market leader by means of brief attacks from different angles: by lowering of prices and intensive promotion campaigns, for example.

Guerrilla strategy

C Followers. Not all organisations strive to become market leaders. Since the market leader is more powerful in a number of areas, attacks have little chance of success in most situations. Followers can, however, use competitive strategies. Every follower can give their product or service a special feature to retain customers or obtain a share of new customers. There are three competitive strategies that market followers can implement:
1   Imitating market leader strategy as closely as possible. The market follower copies the market leader in activities such as segmentation and the use of marketing mix instruments (price, product, promotion, and place).
2   Imitating market leader strategy but at a certain remove. The follower may adopt a certain degree of differentiation in some areas.
3   Mimicking market leader administration in certain areas, but using one's own strategies in others.

Followers

Studies show that a follower's profitability can approximate that of the market leader. This may be explained by the fact that a follower does not need to invest significant resources in basic research in the way a market leader often has to. Instead, a follower can invest in further research and development.

D Specialists. Specialists are organisations that focus on small market niches. They are active in parts of the market that are out of reach for other organisations because of their unusual character.

Specialists

Ideally, such a specialised part of the market has the following characteristics:
- It is a niche market;
- It is large enough to be profitable;
- It has growth potential;
- It lies outside the field of interest of larger organisations in the market;
- It has the ability and means to operate effectively in the specialised part;
- It is able to survive a potential attack from large organisations by means of customer goodwill.

The power of these types of organisations is derived from their specialisation. Many forms of specialisation are possible: for example, geographical specialisation (e.g. operating only in particular regions) and product specialisation (e.g. high-quality products only).

Ad 2 Strategies for a turbulent environment

Turbulent environment

Today, enterprises are operating in a turbulent environment, characterised by:
- various variables undergoing change at an increasing rate;
- having greater mutual dependence on all sorts of phenomena;
- developments having an increasingly autonomous character.

The prediction of future developments becomes more difficult in a turbulent environment. Predictions have a high degree of uncertainty. Instead of predicting, it is therefore much more meaningful to identify an organisation's vulnerable factors. One way of doing so is via a susceptibility analysis.

O&M IN PRACTICE

DSM innovations profitable from 2019

Full steam ahead for DSM. Is the company's growth indeed limitless? For 2019 and 2020, DSM predicts major innovation programmes to go 'on stream'. Examples include the so-called 'Clean Cow'-product, a nutritional ingredient that counters bovine methane production, an important global source of greenhouse gasses. In addition, there is 'Green Ocean', a collaboration with German Evonik. Together, the companies are producing omega 3-fatty acids for animal feed and salmon farming from algae. This means that farmed salmon will no longer need to be fed small fish, thus preventing ocean depletion. And what about the fully recyclable DSM-Niaga carpet, which uses a technique that could also be applied to mattresses or shoes? DSM will be offering the technology under licence. Recently, DSM began a collaboration with bed manufacturer Auping.

Source: *Het Financieele Dagblad*, Thursday 15 February 2018 https://fd.nl/ondernemen/1241998/ innovaties-dsm-gaan-vanaf-2019-geld-opleveren, consulted 7 May 2018

When vulnerable factors in an organisation are detected, it is important to determine how to deal with them on their own terms. In other words, an organisation must try to solve its vulnerability issues with the help of turbulent situation strategies. For this purpose, the organisation has the choice of four strategies:

1 immunisation;
2 adaptation;
3 manipulation;
4 innovation.

1 **Immunisation**. The first and most obvious way of protecting oneself in areas of vulnerability is to make oneself impervious to attack. A possible option is diversification: for example, penetrating new markets with new products, primarily looking for relationships in a new business area and/or new production techniques (concentric diversification). If there is no longer any relationship with existing markets and/or products, this is called 'conglomeration forming'.

The main motive for diversifying is to spread the risks, making the organisation less sensitive to changes in the environment.

In practice, diversification has a number of drawbacks:
- After diversification, organisations might find themselves with components that are scarcely connected. This hampers positive synergy and increases bureaucracy.
- Diversification should be the last option used to escape from a weak competitive position. Diversification can only be successful if the enterprise holds a powerful position.
- The key goal of spreading risks through diversification is seen mostly in financial terms, without considering interactions between new and existing activities.

Immunisation
Concentric diversification

2 **Adaptation**. This strategy relates to an organisation's to adapt itself to changing circumstances – or, in other words, its flexibility. The organisation can be flexible in many areas, including the following:
- products;
- production processes;
- organisational structure;
- financing;
- information retrieval systems.

Adaptation
Flexibility

An increase in the adaptability of organisations can be gained by decentralisation: that is, by using smaller organisational units with shorter decision-making processes and communication lines.

Decentralisation

3 **Manipulation**. Manipulation can be defined as the full or partial recovery of earlier loss of influential power. As mentioned, a characteristic of a turbulent environment is the increasing autonomy of developments: organisations increasingly unable to control what is happening. Trying to win back part of the lost ground is an obvious strategy.

Since control over developments is a consequence of concentration of economic power, other organisations will obviously follow suit. Economic power can be recovered by internal growth and by coalition formation: collaboration with other organisations (see also Chapter 4). A consequence of coalition formation is that organisations have to give up part of their autonomy in order to reach consensus in the area of policy.

Manipulation

Innovation

4 Innovation. To react adequately to change, both a certain degree of flexibility and innovation are required. As with flexibility, an organisation can be innovative in many aspects. These include:

- production techniques;
- organisational structure;
- distribution;
- communication;
- information retrieval.

Technical innovation

Where technical innovation is concerned, organisations have to choose between buying a new product or developing it themselves. Both options have their benefits and drawbacks. Buying a new product can be cheaper, and the introduction time is short. But by developing one's own innovations, one can stay ahead, favouring profitability.

Expansion strategies

Ad 3 Expansion strategies (the product-market matrix)

Organisations have two growth possibilities:

1 New **products** can be developed.
2 New **markets** can be entered.

When the two dimensions are combined, a product-market matrix (Ansoff) arises (see Figure 2.13).

FIGURE 2.13 **ANSOFF'S PRODUCT/MARKET MATRIX**

		Product	
		Existing	New
Market	Existing	Market penetration	Product development
	New	Market development	Diversification

Market penetration

Market penetration

Market penetration occurs when an organisation increases its market share in an existing market with its existing product. The market needs to be a growth market and the organisation needs to have a competitive advantage.

Product development

Product development

Product development is the development of new products while continuing to operate in the existing market.

Market development

Market development

New markets for existing products can be developed: for example, a restaurant opening a takeaway service. Another option is that of selling existing products in foreign markets.

Diversification

Diversification

Diversification refers to organisational growth by developing new products and selling these in new markets.

This leads to the next question of how to shape an organisation's growth. In principle, there are three strategies or possibilities for growth: through autonomous growth, through a collaboration, or through engaging in mergers with or take-overs of other organisations.

Autonomous growth

The organisation takes control of its growth itself. This method of growth often takes up a (very) large amount of time. One advantage is that is does not require or cause the organisation's dependence on a third party, and that all of the company's expertise, such as technological knowledge and skill, remains within the organisation.

Collaboration

The organisation finds one or more partners. Collaboration is an umbrella term for various cooperative forms. Examples are strategic alliances and joint ventures. This type of growth is often much faster than autonomous growth. The increased growth speed is usually the result of the fact that the partners combine specific expertise and are able to learn from each other (quickly).
Growth through collaboration is discussed in greater detail in Section 2.8.

Mergers and take-overs

This form of growth means combining with other organisations. While it is theoretically the fastest way to grow, it is a process which, in practice, turns out to be rather laborious.
Growth through merger and take-over is discussed in greater detail in Section 2.6.

Ansoff's growth model indicates four directions of growth (market penetration, product development, market development, and diversification). There is one growth direction to add to this list: vertical integration. Vertical integration means the organisation takes control of another link in either direction. This process is referred to in terms of forward or backward integration. Forward integration means the organisation takes control of a link in the direction of the final consumer, for example a wholesaler taking over a chain of retailers. Backward integration is when an organisation takes control of a link in the direction of the original producer, for example a wholesaler taking over a manufacturer of finished products.

Combining the five growth directions with the three different forms of growth leads to a matrix that demonstrates all growth possibilities, as shown in Table 2.2.

TABEL 2.2 **GROWTH MATRIX (COMBINING GROWTH STRATEGY AND GROWTH DIRECTION)**

Growth strategy/form	Autonomous growth	Growth through collaboration	Growth through mergers/take-overs
Market penetration	X	X	X
Product development	X	X	X
Market development	X	X	X
Diversification	X	X	X
Vertical integration	-	-	X

Ad 4 Michael Porter's generic competitive strategies

Michael Porter argues that the formulation of a competitive strategy depends on an organisation's position relative to its environment. By environment, Porter specifically means the company's active industry or sector of operation. Michael Porter is of the opinion that organisations that choose a clear strategy are more successful than organisations that do not. In his book 'Competitive Strategy' (1980), he argues that there are essentially three possibilities when choosing a strategy: cost leadership strategy, differentiation strategy, or focus strategy. Only by choosing one distinct strategy can a company achieve competitive advantage. An organisation can only be successful if it manages to distinguish itself from its competitors.

Based on an analysis of the industry, it is possible to choose either of two strategies to optimise the results within the industry:

Undifferentiated strategy

a **Undifferentiated strategy**: the emphasis of this strategy is on developing a product or service and putting on the market, all the while ensuring the costs remain as low as possible. The quality of the product or service certainly also remains of importance under this strategy.

Differentiation strategy

b **Differentiation strategy**: the emphasis of this strategy is on achieving a competitive advantage by focussing products or services on specific customer requirements.

These two strategies can then be finetuned by involving the concept of 'competitive reach'. Competitive reach is an accurate representation of the organisation's targeted client groups, as well as the marketing tools used to reach those target groups. Competitive reach can be broad or narrow.
The various strategies are illustrated in Figure 2.14.

FIGURE 2.14 **FOUR STRATEGIES FOR OBTAINING COMPETITIVE ADVANTAGE**

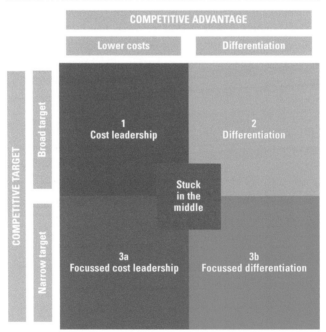

There are three possible generic competitive strategies, discussed in the following paragraphs.

A broad competitive reach (broad target area) means the organisation focusses on the market as a whole. In this situation, there are two possible competitive strategies.

Cost leadership

This competitive strategy entails offering products or services at the lowest possible price. This means that organisations are out to achieve a cost price that is as low as possible. Low cost prices can be achieved through mass scale production (economies of scale), by designing operational processes as efficiently as possible, and by adjusting the cost level downwards using (directed) technological innovations. Cost leadership often means that many standard products or services are offered. If more than one organisation in the same industry chooses this strategy, a scenario of strong mutual competition arises. This usually results in overcapacity, leading to inevitable reorganisations in the industry. Examples of organisations using this strategy are Ryanair and Lidl.

Differentiation strategy

Differentiation means the organisation chooses to distinguish itself from other organisations in the same industry through its products or services. The distinction is based on unique characteristics of the products or services compared to those offered by other providers in the same market. These characteristics can include the quality of materials used, the extent of service provided, sustainability or durability, and product design.
A differentiation strategy does not preclude the success of other providers in the same industry. Each organisation is able to address the requirements of specific customer groups. The unique characteristics of the individual products or services mean that buyers are willing to pay a higher price. Examples of organisations using this strategy are KLM Royal Dutch Airlines and supermarket chain Tesco's.

In the case of a narrow competitive reach (narrow target reach), the organisation does not focus on the target group as a whole, but only on certain buyer groups or segments. This means that, within the market, the focus is on particular buyer groups. Michael Porter calls this strategy the **focus strategy**. Choosing to focus on a particular buyer group makes it possible to address the specific requirements of this group of buyers with even greater precision, resulting in a clear preference. A focus strategy can be further specified into a cost focus or a differentiation focus strategy. An example of an organisation that aims at a cost focus strategy is Euromaster. Examples of differentiation focussed organisations are (expensive) car brand Ferrari and (expensive) perfume brand Chanel.
Michael Porter is of the opinion that an organisation should always make a clear choice for one of these three strategies. Only a clear choice can result in an organisation's success. If the organisation does not decide on one of the strategies, it will not create sufficient distinctiveness or competitive strength as a result. Michael Porter refers to this as being 'stuck in the middle' – an organisation whose profitability will (eventually) decline.

Michael Porter's competitive strategies offer a clear illustration of the product or service positioning of organisations. Michael Porter's opinion that organisations should make a clear decision has received criticism following the publication of the model. In practice, there are also successful organisations that combine a differentiation strategy with strong cost consciousness. Nevertheless, it is still a good conceptual model.

Triodos continuing sustainable investment policy

Companies that do not contribute to be sold

Fighting the effects of global warming requires a stronger approach. To that end, Triodos has decided only to invest in companies that make a positive contribution to the world. Triods' seven sustainable transition themes are:

1 Health and well-being;
2 Inclusive coexistence and empowerment;
3 Sustainable agriculture and nourishment;
4 Sustainable mobility and infrastructure;
5 Renewable resources;
6 Circular economy;
7 Sustainable innovation.

Source: Fondsnieuws, May 2018, edition 9, no. 2 (an FD media group initiative)

Ad 5 Treacy and Wiersema's value disciplines

A model similar to Porter's competitive strategies is the value strategy model by Treacy and Wiersema (1995), known as: 'value disciplines'. Michael Porter is of the opinion that an organisation should make a dedicated decision to pursue one single competitive strategy. Failing to do so means the organisation will run the risk of becoming 'Stuck in the Middle'.

The basis for Treacy and Wiersema's value strategy model is that organisations should score well on all value strategies and, in addition, excel in one selected value strategy. This is the only way for an organisation to create competitive advantage – not on the basis of a single selected value strategy. The reason is that customers always asses the three aspects in relation to each other. Even though a certain group of consumers may focus on quality, that does not mean they place no value on price or service.

Treacy and Wiersema's three value disciplines are:

1 Operational Excellence – cost leadership;
2 Product Leadership;
3 Customer Intimacy – customer relationship.

The three value disciplines are shown in Figure 2.15:

FIGURE 2.15 **TREACY AND WIERSEMA'S THREE VALUE DISCIPLINES**

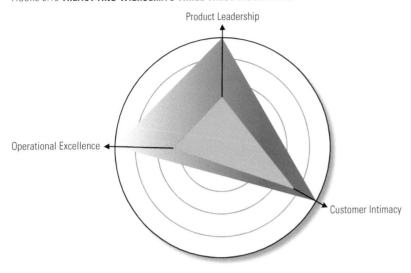

Source: *Business- en Managementmodellen*, Marijn Mulders, Noordhoff Uitgevers, 2018, p. 350

Operational Excellence

Designing all business processes as efficiently and effectively as possible is the most important angle and challenge. On the one hand, the design should focus on quality – on the other, it should be on production at minimised costs. The entirety of the operation management should be optimised. Major attention is paid to quality care, and there is also a high degree of cost consciousness. For buyers, this angle results in low prices and shorter waiting times, among other things.

Operational Excellence

Product Leadership

This value discipline centres on the product or services. The organisation is able to continually introduce innovative products or services onto the market. Organisations adopting this strategy focus heavily on Research & Development activities, the development of creativity, and a business culture that encourages innovation. The 'time to market' is also very important: the period between the moment a new product is designed and its availability on the market. This should be kept as brief as possible in order to stay ahead of the competition in the competitive process.

Product Leadership

Customer Intimacy

This discipline centres on the relationship with customers or buyers. Important elements within the customer relationship are customer loyalty, degree of service, reliability, and specifically addressing customer needs and expectations. This value discipline often relies on Customer Relationship management systems in order to monitor and (specifically) cater to individual customers and customer groups. It also involves developing loyalty schemes for specific customer groups, with the goal of encouraging a long-term commitment from the customer to the organisation. Loyalty schemes may focus on savings, discounts, or attending events or trainings. Customer Intimacy does not operate from the perspective of individual transactions, but more from that of customer-oriented, long-term solutions. In many organisations, account managers are the link between the organisation and its customers.

Customer Intimacy

To ensure that these value disciplines lead to a structural competitive advantage, the organisation should observe the following list of four rules:

1 Excel at one value discipline. There should be one value discipline at which the organisation wants to be the best (excel) on the market;
2 With regards to the other disciplines, the organisation should achieve a basic level (threshold) of quality;
3 The disciplines are not one-time activities, but require continuous attention;
4 The business processes must be designed in such a way as to determine the quality levels of the value disciplines.

Ad 6 Blue Ocean Strategy

In 2005, W. Chan Kim and Renee Mauborgne published '*Blue Ocean Strategy. How to create Uncontested Market Space and Make the Competition Irrelevant*', and introduced the world to a new way of strategy development. They did so by describing two distinct methods of (new) strategy, namely the Red Ocean and the Blue Ocean.

Red Ocean

The Red Ocean

The Red Ocean means the organisation chooses the option of competing in its existing markets. The idea is for the organisation to attempt to outperform its competitors. The authors label this strategy with the colour red because it tends to result in a 'bloodbath' or in severe 'bloodshed'. The pattern is one of intense competition, followed by the emergence of winners and losers. Competition occurs within a particular market space with existing operators. In this market space, organisations opt for a differentiation strategy or cost leadership.

Blue Ocean

The Blue Ocean

The Blue Ocean strategy means the organisation chooses to ignore existing market space in favour of creating a new market using new products or services. This new market space is free of competition, and thus enables the organisation to formulate its own rules. The authors chose the colour blue to represent this process to illustrates its wide-open nature, with 'plenty of fish in the sea' waiting to be caught. Within the new market space, it is possible to choose either a differentiation strategy or cost leadership.

At the core of the Blue Ocean strategy is the aim of value innovation. Value innovation consists of two components:

1 value creation: customers should be offered the highest customer value;
2 low costs: adopting a high level of cost consciousness.

Implementation of the Blue Ocean strategy encompasses six principles, four of which are directional and two are operational (Mulders, 2018).

Directional parameters

1 Re-establish and redefine market boundaries.
2 Keep a broad perspective. Do not focus solely on numbers, but keep an eye on the bigger picture.
3 Look beyond existing clients towards new (potential) clients.
4 Construct a business model that has the potential for sufficient profit.

Operational principles

1 New strategy demands organisational change and leadership.
2 Implementation is closely linked to the strategy selected.

Examples of organisations to successfully apply the Blue Ocean strategy are Apple, Tesla and Cirque du Soleil.

SMEs unable to keep up with innovation race

The manufacturing industry has been experiencing such rapid digitisation and robotisation that many supplying small and medium enterprises are unable to keep up under their own power; thus warns the industry alliance. Cabinet will rapidly need to broaden the criteria for innovation subsidies in order to keep SMEs in the race. If not, too many holes will be struck in the production chain, and the Netherlands will start lagging behind countries like Germany and Belgium.

One of the major deterrents for SMEs is the high and risky investment involved with the modernisation of their business processes and production means, for example in the field of 3D printing. Budget and staff deficiencies are the most important obstacles. The urgency of the matter is apparently such that 'leading players' might start to shift their production to other locations unless Dutch SMEs manage to keep up.

Source: *Het Financieele Dagblad*, 23 April 2018 https://fd.nl/economie-politiek/1251182/metaalsector-mkb-ers-kunnen-de-innovatierace-niet-bijhouden, consulted 7 May 2018

Strategy formation: evaluation and choice of a strategy

After the strategies have been set out, the organisation makes some preliminary choices. These strategies are then evaluated in terms of their medium-term prospects.

An increasingly frequent method for this evaluation is the scenario method. Scenarios can be considered 'qualitatively tested pictures of the future'. Figure 2.16 illustrates the concept of the scenario method.

FIGURE 2.16 **THE SCENARIO METHOD**

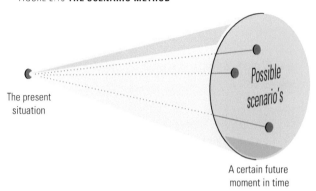

The present situation

Possible scenario's

A certain future moment in time

Scenario method

In the scenario method, the development of a number of factors is predicted in the medium term (the picture of the future). These factors can include competition, prices, market growth, environmental legislation, and economic growth.
Uncertainty and complexity increase with the time span of the predictions. This explains the 'fish-trap' structure of the illustration mentioned. All possible scenarios can take place between the outer limits. Some advantages of the scenario method are:
1 The feasibility of strategies can be tested using future projections;
2 Extra options can be created by means of scenario methods;
3 Scenarios can support decision-making processes relating to choice of strategies.

Decision rules

For the choice of a final strategy, a number of criteria should be formulated. These 'decision rules' are again rooted in the objectives of the organisation. The chosen strategy must be in accordance with the organisation's capabilities.

2.2.3 Planning and implementation

Planning and implementation

What follows is the last and possibly the most important phase of strategic management: planning and implementation (see Figure 2.19).
This section first deals with the planning process and then considers how to implement strategies in organisations.
At a time when flexibility and alertness are increasingly important to the continued existence of organisations, one may be inclined to assume that cutting out all planning is the best and swiftest way of reacting to opportunities and threats emanating from the environment. At least one is not tied to a certain course of action. On closer inspection, however, such a course has the following disadvantages:
1 The organisation has less knowledge of its handicaps and future risks;
2 Future opportunities cannot be systematically explored or prepared for. With bigger and more complex organisations, it is more difficult to keep day-to-day business in order and to react appropriately to stimuli from the environment.

Organisations have an optimal size: beyond a certain limit they can only react quickly and efficiently if the planning procedures are well oiled. Where this limit lies depends on the nature of the industry and the capacities of the top manager. In other words, at some point, planning does become necessary. In most industrial sectors, the most effective term for strategic planning has come down from five or six years to two or three. This is a consequence of the faster pace of changes within the environment.

Planning cycles

The output of strategic management consists of a strategy or a plan.
Implementation of a strategy involves translating it to shorter time frames and
lower hierarchical levels. A cyclical process – the planning cycle (see Figure 2.17) –   Cyclical process
is the result.

FIGURE 2.17 **PLANNING CYCLE**

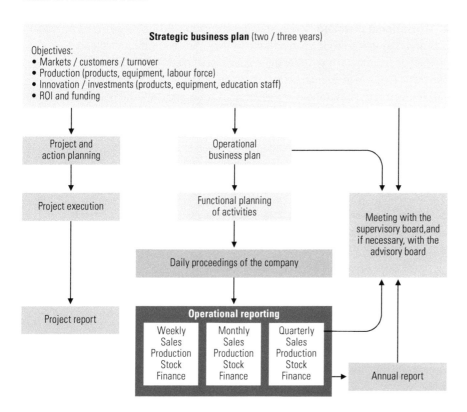

The following steps can be identified in this process:
1 strategic planning;
2 operational planning;
3 function-specific planning.

1   Strategic planning. This is high-level planning, the outcome of strategic   Strategic planning
management as described elsewhere in this chapter. Some relevant questions are:
– What objectives does the organisation want to reach within two to three years
     with regards to product-market combinations, growth, volume of trade, profit,
     and market share?
– How does the organisation to do so in terms of timing, required investments,
     financing, organisation, personnel, and data systems?

These issues need to be addressed yearly or quarterly. It might be sensible to
appoint separate study groups for some activities. These can work through the
various issues, coordinate matters and report back to top management. Among
other things, this might be appropriate for courses of action that:
– involve a number of different functional areas;
– are large in scale and of great importance to the organisation;
– are new to the organisation.

By way of example, there are:
- product development and market introduction;
- information planning and computerisation projects;
- quality campaigns.

Strategic planning should cover a period of two to three years, but should be reassessed each year, or even more frequently if changing circumstances demand.

Operational planning

2 Operational planning. The intended goals should be identified in the strategic plan and reassessed each year in terms of expenses and yields, sale and production quantities, investments, supplies, staff planning, and so on.
The plan results in an annual budget in which production or sales quantities are indicated by sector, together with associated costs and staff members responsible for the execution of the plan. The budget is thereby linked to a degree of delegation to lower managerial levels. In order to reach their targets, the managers need to be sufficiently competent and have adequate means at their disposal.
An operational plan should be worked out in detail each quarter, month, or week – depending on the industrial sector and size of the organisation.

Function-specific planning

3 Function-specific planning. The operational plan should be adapted to the various functional divisions for daily activities. Some examples of these activities are:
- monthly and weekly production planning and programming;
- timetable planning for production teams;
- liquidity planning;
- recruitment and selection procedure planning.

An appropriate reporting system is vital for a planning system to function well. It should give feedback for each phase in the cycle, comparing actual results with intended ones. The information should be available in time for any adjustment needed.
Such an approach gives rise to a continuous cycle of planning and reporting, forcing the organisation to look at the direction it is going systematically and in a structured way, and to maintain its course in daily reality, while leaving room for possible adjustments.
Planning systems are often implemented when an executive manager becomes preoccupied by daily operational concerns. It is useful to start with operational planning and follow this with function-specific planning. If this is successful, management will have time for further explanson of the organisation: that is, for activities at a strategic level.

2.3 CRITICAL COMMENTS ON THE CLASSIC APPROACH TO STRATEGIC MANAGEMENT

The previous sections dealt with the classic approach to strategic management in detail. It should be clear why this strategic management process is seen as a strategic planning process.
In his book *The Rise and Fall or Strategic Planning*, Henry Mintzberg considers the possibilities and limits of strategic planning. In the book, he shows himself not

to be an advocate of abolishing strategic planning either partially or completely. Instead, he discusses its possibilities and limitations.

Firstly, Mintzberg gives his definition of a strategy. He takes the matter further than was done in the beginning of this chapter. Strategy is not only a plan, but also a 'pattern of actions'. The plan can be seen as the intended strategy. The ultimate strategy is a combination of the 'intended strategy' and a number of unexpected actions, thereby becoming more dynamic (see also Figure 2.18).

FIGURE 2.18 **FORMS OF STRATEGY**

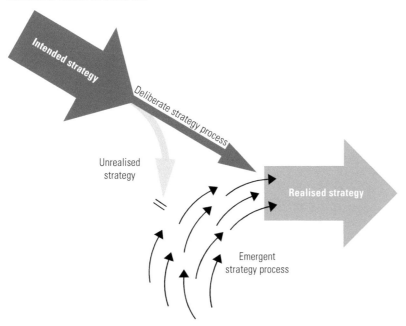

Source: Henry Mintzberg, *The Rise and Fall of Strategic Planning*, The Free Press, 1994

Mintzberg has a lot of difficulty with the concept of strategic planning. As he sees it, planning strategy is impossible. The development of strategies is a creative activity. Its characteristic is its combination of original and unique elements, which give rise to new strategies. According to Mintzberg, the importance of planning lies mainly in the formalising of decision-making.

Supporters of the classic approach to strategic planning are mistaken in thinking that the future can be predicted and that strategic management can be formalised (as indicated in the previous sections). Creativity would be suppressed by the compulsive urge to formalise, leading to insufficient room for the development of alternative strategies. In such a situation, alternatives would only be allowed within the formally fixed framework.

Another of the problems of strategic planning is that planning and implementation are carried out by various different people within the organisation. This could lead to problems.

Mintzberg claims that formalisation of strategic planning in artificial-intelligence systems has failed, as human intuition is difficult to replace.

Despite all this criticism, Mintzberg agrees that strategic planning has an important function. It can make an important contribution to the development of a strategy. But strategic planning should be seen from another perspective. Its focus should be on the learning capability of the enterprise and the influence of the vision held by its employees. Furthermore, Mintzberg supports the integration of analysis (planning) and intuition (view and creativity).

The next section deals with an up-to-date approach to strategic management in line with some of Mintzberg's ideas.

Lidl wants to decrease use of plastics by 20% by 2025

The Lidl chain of supermarkets has developed a strategy for plastics, aimed at reducing the use of plastic, improving recycling, and using innovative packaging. Lidl's goal is a reduction of at least 20% in the use of plastics by Lidl Netherlands by 2025. At the same time, Lidl has announced that, by 2025, all of its plastic packaging will be 100% recyclable. This supports the European strategy for plastics recently suggested by the EU committee.

Lidl's goals are in line with a transition to circular systems. To that end, the chain of supermarkets joined forces with the TU in Delft, the Netherlands, in order to make tangible steps. Lidl's own brand deposit bottles can be returned to Lidl stores and recycled within Lidl's own system. The recycled materials are then used to manufacture new PET bottles. As a result, these bottles currently consist of over 60% recycled materials already.

Source: http://www.levensmiddelenkrant.nl/ nieuws/handel/formules/lidl-wil-20-procent-lager-plasticverbruik-in-2025, consulted 7 May 2018

2.4 STRATEGIC MANAGEMENT IN THE 21ST CENTURY

Competitive position

Those who have followed the competitive position of enterprises in the past years will have certainly seen that major shifts have been taken place. In particular, new enterprises that are in competition with established businesses have arisen, although they have fewer financial means, a smaller market share, limited technological knowledge, and often a less well known name.

Research has shown that the success of these enterprises cannot be explained sufficiently by known factors such as large market share, size of the enterprise, available know-how, geographical spread of activities, and production in low cost countries. It therefore seems as though the classic model of strategic management, where strategic management is synonymous with strategic planning, needs revising.

In the approach to strategic management outlined in the coming sections, the emphasis is on strategic thinking within organisations. Strategic thinking is demonstrated whenever organisations have a vision to share and put into practice, highlighting the enterprise's capability to adapt.

Strategic thinking

Within the new approach, strategic management can be seen as a continuous search for competitive advantage, based on the perpetual learning ability of an organisation. This competitive advantage consists of a combination of a common vision and the development of core competencies. Core competencies are a combination of unique knowledge, experience, skills, values and standards: areas in which an effective organisation is strong. The important keywords in strategic management are leadership and entrepreneurship, while customer needs are central to the process. Hamel and Prahalad are the founders of this new perspective of strategic management.

2.4.1 Strategy model of Hamel and Prahalad

Strategic management in the new perspective follows a continuous cycle of four phases.
A diagram showing the four phases can be seen in Figure 2.19.

FIGURE 2.19 **A NEW PERSPECTIVE ON STRATEGIC MANAGEMENT**

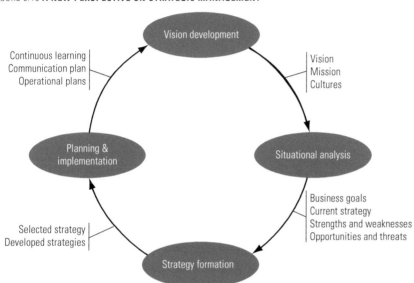

At the core of Hamel and Prahalad's strategy model is 'strategic intent': an obsessive desire within the organisation to become the market leader within a period of ten years, give or take. However, there may well be a gap between the aspirations of the enterprise and its available means. Closing of this gap becomes the main objective (Figure 2.20).

Strategic intent

For it to be effective, strategic intent must inform the daily activities of enterprises. Some characteristics of strategic intent are:
a being consistend with the objectives of the enterprise;
b expressing the collective will;
c radiating a winner mentality;
d providing impetus to activities within the organisation.

FIGURE 2.20 **WHY DO GREAT COMPANIES FAIL?**

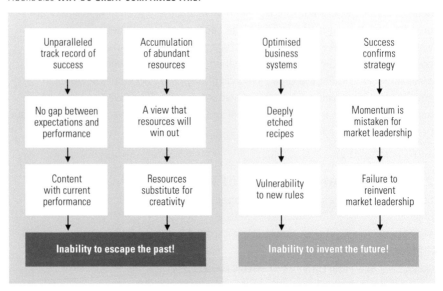

Source: *Competing for the Future*, Hamel & Prahalad, Harvard Business School Press 1994

Compared to a mission statement, a strategic intent is more specific and more directive of activities within the enterprise. Some examples of firms that have a clear strategic intent are:

a Heineken: 'Brewing a Better Future';

b Ahold: 'better choice, better value, better life, every day';

c Honda: 'The Power of Dreams';

d Coca-Cola: 'To refresh the world and to inspire moments of optimism and happiness'.

Corporate challenges

To translate the strategic intent into practice in the short term, objectives (corporate challenges) should be determined for a period of one to three years. The strategic intent can be seen as a marathon run and corporate challenges as sprints. A second important aspect of this model of strategy formation is that it consciously aims for a mismatch between the aspirations of the enterprise and its available means, the so-called Strategy as Stretch. The emphasis lies on the ambition to reach a goal (Figure 2.21).

Strategy as Stretch

FIGURE 2.21 **STRATEGIC MANAGEMENT MODEL**

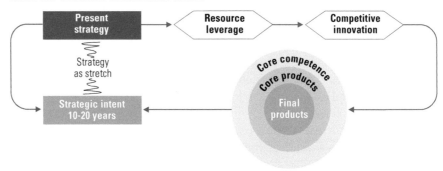

The notion of strategy as stretch is one of the most fundamental differences with the classic approach to strategic management. Prahalad and Hamel point out that enterprises that aim for a balance between the environment and the enterprise can only make marginal changes. The traditional concept of strategic management results in a status quo enterprise. Only by intentionally creating such a gap is the enterprise forced to use all its creativity, make decisive innovations, and impose vital changes. The entire organisation must be convinced that there is only one right way, which requires a winner's mentality: reaching the goal.

Such an ambitious objective can be reached only by:

A Applying available means more effectively (resource leverage);

B Being more inventive than competitors (competitive innovation);

C Seeing the enterprise as a portfolio of core competencies that should be developed, instead of a portfolio of product-market combinations.

These three methods are explained below.

A Applying the available means more effectively (resource leverage). If the available resources needed to reach an ambitious objective are insufficient, they should be made more productive. Some ways of doing so are:

Resource leverage

1 **Concentrating means on strategic intent.** Many resources are lost unnecessarily on administrative tasks and/or are spread out across a large number of activities often not of strategic interest.

2 **Integrating resources and experiences.** This can be done by collaborating with other enterprises and/or by creating a mentality which focusses on learning potential.

3 **Looking for additions from other available means.** Resources from the past can often be applied to the development of new products.

4 **Conserving means for other purposes.** Available knowledge can be applied to different products. Honda keeps its knowledge of motors up to date by using it on cars, motorcycles, chain saws, motorboats, snow scooters etc.

5 **Earning back investments as soon as possible.** This is only possible if the resources have contributed to the development of successful products.

B Being more inventive than competitors (competitive innovation). This second method of implementing a strategic intent involves taking a fresh look at products, markets, competition, and the use of resources. The market leaders need to be challenged by enterprises that are taking a different approach to work. Developing one business after another (competitive space), and doing so quickly and more intensively, leaves the competitors in the dust.

Competitive innovation

In this respect, one needs to have a profound understanding of the needs and lifestyles of the customers of today and tomorrow. When putting new products onto the market, merely listening to the wishes of the buyer is not enough. A few decades ago, there was no need for the CD player, the Walkman, and so on. The point is that consumers have to be led to where they want to go without them realising that they are being led.

Traditional market research has clearly failed in this respect. Only enterprises that succeed in creating really new markets and dominating those market can be successful.

C Seeing the enterprise as a portfolio of core competencies that should be developed instead of a portfolio of product-market combinations. The third method of developing a strategic intent is to consider the enterprise as a set of core competencies. This is a collective learning process that coordinates different production skills and integrates production possibilities.

Core competencies

A core competency has four aspects:
1 technology (hard and software);
2 collective learning (at different levels and functions);
3 uniqueness (for customers and competition);
4 varied applications (for different target groups and markets).

Some examples of core competencies are:
a Apple: user-friendly and futuristic design of electronic devices;
b Intel: complex computer chip design;
c Rolex: design and production of expensive prestige watches;
d Black & Decker: small electronic machine competence.

Core products Core competencies give rise to core products or components that increase the value of the end products. Core products form a link between the core competencies and the final products (Figure 2.22). Future competition could take place on all three levels. It is therefore important for an enterprise to be strong on all levels.

FIGURE 2.22 **RELATIONSHIP BETWEEN CORE COMPETENCE, CORE PRODUCT AND FINAL PRODUCTS**

The long-term success of enterprises depends on their capacity to develop core competencies quickly, to produce products may not even exist yet, and to do so at low costs. It is only when an enterprise views itself as the sum of its core competencies instead of its product-market combinations that new horizons are discovered. An enterprise specialising in semiconductors and displays starts to see products such as watches, calculators, mini-televisions, and so on, in a new light. Working on core competencies demands an entirely new type of organisation. High value is placed on commitment, communication, and staff willingness to function outside its own division.

Strategic architecture Last but not least, enterprises should detail and document their core competencies in a 'strategic architecture': a blue print for the future. This blue print can be used to identify the links between consumer needs and the core competencies that need to be developed, as well as the technologies needed.

2.4.2 Strategy formation in times of disruption and innovation

Strategy formation and strategic planning are becoming increasingly 'open' in terms of their character. This means that increasing numbers of parties are becoming involved in the formation and planning of strategy. This has made the process of strategy formation and strategic planning increasing uncertain and complex for strategic planners. The 'open' character includes the extent of inclusiveness and the extent of transparency of strategy formation. These factors of inclusiveness and transparency have major consequences for the communication between all parties involved (Whittington, Cailluet, Yaakis-Douglas, 2012). These consequences are illustrated using Figure 2.23.

FIGURE 2.23 **OPEN STRATEGY: CONSEQUENCES FOR COMMUNICATION**

	Transparency	Commitment
Internal	E.g. discussing strategy in a blog	E.g. exploring possibilities in a larger group
External	E.g. updating internal and external parties on strategy	E.g. openly attracting ideas (crowd-sourcing)

Open strategy formation/strategic planning ties in with the concept of open innovation. Open innovation takes place in organisations that continually increase the level of integration of their knowledge and ideas with groups of external parties and employees from within the organisation. Furthermore, innovation is no longer only a matter of top-level management and staff developing a planned strategy development (top-down approach), but now, more importantly, also involves a bottom-up approach. There has been increasing attention for strategy-as-daily-practice, visible in the many day-to-day decisions individual employees make themselves. The theory behind this process is that greater support and consensus among employees creates a situation that has a beneficial effect on the implementation of plans.

Another look at current strategy formation and strategic planning notably demonstrates that the process is currently influenced by a group of four forces. In order, these forces within strategy formation and strategic planning are: *Organisational, Social, Technological,* and *Cultural* forces. These four forces lead to greater openness in strategy formation and strategic planning. The four forces, including specific factors, are shown in Figure 2.24.

FIGURE 2.24 **FORCES INFLUENCES STRATEGY FORMATION**

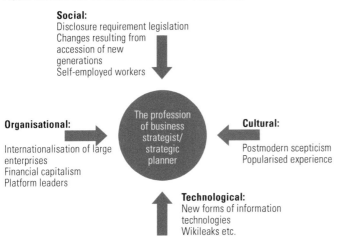

Social:
Disclosure requirement legislation
Changes resulting from accession of new generations
Self-employed workers

Organisational:
Internationalisation of large enterprises
Financial capitalism
Platform leaders

The profession of business strategist/ strategic planner

Cultural:
Postmodern scepticism
Popularised experience

Technological:
New forms of information technologies
Wikileaks etc.

Source: R. Whittington, L. Cailluet, B. Yakis-Douglas, HMR 141, 2012

Organisational forces

Organisational forces

As a result of the increasing globalisation of enterprises, it has become apparent that exclusive centralised control from a global head office is an outdated concept. It is, in fact, decentralised initiatives and local expertise that are gaining ground. These types of organisations are known as 'transnational' enterprises. A transnational strives for a high degree of worldwide integration on the one hand, and applies a high degree of localised differentiation on the other. From an economic perspective, it makes sense to involve the periphery of the organisation in strategy meetings. Moreover, the applied strategy of a more aggressive, financial form of capitalism requires greater openness. A culture of active shareholders and hostile takeovers requires good communication between all parties involved where strategy formation and strategic planning are concerned, thus demanding a high degree of inclusiveness and transparency.

Social forces

Social forces

Social forces are also increasingly causing major business groups to have to answer to the various parties involved in the organisation. Honest reporting (known as 'Fair Disclosure' in the US) leads them to yield more strategic background information to the parties involved. This louder call for transparency of information towards all parties concerned is largely the result of the recent economic crisis, which was initially born from the financial sector. Social changes within enterprises are starting to lead to greater inclusiveness of various parties where strategy formation and strategic planning are concerned.

Technological forces

Technological forces

Technology has had a major influence on both inclusiveness and transparency. Electronic technologies such as PowerPoint, electronic scoring, group discussions about strategy ('strategy jamming') all encourage the communication between and direct involvement of various parties in strategy formation and strategic planning. Governments are also increasingly making use of publicly accessible online resources to set up discussion forums about their policy, as a way of providing more information to make average citizens more involved in public administration, and to create greater consensus and support.

Cultural forces

Cultural forces

Cultural changes have encouraged a wider involvement with strategy formation and strategic planning. This wider involvement was born from a broader spread of knowledge on the one hand, and a greater extent of self-management within the teams of an organisation on the other. Another reason for the growth of this wider involvement is the growing level of employee education. The number of people graduating with an MBA has more than tripled since the 1960s. The number of Bachelor's and Master's students continues to grow every year and is no longer restricted to certain continents. One final factor of influence can be identified as the great respect that has grown for locally available knowledge held by lower-level organisational managers who operate closer to the market. A monopoly on wisdom from a head office is being cast aside in favour of consultants cooperating as part of communal teams with managers who are close to their clients.
All of this indicates that organisations are becoming increasingly entwined in collaborations and organisational networks. Minor disruptions in one organisation have immediate repercussions on all parties involved in the chain. Keeping a sharp eye out for new trends and developments among one's 'neighbours' and anticipating those trends is also a determining factor for the continued success of

organisations. At the strategic level, organisations have no choice but to engage with the partners in their chain, cluster and/or network. Joint strategy formation by committed organisations is being enforced by the four forces. Individual organisations would rather operate for themselves but, in the current time and age, this is no longer a possibility (Van Assen & Van den Berg, 2012). Van den Berg and Van Assen describe strategic conversation as a continuous, action-oriented learning process regarding strategic themes that is developing based on dialogue as well as discussion. Organisations have learned to adjust to the change in their environment because they are processing and interpreting the right information from that environment. A strategic conversation demands openness and mutual communication between organisations to anticipate future trends and developments.

O&M IN PRACTICE

The Netherlands popular with expats

The Netherlands is an appealing country for expats. As a nation, it is ranked as the best destination for expat families. The number 1 position in the 'family' component is due to several factors, including the ease of making new friends and the quality of education available. Less favourable is the score for 'quality of life'. Other countries offer fewer difficulties when it comes to finding accommodation or integrating with the local population.

Source: *Het Financieele Dagblad*, 7 March 2018

FIGURE **THE MOST ATTRACTIVE COUNTRIES FOR EXPACTS**

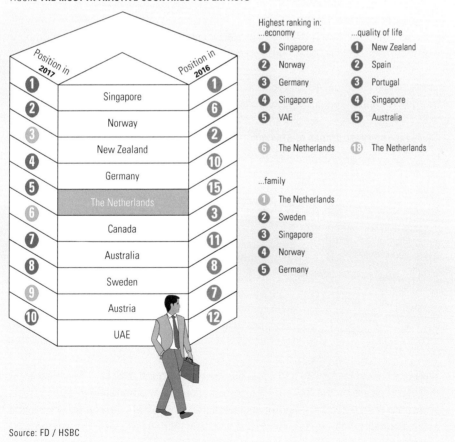

Highest ranking in:
...economy

1 Singapore
2 Norway
3 Germany
4 Singapore
5 VAE

6 The Netherlands

...quality of life

1 New Zealand
2 Spain
3 Portugal
4 Singapore
5 Australia

18 The Netherlands

...family

1 The Netherlands
2 Sweden
3 Singapore
4 Norway
5 Germany

Position in 2017 / Position in 2016

Position 2017	Country	Position 2016
1	Singapore	1
2	Norway	6
3	New Zealand	2
4	Germany	10
5	The Netherlands	15
6	Canada	3
7	Australia	11
8	Sweden	8
9	Austria	7
10	UAE	12

Source: FD / HSBC

2.4.3 Starts-ups and the 'lean' strategy process

Start-ups

Over the past 20 years, there have regularly been new examples of those enterprises known as start-ups. Well-known start-ups include Snapchat, WeWork, Uber, WhatsApp, and Airbnb: all companies which, in very little time, grew into major (multinational) enterprises. But what exactly is a start-up? A start-up is a fast-growing enterprise that is able to meet a certain market need. Start-ups are able to meet market needs because they have developed a business model centred on an innovative product, service, business process, or platform. Start-up organisations often cause disruption in a certain industry or sector. Innovation in this case involves not only a product or service, but also the collaborations in which the start-ups engage. For example, start-ups are shaped by a journey of incubators and coworking.

Incubator

Coworking

An incubator is a company that supports new companies in their start and expansion efforts. They do so by offering services, such as management training, housing, and assistance with financing activities. Coworking is a work method characterised by collaborations in a physical location in order to solve certain problems or issues. The collaborating organisations are usually self-reliant. Start-ups also look for innovative financing methods. Crowdfunding is a frequently used method. Crowdfunding is a financial form which does not rely on the involvement of financial intermediaries like banks. Instead, crowdfunding establishes a link between a (usually) large group of investors and an entrepreneur looking for credit. To facilitate crowdfunding efforts, entrepreneurs use a digital platform.

Crowdfunding

Qredits

Angel investors

Other innovative financing methods are angel investors and Qredits. Angel investors are private individuals interested in investing in new companies. Qredits are foundations whose goal is to help start-up companies secure financing. One way they help out is by offering micro-credits.

Start-ups usually grow according to a certain pattern. The following image displays this growth pattern schematically (Hillesum, 2015).

FIGURE 2.25 **THE THREE STAGES OF STARTUP**

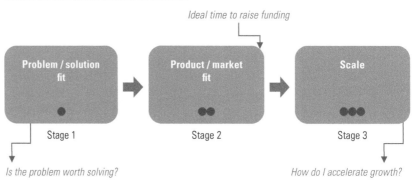

Source: https://www.trumanamsterdam.com/stuff-we-find-inspiring/de-kern-van-lean-startup.

Start-ups should be flexible and agile, but they also require direction. This means that start-ups are on the lookout for a combination of entrepreneurship and strategy. The strategy selected by a start-up indicates the constraints within which innovation and experimentation need to take place. In a lean strategy process, the strategy provides the entirety of the direction and alignment. The strategy is both a test of new ideas and a measure of the success of the experiments used to test out new ideas. The strategy enables employees – indeed encourages them – to be creative

(Collis, 2016). Any organisation with limited resources needs a strategy that limits and restricts their use to prevent unbridled experimentation. This helps companies in determining the extent to which business models or market segments offer long-term appeal before testing their viability. A lean process of strategy formation begins with an essential, immutable aspect of the strategy, being the organisation's vision or end goal. It is the reason for the organisation's existence.

In order to realise this vision, a strategy is required – one that is founded on three pillars (Collis & Rukstad, 2008):
a objective;
b scope;
c competitive advantage.

Objective: when formulating the objective, the start-up company indicates what they feel would constitute success. The period of time in which success is to be achieved is limited: for example, the goal is to become a listed company within 5 years.
Scope: the second pillar defines the company's 'playing field', as well as defining what the start-up will or will not be doing.
Competitive advantage: lastly, a start-up needs a clear idea of how it intends to be victorious on its chosen market. In other words: why clients will want to choose the start-up's products and services instead of those offered by major competitors.

The implementation of a lean strategy means that people make all sorts of (new) decisions for a start-up every day. All of these decisions have their own effects and influence on the start-up and help give shape to the strategy. This is also known as the emergent aspect of strategy (Collis, 2016).

European tech front versus China and America

O&M IN PRACTICE

European artificial intelligence institutes are joining forces in order to catch up with China and the United States. Their goal is to attract top-level scientists in various fields, for example image and facial recognition, and to create a better climate for start-ups.

Source: *Het Financieele Dagblad*, Tuesday 24 April 2018

FIGURE **CHINA DOMINATES FINANCING (EXTERNAL INVESTMENTS IN START-UPS ACTIVE IN ARTIFICIAL INTELLIGENCE BY REGION IN 2017)**

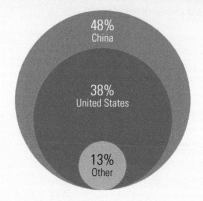

48% China

38% United States

13% Other

Source: FD / CBInsights

2.5   STRATEGIC MANAGEMENT AND BUSINESS INTELLIGENCE

Good information is a boon to the process of strategic management. For some considerable time, organisations have been confronted with rapidly changing environments (both internal and external), demanding quick responses. Decisions have to be made faster on both the strategic, and on the tactical and operational levels.

For good decision-making, adequate management information and analysis are indispensable. Consequently, an increasing number of organisations is using Business Intelligence.

Business Intelligence

Business Intelligence can be defined as all those activities linked to information, analysis, and IT that contribute to effective and efficient decision-making.
In a modern organisation, Business Intelligence involves various parts of the organisation. Within Business Intelligence, an information value chain is present – a process depicted in Figure 2.26.

Information value chain

FIGURE 2.26 **THE INFORMATION VALUE CHAIN**

The chain operates in two directions:
1 from left to right, producing information;
2 from right to left, translating the information needs of the customer into appropriate definitions and sources.

It is important for management to define what kind of information is needed. Information needs are the basis of the information value chain. The information needs of an organisation can be included in a so-called information plan. An information plan can be described as a plan that documents the vision the organisation's management has in terms of information service improvement and expansion, as well as implementation priorities. The information plan derives directly from the general organisation strategy.

Information plan

The various parts of the information value chain listed here are discussed below:
– data;
– aggregation and integration;
– information;
– analysis and interpretation;
– the position of business intelligence in the organisation.

Data
Data deals with sources. Sources can take two forms: internal and external.

Internal sources

Internal sources are customer files and transaction data bases such as:
– An energy provider's consumption data;
– A telecommunication business's call data;
– A bank's transaction data.
Such data is often stored in large databases (production systems). The data will have been designed to support the primary processes. Problems may arise if it

External sources

is used to extract management information. Some examples of external sources are data purchased to enrich one's own data, or customer profiles, which can be obtained by market research.

While internal sources are often managed in an IT environment, external sources are found mostly in marketing departments.

Aggregation and integration

Converting data into information requires a process of aggregation and integration. In this context, aggregation consists of summarising rough data to enhance analysis and interpretation. Consistent definitions are important to the process of aggregation. For instance, the term 'turnover' may be understood differently from the way it was intended in the original data. But the commissioning party or buyer of information will use only one definition. The correct definitions should be defined beforehand and must be maintained.

Aggregation

Integration consists of the mixing and connecting data from various sources to obtain added value: for example, combining data from a call centre with invoice data to optimise a call centre's operations.

Integration

Information

Information lies halfway along the value chain, where all information products become available for further analysis (the information portfolio) and must be managed actively to guarantee quality. New portfolio elements are being added all the time, while older ones seldom disappear. This diminishes the clarity of the available reports.

Information portfolio

Analysis and interpretation

Information obtained via the previous step has to be connected with knowledge and skills. Knowledge is obtained from specialists in the area concerned. They have the skills to analyse the information and to draw conclusions. Important consultancy skills are required, including the ability to handle statistics, as well as 'softer' skills, such as organising good brainstorming sessions or using interview techniques effectively. All these skills are needed to uncover the real needs of the buyer.

Skills

Input for decisions

Once all of the previous steps are taken, the input needed for a decision is present. Decision-making, however, lies outside the scope of Business Intelligence, as it is the responsibility of the decision-maker.

The position of Business Intelligence in the organisation

The maturity of Business Intelligence within an organisation can often be deduced from where Business Intelligence within that organisation is situated.

The best place for a Business Intelligence team is within the business, directly linked to those who are responsible for profit and loss – they are the ones who are able to estimate the value of Business Intelligence for their job. The second best position is within the finance department. Although this department is focussed on the financial side of the business, the finance department is traditionally well aware of the importance of good information.

The most usual, yet not immediately obvious, position for Business Intelligence is within the IT department. Organisations not yet acquainted with modern information systems consider Business Intelligence to be a purely technological field, and therefore locate it within their IT division. Such divisions are mostly dominated by the 'T' of technology – while in Business Intelligence, technological features take a supporting instead of leading position.

The next section looks at the background of a decision that emanates from the process of strategic management, namely: collaboration between organisations.

2.6 TYPES OF COLLABORATION

Collaborative activities

Collaboration is in fashion. Now more than ever, companies are choosing to work with each other at both the national and international level. The decision to engage in some form of collaboration should be a strategic one.

Some examples of strategic issues that may be tackled via collaborative activities are:

a **Competition**: enterprises may try to decrease the number of competitors within their industrial sector through collaboration. This constitutes a horizontal form of collaboration.

b **Risk-reduction**: enterprises may try to reduce their risks by spreading them across a number of different businesses via collaborative ventures.

c **The creation of specific enterprise areas**: one enterprise donates its powers of innovation to a collaborative venture, while another enterprise donates its major sales channels.

d **The removal of specific barriers**: if an enterprise wants to introduce its products into a foreign market, collaboration with a local enterprise in that foreign country can be an effective strategy.

Globalisation of knowledge

One explanation for the large increase in the frequency of collaboration is the globalisation of knowledge.

In the past, the main reason for working together was to gain scale advantages (a production issue). A future trend now becoming increasingly visible is that of collaboration in order to exchange and develop knowledge (a knowledge issue). This is prompted by the fact that knowledge is becoming more global, and that a growing number of countries is making a contribution to new knowledge development. Collaboration is easy. Many forms of knowledge are easy to transmit. Knowledge can easily be shared and therefore be made available globally (via books etc.). Having the edge over one's competitors in the area of knowledge generates a powerful competitive advantage. Developing knowledge together with a partnering organisation is therefore beneficial, though it should be remembered that while most knowledge can be transmitted, some forms cannot.

Knowledge comes about through complex social relationships: for example, via teams of people from jointly working organisations. Individual organisations may not have the resources to undertake such developments alone.

2.6.1 Collaborative organisational forms

Collaboration can take many forms. The main ones are:
- strategic alliances and trade cooperatives;
- joint ventures;
- mergers and acquisitions;
- outsourcing;
- licensing and franchising.

Strategic alliances and trade cooperatives

Strategic alliance

The term 'strategic alliance' refers to two or more different enterprises entering into an agreement to work together without creating a new legal entity. Both businesses continue to exist as independent enterprises. The enterprises work together in particular areas, sharing knowledge, resources and skills with each other.

The objectives of a strategic alliance may vary. Possible objectives include:
- a growth strategy, such as market development and market penetration;
- economies of scale, for example production or service provision;
- cost advantages;
- the development of new products;
- competitive advantages (both national and international).

Strategic alliances can be divided into the following three categories:
- **Horizontally or vertically**: a horizontal alliance means a collaboration within the same link of the industry or sector; a vertical alliance means a collaboration between different links along an industry or sector. In addition to horizontal and vertical alliances, there is also the diagonal alliance, which is a collaboration between different sectors.
- **Offensive or defensive**: an offensive alliance means working from an organisation's strengths, such as technology or distribution. A defensive alliance places the emphasis on defending a particular market or competitive position.
- **Product of process oriented**: a product-oriented alliance is a collaboration in order to manufacture a particular product or service. A process-oriented alliance is a collaboration that does not focus on a product, but on a process (way of working or thinking).

Horizontally or vertically

Offensive or defensive

Product of process oriented

Trade cooperative

Trade cooperative

A trade cooperative is a cluster of interdependent organisations working together to reach a joint target.

As such, a network involves active interaction between (parts of) organisations, with the intention of gaining the benefits of positive synergy. A network exists irrespectively of any competitive relationship between its participants. Gaining the full benefit of a network arrangement is dependent on the manner in which the individual participants operate and influence the direction within the network. Collaboration as part of a network has been simplified following the arrival of the internet. A network has a high degree of flexibility and, as a result, is able to address market and sector developments quickly.

Network of organisations
Active interaction

Networks are attracting more attention because of the increase in the frequency of two kinds of phenomena:
1 strategic behaviour;
2 technology.

Strategic behaviour. As was noted elsewhere, collaboration is becoming increasing popular. It has been shown that, in real life, organisations cannot function independently of each other. This applies equally to sections of organisations. The challenges posed by efficiency and effectiveness force individual organisations to enter into particular relationships, such as those involving distribution, research and development, and production. It is striking how many organisations are now joining such networks. The result is a rich tapestry of different organisations and components.

Strategic behaviour

Technology. The changes that have taken place within manufacturing companies constitute striking evidence of recent changes in technology. Technological changes are causing goods and services to be produced in a different way, thereby also changing the requirements placed on physical surroundings.

Technology

The globalisation of knowledge and rapid developments in information technology have facilitated flexible exchange of business activities. Successful performance in markets today means higher requirements for organisations in future. Therefore, specialist knowledge is indispensable. With organisations focussing increasingly on their core activities and technology being applied to problem-solving in an increasing number of ways, survival now depends on one's participation in networks. To sum up:

a The pace of technological development is accelerating all the time.

b Developmental and production processes are increasingly capital-intensive.

c Products are being offered with ever-increasing diversity.

d The life cycle of products is becoming increasingly shorter.

e Development costs are growing at an increasing rate.

f New technology means that unexpected market product combinations can be met at short notice. Their viability, however, is dependent their uniqueness.

In all, it may be concluded that the commercial risks involved in business activities will continue to increase.

Advantages of being part of a network

Organisations and their divisions can expect to experience significant pressure as they try to operate within a competitive world. Participation in a network offers advantages in such a situation. Within the network, the strengths of organisations can be used to their full advantage. Joining a network can have an added value for individual organisations. However, it also has certain repercussions, including the control that can be exerted over particular business processes.

Being part of a network

Being part of a network can mean the following advantages for an organisation:
– more technological possibilities;
– more products or variations on products;
– better products;
– improved accessibility to more markets;
– better market position;
– better production processes.

Types of network

Eight basic types

There are eight identifiable basic network types. These clearly demonstrate the various aims of collaboration, and are listed in ascending degree of intensiveness:

1 Joint improvement of secondary processes in areas such as logistics and quality. This is achieved by carefully attuning information, organisation, planning and control needs.

2 Joint projects in relation to the primary activities of production, research and development, and sales.

3 Collaboration in marketing and sales activities, such as marketing research, pricing, and promotion.

4 Joint acquisition of knowledge, people and means: for example, joint training courses and purchases.

5 Vertical collaboration in production. In such a situation, production activities are geared to successive links along the business chain.

6 Horizontal collaboration in production. The aim here is to produce goods jointly. Individual organisations produce components that, together, form the end product. Research is performed individually, not jointly.

7 Co-makership, a collaborative form which, in contrast to the previous examples, has research and development processes carried out jointly as well. This form of collaboration is vertically structured.

8 Horizontal collaboration that also involves working together on research and development, but here with a horizontal connection. Both partners are tasked with developing and producing a product.

Phases of network membership

It can be concluded that networks go through a number of phases, and that these are comparable to those of the product's lifespan. Organisations start off becoming aware that there are possibilities for collaboration. This is called the awareness phase. The exploration stage involves the creation of a network. The expansion stage involves further expansion of the network. The commitment stage represents the network's strongest phase. However, most networks are temporary in their nature. The reasons for a network's existence disappear, and thus it is dissolved: the dissolution phase.

Co-makership

Awareness phase
Expansion
Commitment

Dissolution

Philips Lighting gearing up for take-overs

The 'lighting company landscape' is undergoing some changes. Traditional bulbs may be an important source of income, but have been eclipsed by the revenue from LED. Philips has been shutting down plants and announcing plant shut downs at a rapid pace, thus clearing the way to invest in digital innovations. Currently, two-thirds of the turnover is generated by new LED technology. In 2013, this figure was only 25%.

Clever street lighting
The fact that global market leader Philips Lighting (32,000 employees) did not fail

to make the switch to LED is due to its impressive knowledge of the lighting industry combined with its understanding of digital connectivity. An example is the CityTouch smart street lighting platform, which has earned the company over a thousand completed projects.

Source: *Het Financeele Dagblad*, 5 February 2018
https://fd.nl/ondernemen/1240421/philips-lighting-staat-klaar-om-op-overnamepad-te-gaan, consulted 7 May 2018

Joint ventures

Joint venture

A joint venture is when two or more different companies jointly set up a subsidiary in order to develop special joint activities on the basis of equal management responsibility. In most cases, each parent enterprise owns 50% of the subsidiary. Consequently, parent companies have access to each other's knowledge, are not required to use as many resources as normal, and can share any risks.

Mergers and acquisitions

Merger Acquisition
Takeover

A merger is the most far-reaching form of collaboration. Mergers involve two comparable enterprises joining together. In contrast, an acquisition or takeover involves one enterprise completely running its activities to fit in with the objectives and plans of another. The acquisition purchase is made via a favourable or hostile bid. These forms of collaboration are further examined in Section 2.6.

Outsourcing

Outsourcing

Outsourcing can also be seen as a form of collaboration between organisations. With increasing expansion, many organisations are focussing more on their core activities. As a result, a number of activities ceases, while others are outsourced to other organisations. An example of outsourcing of supporting activities is contracting out certain personnel and accounting activities within an organisation.

Licensing and franchising

Licence

A licence allows an enterprise's products to be made by another enterprise in exchange for a fee. A good example is Coca-Cola. They give companies in foreign countries the right to produce Coca-Cola drinks under licence.

Franchising

Franchising is a specific form of licensing that is found primarily in retail businesses. By entering into a franchise agreement, the franchisee (a shopkeeper) agrees to follow the standard guidelines of the franchiser (a brand owner). McDonald's is an example. The agreement between franchisee and franchiser determines such issues as store design, purchasing, sales promotions, marketing, pricing policies, and the range of products on offer. A licence is contractually agreed. A licence contract is a form of knowledge trade: all that is sold is exploitation rights, not ownership rights. The company that obtains the licence is required to pay a fee to the franchiser in exchange for the rights to use the retail model. This fee is known as a royalty.

A franchisee remains self-employed. For both parties, the franchise system has many advantages.

For franchisees, the advantages are:
- taking advantage of the national image of the chain.
- taking advantage of the services of the franchiser (including product range and advertising).
- reduced risk because the retail formula is an established one.
- a single point of focus: sales.

For franchisers, the advantages are:
- that only moderate investment is required to expand a chain of stores, which means relatively rapid expansion is possible.
- a recruit that is likely to be highly motivated, since every franchisees is self-employed.

Collaborating via a franchise agreement works well in practice, and offers small entrepreneurs good future prospects. In short, the franchise system combines the advantages of a large business with those of a small one.

In practice, it has been shown that franchising is an effective way of competing with the large voluntary retail chains in which all retail locations are owned by one enterprise. The success of franchising is also demonstrated by the fact that these large retail chains have also started using the franchise system. Traditional chain stores, such as Ahold and HEMA (a Dutch department store with outlets in the Netherlands, Belgium, France and Germany) now include some franchisees. The previously mentioned buyers' cooperatives are also increasingly following the franchising model. A well-known example of a purely franchise business is McDonald's.

The aforementioned forms of collaboration can be regarded as being successful as soon as they reach the common objectives stipulated at the outset (for example, when combined purchasing ensures a stronger position similar to that experienced by a larger business).

Effective way of competing

Chain stores

Aldi to open physical stores in China

O&M IN PRACTICE

Major supermarket chain Aldi is looking to expand in China. The German discount supermarket has been active on the Chinese online market for well over a year, but now wants to open up physical stores as well. Within the coming years, the company wants to set up around 50 physical locations in the Shanghai region, as well as a large distribution centre.

Aldi (short for Albrecht Diskont) is one of the world's most successful discount supermarkets. Since 1961, the company has consisted of two independently operating companies, Aldi Nord and Aldi Süd. The two brothers who had been heading the chain up to that point, Theo Albrecht and Karl Albrecht, were unable to come to a unanimous decision on the matter of selling tobacco – as a result, they split up the company.

Source: *Het Financieele Dagblad*, 9 March 2018
https://fd.nl/ondernemen/1245105/aldi-wil-fysieke-winkels-openen-in-china, consulted 7 May 2018

Some other forms of collaboration within the retail sector are:
- Collaboration between Interflora florists, whereby a consumer can get flowers delivered to any address.
- Collaboration between a bar and a brewery, whereby the brewery not only supplies drinks, but also provides financial support through interior decorations.
- Collaboration between a petrol station and an oil company in relation to the various oil distribution networks.
- Collaboration between a computer hardware manufacturer and a software company, leading to the installation of complementary programs on computers.

Intensiveness of collaboration

Degree of intensiveness

The forms of collaboration mentioned vary in their degree of intensiveness. Figure 2.27 classifies the various forms.

FIGURE 2.27 **INTENSITY OF VARIOUS FORMS OF COLLABORATION**

Moderate   **Collaboration**   Intense

Flexible arrangements	Contractual relationships	Pooling of assets	Integration
• Networks • Strategic alliances	• Outsourcing • Licensing • Franchises	• Joint ventures	• Acquisitions • Mergers

Source: *Toegepaste organisatiekunde*, Peter Thuis, Noordhoff Uitgevers, 2018

2.6.2   Alliances: motivating factors and the keys to success

There may be various motives for developing inter-company strategic alliances. Figure 2.28 shows these diagrammatically.

FIGURE 2.28 **GENERIC MOTIVES FOR STRATEGIC ALLIANCES**

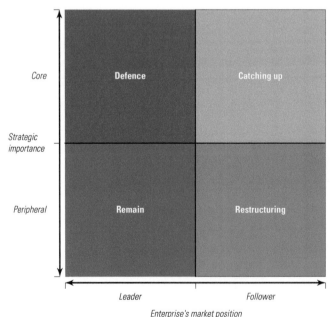

Source: P. Lorange, J. Roos & P.S. Bronn, *Long Range Planning*, December 1992, *PEM-select*, 1993

The term 'defence' is used when the goal of collaboration is the protection of the market leader's core activity in order to secure a future competitive position. An example of a defensive strategy is in IBM developing specific software applications for large customers.

If the activity of the enterprise is not part of its core activities even though the enterprise is still the market leader, the goal of collaboration should be to remain in this position: a defensive strategy, therefore.

When the goal is not to defend the core activity but to strengthen the competitive position, this is known as 'catching up'. Catching up is an offensive strategy. It is linked to the core activity of the enterprise, but only as a market follower.

Another offensive strategy involves setting up a collaborative agreement: a strategy known as restructuring. Such an arrangement indicates that the enterprise is a follower in specific activities rather than occupying a leading position in the market. Restructuring might go so far that the organisation subsequently disposes of these activities.

There are many motives for collaboration. These can be categorised under three headings:

1 **Cost-orientated collaboration.** Here, the principal purpose is to reduce costs. This kind of arrangement has particular relevance for day-to-day activities within the enterprise.
2 **Position-orientated collaboration.** This is particularly linked to the expansion of existing markets or the tapping of new markets, and the acquisition of a particular position within a market.
3 **Knowledge-directed collaboration.** The principal purpose is to learn about each other's capacities and expertise. This usually concerns knowledge related to the core competencies of the enterprise.

Reasons behind successful collaboration

Enterprises who work together both bring something to the arrangement: for example, production capacity, product know-how, distribution possibilities, or knowledge of specific markets. It is important that both organisations benefit, creating a joint lead over competitors, without either having to give away their most commercially sensitive knowledge and skills to the partnering organisation. It would seem that, in many Western enterprises, more is being given away than is obtained.

As a form of collaboration, outsourcing production often leads to a situation where the outsourcing company can economise on capital investments and budgets for product design and research. After some time, though, a dependent relationship can develop – since the partner controls both product development and production. Meanwhile, the partner will have learned a lot about the wishes of the final buyer and gained valuable experience in product development. The introduction of a competing product on the partner's own market may quickly follow, and its success is pretty much guaranteed. This obviously diminishes the competitive strength of the outsourcing company.

The conclusion may be that collaboration can offer a large number of advantages, but that caution is still wise. There is a real danger of one party becoming a victim of the collaboration in the long term.

Defence

Remain

Catching up

Restructuring

Cost-orientated collaboration

Position-orientated collaboration

Knowledge-directed collaboration

Some critical success factors that should be taken into account when entering into a collaboration arrangement are:

a Cultural differences must be dealt with carefully. When people from different countries or continents start working together, it is not unusual for cultural differences to arise on three levels: in addition to differences in national culture, there are also differences in business culture and personal culture.

b The form of collaboration that provides the best 'fit' should be chosen. Enterprise managemen can be influenced by trends. Strategic alliances are 'in'.

c It is very important to remain focussed on the real reasons for the collaboration and its goals. Less rigid and more operational collaboration is frequently a much better alternative to a spectacularly set up strategic arrangement.

d Advantages that look the most impressive on paper rarely materialise. As a telling Chinese proverb would have it: 'Those who walk softly will go far'. Avoid emphasis on form over emphasis on content.

O&M IN PRACTICE

Galapagos looking for protection against take-overs

Galapagos is working on a protective construction to prevent the Dutch-Belgian bio-tech firm from being taken over. Galapagos wants to 'construct a defensive perimeter' to hold off American pharmaceutical concern Gilead in particular. The concern is apparently interested in a take-over of Galapagos. Galapagos announced that it will be looking for a second pharmaceutical company to assume a share interest of 10% or more in Galapagos – the same as Gilead. This would make a take-over by Gilead 'extremely tricky'. Under Belgian law, the US concern would not be able to force a second major

shareholder to sell its shares. Damrak-listed Galapagos has its main headquarters in the Belgian city of Mechelen. Galapagos is looking to expand and become a new European pharmaceutical concern. Over the past decades, no other European bio-tech company has been able to achieve this goal, because their shareholders have always succumbed to the appealing take-over bids made by the traditional, major pharmaceutical concerns.

Source: *Het Financieele Dagblad*, 12 February 2018
https://fd.nl/ondernemen/1241243/galapagos-zoekt-bescherming-tegen-overname, consulted 7 May 2018.

One possibility for the assessment of the success of collaborations between enterprises is by reviewing competitive potential. This is defined as an organisation's ability to develop skills that form the basis for new generations of products.

For most enterprises, product quality is an important indicator for a company's competitive strength.

If a company decides to work with others, it normally has an effect on the whole organisation. Consequences come in the areas of strategy, organisation, and day-to-day operations. So what are the critical success factors in these three areas?

1 Strategy:
- Cooperating businesses understand which factors motivate the other, and they normally have common goals;
- By working together, cooperating organisations create added value;
- Cooperating organisations invest in a shared identity and a clear image.

2 Organisation:
- When two organisations cooperate, all elements of their collaboration agreements and task division are transparent;
- Responsibilities on both sides are clear;
- When leadership is shared, the skills of both management teams are used;
- Differences or disagreements between collaborating organisations can be a source of inspiration and learning;
- Practical arrangements about such things as communication and cooperation are agreed from the start.

3 Day to day operations:
- Collaborating businesses invest in each other;
- Trust grows and conscious steps are taken to maintain this trust;
- Cooperating companies respect the agreed decision-making process and set down clear responsibilities and authorities;
- Learning from each other is a key part of a partnership;
- Flexibility and creativity are important.

In practice, collaborations between organisations are not always successful. Why do some collaborations succeed where others fail? Research shows that some organisations are more skilled at collaboration than others.

Ruben van Wendel de Joode, Edwin Kaats and Wilfrid Opheij, partners at Twynstra Gudde, developed a model to help organisations improve their collaborative skill. The model describes various aspects that are important for collaborative success.

The model comprises three building blocks:
1 Developing a clear collaborative strategy;
2 Developing effective collaborative relationships;
3 Developing an organisation aligned with collaboration.

Figure 2.29 offers a more detailed look at the building blocks.

FIGURE 2.29 **THREE BUILDING BLOCKS OF SKILLED COLLABORATIVE ORGANISATION**

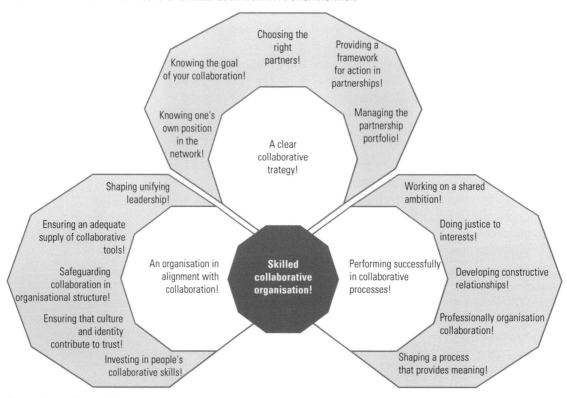

Source: *Holland/Belgium Management Review*, 147/2013

2.7 COLLABORATION BETWEEN COMPETITORS AND PARTNERS

Difference between collaborative ventures

There is a difference between collaborative ventures involving organisations that are in competition with each other, and ventures involving organisations with complementing products or services. However, both types of collaboration between potentially competitive and between non-competitive organisations can

Network

be described as a network.

2.7.1 Collaboration between competitors

At first glance, it might seem rather strange to see competitors working together with each other. Yet this has happened quite a lot in recent years. Some reasons are that:

a independent product development is prohibitively expensive;
b it becomes possible to penetrate new (that is, unexplored) markets;
c it can help to increase production efficiency while also improving quality control.

In particular, the high-tech and automobile industries have had a tradition of collaboration between competitive enterprises. This is especially true between European and Asian companies.

The collaborative agreement is likely to be useful if both parties can answer all of the following four questions in the affirmative:

1 Are the strategies complementary? A collaborative venture has a high chance of success if both partners follow a complementary strategy and the objectives of both partner's complement each other.

2 Is collaboration vitally important for both parties? The greater the interest in collaboration and in the extent to which each side is willing to invest in working together, the more both sides contribute to the process in order to ensure that the plans are really carried out.

3 Will both parties become dependent on each other through collaboration? Developing mutual dependency on each other is often the price that must be paid for working together. At the same time, there is a benefit in reinforcing the competitive position of both sides against outside competitors.

4 Can both parties grow as a result of collaboration? A key goal of collaboration is the strengthening of the competitive position. When trade and growth are more likely to increase with collaboration than without it, the chance of the arrangement being a success will increase.

2.7.2 Collaboration between non-competitive organisations

Organisations that are not in competition with each other can combine their strengths by entering into a collaborative arrangement. The following types of arrangement are explored below:

1 collaboration in retailing;
2 public-private collaboration.

Collaboration in retailing

In recent years, large retail stores and franchisers have grown in strength – to the detriment of small enterprises. Small entrepreneurs who want to survive in the long term must consider joining forces with others for their purchases of stocks and supplies. Such an arrangement will lead to the potential double advantages of lower purchase prices (a large-scale advantage) and local customer orientation (a small-scale advantage). Such collaboration, however, always means that part of the small enterprise's autonomy must be surrendered. The scope of the autonomy to be relinquished depends on the form of collaboration selected. The following section discusses collaborative forms that range from large franchise organisations to small buyers' cooperatives.

Collaboration in retailing

Buyers' cooperatives

A buyers' cooperative is a fairly traditional arrangement whereby retailers of similar products work together in order to obtain a number of advantages. Participating in a buyers' cooperative has special significance if a retailer wishes to take advantage of a full service package offered by a service provider or trade association.

Buyers' cooperative

Such a full service package can include joint marketing and advertising campaigns, sales consultancy, sales technique advice, store design, automation, and administration support. In addition, the entrepreneur receives a purchase discount and is offered special financing and payment terms. The content of a full service package can vary, and entrepreneurs are able to select the elements of which they wish to take advantage. The entrepreneur thus retains a considerable amount of freedom of choice.

Full service package

Voluntary branch operation

Voluntary branch operation

A second collaborative form is the voluntary branch operation: a centrally directed organisation operating under a single moniker, consisting of one or more similar wholesalers and, as a rule, a large number of similar retailers, where ownership and exploitation remain under the control of the individual participants. Voluntary branch operations are most common in the foodstuffs industry.

Public-private collaboration

Public-private collaboration

Collaboration between local or national government authorities and the business world is frequently found in many different areas, including:
- urban renewal;
- infrastructure projects;
- environmental projects;
- education.

The two most important reasons for this type of collaboration are financial and social in nature. The financial and staff resources of government authorities are too restricted to engage in many projects. The business world has an interest in profitable investment projects.

Social benefit

Government authorities aim to secure maximum social benefit. Consequently, projects need to be completed as quickly as possible, and to the highest standards of quality. The advantage to the business world may consist of an acceleration of procedures as a consequence of working together with public bodies. Greater involvement of a public authority in the project makes this possible. In addition, for a private sector business, working along with public institutions reduces the financial risks involved. The authorities look carefully into the viability of the project, and keep the investment risks as low as possible. Take the example of a situation where a private sector company is instructed by a local authority to clear some chemically polluted ground. The local authority is keen to see the work carried out properly and quickly. The private sector company is attracted by the financial potential of the project. The local authority will not place any obstacles in the way of getting the job done. In short, the official machinery is inclined to be obliging towards the private sector organisation.

Privatise

Obviously, not all public-private joint ventures are successful. Some government authority activities are being privatised to improve them and to make them more manageable. As a consequence, collaboration with other organisations is simplified, and the financial rationale for new investments is made clearer. A more effective and efficient system for anticipating social changes will also have been created.

2.8 MERGERS AND ACQUISITIONS

Large scale mergers

Large scale mergers and acquisitions are currently taking place within all industrial sectors. The indications are that this trend will continue in the future.
After some introductory remarks about mergers and acquisitions, this section looks at the following topics in greater detail:
a the motives behind mergers and acquisitions;
b acquisition price and price calculation;

c problems associated with mergers and acquisitions;

d the next step after the merger.

As the terms 'merger' and 'acquisition' are used in a similar context, it is wise to take a moment to define the meaning of each.

A merger is a form of collaboration and joining together of enterprises which, in doing so, completely abolish their economic and legal individuality. The partners join forces to determine how to reach which joint goals. The term acquisition is used when one or more of the parties take sole responsibility on behalf of all partners in the new venture with regards to the venture's objectives and strategies for reaching those objectives. It is only whichever partner has been taken over who will lose their autonomy. Sometimes, a partner does not relinquish their autonomy voluntarily. Figure 2.30 shows the following various merger and acquisition methods.

Merger

Acquisition

1 In this situation (two partners: A and B), A is able to purchase shares in B. It can either pay in cash or in its own shares.

2 Partners A and B put their shares into a joint holding company. They do so in exchange for shares in C.

3 Partners A and B create a new subsidiary (D). A's and B's assets are put into D in exchange for shares.

4 A and B have now started to acquire the character of a holding company.

FIGURE 2.30 **EXPLANATION OF MERGER AND ACQUISITION METHODS**

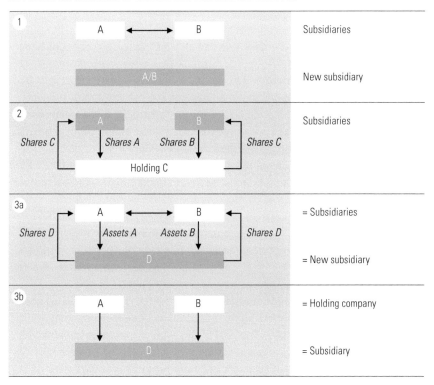

Source: *NRC Handelsblad*, 08-12-1993

2.8.1 The motives behind mergers and acquisitions

Strategic reorientation

With their eye on a growing European market, many organisations are considering a strategic reorientation. Many companies have become stronger in the European market by determining which of their activities are core ones, followed by improving their growth via mergers and acquisitions. These organisations hope that by gaining a larger market share, they will increase their profits. Some try to do so by creating economies of scale and slimming down supporting or staff divisions. One way of doing so is by improving productivity and cash flow. As the consumer market is not expanding dramatically, the only way to grow would seem to be via acquisition purchases or mergers. The organisation's competitive position also plays a very important role. If a market leader enters a new market, its competitors are likely to be seriously considering doing the same. Enterprises need to reduce the chances of competitors seeing a chance they have missed. Of course, it is always possible for the market leader to make a mistake: lurking competitors will then be misled.

Competitive position

Synergy

Synergy is another motive identified by many enterprises as a reason for a merger or acquisition. Synergy means organisations complementing or strengthening each other through features such as joint expertise or the creation of economies of scale (the 1 + 1 = 3 effect).

In addition to commercial motives, personal interests can play a role in a merger or acquisition. A larger enterprise often means greater prestige for management and sometimes an increased remunerations package. Naturally, the larger an enterprise becomes, the smaller the chances of its being taken over.

In addition to these forms of mergers, one can also distinguish a number of types of other mergers:

Horizontal and vertical merger

a **Horizontal and vertical merger**: a horizontal merger is when competitors join forces. These are organisations that manufacture and provide similar products and/or services, and even operate on the same markets. One important reason for this type of merger is to achieve economies of scale and to develop greater competitive strength. A vertical merger is a combination of two organisations that operate on different links of the industry. Vertical integration can take a step either forward or backward (forward or backward integration). A vertical merger affords an organisation greater control over the distribution of products and/or services.

Conglomerate merger

b **Conglomerate merger**: a merger of organisations operating in different industries or sectors. An important reason for this type of merger is to spread risk. Organisations taking part in a conglomerate merger have opted to diversify their activities.

Market or product-extension merger

c **Market or product-extension merger**: a market-extension merger is when two organisations who offer the same products and/or services operate in different geographical markets. The goal of this type of merger is to become a larger global player, thus developing competitive strength. A product-extension merger is a merger between suppliers of different products and/or services that operate on the same market. These products and/or services are usually related.

Nestlé desperately needs Starbucks alliance

Billion-dollar deal to keep JAB the Douwe Egberts parent company, at bay

Nestlé has taken a swing at its competitor, JAB. A billion-dollar deal with the Starbucks chain of coffee bars should enable the Swiss to keep US company JAB at bay. Nestlé has had difficulties where growth is concerned. Now, through its first ever alliance with another heavy hitter in the coffee game, Nestlé has set out to conquer the US luxury coffee market. But the deal has benefits for others besides just Nestlé. Starbucks, which, within the confines of its US home market, is encountering the limits of its growth, will be offered an incredible global growth spurt through the collaboration. Nestlé is in business with virtually all supermarkets and countless hospitality companies. If the Swiss start selling coffee cups, coffee packs, and tea produced by Starbucks wherever they do business, sales for the US company could grow much more quickly than they would without Swiss reinforcements.

Source: *Het Financieele Dagblad*, Tuesday 8 May 2018 (translated)

2.8.2   Dutch Consumer and Market Authority

On 1 April 2013, the Nederlandse Mededingingsautoriteit NMa (*Dutch Competition Authority*), de Consumentenautoriteit (*Consumer Authority*) and the Onafhankelijke Post en Telecommunicatie Autoriteit OPTA (*Independent Postal and Telecommunications Authority)* merged into the new Autoriteit Consument en Markt ACM (Consumer and Market Authority). This independent watchdog organisation advocates the rights of business and consumers.

ACM's mission statement is as follows: 'The Consumer and Market Authority promotes opportunity and choice for companies and consumers. We create opportunities by combatting unfair competitive advantages, and by facilitating market entry for new providers. More providers equal more competition. Competition leads to innovation: new products, services, and companies. This provides consumers with more options. But we also want consumers to be able to make the right decisions, by ensuring that business provide proper information about their products and services. And by informing consumers of their rights so that they may actively rely on those rights. We stand up to businesses who obstruct the opportunities and choices of consumers and other companies.' Figure 2.31 shows the ACM's organogram.

Dutch Consumer and Market Authority

FIGURE 2.31 **ORGANOGRAM OF THE CONSUMER AND MARKET AUTHORITY**

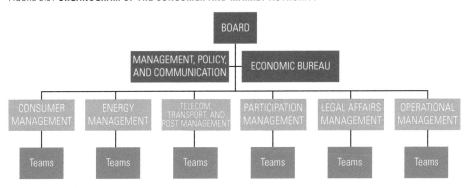

Source: www.acm.nl

To ensure its proper functioning in the Netherlands, ACM collaborates with various bodies, such as ministries, watchdog organisations, scientific institutions, and arbitration committees. Because the problems faced by businesses and consumers are increasingly international in their nature, ACM also frequently collaborates with other foreign watchdogs and institutions.

One of ACM's tasks is to verify and approve the mergers and take-overs of large enterprises. Mergers and take-overs can create such entrepreneurial behemoths as to offer them excessive power in certain industries, thus leading to excessive **Concentrations of** concentrations of power. If one organisation is too powerful, a possible result is **power** unfair competition, with potentially negative consequences for consumers. In order to prevent such concentrations of power, the Netherlands has implemented the Competition Act, established on 1 January 1998. In 2004, the Act was updated with regard to the European Community. Enforcement of the Act is the task of ACM.

Companies interested in mergers or take-overs are subject to an investigation by ACM to determine the possible consequences of the process in question.

Concentrations must be reported to ACM if they meet the following conditions:

1 the merging companies have a combined global annual turnover of 150 million Euros or more; *and*
2 at least two of the merging companies each have an annual turnover of 30 million Euros or more in the Netherlands (www.acm.nl).

ACM may prohibit the companies from merging, or apply a restrictive clause, for example the sale of certain organisational units.

In addition to mergers and take-overs, ACM concerns itself with cartels. A **Cartel** cartel is when two or more companies enter into an agreement in order to limit mutual competition. Under Dutch legislation, cartels are prohibited (based on the Competition Act). ACM may impose fines if a cartel is uncovered.

As many companies operate internationally, enforcing competition law is no longer a national affair. Dutch competitive law is based on its European counterpart. The influences on Dutch competition law, however, are not restricted to European ones. The rest of the world is continually subjected to developments that impact the legislative field of competition and the economic world in which ACM operates. Developments in the US, for example, occasionally call for trans-Atlantic deliberations.

This means that ACM is part of a collection of European and international alliances with regard to competition law (such as the International Competition Network and the Organisation for Economic Collaboration and Development). ACM provides an active contribution to these alliances.

A proper understanding of the international aspects and work of ACM depends on separating European collaboration from the international kind. International (multi- and bilateral) collaboration takes places based on the mutual acceptance of sovereignty, and therefore restricts itself to the exchange of experiences and ideas.

European Commissioner wary of Apple's power following music service take-over

The Danish European Commissioner for Competition is set to conduct a careful investigation into Apple's take-over of music service Shazam. The European Commission is wary of the fact that the take-over may impinge on the freedom of choice for music fans. The Committee states that Apple's take-over has presented the company with sensitive client and competitor data; a result of Shazam's practice of referring its users to music stream providers. Using this data, Apple could attempt to directly address clients making use of their competitors' services in an attempt to encourage them to switch providers.

Source: *Het Financieele Dagblad*, Tuesday 24 April 2018

A cartel is when participants exchange competition-sensitive information. Sharing competition-sensitive information may occur in various fields. The ACM website lists the following:
– proposed deals, discounts, or product innovation;
– proposed prices and rates;
– distribution of markets and clients;
– turnover information;
– market share.

Cartel formation is subject to serious fines. For companies, these may amount to tens of millions; for individuals, figures may run as high as 900,000 Euros.

At the European level, however, collaboration between EU member states and the EC does occur. In addition, there is collaboration between individual EU member states, for example with respect to the European Competition Authorities (ECA) and European Competition Network (ECN).

ECA
ECN

One of the most important pillars of the European Union is that, within the internal European market, there is a single competition policy. Disruptions in the field of competition between companies from the various member states must be avoided. This gives rise to a situation where, within the internal EU market, equal conditions for competition are established and applied for all companies.

2.8.3 Problems associated with mergers and acquisitions

Mergers and acquisitions are not always as successful as was once thought. It appears that approximately 40% of new mergers fail to get off the ground, while half of the acquisitions are overturned within six years. Nor do the expected advantages of a merger always measure up to the disadvantages. In fact, a large number of intended mergers do not materialise. Because very large companies arise as a result of mergers, and because there is consequently less competition, management might fall into the trap of becoming complacent. Scale advantages disappear when a company reaches a size at which growth generates more problems than benefits, because efficiency improvements have already been instigated.

Scale advantages

It is worth taking a moment to consider some of the main problems associated with mergers and acquisitions. One of the biggest problems posed by attempts to fuse two enterprises together is the existence of different organisational cultures. An organisation can be recognised through its customs, its way of thinking, the existence of rituals, and the maintenance of particular norms and values. If two or more totally different cultures exist, it is sensible to start with a joint venture, so that each part of the new organisation can gradually get to know the other. All parties will need to make some concessions and must come to understand that clinging to individual organisational cultures will stand in the way of a successful new operation – as well as having a negative effect on individual prospects within the organisation. The subject of organisational culture is treated in more detail in Chapter 12.

It is vital that the management and staff of the enterprise that has been taken over are kept fully up to date. If information is not always provided and if there is a lack of clarity, a vacuum will tend to be created – and this is likely to have undesirable consequences. Management will become demotivated as a consequence of uncertainty about job security, position within the company, salary scaling, and so on. Staff will be even less motivated and, as a result, talented employees may be tempted to leave. Takeovers attract headhunters all too frequently. It is not unusual for between 5 and 10% of the employees of a company to leave voluntarily when there is a merger or acquisition. This naturally depends on job scarcity and staff quality.

Particularly in organisations with an informal character, loss of management and staff with experience and knowledge can have disastrous consequences. Filling the resulting vacancies with new staff and managers can be very costly, as a lot of recent experience and knowledge will not have been written down, and is therefore very difficult to transfer.

Lastly, expectations in relation to the merger may be overly optimistic from both a quantitative and a qualitative point of view, especially if major results are expected within a short time.

The above-mentioned common problems must be taken seriously when considering a merger or acquisition. The chances of a successful merger or acquisition are improved if:

a a strategic plan exists in which the objectives of the enterprise are clearly stated and the strategy for reaching these objectives is explained.

b management leads the process properly and keeps staff well informed of developments.

c the process is supported by a thorough and well-thought-through plan.

d an accurate financial and feasibility analysis has been carried out in advance, identifying expected short, medium and long-term results.

2.8.4   After the merger

Once the merger contract or memorandum of collaboration has been signed, it is time to start its implementation. A number of necessary tasks must be systematically carried out in each part of the business. Here, management plays a central and guiding role. Figure 2.32 shows a number of business areas that requires attention. A practical first step to take is setting up task forces for each different part of the business with the purpose of creating an integrated plan for the entire operation. The activities that should be undertaken in each business unit are discussed below.

FIGURE 2.32 **THE POST-MERGER IMPLEMENTATION PHASE PER BUSINESS UNIT**

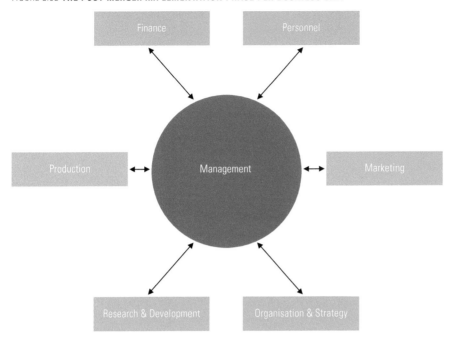

If there is not enough attention paid to the post-merger phase, the expected
results are fierce disappointment among employees and a level of profitability
that is below expectations. Afterwards, these issues will require additional time
and energy. This means the merger will have missed its mark, causing more
disadvantages than benefits.

Post-merger phase

Organisation and strategy

As mentioned, a clear strategy must be drawn up and communicated to those
inside the organisation as well as to external interested parties such as customers,
shareholders, and competitors as soon as possible. From here on, it should be
clear what the objectives of the enterprise are, which products will be launched on
which markets, what the competitive advantages are, and what the plans for the
short and medium term are.

Strategy

The next step is the new structure, with the most important positions needing to
be identified and filled. The progress and the results of the various task forces can
be negatively influenced by extended periods of uncertainty.

The danger of individual's own interests taking priority over those of the enterprise
should not be ignored. Finally, all bookkeeping procedures should be matched and
contracts harmonised.

Finance

It is important that financial reporting procedures throughout the various parts
of the new organisation are aligned with each other quickly, so that it remains
possible to stay abreast of the overall results of the new enterprise. The integration
of different automations systems can be a complicated, time-consuming, and
costly matter. Attention must be given to planning procedures and the distribution
of budgets.

Financial reporting

Personnel

On the personnel side, steps should be taken to harmonise job functions and employment conditions. Next, it is necessary to look at any duplications that may have occurred as a result of the merger or acquisition. If there are too many staff members, it will be necessary to transfer some employees or to let them go. These employees may require support and assistance.

The various personnel functions in the new organisation (such as recruitment and selection, evaluating and rewarding, career planning and training) must also be geared to each other.

Marketing

Own image

External communications

The new organisation must develop its own image. This should begin with a new name. Frequently, the choice is for a name in which the names of the old companies are still recognisable. All external communications, such as advertising and public relations, must be geared to the new enterprise.

Production

Production facilities

By combining their resources, organisations can make use of each other's production facilities. These must be examined carefully to see how they can be matched to each other. Additionally, materials and goods purchases can be combined. To select the best supplier for the future, a comparison of current suppliers should be carried out.

Research and development

The exchange of know-how can generate significant advantages in the long term. Research projects that overlap should be integrated.

Post-merger phase

If too little attention is paid to the post-merger phase, productivity and output are likely to be disappointing. As a result, even more time and energy must be put into the project. The merger will not then reach its target and as a result, there will be more sorrow than satisfaction.

Summary

- Strategic management: ensuring the proper alignment to the environment as well as continuously maintaining and developing the skills required to implement any potentially required changes in an organisation's strategy.

- Multiple approaches: the 'classical' approach and the 'new or modern' school to strategic management. The classical style equates strategic management to strategic planning, whereas the new style equates strategic management to strategic thinking.

- The classical process of strategic management consists of three phases
  1 Situational analysis:
  a Establishing current vision, goals, and strategy;
  b Internal exploration of strengths/weaknesses (based on functional areas or results): internal exploration of potential results through portfolio analysis, for example using the Boston Consultancy Group matrix;
  c External exploration of opportunities and threats: the objective of the external exploration is not to uncover the influence of each individual party or factor, but to establish their mutual connectedness.
  2 Strategy formation
  a Establishing vision;
  b Developing various strategies. There are six strategy groups:
    – strategies depending on market share (market leaders, challengers, followers, specialists)
    – strategies depending on market turbulence (immunisation, adaptation, manipulation, innovation);
    – expansion strategies (Ansoff's product-market-matrix).
    – Michael Porter's generic competitive strategies
    – Treacy and Wiersema value disciplines
    – Blue Ocean strategy

  c Strategy selection and evaluation
  Scenario method: a medium-term future prediction is made for a number of factors based on the current situation
  Strategy formulation according to Porter: in order to formulate a competitive strategy, it is important that the enterprise is considered from the perspective of its environment (industry or sector). Within an industry, there are five distinct competitive forces.
  3 Planning and implementation
  Implementing the strategy
  a To implement the strategy, it must be translated into the shorter period and lower hierarchic levels of the organisation. This lends shape to a cyclical process (the planning cycle);
  b The three steps of the planning cycle: strategic, operational, and function-oriented planning;
  c Strategic planning relates to periods of two to three years, but is implemented again every year;
  d The operational planning details the goals achieved by the strategic planning into one year periods, and indicates costs and returns, sales and production quantities, investments, inventories, etcetera;
  e The function-oriented operational planning details the operational plan to the daily activities within the various functional departments.

- Mintzberg: strategy cannot be planned. Mintzberg argues a link between analysis (= planning) and intuition (= vision and creativity).

- Hamel and Prahalad: at the core of the 'new' school of strategic management is 'strategic intent'. Enterprises create an obsession in order to be market leader for a period of ten to twenty years.
  Implementation through:
  – a more productive utilisation of available means;
  – greater inventiveness than the competition;

- viewing the organisation as a portfolio of core competences that is to be expanded (instead of a portfolio of product-market combinations).

▶ Strategy formation and strategic planning are becoming increasingly 'open'. This 'open' character is demonstrated through the degree of inclusiveness and the degree of transparency of strategy formation.

▶ Open strategy formation/strategic planning is related to the concept of open innovation. Open innovation is when companies increasingly make use of a combination of groups of external parties and the organisation's own employees to pool knowledge and ideas.

▶ Current strategy formation and strategic planning are influenced by four forces: organisational, social, technological, and cultural forces.

▶ A start-up is a fast-growing enterprise that meets a market need. Start-ups are able to meet market needs because their business model has been developed around an innovative product, service, business process, or platform.

▶ Start-ups need flexibility and agility, but also direction. This means that start-ups try to combine entrepreneurship and strategy.

▶ A lean strategy process is one where the strategy provides the entirety of the course and alignment. The strategy is both a test of new ideas as well as a measure for the success of experiments used to test the new ideas.

▶ A lean process of strategy formation starts with the organisation's vision or final goal: the reason for which the organisation exists. In order to realise this vision, the formulation of a strategy is required. This strategy must be founded on the 3 pillars of objective, scope, and competitive advantage.

▶ The decision to join in a collaboration is of a strategic nature.

▶ The various goals of collaborations: reducing competition, spreading risk, collaborating in specific entrepreneurial fields, or removing specific barriers.

▶ The decisions to engage in a collaboration is based on the exchange and mutual development of knowledge with increasing frequency. A knowledge advantage is a good basis for a powerful competitive position.

▶ Forms of collaboration are: strategic alliance and organisational network, take-over and merger, outsourcing and licencing and franchising.

▶ Motives for collaboration can be offensive (catch-up and restructure) or defensive (defend and maintain) in nature.

▶ Reasons for engaging in collaboration: cost oriented, position oriented, and learning oriented collaboration.

▶ When assessing the success of a collaboration, attention is focused particularly on the attained competitive power. This is the organisation's strength to develop skills that form the basis for the development of new generations of products.

▶ A strategic alliance can be divided into one of three categories: horizontal or vertical, defensive or offensive, and product- or process-oriented.

▶ Organisational networking is a cluster of independent organisations, a combined collective. There are eight basic types of network, ascending in order of cooperative intensity.

- A merger means both partners lose their full economic and legal autonomy. Together, they determine the goals of their collaboration, as well as the intended realisation of those goals.

- Synergy is an often-heard motive for merger or take-over (the 1 + 1 = 3 effect).

- It is possible to distinguish between several kinds or types of mergers: horizontal and vertical merger, conglomerate merger and market or product extension merger.

- Mergers and take-overs of large enterprises require the approval of the Consumer and Market Authority (Dutch: Autoriteit Consument en Markt, ACM). ACM's guidelines are based on European competitive law.

- A cartel is when participants exchange competition-sensitive data.

- Following a merger or take-over, a great deal of emphasis should be placed on the post-merger period, the implementation period.

3
DIGITAL TRANSFORMATION

Contents

After studying this chapter:

- you will have gained insight into the significance of digital transformation for organisations;
- you will have been familiarised with the most important technologies involved in digital transformation;
- you will be able to offer examples of the impact of digital transformation in various industries;
- you will be able to list the factors involved in success digital transformation.

Deskbookers, for the perfect workspace

Deskbookers connects office space and professionals, their website proudly proclaims. Founded in Nijmegen, the Netherlands, in 2013, the company has since shifted its base of operations to Amsterdam. Following its inclusion in Rockstart Accelerator, a programme for start-up companies, the company experienced rapid growth. Deskbookers is one of the first online market places for workspace, and it is the current market leader in Germany and the Netherlands, providing an online booking platform for unique work and meeting places. With a growing portfolio of available locations, currently numbering 10,000 across the Netherlands, Deskbookers is the simplest way of finding and booking work or meeting space, for example for a meeting, seminar, training session, conference, or presentation – all on one convenient website.

It is easy to find the perfect meeting or working space by entering a city, date, time of day, and number of participants. Deskbookers is part of a market that is slowly moving from offline towards online, and thus presents a disruptive business model in a market that is mostly directed by supply. Deskbookers focusses on addressing client demand by offering flexibility in booking a selected work place. Another one of a kind feature is that clients pay not by appointment, but by time of use – accurate to the minute.

Deskbookers is the Airbnb of office space. Its revenue model is relatively simple: Deskbookers earns a commission for every room booked. The company is ambitious: Deskbookers wants to be world leader in helping organisations and employees reduce housing costs, transport costs, and travel times, thereby improving productivity. The result is a sustainable working method that puts (office) space to more efficient use, that reduces commuting times and particulate and CO_2 emissions, and that improves working conditions and the balance between private and professional life.

Source: www.deskbookers.com, www.sprout.nl, www.quotenet.nl

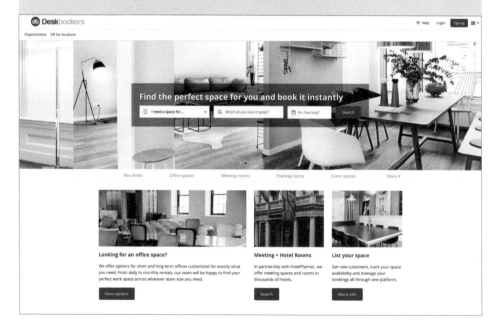

3.1 INTRODUCTION

The world is experiencing a breakthrough in the digital revolution. Companies are implementing digital transformations with strategic considerations for improving the efficiency of their organisation and production processes. Business life has begun digitising rapidly, and new technologies are changing products, processes, business models, and business cultures. Digital Darwinism is key: 'adapt or die'. Old revenue models are disappearing; others are taking their place. Digitisation offers consumers increasing convenience, for example in doing their shopping, taking care of their finances, scheduling appointments, booking trips, etcetera.

Chapter 1 on Environmental Influences briefly addressed the enormously important role that new technologies play in innovation, and thereby on the success and continued existence of organisations. Most organisations were used to a business model based on incremental improvement, standardisation, and economies of scale offering baby steps forward. This was founded mainly on many

Innovation is a hygiene factor

O&M IN PRACTICE

Dutch bank ABN AMRO has turned its gaze outward. According to CEO Kees van Dijkhuizen, the quality of the results is all down to how the bank's internal affairs are organised. Speed is an important component of the digital services provided. The bank is hard at work on its digital transformation. Following the 2008 financial crisis, the Dutch government still has a controlling interest of approximately two-thirds of the bank, which has been downsized from 110,000 employees worldwide to somewhere over 20,000 today. Dijkhuizen: 'We can cut costs through efficiency-improvement measures, such as the application of new technology and downsizing the office network. We have also looked at internal bank support: the back office and our overhead.

Speed is a very important component of digital service provision. Being able to offer a mortgage loan within 24 hours has allowed us to establish a firm hold on the Amsterdam housing market, for example. The increased use of webcasting, online video conferences between customers and employees, is part of this process. The massive banking IT-systems have meant a minor setback, which is why we launched Moneyou, for example: a subsidiary that offers full financial services online. Moneyou has its own IT-platform, and changes can be implemented very quickly. We have to make sure that we are both quick and able to safeguard our innovative strength.'

Source: www.managementscope.nl, 02-11-2017

years of experience and the development and retention of professional expertise, and is referred to as improvements resulting from an **experience curve**. Digital technologies force organisations to reinvent their business models and business operations, for example creating value chains where new competitors emerge among companies that formerly had no such competitors. Dutch publishing house Wolters Kluwer, for example, transformed its role from publisher to supplier of software solutions, even taking on board some of the legal administration. Progress is no longer measured in steps but in leaps and bounds, giving rise to the concept of the exponential curve in operational improvement: a curve that is much steeper than the experience curve. Across nearly all industries, the speed and impact of so-called disruptive technologies is forcing businesses to review their business and value creation models.

This chapter pays attention to the (future) role of technology in organisations, and to the way in which organisations are transforming, or digitising, themselves.

Digitisation According to a definition by the Vlerick Business School, digitisation is: 'an integral business transformation dominated by digital technologies'. Other definitions add the fact that the changes involved are fundamental adjustments to customer interactions and the customer experience. The focus is now 100% squarely on the customer and their organisational interaction at all times. Digital is not a channel, but digital thinking ought to become part of the DNA of any organisation, and is naturally accompanied by a new way or working and communicating in organisations.

3.2 PHASES OF DIGITAL TRANSFORMATION

Phases of digital transformation Across nearly all industries, the speed and impact of new (disruptive) technologies is forcing businesses to revisit business and value creation models. There are three distinct phases of digital transformation (Caudron, van Peteghem, 2016):

FIGURE 3.1 **PHASES IN DIGITAL TRANSFORMATION**

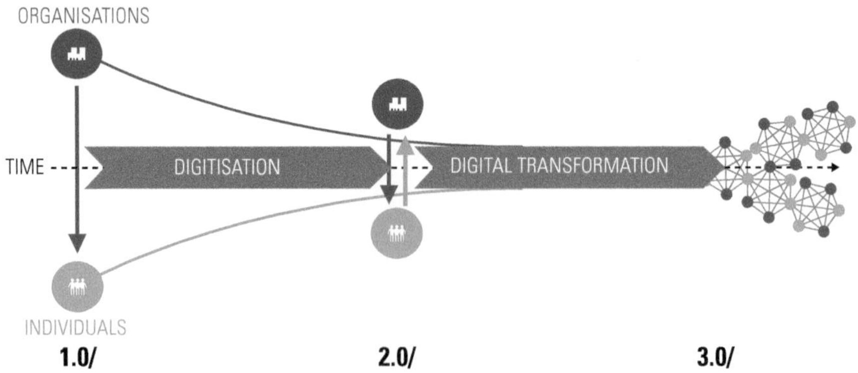

Source: Marco Derksen, 2018

Phase 1.0: Traditionally driven
This concerns traditional, hierarchically directed organisations with a number of different divisions (or business units) and departments that are directed from a top-down leadership philosophy. People's functions are demarcated: their task packages are fixed, and they work together in assigned teams. The use of

technology, software applications including the use of social media, is restricted by rules and procedures. There is great clarity about intended working methods, career perspectives, and salaries.

Phase 2.0: Transitional phase from traditional to digital

This phase is characterised by an active application of digital resources while still adhering to the existing organisational structure as described in phase 1.0. However, there is some experimentation with self-managing teams or matrix organisation. Characteristics are that clear hierarchic management is being abandoned in favour of working on a new business model – nevertheless, for the moment, the old model is maintained. One of the challenges of this phase is that there are both people who want to work according to the traditional methods and people who want to embrace new working methods, which they find to be a source of inspiration. This combination can lead to great confusion and miscommunication.

Phase 3.0: Radical shift to digital transformation

A digital transformation is complete only once the organisation succeeds to achieve the third phase of radical shift to digital transformation. This refers to organisations that use new revenue models, business processes, and organisational models, allowing them to work much more quickly and cheaply than their competitors. People in these organisations work in self-managing and flexible teams without managing individuals, which is made possible by the use of digital technologies that facilitate communication and collaboration. People in various areas of expertise work together as equals, and are encouraged to apply their creativity and continue to work on their own improvement. Previous organisational structures are abandoned, and people work together in networks.

Traditional organisations usually start their digitisation in phase 1.0, then to arrive at phase 2.0, followed by a development into the direction of phase 3.0, which concerns a full digital transformation. Internet companies such as Amazon began as phase 2.0 companies but have not yet fully completed phase 3.0: they do use digital technologies, but are still traditionally structured, using departmental and organisational demarcations.

Organisations whose business model is based on digital technology are much quicker to make the step from 2.0 to 3.0, with well-known examples being Netflix, Airbnb, Coolblue, and Booking.com.

Change is not a goal, it is a means to a end. The most important motives for business digitisation are shown in Figure 3.2.

FIGURE 3.2 **REASONS FOR DIGITISATION**

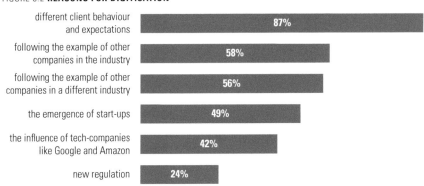

different client behaviour and expectations — 87%
following the example of other companies in the industry — 58%
following the example of other companies in a different industry — 56%
the emergence of start-ups — 49%
the influence of tech-companies like Google and Amazon — 42%
new regulation — 24%

Source: FD Transformers, edition 2018

Additionally, companies list internal pressure as a change agent: pressure to work more efficiently, to offer better customer service, and to work from a digital workspace.

3.3 KEY TECHNOLOGIES FOR DIGITAL TRANSFORMATION

Important digital trends, discussed below, flow from one into the next and reinforce each other. Organisations need to develop a digital quotient which mergers strategy, culture, people, and capability. Digital transformation has changed the entire playing field, and this change is expected to continue, since digital capabilities are continuing on a path of exponential growth. Figure 3.3 illustrates several milestones of digital evolution.

FIGURE 3.3 **MILESTONES IN THE DIGITAL REVOLUTION**

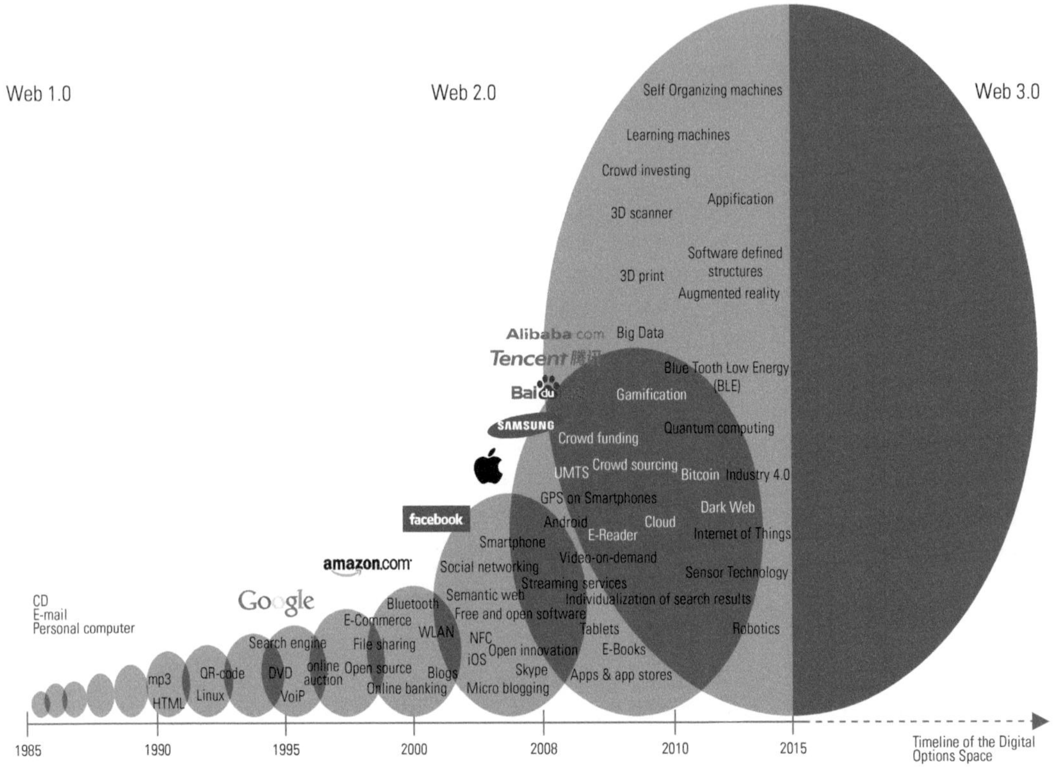

Source: Roland Berger, Trend Compendium 2030 Megatrend 5: Dynamic technology & innovation Digital Transformation has, 2017

The following technologies are briefly discussed below:
– Mobile Internet;
– Cloud Technology;
– Internet of Things;
– Artificial Intelligence;
– Robotisation;
– 3D Printing;
– Virtual and Augmented Reality;
– Big Data.

3.3.1 Mobile Internet

Mobile internet refers to the use of smartphones, tablet PCs, and mobile applications. Companies are mainly embracing mobile technology as a way of letting their staff work more efficiently: having employees who are continuous connected to the internet, even on the go, increases productivity. In terms of application, the most important need is for mobile access to email. Collaboration with colleagues, project management, and video conferencing are also considered important. Mobile technology is often used to innovate the business model: marketing using mobile technology has a positive influence on turnover. Smartphones have revolutionised the way in which, for example, holiday makers do business with travel organisations. Dates are shared with travellers, voice commands are implemented, organisations try to approach customers through WeChat, blockchains are the latest buzzword: all examples of the intensive use of mobile internet by the industry.

Mobile internet

The Netherlands is the European leader in the field of mobile internet, TV, and telephone network speeds and availability. The national policy for access and speed in the Netherlands emphasises the point, even for future technologies such as 5G networks. At the same time, Dutch companies, particularly in the SME sector, are failing to put mobile digital technology to its best possible use. 82% of Dutch citizens shop online, whereas only 15% of SMEs offer their services or products this way (figures date May 2018). Digital business is in need of a boost. In addition, organisations have not yet sufficiently developed mobile strategies for coping with these changes.

Is IKEA's future found online?

Fewer and fewer consumers are willing to trudge over to a squarehouse on an industrial site. We prefer cheap online goods (e.g. Amazon or Alibaba), or exclusive, trendy lifestyle stores (e.g. Zara and H&M). Ikea has noticed the shift, and is working on a new strategy.
Albeit rather late in the day, Ikea is going to start selling its merchandise online: by 2020, 10% of its turnover is expected to be generated by online sales. And IKEA is also making plans to position itself closer to its customers, as more and more residents of urbanised areas do not have access to a

car. These new locations, approximately 1/10th the size of a regular IKEA centre, offer mainly the collection's decorative items; but they are also experimenting with showrooms with kitchens and beds. IKEA products are even being sold through other partnering websites. The company is still ascertaining whether this new approach will not cause the collapse of the IKEA identity. Only time will tell.

Source: *Het Financieele Dagblad*, Transformers edition 2018

O&M IN PRACTICE

3.3.2 Cloud Technology/Cloud Computing

Cloud Computing or Cloud Technology is the use of computer hardware and software supplied via an online resource, usually in the form of a service. A cloud is a network of servers, and consists of three layers: infrastructure (servers, storage, and network cables, for example), the platform (the 'building blocks' which developers can apply: the place where data is gathered), and applications. Cloud service providers offers these three different layers as individual products: Infrastructure-as-a-service, Platform-as-a-service and Software-as-a-service. The customer is in charge of assigning the cloud to run the application: either publicly, privately, or in a hybrid form.

Cloud Computing
Cloud Technology

Some servers use computing power to run applications via the internet, others to provide a service, for example website hosting. Still other servers are only useful for storing data. The function of a server depends on the cloud layer. The cloud is, in effect, not always tangible (Figure 3.4).

FIGURE 3.4 **CLOUD ARCHITECTURE**

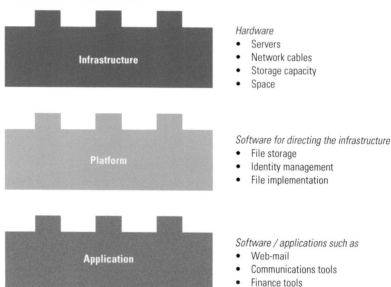

Source: Wat is cloud computing nou precies?, Workflowise.nl (2018)

Whereas data, applications, and software were formerly only accessible and storable at a physical location, storage is now possible via an external online cloud. Among other things, this means that companies do not need to update their own software, nor to they need to invest in additional storage capacity. Another advantage of cloud computing is that anyone with a business idea can sign up for a platform-as-a-service, swiftly enabling them to compete with existing companies. Start-ups, for example, can offer their products or services all over the world in a matter of days. Since the emergence of cloud computing, big data software has no longer been restricted to big businesses only. Hardware and IT companies are experiencing the resulting issues, particularly the strain it puts on their income. For many companies, the switch from local hosting to cloud services is a cost-cutting measure: there is no longer a need to invest in one's own server or software. Instead, these are rented through providers. Heavy-duty computers are also no longer required, since all processes are run online.

Cloud computing makes it possible for any location to become a work place. With data and applications accessible anywhere, flexible and location-independent work becomes possible. Moreover, data is stored at a secure data centre that houses the cloud servers. Cloud computing uses online software which providers update automatically, saving time and money that would otherwise be spent on man-hours. Cloud services can be scaled, meaning price depends on use. Capacity and price scale up as the company expands, so that active budgeting of or investing in software and hardware is no longer necessary.

3.3.3 Internet of Things

The internet is most commonly used as a means of finding information or communicating with others. But in addition to people, the internet also helps to connect objects (things): a network of devices connected to the internet to gather and exchange data. Devices are connected to the rest of the world, and can even include domestic appliances (so-called embedded systems). Everyday objects are thus made into online entities that can communicate with people and other objects, forming a basis for autonomous decision-making.

Internet of things can be defined as the 'networks of cheap sensors and actuators for data collection, monitoring, decision-making, and process optimisation.' The name 'internet of things' refers to a situation where online computers will outnumber the people that they serve. Smart fridges letting people know they are about to run out of milk, fitness wristband showing them their health levels, cars with sensors monitoring driving behaviour, self-directing grass cutters and hoovers: all examples of the Internet of Things (IoT). IoT interconnects the digital with the physical through sensors or computer chips built into physical objects. These developments happen quickly; therefore, companies should make it a priority to consider their stance on the issue. IoT is increasing the acceptance of cloud technology, big data, and mobile internet, leading to organisations digitising even more quickly, using smart software, mobile devices, and apps. The demand for IT services is expected to continue to grow. The production industry (particularly heavy industries), the transport and logistics industries, and energy companies are major IoT clients. The government is also ramping up its investments in, for example, smart traffic management solutions and energy-friendly solutions in so-called smart cities. It is expected that companies will be using IoT to increase their focus on external, customer-oriented objectives. Initially, the majority of companies has focussed on implementing internal operational improvements.

3.3.4 Artificial Intelligence (AI)

AI is a technological innovation in which computers perform tasks that, ordinarily, would require human intelligence. There are two versions of artificial intelligence: the Narrow-variant and the General-variant. The Narrow-AI has been present as part of daily life for some time now, in the form of search engines, robotic hoovers, and grass cutters. Narrow-AI is applied large scale to, for example, facial and voice recognition, pattern detection, and investigative research. The General-variant is a fully developed AI which, in the future, will be able to exist separately from human intervention. This has been the subject of years of study: the possibility of imitating human thought and converting it into computer language.

AI, however, does not mean that the appliances are aware of the tasks they are performing. They follow algorithms and recognise patterns. Through learning from their mistakes, their results improve. Another term for this is **Machine Learning** – a process that allows AI devices to work even smarter.

Artificial intelligence can offer humanity enormous benefits. Recognition of speech, images, and patterns, self-managing systems, translation machines, walking robots, and question-answer systems can help to improve comfort, user experience, and efficiency. Healthcare is also looking towards AI to solve many issues: an intelligent computer might, for example, be much more accurate at recognising minor deviations and changes than a (human) doctor would. And fatigue does not come into play for an AI performing very complicated operations. There are advantages to AI in terms of accuracy, precision, repetition, ease, and accessibility. But AI does come with substantial risks. There is a call for more research into the 'self-learning' aspect of human intelligence. This is the only to ensure that the systems that are developed will continue to do as humanity tells them to.

New technologies in healthcare

The healthcare sector could benefit from the effective implementation of data in the form of benefits to both the industry and general interest. As of yet, a lack of cooperation is impeding this process. The multitude of technological innovations and high-potential developments has resulted in new, often potent players joining the care market. In addition, care institutions are faced with a number of fundamental digital changes; examples are digital scanners for medical purposes, and electronic, digital patient files. It is of crucial interest for the care sector to find collaborative forms that properly mesh with the digital developments and organisations marketing these innovations.

Assigning a Chief Digital Officer (CDO) or a department focussed on digital developments in the care sector would be a good first step. Every care organisation should focus on which new digital trend, be it Artificial Intelligence of Big Data, they should be focussing their efforts, without losing sight of patients', or customers', interests. The biggest dilemma for the care sector may be the classic balance between costs and quality of care. Digitisation may improve quality of care substantially, but does not come free. After all, medical assessment and personal contact will always remain at the heart of any care process.

Source: www.managementscope.nl, 12 April 2018

3.3.5   Advanced Robotics/Robotisation

A robot is a programmable machine that often not only processes information, but can also perform physical tasks. A robot may also be equipped with artificial intelligence and self-learning capabilities, increasing its autonomy. Robotics is the scientific branch concerned with developing and studying robots. Robotisation is the term used to describe how a number of tasks first performed by people are now being carried out by robots. Heavy industry and aeronautics were the first industries to use robots to perform tasks quicker, cheaper, and more accurately – for example the implementation of welding robots in the automobile industry. Robots and drones are often deployed in reconnaissance missions in hostile situations. Aeronautics uses advanced robots for perfoming autonomous tasks and relaying observations to earth. The International Space Station also uses the robotic

Robotics
Robotisation

arm. More and more industrial branches are coming to rely on robotics: in elderly care, robots are providing a social aspect to combat elderly solitude, for example. In surgical wards, robots are used in keyhole surgery. In this case, they usually rely on remote manual input.

Combined with artificial intelligence, a robot could, theoretically, be equipped with continually expanding autonomy – with resounding consequences. Fukoku Mutual, a Japanese insurance company, uses IBM's Watson artificial intelligence software. AI robots rapidly calculate the amount the insurance company has to pay to customers who have signed a life insurance contract. According to the company, the entire process revolves around the customer: because robots do not make mistakes, people are always paid the correct amount. On top of that, the company saves 140 million Yen, which comes to 1.5 million Euros, every year. As a consequence, 30 employees have already lost their jobs.

Experts predict that the changes to the labour market will turn it onto its head, costing millions their jobs. Middle class jobs, in particular, are vulnerable. US department store Walmart uses self-driving scanner robots: new, rolling employees/robots that check to see whether shelves require stocking and whether information labels are correct. The result is a reduction in human error, and employees can focus more on service tasks. In Chapter 6 on The Future of Work, the consequences of digitisation for employment are addressed in greater detail.

3.3.6   3D printing

3D printing, or additive manufacturing, makes it possible to produce objects in various different materials and components as a single whole, one layer at a time. A 3D-printer is a device that uses digital 'blueprints' (computer files) to produce three-dimensional objects by reconstructing an object from compound layers. A frequently used 3D-printing methods is to use a fine powder (such as plaster or polyurethane) like that used in inkjet printers, with different layers of this powder being stuck together to create a fixed shape. Fluids or gels are also used. 3D-printing is particularly prevalent in machine construction, aviation and aeronautics, the automobile industry, and in the manufacture of medical tools. Many everyday products are made by 3D-printers: tooth prosthetics, hearing aids, artificial hip joints.

3D printing

One of the industries changed drastically by the digital transformation is the world of the designer and engineer. Trends like digital design, in the form of 3D-printing, are changing the nature of their work enormously. The manufacturing industry in particular needs to utilise these new opportunities to speed up the industry's digitisation. Entirely new supply chains are being created by digitisation and 3D-printing in particular. Flexibility is improved; design restrictions are removes; distribution limits are abolished. Production in small, personalised quantities is made possible; using little to no capital investments, service component scan be reconfigured. Unnecessary stock will become a thing of the past: 3D-printing will change production capacity.

This will have major repercussions on product distribution in the future. Because 3D-printing allows products to be manufactured locally, there will be many substantial shifts in the transport process. Internal trade flows, as a result, will dwindle.

The impact of the digital transformation on various societal sectors is addressed in the next paragraph.

3.3.7   Virtual and Augmented Reality

Virtual Reality

Virtual Reality (VR) is a simulated form of real life. It is a computer-generated environment that can be experienced using special VR goggles or headsets. Users see and hear a lifelike experience that is often interactive. The generated environment can be explored and manipulated.

Augmented Reality

Augmented Reality (AR) visualises digital information. All data now accessible using the online or physical resources can be visually integrated with the real world. This makes gathering, learning, and implementing information much simpler. **Augmented reality** does not remove the real world from the view of the observer. Instead, it is blended with holograms. **Virtual reality** places the viewer in a virtual world, obscuring the real one.

In terms of its applications, Virtual Reality is suitable for training in healthcare, the service industry, education, defence, and heavy machinery plants. Examples are reanimation courses, fear therapy for psychiatric patients, detectives reviewing a crime scene in VR, or experiencing military life under simulated conditions. Augmented Reality aims at the intersection of reality and virtual reality, with its most important feature being that it adds a digital layer to the real world. The advantages of AR are numerous, and include:
- The ability to interpose information on the live image of a camera or AR head-set, thus showing traffic information, route navigation, etc.
- The possibility of manufacturing AR 'smart glasses', meaning one's hands are free to perform other activities. The software can often also recognise gestures, making hardware controllers superfluous.
- The integration of smartphones and tablet PCs. The fact that these devices already come equipped with cameras means that they can already make use of AR technology, thus drastically lowering the threshold.

3.3.8   Big Data

Big Data

Big Data (or data analytics) is the term for the use of one or more datasets that are too large for regular database management systems to maintain. According to the Gartner research institute, big data involves three factors: data amount, data arrival/requisition speed, and data diversity. Mainly, this is given to mean that the data is not structured, and cannot be stored in a traditional database. Three other factors are data variance, data quality, and data complexity. Big data is becoming increasingly important; the amount of data stored is growing exponentially, thus lowering costs as the technology becomes increasingly imbedded in society. Data-driven companies earn double the value of their competitors, thus substaintially increasing their turnover. Using data like predictive algorithms offers a better insight into, for example, customer requirements. This makes it possible to tailor to consumer requirements, and thereby increase sales. Big data, therefore, offers a competitive advantage. Having data means physical means are no longer required to ensure innovation or competitive strength. Organisations like Uber and Airbnb do not have physical resources, but fare better than their competitors in terms of market value.

A data-driven organisation can upscale more easily. Uber, for instance, achieved a value of a billion dollars in less than four years. By comparison, this used to take companies at least ten years. Amazon, for example, started with book sales, moved on to include retail, then foodstuffs, and will probably begin focussing on logistics next. This expansion is possible because the company's data knowledge can easily be transferred from one domain to the next. The same applies to Tesla, which uses its knowledge of energy and batteries for clean-energy solutions. Big data has meant a surge for the industry, and has led to a renewed interest in the job of data-analyst.

The impact of blockchain on sustainability

O&M IN PRACTICE

What exactly is blockchain? According to Paul Aelen-Ensie, blockchain is a distributed database which maintains a steadily growing list of data items safeguarded against manipulation or forgery. Blockchain came to the public interest as a result of bitcoin trading, where it served as a database for online transactions. In short: blockchain is a way of safely storing data, such as contracts and value transactions.

Several transformations enabled by blockchain:
- **Blockchain enables sharing economy**: we will no longer have need for companies in the style of Uber or Airbnb if blockchain transactions are possible.
- **Blockchain clarifies the coffee chain**: the majority of coffee plantation farmers lives below the $2 per day poverty threshold. Distributors make vast sums of money on the trade. Blockchain is

the best possible way of creating and improving trust in the chain.
- **Blockchain improves care efficiency**: there are care providers working with blockchain trials in maternity care. Maternity specialists and mothers both register support hours on a smartphone app, thus shifting control of care supplied to the people concerned: the mothers.

Blockchain is often described as a disruptive technology that might wipe existing market parties off the stage. Business life, however, views blockchain more in terms of opportunity than threat: it offers a possibility for making existing business cases more relevant, for reducing costs, and for increasing service value.

Source: *Het Financieele Dagblad*, Duurzaam Bedrijfsleven, nr. 14 2018

3.4 THE IMPACT OF DIGITAL TRANSFORMATION

Digitisation seems inevitable across all economic sectors. It disrupts existing revenue models and even embodies the revenue model of companies like Uber and Airbnb. Over the coming ten years, 40% of all major companies may disappear as a result of failing to adapt to the market. This includes Fortune 500-companies. According to John Chambers, former CEO for Cisco, a third of these companies will disappear. This digital disruption leads to successful new companies, like Spotify, Google, Facebook, Amazon, Tesla and many others. Digitisation represents not only an increase in capacity, computing power, and speed, but also in connectivity. Quick action and flexibility in addressing changing customer demands is a must. The following list describes the impact and the effects of digital transformation on a number of sectors.

The figure below lists the leaders in digital transformation.

Which companies and sectors are ahead in terms of the digital transition? And which companies should function as one's example where specific digital skills are concerned?

TOP 5 LEADERS

1	ABN AMRO	(financial services)	ABN·AMRO
2/3	KPN	(ICT/telecommunications)	kpn
2/3	Vopak	(oil/gas/energy)	Vopak
4	Wolters Kluwer	(media)	Wolters Kluwer
5	GrandVision	(retail)	GrandVision

KPN and Vopak share second place, followed closely by the other companies. The diversity of the industries is remarkable: Arcadis, Coolblue, Eneco Group, ING, Port of Rotterdam, PostNl, Randstad. (FD.nl 23-06-2017)

3.4.1   The financial sector

Following the 2008 financial crisis, the bank sector continues to be viewed with some measure of distrust. This makes the sector susceptible to change and disruption. Millennials in particular are looking for alternatives in the form of, among other things, new payment systems and cryptocurrencies. The latter is a new method of exchanging virtual currencies (e.g. Bitcoin).

The new generation demands greater transparency and flexibility in banking: they want to be able to have access to swift and cheap mobile banking anywhere, anytime. They have greater confidence in the new technologies and see opportunities for taking control. The result: the emergence of new banks and crowdfunding platforms. Crowdfunding is an alternative means of financing a project by creating direct lines of contact between investors and entrepreneurs (private individuals). The rise of fintech companies is a logical consequence of this disruption. Fintec is a combination of 'financial' and 'technology'; fintech companies combine financial services and products with innovative technology. The Adyen company is an example: an online payment system which lets companies handle all payments. Various apps for payment requests via WhatsApp linked to one's bank account are also available. These have become the alternative options to banks, capital managers, and insurance companies. The blockchain technology is assuming the role of the traditional third party: banks and notaries. Blockchain is the internet's cash book; the technology inspires trust, allowing users to do business (settle contracts or loans, for example) without the need for an intermediary.

It is important for the financial sector to stay abreast of the developments in digitisation, automation, and robotisation in order to remain a competitive force on the international market.

3.4.2 The retail industry

Business is difficult for the retail sector: physical stores are seeing a drop in turnover, whereas online stores are seeing their sales and income grow. The wider assortment, lower prices, and more favourable purchasing policies (including the right to free returns in some cases) mean that online stores do see a rise in turnover, but hardly in profit. Amazon, one of the world's first and largest online stores booked its first profit only in 2015. Store chains who began as physical chains, however, seem to be upping their profit exactly because they offer a physical alternative. This has caused a number of online stores to decide to start experimenting with physical locations, such as flagship or pop-up stores. These experiments show that the shopping experience and personal attention are still appreciated. A reasonably common phenomenon is that of the online ordering and at home delivery of one's daily shopping. It is a matter of convenience, particularly where heavy or bulky purchases are concerned. New online supermarket chains, such as Picnic, offer products free of charge, and are even looking into making delivery times more specific.

The rise of the sharing and trading economy has also had a major influence on retail. Consumers have decreased their purchases following the rise in popularity of trading or borrowing products – eBay, for example, is doing well. Online website Peerby offers neighbourhood or area functionality: tools can be borrowed or rented from people nearby. This, in turn, has major repercussions for do-it-yourself stores, who are registering a drop in turnover as the result of this change in behaviour.

3.4.3 The healthcare industry

Digitisation and new technologies are causing major changes to healthcare with respect to the organisation and methods of treatment. Using digitisation, treatments can be streamlined better, and the focus can be shifted towards the patient. Digitisation improves quality of care because it makes it possible to better apply the available information. Moreover, it improves efficiency by streamlining the flows of information, being medical data. Quality, affordable, and accessible care are made possible through the use of innovative IT-applications. Digitisation of healthcare enables doctors and nursing staff to review and analyse patient data at a glance. It also offers patients permanent access to their own medical records, allowing them to better monitor their own health levels. It also prevents the silo-effect in hospitals, thus making it impossible to overlook important information that would benefit patient health. The result is a personalised digital world which patients themselves maintain. All available health data becomes ownership of the patient, and patients and doctors are linked at all times.

Picnic: Retail trade transition at rocket speeds

Popular Dutch online supermarket Picnic, which claims to offer daily shopping at competing prices with delivery to your door at no extra costs, wants to use a new distribution chain to disrupt the supermarket chain. Founder Joris Beckers hopes to increase the market share to 50%. Picnic is a trendy, rapidly growing start-up. The company's turnover was 100 million Euros in 2017, with 150,000 returning customers and 50,000 weekly orders. They are looking to change the distribution model of Dutch food delivery using four national distribution centres used to assign orders to dozens of local hubs. Deliveries are free, and the company claims, despite the fact, that shopping at Picnic is no more expensive than in the physical stores of their competitors. Picnic is the major 'disruptor' in the supermarket industry. The fundamental difference is one of supply: customers place tomorrow's orders today, allowing for cost-saving on purchasing and reducing food waste by 70% compared to regular supermarkets. This means substantial flexibility. In addition, there are no extended lease contracts like those regular supermarkets have to deal with. Picnic has invested heavily in quality of service, in this case delivery. Following consumer polls, they concluded that customers would rather do business with a female delivery driver: customers placing the order are usually women, who would prefer not to let a male delivery driver into their home. The company uses self-managing teams who know their customers personally; there are no managers. Sales follow the pareto-principle: 20 percent of the assortment – being, for example, eggs, bread, vegetables – accounts for 80% of sales. As a result, the company does offer niche products. Their major current barrier is to continue their growth while retaining the existing level of quality. This explains Picnic's new customer waiting list.

Source: www.managementscope.nl, 06-09-2018

Introducing the digital self-diagnostic

The Orikami company specialises in the use of data in healthcare. By looking for new connections and patterns in large data files, they try to predict individual patients' symptom progression. These predictions serve as the basis for improved treatment and care.

Founder Bram Teuling developed an app which can be used to monitor MS-patients continuously, instead of having a neurologist review their case once every year. Using two tests, the app lets patients see how their illness is progressing. One test measures the patient's ability to concentrate and remember by checking for symbol recognition. A two-minute walking test is used to assess patient mobility. By having patients conduct regular measurements with the app, doctors are offered more insight into whether the expensive medication has any effect. Using large quantities of data gathered by the app, the company hopes to be able to offer even more accurate MS prognoses in future. Or, even better: to provide doctors with timely updates to let them adjust treatments to prevent patient relapses.

Source: FD.nl 22-06-2018

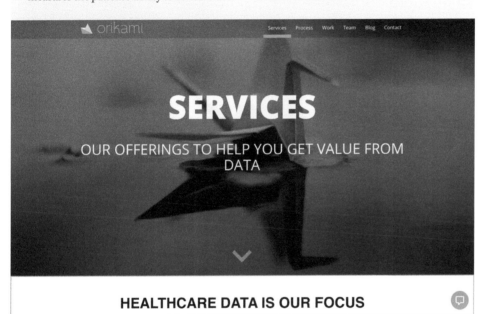

HEALTHCARE DATA IS OUR FOCUS

3.4.4   The automobile industry

Changes in consumer behaviour lead to massive changes for the automobile industry. Moreover, the industry has seen major technological change, putting enormous pressure on companies to continue to innovate.

Private car ownership will largely be replaced by the borrowing, renting, and sharing of cars: on-demand, tailored access to cars. The **Economist** has calculated that sharing 1 car means 15 fewer will be necessary for private ownership. Moreover, car owners need to make a decision based on the type of fuel consumed: hybrid, fully electric, or hydrogen? Denmark wants to prohibit the use of combustion engine cars on the roads. Therefore, no pure gasoline or diesel-powered cars will be allowed on sale from 2030. Norway even wants to prohibit gasoline and diesel cars from 2025.

The industry is also hard at work on developing self-driving, autonomous vehicles. The development of the self-driving car is powered less by the consumer, but by disruptive economic forces, such as the Uber company. Car owners will no longer need to continue their role as drivers, allowing for greater profit. Other autonomous vehicles are also being developed: recreational and professional drones. Agricultural robots, self-steering vessels, self-driving undergrounds and trains, mail drones: mobility will change drastically in terms of function and form.

3.4.5 The agriculture and nutrition industry

This industry has also undergone significant changes following the introduction of advanced IT-solutions and digitisation.

Data and sensors will offer livestock farmers improved insight and effectiveness. Linking sensors and computer chips to animals or installed subterraneously, for example, would offer a lot of information, thus enabling more precise and customise activities. This data comes with more efficient and sustainable business operations, limiting wastage where possible. Consider soil quality, animal welfare, revenue per acre, for example.

O&M IN PRACTICE

Digital is the new 'level playing field' for Royal FloraHolland

Using 4 auction locations and 35 auction clocks, the Royal FloraHolland corporation is the world's largest flower auction, generating 4.7 billion euros in trade. Since its founding in 1911, member plant breeders have continued to invest in upscaling and improving infrastructure. Now, the time has come to develop an accompanying digital infrastructure, allowing growers to join the digital world. This is taking place in terms of three dimensions: business model digitisation, company digitisation, and industrial digitisation. The aim of Royal FloraHolland is to become the leader across the board, making them the digital ecosystem for global horticulture.

This way, digitisation attracts new contenders, whose business models enrich the industry as a whole. The application of digital and data makes it increasingly easy for international parties to connect. A couple of clocks and a grower can broaden their sales market; a buyer can source worldwide. If these changes are facilitated using a digital, data-driven structure, using new standard values, a new 'level playing field' is created. Known as Floriday, it is a global, digital ecosystem for plant breeders.

Source: *Het Financieele Dagblad, Transformers* 2018 edition

Consumers are also becoming more interested in the origin of products, which can also be facilitated by digitisation. Transparency is desired, also in the interest of public health. For example: Has the farmer used pesticides? If so, which? What is the product's provenance? It becomes possible to better and more frequently address customer demands. In turn, the food industry is kept more up to date on trends in food and nutrition habits.

3.4.6   The manufacture industry

The manufacture industry is the part of the industry that converts materials into new products. It includes machine construction, electronics, and textiles, among others. Companies in this industry mostly focus on production. The manufacture industry mainly uses IT to improve the efficiency of business processes, thus optimising production and enabling large-scale custom production. Autonomy and self-management are achieved through digitisation; including more dynamic and flexible production. It becomes easier to address market changes, and to manufacture more intelligently. Industries dedicated to consumer products can use vast quantities of data (big data) to better address specific customer preferences. As of yet, the manufacture industry is mainly concerned with economies of scale: the greater the produced quantity of a single type of product, the lower the fixed costs per unit, the higher the profit. Product diversity, as a result, is limited. This opens the door to micro plants and 3D-printing, limited editions, and custom products. The summary conclusion should be that the focus continues to shift towards to consumer, that robotisation and automation have had their introduction, and that a more efficient business model will allow companies to continue to remain competitive.

3.4.7   Transport and logistics

This is another sector where digitisation has resulted in greater efficiency and transparency through the application of ICT applications, such as transport management system (TMS) and warehouse management systems (WMS). This has meant a significant improvement in terms of route planning, parcel tracking, communications, fleet management, order admin, and financial admin capabilities. Continued and frequent online consumer shopping has required the industry come up with an even more flexible and efficient approach. This has resulted in smart solutions and arrangements. Means of transport are equipped with sensors, allowing better insight into cargo whereabouts and contents. This data is critically important, because it can be shared internationally, benefitting governments and companies alike. Customs can also access a central ICT gateway, which handles government messages, to retain insight into the flow of goods.
Amazon's distribution centres, for example, frequently use automatically guided and driving order collection robots, thus minimising handling fees. Moreover, physical and relatively intense human labour is replaced by robots. Relevant technological developments such as digitisation, automation, and robotisation are improving the integration of the various applications. Transport and logistics industry processes are increasing in complexity, but the ICT technologies used to cope with these changes are also improving in terms of efficiency and accessibility, allowing for the optimisation of internal business operations.

Digital transformation creates value for business on multiple levels, in the form of:
- e-commerce, social media and mobile networking leading to increased turnover
- improving connectivity
- ensuring the automation of manual activities
- ensuring better, more efficient decision-making
- leading to product and service innovation.

3.5 CONDITIONS FOR SUCCESSFUL DIGITAL TRANSFORMATION

Although new technology is the driving force behind any digital transformation, this does not mean that it is only technology that ensures that digital transformation is successful
There are four distinct strategic pillars that contribute to successful digital transformation. These are summarised in the abbreviation PACT: People, Actions, Collaboration, and Technology.

© marketoonist.com

People
The success of a digital transformation hinges on the right knowledge and skills of the people involved. Knowledge refers to the implementation and use of new technologies as well as to digital awareness, new business models, business processes, and work methods. Continued development and education in these areas is seen as one of the most important pillars. Chapters 6 and 7 address the future of work and human development in greater detail.

Actions
Processes and conduct (actions) needed to make the digital transformation into a success are described in a clearly developed digital strategy. This involves a link to the encompassing business strategy. The choice is between developing these actions inside or outside of the organisations.

Collaboration

It is important for an organisation to collaborate with both internal and external stakeholders. This could involve various departments, customers, and partners including consultancy firms, education institutes, etcetera. A digital transformation is accelerated when the missing knowledge and ideas are provided and implemented.

Technology

The application of the right technology is what ensures a successful transformation. As discussed in the previous sections, there are many new technologies awaiting application. As the development of new technologies takes place at lightning speed, it is of the utmost importance that this development is monitored continually.

Research by Fujitsu shows that the success of a digital transformation depends mainly on human aspects, including people, actions, and collaboration. The role of technology accounts for only 20%. Therefore, it is of critical importance that investming in people takes precedence over everything else.

FIGURE 3.5 **SUCCESS FACTORS OF DIGITAL TRANSFORMATION**

People

31 %

Having the right knowledge and skills

Actions

32 %

Having the right processes, attitudes, and behaviours

Collaboration

16 %

Collaborating with partners to achieve innovation

Technology

20 %

Having the right technologies

Source: The Digital Transformation PACT, Fujitsu (2018)

Many organisations proceed with digital transformations with great success, whereas other organisations stay grounded and make little progress. In the book 'Leading Digital', the authors offer a number of reasons for this principle.

The first is that organisations often have unrealistic expectations. Many organisations are initially too optimistic, becoming blinded by the many possibilities that new technologies present. Their enthusiasm appears to mainly involve 'digital technology' versus 'transformation'. Many people realise that transformation is, in fact, more important than technology. A second reason corresponds with the earlier cited study: underdeveloped talent. Companies are short on people with the right expertise and experience. Additionally, properly educating existing staff appears far from simple. Poor communication is the third reason. Many business teams and technology teams restrict themselves only to their own domain. Collaboration and cross-pollination, however, are prerequisites of digital transformation. A fourth reason is the lack of a so-called 'digital culture', which has to do with the fact that many employees fail to see the benefits of digital transformation either to the industry, the company, or to themselves personally. Lastly, another challenge is that of competitor pressure. Customer expectations continue to grow, thereby continually raising the bar. The best app for travel booking comparison websites, for example, becomes the de facto norm. Solutions should always be assessed from the perspective of 'the best' experiences. Chapter 13 pays greater attention to the recommended direction of changes in organisation.

Why to bring the board on board with digitisation

Top-level managers are all looking for that bit of security in times of disruptive innovation: what are the secrets to a successful digital transformation? According to Stijn Viaene, full professor and partner of Vlerick Business School, the digital transformation is, first and foremost, a business transformation.

Viaene: 'It is, in fact, a holistic, end-to-end business change. It is not sufficient to adjust the IT or Marketing department alone. The entirety of the business operations must undergo a digital transformation: not merely the strategy, but also the organisational design, the processes, and

the HR and reward systems. Technology plays a dominant role in fundamentally reimagining business operations. Another misconception is that digitisation is the domain of a specific organisational role. The entire board has to join in with the process: not just the CEO, but their management team as well. Only with a board that is forged into a 'band of brothers' will an organisation be able to really transform and sweep up the employees in the process. The entire process depends on refusing to accept managerial laziness.'

Source: www.managementscope.nl, 17-04-2017

Summary

► Organisations must transform, or digitise, in order to retain their right to exist.

► Digital transformation is only effected once there has been an integral business transformation which is dominated by digital technology. The business centres on the customer, and digital thinking must become part of organisational DNA.

► There are three distinct phases of organisational transformation:
Phase 1.0: a traditionally driven organisation;
Phase 2.0: a transitional phase from traditional to digital;
Phase 3.0: a radical shift towards digital transformation.

► Important technologies for digital transformation are mobile internet, Cloud Computing, The Internet of Things, Artificial Intelligence, Robotisation, 3D-printing, Virtual and Augmented Reality, and Big Data.

► Digital transformation has had an impact on all sectors of industry, including the financial sector, retail, healthcare, the automobile industry, the agriculture and food industry, the manufacture industry, and transport and logistics. Key words for impact are customer-orientation, organisational agility, rapid response to change, new business models, cost cutting, and new product and service development.

► There are four distinct pillars that contribute to successful digital transformation. These are summarised by the term PACT: People, Actions, Collaboration, and Technology.

4

INTER- NATIONALISATION

After studying this chapter:

– you will have gained insight into the reasons and motivations behind internationalisation;
– you will have gained knowledge of and insight into five forms of economic integration;
– you will have familiarised yourself with the function and organisations of the European Union;
– you will have familiarised yourself with the most important international organisations;
– you will have familiarised yourself with a number of basic theories on internationalisation;
– you will have gained knowledge of and insight into the motives for and forms of outsourcing

Tunga: websites and apps built by Africa's youths

Programmers are a scarce resource, which start-up company Tunga has now found in Africa. Tunga links companies to software-programmers and organisations looking to have software built. Using support from organisations like Stichting DOEN, Dioraphte, and Oxfam Novib, over the past 2.5 years, the company has built a network that employs Africa's youths as software programmers on international projects. This gives companies access to the well-trained, affordable software programmers who are increasingly difficult to come by in many western countries.

The start-up company, owned by Ernesto Spruyt (42) and Michiel Huisman (35), wants to use this approach to contribute to the creation of a well-paid job structure for Africa's younger generation which, despite being well-trained, has barely any access to the labour market. Tunga is a member of the *Fairtrade Software Foundation*.

Tunga focusses on SMEs as well as larger organisations and NGOs. The company's clients can be found on all continents, but it is focussed on the EU, where the Netherlands is heavily represented. This is due, in part, to the entrepreneurs' network, as well as the country's strong digital development.

Tunga offers its clients three options: implementing software projects, secondment of software programmers (at a distance), or recruiting programmers. Projects and secondment come in at 20 Euros per hour, which includes a margin for the start-up. Recruitment is available for a fixed fee per candidate.

In addition to their own IT experience, the founders have a background in the hospitality industry and in developmental aid. They say this is reflected in their work methods, with a high level of service for clients on the one hand, and proper care for developers on the other.

Source: www.sprout.nl, www.tunga.io, www.social-enterprise.nl

4.1 INTRODUCTION

Since its early days, the Netherlands has been an internationally oriented country. Consider its Golden Age (1600-1700 AD), during which the Republic of the Seven United Netherlands knew enormous prosperity. In those days, the Dutch government had founded the East India Trading Company, usually known by its Dutch abbreviation VOC. Its ships sailed and traded across the world's seas and oceans, with a particular focus on gold and spices. In the 20th century, internationalisation took off enormously following World War II. More and more countries and companies began to join in the trade. International investments grew, and many organisations went from nationally-oriented to multi-nationally-oriented, with the borders dividing nations becoming increasingly meaningless. The development of the internet has meant that this transformation has only grown in scale and speed. Online stores like Amazon and Alibaba operate on a global scale.

Internationalisation

One aspect addressed in Section 4.4.4 is the relocation of activities to low-wage countries, such as India, Vietnam, and China. This is known as outsourcing. Through collaborative agreements, (parts of) business operations, such as IT, admin, and clothing, are transferred to a low-wage country. The term 'low-wage country' is used for countries where production is cheaper than in, for example, European or American countries, mainly due to the significant difference in wage costs compared to Europe or the US.
From the perspective of the Netherlands, there are organisations that operate on a global scale, with on the one hand organisations based in the Netherlands (with examples including Unilever, AkzoNobel, Philips and Shell), and on the other hand foreign organisations operating in the Netherlands (including Google, Cargill, IBM and Bank of Scotland).

Low-wage countries

Two concepts that are often mentioned with respect to internationalisation are import and export.
Reasons for companies and countries to engage in import are that:
- products are cheaper to produce abroad (for example due to lower wage costs);
- the product quality of foreign products is superior to that of domestic products;
- the imported products are not manufactured domestically.
Reasons for companies and countries to engage in export are that:
- they are looking to expand the market field, allowing for improved economies of scale and competitive advantage;
- the product quality of domestic products is superior to that of foreign products;
- the domestic market is subject to overcapacity.

Import
Export

These days, another frequently used term related to internationalisation is globalisation. Whereas internationalisation is actually only concerned with products or services, globalisation focusses less on those aspects but much more on a process of global economic, political, and cultural integration between countries and continents. Not only the production of goods and services plays a role in this process – other important aspects are the global transfer and localisation of labour, knowledge, and capital. Countries and continents are still connected on many fronts and partially depend on one another. Consider environmental issues and counterterrorism efforts. Developments in information and communications technology can only lead to even more expansive globalisation in years to come.

Globalisation

The world of robotics

Employees in Dutch industries can look forward to new robot companions. Robot-density in the Netherlands has grown by 65% – a much higher figure than in the rest of the world. The only exception is China, which experienced an even greater robotic expansion. According to the International Federation of Robotics, 294,000 robots were installed worldwide in 2016 – of which around 100,000 were in the car industry and 90,000 in the electronics sector. In 2020, the total number is expected to grow to 521,000.

Source: *Het Financieele Dagblad,* 23 May 2018

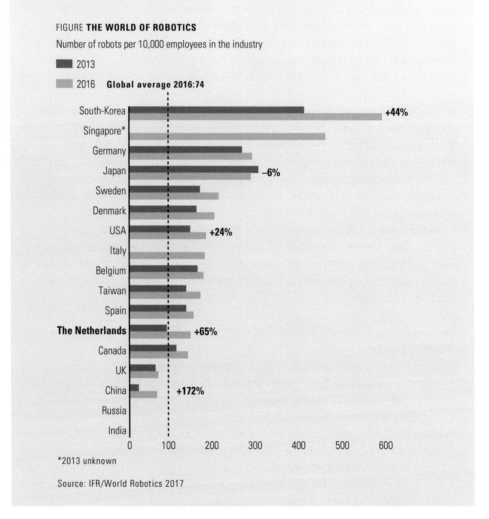

FIGURE **THE WORLD OF ROBOTICS**

Number of robots per 10,000 employees in the industry

Source: IFR/World Robotics 2017

Globalisation is related to the following themes:
- **Trade**: trade between the world's nations is growing. Global trade also means a global redistribution of labour.
- **Transport**: global transport of good and people is becoming increasingly aligned.
- **International** trade policy: more and more agreements on the nature of global trade are being made between countries and continents on the government level. Consider policies involving the size and scope of tax territories for import and export, and customs legislation.

- **International finance and capital flows**: more and more agreements on the proper monitoring and managing of cash flows are being made between countries and continents at the government level. Consider interest restrictions and agreements in terms of bank or insurance company buffers.
- **International organisation of production of goods and services**: organisations continue to look for the most efficient and effective method of organisating of their global business activities. Economies of scale play an important role, as do participations in strategic alliances/networks, or participations in take-overs or mergers. This has a strengthening effect on the connectedness of corporate life.
- **Information and communications technology**: developments in this field have made the world 'smaller and nearer'. Physical movement is often less necessary, and sharing of knowledge has become much easier.
- **Politics**: globalisation has also had consequences on how countries and continents align their legislation. Within Europe, countries have relinquished part of their sovereignty to a higher body within the European Union, in order to improve the harmonisation of the rules of the various member states and other parts of the world.
- **Tourism**: More and more of the world's citizens are seeing travelling as a fine and useful activity. Global travel is increasing. A special organisation within the UN is concerned with global tourism: United Nations World Tourism Organisation (UNWTO). They gather and analyse statistical information on global tourism. An example of one of their overviews can be seen below:

FIGURE 4.1 **DEVELOPMENT OF GLOBAL TOURISM**

Number of international arrivals worldwide
(x million)

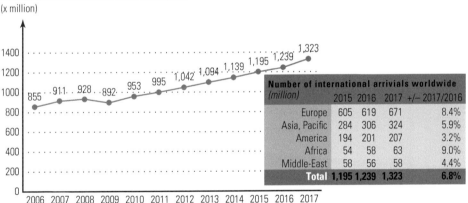

Number of international arrivals worldwide (million)	2015	2016	2017	+/– 2017/2016
Europe	605	619	671	8.4%
Asia, Pacific	284	306	324	5.9%
America	194	201	207	3.2%
Africa	54	58	63	9.0%
Middle-East	58	56	58	4.4%
Total	**1,195**	**1,239**	**1,323**	**6.8%**

Source: UNWTO (July 2018)

Source: **Toerisme in perspectief**, January 2018, **NBTC Holland Marketing**, Afdeling Market Insights, www.nbtc.nl/nl, consulted 4 June 2018

This chapter pays attention to the five forms of economic integration that are possible between countries. These five forms of economic integration encourage the mutual internationalisation of countries. Internationalisation is also encouraged from an institutional perspective. To that end, various international organisations, such as the United Nations, have been established. The most important of these international organisations are covered in a later paragraph, which is followed by a discussion of the organisational issues of internationalisation, emphasising basic organisational forms and strategies.

4.2   FORMS OF ECONOMIC INTEGRATION

Based on its political responsibility, the Dutch government tries to direct the state of affairs of the economy. For example, it may influence pricing, income distribution, the labour market, the balance of payments, monetary issues, and economic growth.

In past years, there has been an increase in the amount of political power and influence that can been exerted on national economies by outside bodies. Within Europe, this has partly been brought about by the removal of borders between the Member States of the EU (European Union), in line with their goal of creating a single common internal market.

Unification of Europe
The Unification of Europe and a shift in political power are factors likely to challenge organisations in the near future. The only way of attaining true unification is by having member states relinquish their national economic and political sovereignty to one or more communal institutions the result is an economic union.

In general, five forms of economic integration can be identified. In ascending order of intensity of integration, these are the free trade zone, the customs union, the common market, the economic union and the complete political and economic union. All five are described below in brief:

Free trade zone
1   The free trade zone. Only the mutual trade restrictions (import and export rights) are repealed by participating countries. Each country determines its own import tariffs for products imported from outside the free trade zone. As a result, the trade policy for members is not harmonised. A certificate of origin is therefore necessary to prevent products being imported via the country with the lowest import tariffs. The advantages of the free trade zone are (Jethu-Ramsoedh & Hendrickx, 2015)
– efficient implementation of production factors;
– encouragement of competition;
– prevention of trade war;
– strengthening of trade and investment;
– encouragement of growth of prosperity.

Some of the world's best known free trade zones are:
a **European Free Trade Association** (EFTA): Founded in 1960, EFTA encompasses the countries of Iceland, Liechtenstein, Norway, and Switzerland;
b **Mercosur**: founded in 1991, the participating countries of this South-American free trade zone are Argentina, Brazil, Paraguay, Uruguay, Venezuela and Bolivia;
c **NAFTA**: founded in 1994, its participating countries are Canada, Mexico and the US;
d **ASEAN**: founded in 1967, this alliance comprises Indonesia, Malaysia, Singapore, Thailand, the Philippines, Vietnam, Brunei, Laos, Cambodia and Myanmar.

Customs union
2   The customs union. A customs union also repeals mutual import and export rates. As a result, there is free trade between participating countries, who also apply a common outside tariff. The same import/export rate is applied to imports from non-participating countries.

Examples of customs unions are:
a **Swiss Toll Zone**: Switzerland and Liechtenstein;
b **Southern African Customs Union** (SACU): founded in 1910, this customs union comprises the countries of Botswana, Lesotho, Namibia, Swaziland and South-Africa. SACU is one of the world's oldest customs unions.

3 The common market. Also referred to as the internal market, the common market is based on a customs union that has no economic interior border but applies one common exterior border. In addition, there are no restrictions with respect to production factors. Within a common market, there is free movement of goods, people, capital, and services.

Common market

To qualify as a free open market, countries need to remove a number (6) of restrictions, including:
- physical limitations: customs checks, and associated paperwork and border crossing delays;
- technical limitations: differences in product norm definitions, entrepreneurial rights provisions, and government acquisition restrictions;
- fiscal limitations: differences in VAT and excise rates which require settlement at the border.

A common market exists within the European Union. In addition, 19 of the 28 member states also comprise an economic and monetary union. As discussed, ASEAN is currently a free trade zone, but aims to become a common market in the future.

4 The economic and monetary union. An economic union with not just the characteristics of a common market, but a harmonisation of monetary policy and its financial government politics. This requires the implementation of central institutions, such as a single Central Bank.

Economic and monetary union

5 The full political and economic union. A complete merger of countries. One example is the formation of the United States of America.

Full political and economic union

A well-known example of a common market is the **European Union**, of which the Netherlands is a member. The European Union (EU) comprised of 28 (or 27) countries. In 2016, the United Kingdom decided to leave the EU.

Countries in the EU enjoy free movement of goods, people, services, and capital. Within the EU, these four freedoms are defined as follows:
1. **Free movement of goods.** Goods are no longer subjected to checks when crossing interior EU borders; the EU comprises a single territory.
2. **Free movement of people.** EU residents can travel to other EU member states unrestrictedly. This includes countries that are not EU members but are part of the European Economic Area (EEA): Liechtenstein, Norway, and Iceland. The 'new' member states are subject to a transition period. Independent entrepreneurs are also free to settle in any of the member states.
3. **Free movement of services.** All EU citizens are free to work where they want. Restrictions apply to new member states.
4. **Free movement of capital.** Free movement of capital offers European citizens countless freedoms. The European Commission made a start on establishing a true European capital market union. The goal of a capital union is to encourage cross-border investments within Europe and to improve access for (small) companies.

Free movement of goods
Free movement of people
Free movement of services
Free movement of capital

The development of a common internal market has led to the formation of an economic block at the European level, thereby possibly improving the competitive position compared to other power blocks, such as Japan, the United States, and South-East Asia.

The unification of Europe will have significant consequences for many organisations. It is anticipated that increased competition will put pressure on production costs, which in turn will lead to a fall in prices. Lower prices generate increased turnover, which leads to economies of scale, and possible business expansion. Larger scale production makes innovation affordable, leading to better products which will more easily find their way to consumers. Thus, there will be a chain reaction of reinforcing effects which will influence Europe's competitive position compared to countries like the United States, Japan, and South-East Asia.

The Netherlands heading for the top of most competitive countries, Germany lagging

A study by Swiss Business School IMD shows that the Netherlands does not particularly excel in any field, in contrast to the US – which has excellent universities and is well equipped to draw in research funds. However, the Netherlands is characterised by a considerable and balanced performance across a wide front.

Source: *Het Financieele Dagblad*, 24 May 2018

FIGURE **THE NETHERLANDS IN A CONVINCING FOURTH PLACE**

The world's most competitive countries according to Swiss business school IMD

Total score

2017		2018
1 Hong Kong		1 USA
2 Switzerland		2 Hong Kong
3 Singapore		3 Singapore
4 USA		4 The Netherlands
5 The Netherlands		5 Switzerland
6 Ireland		6 Denmark
7 Denmark		7 UAE
8 Luxembourg		8 Norway
9 Sweden		9 Sweden
10 UAE		10 Canada
11 Norway		11 Luxembourg
12 Canada		12 Ireland
13 Germany		13 China
14 Taiwan		14 Qatar
15 Finland		15 Germany

Source: FD, IMD

The Netherlands

Total score ranking: '13 14 – '14 14 – '15 15 – '16 8 – '17 5 – '18 4

Economy: '13 17 – '14 15 – '15 25 – '16 9 – '17 9 – '18 6

Governmental efficiency: '13 14 – '14 18 – '15 13 – '16 15 – '17 12 – '18 8

Corporate efficiency: '13 14 – '14 12 – '15 12 – '16 10 – '17 4 – '18 6

Infrastructure: '13 9 – '14 11 – '15 8 – '16 7 – '17 8 – '18 9

Organisations and their environment
PART A

There are around 500 million people living in the European Union. China (1.4 billion) and India (1.3 billion) are the only countries with more inhabitants. In addition to having many residents, the EU also has significant economic power when viewed from a global perspective. The EU accounts for approximately 25% of the world's imports and exports.

Originally, the EU dealt with issues of trade and economy. This has since been expanded on, with the EU currently also dealing with issues of freedom, security, civil rights, employment opportunity, environmental safety, and consumer protection. The EU houses five common institutions that sort out all affairs within its borders. These five institutions are:

1 **The European Commission.** On the one hand, the European Commission engages in initiatives for (new) rules and legislation; on the other, it is concerned with supervising the fact that relevant treaties are upheld by the EU. The European Commission ensures 'daily management' of the EU. It is located in Brussels, Belgium.

2 **The European Council.** The European Council is responsible for the political decision-making within the EU. Thus, the European Council determines the political development of the EU. In principle, all decisions need consensus. The European Council convenes in Brussels at least twice per year. The European Council is the only body within the EU authorised to sign or adjust treaties. The European Council is located in Strasbourg, France.

3 **The Council of the European Union.** Also known as 'the Council', this body is concerned with legislation and budgeting, in tandem with the European Parliament. Every proposed legislative or budgetary adjustment requires the Council's consent. In addition to these two important tasks, the Council also makes decisions with regard to foreign policy and safety policy. The Council of the European Union is located in Brussels, Belgium, and Luxembourg, Luxembourg.

4 **The European Parliament.** Members of the European Parliament are elected directly by residents of the 28 (or 27) EU member states every five years. The European Parliament has 750 elected members, 26 of whom are from the Netherlands (2019). The European Commission presents its proposals, which are the basis for debates held in Parliament. The European Parliament eventually makes its decisions together with the Council of the European Union. The European Parliament is located in Strasbourg, France; Brussels, Belgium; and Luxembourg, Luxembourg.

5 **The European Court of Justice.** The task of the Court is to ensure that the laws and rules established in the EU are properly adhered to. The Court also passes judgement if member states fail to follow, or even break, a law, rule, or obligation following from a treaty. Another important aspect of the Court is that, within the European Union, its authority outranks that of the individual member states. The European Court of Justice is located in Luxembourg, Luxembourg.

Within the European Union, currently 19 of the 28 (or 27) countries are participating in the economic and monetary union (EMU). These 19 member countries use the Euro as their currency (the Euro zone). Economic and financial politics are also coordinated within the EMU. The 19 EU member states participating in the EMU have transferred their authorities with regards to monetary issues to the European System of Central Banks (ESCB). At the head of all of the Central Banks is the European Central Bank, located in Frankfurt am Main, Germany. The objective of the EMU is to create a complete free common market with a common currency and high price stability. In addition to the 19 EU member states, a number of microstates and oversea territories use the Euro as legal tender. The countries using

The European Commission

The European Council

The Council of the European Union

The European Parliament

The European Court of Justice

EMU

the Euro as a currency are: Andorra; Belgium; Cyprus; Germany; Estonia; Finland; France; Greece; Ireland; Italy; Latvia; Lithuania; Luxemburg; Malta; Monaco; the Netherlands; Austria; Portugal; San Marino; Slovenia; Slovakia; Spain and Vatican City.

4.3   INTERNATIONAL ORGANISATIONS

Section 4.1 discussed internationalisation and globalisation. Various organisations have been established in order to pave the way for these developments. To illustrate the nature of these organisations, the most important ones are discussed below:
1 **The United Nations** (UN), including the **World Bank** and the **International Monetary Fund** (IMF);
2 **The World Trade Organisation** (WTO);
3 **The Organisation for Economic Collaboration and Development** (OECD);
4 **The World Economic Forum** (WEF);
5 **The BRICS countries** and the **New Development Bank** (NDB) and **Contingency Reserve Arrangement (**CRA).

United Nations (UN)

United Nations

A nearly universally known organisation is the United Nations (UN). Founded in 1945 by 51 member countries, the UN currently encompasses all internationally recognised and independent countries as its members. Within the US, the governments of the member states collaborate in terms of international legislation, security, human rights, global economic development, and the study of social and cultural development. The organisation's 'constitution' is recorded in the 'UN Charter'. The Charter documents the rights and obligations of the member states, as well as the functions and procedures of the various bodies within the UN. Another important UN declaration is the 'Universal Declaration of Human Rights'. Following World War Two, a great deal of attention was paid to international human rights, which eventually led to the drafting of the aforementioned declaration in 1948.

The UN has established five core activities. These activities are:
1 maintaining international peace and safety;
2 developing friendly relationships founded on a respect for equal rights and the right of self-determination of peoples;
3 achieving international cooperation by solving global issues that are economic, social, cultural, and humanitarian in their nature;
4 promoting respect for human rights and basic freedoms;
5 serving as a central point for peoples' attempts to achieve and align common goals.

Financing for the UN is largely comprised of contributions made by its various member states. The contributions encompass an assigned componenet and a voluntary component. Six governing bodies operate within the UN. Well-known examples are the 'General Assembly', the 'Security Council', and the 'International Court', located in The Hague, the Netherlands.
Since there are many different languages spoken by the countries of the UN, all formal meetings and documents are in six languages: English, French, Russian, Spanish, Chinese, and Arabic. There are various specialised organisations operating within the US. A selection of these organisations is:

- International Atomic Energy Agency;
- International Civil Aviation Organisation;
- International Maritime Organisation;
- Food and Agriculture Organisation;
- World Bank;
- World Health Organisation;
- International Monetary Fund.

The UN pays a great deal of attention to sustainable business. To that end, the UN has established a list of Sustainable Development Goals (2015-2030), which are discussed in detail in Section 5.1.3.

Section 5.1.8 addresses an international collaborative alliance in the field of MVO: Global Compact. Global Compact is a collaboration between the UN, companies, and other stakeholders.

In the context of internationalisation, separate attention is paid to the IMF and the World Bank.

World Bank

The World Bank is the world's major institution for developmental collaboration. World Bank
It provides loans for developing countries and middle-income countries, with the most important goal being the fight against poverty. The World Bank was founded during the Bretton Woods Conference. The International Monetary Fund (IMF) was founded at the same time. The World Bank and the IMF each have their specific objectives. Initially, the goal of the World Bank was to encourage the reconstruction of Europe following World War Two. Later, the World Bank shifted its focus to developing countries. The IMF's goal is to ensure monetary stability. The World Bank is comprised of two components: The International Bank of Reconstruction and Development (IBRD), and the International Development Association (IDA). Founded in 1944, the IBRD is the oldest of the two. It focusses on creditworthy poor countries, which are offered a loan at more favourable conditions than those offered by a commercial bank. The advantages of these loans generally include lower interest rates and longer maturities.

International Monetary Fund (IMF)

The International Monetary Fund (IMF) was founded at the same time as the World Bank. The IMF currently has 189 member countries, all of whom participate in the IMF's goal of monitoring and promoting the stability of the international monetary and financial systems. Therefore, the IMF has both an analytical and a strongly advisory task. The IMF also helps member states to solve shortages on their balance of payments. A final notable function is the fact that the IMF helps member states to prevent and resolve economic and financial crisis situations.

The IMF is provided with means and finances in two ways:

1 All member countries pay a sort of 'membership fee', based on each individual country's Gross Domestic Product (GDP) and its monetary and financial situation. Every five years, the membership fee is re-established. The amount a country pays also determines the weight of its vote: the higher the membership fee, the higher the weight of the country's vote.
2 The IMF is able and allowed to borrow funds from other channels.

Does the world feel safe?

The Dutch have a relatively high level of trust of the police, have little fear of going out at night, and report few thefts.

Source: *Het Financieele Dagblad*, 14 June 2018

FIGURE **HOW SAFE DOES DO THE WORLD'S NATIONS FEEL**

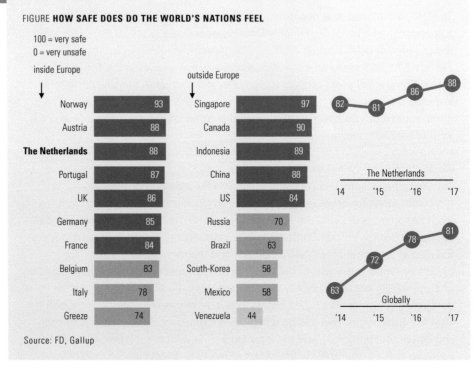

100 = very safe
0 = very unsafe

inside Europe

Norway	93
Austria	88
The Netherlands	88
Portugal	87
UK	86
Germany	85
France	84
Belgium	83
Italy	78
Greeze	74

outside Europe

Singapore	97
Canada	90
Indonesia	89
China	88
US	84
Russia	70
Brazil	63
South-Korea	58
Mexico	58
Venezuela	44

The Netherlands
82 — 81 — 86 — 88
14   '15   '16   '17

Globally
63 — 72 — 78 — 81
'14   '15   '16   '17

Source: FD, Gallup

World Trade Organisation.

World Trade
Organisation

Founded in 1995, the World Trade Organisation (WTO) is governed centrally from Geneva, Switzerland. A governmental organisation, the WTO is a collaboration between countries who have retained full sovereignty. The organisation has over 160 member states. The WTO continued on the foundations laid by the General Agreement on Tariffs and Trade (GATT), established in 1947. The task of the WTO is to promote global trade, resolve trade conflicts, and remove trade barriers. The WTO strongly believes in international free trade, which the organisation feels is the best way of improving global prosperity. The WTO cannot implement rules itself; decisions can only be made if all member states agree. The member states are therefore the 'boss' of the WTO. Meetings take place once every two years. This meeting is known as a Ministerial Conference; it is intended as a way of arriving at new legislation regarding any trade issues involving the member states. A consensus at this conference results in legislation which all member states must implement. It is possible for members of the WTO to take other members to court if the agreed upon rules are not followed. The WTO uses several working groups to prepare for the biannual Ministerial Conference; these groups include the Goods Council, the Services Council, and the Intellectual Property Council. The requirement of unanimous decision-making makes the WTO a cumbersome organisation; getting all member states on the same page can take years. As a result, the formal meetings are generally complemented by various informal ones to influence the decision-making – so-called backroom, corridor, or shadow meetings.

Organisation for Economic Collaboration and Development (OECD)

Founded in 1948, the OECD is a collaboration between 35 European and non-European countries. Originally focussed on the reconstruction of Europe following WWII, like the World Bank, the OECD was then known as the 'Organisation for European Economic Cooperation' (OEEC). The name was changed to OECD in the 1960s.

In addition to the 35 collaborating countries, the OECD also has several partners (including Russia, China, and India). All collaborating countries in the OECD are countries with a market economy driven by democratic principles and respect for human rights. The OECD was created to study and coordinate social and economic policy on the one hand, and to sole common problems and align international policy on the other.

Organisation for
Economic Collaboration
and Development

The objectives the OECD has set for itself are:
- stimulating sustainable economic growth;
- improving employment;
- improving living standards;
- safeguarding financial stability;
- supporting economic developments in other countries;
- contributing to the growth of global trade.

The most important body within the OECD is the 'Council'. This council is comprised of ministers from the collaborating countries, and permanent representatives. In addition to the council, there is the 'Executive Committee'. OECD decisions are made based on unanimous agreement. Once a decision has been made, all collaborating countries are bound to uphold it. The OECD is financed by the collaborating countries. In contrast to the World Bank and the IMF, the OECD does not award loans to countries. The OECD has developed a 'Better Life Index': a tool that offers an insight into the personal wellbeing of citizens of the various countries. When measuring wellbeing, various factors are considered, including education, income, milieu, housing, health, crime, balance between work/private life, and happiness. In 2017, the following countries made the top 10:

Better Life Index

TABLE 4.1 **TOP TEN BETTER LIFE INDEX (2017)**

Position	Country
1	Norway
2	Denmark
3	Australia
4	Sweden
5	Canada
6	Switzerland
7	Iceland
8	USA
9	Finland
10	The Netherlands

World Economic Forum (WEF)

The World Economic Forum was founded in 1971. It is not a collaboration between countries, like the UN, but a collaboration between various different parties. The best-known WEF meeting is the annual one in Davos, Switzerland, where the chairpersons of the board of directors are joined by presidents, heads of state, country ministers, journalists, and intellectuals. The annual meeting in Davos addresses important global problems and issues. As those in attendance are highly influential individuals, the WEF has a certain reputation and influence.

Since the WEF is largely comprised of representatives of some of the world's largest enterprises, anti-globalists view it as a sort of business forum.

To change this image, the WEF has gone to even greater lengths than in earlier years to invite a diverse group of attendees to their annual meeting. Scientists, media, young people, and non-profit organisations are also welcome. The atmosphere of the annual meetings in Davos is one of informality. The WEF's results are in various fields, such as corruption, socially responsible enterprising, and healthcare.

BRICS countries and the New Development Bank (NDB) and Contingent Reserve Arrangement (CRA)

The five emerging economies of Brazil, Russia, India, China, and South-Africa founded their own counterpart to the World Bank and the IMF in July 2014. The five emerging countries feel that the World Bank and the IMF place too much importance on defending Western interests (United States and Europe). In 2014, approximately 40% of the world's population lived in one of the five BRICS countries, with the five sharing over a quarter of the world's surface between them. The BRICS countries have elected to introduce two new initiatives:
– the New Development Bank (NDB);
– a Contingent Reserve Arrangement (CRA).

The New Development Bank (NDB)

The goal of the NDB is to offer resources to improve infrastructure and other projects, with specific focus on the BRICS countries. The result should be a more balance global economic order, emphasising the new economic centres of power. The NDB's starting capital was 50 billion dollars. All five countries donated 10 billion dollars. The countries have not yet offered any other guarantees for the coming years.

Contingent Reserve Arrangement (CRA)

The new CRA development bank aims to help countries experiencing financial difficulties, for example in the form of the necessary support in case of issues with the balance of payment. These countries, in turn, are made less dependent on other powers, such as the United States and Europe. The CRA's starting capital was 100 billion dollars, most of which was donated by China. The CRA's capital is also intended to increase over the coming years.

O&M IN PRACTICE

GDP – the costs of terrorism in the EU

Terrorism related costs across the European Union amount to approximately 179.8 billion dollars over the period from 2014 to 2016. Three countries (the United Kingdom, France, and Spain) have suffered for nearly 71% of total terrorism related costs.

Source: *Het Financieele Dagblad*, 13 June 2018

FIGURE **GDP-COSTS OF TERRORISM IN THE EU**

	estimated total costs in € billion, 2004 - 2016	per resident
UK	€ 43.7	€ 699.10
France	€ 43.0	€ 665.60
Spain	€ 40.8	€ 894.90
Germany	€ 19.2	€ 234.90
Greece	€ 10.4	€ 945.20
Belgium	€ 7.8	€ 721.10
Ireland	€ 4.3	€ 974.00
Sweden	€ 2.9	€ 306.70
Italy	€ 2.2	€ 37.40
The Netherlands	**€ 1.7**	**€ 102.50**
Austria	€ 0.9	€ 103.00
Cyprus	€ 0.9	€ 1071.10
Denmark	€ 0.7	€ 122.30
Finland	€ 0.5	€ 89.90

Source: FD, European Parliament

4.4 INTERNATIONAL MANAGEMENT

Many theories have been developed as to why organisations or countries take part in internationalisation. These theories can be subdivided into three group-theories (Hessels e.a., 2005). These groups are:

1 **Trade theories.** Trade theories attempt to explain why international trade between countries occurs. Well-known theories on this subject are the theory of absolute advantage, the theory of comparative advantage, and the new trade theory.

Trade theories

2 **Static theories.** Static theories attempt to answer the question of why organisations engage in international activities. It does not focus on why countries enter into trade, but why organisations produce and invest abroad. Examples of static theories are the theory of the growth of the firm, the product life cycle approach, and the internalisation theory and transaction cost approaches.

Static theories

3 **Process theories.** Process theories attempt to show how organisations take part in internationalisation. Theories in this group are the most recent. Process theories view internationalisation as a process. In other words: organisations

Process theories

that take part in internationalisation proceed through a number of phases. Well-known theories that are part of this group are the 'stage model theory of internationalisation,' the so-called 'Born Globals', the 'international new ventures', and network models.

This book uses process theories as a foundation, and discusses two important theories within that group: the 'stage model theory of internationalisation' and 'Born Globals'.

4.4.1 Stage model theory of internationalisation (Uppsala model)

Stage model theory of internationalisation

Developed in the 1970, this theory is the result of studies by Swedish researchers Jan Johanson and Jan-Erik Vahlne. They found that internationalisation (of Swedish organisations) developed as a process during which organisations proceeded through a number of stages, depending on the organisation's available knowledge level and experience with regards to internationalisation. According to this theory, internationalisation does not take place in leaps and bounds, but by taking baby steps. Learn as you go! Depending on the knowledge and experience available, the organisation selects the appropriate entry strategy. An overview of this succession of entry strategies is as follows (see Figure 4.2):

FIGURE 4.2 **OVERVIEW OF VARIOUS ENTRY STRATEGIES UNDER STAGE MODEL THEORY**

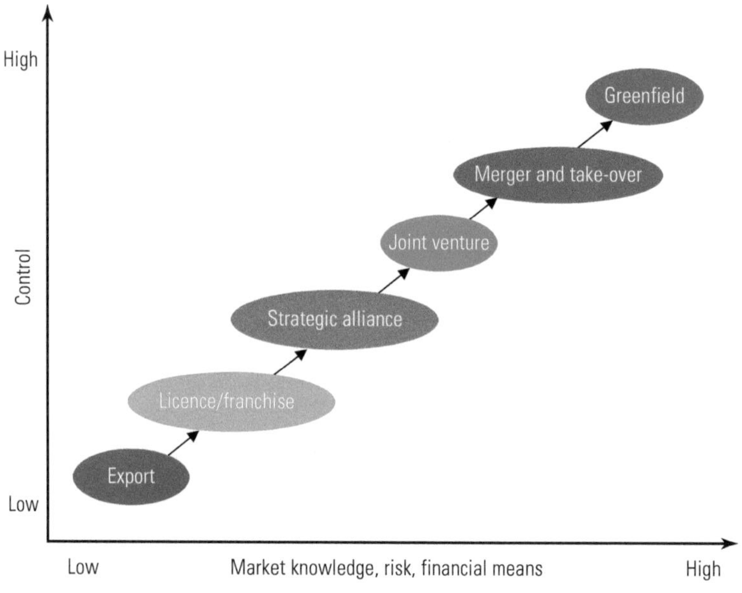

Source: Ebbers, H. (2016), *Internationale bedrijfskunde en globalisering*, Groningen / Utrecht Noordhoff Uitgevers, p. 148

This figure shows that an improvement in market knowledge creates greater control over international activity. This link is also evident from the entry strategy selected.

Export-oriented entry strategy

The organisation will initially opt for an export-oriented entry strategy, with a choice of indirect or direct export. Indirect export means export is handled by the external party – for example through the use of a trade agency, distributor, or trading firm.

Organisations and their environment
PART A

© Noordhoff Uitgevers bv

Direct export is when, for example, the organisation chooses to establish its own export department or foreign branch. The advantage of indirect export is decreased risk, which is offset by a reduced development of market knowledge. The risks of direct export are greater but, in contrast, it generates greater knowledge of internationalisation.

The next step is licensing or franchising. The income from these ventures is mostly in the form of royalties. The risks in this phase are still limited. Through a strategic alliance, a company can eventually arrive at a joint venture – generally a good entryway into local culture. The logical sequel to a joint-venture is the take-over of or merger with a foreign party. A merger or take-over means a directional investment. The organisation's commitment to international activity increases, as do its (market) knowledge and risks. Eventually, the organisation may decide to construct their entire operation abroad, including R&D activities – for example by setting up a plant without taking over another company. This final step is known as 'Greenfield'. The entry strategies mentioned are covered in greater detail in Section 2.5.1 (forms and intensities of collaboration).

Licensing
Franchising

Merger
Take-over

Looking at the different phases of internationalisation, studies have also shown that, in terms of physical and cultural distance, organisations also shift their boundaries outwards. Initially, an organisation may select a neighbouring country, or one that is close to it in physical and cultural terms. At a later stage, it may move to outlying markets, whose cultural characteristics are also different from those of the home country. This development is shown in Figure 4.3:

FIGURE 4.3 **PHYSICAL AND CULTURAL DISTANCE**

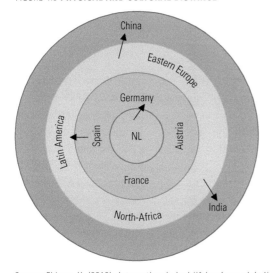

Source: Ebbers, H. (2016), *Internationale bedrijfskunde en globalisering*, Groningen/Utrecht Noordhoff Uitgevers, p. 148

A 2016 study by the Dutch Chamber of Commerce (Kamer van Koophandel – KvK) shows that entrepreneurs are driven by the following factors when considering international business:

FIGURE 4.4 **MOTIVATION OF ENTREPRENEURS FOR INTERNATIONALISATION**

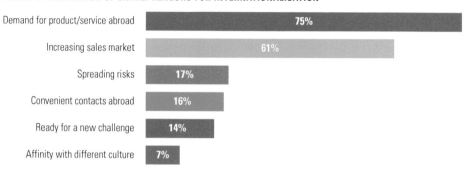

Demand for product/service abroad	75%
Increasing sales market	61%
Spreading risks	17%
Convenient contacts abroad	16%
Ready for a new challenge	14%
Affinity with different culture	7%

The same study by KvK also asked about the entrepreneurs preferred form of internationalisation, with the top ranking forms being:

FIGURE 4.5 **SELECTED FORM OF INTERNATIONALISATION**

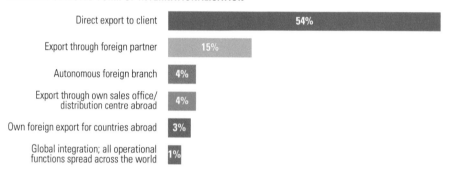

Direct export to client	54%
Export through foreign partner	15%
Autonomous foreign branch	4%
Export through own sales office/ distribution centre abroad	4%
Own foreign export for countries abroad	3%
Global integration; all operational functions spread across the world	1%

4.4.2 Born Globals

The previous paragraph indicated that organisations set on internationalisation go through the process one small step at a time. This is supported by the KvK study (2016). However, there are organisations that have an international orientation from the outset, skipping the development phases. Such companies are called

Born Globals

'Born Globals'. A Born Global can be described as 'a firm which, from its creation, strives for rapid internationality and is able to globalise quickly without requiring a long period of trade on the domestic market or an extended process of internationalisation' (Hollensen, 2010). From the outset, these types of companies already have a clear, international vision; their entrepreneurial activities are aimed at other countries and continents from the start. Chetty, S. and Campbell-Hunt, C. (2004) describe the most important characteristics of Born Global organisations:
– The domestic market has no relevance;
– The experience of the founding party/parties on international markets is extensive;
– International markets are developed simultaneously;
– The utilisation of technology is essential to success. Technology may refer to computer, communications and/or transport technology;
– There is extensive and intensive collaboration with foreign partners, and the company is part of alliances and network structures.

Examples of Dutch Born Globals are Booking.com, TomTom and WeTransfer. Well-known US Born Globals are Google and taxi company Uber; from China, there is internet company Alibaba.com. Born Globals are found in all economic sectors.

4.4.3 Basic forms of international organising

Enterprises involved in internationalisation should consider the organisation and alignment of their activities. These considerations should be viewed in terms of a strategic angle. When defining that strategic angle, two perspectives are of importance:

1 degree of local differentiation of activities (low or high);
2 degree of global integration of activities (low or high).

Combining these dimensions results in four combinations: basic forms of international organising. These four basic forms are shown in Figure 4.6.

FIGURE 4.6 **BASIC METHODS OF ORGANISING AN INTERNATIONAL BUSINESS**

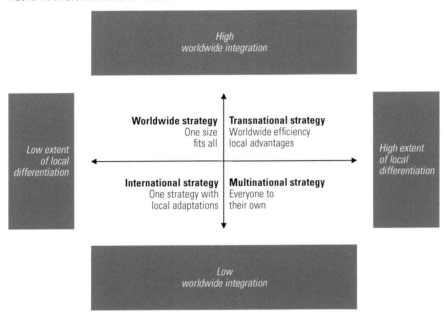

Source: FD

The multinational strategy was the popular choice in Europe for a long time. In this basic form, the international business components are autonomous. This vision holds that each country/region is unique and responsible for its own success, as well as the way in which it arranges for its uniqueness and success to be given shape. The different countries/regions therefore apply their own strategies. The different business components are responsible in terms of operations and results. The function of the head office is mainly concerned with coordination. From a practical perspective, this form of organising comes with its disadvantages:

- relatively few possibilities for economies of scale;
- the emergence of 'fiefdoms' in the various countries/regions.

In practice, European companies are showing a strong tendency towards reconsidering their multinational strategy and changing it into a transnational one. A transnational strategy is a clear choice for the global integration of business components, allowing for global efficiency. It also places greater emphasis on centralisation and control. European companies remain in favour of striving for a high degree of local differentiation.

Multinational strategy

Transnational strategy

In other parts of the world, other choices are being made with regard to the basic form of international organising. Japanese companies frequently choose a worldwide strategy, with a central strategy implemented in all countries/regions. This results in a single strategy that does not allow local differentiation.

Worldwide strategy

International strategy

Lastly, US companies frequently opt for the international, central strategy. In contrast to Japanese companies, local differences are possible.

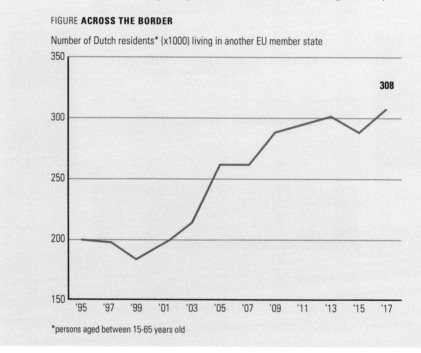

O&M IN PRACTICE

More Dutch citizens living abroad

International mobility among the Dutch is growing. The number of Dutch citizens living abroad is relatively high compared to citizens of other West-European countries. Germans are the most sedentary Europeans, with a share of only 1.0% of the population. The United Kingdom, Belgium, and France also score lower than the Netherlands.

Source: *Het Financieele Dagblad*, 31 May 2018

FIGURE **ACROSS THE BORDER**

Number of Dutch residents* (x1000) living in another EU member state

308

*persons aged between 15-65 years old

4.4.4   Outsourcing

Outsourcing

Outsourcing may be considered a form of cooperation between organisations. As economies of scale increase, more and more organisations reflect on their core tasks. As a result, certain activities are divested of; others are outsourced to other organisations. Activities performed by supporting departments in particular are being outsourced with greater frequency. The resulting problem is that it creates high additional costs as well as making it hard to relate the activities to the primary activities of the organisation that these supporting activities are designed to benefit. An example of the outsourcing of supporting activities is the outsourcing of part of the functions of HR and Financial Admin.

Small to medium enterprises will also begin outsourcing part of their supporting activities over the coming years, particularly in the field of specialised service provision. In general, one may state that there is a (strong) increase with regards to the demand for organisation and automation consultancy, catering services, research staff, and personnel training and development.

Motives for outsourcing

'Concentrate on your core activities and outsource what you can' has been a prevailing strategy for the past decades. But how far to take this principle? If everybody outsources everything, nobody does anything. There is a necessary limit, but when will that be reached?

In the 1980s, it was mainly Michael Porter who, in his books on competitive strength, discussed the notion that it is better to do a few activities very well. Since then, the focus on one's own core activities became a mainstay, and businesses began outsourcing more and more. The results are well-known: an increasingly large share of the sales turnover arrives through acquisition.

Core activities are not constant fixtures, but change over time, sometimes even very strongly. A company that is too slow to adapt to changing circumstances and fails to define new core activities may very well simply cease to exist! The maintenance of buildings, security, catering, and health and safety are obviously not part of the core activities, and have been outsourced by many companies.

The motives for outsourcing are often summarised using the four Cs:

1 **Costs.** If suppliers can provide the activities to be outsourced at lower costs, cost reduction is possible.
2 **Capital.** Outsourcing can free up capital or retain it for investments in core activities.
3 **Capability.** Making use of the knowledge of suppliers is an important means of improving quality.
4 **Capacity.** Being able to call on suppliers means the outsourcing company can respond to market fluctuations more flexibly.

An increase in knowledge and an advancement in technical development means specialisation becomes the most frequent reason for outsourcing. Specialisation, of course, is all to do with which core activities a businesses choose (not) to focus on. Thus, it becomes possible to define the three goals of outsourcing:

1 **flexibility**: …the ability to respond flexibly to market fluctuations…
2 **specialisation**: …using optimised expertise and production techniques to achieve maximum quality…
3 **cost reduction**: …while making sure costs are kept to a minimum.

Forms of outsourcing

Practical forms of outsourcing are varied. The following is a list of four frequently encountered forms of outsourcing:

- **Full outsourcing.** All actions required for a certain activity are performed by an external party. This is the most frequently seen form.
- **Collaborative effort.** The outsourcing company enters into an agreement with a supplier. Together, the manufacture a service of product. The most frequently seen type of collaboration is the joint venture.
- **Assigning activities to specialised departments or separate companies.** Certain business processes are assigned to a separate department or company. An important caveat is that the control of the activities must be retained. The separate department or company may also choose to become a supplier for external parties, at which point it becomes known as a 'shared service centre'.
- **Partial outsourcing.** Some parts of the business processes are outsourced, whereas other are performed internally. Proper alignment is crucial in this scenario.

Outsourcing and offshoring

Offshoring

The concepts of outsourcing and offshoring are often used interchangeably – and unjustly so. Offshoring always refers to the transferring of activities across (national) borders. Outsourcing relates to having others perform activities, either domestically or abroad. 'Captive offshoring' is when activities are currently performed by a company's own staff, but are intended to become or benefit cross-border practices (for example if a Dutch company were to set up a call centre in India for Dutch clients). It is also possible to assign activities to other (foreign) organisations (offshore outsourcing). Figure 4.7 indicates the differences between the varieties of these concepts.

FIGURE 4.7 **OFFSHORING AND OUTSOURCING**

Location / Company	National	Abroad
Internal – direct control	Insourcing	**Captive Offshoring**
External – via a third party	Outsourcing	**Offshore Outsourcing**

Source: *Holland Management Review*

Low wage countries

A frequently heard term in the context of offshore outsourcing is that of the 'low wage country'. The introduction to this chapter indicated that this term applies to countries where production is cheaper than in many Western European or American countries. This is because the wages in low wage countries are significantly lower. Relocating (part of) the production process is an important facet in the development of globalisation. The concept of the low wage country, however, is nothing new. Even in the 1960s, a large share of the Dutch textiles industry was shifted to countries and regions such as Turkey or North Africa. When wages in these countries went up, production was relocated to other, cheaper alternatives.

Goods and services

A large part of the traditional manufacturing industry has been relocated to low wage countries. Examples are the clothing industry, the shoe industry, and the IT industry. Parts of the automobile and aircraft industries are also outsourced to low wage countries. In a number of cases, assembly still takes place in more expensive regions. The reason for this is the high taxation on the import of finished products; by having assembly take place closer to home, these costs can be prevented or minimised.

In addition to products, some services are also outsourced to low wage countries, like Dutch call centres set up in Suriname or South Africa, due to the low language barriers between the countries. The UK and USA have transferred many services to India, since a large part of the Indian population speaks English and is qualified to do the work properly.

Examples of low wage countries are India, China, Thailand, Vietnam, the Philippines, and Mexico. There are also low wage countries in Europe. In this context, relevant countries are Poland, Romania, Bulgaria, Slovakia, and the Czech

Organisations and their environment
PART A

© Noordhoff Uitgevers bv

Dutch IT Outsourcing Study 2018

A Dutch study, part of the annual studies into IT-outsourcing, claims that the most important reasons for Dutch organisations to choose outsourcing are: focussing on core activities, improving quality of service, and reducing costs. Outsourcing companies are generally satisfied with the quality of services offered by their suppliers, which has been true for years. Targets are usually met. An important finding in the study is that companies in the Netherlands are still very interested in outsourcing. 81% of companies participating in the study confirms that they intended to continue to outsource at least the same amount of IT activities. One in ten customers says they will be outsourcing less over the coming two years.

Source: BoardroomIT, Strategic sourcing, commercial edition of ICT Media by *Het Financieele Dagblad*, May 2018

Republic; even though wages in these countries are higher than those in East Asian countries, the transport costs from European countries are lower, and there are no import duties within the European Union.

Social development and outsourcing

The relocating of goods and services to low wage countries is subject to great criticism. This criticism involves two important factors: employment opportunities and labour conditions. By shifting work to low wage countries, many employees in the more prosperous countries lose their jobs, which cannot (all) be compensated for with jobs in other industries. Rising unemployment is the result, as is higher government expenditure.

There is also criticism of the labour conditions and income generation in low wage countries. Several initiatives have been developed in order to address and prevent these international social issues. Examples are the Agreement on Sustainable Garment and Textile and the Fairtrade seal.
The *Agreement on Sustainable Garment and Textile* means that companies that sign the agreement (or covenant) agree to combat discrimination, child labour, and forced labour. In addition, they encourage the right to free negotiations by independent unions, living wages, and safe and healthy working conditions for

employees. The goal is to have around 80% of companies in the Dutch clothing and textiles industry sign the agreement by 2020.

The goal of the *Fairtrade seal* is to help farmers and labourers in developing countries to improve their position on the international commercial chain, helping them to make their work a source of living income while working on a sustainable future. In addition to a seal of approval, Fairtrade is also a global movement. The Max Havelaar foundation in the Netherlands is the owner of the Fairtrade seal. Well over 25,000 products with the Fairtrade logo are sold in 30 countries worldwide, and over 1.5 million farmers are involved in the initiative. (www.maxhavelaar.nl)

Summary

- Two important concepts in internationalisation are import and export.

- Globalisation refers not only to products or services, but rather a process of global economic, political, and cultural integration between countries and continents.

- Globalisation and internationalisation intersect with the themes of trade, transport, international trade policy, international finance and capital flows, international organising of production of goods and services, information and communications technology, politics, and tourism.

- There are five forms of economic integration. In ascending order of intensity of integration, these are: the free trade zone, the customs union, the common market, the economic and monetary union, and the full political and economic union.

- The European Union (EU) comprises 28 (or 27) member states; the European Monetary Union (EMU) comprises 19 countries.

- Within the EU there is free movement of goods, services, people, and capital.

- The five common institutions of the EU are: The European Parliament, the European Commission, The European Council, the Council of the European Union, and the European Court of Justice.

- International organisations encouraging internationalisation are: The United Nations (UN) including the World Bank and the International Monetary Fund (IMF), the World Trade Organisation (WTO), the Organisation for Economic Collaboration and Development (OECD), the World Economic Forum (WEF), and the BRICS countries with the New Development Bank (NDB) and Contingency Reserve Arrangement (CRA).

- Theories on internationalisation fall into one of three theory groups: trade theories, static theories, and process theories.

- The stage model theory says that internationalisation in organisations develops as a process, through baby steps, depending on the available knowledge level and experience with regard to internationalisation within the organisation. Depending on the phase of internationalisation in which an organisation finds itself, it chooses an entry strategy.

- Entry strategies are export, licensing franchising, strategic alliance, joint venture, merger or take-over, and greenfield.

- 'Born Globals' are organisations that strive for rapid internationalisation and globalisation from the moment of their founding, without requiring a long period of trade on the domestic market or a long process of internationalisation.

- Four basic forms of internationalisation strategy are: multinational, transnational, global, and international.

- Outsourcing is when organisations have other organisations perform certain of their activities.

- Motives for outsourcing are the four Cs: Costs, Capital, Capability, and Capacity.

- Goals of outsourcing are improving flexibility, specialisation, and cost reduction.

- Four forms of outsourcing are full outsourcing, collaborative effort, assigning activities to a specialised department or company, and partial outsourcing.

- Offshoring always relates to relocating activities across (national) borders. Outsourcing relates to having others perform activities, either domestically or abroad.

- A low wage country is a country whose wages are significantly lower.

5

CORPORATE SOCIAL RESPONSIBILITY, CORPORATE GOVERNANCE, AND ETHICS

Contents

After studying this chapter:

- you will have familiarised yourself with the most important concepts in the fields of corporate social responsibility, social enterprise, and sustainable development;
- you will have gained insight into the most important concepts and approaches related to corporate social responsibility;
- you will have familiarised yourself with important Dutch and international CSR organisations;
- you will have familiarised yourself with important concepts related to Corporate Governance and Corporate Governance code;
- you will have familiarised yourself with key concepts, sources, approaches, and corporate code regarding business ethics.

Social entrepreneur Swink

Swink is an online marketing agency and one of the first Social Enterprises in the Netherlands. The company's unique feature is that it uses the extraordinary talents of people with autism to provide exceptional online services to clients (in particular large companies, governments, and institutions). The benefits are twofold; the company provides high quality service and creates permanent jobs for people with autism (Social Return).

Niels van Buren is the commercial director for Swink.
Niels: 'Swink focusses on online marketing. Swink employs people with autism exclusively. Their strong analytical skills, higher than average intelligence, and attention to detail are talents that, when properly applied, allow them to become full-fledged members of the labour process.'
'We give our employees clear assignments, offer continuous coaching, make sure working pressure is kept low, and ensure there is a relaxed atmosphere at work. We talk to our people all the time.'

Coping with stress or noise pollution are not among the strong suits of the autistic, who benefit from a low-stimulus office. There are sound-proof rooms for phone calls, and noise-cancelling headphones available for all.

Partnering with Swink has a direct social impact: the more assignments, the more autistic people can get to work. This way, the company contributes to paid jobs for people who are restricted in terms of job market possibilities, and contribute to society (social return).

The Dutch government also feels social return is important, leading to the introduction of the Participation Act, whose goal is to ensure that, by 2026, 125,000 jobs are incrementally created for people with an occupational disability. Various governmental organisations, such as the Amsterdam municipality or the Central Government, have made social return a condition in a number of their procurements.

Source: amsterdam.jekuntmeer.nl, swinkwebservices.nl

5.1 INTRODUCTION TO CORPORATE SOCIAL RESPONSIBILITY

Corporate social responsibility (CSR) has attracted growing attention in recent years. Sustainable entrepreneurship, sustainable development, and social enterprise are other terms referring to the same concept.
What is the role and responsibility of business in society? Societies have grown to increasingly expect organisations to be transparent about their responsibility regarding their business operations, and the effects of those operations not only in terms of financial data, but also in terms of environmental and social consequences.

5.1.1 Two perspectives on Social Responsibility

With regards to CSR, there are two distinct perspectives (Source: Robbins, S and Coulter, M (2015), **Management**, Benelux: Pearson): the classic perspective and the social-economic perspective.

The **classic perspectives** on CSR is that the onle responsibility of management is to create profit. The most important stakeholders, after all, are the shareholders, who are only interested in maximising profits. CSR does exist in this perspective, but should always lead to profit maximisation for the shareholders. An important advocate of this perspective is Nobel prize winner (1976) Milton Friedman. Friedman is seen as one of the 20th century's most important and influential economists. The classic perspective is comparable to the Anglo-Saxon way of thinking, and originated in the US and England.

Classic perspective

The **social-economic perspective** places much greater emphasis on the social and responsible aspects of CSR. Organisations have a responsibility to do more than just turn a profit, but to make a positive contribution to society as a whole. This perspective is comparable to the Rhineland way of thinking. Many organisations in countries like Switzerland, France, Germany, the Netherlands, Belgium, Luxembourg, as well as in several Scandinavian countries, have concretised this perspective as part of their business operations for some time now.

Social-economic perspective

Today, more and more organisations across the world have recognised the social-economic perspective, and are organising and performing their activities in alignment with this perspective. Organisations who recognise and implement the social-economic perspective do so in phases (Robbins & Coulter, 2015). Table 5.1 illustrates these phases schematically:

TABLE 5.1: **DEVELOPMENT PHASES OF CORPORATE SOCIAL RESPONSIBILITY**

Less	Corporate Social Responsibility		More
← · →			
Phase 1	Phase 2	Phase 3	Phase 4
Owners and management	Employees of the company	Stakeholdera	Society as a whole

Source: Robbins, S en Coulter, M (2015), *Management*, Benelux: Pearson.

5.1.2　Social enterprise

An increasingly visible trend in the past years has been the emergence and growth of social enterprise. This trend is seen in many countries the world over. The 2016 'Social Enterprise Monitor' shows that, between 1 January 2014 and 1 January 2016, employment growth in social enterprises grew by 24%. Another figure is the percentage of European employment accounted for by social enterprises: 6%.

Social enterprise

A social enterprise can be identified by the following characteristics, namely that it:
1 has a primarily socially responsible vision;
2 realises its vision as an autonomous enterprise providing a product or service;
3 is financially self-reliant based on trade or other forms of value exchange, and is therefore barely if at all limited by gifts or subsidies;
4 is social in the way it is managed. In this context, social refers to the fact that the financial targets are aimed at increasing social impact, that there is a balance of authority in the organisation, and that the organisation is aware of the ecological footprint of its activities. (www.social-enterprise.nl, consulted 9 July 2018)

From these characteristics, it becomes clear that a social enterprise occupies the spectrum between a commercial and a charity organisation. This is shown schematically in Figure 5.1.

FIGURE 5.1 **POSITION OF SOCIAL ENTERPRISES**

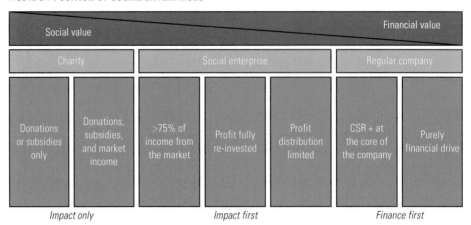

Source: www.social-enterprise.nl

The goal of a social enterprise is to resolve a social issue and, in doing so, create additional social value. Thus, a social enterprise creates a conscious change in society. In order to achieve this change, a social enterprise needs a model for the change known as the 'Theory of Change'. This model is one in which the enterprise describes how it intends to achieve a particular change. By implementing resources and their output in a certain manner, the model describes the eventual positive effects on consumers and society. In point of fact, by demonstrating the positive impact on consumers and society, the social enterprise creates its own raison d'etre.

The 'Theory of Change' is shown schematically in Figure 5.2:

Theory of Change

FIGURE 5.2 **THEORY OF CHANGE**

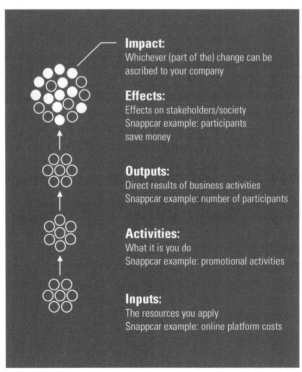

Source: www.social-enterprise.nl

Share and share alike

The average car spends 23 hours per day standing still. Nevertheless, new cars roll off the assembly line every day. What a waste! Why don't we make better use of the cars we already have? This is the idea behind SnappCar, a peer-to-peer car-sharing platform. Private individuals can rent their car out to others using SnappCar easy and insured. There are currently over 75,000 people using the convenient app. SnappCar improves people's social and financial-economic position. After all: sharing a car connects people, and earning a little extra helps them reinforce their financial position. This way, SnappCar wants to have a positive effect on more than just the environment – it wants to have an influence on people. SnappCar wants to be a catalyst for a sharing economy, with less emphasis placed on personal property.

Source: www.social-enterprise.nl, consulted 9 July 2018

5.1.3   Sustainable development

Another important step in this respect was made with the publication of the Brundtland-report in 1987. Written by the World Commission on Environment and Development (WCED), it was given the name of the Norwegian prime minister at the time, Gro Harlem Brundtland. The report, officially entitled *Our common future*, concludes that important global environmental problems were caused not just by poverty in one part of the world, but also by unsustainable consumption and production in other parts of the world. The only way of combating these global environmental issues is to agree to and achieve (global) sustainable development. This sustainable development was defined as 'a development that meets the needs of the present generation without compromising on the opportunities for future generations to meet theirs'.

Sustainable development

The concept of sustainability is related to the scarcity of non-renewable natural resources. Current prosperity as well as future prosperity are based largely on these scarce resources.

Originally used in the forestry and fishery sectors, the concept of sustainability in these sectors means that nature should be managed in such a way as to prevent naturally occurring structures and processes from being affected. Through a sustainable utilisation of these two natural resources, future generations would also be able to benefit from them. In other words: sustainable development is when ecological, economic, and social interest are in balance.

Sustainability

How sustainably do companies operate?

The Dow Jones Sustainability World Index shows an insight into the sustainability practices of the world's largest companies. It is an important measurement in the field of social and environmental/sustainability issues, and an important guiding principle for many investors interested in sustainability.

The Index was introduced in 1999 and shows the sustainability scores of the world's largest listed companies. The 16 Dutch companies on the Dow Jones Sustainability World Index are ABN-AMRO, ING, Koninklijke Philips, Philips Lighting, Randstad, SBM Offshore, Koninklijke Ahold Delhaize, Unilever, Aegon, NN Groep, Akzo Nobel, Koninklijke DSM, ASML, Koninklijke KPN, Air-France-KLM and PostNL.

Source: https://executivefinance.nl/2017/09/16-nederlandse-bedrijven-dow-jones-sustainability-index

In addition to the 1987 Brundtland-report, there have been various other milestones on the path to sustainable development.

Consider the Convention on Biodiversity held in Rio de Janeiro in 1992. Biodiversity is the term for the variety of life forms in a certain ecosystem (for example: a forest) or on the entire planet. Biodiversity is an indicator used to represent the health of an ecosystem. The higher the level of biodiversity, the healthier the ecosystem. Countries with the highest level of biodiversity are all found in South America. The treaty that followed the convention was signed by members of the United Nations (UN) who agreed to develop new policies with regard to environment and development. The UN declared 2010 the International Year of Biodiversity.

Biodiversity

Three important developments covered in detail in the following paragraph are:
1 Sustainable Development Goals for the United Nations (2015 – 2030);
2 The Paris Climate Accord (2015);
3 Sustainable development in the field of consumption.

Sustainable Development Goals for the United Nations (2015 2030)

Sustainable Development Goals for the United Nations

The 193 UN member states formulated new global objectives for the 2015-2030 period. These Sustainable Development Goals (SDGs) are intended to end (extreme) poverty, inequality, and climate change the world over by 2030.

FIGURE 5.3 **THE 17 SUSTAINABLE DEVELOPMENT GOALS UN 2015-2030**

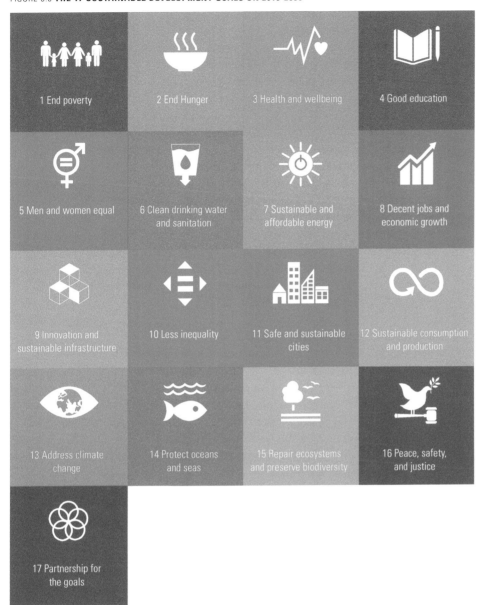

The SDGs are the follow-up to the previously formulated millennium norms (2000). In order to achieve the global objectives, the UN has set an agenda with the following 17 goals (see Figure 5.3):

1 Eradicating all forms of (extreme) poverty
2 An end to hunger, ensuring food security and sustainable agriculture
3 Healthcare for all
4 Inclusive, equal, quality education for all
5 Equal rights for men and women and empowerment of women and girls
6 Clean water and sanitaire facilities for all
7 Access to affordable and sustainable energy for all
8 Inclusive economic growth, employment opportunities, and decent work for all
9 Infrastructure for sustainable industrialisation
10 Reducing inequality in and between countries

11 Making cities safe, resilient, and sustainable
12 Sustainable consumption and production
13 Addressing climate change
14 Protection and sustainable use of oceans and seas
15 Protection of ecosystems, forests, and biodiversity
16 Encouraging safety, public services, and rights for all
17 Reinforcing the global partnership to achieve goals

Achieving these ambitious goals requires close cooperation between the member states across the globe, as well as, for example, between the United Nations and the European Union. Agreements have also been made on how progress should be monitored and measured. Based on their progress, member countries can submit their reports to the UN and be held accountable. In the Netherlands, there are various collaborations between different ministries and other socially active agencies, like socially conscious organisations and companies. All countries report their results to the United Nations. The goals can only be achieved through the financing of various activities and projects. This financing comes from various sources – consider member ship tax payments, trade and investments, developmental aid, and contributions by companies.

Paris Climate Accord (2015)

2015 United Climate Change Conference

Between 30 November and 12 December 2015, the United Nations hosted a conference on global climate in Paris. Officially known as the *2015 United Climate Change Conference*, this conference resulted in the signing of the Paris Accord on 22 April 2016 by all countries except the United States. The precursor to the Paris Accord was the 1997 Kyoto-protocol. The first climate treaty, officially the *United Nations Framework Convention on Climate Change*, was ratified in 1992, and also fell under the responsibility of the United Nations. It was signed by many countries at the 'Earth Summit' in Rio de Janeiro.
The climate accord requires the governments of many countries to take joint steps to ensure the changes in the earth's climate do not get further out of hand. The participating countries recognise their responsibility for the earth's climate, and that the negative effects of human activity should be prevented as much as possible. The aim of the accord is as follows: 'to stabilise the concentration of greenhouse gasses in the atmosphere at such a level as to prevent a dangerous human influence on climate'.

Countries participating in the accord fall in one of two groups: the industrialised countries, largely the same as those that are part of OECD (the Organisation for Economic Collaboration and Development), and the developing countries. This split between the groups is very important, because not all countries have the same obligations towards the Climate Accord.
The industrialised countries have obligated themselves to reducing the emission of greenhouse gasses. The obligations for the developing countries are less severe. They are not obligated, for example, to reduce their emissions. In addition, some industrialised countries have obligated themselves to financially supporting the developing countries in their activities.

Global air quality

According to the World Health Organisation (WHO), 32 percent of the victims of air pollution die as a result of heart conditions, and 1 in 5 victims of pneumonia.

Source: *de Volkskrant*, Thursday 3 May 2018

FIGURE **FATALITIES FROM AIR POLLUTION**

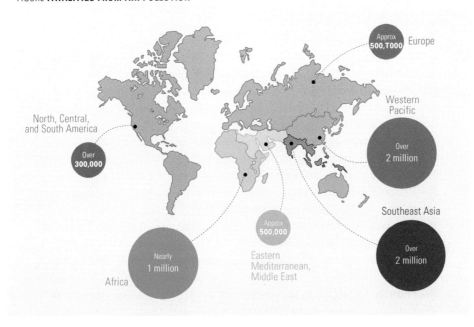

The key issues of the Paris Climate Accord are:

1 The average global temperature must not increase by more than two degrees Celsius (compared to temperatures during the pre-industrial age, roughly between 1500 and 1870 AD). Countries make every effort to strive to limit the temperature increase to a maximum of 1.5 degrees Celsius. Scientists agree that an average increase of over 2 degrees would severely disrupt the Earth's climate systems.

2 Participating parties will make every effort to reduce the emission of greenhouse gases and other harmful agents in combination with whatever technology is available. This takes into account the differences between countries.

3 Addressing the negative consequences of climate change and reducing the emission of greenhouse gases, while simultaneously preventing negative consequences for food production, requires additional effort.

4 All parties must make financial contributions to lowering the amount of greenhouse gases and researching climate-proofing developments.

5 The parties of the Paris Accord have set themselves the goal of setting aside at least 100 billion dollars (91 billion Euros) per year until the next climate conference in 2025, for use by poorer countries experiencing economic difficulties in achieving the goals set in the climate accord. The money should become available from 2020.

6 The Accord is binding and the countries have obligated themselves to uphold it.

The countries also agreed to a global evaluation every five years from 2023. This evaluation ("Global Stocktake") will review the reduction in emissions. The 'Conference of Parties' is the most important decision-making body within the Accord, as this is where the countries in the Accord discuss the results achieved by all participating countries each year. The participating countries also report to this body.

Sustainable development with respect to consumption

Sustainable development with respect to consumption

Sustainable development with respect to consumption currently involves various aspects or topics, including:

a **Agricultural innovation**: by the year 2050, the Earth's population will number in the 9 billion. The demand for agricultural meat and produce will likely have doubled. New forms of cultivation are required. Examples are aquaponics (a combination of aquaculture and hydroculture) and eco-villages. Eco-villages are small communities of between 50 to 150 people whose goals is to be socially, economically, and ecologically sustainable.

b **Alternative nourishment**: the future should be an age of new, sustainable, and nutritious food sources. Consider lab-grown, synthetically produced meat. People must come to the realisation that alternative nutrition is a necessity and that human food consumption patterns need to be adjusted. The popularity of veganism is likely to grow.

c **Ecovenience**: a combination of eco-friendly products that are also convenient. This trend is expected to grow. An important related development is minimising the utilisation of packaging materials. For example, consider putting cleaning agents like soap on tap.

d **Reconomie**: for 'recycling economy'. With increasing frequency, consumer products are put to a new or different use instead of being thrown out or destroyed. The re-use of products is a helpful way of (partly) reducing human produced waste (www.bedrock.nl).

5.1.4   Corporate Social Responsibility (CSR)

The Dutch Sociaal Economische Raad (Social Economic Council, SER) describes Corporate Social Responsibility as follows (SER, De winst van waarden, 2000):

Create value

'The conscious direction of business activities to create value in three dimensions of profit, people and planet, thus contributing to long-term social welfare'.

A company's right to existing, in this context, is not only seen in terms of whether it is profitable. In fact, the most important aspect of companies is that they achieve a balance between turnover (profit), the environment (planet), and staff and other human parties affected by their activities (people). Companies are to be held

Profit

accountable for all three of these aspects. Profit refers to a socially responsible attitude towards business activities which, naturally, should be profitable –

Planet

otherwise the company would not be viable. Planet refers to a socially responsible attitude towards the environment and/or the environmental effects of a company's

People

business activities. People refers to a socially responsible attitude towards human beings, both inside and outside of the organisation – 'outside' here intended to refer to society as a whole.

An example of the possible implementation of CSR policy is the 'cradle-to-cradle' principle developed Michael Braungart and William McDonough. In their book *Cradle to Cradle: Remaking the Way We Make Things* (2002), they describe a system whose aim is to provide the current generation with its own needs, as well as providing future generations with additional possibilities. At the core of the cradle-to-cradle principle is the concept that materials used in the lifecycle of one product must usefully be applied to (create) another product. This principle does not refer to the usual recycling of materials which leaves behind residual materials. Cradle-to-cradle means that no loss of quality and no residual products occur following re-use. Cradle-to-cradle refers to the entire chain of creating to utilising to discarding.

Cradle-to-cradle

In their book, the authors use the cherry tree as a metaphor for their cradle-to-cradle principle. A cherry tree represents the ideal cycle of re-use. The tree supplies its own maintenance, nutrition, and offspring. The cherry tree as a metaphor means that it is also a natural source of nutrition for insects and birds, that it replenishes the earth, and that it purifies the air.

Important concepts that are part of the 'cradle-to-cradle' principle are Downcycling and Upcycling. Many of the current forms of recycling are examples of Downcycling: the recycled product loses part of its original value. Under the principle of cradle-to-cradle, the idea is in fact to ensure that the recycled product retains or improves on the value of the original product. This is known as Upcycling. The original English language edition of *Cradle to Cradle: Remaking the Way We Make Things*, for example, is printed on recyclable plastic instead of paper. Using a simple process, this plastic can be reused as a fine, clear white paper. The ink used to print the book can easily be separated from the plastic, after which it, too, can be reused.

Downcycling

Upcycling

Apple leading other companies in sustainability?

O&M IN PRACTICE

Apple claims to have finally done it: all of its buildings are run using renewable energy. The tech giant is now attempting to sway suppliers. In 2014, the last of Apple's energy-draining data centres went fully green. Now, the same applies to all of Apple's offices, stores, and shared facilities. Most buildings use power from giant windmill parks or solar powerplants which either Apple has had constructed, or with which it is under long-term contract.

Nine of Apple's suppliers have made the move to clean energy. Over 10% of Apple's production partners now use renewable energy and if Apple has anything to say about it, we can expect this number to reach 100%.

Source: *de Volkskrant*, Friday 13 April 2018

5.1.5 Basics and perspectives of CSR

Stephen P. Robbins and Mary Coulter's 'Management' lists four basic premises for CSR:

1 CSR is an integral vision of entrepreneurship, with the company creating value in an economic (profit), an ecological (planet), and a social (people) sense.
2 CSR is ingrained in all business processes. Each business decision requires an assessment weighing the different stakeholder interests.
3 CSR is a customised process. CSR activities are different for all companies, depending on company size, sector, culture, and business strategy.
4 CSR is a process, not a destination. The goals it strives for change over time and as a result of implemented decisions. Companies make plans and take steps to (further) shape their social responsibility.

Looking at the practice in organisations, CSR is usually translated into one of its following dimensions:

1 What are the **norms and values** a company represents? These norms and values are often documented in a code of conduct and so-called 'rules of compliance'.
2 **The company's social responsibility**: this deals with the way an enterprise organises and implements its activities while, at the same time, assuming its responsibility with respect to the environment and social issues. Organisations provide an insight into this information through a 'Sustainability Report'.
3 **The company's social commitment**: this refers to what and how a company gives back to society; a concept which, of course, is subject to a variety of interpretations. Some examples are: contributing to a charity, for example through enlisting staff (offering developmental aid on a voluntary basis); sponsoring (of sports activities, for example); contributing to a certain aspect of social improvement (for example Unilever's food department)

In order to offer stakeholders an insight into an organisation's involvement in sustainability, and an assessment of the organisation's score in that regard, is by using a CSR scorecard. A CSR scorecard documents all the dimensions of an organisation's policy and practices in a single file. Each dimension is comprised on ambitions, objectives, and performance indicator. An example of a CSR scorecard is shown in Figure 5.4:

FIGURE 5.4 **EXAMPLE OF A CSR-SCORECARD**

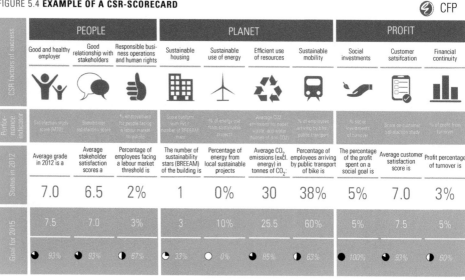

MVO dashboard © CFP 2013

Source: http://www.cfp.nl/mvo-scorecard-als-instrument-voor-integrale-prestatiemeting

Organisations and their environment
PART A

Companies are also increasingly seeing the opportunities offered by sustainability. Whereas CSR was initially viewed as a form of accountability or something requiring intrinsic motivation, it is now increasingly appreciated as a competitive tool and an image-improving instrument. CSR, it turns out, contributes to satisfied customers, motivated staff, and committed stakeholders. In addition, sustainability performance is seen as an increasingly important factor for investors and credit providers. Moreover, companies are becoming aware that their sustainability is a prerequisite for their future existence. From this perspective, CSR is a source of innovation: consider the emergence of circular business models, cleantech (technological improvements that contribute to a cleaner environment and/or save energy), tapping new markets by developing products for the Bottom of the Pyramid (an economic model that focusses on the bottom of the global income pyramid) and new, clever ways of collaborating (social innovation). There is now a growing conviction that CSR pays off.

Transparency is an important condition for CSR. It ensures that stakeholders can join a company in thinking about solutions and improvements, that customers know where a company stands, and that a company can be held accountable for its business operations after the fact. The government also asks that companies

A how-to of sustainable investment

Pension funds set three types of goals
The following example lists three pension funds and their targets in three different areas.

CO₂-reduction	Sustainable solutions*	Portfolio breakdown
FIGURE CO₂-reduction	FIGURE SUSTAINABLE SOLUTIONS	FIGURE PORTFOLIO LAYOUT

ABP	**ABP**	**ABP**
CO₂-footprint of share portfolio to be reduced by 25% before 2020	Aims to have invested € 58 billion in sustainable solutions by 2020. Per the end of 2017, the invested amount was at €49.8 billion.	Wants to have classified 10,000 companies into 'leaders' or 'stragglers' by 2020. 593 companies have been tested thus far.
PFZW	**PFZW**	**PFZW**
Co₂-footprint of all investments to be halved by 2020 compared to 2014. Per the end of 2017, reduction was at 27%.	By 2020, € 20 billion is to have been invested in sustainable solutions. Per the end of 2017, this invested amount was at 12.8 billion.	Engaged in dialogues with 361 companies out of 2,500 listed companies in which the fund has invested.
BPL	**BPL**	**BPL**
Co₂-footprint of share portfolio to have been halved by 2020. Target already met.	Invests in green bonds and real estate with green energy labels. Restricts construction to energy-neutral homes.	Entire share portfolio restructured, meaning that 30% of companies with the lowest level of EG criteria compliance have been excluded.

*Such as windmills, improved water quality, improved education, famine relief
Source: *Het Financieele Dagblad*, 14 May 2018

are transparent about their CSR policy and activities. Using the so-called
Transparantiebenchmark (Transparency Benchmark), the Dutch Ministry of
Economic Affairs and Climate offers interested parties an insight into the way in
which Dutch companies report on their CSR activities. The best report is awarded
the Kristalprijs (Crystal Award, for being 'crystal clear'). Transparency can be
created through various means, for example by publishing facts and figures on a
website, in a brochure, or in an annual report. Transparency also deals with clear
and honest product information on packaging, tracking details that show where a
product is located, and quality client and guarantee arrangements.

Transparency Benchmark

The theme of the 2018 Kristalprijs involved supply chain transparency. Supply chain
transparency plays an important role in CSR; not only at the national but also at the
international level. For example, supply chain transparency is documented in the
OECD guidelines for multinationals and in the Guiding Principles for Business and
Human Rights established by the United Nations.

Supply chain transparency

Every company is part of a particular (combination of) supply chain (or chains). As
a result, CSR not only relates to the activities in a company itself, but also to the
activities of the suppliers and clients with which a company is in business. The
central issue for the 2018 Kristalprijs was the extent to which companies reported
not only on themselves but on the supply chain(s) in which they operated, as well
as the resulting risks for the company itself and for people and the environment in
general.

Seals or certificates are a way of showing whether a product is sustainable. If a
company is dishonest about its sustainability performance, then this is sometimes
known as greenwashing – a practice that leads to scepticism of and loss of faith in
a company.

All of this illustrates that transparency in accountability on business operations is
not merely an internal matter – it is also an external one. A company is seen as a
collection of stakeholders; not just direct stakeholders, but also indirect ones. The
direct stakeholders are shareholders, clients, employees, banks, and suppliers.
Indirect stakeholders are local residents and environmental organisations, to name
just a few.

Dividing the stakeholders according to the three dimensions (3Ps) offers the
following distribution:
1 **profit**:   shareholders – tax payers – society – banks;
2 **people**: employees – consumers – neighbours – local communities – human
rights (organisations) – local residents;
3 **planet**: nature and environmental organisations – governments – United
Nations.

5.1.6   Stances on Corporate Social Responsibility
This paragraph focusses on two possible approaches to Corporate Social
Responsibility:
1 stances on social responsibility;
2 natural resource-based view.

Stances on social responsibility
In practice, companies handle CSO in different ways (Hupkes, 2010). This has
to do with the fact that different companies can have different visions of what
constitutes 'social responsibility'. Socially responsible for what? Theoretically, there
are four possible stances on social responsibility:

Social responsibility

1 **Minimal social responsibility**: this is the stance that says a company is only beholden to execute its task adequately and efficiently within applicable legal parameters. The organisation carries no other additional social responsibility.

Minimal social responsibility

2 **Social acceptability**: this stance also pays attention to the development of support and consensus for the decisions made or to be made by the company, in addition to the legal framework. Alternatively, this could be called 'good citizenship'.

Social acceptability

3 **Broad social responsibility**: this stance considers all of the effects on a company's actions in terms of social responsibility. The organisation feels that it has a broad social responsibility, even in those fields to which no particular legislation applies. This notion attempts to involve all relevant parties (stakeholders).

Broad social responsibility

4 **Social activism**: a company operating under this stance experiences such lengths of social responsibility that it feels compelled to encourage social progress. The company feels obligated to right wrongs, even if this results in complications for business operations.

Social activism

Natural resource-based view

An international expert in the field of sustainable development and development strategy, Stuart Hart is also the founder of the American 'Center for Sustainable Global Enterprise'. He developed the 'natural resource-based view of the firm', a theory based on a movement in strategic management which emerged around the 1980s the 'Resource-based view (RBV)'. This movement considers an enterprise to be a collection of tangible and intangible means or assets and business processes or capacities. Examples are:

Natural resource-based view

a tangible means or assets: machines, land, buildings, raw materials, and employees;

b intangible means or assets: image, patents, brands, and influence;

c business processes: acquisitions and sales, production, and product development.

The movement dictates that organisational strategies should be based on an organisation's available means or resources. Only through the implementation and combination of resources can an organisation develop a sustainable competitive advantage.

Using RBV as a bases, Stuart Hart added the CSR element to create the 'natural resource-based view'. Hart's perspective is that an organisation's CSR policy should, on the one hand, minimise the impact of its activities on its environment while, on the other hand, helping to create value in environmental, social, and economic respect. It is through the creation of value in one or a combination of these fields that an organisation may develop a sustainable social competitive advantage. An important facet is the environmental pressure on the organisation. According to Stuart Hart, an organisation can develop and employ one of three tactics with regard to lowering environmental pressure. These three tactics are (Bossink & Masurel, 2017):

1 **pollution prevention**: reducing/minimising emissions and waste;

2 **product management**: lowering environmental pressure resulting from products or services offered;

3 **sustainable development**: all organisational activities aimed at contributing to cleaner production and a better society.

In order to realise these tactics, organisations tend to use one of the following basic strategies for CSR value creation. In practice, an organisation may choose to combine two or more of the six basic strategies. The following table, 5.2, demonstrates the core principles of each strategy.

TABLE 5.2 **SIX BASIC STRATEGIES FOR CSR VALUE CREATION**

Characteristics	CSR basic strategy					
	Design strategy	Planning strategy	System strategy	Goal strategy	Positioning strategy	Interaction strategy
Core strategy	Inventing new, sustainable processes, products, and services	Systematically introducing sustainable processes, products, and services	Managing a coherent whole of sustainable processes, products, and services	The focussed strive for sustainability goals	The conscious profiling of the sustainability characteristics of the organisation's market position	Collaborating and cooperating with various stakeholders of the organisation to work on sustainable processes, products, and services

Source: Bossink, B & Masural E (2017), *Maatschappelijk Verantwoord Ondernemen*, Groningen/Utrecht, Noordhoff Uitgevers

5.1.7 Dutch CSR organisations

MVO-Platform

The Netherlands knows an active network in the field of CSR: the MVO (short for Maatschappelijk Verantwoord Ondernemen, the Dutch term for CSR) Platform. The MVO-Platform is a network of Dutch social organisations and unions who have joined forces make a communal effort in this field. The following organisations are some of those involved in the Platform: Amnesty International, CNV International (union), FNV (union), Consumentenbond (consumer watchdog organisation), Cordaid, Greenpeace Nederland, Max Havelaar (Fairtrade organisation), Milieudefensie (environmental protection organisation), Oxfam Novib and Stichting Onderzoek Multinationale Ondernemingen (knowledge centre on multinationals). The MVO-Platform uses the following definition of CSR: 'CSR is a results-oriented process in which a company takes responsibility for the entirety of its business processes and its relative position along the supply chain in terms of the effects it achieves in social, ecological, and economic respect, for which it considers itself to have a responsibility of transparent accountability to all stakeholders.' The emphasis in this context is on socially responsible entrepreneurship by companies operating in developing countries.

MVO-Platform The MVO-Platform has formulated two goals:
1 Platform participants aim to reinforce their influence on companies, both individually and communally;
2 The Dutch government fulfils a strong role in both a national and an international context by, on the one hand, encouraging corporate social responsibility in an ambitious manner and, on the other hand, enabling regulation that can be used to hold companies accountable.

The MVO-Platform's three main topics are transparency, supply chain responsibility, and accountability. The MVO-Platform is a co-founding member of *the European Coalition for Corporate Justice* (ECCJ). The ECCJ network has more than 250 organisations in fifteen European countries.

Heavy industry presents ambitious climate plan

By 2050, eleven energy-intensive industrial concerns in the Dutch regions of Zeeland and West–Brabant and the Belgian regions of Flanders are joining forces to reduce their combined CO 2-emissions by 85% to 95% compared to emission levels in 1990. To that end, the concerns have drafted a plan requiring 700 million Euros in investments in plants and pipe networks.

Source: *Het Financieele Dagblad*, 18 April 2018

FIGURE **OVERVIEW OF INDUSTRIAL CONCERNS IN THE PROVINCES OF ZEELAND AND WEST-BRABANT AND THE COMMUNITY OF FLANDERS PARTICIPATING IN THE CLIMATE SCHEME**

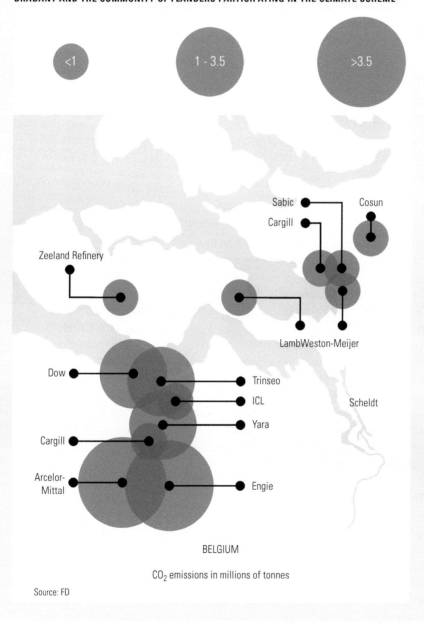

CO_2 emissions in millions of tonnes

Source: FD

MVO-Nederland

MVO-Nederland

MVO-Nederland is an organisation aimed at encouraging business CSR. Founded by the Dutch Ministry of Economic Affairs in 2004, members of the organisation include beginning, advanced, and leading players in both SMEs and major corporations. MVO-Nederland shows them the market opportunities offered by CSR, facilitates mutual collaboration, and provides practical information for concretised CSR operations. At the European level, CSR Europe provides similar services, and other countries have similar organisations. The mission of MVO-Nederland is: 'to inspire, connect, and expedite as many companies and organisations as possible on their road to climate-neutral, circular, and inclusive business models and strong and stable business results. MVO-Nederland's four key issues:

1 Climate neutral enterprise;
2 Circular economy: waste-free enterprise;
3 Inclusive enterprise: enterprise which recognises and utilises all talents, with or without any associated limitations;
4 Inclusive and sustainable enterprise on the supply chain (International Corporate Social Responsibility or ICSR): enterprise with additional value for people and planet developing along the supply chain, with human rights and good labour circumstances being the standard.

Over 2,200 sustainable companies are a member of MVO-Nederland. These companies vary in size and operational sector.

5.1.8   International CSR

CSR is a trending topic not just in the Netherlands, but across the globe. As more and more organisations are operating on a global scale, it may, in fact, be better to start referring to CRS as ICSR – International Corporate Social Responsibility.

Organisation for Economic Collaboration and Development (OECD)

OECD

The OECD, for example, has compiled a code of conduct which offers recommendations regarding the practical interpretation of CSR. This behavioural code includes recommendations in the fields of child labour, employment relationships, environmental damage, and corruption. The OECD is mainly a collaborative effort of 'prosperous' nations, including European countries, the United States, Japan, South Korea, and Australia. Participating countries are obligated to found a National Point of Contact (NPC).

NPCs have two tasks: on the one hand, they ensure that companies are familiar with the guidelines; on the other, they deal with complaints regarding perceived violations of the code of conduct.

Global Compact

Global Compact

Another international collaboration in CSR is the Global Compact. Global Compact is a collaboration between companies, stakeholders, and the United Nations. Their objective is to make the world more sustainable and more social. Global Compact's code of conduct comprises ten principles covering the environment, human rights, and employment conditions. Internationally active companies should uphold these principles. Companies can endorse the principles and, in doing so, join the others in the Global Compact. There are around 9,000 companies from 162 countries participating worldwide, including 130 from the Netherlands. Each of the 10 principles is categorised into one of four pillars. The four pillars and ten principles of the Global Compact are listed below (www.gcnetherlands.nl).

Human Rights pillar

1 Companies must uphold and respect internationally accepted human rights; and
2 continually advise themselves on whether they are still in compliance with these rights.

Labour pillar

3 Companies must support the freedom of association and the effective recognition of the right to collective bargaining;
4 endeavour to eradicate all forms of forced or compelled labour;
5 effictively abolish child labour;
6 and eliminate discrimination in labour and professions.

Environment Pillar

7 Companies should be cautious in their approach to environmental challenges;
8 take initiatives to improve their environmental responsibility; and
9 encourage the development and distribution of environmental technologies.

Anti-corruption pillar

10 Companies should prevent and oppose all forms of corruption, including (but not limited to), bribery and extortion.

Both the OECD and Global Compact codes of conduct are unenforceable.

ISO 26.000

Another development in this field is the ISO 26.000 guideline, globally applicable to organisations implementing CSR. The international guideline was created through a global multi-stakeholder process which also included the Dutch MVO-Platform. The advantage of ISO 26.000 is that it described basic CSR concepts which enjoy a broad global consensus. ISO 26.000 goes far beyond the previously described codes of conduct, and encompasses the following factors: good governance, human rights, labour conditions, the environment, fair and honest trade, consumers, and social commitment. ISO 26.000 knows four important fields. The MVO-Nederland website indicates: 'The basis of ISO 26.000 is that an organisation uses a basic approach (CSR principles) and joins its environment (stakeholders) to review which social themes (CSR core topics) to address (implementation).'
The website offers further information on how to concretise these four fields:

ISO 26.000

1st field: CSR principles:

The guideline indicates how an organisation can concretise each principle:
1 Accountability;
2 Transparency;
3 Ethical conduct;
4 Respect stakeholder interests;
5 Respect legislation and regulation;
6 Respect international codes of conduct;
7 Respect human rights.

2nd field: Stakeholders

ISO 26.000 indicates the environment's interest in the organisation, and the organisation's interest in the environment. To that end, the guideline describes how an organisation should inventory which stakeholders represent the environment, and how it should involve these stakeholders to obtain their input on the organisation's expected performance in terms of CSR.

3rd field: CSR core themes

Aside from the CSR principles, ISO 26.000 also lists 7 CSR core themes that should be given attention by all organisations. These core themes are subdivided into 37 sub themes, the so-called CSR issues. It is left to the discretion of organisations to determine if and to what extent they prioritise each CSR issue. Per sub-theme, ISO 26.000 offers a guideline for concretising the themes.

1 Organisational governance;
2 Human rights;
3 Labour circumstances;
4 Environment;
5 Fair trade;
6 Consumer affairs;
7 Commitment to society's development.

4th field: Implementation

The eventual goal is to address the aforementioned themes on a structural basis, and to integrate CSR into the way a business is managed. A well-known management approach to the systematic approach is the plan-do-check-act-cycle. The different ISO 26.000 components are addressed in this management cycle.

Shell oldest Dutch royal listed company

On average, it takes 55 years before a Dutch company can fly the Royal Crown of the Netherlands in its logo, while the average company to do so is nearly 211 years old. Shell got the 'Koninklijk' label 128 years ago, while the company was founded in 1890. Shell is the oldest company to have been awarded the 'Koninklijk' ('Royal' in Dutch) label; at 16 years old, DSM is the youngest company to do so. Out of all 126 Dutch listed companies, there are fourteen that are allowed to display the little crown.

Source: *Het Financieele Dagblad*, 30 April 2018

FIGURE **YEAR IN WHICH CURRENT SHARE MARKET LISTED FUNDS WERE AWARDED THE TITLE OF 'KONINKLIJK' (ROYAL)**

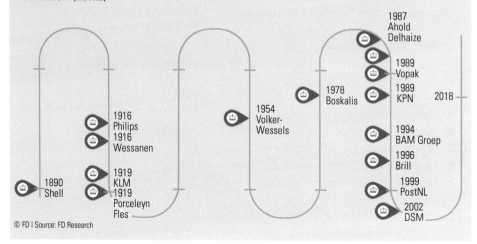

1987 Ahold Delhaize
1989 Vopak
1989 KPN
1978 Boskalis
2018
1954 Volker-Wessels
1916 Philips
1916 Wessanen
1994 BAM Groep
1996 Brill
1890 Shell
1919 KLM
1919 Porceleyn Fles
1999 PostNL
2002 DSM

© FD I Source: FD Research

5.2   INTRODUCTION TO CORPORATE GOVERNANCE

Corporate governance is described as the system used to manage and control companies, with transparency and responsibility seen as the most important characteristics of good accountability. Corporate governance signifies 'decent management': corporate management of a kind that makes politically, socially, economically, and ethically responsible decisions.

Corporate governance

In his book *Corporate governance* (2017), Frans van Luit explains that 'good or decent management' consists of agreements covering the following areas: managing, controlling, auditing, informing, and supervising. Based on these areas, Frans van Luit developed the so-called circle of governance, shown in Figure 5.5. The various components of the circle of governance are described below.

Circle of governance

FIGURE 5.5 **CIRCLE OF GOVERNANCE**

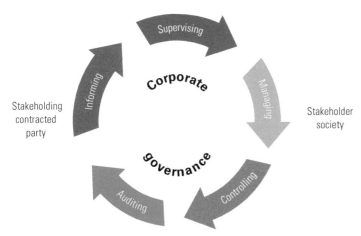

Source: Luit, van, F (2017), *Corporate governance*, Groningen, Noordhoff Uitgevers

Managing
Organisational management should assume responsibility in making decisions. Management is awarded a fitting reward for its efforts.

Controlling
All sorts of processes take place in an organisation, and come with specific risks. Consider strategic, financial, and operational risks. The goal of controlling is to make the multitude of risks manageable, and to ensure that the organisation can continue to make use of adequate buffers (capital).

Auditing
Auditing has both an internal and an external aspect. Internal auditing refers to various (internal) investigations whose goal is to establish whether the processes have been properly managed and controlled in striving to achieve the established goals. In larger organisations, this process takes the form of multiple investigations: financial, operational, IT, and compliance audits. External audits are performed by accountants as part of a legally required procedure. An accountant's task is to perform an audit to establish whether a company's annual account is a truthful reflection of its performance. To that end, the accountant issues a report. The annual account comprises an organisation's financial data; the balance sheet,

the statement of income, and the notes to both financial overviews. Another tool is the annual report, used by management to report on the past year. The accountant's report only refers to the annual account.

Informing

Organisations have multiple stakeholders. In addition to the organisation's owners, there are employees, suppliers, banks, environmental organisations, media, local residents, and government institutions. All of an organisation's stakeholders want to be kept up to date on all sorts of matters pertaining to the general assembly. An important way of providing information is through the annual report. The Dutch Council for Annual Reporting uses guidelines to indicate the conditions that an annual report should meet. The Council (Dutch: Raad voor de Jaarverslaggeving, or RJ) is an advisory body, whose goal is to improve the quality of external reporting in the Netherlands. The Council also offers advice with respect to legislation to the Dutch government. Council members are appointed by FNV and CNV (unions), VNO-NCW (employee organisation), NBA (professional accountants' organisation), VBA (association of investment analysts) and Eumedion (corporate governance and sustainability interest group).

The board or management of an organisation is obligated to publish an annual report. This annual report is the board or management's way of reporting on the most important facts and events of the financial year. According to annual reporting guidelines, paying attention to CSR and social aspects is also necessary.

In practice, this is exemplified in the following components of the annual report:

a **Sustainability report**, paying attention to environmental aspects (incl. pollution and environmental performance), social aspects (incl. employment opportunity, safety, human rights, and integrity), and economic aspects (incl. contributions to research & development).

b **Governance reporting**: the board should report on how the principles and best-practice provisions in the Corporate Governance Code have been applied. It should explicitly state whether and why any deviations from the Code have occurred.

c **Supervisory board's report on board and management remuneration**: remuneration encompasses two aspects: remuneration policy and remuneration policy implementation. In its report, the supervisory board should explain what the remuneration policy is, why this remuneration policy has been adopted, and how the policy relates to the value development of the organisation as a whole. The annual report itself offers a detailed insight (summary) into the actual remuneration: what have the specific rewards over the past year entailed and how have these rewards been constructed?

Supervising

An organisation's board or management is responsible for making decisions and implementing daily policy. The supervisory board is responsible for monitoring the implementation of this policy. The Dutch Civil Code has the following to say about the supervisory board's task: 'the task of the supervisory board is to supervise the board's management as well as various general matters pertaining to the company and any joint enterprise. The supervisory board offers its advice to the board. In performing its task, the supervisory board conforms to the interest of the company and any joint enterprise'.

Unilever boss earns 292 times as much as employees
Gap between top level executive and average employee is largest in foodstuffs company

As of this year, the code of good governance demands that companies explain their internal payment ratios. The underlying idea is that, when establishing salaries for top level executives, the supervisory board does more than simply compare figures with other board members both foreign and domestic, but to also consider the effects of a policy within the company.

Source: *Het Financieele Dagblad*, 23 March 2018

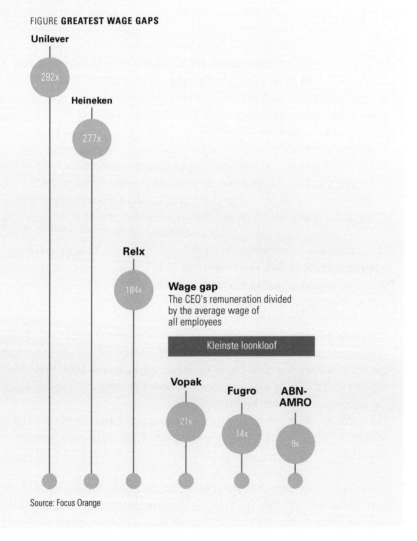

FIGURE **GREATEST WAGE GAPS**

Unilever
292x

Heineken
277x

Relx
184x

Wage gap
The CEO's remuneration divided by the average wage of all employees

Kleinste loonkloof

Vopak
21x

Fugro
14x

ABN-AMRO
9x

Source: Focus Orange

In larger organisations, the task described above is performed by a combination of three committees. These committees, assigned by the supervisory board, are:

Auditing committee

a **the auditing committee**: this committee maintains contact with external accountants (auditing);

Remunerations committee

b **the remunerations committee**: a synonym for remuneration is 'payment'. This refers specifically to the organisation's reward policy. The board's reward occupies a special place in this policy. The Dutch Corporate Governance Code 2016, Principle 3.1, states the following about remuneration policy: 'Remuneration policies for management should be clear and accessible, focussed on long-term value creation for the company and any joint enterprise, and take into account internal remuneration ratios as they exist in the company. Remuneration policy must not encourage management to ignore other interests in favour of its own, nor to take risks that do not correspond to the formulated strategy and established risk tolerance. The supervisory board is responsible for the formulation and implementation of the remuneration policy';

Selection and appointment committee

c **the selection and appointment committee**: this committee is concerned with appointing and reappointing supervisory board and management members.

5.2.1 Development of Corporate Governance Code in the Netherlands

In 1997, the Peters committee issued forty recommendations with regard to 'good governance, adequate supervisions, and accountability'. The reasons for these recommendations were that:
– faith in governance had been shaken due to reporting scandals;
– the share market had seen poor development, which caused problems like poor or overly aggressive take-over or financing policies to rise to the surface;
– there was an urge for greater transparency and accountability, prompted in part by growing shareholdings and the awareness of shares in pension rights.

Many companies ignored the recommendations by the Peters committee. Internationally speaking, there have also been changes in insight. Therefore, the **Tabaksblat Committee** Dutch government created the Tabaksblat Committee, headed by the eponymous former chairman of the board of Unilever.

On 1 July 2003, the Tabaksblat committee published a code of conduct for Dutch Corporate Governance. Committee members included experts in the fields of business, science, accountancy, institutional investment, private shareholding, and the share market. The code came into effect on 1 January 2004, and calls for self-regulation. If this code was to prove insufficient incentive, the government retained the ability to enforce certain matters by law.

The code was intended for listed companies and is based on the principle of 'apply or clarify'. Companies that do not follow (part of) the code must motivate such deviations.

Monitoring Committee

An updated code came into effect on 1 January 2009. The Dutch Monitoring Committee for Corporate Governance Code, established by the Dutch Minister of Finance, updated the Dutch 2003 Corporate Governance Code. The Monitoring Committee's most important task has always been to improve the applicability and usability of the code, and to monitor Dutch listed companies' and institutional investors' compliance with the code. A new feature of the updated code is that it contains principles and best-practice provisions which establish the relationships between management, the supervisory board, and the general assembly of shareholders.

The principles contain general notions on good corporate governance, concretised in the form of best practice provisions that offer a norm for the behaviour of managements, boards, and shareholders. The best practice-provisions are oriented both nationally and internationally. The idea is that, every year, a company uses part of its annual account to report on how the company has applied the principles and best practice provisions over that year. If the company chooses to deviate from the code, they are required to motivate their deviations. The task of the shareholders is to ensure that management and the board uphold the code, since it is management and the board who are responsible for the code's implementation. The updated code ties in with existing legislation and developments in the field of corporate governance both domestically and abroad.

Examples of best practice provisions in the field of governance:

a Managers are appointed for periods of no longer than four years. Any reappointment should also be limited to a four-year period.

b The company creates and implements its own custom internal risk management and supervision system (integral risk management).

c Managers should be part of no more than two directorates with listed companies. A manager cannot be a chairperson of the supervisory board of a listed company.

d Management submits the following for approval by the supervisory board: the company's business and financial objectives; the strategy intended to the realisation of these objectives; the conditions applied to this strategy; the social aspects of enterprise as relevant to the company.

In 2016, the Corporate Governance Code received another update. It now centres on the long-term value creation of organisations (sustainable operations). Culture has also been given a role in good corporate finance. Other updates are in the field of supervisory board member appointments and management structure. The basis for the appointment period for supervisory board members is four years, with one possible reappointment for four years, and any further reappointments limited to two years. The code no longer applies only to two-tier-board management structures, but also for one-tier-board management structures.

5.2.2 Corporate governance abroad

As discussed, corporate governance is not limited to Dutch business life. As many companies operate internationally, they are regularly required to be in compliance with more than one corporate governance code. Dutch companies that are also listed on US share exchanges, for example, need to be in compliance with both the Dutch and US Code of Corporate Governance.

There have been various attempts at a single international code. One example is the OECD's 'Principles of Corporate Governance', last updated in 2015. The Dutch Code by the Tabaksblat committee was based on this code. The 'Principles of Corporate Governance' can be divided into five main groups (Van Luit, 2017):

1 publication and transparency;

2 management responsibilities;

3 shareholder rights;

4 equal treatment of shareholders (certificate holders and share certificate holders);

5 the role of stakeholders in het corporate governance process; company management (board of directors).

The OECD guidelines apply to multinational companies and contain recommendations from all participating governments.

Sarbanes-Oxley Act

As stated, the Dutch Corporate Governance Code operates on the basic principle of 'apply or clarify'; in other words: self-regulation. The same principle is also applied in other countries, such as the United Kingdom. There are also countries whose legislation dictates the Corporate Governance Code. An example is the United States, where the 2002 Sarbanes-Oxley Act was implemented in response to some of the country's major accounting scandals (incl. Enron). It is largely aimed at the reliability of financial reporting. If company management purposefully issue incorrect financial information, the Sarbanes-Oxley Act makes prosecution possible, possibly leading to extended jail time and large fines. There is also the 'Disqualification' tool: if a manager tries to pull a fast one and is caught, they are prohibited from fulfilling a similar function for a number of years. The law also stipulates tightened requirements for external accountants. The Sarbanes-Oxley Act applies to all companies that are listed on US share markets, no matter the country or location of their registered office. Ahold Delhaize, for example, is listed on the New York Stock Exchange, but has its registered office in Zaandam, the Netherlands. As such, Ahold Delhaize must comply with both the Sarbanes-Oxley Act and the Dutch Corporate Governance Code. The most important legal articles are articles 302 and 404.
Article 302 applies to the supervision on the spreading of information (disclosure). Company management is expected to provide periodic reports on the effectiveness of its supervision, both at the design and design implementation levels (design effectiveness), and at the level of operating effectiveness.
Article 404 applies to the rules for internal auditing and financial reporting. Of note is the fact that management is required to offer a qualitative assessment of the reliability of its internal audits. Both the Chief Executive Officer (CEO) and the Financial Executive Officer (CFO) are to declare, in writing, that the audits are impeccable. In addition, the accountant (auditor) must provide a written declaration with regard to the reliability of the financial data and internal audits, as well as company management's honesty and reliability.

The implementation of the Sarbanes-Oxley Act (or SOX Act) is the responsibility of the Public Company Accounting Oversight Board (PCAOB), a government agency that develops the auditing norms. In addition, the agency verifies the audits performed by accounting firms.

5.3 INTRODUCTION TO BUSINESS ETHICS

In recent years, increasing attention has been paid to the ethical aspects of entrepreneurship and management. The internal and external stakeholders of the organisations of today are interested not only in the fiscal performance of an enterprise. So-called 'non-commercial goals' – greater involvement in environmental issues – are playing an important role in enterprises that wish to maintain a good relationship with their wider environment. Issues relating to personnel policy, environmental pollution, discrimination, trade with less developed countries, tax policy, religion and so on, cannot be approached solely from the perspective of maximising profit. Practical ethics may involve (painful) choices and dilemmas. A moral choice may (often) cost more and even work against the purposes of an enterprise. Despite this, many enterprises make decisions

246   Organisations and their environment
PART A   © Noordhoff Uitgevers bv

that negatively impact their maximum profit but which represent a compromise between aiming for profit growth on the one hand, and promoting socially acceptable activities on the other.

Many organisations have goals which show the influence of ethical motives, thus clearly profiling their position.

Management at all levels is also often faced with decisions in which ethical issues play an important role: for example, selecting employees to be made redundant because of restructuring requirements – should management favour an employee who is single or one who has a family to support? And what to do when deciding between a Western or non-Western applicant? A male or a female applicant? One way or another, 'ethical aspects' play a role in almost every decision a manager has to make. The way a manager behaves or interacts with their employees reveals something about their values, norms and sense of ethics.

It is important to note that 'ethical' is not the same are 'lawful'. The law can be enforced; ethics cannot.

Another mistake is the interchangeable use of the words 'ethical' and 'moral' as though they mean the same – they do not. 'Moral' describes the general rules that illustrate what people consider to be the 'right thing to do'. Moral refers to all norms and values that are important to an individual. It is an abstract concept that does not take situations into account. A moral can be used to help a person decide if something is right or wrong. To an important extent, morals are determined by the traditions, norms and values of a person's society.

Moral

The corruption index

Every year, Transparency International (TI), a non-profit organisation, studies global corruption. The higher the score, the more corrupt the country. Corruption here is defined as 'the abuse of entrusted power to further personal gain.'

Source: https://www.transparency.nl/nieuws/2017/01/corruption-perceptions-index-2016-ongelijkheid

Ethics Ethics, on the other hand, involves critical thought about morals. It is therefore a much more subjective notion than moral. Ethics always refer to the application of a moral to a situation. 'I behaved a certain way, but should I have behaved differently?' Is the morality one has demonstrated really that obvious for one's circumstances? Morals, therefore, are the basis of ethics.

The concept of ethics is nothing new – consider some of the best known Greek philosophers, like Socrates (469 BC - 399 BC), Plato (427 BC - 347 BC) and Aristotle (384 BC - 322 BC), who concerned themselves with issues of ethics, the nature of virtue, and right or wrong.

5.3.1 Sources of ethical conduct

Ethical organisational conduct can be influenced by various sources (see Figure 5.6). Most of this influence comes from the norms and values generally held to be acceptable by society, in relation to topics such as honesty, justice, privacy, manners, habit, and tradition.

FIGURE 5.6 **FACTORS INFLUENCING THE ETHICAL ORGANISATIONAL CONDUCT**

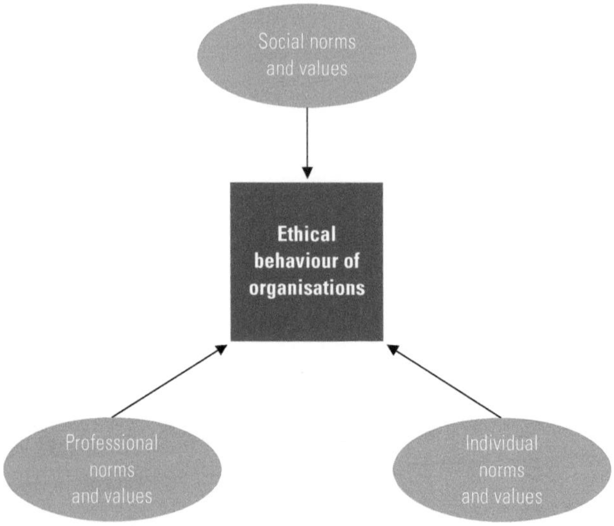

Societal norms and values These **societal norms and values** develop over time and are not the same across all countries and continents. Ethical conduct in organisations is determined by society to a large extent, as an organisation is part of a society, and does not exist outside of it completely.

Professional norms and values Next, **professional norms and values** play in important role. Various professions have their own codes (medical personnel, accountants, business consultants, etc). Deviation from those established codes of conduct may even lead to expulsion.

Personal norms and values Lastly, **personal norms and values** also play an important role. These values are strongly influenced and shaped by one's upbringing and referential groups.

5.3.2 Responsibility, accountability and integrity

A frequently heard word in the context of ethics is 'responsibility' or 'accountability'. Ethical conduct and responsibility, or accountability, are interwoven concepts. Wieger van Dalen's *Ethiek de Basis* (Ethics, the basics) describes three types of responsibility. The first is the responsibility that is imposed, in the form of legislation. A driver who fails to wear their safety belt while driving may be fined – what they are doing (or rather, failing to do) is punishable by law. This is the type of responsibility that is known as **liability**. If responsibility stems from workplace agreements, it is known as **task responsibility**. Another possibility is that of a situation which, even though it is not subject to prior agreements, demands people behave a certain way simply because they are expected to do so. This type of morality-related responsibility is called **virtue responsibility**. An example: while on a skiing holiday, a holiday maker catches sight of someone who seems to have fallen over in the snow. In such a case, they are expected to help or to ensure that help comes. Ethical conduct has strong ties with the concept of virtue responsibility, because this is the type of responsibility that comes with the greatest amount of individual freedom of choice. It is an important feature of the latter type of responsibility in particular that the responsibility does not merely apply to a person; they must also experience a sense of responsibility and act accordingly. Responsibility as a virtue means that a person should take measured and reasoned decisions. *Ethiek de Basis* lists five criteria that a person of virtue responsibility should fulfil. It is important to note that virtue responsibility is a relative concept: virtue responsibility applies to people in degrees, not in terms of 'yes' or 'no'. The five criteria are (Van Dalen, 2017) that:

1 people take autonomous decisions;
2 people take their obligations seriously;
3 people weigh up different norms;
4 people recognised the consequences of their actions and
5 people are personally accountable for their decisions.

In practice, the three types of responsibilities tend to intermingle and should not be approached as though they were fully distinct aspects.

Another concept with close ties to ethics and responsibility is 'integrity'. Complimenting a person's integrity means making a statement on two important personal characteristics: honesty and reliability. In *Ethiek de Basis*, integrity is described as being able to apply moral self-determinism. The book describes this concept of moral self-determinism as 'considering one's actions as a person from a moral perspective, and behaving accordingly'. In order to develop and apply moral self-determinism, *Ethiek de Basis* indicates the following three required skills:

1 **Identifying moral obligations**: people can sense a moral obligation to address or act on a situation. It is important that this moral obligation is experienced from within (intrinsic), and has not been imposed by an outside factor (extrinsic).
2 **Balancing moral obligations**: moral obligations may be related to various aspects of human life. They may arise from a person's work, social status, or personality. In specific situations, a person must find the correct balance between the multitude of (potentially) relevant moral obligations.
3 **Maintaining personal moral**: over the course of their lives, people continue to develop their moral obligations. This development can take the form of a retention of certain moral obligations or their adjustment or dismissal as a result of (personal) experience. Moral self-determinism means that a person is conscious about their moral obligations and make their own decisions with respect to those obligations (Van Dalen, 2017).

Rabobank paying through the teeth for US violations

American Rabobank-subsidiary RNA pleaded guilty to obstructing an investigation into money laundering in front of a San Diego court. RNA paid approximately €298 million ($369 million) to the US Prosecutor's Office and bank watchdog OCC. 'When Rabobank found that a substantial number of client transactions appeared to indicate drug smuggling, organised crime, and money laundering, the bank chose to turn a blind eye and to obfuscate shortcomings in its anti-laundering program,' says the prosecutor in a press statement. 'What is worse, Rabobank took steps to obstruct an investigation into these shortcomings by regulatory authorities.' Financial institutions are legally required to report any cash withdrawals over $10,000 and unusual transactions that may point to money laundering, tax evasion, or other criminal activity, to regulatory authorities.

Source: *Het Financieele Dagblad*, 8 February 2018 https://fd.nl/ondernemen/1240947/rabo-tast-diep-in-de-buidel-voor-overtredingen-in-de-vs, consulted 7 May 2018.

5.3.3 Approaches to ethics

With regard to ethics and responsibility, there are different approaches. In the context of this book, the following two perspectives are discussed:

1 four stances on ethics;
2 social approach to responsibility.

Four stances on ethics

There are four distinct visions of or approaches to ethics: the utilitarian stance, the individual stance, the egalitarian stance, and the moral stance. A person confronted with an ethical dilemma may approach this issue from any of these four points of view.

Utilitarian stance on ethics

Utilitarianism | Utilitarianism is derived from the Latin 'utilis', meaning useful. The founder of utilitarianism was British, Jeremy Bentham (1748-1832).
The utilitarian stance is that ethical decisions should be based on the outcomes and effects of the decision. The criterion is that of the costs weighed up against the benefits, and the best decision is whichever one benefits the greatest number of people. Closing a department because that is the best way to guarantee the continuity of an organisation is an example of such a decision.

Individual stance on ethics

Individual
Liberal | The focus of the individual or liberal stance is on the individuals, whose rights and freedoms must be protected and respected. In organisations, this means that the individual and the development of the individual are of crucial importance. Decisions need to be made with the (long-term) interests of the individual in mind. Honesty and integrity are important aspects of this approach.

Egalitarian stance on ethics

Egalitarian | The egalitarian stance is that the costs and profits resulting from an ethical decision should be divided between the interested parties and/or individuals as proportionally and impartially as possible. A remuneration policy, for example, should not distinguish between different employees doing the same work. The same is true of equal efforts; 'what is good for the goose is good for the gander'.

Moral stance on ethics

According to the moral stance, a decision is ethical when it is in line with fundamental human rights. These rights should be respected and protected when making decisions. They include the right to live freely, to receive fair treatment, to respect for one's privacy, to equality, and to the freedom to express one's own opinion. The 'Universal Declaration of Human Rights' (United Nations, 1948) may serve as a moral guideline.

Moral

Social responsibility

Peter Thuis (2017), in his book *Toegepaste Organisatiekunde* (Applied Organisational Management), describes an approach that views responsibility from a social context (the organisation). Known as the social responsibility approach, it does not look at the individual context of ethical dilemmas or issues, but places them in a broader frame of reference. Social responsibility is an organisation's obligation to maximise the positive societal consequences and minimise the negative societal consequences of its actions. Social responsibility and ethics are therefore not synonymous. Ethics comes down to individual decisions and actions; social responsibility is much more to do with the collective effects of organisations on society. Ethics and social responsibility are strongly related, however, and are often in line with each other. Consider the individual employee that sells the wrong products to a group of customers (individual context); the organisation will likely ensure that the customers are refunded or offered a replacement product (social context).

Social responsibility

Social responsibility can be implemented as a number of different concepts: the traditional concept, the social-responsibility concept, and the empowerment concept.

The **traditional concept** of social responsibility operates on the basis that both organisation and management should serve at the discretion of the shareholders, who own the company. The interests of the shareholders are all that matters.

Traditional concept

If the shareholders are only one of several relevant parties, and there are other stakeholders with an interest in the organisation, the applicable concept is the **social-responsibility concept**. In this case, organisation and management should serve the interests of all stakeholders, not merely thos of the shareholders.

Social-responsibility concept

If one shifts the line of responsibility even further along, oen arrives at the **empowerment concept**. Empowerment means that not only the organisation's stakeholders are served, but that the organisation itself also actively engages in initiatives for a better society. This is the broadest interpretation of the concept of social responsibility.

Empowerment concept

5.3.4   Company code

Many organisations describe their ethical principles in a company code, a type of code of conduct. Ninety percent of all major Dutch organisations have a company code. A company code can be described as follows: 'a list of general business principles and ethical behaviour principles established by an enterprise, aimed at the acceptability of employee and organisational practices'. Company code is not legally enforced, but is used to direct organisational behaviour.

Company code

A company code usually comprises of four components or layers (De Leeuw & Kannekens, 2013):

1 **Mission**: describes an organisation's strategic objectives and values. The mission is usually phrased in the form of a 'mission statement'.
2 **Core values**: the core values make up an organisation's ethical compass. They offer a revealing insight into an organisation's culture and the operational directives for its employees. In defining its core values, an organisation establishes its identity. The core values are often documented as part of a 'value statement'.
3 **Responsibilities**: the mission and core values are used to define the responsibilities towards the organisation's most important stakeholders. These responsibilities are often phrased as 'business principles'.
4 **Rules and standards**: these offer an insight into the behaviour expected of all organisational members, both inside and outside of the organisation. The rules and standards are often defined in a behavioural code or code of conduct, or simply as part of the house rules.

The structure of a company code is shown below in Figure 5.7.

FIGURE 5.7 **COMPANY CODE STRUCTURE**

In practice, some organisations include all four components or layers in their company code; other organisations restrict themselves to a selection when defining their company code.

In their book *Bedrijfsethiek en MVO* (Business Ethics and CSR), Jan de Leeuw and Jacinta Kannekens list the various functions and goals of a company code, distinguishing between internal and external functions and goals:

Internal (personnel and management)
a **Exploratory function**: the code provides all employees with an insight into the organisation's most important policy principles. The company code is a way of getting to know the organisation.
b **Explicating function**: writing a business code means making choices, in the sense that a company code explains what kinds of behaviour are and are not tolerated. The company code offers direction with regard to how certain matters and issues should or should not be addressed.
c **Directive function**: a clearly defined company code offers employees a guideline for how to act (in specific situations).
d **Internally corrective function**: a company code offers employees a basis for discussion and correction when it comes to certain behaviours.
e **Engaging function**: a company code improves employees' commitment to the organisation, and encourages them to apply themselves to the organisation's mission and core values.

Organisations and their environment
PART A

DSM Core Values

O&M IN PRACTICE

Sustainability is our core value. We offer our direct customers and consumers scientifically based solutions in response to the demands posed by the challenges of our time. We are convinced that businesses have a responsibility to contribute to a better world using the United Nations' Sustainable Development Goals as a guiding principle. Nutrition, health, circular economy: these are major social challenges to which we are fully committed. We are always hard at work to improve our environmental and societal impact, and our innovative Brighter Living Solutions offer just that solutions and products, that are quantifiably better for both people and planet than the products they are intended to replace. These enhanced products and technologies are becoming a steadily growing part of our portfolio.

Source: http://www.dsm.com/countrysites/dsmnl/nl_NL/visie-strategie.html

f **Initiating function**: a company code can have a positive effect on a company's image and identity. A company code ensures a widely supported similarity of employee behaviour towards clients, demonstrating to those clients what they should or should not expect from the organisation.

External (other stakeholders)
a **Distinguishing function**: in its company code, a company makes certain decisions that distinguishes them from other organisations. This allows various parties to distinguish one company from another in the same sector or industry.
b **Legitimising function**: the company code offers an insight into the behaviour that employees and management are or are not expected to demonstrate. This informs stakeholders of what (not) to expect from the organisation which can have a positive effect on stakeholder confidence in the organisation.
c **Externally rectifying function**: a company code offers a description of what stakeholders and other groups in society should (not) expect from the organisation. This means that stakeholders or other groups in society can 'obligate' the organisation to uphold its code, or to offer positive or negative criticism on the organisation based on the comparison between its company code and the behaviour of its employees.

Summary

- There are two approaches to corporate social responsibility: the classic and the social economic approach. The classic approach states that the sole responsibility of management is to maximise profit. The social economic approach states that organisations are responsible not only for generating profit, but also for offering a positive contribution to society as a whole.

- A social enterprise has the following four qualities: it has a primarily social mission; it is implemented as an independent enterprise offering a product or service; it is self-sufficient, based on trade or other forms of value exchange; it therefore barely relies (if at all) on gifts or subsidies; and it is social in the way the organisation applies itself.

- Sustainable development is defined as 'a development that meets the needs of the present generation without obstructing the opportunities for future generations to meet theirs'.

- Sustainable development is development that properly balances ecological, economic, and social interests.

- Important developments with regard to sustainable development are: the United Nations' development goals (2015 -2030), the Paris Climate Accord (2015), and sustainable development in the field of consumption.

- The Nederlandse Sociaal Economische Raad (SER), or 'Dutch Social Economic Council' defines Maatschappelijk Verantwoord Ondernemen (Dutch for Corporate Social Responsibility) as: 'consciously directing business activities to create value in three dimensions – profit, people, planet – thereby contributing to long-term societal well-being.'

- At the core of the 'cradle-to-cradle' principle is that, at end of their lifecycle, materials used as part of one product can be put to good (or better) use in a different (new) product.

- The four basics of CSR policy are:
    - CSR is an integral take on entrepreneurship, with a company creating value in economic (profit), ecological (planet) and social (people) terms;
    - CSR is embedded in all business processes;
    - CSR is fully customised;
    - CSR is a process and not a destination.

- Companies are increasingly coming to grips with the opportunities presented by sustainability. Whereas CSR was initially viewed as a way to hold organisations accountable or as something which required intrinsic motivation, it is now increasingly seen as a competitive, image-reinforcing tool.

- A company is a seen as a collection of interested parties: stakeholders. These stakeholders are not only directly but also indirectly connected to the company. Direct stakeholders are shareholders, buyers, employees, banks, and suppliers. Indirect stakeholders include local residents and environmental organisations.

- Two approaches to Corporate Social Responsibility are: four stances on social responsibility and the natural resource-based view.

- The four stances on CSR are: minimal social responsibility, social acceptability, broad social responsibility, and social activism.

- According to the natural resource-based view, the CSR policy of a company should minimise the impacts of company activities on its surroundings on the one hand, and help to create value in environmental, social, and economic terms on the other. In fact, it is through the creation of value in one or more of these fields that an organisation may develop a sustainable social competitive advantage.

- Important Dutch CSR organisations are the MVO-platform and MVO-Nederland.

- ▶ Important international CSR organisations are: the Organisation for Economic Collaboration and Development (OEC), the Global Compact, and ISO 26.000.

- ▶ Corporate governance means 'decent management': management which makes responsible decisions both in political, social, economic, and ethical terms.

- ▶ Decent or good governance comprises agreements in the following fields: managing, controlling, auditing, informing, and supervising.

- ▶ According to Dutch Annual Reporting guidelines, companies are required to pay attention to CSR and soci(et)al aspects. In practice, this is demonstrated by the following aspects of the annual report: the Sustainability report, the Governance report, and the Supervisory Board's report on management remuneration.

- ▶ The Tabaksblat committee published a Dutch code of Corporate Governance on 1 July 203. The code is intended for listed companies and is based on the principle of 'apply or clarify'. Companies that do not uphold (part of) the code are required to motivate their decision to deviate from the code. There are also companies where the Corporate Governance Code is legally binding, including the United States (Sarbanes-Oxley Act).

- ▶ It is important to note that 'ethical' is not the same are 'lawful'. The law can be enforced, ethics cannot.

- ▶ Morals can be described as general rules which people use to define the correct way of behaving. Moral means all the norms and values a person holds to be important. Moral is an abstract notion that does not take specific circumstances into consideration. Ethics, on the other hand, relates to the critical assessment of morals. Ethical is therefore a much more subjective notion than moral. Ethics always deal with specific situations or circumstances.

- ▶ Sources of influence on ethical organisation conduct: social, professional, and individual norms and values.

- ▶ Three types of responsibility are: accountability, task responsibility, and virtue responsibility.

- ▶ Five criteria that establish a person's virtue responsibility are that they: make autonomous decisions; take their responsibilities seriously; weigh up different norms; anticipate the consequences of their actions; are personally accountable for their decisions.

- ▶ Moral self-determinism requires the following three skills: identifying moral obligations; balancing moral obligations; preserving the personal moral.

- ▶ Two approaches to ethics are: the four stances on ethics, and the social approach to responsibility.

- ▶ The four stances on ethics are: the utilitarian stance, the individual stance, the egalitarian stance, and the moral stance.

- ▶ The social approach to responsibility does not take into account the individual context of ethical dilemmas or issues, but places them in a broader framework (organisational framework). Social responsibility is an organisation's obligation to maximise the positive influence of its policy on society, and to minimise the negative influence of its policy on society.

- ▶ Social responsibility and ethics are not synonymous. Ethics deals with individual conduct and behaviour; social responsibility is more concerned with the collective effects of organisations on society. Ethics and social responsibility are very intertwined.

- ▶ Social responsibility can be expressed through the following concepts: the traditional concept, the social-responsibility concept, and the empowerment concept.

- ▶ A company code is 'a company's documented collection of general principles and ethical codes of conduct, aimed at defining the acceptability of the conduct of employees and the organisation as such'.

- ▶ A company code usually consists of the following four layers: mission, core values, responsibilities, and rules and standards.

- ▶ A company code has both internal and external functions and goals.

The previous section described an organisation as a means of human cooperation towards a common purpose. People determine whether an organisation will achieve its purposes. People play the principal role in every organisation. In this section, various angles of this role are discussed.

PART B
PEOPLE AND ORGANISATIONS

INTERVIEW WITH PETER WENNINK, CEO FOR ASML, AND HARRY DE VOS, CHRO FOR ASML

ASML is one of the few companies in the world manufacturing machines (wafer steppers) used to manufacture chips (semi-conductors). ASML supplies these machines to major chipmakers, such as Samsung and Intel. Eventually, chips made using ASML machines end up in smartphones and computers, as well as cars, planes, and domestic appliances. Around 85% of the chips in these devices have been manufactured using an ASML machine. For such a billion Euro

company, (a turnover of 9.05 billion in 2017), ASML is rather obscure. The reason for that is that the company does not make products used by consumers. The machines they produce are huge and exceptionally complex, costing over 100 million Euros each. Importantly, ASML's machines are able to create increasingly smaller transistors: the key building-blocks of a micro-chip. The company, founded in Veldhoven, originates from Philips.

Peter Wennink (1957) was originally a chartered accountant for Deloitte, where he specialised in high technology and the semi-conductor market before transferring to ASML in 1999 – where he first became the financial director and then, in 2013, the CEO.

Every since you became CEO, ASML has been offering scholarships to Master's students. What is ASML's reason for doing this?
'For a period of two years, a student can get financial support without being required to intern or work at ASML. This is ASML's way of combatting the deficiency in highly-trained technicians in the Netherlands. The company is currently forced to recruit those technicians from abroad; they are generally less loyal than their Dutch counterparts, even though loyalty is important to a knowledge-intensive company like ASMLs.'

How does ASML create loyalty?
'Loyalty should be to the team, not to me. That is why it is so important to create a safe culture. For that reason, groups are very important. Employees

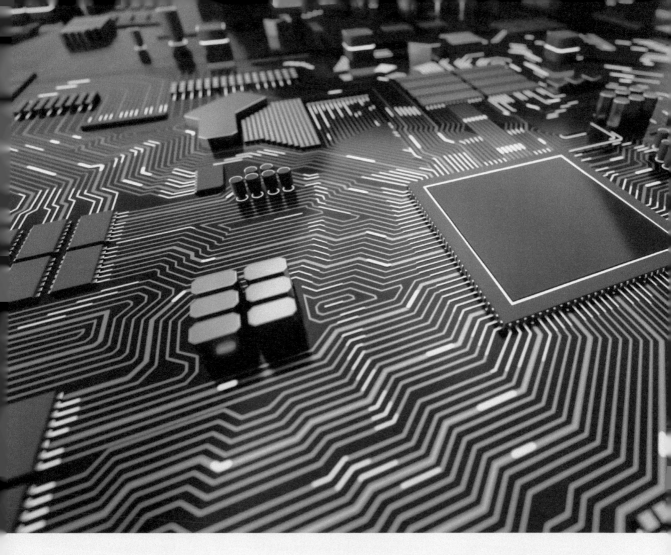

never find themselves one-on-one with the CEO. A group lets people voice their opinions. It also helps that ASML is so complex that people have no choice but to huddle up. We have managed to retain a start-up culture, in a sense. We have also decided to convert a large portion of flexible contracts into fixed ones; not just to boost company growth, but also to afford people greater security.' (Ed. – The company formerly, and for a long period, used a flexible organisational model in order to be able to downsize at a moment's notice if market conditions demanded.)

What other ways of creating employee commitment do you use?
'The engineers are a bit more patient than people in the support departments, or they are more realistic. Up until a few years ago, we mainly moved people around based on intuition. Now, we take a more structured approach. We test people, particularly in terms of behaviour. In our company, connectors are crucial. I am often asked: "How do I become a good manager?" My response would be: "First, try to be a very good engineer."

Nowadays, 'customer' is the central theme of CEOs everywhere. What has changed in the relationships with clients?
'These days, the most important force is productivity improvement. Clients are pushing us to provide better, faster, more accurate machines that can make increasingly versatile

chips. There is an insatiable need for computing power. The pressure is huge. Clients are willing to invest millions in the latest technologies. They try to transfer part of the complexity of their business to their suppliers. They want me to provide more than a machine: they want to know how to combine machines and software to improve their productivity. Our clients, for example, share their roadmaps for the coming ten years with us so that we know what it is they will need. Conversely, we are very transparent to our client, in terms of our investments, risks, margins on machines, and reasons for those margins. It is a way of investing mutual trust.'

And what is the CEOs role towards clients?

'Clients want my guarantee. Our clients – particularly in Asia – want to get to know me. The kind of person I am. Whether I am competitive, can be trusted, will deliver. I am the team's main negotiator. On the one hand, I am the one in charge of the financial aspect, the one who has to

have our technologies explained to him. On the other hand, I talk to the CEO on the other side of the table about issues that are not addressed in regular negotiations. Their greatest fears, for example. My most important assignment is to ensure that our suppliers, partners, and clients are all on the same level in terms of expectation. That balance is crucial. If one of my clients is experiencing an 'issue' with a chip machine, I am already on a plane there.'

Harry de Vos (1956) has 39 years of experience in various HR-functions with companies like General Electric, Electrolux AB, and , since 2007, with ASML NV as the SVP-HRO. Being the director of HR, De Vos is responsible for developing team management and negotiating contract conditions, among other things.

How does a high-tech company like ASML attract the right people?

'The supply of talent from Dutch universities for ASML's industrial field is not big enough, resulting in our having to attract a large number of employees from abroad. On average, we hire 150 new employees every month. Of those new recruits, 30 to 40% are from countries abroad. The extreme volatility (turbulence) of the chips market requires an appropriate response in terms of employee policy. Around 20% of all labour is performed by flexible workers. The well-known HR motto of 'inspire and retain' applies to both our fixed employees and our flexible ones. We want to ensure ASML employees remain employable for as long as possible.'

Clients like Intel, Samsung and TSMC have already consented to a 1.4 billion Euro investment for ASML's research and development. Are you allowing employees to cross-pollinate in order to share knowledge?

'This programme of co-investment is an important step for ASML. The three companies mentioned are our most important clients. Using the funding they provide, we can accelerate joint technological development, leading to 1,500 extra additional FTEs in our supply and demand chain in the short term alone; half with us, half with suppliers. Employee exchange is still limited for now, but the investment programme does improve the force of our labour market capacity; whereas we used to show some good candidates the door, we can now refer them to our suppliers.'

How does that work in terms of organisation?

'We have launched a Recruitment Box in collaboration with a number of suppliers, including TNO. This allows us to match supply to demand, which is good news for our entire operational chain. We can exchange knowledge more easily; an important aspect,

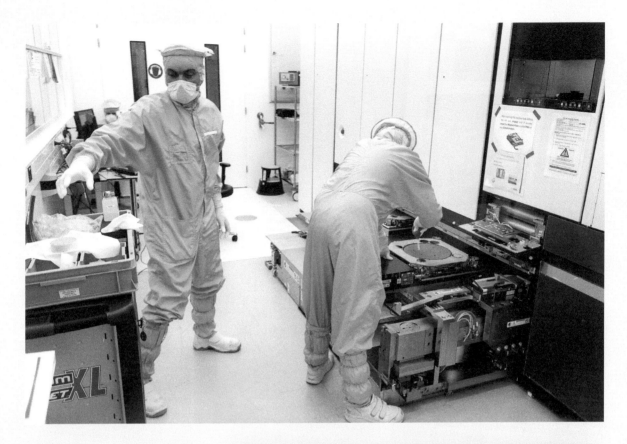

because the required specific qualities of our employees will only continue to grow in years to come.'

What are ASML's challenges in terms of HR policy?

One challenge is the continuous updating of knowledge, which will always be tricky considering the increasing complexity of our business and applied technologies. Another problem is that of diversity; out of all our technicians, no more than 7 percent is female. Technology and women, it still appears to be a challenge in the Netherlands.'

Source: www.mt.nl, 24-07-2017, *Het Financieele Dagblad*, 23 December 2017, www.management-scope.nl, www.schaappartners.com

6
THE FUTURE OF WORK

Contents

After studying this chapter:

- you will have gained insight into factors that influence the future of work;
- you will have been familiarised with the most important competences for the future;
- you will have been familiarised with jobs that will (partly) be automated or roboticised and/or replaced with new jobs;
- you will have gained insight into the importance of a lifetime of learning, and into the steps needed to remain employable in the job market.

Psylaris: the virtual therapist of the future

Psylaris wants to use virtual reality to make psychological aid more efficient and accessible. The company is developing Virtual Reality-applications for the treatment of psychological issues. VR-modules can help patients faster, better, and more effectively, argues the start-up company from Maastricht, the Netherlands. Psylaris' initial service is aimed at reducing the intensity of negative patient emotions. This is done through Eye Movement Desensitisation and Reprocessing (EMDR), a clinically proven method of treatment which has been around for more than 25 years. It is designed to combat largely psychological complaints resulting from a concrete, traumatic event, the memory of which still invokes an emotional response. Consider a heavy accident, or sexual or physical violence. Remembering the incident, combined with a form of distraction, such as eye-movement, is said to encourage the natural processing system. Founders Christoph Lynen (29) and Mike Verhiel (29) helm the company. Lynen holds a master's in Cognitive Neuroscience, Verhiel a master's in International Business, as well as broad, innovative product management experience. They registered for Y Combinator in early 2018. They were stunned when the most successful start-up-accelerator in the world invited them,

the third ever Dutch company. 'Over three months, we submerged ourselves in the program and were offered 120,000 Euros and, more importantly, access to the network. The name Y Combinator alone opens many doors,' says Lynen. The use of software helps keep costs relatively low, potentially making the technology accessible to patients in need of mental care in developing countries as well. 'All that is needed is a VR headset combined with the application. This makes it a potential alternative in refugee camps, where barely any psychological aid is currently available,' argues Verhiel.

Psylaris has already sold its first licences to clients.

Psylaris is currently focussing mainly on mental healthcare institutions in Europe, many of which are dealing with growing patient numbers, making it impossible to optimise treatment. The start-up's application can help relieve their efforts. An institution orders the headsets, after which Psylaris provides the app licence according to the SaaS principle. Clients pay a monthly or annual fee, depending on the number of licences, patients, and specialists using Psylaris.

Source: www.sprout.nl/juli 2018, www.psylaris.com

✳ Psylaris   EMDR-VR app   Benefits   FAQ   Contact   Blog

Psylaris
Therapy in virtual reality.

6.1 INTRODUCTION

Organisations in the 21st century are faced with exceptional challenges. Never before has the world seen change take place at such a rapid rate as today. Over the coming 15 years, many technologies will ensure that people will need to acquire a great deal of new knowledge and develop many new skills. It is expected that substantial numbers of jobs will be replaced by machines, but that new jobs will be created as well. Employment in the Netherlands will continue to grow until 2030, as long as organisations continue to advance in the use of new technologies, and people continue to be (re)trained and (re)educated. The field of Learning & Development is therefore expected to take on an increasingly important role. The challenge for this book is to offer insight into the form that organisational learning and development will take in the 21st century. This chapter mainly addresses work developments, and the meaning of those developments for people and organisations.

6.2 EMERGING DISRUPTION

Over the past 250 years, there have been three industrial revolutions. The **First Industrial Revolution** (circa 1760-1840) was one that spread internationally from the United Kingdom. It was a period driven by technical inventions, particularly the steam engine, and improved the effectiveness and efficiency of machinery. The mechanisation of the agricultural world also led to new processing and refinery plants, such as for sugar, potato, flour, and straw. Up until the 19th century, agriculture remained the largest economic industry in the Netherlands.

Industrial revolutions

The **Second Industrial Revolution** (1870-1914), or the 'technological revolution', began towards the latter part of the 19th century. At the time, new technologies, along with the introduction of assembly lines and electrical installations, led to mass production and rapid industrialisation. Once again, many new factories were opened. The period also gave rise to the creation of many new jobs, often with people operating machinery. Existing work was also replaced. With increasing frequency, agricultural machines were used to handle the work formerly performed by humans and animals alike.

The **Third Industrial Revolution** (1960-1990) brought mainframe computers (1960), personal computing (1970s/80s) and the internet (1990s). This revolution changed the interaction between individuals and businesses. Technological progress put pressure on the traditional middle classes, they being the people who handled the transactions. Examples of jobs which were more or less rendered obsolete through automation in the 1970s to 2010s were general office work (-37%), administrative work (-43%), secretarial work (-59%) and the tasks performed by typists (-80%) and phone operators (-86%). On the other hand, business life gained many new non-transaction-related functions and non-production-related functions that required complex problem-solving skills, thorough experience, and specific contextual knowledge, such as the work performed by software developers, computer designers, PC network specialists, printer technicians, and IT consultants.

A robot in control of accounting

Deloitte is putting computers in charge of part of its accounting. Does this mark the end of the era of the accountant? Accountants will retain final responsibility, but if their verdict differs from that of the computer, they will have some explaining to do. From now on, digital technology will play a huge role. The issue is with 13 frequently seen verification-related activities, such as accounting work for position/task packages in supplies, debtors, and cash positions. All low

risk positions, and still modest in number for now: 160 task packages have been identified. High risk positions, such as turnover, are still verified according to the traditional method. At the core of the new working method is the application of data-analysis: the 'risk-guided analysis', establishing the risks that verification should focus on. This method instructs each accountant what to do and how thoroughly to do it for every company.

Deloitte has already set its sights elsewhere. The firm is experimenting with artificial intelligence in data-analysis, and with roboticised control activities – thanks to the advanced digital environment in the Netherlands, and to the mind-set of clients and accountants alike.

Source: *Het Financieele Dagblad,* Transformers 06, June 2018

6.2.1 The Fourth Industrial Revolution

Today, the world is on the cusp of the *Fourth Industrial Revolution* (2012-), powered by 'cyber-physical systems' that require entirely new capabilities from human and machine alike. A cyber-physical system is a mechanism that is controlled or monitored by computer-controlled algorithms that have been deeply integrated with the internet and its users. This fourth revolution has been enabled through smaller and more powerful sensors, the mobile internet, machine learning, and artificial intelligence.

Fourth Industrial Revolution

In 2016, the Fourth Industrial Revolution was the theme of the *World Economic Forum* (WEF) in Davos. Professor Klaus Schwab, founder and chair of the WEF, published a book on the subject: *The Fourth Industrial Revolution* (2016). Some see this revolution as a combination of 'Industry 4.0' and smart services; others see a combination of developments from the second and third industrial revolutions, and continue to file the current age under the headings of 'third industrial revolution', or 'digital revolution'. Schwab, however, offers three reasons why Fourth Industrial Revolution should be considered to be fundamentally different from the third:

Industry 4.0

Digital revolution

1 **Speed**: The Fourth Industrial Revolution is developing exponentially rather than linearly.
2 **Breadth and depth**: This revolution continues to build on the Third Industrial Revolution while at the same time combining technologies leading to previously unknown paradigm shifts in terms of the economy, business life, and society.

3 **Impact on systems**: The fourth revolution leads to a transformation of entire systems, at various international location, industries, and societies as a whole.

6.2.2 New technologies

The Fourth Industrial Revolution is powered by technological developments whose potential for disruption is substantial. Technological break-throughs have come with increasing frequency over the course of history. The importance and use of new technologies are part of organisational strategy, and are therefore addressed in Chapter 2. Add to that the fact that new technologies are also adopted increasingly quickly. The time it takes for an invention or a technological novelty to garner 50 million users is becoming shorter and shorter; for radio it was 38 years, for TV is was 13 years, for the iPod it was four years, for Facebook it was one year, for Twitter it was nine months, for Angry Birds it was 35 days, for Pokémon Go it was 19 days.

Disruption

The *McKinsey Global Institute* identified twelve technologies that would have the potential for economic disruption in 2013 (see Table 6.1).

TABLE 6.1 **TWELVE TECHNOLOGIES WITH THE POTENTIAL FOR ECONOMIC DISRUPTION**

Technology	Examples of people, products, and resources the technology may impact
Mobile internet Increasingly cheap and versatile mobile (computer) devices with internet connectivity	**4.3 billion** people not yet connected to the internet, potentially to be connected via mobile internet **1 billion** people working in transaction and interaction jobs (nearly 40% of all potential labour)
Knowledge network automation Intelligent software networks that can perform knowledge work tasks, for example unstructured assignments and subtle assessments	**230+ million** knowledge workers (9% of global labour potential) **1.1 billion** smartphone users potentially using apps for automated digital support
Internet of things Network of cheap sensors and actuators for data collection, monitoring, decision-making, and process optimisation	**1 trillion** devices potentially connectable to the internet in industries such as manufacture, healthcare, and mining **1 million** machines and devices communicating worldwide, in industries such as transport, security, healthcare, and utilities
Cloud technology Use of computer hardware and software supplied via the internet, generally as a service	**2 billion** global users of cloud-based email services like Gmail, Yahoo and Hotmail **80%** of North American organisations hosting or intending to host essential applications in the cloud
Advanced robotics Increasingly superior and intelligent robots with more senses and greater agility, implemented to perform human tasks or augment the human body (*augmented humans*)	**320 million** labourers in the manufacture industry (12% of global labour potential) **250 million** major surgical procedures per year
Autonomous and near-autonomous vehicles Vehicles that work and navigate with no (or reduced) human intervention	**1 billion** cars and lorries worldwide **450,000** aircraft in general, civil, and military aviation worldwide
Next-generation genomics Fast and cheap sequencing (Next Generation Sequencing/NGS), advanced big-data-analyses and synthetic biology	**26 million** casualties from cancer, cardio-vascular conditions, and Type II diabetes every year **2.5 billion** people working in agriculture
Energy storage Devices or systems that store energy for future use, including batteries	**1 billion** cars and lorries worldwide **1.2 milliard** people without access to electricity worldwide
3D-printing Additive manufacturing technology used to produce objects consisting of layers of materials printed based on digital models	**320 million** labourers in the manufacture industry (12% of global labour potential) **8 billion** toys manufactured globally every year
Advanced materials Materials developed for their superior properties (strength, weight, conductivity) or functionality	**7.6 million** tons of silicone used per year **450,000** tons of carbon fibre used per year
Improved oil and gas detection/retrieval Detection and retrieval technology that would make the extraction of unconventional sources of oil or gas feasible	**22 billion** BOEs (*barrel of oil equivalent*) of natural gas globally per year **30 billion** barrels of crude oil globally per year
Renewable energy Energy generated from renewable sources with a less detrimental impact on the environment	**21,000** terawatt-hours of electricity used every year **13 billion** tons of CO2 emitted through electricity generation every year; more than the emissions of all cars, lorries, or aircraft combined

A WEF-list (2016) of expected turning points of various technologies in 2025 shows, for example (see Table 6.2):

TABLE 6.2 **EXPECTED TURNING POINTS OF THE APPLICATION OF VARIOUS TECHNOLOGIES**

Prediction (2025)	Probability (in %)
10% of people wear clothing connected to the internet	91.2%
90% of people have free unlimited data-storage	91.0%
1 billion sensors are connected to the internet	89.2%
The first robotic US pharmacist	86.5%
10% of reading glasses are connected to the internet	85.5%
5% of consumer goods are manufactured using 3D-printing	81.1%
90% of the population uses a smartphone	90.7%
10% of cars on US roads are self-driving	78.2%

Source: WEF, 2016

6.2.3 Organisational lifespan

New technologies, apart from being a disruptive agent, also impact economic growth. Early 20th-century economist Joseph Schumpeter (1883-1950) studied the rise and fall of companies in Europe and the US. He found that important industrial developments go hand in hand with a process of *creative destruction*, which leads to shifts in the origin of profit along the value chain, to a restructuring of industrial structures, and to the repression of established enterprises. Schumpeter believed that 'economic progress – in a capitalist society – comes with turmoil.' Yale professor Richard Foster applied Schumpeter's theory to modern management and innovation practices in his book *Creative Destruction* (2001).

Joseph Schumpeter

Creative destruction

Richard Foster

Foster studied the lifecycles of the most prestigious companies in Standard & Poor's top 500. Foster noted that the lifespan of companies has experienced a very sharp decline: from 90 years in 1935 to 18 years in 2011 (see Figure 6.1). He predicts that the lifespan of any S&P 500-company will be no more than 13 years by 2027. This does not necessarily mean that all companies will be consigned to the graveyard at age 13: they may just as well undergo split-offs, mergers, or take-overs, leading to their removal from the S&P 500.

According to Foster (2001), organisational lifespan is related to the matter of balance between three managerial commandments: 1) effective business activities, 2) the creation of new business that meets consumer needs, 3) discharging formerly important business that no longer meets company growth and profitability standards.

FIGURE 6.1 **THE LIFESPAN OF ENTERPRISES HAS SEEN A SHARP DECLINE IN THE PAST CENTURY**

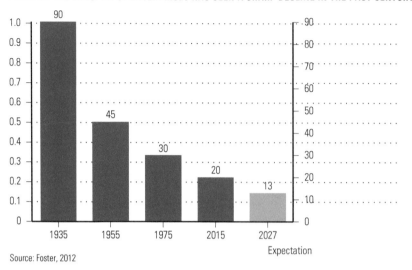

Source: Foster, 2012

The challenge is in the fact that companies need to innovate in order to create new business, but that investments in innovation often clash with business effectiveness (in the short-term). As a consequence, major companies are not quick enough to align with a changing external environment, and thus start to lag behind before eventually dwindling. The implication for employees is that the concept of a job for life, or working for only two or three companies, will become a thing of the past. Additionally, the Fourth Industrial Revolution will impose drastically different demands on people's skills. Employees will need to prepare for a career spent working for multiple companies, and ensure that they acquire combinations of skills and experience that make them valuable on the market. The biggest difference between the Fourth Industrial Revolution and the three preceding ones is everyone and everything's continuous commitment, and the speed with which the change is unfolding.

6.3   THE FUTURE OF JOBS

'There has never been a better time than the present for professionals with specific skills and the correct training, because these people can apply technology to create and retain value. At the same time, there has never been a worse time for workers with only 'standard' skills and capacities, because computers, robots, and other digital technologies are continuing to master these skills and capabilities at extraordinary speeds.' (Erik Brynjolfsson & Andrew McAfee, MIT Initiative on the Digital Economy).

Many new technologies disrupt labour markets. Developments in the field of technology and new business models are expected to have a fundamental impact on existing and future jobs, varying from job creation to job disappearance. The same happened during the first, second, and third industrial revolutions, when jobs in one sector vanished (as with agriculture), while jobs in new sectors where created (as with manufacture and servicing). Over the course of history, various economists have concerned themselves with the impact of technology on labour potential. Economist David Ricardo (1772-1823) predicted that the use of machines would have a destructive influence, particularly on the labour class. John Maynard Keynes (1883-1946) predicted universal unemployment resulting from technological developments 'because we are finding new means of saving on labour force more quickly than we are finding new uses for that labour force'. The new generation of technologies of the Fourth Industrial Revolution may threaten jobs that, previously, were not influenced by new technologies. Researchers at Oxford University (Frey & Osborn, 2013) predict that 47% of all US jobs have a 70% likelihood of disappearing over the coming two decades (see Table 6.3).

TABLE 6.3 **HOW SUSCEPTIBLE ARE THESE JOBS TO AUTOMATION?**

Telemarketers	99
Accountants and bookkeepers	94
Sales assistants	92
Technical writers	89
Realtors	86
Typists	81
Machine operators	65
Economists	43
Dentists	0.4

Source: Frey & Osborne, 2013

Another study (Bowles, 2014) shows that the percentage of European jobs susceptible to automation fluctuates between 45% and 60% (see Figure 6.2). The professional population in Southern Europe runs the highest risk of their jobs being automated. Employees in the Netherlands expect that 22% of existing jobs will be automated over the coming three decades (Blom, 2014). Dutch employers are more pessimistic: they think 37% of jobs will have become obsolete by 2046. OECD researchers, on the other hand, take a more optimistic view: for the Netherlands, they predict that only 10% of all jobs stand any major risk of becoming automated. The OECD researchers consider technological development to be less of a threat because they also take into account the heterogeneity of activities that comprise jobs instead of basing their estimates only on jobs as a whole.

FIGURE 6.2 **NUMBER OF MAN HOURS VERSUS MACHINE HOURS**

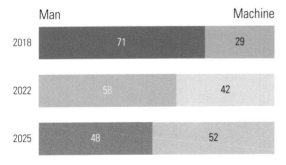

In their 2018 report *The Future of Jobs*, the WEF predicts that approximately 52% of all labour hours will be performed by machines by 2025. The WEF does not expect unemployment to rise; instead, new technology will make people more productive. Jobs, however, will begin to take on very different forms, and a growing need for (re)training and (re)education is predicted.

Researchers at the McKinsey Global Institute (Chui & Manyika, 2016) have compared activities in jobs against jobs as a whole. Their conclusion: the existing technologies they studied could automate 45% of *activities* that employees perform for pay. And for approximately 60% of jobs, over 30% of activities could be automated. The OECD study identifies a major chance of automation for jobs currently performed by lower schooled employees with lower incomes (See Figure 6.3).

FIGURE 6.3 **EMPLOYEES AT HIGH RISK OF AUTOMATION, PER LEVEL OF EDUCATION**

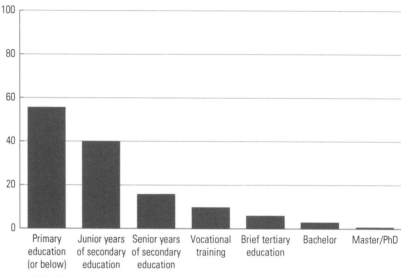

Source: OECD, 2016

The *McKinsey Global Institute* has made a detailed analysis (Arntz et al., 2016) of over 2,000 activities in over 800 professions in the US. The researchers reviewed whether it was technically feasible to automate the professional activities using existing technologies (see Figure 6.4).

FIGURE 6.4 **TYPES OF ACTIVITIES WITH TECHNICAL POTENTIAL FOR AUTOMATION**

Source: McKinsey Global Institute, 2016

Professions comprise various kinds of activities, all with varying potential for automation. Another factor is that the time people spend on those activities differs per profession. Approximate one fifth (18%) of the time that US employees spend at their workplace is spent on predictable physical activities that are highly susceptible to automation. But there are major differences from one industry to the next. For example, employees in the manufacture industry spend around one third of their time on physical activity. Around 73% of activities of employees in catering and the hospitality industry stand a chance of becoming automated. Consider burger making devices, self-service, and robotic staff. The finance and insurance industry spends around 50% of its time gathering and processing data, which are activities very well suited to automation. Major changes in the various industries and their components are expected. The Citigroup (Noonan, 2016), a multinational US investment bank, predicts that, over the coming ten years, European and US banks will reduce their staff by over 30%. The potential for automation in healthcare is at around 36%, though this percentage is much lower for professionals whose daily activities require expertise and direct patient contact. Figure 1.7 shows that there is a shift when it comes to activities that appeal to communication, expertise, and people management skills.

Physical activities

FIGURE 6.5 **THE NEED FOR SPECIFIC HUMAN ACTIVITY BETWEEN 2003 AND 2030**

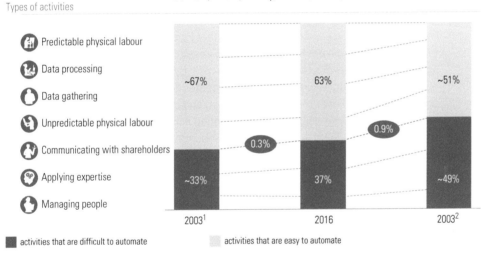

Source: *Shaping the future of work in Europe's digital front runners*, McKinsey Global Institute, Bughin et al., 2017

It is expected that every employed citizen of the Netherlands will be faced with increasing automation and robotisation. This expectation is shown in Figure 6.6.

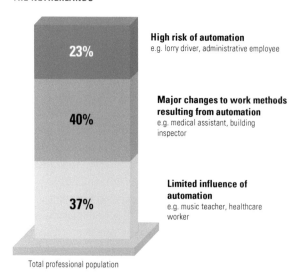

High risk of automation
e.g. lorry driver, administrative employee

Major changes to work methods resulting from automation
e.g. medical assistant, building inspector

Limited influence of automation
e.g. music teacher, healthcare worker

Total professional population

Source: McKinsey, Bughin et al., 2017

In short, the study shows that technological developments will come to replace existing jobs. But there are differences between the extent of replacement (for example between 10 and 49%), the changes per economy (for example Dutch versus Japanese economy), the impact speed (short-term, medium-term, or long-term), and whether jobs are wholly or partly replaced (based on specific activities). Numerous factors are used to predict whether jobs can be automated, including technical feasibility; hardware and software development costs for automation; labour costs and associated supply-and-demand dynamics; other advantages apart from substitution of labour (such as greater output and quality, and fewer errors), and issues with respect to legislation and social acceptance. This is not to say, however, that the possibility of automating activities or jobs will not continue to increase. It will do so, no matter whether current technological development continues along its exponential rate of development. Studies also show that automation can lead to new jobs, as shown in Figure 6.7.

FIGURE 6.7 **THE EFFECTS OF AUTOMATION ON THE DUTCH LABOUR MARKET BETWEEN 2016-2030**

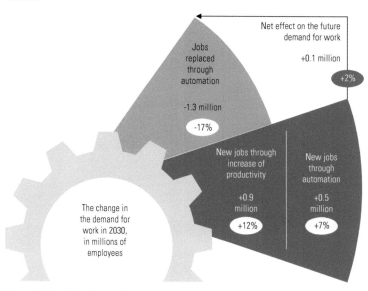

Source: McKinsey Global Institute, Bughin et al., 2017

The conditions for the realisation of the positive scenario are that organisations need to rapidly embrace new technologies (becoming automation innovators), and that the workforce needs to rapidly engage in (re)education and (re)training. If either party fails to do so, there is an increased chance that employment opportunities will decrease, resulting in increased unemployment and a strong decline in national income growth.

'There are human qualities to Amelia already'

IPsoft, developer of the virtual assistant Amelia, owned by Chetan Dube, is doing well. The company has specialised in the automation of office environments using artificial intelligence. Companies like BMW, Credit Suisse and Dutch insurance agency VGZ are listed as their clients, and are making use of Amelia. You can trouble her with all your consumer questions: from needing a new password to checking you are covered for new glasses. Because a satisfied customer is what matters most, argues Dube. Dube: 'Europe is always fretting about new developments. "Does this technology benefit society?" I would pose a question in response: as a company, are you even able to refuse joining in? Europe is behind in the field of artificial intelligence. The US and Asia (India) are simply barrelling along. The

Netherlands is a digital country, but with respect to AI, there are only few significant companies.'
IPsoft has already made its first move: they have founded the Doctor Amelia project in India. 470 million people in India own a mobile phone, but over half of them do not have access to decent health care. Amelia functions as a mobile phone powered doctor. You can ask her questions, after which she offers a diagnosis; she can also prescribe treatment or medication. This is not possible in Europe. Dube: 'European legislation will need to keep up; technology can free up a doctor's time spent on writing prescriptions, allowing them to spend more hours on true research and examination.'

Source: *Het Financieele Dagblad*, Weekend, 23 June 2018

6.4 NEW COMPETENCES

Most of the technologies discussed have already had a significant impact on employee skills. This certainly holds true for mobile internet, cloud technology, increasing computer processing capabilities, sharing economy, and crowdsourcing.

Other technologies are expected to grow in impact between 2018 and 2025; examples are the internet of things, robotics, autonomous transportation, artificial intelligence (AI), advanced production, 3D-printing, advanced materials, and biotechnology. The acceleration in the field of technological development will shorten the life expectancy of expertise, knowledge, and skills, and will require employees to acquire new capabilities. If certain activities in a job become automated, employees need to focus on new activities that require different skills.

Technological skills are changing the swiftest. An expected 50% of all substantive knowledge gained in the first year of a technical study will be obsolete by the time of graduation. Aside from technical or 'hard' skills, employers are concerned about work-related practical skills, such as creating content or assessing the goal and importance of information; these skills are also expected to become subject to drastic change over the coming years.

Creativity · Creativity will become one of the top three employee skills required for professionals. An avalanche of new products, technologies, and ways of working are intended to make people more creative if they are to profit from the changes. It is estimated that, by 2022, one third of the core skills in any profession will consist of skills not yet deemed crucial to those professions at this point in time (see Figure 6.8).

FIGURE 6.8 **THE TOP TEN OF COMPETENCES IN 2022**

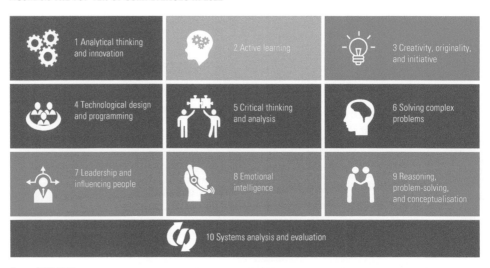

1 Analytical thinking and innovation

2 Active learning

3 Creativity, originality, and initiative

4 Technological design and programming

5 Critical thinking and analysis

6 Solving complex problems

7 Leadership and influencing people

8 Emotional intelligence

9 Reasoning, problem-solving, and conceptualisation

10 Systems analysis and evaluation

Source: WEF, 2018

Digital competences · As stated, the Fourth Industrial Revolution is also known as the 'digital revolution' or the 'digital age', indicating the need for the development of digital competences (see Table 6.4). EU-studies argue that 'digital skills are essential in nearly all professions that use technology to help perform existing tasks' and that '90% of jobs will, in the near future, come to rely to some extent on a certain level of digital skill.' In 2015, around one third of Europe's population between the ages of 16 and 74 was insufficiently digitally skilled to participate in society and the economy. Purely from the perspective of the professional population (employed and unemployed alike), this concerns over a third of the population (37%). Lacking the necessary digital competences will have direct consequences for one's employability.

In the EU, 42% of people lacking in computer skills are inactive on the labour market. Many of these people face social isolation. Moreover, they most likely do not have access to online government, banking, healthcare information, or other resources.

The EU has developed DigiComp 2.0, a European framework for digital skills. It is intended to be a tool for the improvement of civilian digital skills, for helping policy makers formulate a policy that encourages the development of digital skills, and for programming education and training initiatives for the improvement of digital literacy. DigiComp lists five areas of competence, 21 individual competences, and three levels of skill (basic, moderate, skilled).

TABLE 6.4 **EUROPEAN FRAMEWORK FOR DIGITAL COMPETENCE**

Areas of competence	Competences
1 Information	1.1 Browsing, searching, and filtering information 1.2 Evaluating information 1.3 Storing and recovering information
2 Communication	2.1 Interacting via technology 2.2 Sharing information and content 2.3 Participating in online citizenship 2.4 Collaborating through digital channels 2.5 Netiquette 2.6 Managing one's digital identity
3 Content creation	3.1 Developing content 3.2 Integrating and (re)developing 3.3 Copyrighting and licencing 3.4 Programming
4 Safety and Security	4.1 Securing equipment 4.2 Securing data and digital identity 4.3 Securing health 4.4 Securing the environment
5 Trouble-shooting	5.1 Solving technical issues 5.2 Explicating needs and determining technological solutions 5.3 Innovating, creating, and trouble-shooting using digital tools 5.4 Establishing gaps in digital skill

Source: EU, 2014

6.5 NEW JOBS

The Fourth Industrial Revolution requires the professional population to have a broad arsenal of thorough knowledge and skills that can easily be converted to new jobs. Interestingly, 65% of children currently attending primary school will eventually hold positions fulfilling jobs that do not currently exist (WEF, 2016). This illustrates that, as of yet, it is not yet clear what future jobs will look like. Some of today's jobs did not exist ten years ago. For example, *app developer* only became a legitimate function following the introduction of the first smartphone in 2007. In 2017, there were 6.7 million available apps found across various app stores (Statistita, March 2017. The increase in the prevalence of social media and social media applications gave rise to the function of *social media manager*. Since Uber's founding in 2009, people have been listing *Uber-driver* as their job description. Google makes substantial investments in self-driving cars, and is recruiting *self-driving car engineers*. Cloud computing was born in 2000. Now, *cloud computing specialist* is a profession that is rapidly gaining ground. More examples of new jobs are *big data analyst or specialist, sustainability manager, YouTube content maker, drone instructor or operator, millennials expert, digital marketing specialist, SEO specialist* (search engine optimisation), *user experience specialist, 3D-designer, offshore windpark engineer, web-analyst, green deal assessor* (assessor for sustainable technology), *mobile service engineer*, and *robots coordinator*.

Between 2018 and 2022, the Word Economic Forum (WEF) concludes that robotisation is resulting in a net creation of jobs. Up to 2022, around 75 million could disappear, but 133 million new jobs could be created through the introduction of machines to take over physical labour. The WEF emphasises that these estimates should be treated with care. A report questioned employers with a total of fifteen million employees as to their expectations. Accountancy, industry, client management, and secretarial functions in particular should expect jobs to be "taken over" by machines. But the number of jobs in, for example, data analysis, software applications, and online sales, on the other hand, will grow. These branches are actually enjoying the support from robotisation. Other industries that value "human competences", like marketing or sales, are likely to see an increase in the number of jobs.

A large portion of current employees will need to school up on their skills, says the WEF. By 2022, around 54 percent of all current employees would need to acquire new skills. Around 35 percent of employees needs six months in additional training; 9 percent will need to be reschooled for a period between six and twelve months. Another 10 would even need more than a year's training. According to the writers of the report, by 2025 around 52% of all currently existing work will be fulfilled by machines. They currently place this percentage at 29%.

FIGURE 6.9 **54% OF ALL EMPLOYEES WILL NEED RETRAINING BY 2022**

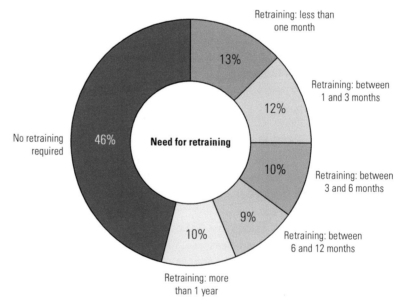

Source: *Future of Jobs Survey 2015*, World Economic Forum

New jobs   Over the coming decade, new jobs will come into being. Futurologists have compiled a list of jobs that are likely to come into vogue by 2025 (Moran, 2016), including: *virtual reality-experience designer, triber* (a professional managing consultant available for creating teams for very specific projects), *urban farmer, end-of-life planner, long-distance care specialist,* and *smart-home handyman.*

The rapid rise of new jobs related to the introduction of new technologies has enormous implications for *how* and *what* people learn. Chapter 7 addresses in detail the issues of preparing people for the concept of fulfilling various roles and jobs throughout their working life: sustainable human resources management.

6.6 A LIFETIME OF LEARNING

A lifetime of learning can be defined as: *an internal motivation to voluntarily continue to acquire knowledge for personal or professional reasons throughout the entirety of one's natural life.* The encompassing goal of learning is to improve one's knowledge, skills, and competences.

Lifetime of learning

One motivation to keep learning is the change in global pension policy, related to the continued increase in global life expectancy. Data gathered shows that life expectancy has increased by three months on average for every year since 1840 (see Table 6.5). Factors leading to growing life expectancy are improved health, swifter diagnoses, improved nutrition, improved medical care, improved education, and the combatting of age-related disease.

TABLE 6.5 **HIGHEST EXPECTED AGE FOR 50% OF BABIES BORN IN 2017**

US	104
UK	103
Japan	107
Italy	104
Germany	102
France	104
Canada	104

Source: Gratton, 2016

The issue of people becoming 100 years old poses a number of interesting financial challenges. Wanting to retain 50% of one's last annual income every year following retirement, at an annual pension saving of 10% of one's income, means full retirement is only possible at age 80+. More and more countries have adjusted the legal age for pensioners upward to 67 years old; this age threshold is expected to increase. Based on current pension legislation in the Netherlands, the retirement age for people who have just finished high school is around 72 years old. In other words: this generation is likely to remain part of the professional population for more than 50 years.

It used to be the case that people grew up in the context of more stable job markets and companies with a relatively long life expectancy; thus, they could rely on the skills they had acquired by age 25 to last them throughout their professional career. The current and future labour markets, however, force people to invest an essential part of their time and money in gaining new skills and updating their existing ones if they want to avoid the risk of missing out. The Dutch government has the ambition for the professional population to continue to work for a long time, and to apply themselves to a lifetime of learning. But everyday reality is different. According to the 2013 report *Naar een lerende economie* (Towards a Learning Economy), written by the Wetenschappelijke Raad voor het

Regeringsbeleid (Scientific Council for Government Policy), the Netherlands pays little attention to post-initial education; the country scores low on the concept of a lifetime of learning. Only 16% of the professional population of the Netherlands participates in education or training programmes outside of their everyday work.

In its *Human Capital Report* (2016), the World Economic Forum concludes that the Netherlands is insufficiently prepared for the future. The report ranks 130 countries by their level of *education and skills*, and based on *employement possibilities for five age groups*. The Netherlands retained its sixth position in 2016, even though it had dropped four places in 2015. Of particular concern is the low degree of labour participation (80%) and the high unemployment (20%) among residents aged 55 and up. The top three countries on the list are Finland (1), Norway (2) and Switzerland (3). The Netherlands scores slightly higher than the OECD average with respect to education investments, but scores poorly with respect to a lifetime of learning. The following context section includes a DHL casefile which describes how employees are encouraged to engage in sustainable learning.

O&M IN PRACTICE

Become inspired by your own development

Behavioural scientist Ben Tiggelaar follows Human Resource developments very closely; he writes about the latest developments and consults organisations.
In order to improve people's sustained employability, it is essential for employees to continue to developed in an increasingly data-driven HR industry. Employers indicate that it is difficult to 'get employees on board'. Employees, on the other hand, indicate that they cannot get round to their personal development. An often cited reason is the lack of urgency; in times of work stress, personal development is often placed on a back burner. According to psychologist Carol Dweck, there are two attitudes towards development. People with a so-called fixed mind-set do not have much faith in the effect of learning, and are often scared to fail. The other group is that of people with a growth mind-set: they do believe in self-development, and are also prepared to make an effort to that effect.

The brain is a habituated machine: it tries to use as little energy as possible to achieve maximum results. In working with continuous change and a rapidly transforming labour market, it is important to learn how our behaviour works, and what we can do to shape our own development. People need to understand how they can plan, shape, and implement their development. There are various factors at play: motivation, capacity (learning), and the environment. By transporting yourself into another work environment, you can advance more quickly. Attempt something novel, take part in an internship, talk to somebody whose job interests you. Actually try out new things and experience them 'live'; that is much more effective than merely pondering your own development.

Source: Mediaplanet, June 2018

The rapid rise of disruptive technologies, jobs threatening to disappear following robotisation, digitisation, and automation, shifts in the demand for new jobs and new skills across various industries, continued outsourcing, the need to acquire new skills at the same pace as the developments in business life combined with insufficient expenditure and utilisation of education and training budgets and the fact that people are insufficiently aware of the importance of learning: all of these tumultuous circumstances combine into a *perfect storm* for changing people's attitude and ensuring they invest in a lifetime of learning.

Organisations across the world are seeing rapid and drastic changes to what, how, and even why they are doing things. Mastering the current and future realities requires far-reaching learning capabilities. The people who are and will continue to be successful in the 21st century are those who embrace the new world of learning, and who are motivated to master new skills and competences. But no matter the fact that this is generally also an individual's responsibility, organisations play a crucial role in the continued education of their people and in the creation of new leaders. This is not a simple task, but the development of human capital is crucial for organisations looking to stay ahead of their industrial pack. The context section below offers an example of one such initiative, which makes use of 'ambassadors of learning': learning representatives.

6.7 EPILOGUE: LEARNING OR STAGNATING IN THE 21ST CENTURY

At the time of the first and second industrial revolutions, the forefathers of people currently at work were engaged in professional activity at least six days per week. The working week for most people across the various industries amounted to 75 hours. In 1960, the Netherlands implemented legislation that proposed a free Saturday, following an example set by the US in 1954. Since then, the working week in some industries has decreased from 48 hours to 32. Today, the working week in most sectors is between 36 and 40 hours long. According to the OECD's annual statistics, the Netherlands and Germany are the countries with the lowest number of working hours per year per employee: 1419 and 1317 hours respectively (US figure, by comparison, average 1790 hours).
It is forseeable that the Fourth Industrial Revolution, combined with an estimated 45-year working life in the near future, will culminate in a need for people to continually improve and revisit their skills. People will need to adopt the mind-set of a lifetime of learning, and allocate around 4 to 8 hours every week outside of working hours to continue learning. This will establish a new standard *working-learning week* of 40 to 48 hours. The Netherlands does not have a culture of employees recognising the need for a financial investment in their own development. Ninety-six percent of investments into learning & developing are made by employers. It should be expected that, in the near future, more and more people will make their own personal investments into learning and their development in order remain relevant to the workplace.

Governments ought to improve tax advantages with respect to learning & development if they view a lifetime of learning as a topic of importance. In addition, education and development funds should be applied to help people develop in the direction of (future) functions in other industries. Employers should create an organisational culture aimed at learning for everyone, and should

The importance of learning representatives

The idea for ambassadors of learning derives from the 'Learning Reps' project successfully implemented in thousands of UK companies by the TUC union in the mid-1990s. Learning representatives (or 'learning reps') are lower educated employees respected by their colleagues. They receive training to be a learning rep in their organisation. These representatives then try to encourage other lower educated colleagues to engage in (additional) education.

The results of a learning rep experiment in the Netherlands suggest that this approach improves the motivation for learning among lower educated employees. The tasks fulfilled by a learning representative include:

a removing the fear of learning from lower educated staff;
b promoting the benefits of learning;
c charting learning and training needs;
d providing information and advice on learning and training;
e organising and supporting learning and training.

Source: http://www.raadwerkinkomen.nl

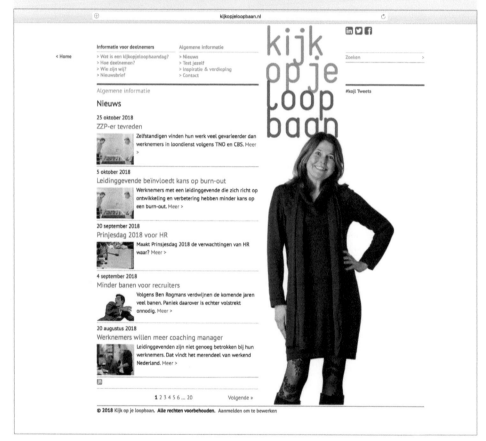

help people to develop skillsets that are important to current and future jobs. Companies should professionalise and modernise their L&D functions, and attract people with thorough expertise in this area. Unfortunately, there are still far too few people who are learning *on* the job. Therefore, organisations will need to redesign their work, and turn every working space into a learning space. Lastly, companies will also need to apply themselves to the (re)education and (re)training of groups of people on the verge of losing their job. Embracing new technologies will help enable organisations to create new jobs.

To sum up: in order to reap the benefits of automation, various stakeholders (employers, governments, and organisations) will simultaneously need to implement several actions as demonstrated in Figure 6.9. People engaging in a lifetime of learning are more successful in their work, and lead happier and more fulfilling lives. The authors of this book are optimistic about the prospects of more people adopting the lifetime of learning mind-set, and about the growing number of organisations set to implement a culture that promotes the continued thriving growth of employees.

FIGURE 6.10 **ACTIONS OF VARIOUS STAKEHOLDERS TO ACHIEVE ADVANTAGES THROUGH AUTOMATION**

Employees

Engage in a lifetime of learning

A Be aware of your employability value

B Spend 4-8 hours per week on learning something new

C Invest time and money in your own development

Governments

Retraining and reeducating are becoming the new norm

A Initiate industrial and geographical retraining schemes

B Provide financial support

C Turn participation in post-regular education into the new norm

Organisations

Embrace technology and strategic learning policies

A Adopt new technologies and create new jobs

B Turn every workplace into a place of learning, modernise the L&D function

C Invest in industrial and geographical retraining

Source: Van Dam, 2017

Summary

- Technological progress has an enormous influence on organisational success, professional qualifications, the future of work, and the importance of a lifetime of learning.

- The world is on the cusp of the Fourth Industrial Revolution (since 2012), also known as the digital revolution. There have been three industrial revolutions preceding it over the past 250 years: the First Industrial Revolution (1760-1840); the Second Industrial Revolution (1870-1914) and the Third Industrial Revolution (1960-1990).

- The life expectancy of organisations will continue to decrease.

- Robotisation and automation have an effect on virtually every job, with some jobs disappearing and others being created: new jobs that demand different knowledge and skills.

- Important new competences for the future are cognitive, social, and digital skills.

- In order to remain relevant on the labour market, employees will need to engage in a lifetime of (re)training and (re)educating.

- Organisations will need to reinforce the role of learning & development, and employees will need to develop a practice or mind-set of a lifetime of learning.

- Investments in the (sustainable) employability of employees has an enormous impact on business results.

- A 'developmentally conscious organisation' offers possibilities for the personal growth and development of all employees.

- A lifetime of learning begins and ends with the individual.

- Mind-sets for a lifetime of learning are:
  - focussing on growth;
  - striving for serial mastery;
  - stretching oneself;
  - building on one's own brand and network;
  - becoming the owner of one's own developmental journey;
  - doing what one loves doing;
  - staying vibrant.

7
HUMAN RESOURCE MANAGEMENT

Contents

After studying this chapter:

– you will have gained insight into the importance of Human Resource Management in organisations;
– you will be able to list the tools used in Human Resource Management;
– you will have been familiarised with the implementation methods of the tools used in Human Resource Management;
– you will have gained insight into the meaning and role of talent management in organisations;
– you will have been familiarised with the applications of Agile Human Resource Management.

Talmundo: onboarding app

Talmundo offers an app for introducing new colleagues to the work and workplace (*onboarding* in the parlance of the field). Everyone is familiar with those first few unfamiliar days with a new employer, not yet fully understanding company culture or company customs. This is usually not a great time for an employee, but it is not too brilliant for employers either. An unaccustomed employee is not a particularly productive one. The company wants to combine HR best practices with company culture from the moment a contract is signed until the end of the first six months on the job. People are always enthusiastic when starting a new job, and employers should use that positive energy to their advantage. The app lets new employees get acquainted with their team, sorts out any administrative hassle before the employee sets to work, and can answer questions on, for example, parking policy or dress code in advance. Managers can use the app to monitor their new team members' introduction process.

Talmundo was founded by Dutch Menno Thijssen (38) and Patrick Bouwens (39), who had been running an e-learning company before starting on Talmundo, and Belgian Stijn de Groef (39). Talmundo is a SaaS: *Software as a Service*. Clients are given access to the app in exchange for an annual licence fee, with the amount payable depending on the number of new employees introduced to a company using the software. In addition, clients pay a one-time app configuration and set-up fee, allowing for a scalable custom fit. The product has been available on the market for a few years, and includes around 100 major employing companies among its clientele, ranging from ABN-AMRO, to Lidl (the Netherlands), to Engie, and Deloitte. The team expects to triple their turnover and number of customers this year. Talmundo operates in four countries; in addition to its home countries of the Netherlands and Belgium, these are France and England.

Source: www.sprout.nl, www.talmundo.com, 2018

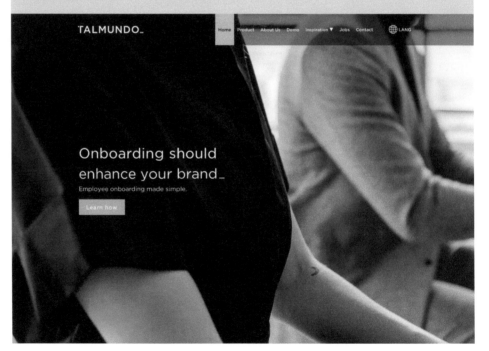

7.1 INTRODUCTION

As discussed in previous chapters, organisations are increasingly confronted with external developments taking place much more rapidly and intensely than before. These developments involve technology, globalisation, changing market circumstances, increasing competition, demographic and social-cultural aspects, new regulations and legislation, and geo-politics – highly meaningful developments for the people in an organisation, also referred to as its human resources. The 2015 Harvard Business Review article 'People Before Strategy' argues that CEOs must remain conscious of the fact that the success of an organisation depends entirely on the quality, motivation, and method with which it implements its manpower. This is emphasised in McKinsey's book (2018) *Talent Wins: The New Playbook for Putting People First*. Financial share markets also immediately tend to respond to the news of organisations recruiting or losing very good people.

Technological developments have a major influence on the amount and contents of work. As discussed in the previous chapter, many new functions will begin to emerge, and nearly everyone will need to acquire new knowledge and skills in order to remain in the game. The internet has made it increasingly easy to recruit quality personnel from all over the world to perform their work from any location. Many call centres and software development centres are located in low wage countries, like India.

Clients are becoming increasingly critical and demanding of both the quality and price of the goods and services companies offer. These changes in market circumstances are forcing organisations to change from a product-oriented approach to a market-oriented or even client-oriented one. Design Thinking is a problem-solving-oriented method applied by many organisations; it centres on the expected needs, wishes, and experience of clients who interact with organisations. As a result, organisations are implementing agile ways of organising; authority, responsibility, and decision-making are left to individual teams. Employees are thus expected to offer greater commitment as well as broader and more flexible employability.

Design Thinking

Social-cultural developments are expressed through advanced individualisation, changes in prevailing thoughts about the meaning of work, changes in the role patterns of men and women, and the presence of increasingly well-educated employees. This has consequences for work-design: part-time work, remuneration, mobility, working from home, etc., as well as for the style of management.

Lastly, there are political decisions with regard to the nature and scope of the system of social security, job protection, pension agreement, minimum wage levels, regulation and legislation for the self-employed, all influencing the scope and structure of the labour market. The Dutch Research Centre for Education and Labour Market (Researchcentrum voor Onderwijs en Arbeidsmarkt – ROA) predicts a growth in employment opportunity of an average of 1% per year until at least 2022. Employment opportunity growth will mainly centre on the care, wholesale, specialist business service, and construction industries. The quality of the recruitment is expected to continue to improve given the increasing inflow of the number of graduates from institutions for higher vocational and scientific education. Nevertheless, shortages of technicians, ICT experts, and nursing staff in particular are expected to continue to grow.

These developments are imposing new or higher demands on organisations, one of the most important of which is the demand for flexibility or agility. The most essential organisational characteristic is the fact that people work together to achieve a common goal. To that end, the production factors (labour, nature, capital, enterprise, and information) will need to be calibrated in the best possible way. This process of calibration is decided by human action – therefore, it is people who are the determining factor of organisational success.

In order for an organisation to be successful, it is essential that it creates an internal environment focussed on increasing the flexibility and mobility of its people. This hinges on the commitment and motivation of those people, and the extent to which their talents and creativity are put to (their best possible) use. Making optimum use of peoples' qualities depends on a human resource policy that is integrated with strategic management, thus creating a close relationship between the organisation's alignment to its environment and the appropriate HR policy. The managerial approach aimed at an integrated approach to strategic management and people's qualities in an organisation is known as Human Resource Management (HRM).

This term, first used in 1984, refers to the publication of books including *Strategic Human Resource Management* and *Managing Human Assets* by Harvard professor Michael Beer.

HRM is defined as: the overall norms and values related to humans at work, and the translation of those norms and values into fundamental approaches, techniques, and methods aimed at utilising people's qualities in the context of intended organisational objectives.

Important aspects of Human Resource Management are:

a top-level management recognising the importance of the human factor;
b an HRM policy in line with the organisation's strategic planning;
c the idea that people do not comprise a cost but a benefit;
d the conviction that people's quality can be put to better use;
e the conviction that realising organisational strategy hinges on its relationship to people's qualities and motivations;
f the need for the professional and planned implementation of systems and instruments, aimed at utilising people's qualities in the context of realising organisational objectives.

Human Resources philosophy has experienced tremendous development over the past century. Initially, the idea was to implement people in such a way as to maximise efficiency. Nowadays, the goal of HR is to implement people sustainably. According to Belgian professor Peggy de Prins, sustainable HRM draws its inspiration from corporate social responsibility. There is a so-called Triple REC at the heart of sustainable HRM: R for Respect, E for Environmental awareness, and C for Continuity.

TABLE 7.1 **THE EVOLUTION IN THE APPROACH TO HUMAN RESOURCES IN ORGANISATIONS**

	Scientific management	Human relations	Revisionism	Strategic HRM	Revisionism bis: sustainable HRM
Period	c. 1918-1945	c. 1945-1965	c. 1965-1980	c. 1980-now	c. 2010-?
Focus	Far-reaching division of labour and rationalisation	Social function of work, social fabric of organisations	Employee participation and commitment	Strategic alignment/ managerial orientation	Outside approach stakeholder orientation
Component	Efficiency	Collaboration	Autonomy	Performance	Sustainability

Source: *Handboek Leren en Ontwikkelen in Organisaties* (2018), Mooiman, Rijken en Van Dam.

HR functions in an organisation comprise the following instruments: recruitment, career development, learning and development, assessment, and offboarding of employees.

A characteristic of Human Resource Management is that these personnel instruments are integrated with an organisation's strategic management. As a consequence, the responsibility for strategic HR rests with the organisation's top-level managerial layer. The direct managers of employees are responsible for the implementation of this policy – it is their task to encourage and coach employees and help them to maximise their development. Assessing employees, compiling training plans, and coaching employees through periods of illness are tasks explicitly assigned to management. The HR department's role is mainly one of supporting and consulting on policy. The relationship between the HRM instruments is shown in Figure 7.2.

Personnel instruments

FIGURE 7.2 **THE HRM TOOLS**

This chapter pays attention to the following Human Resource Management instruments:

a recruitment (section 7.2);
b career development (section 7.3);
c learning and development (section 7.4);
d assessment (section 7.5);
e reward (section 7.6);
f offboarding (section 7.7);
g talent management (section 7.8).

The chapter concludes with a reflection on Agile Human Resource Management (7.9).

Growing a better world together

Janine Vos is chief human resources for Rabobank as well as a member of the Rabobank's board of directors. She is coaching the organisation through a process of downsizing that means the end of 12,000 jobs.
Janine Vos: 'I joined Rabobank just as it had begun the implementation of the largest reorganisation in its history. People feel married to the bank, experience a connection to its notion of cooperation, are loyal. To many, the process is like a divorce. The world is no longer what it was, you have to make a decision that will ensure the bank remains healthy. Change needs to happen faster than light, these days; client behaviours change, technology is turning our business model on its head.

All you can do is be careful with your people. You need to have a good social plan, offer guidance, also in terms of training. Around 80% of the available attention is on people leaving. But we also need to look at those staying with us. We have allocated an additional training

budget, for example. The three crucial factors are professionalism, vitality, and capacity for change.
We find ourselves in the middle of a period of major digital transformation. A transformation is effected through contributing individuals; not through a top-down message saying the collective needs to get to it. The issue is not one of knowledge being power; the issue is one of collaboration, of coaching, of self-managing. The hierarchical relationships will change even more extensively over the coming years, in the direction of human-to-human. It used to be the case that management decided who was or was not talented. Now, the principle is: if you think you are talented, sign up. Particularly those with a developed sense of professionalism, vitality, and capacity for change – the people with a lot of energy; they are what you want.

With respect to digital transformation, I feel human behaviour and culture are the key to success. The people

in an organisation truly matter: happy people, happy customers. The employee's personal touch is becoming increasingly important. Digital issues lend themselves to the application of robotics, but in the case of major life events, it feels better to have another person offer you their advice; a person who sees and recognises you for who you are.'

Source: *Management Team*, March 2018, Main interview

7.2 RECRUITMENT

The quality of an organisation is largely determined by the quality of the people it employs. Because functions change rapidly over time, organisations are now increasingly prone to selecting their people based on a broad range of competences and career paths, instead of for highly specialised functions. Therefore, it should not come as a surprise that, for many organisations, the recruitment and selection of staff is a professional process that takes place along carefully established procedures. A well-designed recruitment and selection procedure has major benefits for both the organisation in question and for applicants subjected to that recruitment and selection procedure. The organisation benefits from the possibility to get the right people for the right jobs; the applicant benefits from the possibility to properly establish whether or not they would want to work for a particular organisation and/or in a particular function. The advantage of taking part in many conversations with various employees, at the same time, is

Onboarding

'good' onboarding' should the applicant end up working for the organisation. Initially, the organisation should determine whether the purpose of the selection process is to look for potential candidates inside or outside of the organisation. Many organisations apply a policy of first implementing an internal procedure, with vacancies placed on an internal vacancy site, or people actively approached by HR for a possible new role. The benefit of using an internal recruitment procedure is that employees are offered an opportunity to improve their career development, possibly leading to promotion.

If there is no internal possibility of filling the vacancy, the next step is to trigger an external procedure. External recruitment agencies, also known as (executive) search firms, take up an important role in the recruitment and selection of personnel. Recruiting and selecting the right people is seen as an activity that requires specialists (recruiters), because an organisation's expertise in this field is often limited. Important recruiter competences are:

Recruiters

a knowledge of a number of business disciplines, such as marketing, sales, ICT, etc.;
b thorough knowledge of the organisation and its culture;
c the ability to comprehend and communicate to organisational management at the strategic level;
d the analytical skills needed to, for example, analyse data generated by recruitment systems;
e the ability to ascertain a candidate's competences;
f the ability to listen: describing the applicant profile required, as well as verifying whether potential candidates meet this profile.

It is also possible for employees to approach recruitment agencies, for example when looking for a new job.
Once the recruitment period is over, the next step is to implement the selection process. The objective of selection is to ensure the correct alignment between applicant, function, and organisation. This alignment presupposes that the demands imposed on the applicant from the perspective of both function and organisation are known.

The procedure is completed through the appointment of an application, which includes resolving the following issues:

a employment conditions: wages, holiday pay, bonuses, travel expenses, pension, etc.;
b date of hire;
c terms of notice;
d function description;
e work location;
f trial/contract period;
g competition/confidentiality clause (where applicable);
h emoluments, such as reimbursement of study costs or use of smartphone (where applicable).

Once a candidate has been contractually hired, it is important to pay attention to their onboarding. This process is essential: the sooner a new employee is up to speed, the greater their satisfaction, motivation, and contribution to the organisation. A study by Google shows that it is very important for new employees to create a supporting network and take part in regular evaluations. In principle, onboarding should comprise 5 Cs:

1 **Compliance**: what are the basic rules everyone needs to follow? These rules are both legislative and organisational, and refer to safety and confidentiality, behavioural conduct, anti-bullying policy, reporting absenteeism, etc.
2 **Clarification**: What will be the new employee's role? How should they be expected to perform/contribute? What are their personal targets? What should be expected from the organisation?
3 **Culture**: New employees should be immersed in the organisation's culture from day one. Everyone should be familiar with the organisation's mission, vision, and values.

4 **Connection**: Every organisation has its groups, sub-groups, and networks. It is important for new employees to recognise and understand the organisation's social structure. Organisation also often implement a 'buddy-system', with a new employee being assigned a more senior colleague as a go-to.

5 **Check back**: Request a response following the onboarding period. It is important for supervisors to check back with their new employees regularly. It is a known fact that particularly Millennials and the new Generation Z thrive on daily feedback with regards to their performance and points for improvement.

Many organisations use formal teaching programmes as part of, of example, a '6-month onboarding journey', during which they discuss the aforementioned topics. The smaller the organisation, the more restricted the degree of professionalism in the onboarding process tends to be.

Technology is playing an increasingly important role in the recruitment and selection of candidates; consider technology used to automate the selection or candidate screening process, the use of chat boxes for answering applicants'

O&M IN PRACTICE

Proving yourself to a robot

More and more employees have become sold on the idea of digitising their personnel selection process. The benefits are better candidates, and a lot of time and money saved. And the automated assessment of CVs is also said to improve diversity. Robotics and algorithms continue to reduce the load for the personnel department. The first selection of applications in particular is experiencing a huge rise in the use of digital technology and artificial intelligence. Candidates are initially assessed by a machine, and not by a person.

Call centres, department stores, Unilever: all are making use of digital technology at a massive scale. The use of 'serious' gaming and digital interviews has become prevalent. Unilever uses a balloon game for the selection of management trainees: blow up a balloon as large as possible without causing it to explode. This game is said to offer a good insight into a person's preparedness to take risks. In another example, questions answered via smartphone are subjected to a facial expression and speech pattern analysis. The CV has become more or less irrelevant for trainees. Unilever expects that 80% of staff selection will eventually be digital.

The ancient principle of the human element of the application interview, however, will not be removed altogether. The data gathered throughout the preliminary process is, in fact, used as the basis for an interview with an improved focus on both the person and the job. Data, therefore, is a holy grail – certainly in a world where the war for talent is waged at the international level. The advantage of artificial intelligence is a degree of objectivity, claim employers. The aim is to have the workfloor reflect society. Staff diversity is improved by, for example, having a system in place that does not look for foreign (board) experience.

Source: *Het Financieele Dagblad, Transformers* edition 2018

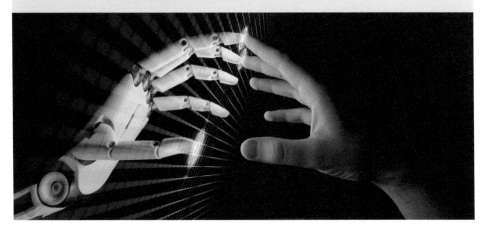

People and organisations
PART B

questions, software that automatically schedules and books appointments, and games used to assess people's (levels of) competence.

7.3   CAREER DEVELOPMENT

Maintaining organisational flexibility demands employee mobility. Remaining entrenched in a certain function for years on end is therefore neither desirable nor frequently possible because of the many changes organisations are faced with. A study by BCG (2018) shows that most people retain the same function for an average of slightly under 5 years. For millennials, the average is 3 years. It is with this information in mind that new employees are often no longer recruited with a specific job but a career in mind. This serves to indicate that employees must have the potential for performing in various future functions. A career is comprised of a number of (horizontal and/or vertical) movements within an organisation over the duration of an employee's working life. In recent times, a great deal of attention has been paid to career sustainability, burn-outs, the balance between personal-professional, post-retirement age careers, and employability. There is a distinction between individual career development and organisational career development. Individual career development deals with activities developed by employees themselves as a way of furthering their career in the direction of a desirable target (Sturges et al., 2010). Organisational career development refers to the activities and practices implemented by an organisation to help support, facilitate, and develop employee careers (Baruch & Peiperl, 2000).

The traditional view of career development is of climbing one's way to a function   *Career development* at the top of a pyramid. A frequently heard metaphor is of a race up a mountain, with winners (those who reach the summit) and losers (who get stuck or forfeit the race along the way). Modern-day career development has to do with employees performing a number of roles that allows them the opportunity to personal growth and development. Many roles are horizontal instead of vertical.

Career development is an important component of Human Resource Management; it is an interplay between manager, supervisor, and employee.

An important HR-task is to clearly communicate the importance of career management.

Defining a proper career development policy requires an organisation to have a good and reliable assessment system. A balanced assessment system is needed to properly assess the capabilities of employees, which is of paramount importance. The lack of a reliable assessment systems presents the organisation with a risk of assigning employees to the wrong functions, or reassigning them at the wrong times: situations best avoided for the sake of the organisation and the employee alike. Furthermore, a balanced assessment system offers employees an insight into their own performance and the resulting possibilities, both inside and outside of the organisation. From the perspective of career development, an organisation can also support employees in their strive for further development by offering some degree of coaching or training. Human Resource policy with regard to career development is inspired by the answers to the following questions:

1 What is the organisation's vision on Human Resource career development? (Who is responsible for what; to what extent is the organisation willing and able to offer support?)
2 What are the organisation's needs in terms of personnel for the coming years?
3 What are individual employees' ideas about their own career development?

In order to answer the second question, the organisation needs to have insight into its near-future development. Only then can the question of the expected needs in terms of personnel be answered. HR can use a number of tools to improve employee development:

a **Mentoring**: employees who are mentored are more committed to both the organisation and career.

b **Career counselling**: Many people need a sounding board where career development is concerned. This is where HR or an external agency can lend a hand.

c **Assessment centre**: A method that is used by a quarter of Dutch institutions to assess employees' capabilities relevant to career development.

d **Self-study**: Workshops or methods used to help people detail their career (plans). The book 'Designing Your Life' by Stanford's Bill Burnett and Dave Evans offers an innovative and scientifically inspired method to help people share their lives and careers.

O&M IN PRACTICE

Vitality and Sustainable Employability at DHL

Starting 1 January 2016, every DHL employee has been assigned a personal budget assigned for their development (including studies, workshops, courses, career advice, external coaching) and/or vitality (including life style advice, healthcare costs like physiotherapy). Employees are free to choose how to allocate their budget as long as it contributes to their development and/or vitality. Starting 1 January 2016, the right to supplementary vacation days is lowered by one day in order to finance this personal Vitality and Sustainable Employability budget. The budget is financed annually as follows: Employees trade in one vacation day, the value of which is matched by the employer. The budget thus created can be spent to improve one's vitality or sustainable employability. Any expenditure above the budget created as a result can be financed from the collective labour agreement's á la carte-budget. If, during any consecutive 3-year period (starting 1 January 2016), at least one vitality or sustainable employability-related cost is financed using the created budget, the employee is awarded three days off as a reward for their commitment to sustainable employability. These three days off are awarded only once per 3-year period. After three years, any remaining budget or bonus days off will expire.

Source: SER, 2017: *Leren en ontwikkelen tijdens de loopbaan een advies over postinitieel leren.*

Career policy and salary structure

In practice, promoting an employee means assigning higher wages. With regard to wage sums, there may be substantial differences between organisations. On the one hand are the organisations with a flat salary structure; on the other are the organisations with a steep salary structure.

Salary structure

Organisations with a flat salary structure are characterised by only minor differences between the salaries of the various organisational functions. Organisations with a steep salary structure apply substantial differences between the salaries of the various ranks. It is important to consider the relationship between the policy of promotion and the salary structure in an organisation.

Why sustainable employability matters

Professor of Strategic Human Resource Management Judith Semeijn studies career sustainability.
Semeijn: 'Our children are on the brink of choosing their next level of education and we are almost certain that they will find their employment in functions that do not yet exist. Over the course of our careers, we will need to choose between difference (career) paths, and we will need to keep learning. Development is not a finite process; the development of the individual should go hand in hand with the development of the organisation.
Managers are an important link between individuals and organisations. It is within their possibilities to coach the process surrounding sustainable employability, for example using experienced career professionals.
Self-management matters to employees. In the end, the only person responsible for your employability is you.

The self-employed cannot rely on an organisation to help them develop. What do you want to achieve? What do your motivation and talents allow you to do? You will need to organise this for yourself.
A career-oriented mind-set and a focus on development should not, however, be introduced at the start of your professional career; they should be taught as early as primary school. Continuing to teach children that other people dictate what you can learn will never let them have success. Traditional education cannot adequately provide for a changing world. Sustainable employability has to start at the basis, with our children.'

Source: TVOO, 09-2018

O&M IN PRACTICE

A steep salary structure usually means that a promotion comes with an inherent risk to the employee. If they fail to perform in their new function, they can expect to be shown the door. This is offset, however, by a substantial improvement in terms of salary. The atmosphere of such organisations is generally characterised by fierce competition. Every employee knows they need to fully realise their potential. The employees concerned tend to be dominated by an ambitious or competitive streak. A flat salary structure usually means that promotion comes with an inherent risk to the organisation instead. The risk to the employee is reduced, resulting in a less steep salary improvement. In other words: the function, and thus indirectly the organisation, is adapted to the new situation. Such organisations often apply a strict policy with regard to internal promotion. At the foreground is the promotion based on employee seniority or age. It is commonplace for decision-making in this situation to take place in committees; higher ranks are dominated by a cooperative spirit. Studies also show that profitability is highest among organisations with a steep salary structure.

7.4   LEARNING AND DEVELOPMENT

Learning and Development (L&D) is an important instrument for Human Resources. In many organisations, the role of L&D has become more important because shareholders are increasingly reviewing the role of a knowledge organisation's intangible assets when assessing its value. According to *Forrester Research*, 85% of the market value of a typical Standard & Poor 500-company stems from its intangible assets. And the bulk of these immaterial assets is people: a company's human capital. Investments in L&D earn results. Consider the value of investing in leadership capabilities; a subject sometimes met with scorn. Studies show that organisations are greatly rewarded for showing good leadership; the companies who scored in the top quarter for leadership qualities scored twice as highly as other companies in terms of their EBITDA (a company's earnings before interest, taxes, depreciation, and amortisation) (De Smet et al., 2014). Organisations investing in the development of their leaders during important changes are 2.4 times more likely to achieve their targets.

As shown in Figure 7.3, organisations invest in L&D for various reasons. The first is because people tend to favour organisations that help them to grow and develop, as market-valuable competence is the new currency. Since there is a shortage of talent in various areas of competence, L&D contributes to both organisational appeal and employee retention. L&D also reinforces the *employee value proposition* (EVP), allowing the organisation to become a sought-after employer.

The second reason for companies to invest in L&D is that issues such as the rise of digital technology, innovation, the reduced lifespan of knowledge, new business models, globalisation, an aging professional population, new legislation, and changes in labour potential to name just a few are having an enormous impact on the need for the development of skills at the same pace as the speed of all of those developments. This is discussed in detail in Chapter 6. Human capital is an essential production factor that requires continuous investments in L&D in order to retain its value. This value of human capital can be determined using the following formula:

The value of human capital = (the sum of one's) education +
collected work experience

FIGURE 7.3 **THE STRATEGIC ROLE OF LEARNING & DEVELOPMENT**

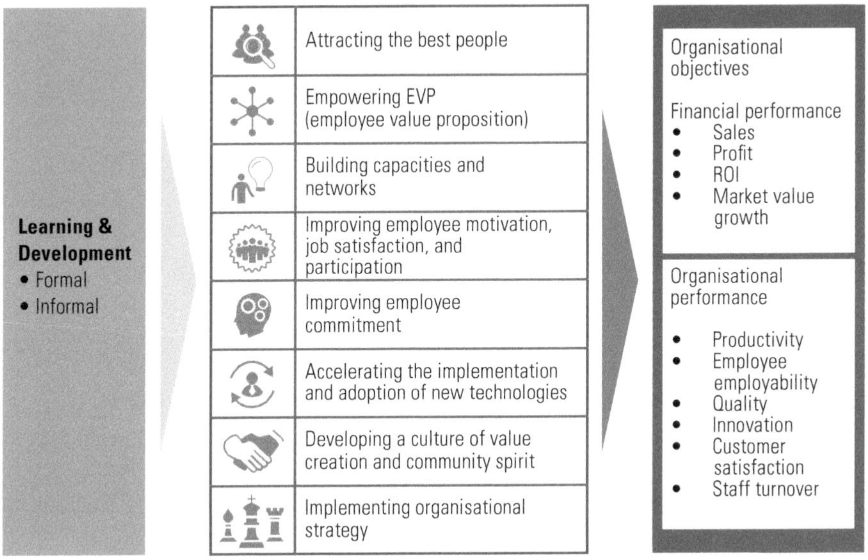

Learning & Development		Attracting the best people	Organisational objectives
• Formal		Empowering EVP (employee value proposition)	Financial performance
• Informal		Building capacities and networks	• Sales
		Improving employee motivation, job satisfaction, and participation	• Profit
		Improving employee commitment	• ROI
		Accelerating the implementation and adoption of new technologies	• Market value growth
		Developing a culture of value creation and community spirit	Organisational performance
		Implementing organisational strategy	• Productivity • Employee employability • Quality • Innovation • Customer satisfaction • Staff turnover

Source: *Learn or Lose*, Nick van Dam (2016)

The value of human capital *increases* by having people with a finished education build up work experience. The value *decreases* because knowledge is quickly dated and forgotten, and because it needs to be supplemented using new learning and work experience.

Thirdly, L&D can improve motivation, job satisfaction, and employee commitment. It is a widely recognised fact that the best way of ensuring employee commitment is by offering employees the possibility to learn and develop new competences. Studies show that a highly motivated and committed workforce is of great value for the rapid and successful implementation of new technologies and other innovative work methods. Once can add to this the fact that committed employees tend to stick around longer with organisations that offer them a challenge, and where they can acquire the skills needed to grow and develop over the course of their career.

A fourth reason for organisations to invest in L&D is that it can help them to construct a value-creation-based culture and community, now that many companies have increased their extent of virtual working and globalisation. There are indications that millennials in particular are keen to work in this type of culture, as well as in a sustainable organisation that contributes to society. They also have a need for respect for the talents of the individual, as well as for open communication with management. Their private lives matter as much to them as a challenging work environment.

Lastly, and most importantly: companies can use training programmes to support the implementation of their business strategy. The classical view of learning is that training programmes should focus exclusively on improving *productivity*. Today, the view is that learning also adds to people's employability. Good employability means that a person can easily find a new job inside or outside of their organisation. An extensive study of relevant literature shows that highly skilled or professionally capable employees can have a positive impact on an organisation's financial and organisational performance by positively affecting customer satisfaction, profit, market growth, and innovation.

7.4.1   An L&D function for the 21st century

Companies like General Motors and General Electric began offering employees the possibility of taking part in in-house training programmes a century ago. These days, thousands of organisations all over the world host their own *corporate academies* or *universities*. These 'organisational' universities constitute 'specialised business components or initiatives whose goal is to develop and maintain institutional and individual capabilities used to align performance to organisational strategy'. Companies like Apple, Disney, Danone, Nike, Deloitte, McDonalds, Philips, McKinsey & Company and Vanguard have all founded such universities, which play an important role in developing a culture of learning.

Various studies confirm that the development of employee capabilities is a high priority for many organisations the world over. Globally, 8 in 10 employers consider learning to be an important or extremely important theme. Senior executives are reporting that their organisations are not developing skills quickly enough, or that their organisations are not maximising the development of leadership. It should, therefore, not come as a surprise that 60% of companies are looking to increase their L&D-expenditure, and that more than 66% of companies are looking to increase their formal number of training hours.

Additionally, many organisations are dissatisfied with their current L&D functions (Benson-Armer et al., 2016). They are therefore expecting their L&D functions to change drastically over the coming years, adding new L&D functions that will demand new qualities and a more rapidly paced and effective work trend to keep up with such a high-speed business life. The most important areas of attention in this respect are: aligning educational priorities to business, determining skill gaps among employees, improving the effectiveness of existing training initiatives, increasing the use of digital education solutions and learning platforms, improving insight into the impact of educational programmes, offering *blended learning* (a mixture of online and face-to-face instruction), integrating working and learning, and personalising and customising learning & development. Companies that take the modernisation of their efforts in the field of skill development seriously should attract people reflecting that attitude, and ensure they hire people whose experience in this area is thorough.

7.4.2   Learning programme quality

Training and education involves substantial investment, particularly considering the costs of employee absenteeism. One could therefore wonder whether there is a maximum threshold for worthwhile expenditure where training is concerned. In order to answer this question, the first step is to list a number of objectives that are generally offered as the reasons for employees participating in training. Possible motives are:

a reducing a knowledge gap;
b re-schooling or re-training due to changing job requirements;
c increasing their commitment to the organisation;
d being offered training as part of a remuneration policy;
e improving employee motivation.

In general, the first two aspects are the most successful in the assessment of a training. The extent to which training is considered to be successful depends on the extent to which the knowledge and/or skills that have been acquires are applicable to the employee's work situation. In practice, this applicability is disappointing, because many trainings tie in with neither the employee's function requirements nor the organisations working methods: an important motivator behind the market's increasing need for function and company-oriented training. Another tendency is that taking part in training is no longer the open-ended activity it used to be. Many companies expect employees to undergo an assessment of their newfound knowledge and insights after they have completed a training course.

Permission to take part in training is often made contingent on a need for training or a requirement for acquiring knowledge and skills. The concept of the need for training generally includes training that is not directly related to performing in the employee's current function, but which does complement their development and anticipates on a possible future function. This is different from a training requirement, where direct functioning is the reason for taking part in training. For example, a conflict management course could be considered a training need for a member of sales staff; for a sales manager, on the other hand, it would be a training requirement. The Human Resource Management-approach places the responsibility for the proper development and training of employees squarely with the direct line manager. Naturally, however, employees are also expected to indicate their own ambitions and the effects of those ambitions on their desired (re)training.

In practice, the quality of a training is difficult to measure, as the concept of quality is defined in different ways: the participant's experience (training as an event), the participant's manager (the outcome for the work situation) and the trainer (contents and tools used).

The quality of a training must therefore be considered from various perspectives, all of which should be evaluated – since this is the only way of making a nuanced assessment of its quality – before answering the question of whether it was money well spent.

Every place of work as a place of learning

O&M IN PRACTICE

A lifetime of learning as the new social security: that is the vision held by Nick van Dam, Professor of Corporate Learning & Development at Nyenrode and IE University. Continued learning is seen as more and more of a necessity in order to stay employable in a world of rapidly changing organisations and a severely dynamic labour market.

In order to remain 'in shape' for the future, employees will need to actively invest time in their continued learning, development, and follow-up – both in their current role and any potential future one. Among other things, this means that one's work should be designed in such a way as to offer a new learning experience every day, thus transforming a place of work into a place of learning. This development implies an employee mind-set focussed on a lifetime of learning, and also demands that employee regularly step out of their 'comfort zone' as well as develop a personal 'brand' and network.

The role of the employer is also crucial in this process; employers can prepare and support employees along their (changes in) career, and help them to get ready for a next big step.

The HR&Development department used to focus on formal learning, which makes up only a fraction of an employee's total working hours. It is more meaningful to assess the actual work: could it be redesigned to make it more of a learning experience, or to design it to enable people to learn from each other and from themselves while working? It is important for HR&D to engage with employees about their working lives: what do they want to achieve, what personal identity do they want to develop through their work? This calls on an active approach to HR&D.

Source: *PW.magazine*, issue 10, 2017

7.5 ASSESSMENT

Assessment

Assessment is the valuation of an employee's functioning over a certain period. This valuation can be expressed as a numeral value (for example 1-5) or through some other means of qualification (for example: excellent, very good, good, sufficient, or insufficient). An assessment may be supported by the use of measuring instruments, such as 360 feedback tools, interviews and/or feedback forms.

The assessment of employees in their organisational functioning is a daily occurrence. Assessments are used to answer the question of whether someone is eligible for promotion, a salary increase, a fixed contract, or a dismissal.

In addition, an assessment offers an employee an insight into their own functioning. Assessments offer guidelines in terms of focal issues, demonstrate strengths and weaknesses with regard to functioning, and serve to indicate the direction for improvement or development. This approach to assessment dictates that it demonstrates the organisation's commitment to the functioning of an individual.

Broadly speaking, assessments deal with discussing, interpreting, and evaluating the performance of whomever is being assessed. Naturally, assessments must be completed using the highest possible level of objectivity. In order to help realise this level of objectivity, an assessment system must fulfil three criteria:

1 **Fair**: an assessment needs to be substantiated, and there has to be a possibility for appeal.
2 **Uniform**: an assessment should rely on assessment criteria, assessment forms, and assessment procedures; whomever is being assessed should be notified of the contents of these components.
3 **Diligent**: an assessment system must include a control for completeness and accuracy of an assessment.

Assessment interview

A standard component of any assessment system is the assessment interview, where one or more assessors clarify their assessment. The interview should also pay attention to encouragements or possibilities for the assessed to improve their performance in future.

Performance review

Lastly, an assessment interview should not be confused with a performance review. In contrast to an assessment interview, a performance or coaching review is not based on hierarchy but on equality. The goal of the performance review is to discuss the perceived functioning and to arrive at agreements for the near future; therefore, the term coaching review may be more appropriate. A frequently found practice among organisations is to first conduct a number of performance reviews before engaging in a final assessment. A study by Raet (2015) shows that over a quarter (27%) of people feel that assessments do not contribute to their personal development, and that they would therefore rather avoid them. According to 24% of Dutch employees, the performance review is also on its last legs. These percentages are similar across the various generations. In his 2017 book *Het nieuwe beoordelen* (The new style of assessment), author Jacco van der Berg describes four basic principles for a new method of employee assessment:

1 **Focus on talent**: see what people are good at and help them to make even better use of their talents in a suitable role.
2 **Ask for feedback**: much of what an employee does lies outside their supervisor's view. It is important that supervisors obtain information from people that *do* see everything an employee does, such as a project leader, a customer, or a colleague.

3 **Engage in continued dialogue**: short updates should be asked for regularly (weekly if possible) instead of once or twice per year. After all, top athletes also receive daily coaching in terms of how to improve their performance.
4 **Offer enabling management**: managers should create a climate that allows employees to maximise their development to achieve success.

Assessment reviews need a radical change

O&M IN PRACTICE

The annual assessment review is a frustrating ritual for manager and employee alike – and one that has barely any positive influence on performance or motivation at that. It needs updating. A single review once a year, with so much depending on it. Year-round evaluations of possible outdated targets. And moreover, an interview is by definition a snapshot.

Organisations with excellent teams work on continuous coaching. Team members are kept abreast of their performance and their potential for improvement year round, with neither assessment scales nor forms. The result: improved performance and a reduced risk of stress or burnout. Focussing on continued employee development through brief meaningful conversations and an open dialogue about performance and development is a better way. Supervisors are not always the right people to ask for feedback regarding employee performance: let employees obtain their own feedback from colleagues, thus placing more responsibility on employees' shoulders. Bottom-up instead of top-down. Moreover, most experts agree that positive feedback beats negative feedback in terms of effectiveness. It has also been shown that developing one's strengths leads to improved performance, innovation, and collaboration more effectively than improving one's weaknesses. The experts are fully agreed: we should go back to real discussions, and tell our colleagues sincerely how we feel.

Source: *Management Team*, March 2018

7.6 REWARD

Reward is defined as all tangibles and intangibles that direct employee behaviour and contribute to their performance. Examples are wages, training opportunities, vacation time, other secondary benefits (such as laptops, smartphones, etc.) as well as work autonomy or working from home.

Performance Reward

The relationship between performance and reward is an important one. It should not be one-sided; performance and reward should definitely be characterised by interaction. The issue is: which elements of one's performance are identifiable in one's reward? In practice, this relationship takes the form of many different reward systems. On the one hand are reward systems that establish a monetary stimulus as the basis for the relationship between performance and reward; on the other are those systems that include other elements in the relationship (such as responsibility and collaboration).

The differences between reward systems boil down to different human dimensions on the one hand, and different philosophies regarding production regulation and organisational maintenance on the other. In order to better structure the resulting issues, it is helpful to consider the two basic factors that influence rewards:

1 one's work (the function);
2 one's implementation of one's work (the performance);

The first issue is one of job rating, the second of reward determination.

7.6.1 Job rating

Job rating deals with establishing justifiable wage ratios, which requires the analysis, description, and grading of the functions in an organisation. The resulting methodology provides a more objective form of wage determination (a job rating system). In addition to systematic determination and justification of wage ratios, job rating can also be applied to personnel assessments, career planning, recruitment and selection and organisation (re)structuring. The basic principle

Job rating system

of a job rating system is the way the organisation and its functions ought to be designed given its relevant organisational objectives. The organisational objectives and derived objectives (such as industrial or departmental objectives) are the framework used to define the functions. Moreover, the job rating system should be inherently flexible enough to enable any adjustments demanded by the market or market environment. Therefore, an organisation must ensure that its system is kept fully up to date.

In practice, a versatile set of instruments for job rating methods has been developed. Four of these are discussed below.

1 **Ranking method.** This method distinguishes between a number of main functions, whose salary is established. Other functions are subsequently ranked and valued using the values of the main functions. In essence, the functions are compared and weighed using the main functions, and then assigned a rank.

2 **Factor comparison method.** This method describes a number of key functions that are assigned wages which are considered acceptable compared to similar functions in other organisations. The frame of reference of this method is therefore not a strictly internal affair, but partly shaped by external organisation. The selected key functions are described in terms of job content. Other functions in the organisation are subsequently compared and integrated using these descriptions.

3 **Classification method.** Here, the basis for the determination of wages is the description of so-called job categories. The various categories are grouped around standard functions whose salaries are established. The standard functions can be oriented both internally and externally. Subsequently, the other functions are also compared to these standard functions and assigned to one of the established job categories.

4 **Points method.** Every function in the system that requires a new value is, as it were, decomposed into its constituent factors, and each factor is valued individually.

TABLE 7.4 **POINTS METHOD EXAMPLE**

Factor	Grade	Weighting factor	Points
1 Knowledge	3	4	12
2 Conduct	6	7	42
3 Authority	5	8	40
Total points			94

Some advantages of job rating:

a It systematically pays attention to all functions. This helps uncover (unknown) errors in function descriptions and job ratings. The recommended course of action is to regularly compare the functions in departments internally, as well as comparing departments to others.

b A systematic approach makes the mutual discussion and comparison of functions less of a hurdle.

c The results of job rating can be applied to rewards as well as other goals, such as assessment, recruitment, and selection.

Some disadvantages of job rating:

a Functionaries who are too rigid about job descriptions spread that rigidity throughout the organisation. Therefore, the wisest course of action is to design the system to be as flexible as possible.

b The introduction of this type of system can cause unrest among staff.

c The intended and expected justifiable rewards fail to deliver in practice, as no existing excessive rewards can easily be retracted.

d Designing and implementing a job rating system tends to take up a lot of time and money. Organisational structures and functions tend to change rapidly; as a result, job ratings sometimes quickly go out of date. An example is the automation industry, where the contents of functions continually change as a result of new technological development, thus imposing new demands on employees. The existing job rating system will no longer be aligned to the newly created function contents.

7.6.2 Reward determination

Determining a reward is possible using one of the following methods:

1 **Market value method.** Here, the reward is based on an external factor; specifically, what the person concerned might earn externally. This situation is one where there is no wage policy: there is barely any relationship between various wages. This method is nevertheless a popular one with small and medium organisations. Rewards can usually be compared to those of other employees or employee organisations.

2 **Systematic method.** In addition to market value, this method also looks for a certain systematic relationship between employee rewards. The goal of this method is to create a systematic wage structure for the entire staff, with differences in reward levels being logical and effective. A reward level is logical and effective if rewards are competitive on the one hand, and internally acceptable on the other. Large organisations in particular design their reward policy around the guidelines of a systematic method.

The creation of the European Union gave rise to interesting issues related to reward policy – a development that could result in important changes in the fields of reward and labour conditions for the coming years. The issues in this regard are twofold: first, there is the question of whether employees might not move to companies across the border if the reward structure elsewhere is more favourable. Second, there is the fact that, in the near future, there is an expected deficit in the labour market for staff in a number of specific functions.

In order to be able to sign up and retain the right people in the right positions, companies should expect to have to deal with a development along two dimensions:

1 **Results-orientation: performance-based and variable reward.** Performance-based reward is any reward that depends on an employee's functioning. The reward in question is generally an addition to base wages. Variable rewards may also become an extension of individual functioning. Rewards can also depend on the performance of the organisation as a whole, usually in the form of a particular allocation of reward components, meaning little to no change in costs for employers.

2 **Flexibilisation of labour conditions.** A number of organisations uses the collective agreement as the basis for an agreement that is completed at the individual level. Most collective agreements already cover various options with regard to individual choice, such as bicycle facilitation schemes, health insurance schemes, saving schemes, additional days off, and pension schemes. In general, reward packages are judged to be fairer and more meaningful, as there is greater room for choice and insight into possible options. The absolute sum is generally not the most important reward assessment criterion for employees; a reward's relative value tends to be more important. Employees are curious about the position of their own rewards in relation to those of other employees.

One of the most frequently discussed differences between men and women on the job market is the wage gap. In the Netherlands, this gap is on average 5% (2016); in the United Kingdom, however, the figure is 22%, and even 25% in Germany. The Dutch Minister for Education, Culture, Science, and Emancipation aims to reduce the differences between the wages for working men and women. The number of self-employed in the Netherlands doubled between 2007-2017; the current figure is over 1 million. This is a group that needs to establish their

Market value method

Systematic method

Performance-based reward

Variable rewards

Collective agreement

own rates (and, by extension, rewards). The amount of money a self-employed individual charges depends on a number of factors, including the market value of the provided services (based on one's education, experience, and specialism), the ratio between the need for and scarcity of the provided services, and, lastly, the industry in which the work takes place. An indicative hourly rate for an IT consultant averages at €90; for an accountant, this figure is €55. Figure 7.5 indicates the average annual income of self-employed individuals by industry.

FIGURE 7.5 **AVERAGE INCOME OF THE SELF-EMPLOYED PER INDUSTRY**

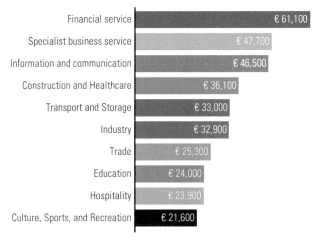

Source: FD. Weekend, 23 June 2018

Lastly, there is a misconception that the worse the economy, the more companies make use of self-employed individuals. This is incorrect. It is not so much self-employed numbers as it is self-employed income that is susceptible to economic changes.

Reasons for self-employment

FIGURE **SELF-EMPLOYED**

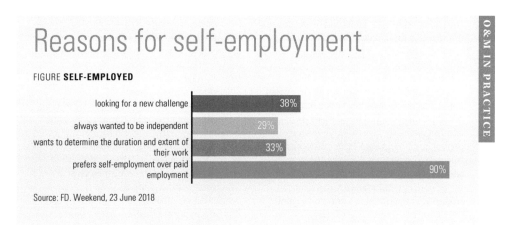

Source: FD. Weekend, 23 June 2018

O&M IN PRACTICE

7.7 OFFBOARDING

Following the discussion of the recruitment and throughput of employees over the previous paragraphs, the current section focusses on support during the offboarding. Employees may leave an organisation for one of various reasons, including:

Offboarding

a reaching retirement age;
b the ending of a (temporary) contract;

c termination of employment due to long-term illness;

d labour conflict;

e finding employment elsewhere.

There are other reasons for employees to (either forcibly or voluntarily) leave an organisation (such as the implementation of automation, resulting in overstaffing). This has financial and social consequences for both employer and employee. The employee may be faced with a decrease in income or a drop in social status. For employers, the dismissal of personnel may be subject to an inherent stigma or to decrease in turnover.

Outplacement Outplacement is a tool that can be helpful in many circumstances. Outplacement is defined as a planned coaching process for forcibly dismissed or voluntarily resigning employees to help them find new, suitable employment or other future orientation in a way that is considered responsible for employees and organisations alike. This description implies that outplacement may refer both to individuals and to groups of employees. In outplacement, employees are counselled by professional consultants contracted by the organisation. Firms that offer outplacement as a way of helping departing employees find a new job are not themselves employment agencies that offer jobs; rather, they aim to put job seekers on the right path. Practice shows that outplacement is characterised by a high degree of success; the number of organisations using outplacement is growing every year. Outplacement is at its most effective in situations where the employee is still employed, and becomes less effective the longer candidates are between jobs.

O&M IN PRACTICE

Outplacement as a form of Corporate Social Responsibility (CSR)

Outplacement is the coaching of employees undergoing, for example, a situation of redundancy, in finding new employment. Any organisation that deals with large-scale reorganisation generally benefits from outplacement. Among European countries, the Netherlands is rather advanced in terms of the philosophy and implementation of outplacement, says Ronal Jeurissen, professor of Corporate Ethics at Nyenrode Business Universiteit. Collaboration with social partners is the guiding thread; based on a certain mutually experienced responsibility, employees and employers are expected to create 'work security' (as opposed to job security) in a flexible economy. This does demand, however, that new safety nets are implemented in the socio-economic system.

The common factor of outplacement and CSR (corporate social responsibility) is the process of globalisation. A globalising world has placed critical emphasis on continuous change and reorganisation in order for European businesses to remain sufficiently innovative and competitive. With increasing frequency, these organisational changes are leading to career switches, job losses, and even unemployment. CSR applies to the social and ecological impact of entrepreneurial business.

In 2010, Jeurissen conducted a study among general managers and HR managers from Belgium, Germany, and the Netherlands, who were, at the time, working for companies engaged in large-scale reorganisation and mass-outplacement. The results of the study showed that, if outplacement is considered a CSR aspect, it is important for businesses to emphasise that outplacement is a company's duty, and one that should be fairly upheld and be profitable at that.

CSR is now an expected role for companies to fulfil; an element integrated in a company's business strategy. Managers are aware of their important societal role, and of their duty to direct their company and steer their employees safely through this new age of ultra-competition. Outplacement is seen as a helpful tool and a practical way of upholding CSR. From this perspective, coaching employees through career changes and offering a responsible dismissal policy seems appropriate. Companies feel a sense of responsibility when it comes to supporting their employees. However, the employee's own (major) responsibility should not be overlooked: they are the party that is primarily responsible for their own employability and for the success of outplacement. Employees are expected to show an active attitude towards the acquisition of new skills and the search for new functions, either inside or outside of the company.

Fairness is another important dimension of the CSR concept. Employees have a right to information, in order both to protect their own interests and to take timely necessary measures. Moreover, there should be clear and objective rules and criteria for the selection of employees who qualify for dismissal. A company's market reputation, after all, is of major interest including with regard to the loyalty of employees spared following a reorganisation.

Organisations practising CSR support their decision using a combination of moral and business motives, expressed in the form of slogans like 'win-win' or 'doing well by doing good'. Companies have learned to view their moral responsibility from the perspective of their business interests.

Source: R.J.M. Jeurissen, *Tijdschrift voor HRM*, 2, 2010

The forms taken by outplacement coaching when offering support to a candidate can be manifold, and include:
a offering moral and psychological support;
b offering career analysis;
c helping in defining a career strategy and help in finding organisations where the candidate might profile themselves;
d helping in the correspondence with organisations, documentation on organisations, etc;
e supporting in negotiating conditions of employment and assessing conditions of employment or, in the case of self-employment, support during the start-up phase of the new organisation or business;
f introducing the employee to a new employer;
g charting the employee's strengths and weaknesses;
h teaching (the application of) communicative skills, such as job interview techniques;

i supporting and training in interview techniques and psychological testing;
j assisting with writing effective letters of application;
k consulting the network of contacts of the outplacement agency;
l offering advice during salary negotiations.

Most organisations choose to outsource outplacement activities to a firm, the reason for which is found in the desire to avoid conflicts of interest (with an employer also functioning as a consultant), and in the lack of knowledge of application techniques or the labour market. Another issue is that most organisations are not equipped with a well-structured network of information or contacts.

Lastly, an organisation making use of the services of an external agency will need to choose between the various such agencies available. A well-reasoned decision for a particular outplacement agency should be based on:
a integrity (what is the agency's reputation?);
b continuity (how long since the agency was founded, and how many people does it employ?);
c professionalism (including its number of current assignments in the industry and at the level of interest to one's organisation);
d methods (including the indicated theoretical foundation for its expertise, and the methods and techniques applied by the organisation);
e facilities (including the accessibility, availability of relevant staff).

In the past, people who left an organisation for whatever reason were shown the door, which was shut and locked behind them. Contact with former employees was usually terminated. This is no longer the case for the 21st century organisation that practices human resource management. It is generally held to be important for an employee to leave an organisation on a positive note; they may continue as stakeholders in the form of, for example, a client or 'ambassador', representing the organisation's image through their former association.
For example, the reputation of McKinsey & Company with regard to its investments in alumni (people who left the organisation) is very good. In McKinsey's view, these are people who may be called upon to work for their new organisation. In addition, there is an increasing number of 'boomerangs'; people who have worked for another organisation or who have spent some time out of work caring for children or parents, now choosing to return to work. There is also the issue of 'applicant's remorse', as it were: people who, shortly after having left one employer for another organisation, come to realise that the grass may have only looked greener. These people are even more strongly motivated than before when they re-join the organisation they left. This also has significant financial benefits for the organisation. A study by BCG (2018) shows that the costs of the recruitment, selection, and training of a new employee corresponds to 6 to 9 months' worth of salary.

The importance of offboarding

Offboarding, or 'a decent farewell to employees', matters. The administrative processes surrounding voluntary or forced departure, such as taking care of outstanding payments, exit interviews, transferring equipment, providing references etc. must be carried out effectively. The size of the impact is influence by:

1   The emergence of alumni-networks. Social networking sites make it possible to recruit former employees as organisational ambassadors if their departure was arranged adequately.

2   Viewing former employees as talent scouts. Former employees are excellent recruitment agents for an organisation that has treated them well. They understand how the organisation works. Referral recruitment is an effective means of personnel recruitment.

3   Boomerang recruitment. A quality offboarding process contributes to employees' potential willingness to return.

4   A good exit interview. A good exit interview provides valuable feedback about the organisation's role as employer and about its HR policy. It can also be used by employers to emphasis a departing employee's duties with regard to issues of non-solicitation, confidentiality, and privacy.

Source: www.pwnet.nl

7.8   TALENT MANAGEMENT

In recent years, organisations have begun to pay more attention to people occupying key positions – positions with a high degree of responsibility that demand complex and specific skills and have a disproportionally large influence on business results and/or the success of initiatives. Research by McKinsey shows that talented employees in roles with high complexity are around eight times more productive that employees whose performance is average. This difference is 50% where roles with a low degree of complexity are concerned. Bill Gates, the founder of Microsoft, is known to have said that 'a great writer of software code is worth 10,000 times the price of an average software writer'.

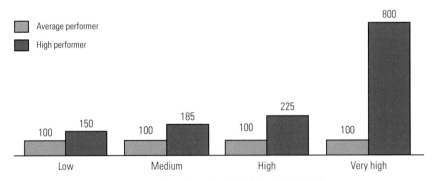

FIGURE 7.6 **% PRODUCTIVITY GAP BY PERFORMANCE AND JOB COMPLEXITY**

Source: 'The war for Talent 2000: McKinsey Global Survey Results,' refreshed in 2012: McKinsey.com

Key roles are not determined based on hierarchy (for example only people at the top), but on the basis of their potential for creating value. Therefore, key positions can be found in all organisational layers.

It is essential that these key positions are held by talented individuals – or talents, referring to people's *skills* or *talented nature* (Van der Sluis 2008). Talent management can be seen as a type of Human Resource Management instrument that encompasses the other discussed instruments but is applied to a very specific target group. There are many definitions of talent management in circulation, one of the most frequently used being that talent management is: 'a systematic and strategic effort to attract, retain, develop, and motivate highly qualified employees.' (Noe, Hollenback, Gerhart & Wright, 1997).

Talent management

Talent management is expressed in various different ways, varying from one organisation to the next. Some organisations propose a highly inclusive approach to talent management. Examples include ING, Deloitte and McKinsey, where all employees are involved in talent management. Others prefer to focus on a small group of employees in the organisation. It should be noted that, even using the inclusive approach to talent management, it is still possible to differentiate with regard to the approach to specific individual talent segments (also known as talent pools).

Talent management pays particular attention to the following activities: finding and hiring talent; continuing to develop talent; creating insight into future accession into key positions. But career development, assessment, and reward also play an important role in retaining talent. As mentioned, a properly maintained relationship with alumni can also be part of the talent management process, as these people may consider returning to the fold.

The implementation of talent management activities depends on an employee's *potential* and *performance*. High potential employees demonstrate this potential through, among other things, high learning agility: they have a willingness and an ability to learn new competences and are able to continue to perform under continually changing circumstances (Lombardo & Echinger, 2000). Using these criteria (potential and performance), all employees can be divided into one of the nine different compartments of the TalentMatrix shown in Figure 7.7.

FIGURE 7.7 **THE TALENT MATRIX**

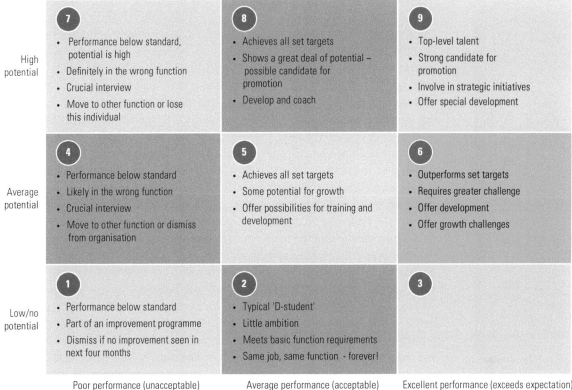

Source: Mölnlycke Health Care/Mercuri Urval (2012)

An individual's location in this matrix indicates a potential talent management/ human resource management approach to their functioning:

a Initiate an improvement programme or even dismiss the employee (1)

b Engage in conversation or transfer to a different function (7)

c Offer specific development and coaching (8)

d Involve in other projects, focus strongly on development, or even offer a promotion (9).

In practice, there are people whose qualities are unique and whose potential is high, but who perform below standard – if at all. There are various possible motives for this issue, both work-related (role, supervisor, organisational culture, etc.) or personal (health, attitude towards work, personal circumstances, etc.). These motives are all subject to potential change throughout a person's life. Therefore, it is not always the 'potential crown princes and princesses' who end up in key positions. On the other hand, it is not all that simple to objectively assess employee performance in a comparative manner.

This does not mean that, from the perspective of talent management, it is not important to chart key positions and the appropriate talent recruitment methods, talent development methods, or talent retention methods to be used by the organisation.

7.9   AGILE HUMAN RESOURCE MANAGEMENT

The final section of this chapter pays attention to the development of agile Human Resource Management.

Human Resource Management (HRM) touches on every aspect and every employee in an organisation. For HR, switching to an agile approach may therefore be a more substantial procedure than for other organisational functions.

For reasons of flexibility and innovation, working in teams and projects is becoming increasingly popular. HRM will also need to be able to shift gears more quickly. GE, Johnson & Johnson, IBM and Procter & Gamble are some of the bigger names who have drawn inspiration from Silicon Valley's agile methods for use in their approach to HR. Long-term planning of core activity processes has slowly but surely given way to a more flexible approach that enables rapid innovation and

Agile approach

adjustment. Following this example, the agile approach is now also found in the field of the workforce. The recruitment and selection, development, and direction of employees is subject to many new changes: a 'light' version of agile. The general principles of agile are applied, without all of the tools and protocols used in the technology industry. The traditional regulating and planning approach is giving way to a less complicated and faster approach based on participant feedback: 'agile performance direction'. Change has been slow to come to HR. Towards the 1990s, markets began to grow less predictable; companies had to obtain personnel with new skills fast. Internal development and promotion were partly replaced by external lateral entry in order to benefit flexibility. Nevertheless, like the other business functions, HR remained focussed on the long-term: good old staff deployment, career planning, and end-of-year reviews were retained. These days, rapid innovation has become a strategic necessity.

To achieve this, organisations turned to Silicon Valley in particular, its software companies. In doing so, the top-down planning approach is replaced by a user-determined work method which makes it easier to implement change. Consider rapid prototyping, iterative feedback, team decision-making, and task-oriented 'sprints'.

This section discusses the changes in human resource policy in a number of areas: performance assessment, coaching, teams, rewards, recruitment and selection, and training and development.

Performance Assessment

The first traditional HR-practice discontinued under the agile approach was the standard end-of-year assessment, together with annually established targets for individual employees based on company or department goals. After all, employees were working in short projects of irregular duration – which, moreover, were often headed by various different people in team formation. Therefore, more and more frequent assessments by different people were needed. In answer, many companies have switched to frequent assessments (or continuous dialogue), often per project. Direct feedback is provided across the year, helping teams to improve their agility and recover from mistakes as they go.

Coaching

Companies with an exceedingly effective agile HR approach invest in improving the coaching abilities of their managers. Examples are coach training for supervisors through weekly video tutorials to be enjoyed at one's own discretion, participating in teaching sessions for agile project management, and collegial peer-to-peer feedback. The latter sees colleagues join in learning cohorts in order to exchange ideas and work approaches without having to fear formal 'judgement'. Another possibility is a professional coach, employed fulltime to coach managers to offer better workplace feedback to their employees. The idea behind this is that a person who has been properly coached is more likely to become a proper coach.

Teams

Since its creation, HR has been focussed on the goals, performance, and needs of individual employees. Because so many companies have now implemented project-based working methods, management and personnel systems are also become more team-oriented. Groups set goals and tasks, implement these tasks, revise them in scrums (a term from the game of rugby used to indicate a tangle of players as the basis for resuming the game). Teams also keep track of their own progress, identify obstacles, assess their own leadership, and develop insight into possible performance improvement. In this context, organisations must learn to cope with 360-degree feedback, workplace control, and complex team dynamics. An agile organisation places a high value on 'upward' feedback from employees to team leaders or supervisors. Changes in workplace control use 'retrospectives': reflection and feedback sessions following every iteration. All personnel are required to be part of these processes with the goal of continual improvement. In terms of team dynamics, the supervisor's task has become complex: they no longer direct individual employees only, but are also charged with ensuring a productive, healthy team dynamic. There is a lot of focus on 'Team Intelligence': identifying the best performing teams in an organisation, analysing their methods, and then using the newfound knowledge to help other teams.

Reward

Reward is also subject to change. As it turns out, rewards mainly encourage motivation if they are offered swiftly following the desired behaviour. The introduction of a bonus is a simple adjustment: tangible recognition instead of an end-of-year wage increase. Direct rewards emphasis direct feedback. Wage increases are frequently implemented based on market conformity. Employees can also be offered a wage increase if they engage in difficult projects or distinguish

Agile HR and TomTom

After years of pioneering and exponential growth, TomTom took a substantial hit to its profits. The crisis and an increase in competition convinced TomTom, manufacturer of satnav systems, to take a different approach.

In several of its departments, the company introduced the concept of agile working, using self-managing teams. But the HR department was also thoroughly revised: considerable downsizing and change from function to role and project-based working. As a result, the company became flexible enough to ride the waves of change. The organisation became flatter.

For HR staff, this means an assignment to one of three function pillars: a service desk for administration and contracts, coach and support for line managers, and a talent acquisition team. The latter pillar is responsible for developing the distinctive solutions that characterise the TomTom experience. HR employees are expected to be enormously flexible: agility, the ability to cope with changing goals, and continually receiving, offering, and processing feedback. TomTom prefers employees being pragmatic and having commercial and business experience to having a traditional background in HR.

Source: www.pwnet.nl

themselves in other ways. A potential disadvantage is the notion that employees will not be fair in their feedback because of the negative impact this may have on their colleagues' rewards. As a result, companies sometime opt to abolish bonuses in favour of a higher base salary: a conscious decision intended to avoid internal rivalry.

Recruitment and Selection

In times of economic prosperity, the pressure on recruitment and selection increases, thus increasing its need for agility. It is possible to create a multifunctional team for all requests for additional staff – a team that would focus on fully greenlit applications: no vacancy is published until candidate requirements are fully established, and only the vacancies with the highest priority are given primacy. Companies are also making more use of technology in order to find and follow colleagues that are better suited to the agile work environment, and there are various online (software) tools on the market to achieve just that.

Training and Development

The training branch also needs to undergo change in order to help the organisation in its quest for personnel with the right skills in as little time as possible. Most organisations can already rely on a broad selection of online training modules. A more novel approach is to use data-analysis to determine the skills needed for specific jobs and promotions. These are then shared with individual employees so they can take part in meaningful training sessions, also from the perspective of possible future job switches. Artificial intelligence is also frequently applied to employee profiles: previous and current functions, expected career trajectory, and completed training programmes.

Naturally, not every group or organisation is engaged in a race for innovation. For some functions, rules are always the deciding factors. And the potential for resistance to change is substantial, particularly in HR. Converting a linear model to a flexible, adaptive one naturally comes with a great deal of change. The human aspect is always tricky. Many HR tasks, such as the traditional approach to recruitment and selection, introduction, and programme-coordination can be expected to become obsolete. The same goes for the expertise required for these tasks. But new tasks will be added. Supervisors will need to make the switch from monitoring to coaching. Management will need to shift its attention from individual employees to employee teams. And, on top of that, there is going to be an increase in IT support, requiring a certain level of knowledge. The pressure to change because of business activities is now growing to such an extent, however, that retaining the traditional working methods will be difficult.

Summary

- Human Resource Management strives for an integrated approach between strategic management and the human qualities in an organisation. This creates a tight relationship between organisational alignment, the organisation's environment, and appropriate staff policy. In doing so, the traditional HRM instruments are integrated into the organisation's policy.

- The HRM instruments discussed are recruitment, career development, learning and development, assessment, reward, offboarding, and talent management.

- Recruitment deals with the recruitment and selection of new employees, and pays attention to the so-called onboarding of new personnel.

- It is now more common for employees to be recruited with a certain career in mind, thus indicating that employees should have the potential to perform in various functions in future. A career is comprised of the roles fulfilled across various organisations by an employee during their working lifetime.

- In many organisations, learning and development has come to play a more significant role because shareholders are increasingly looking at the role of intangible assets when determining the value of knowledge organisations. With jobs changing faster than ever, people will need to keep (re)training and (re)educating continually.

- Assessments are used to answer the questions of whether an employee is eligible for promotion, an increase in salary, a fixed contract, or even dismissal. In addition, an assessment offers an employee insight into their own functioning, and can be used to help guide employees along the path to improvement, to clarify strengths and weaknesses, and to suggest possibilities for further development.

- A person's function and performance are two key factors that influence their reward.

- Offboarding involves employees leaving an organisation for any of various reasons, with the initiative held by either the employer or the employee. Both parties benefit from an employee's departure taking place on a positive note.

- In recent years, organisations have begun paying more attention to people in key positions. Talent management is mainly concerned with searching for and hiring talent, continuing to develop talent, and creating insight into future succession into key positions.

- Because organisations are having to deal with external changes at increasing speeds, HR is expected to increase the agility of its approach.

8

INDIVIDUALS AND GROUPS

Contents

After studying this chapter:

–   you will have become acquainted with the interests of individuals and groups in organisations;

–   you will have gained knowledge of and insight into general concepts related to individuals, such as motivation and personality;

–   you will have gained knowledge of and insight into specific aspects of individuals, such as emotional intelligence, overburdening, and core qualities;

–   you will have gained knowledge of and insight into general concepts related to groups, such as group types and group characteristics;

–   you will have gained knowledge of and insight into specific aspects of team management and characteristics of successful teams, such as personality styles, high performance teams, and RealDrives;

–   you will have gained knowledge of and insight into organisational conflict.

Magioni: vegetable pizzas

Entrepreneur Manon van Essen (30), owner of Magioni, is heading onto the UK market with her vegetable pizzas, to be offered by 300 Waitrose supermarkets.

A non-fatteing pizza, might such a thing be possible? That is what Van Essen and her friends were wondering one-night dining outside in 2016. After many attempts, all Instagrammed, to use vegetables as the basis for many different experimental pizzas, Van Essen started to develop her own recipes for veggie pizzas. The end result was Magioni, her brand of nearly 50% vegetable pizzas.

In two years, Van Essen was able to market her pizzas to a multitude of Dutch supermarkets, starting with Albert Heijn and followed by Jumbo, Plus, Deen and DekaMarkt. Since 2018, the pizzas can be found in Spanish supermarket chain Mercadona – by way of a pilot project. The 30-year-old owner says her success is due to the appeal of healthier products to her generation, the so-called millennials.

Manon: 'This is such a millennial product. We are becoming more aware of our world. The living practices of the previous generations are unsustainable to us. So, we have to take steps, but nobody wants to take their healthy diet to the extreme – and my product offers a happy compromise.' Magioni pizzas are 40 to 50% vegetables, a compromise between a ultra-healthy and cheap snack food. There is a vegetarian option, but the other pizzas of the brand also come with less healthy, non-sustainable elements, such as meat or cheese.

To market her product, Van Essen uses a prolific Instagram-channel with over 52 thousand followers, where she provides pictures of new pizza creations, among other things.

This was the start of Manon's dream: Philosophising about an ideal world where a pizza is as good for you as a salad.

Source: www.sprout.nl, www.magioni.com

8.1 INTRODUCTION

In the introduction to this book, an organisation was defined as 'any group of people cooperating to achieve a common purpose'. This definition highlights the fact that cooperation between people is a feature of any organisation. For many organisations, the human effort that goes into activities is crucial for the survival of the organisation. This applies not only to the strategic level, but also to the tactical and operational levels. In this chapter, the focus is on the people who 'inhabit' organisations. A large part of their active life takes place within organisations. What motivates them? In what terms can their behaviour within organisations be described? How can management within organisations encourage a particular type of behaviour? The purpose of this chapter is to give an insight into individual and group behaviour, including how to predict and influence it.

8.2 PEOPLE IN ORGANISATIONS

People in organisations can be considered from various perspectives. This chapter focusses on people at the level of the individual and of the group. Regarding the former, initial attention is paid to general concepts, such as motivation, personality and attitude. In addition, the following specific subjects are discussed:
a motivation;
b emotional intelligence;
c overloading, stress, stress prevention and burnout;
d intuition and creativity;
e core qualities.

Subsequently, group behaviour is discussed. Within organisations, people nearly always operate in groups. Aside from having individual tasks, people also form part of a group or various different groups. Organisational goals are largely realised through appropriate forms of cooperation. This part of the chapter initially deals with general structural definitions, such as what constitutes a group, possible kinds of groups, and different group characteristics. Then, more specific issues are addressed, being:
1 team management and characteristics of successful teams;
2 organisational conflict.

8.3 MOTIVATION

Organisations prefer to attract motivated employees. Motivated people are good at their job and therefore add extra value to the organisation. But what is motivation? The word 'motivation' comes from the Latin word 'movere', meaning 'moving'. Motivation is what gets people moving. Motivation can be described as the inner readiness of a person to perform certain actions.

Motivation

The introduction chapter of this book described some general theories of motivation: those by Abraham Maslow (the Hierarchy of Needs), Elton Mayo (Human Relations Movement), Frederick Herzberg (Revisionism) and Douglas McGregor (Theory X and Y).

The distinction between work-related motivation and non-work-related motivation is a crucial aspect of the concept:

Job intrinsic motivation

– **Job intrinsic motivation.** This is motivation that derives from the work itself. People who are thus motivated see their job as a challenge. For these people, work is an important part of their life. Translating this motivation into the terms of Maslow's Hierarchy of Needs leads to more fundamental needs: the need for acknowledgement and self-fulfilment. Having responsibility, expanding one's skills, and living up to performance expectations constitute important motivating factors. Work-related motivation seems to provide long-term stimulation.

Job extrinsic motivation

– **Job extrinsic motivation.** Motivation of this type does not derive from the work itself. It derives from items extrinsic to the job, such as work circumstances, rewards, bonuses and status. These are the job's 'perks', so to speak. People whose motivation is job extrinsic have a pragmatic attitude to their work. In practice, this form of motivation is short term.

Many new theories of motivation have developed from the original ones. These theories consider motivation from certain perspectives and give further insights into particular aspects of motivation. Three of these theories are reviewed in this section: Alderfer's theory, McClelland's theory and Vroom's expectancy theory.

8.3.1 Alderfer's theory

Maslow discussed five needs. Alderfer's theory (1969) identifies a more limited number of needs:

Existential needs

– **Existential needs.** These concern material security, corresponding to the physiological needs and security defined by Maslow.

Relational needs

– **Relational needs.** These concern good relationships with other people. Social acceptance, appreciation and acknowledgement are important. Translated into Maslow's terms, these are the need for acceptance and the need for acknowledgement.

Growth needs

– **Growth needs.** These needs are directed towards personal growth and self-fulfilment and equate to Maslow's main need within the pyramid: the need for self-fulfilment.

In its simplified form, this is known as the ERG theory (the abbreviation standing for the three groups of needs). While the theory strongly resembles that of Maslow, there are some significant differences.
Alderfer's needs are not hierarchical. Maslow believed that satisfied needs no longer form effective stimuli. Alderfer is of the opinion that various different needs can be in effect simultaneously. Additionally, there is no question of a fixed order.

Frustration-regression hypothesis

Alderfer also introduces a new element: the frustration-regression hypothesis. His suggestion is that a need on a lower level becomes more significant if higher-level needs are frustrated or are not feasible. But Alderfer has the same opinion as far as deprivation of needs is concerned: he too believes that people are prompted into action if they experience a deficiency (that is, if their needs are deprived).

8.3.2 McClelland's theory

Maslow and Alderfer assume that everyone's needs are fixed, and therefore innate. McClelland has a different opinion: needs are learnt. He believes that, in the first years of a human life, a personal need profile is developed. During the development of this personal profile, a particular need becomes dominant. As one's life develops, this functions as a 'steering' instrument. McClelland identifies three needs profiles (1971):

1 **Performance need.** This need is directed toward providing a good performance. A person looks for challenges, both during work and in other activities.
2 **Power need.** This is a need to obtain influence and control over people.
3 **Affiliation need.** This mainly concerns the building up of good relationships.

Performance need

Power need
Affiliation need

Research has shown that one can indeed discern a dominant need within the needs profile. At the start of the 1980s, Kotter and Kolb investigated higher and lower management and hypothetical dominant needs. The investigation showed that, within higher management, performance and power needs were particularly dominant, but that lower management chiefly possessed an affiliation need. McClelland is of the opinion that the acquisition of a needs profile takes place mainly during the first years of one's life. The profile does not change once it is established. Other researchers do not endorse this view. They believe that the needs profile can develop further during life, depending on situations and experiences: the needs profile is situation-dependent.

McClelland's theory could have particular significance if applied to determine the kind of needs profile required in order to effectively carry out particular functions within organisations. For a salesperson, is the performance need particularly essential? For a private banking account manager, is the affiliation need most important? The dominant need profile could form an important criterion in employee selection procedures or assessment.

8.3.3 Vroom's expectancy theory

For his approach to motivation, Victor Vroom has chosen another perspective: process orientation. A process-oriented motivational theory deals with the issue of the motivational processes of employees, and attempts to explain why these processes take the form they do. Gaining an insight into this allows motivation to be influenced.

Process-oriented
motivational theory

Vroom assumes that an employee acts to achieve a certain goal. For Vroom, the real motivation is not important. Expectancy theory (1964) states that an employee is inclined to act in particular way based on the expectation that their actions have a particular outcome. The motivational process is comprised of three variables, or steps:

Expectancy theory

1 **Expectancy.** This variable indicates how effort relates to performance. How does the employee estimate what is required for their efforts to produce the desired performance?

Expectancy

2 **Instrumentality.** This variable indicates how performance and reward are related. Will a good performance indeed yield rewards to the employee?

Instrumentality

3 **Valence.** This variable indicates the attractiveness of the reward.

Valence

The motivational process is shown in Figure 8.1.

FIGURE 8.1 **VROOM'S EXPECTANCY THEORY APPLIED TO AN EXAMPLE**

Source: Peter Thuis, *Toegepaste organisatiekunde*, Noordhoff Uitgevers, 2014

According to the expectation theory, an employee performs better:

a the greater they estimate the chance of good results;
b the greater their chance of obtaining certain rewards;
c the higher the rewards.

The Dutch spend relatively little time working

FIGURE **AVERAGE WORKING WEEK IN HOURS, EXCLUDING VACATION TIME**

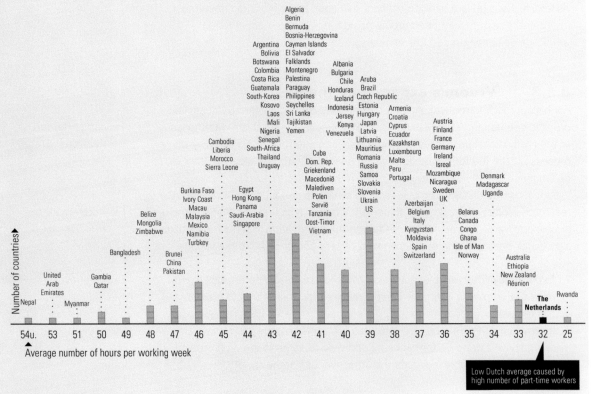

Source: *de Volkskrant*, Sir Edmund, 12 April 2018, CBS, OECD

According to the expectancy theory, the extent of motivation can be expressed by the following equation:

Extent of motivation = expectancy × instrumentality × valence

It is important to realise that these variables cannot be seen as being separate. Instead, they form a trinity. Managers wanting to exert an influence on an employee must therefore keep the entire picture in mind.

8.4   PERSONALITY

When one talks about a person, one usually has a picture of that person in one's mind. People may be describes using concepts like 'persevering' or 'difficult to work with' or 'somewhat volatile'. What this description is in fact doing, is characterising a person: summarizing their character by attaching labels based on one's experiences with or information one has obtained about a person. People also connect an impression of certain behaviour to a certain personality. This behavioural image allows one to explain or predict others' behaviour.

O&M IN PRACTICE

The 10 happiest countries

Happiness is one of world's most frequently described, serenaded, and researched emotions. It is prized and sought-after the world over and, apparently, there are some countries where residents are happier than in others. According to the World Happiness Report 2018, Finland is currently the happiest country in the world.

Source: https://www.trendalert.nl/dit-is-het-gelukkigste-land-ter-wereld-in-2018, consulted at May 18, 2018

1. Finland
2. Norway
3. Denmark
4. Iceland
5. Switzerland
6. The Netherlands
7. Canada
8. New Zeeland
9. Sweden
10. Australia

Individual An individual can be defined as a combination of psychological characteristics that are characteristic of that person. Just as with motivation, people usually look at personality from various angles. It is particularly important for organisations to be knowledgeable where personality characteristics are concerned, as the charactersitics of a person and the characteristics of their function must match each other. Researchers have developed many different personality models. This section focusses on two of these models:

1 the Enneagram;
2 the Myers-Briggs Type Indicator.

8.4.1   Enneagram

Enneagram The Enneagram is an ancient model. The word itself is Greek, and consists of the components 'enneas' and 'gramma', meaning 'nine' and 'what has been written' respectively. The model is used to describe human personality and explain behaviour. In the 1960s and 70s, US psychologists adapted the model to fit modern times. The Enneagram is shown as a nine-pointed figure within a circle. Each point represents a type of personality (Figure 8.2).

FIGURE 8.2 **THE ENNEAGRAM**

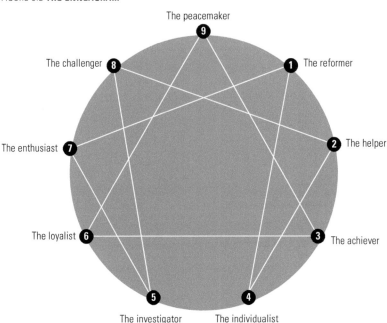

According to the Enneagram, every person has one basic type of personality, which is immutable. However, while the basic type remains unaltered, it can be expanded upon and given depth in order to develop it.

The Enneagram consiste of nine personalities.

Reformer **1 The reformer :**
 – is good at evaluating;
 – believes in corroborating things in a responsible and rational way;
 – is critical when phrasing questions, especially those concerning definitions and underlying principles;

- is good at reasoning, arguing and discussing;
- surveys the consequences of words and actions;
- is irritated by people who pretend to be experts;
- does not want to make mistakes and is afraid to make mistakes;
- does not like self-satisfaction in colleagues;
- is particularly annoyed by ignorance, nonchalance and stupidity;
- has difficulty with emotional expression.

2 The helper :
Helper
- is spontaneous and expresses what bothers them;
- senses what others need;
- has social skills;
- has ready access to their emotions;
- is personally committed and brings depth into important personal relations;
- finds it hard to limit their helpfulness;
- finds it hard to recognise and respect the others' borders;
- finds it hard to put a lid on their emotional outbursts;
- pays a lot of attention to the needs of others, sometimes neglecting their own;
- needs to be mindful of not seeking too much appreciation.

3 The achiever :
Achiever
- finds success to be important: the sky is the limit;
- has will power: where there is a will, there is a way;
- is effective and efficient: fastest is best, irrespective of the consequences;
- is good at realising goals;
- can reduce the complex to the simplistic;
- senses what is 'in', what has potential, and can anticipate on both;
- has a positive way of speaking, thinking, and acting, and appears dynamic and energetic;
- believes that something has value if it is useful;
- cannot stand failure;
- finds it hard to acknowledge when things are not going well.

4 The individualist :
Individualist
- feels compassion is important in this world;
- has a sense of aesthetics: things must be beautiful;
- finds authenticity to be important;
- can analyse well and identifies problems quickly;
- has a rich imagination and ethical vision;
- is alternately introverted and extroverted;
- talks with intense expression in their words and gestures;
- does not like superficial contact or small talk;
- has a creative way of life;
- is not always capable of sketching a positive self-image.

5 The investigator :
Investigator
- is detached, does not pay mind to other people's business;
- values self-determination highly: deciding whether to share private details with others is up to oneself;
- values autonomy;
- can thoroughly invest themselves in certain subjects;
- patiently acquires expertise;

- is good at being alone;
- is good at enforcing order on complex matters;
- is discreet and can keep a secret;
- cannot stand dependence.

Loyalist

6 The loyalist :
- finds loyalty to be very valuable: one has to keep one's appointments;
- finds practical applicability to be important: one has to know what one can do with it;
- finds strength to be important: in this society, one has to be strong;
- is punctual when performing tasks;
- is good at spotting mistakes;
- has a talent for designing structures and procedures; looks for concrete solutions;
- thinks, and generally acts and speak, at a rapid pace
- can quickly scan an environment to identify events, individuals, and issues;
- finds it hard to make mistakes;
- finds it hard to admit their shortcomings.

Enthusiast

7 The enthusiast :
- find the world fascinating;
- functions less well when they are not enthusiastic;
- is attracted to the extraordinary and finds the ordinary too restricting;
- is versatile and sees many ways of approaching things;
- sees various options and is not easily caught out;
- is a fluent speaker and a fascinating narrator;
- can generate ideas;
- opens up new horizons, focusses on possibilities, sees potential, develops a new vision easily;
- has trouble with routine, limitations, measures, seriousness and borders;
- talks a lot about emotions, but rarely shows them.

Challenger

8 The challenger :
- finds results to be important;
- is direct: to postpone something is to renounce it;
- needs a challenge;
- has will power: if one wants something, one should get it done;
- is a natural leader: delegates well;
- is good at detecting others' weaknesses;
- is a witty, humorous speaker;
- is protective: stands up for themselves and friends;
- has respect for opponents that dare to resist and fight them;
- does not want to be emotionally vulnerable.

Peacemaker

9 The peacemaker :
- values solidarity and unity in a group;
- strives for harmony, balance and equilibrium;
- feels uncomfortable if the atmosphere is not good;
- believes that people are equal: basically, every human being is equally important;
- believes in the goodness of human beings: there is something good in everyone;
- is helpful, caring, and attentive, and knows how to be impartial;
- is a patient, and usually also a hard worker, and is versatile and sees things in perspective;

- is usually kind-hearted and slow to anger, with those around them feeling they radiate peace;
- has trouble with conflicts in which they is personally involved;
- finds it hard to say 'no' and show their limits.

According to the Enneagram, humans percieve the world in three ways: via thinking, feeling and instinct. These three intuitions are related to body parts:

1 **thinking** → the head;
2 **feeling** → the heart;
3 **instinctive** → the belly.

While every person makes use of all three ways of looking at the world, one perception dominant for each individual. Based on these perceptions, nine personality types can be identified. Without intending to stereotype, the general categories are:

a Personality types 5, 6 and 7 are focussed on the head. They have a strong tendency to think, and their basic emotion is fear.

Head

b Personality types 2, 3 and 4 are focussed on the heart. These types have a strong tendency to feel. Relationships and the opinions of others are important for them. The basic emotion for these personality types is shame.

Heart

c Personality types 1, 8 and 9 are focussed on the belly. They are directed to the 'being' of things and themselves. They have a strong urge to show their importance, their significance. People of this type quickly feel guilty. Their basic emotion is anger.

Belly

See Table 8.1 for an overview of the nine personality types and their specific characteristics.

TABLE 8.1 **THE NINE PERSONALITY TYPES AND THEIR SPECIFIC CHARACTERISTICS**

Type	Good at	What gets in the way	Leadership style	Growth challenge
Type 1 The reformer	Reasoning, evaluating	Being afraid making mistakes	Deliberate, well-argued, correct, demanding	Type 7 More easy-going, allowing humour, joy as a goal in itself
Type 2 The helper	Empathy, emotional expression	Needing to be liked	Emotional, wants to receive explicit appreciation. Not a typical leader	Type 4 Genuinely sensing another's pain
Type 3 The achiever	Results-oriented, enthusiasm	Having to score	Positive, dynamic, the end justifies the means	Type 6 More loyal, more critical
Type 4 The individualist	Ethical vision, rich imagination	Seeing another's misery	Not very structured, not a leader by nature	Type 1 More rational
Type 5 The investigator	Specialisation, discretion	Invasion of one's privacy	Focussed on content, not a leader by nature	Type 8 Standing out more
Type 6 The loyalist	Solving problems	Not being in command of a situation	Based on rules and procedures, loyal, finds it hard to delegate	Type 9 More relaxed, having more faith in the environment
Type 7 The enthusiast	Generating ideas	Being limited in their freedom	Loose, no strong need to lead	Type 5 Holding back, more discrimination
Type 8 The challenger	Removing obstacles, delegating	Own weakness	Natural leader, confident, impatient	Type 2 More empathic, more emotional expression
Type 9 The peacemaker	Maintaining harmony, mediating	Conflict, having to say no	Reassuring, uniting, not always clear	Type 3 More purposeful, more assertive

Source: www.intermediair.nl

How useful is the Enneagram? Firstly, the Enneagram offers a potential insight into the self. "Which type am I? What are my personality characteristics, what are my strengths? How can I develop my basic type further, and how can I become more aware of my less pleasant sides? Which leadership style best fits my type? Where are my stress pitfalls?" The Enneagram can be used for these situations, thus being applied on an individual basis.

There are other ways of using the model, as well. It is a good instrument for relationships with others. When one works together with others, one is confronted with people who are likely of another basic type. Just being aware of this fact is already a step in the direction of improved communication and cooperation. It also constitutes a good tool for managers. Which types are successful in particular functions? Which types need to be represented in a team in order to realise its goals? The Enneagram also offers way of coaching employees, and of obtaining better insight when directing people.

8.4.2   Myers-Briggs Type Indicator

Myers-Briggs Type Indicator

A frequently applied model is the Myers-Briggs Type Indicator (1980). Psychiatrist Carl Jung laid the basis for this model around 1920. Myers and Briggs used Jung's results to develop the model further. The model can be used to estimate a person's personality. It is based on the assumption that individual preferences exist. Differences in individual behaviour can largely be explained in terms of these preferences, which are as follows:

1	social interaction:	extravert or	introvert;
2	data collection:	sensing or	intuitive;
3	decision-making:	thinking or	feeling;
4	styles of decision-making:	judging or	perceiving.

People exhibit a preference for one of each of these alternatives, choosing either the former or the latter. It should be emphasised that one preference is no better than any ohter.

The various options and their implications are discussed below. Myers and Briggs abbreviated each to the first letter of the term used where possible.

1 Social interaction or 'uploading':

Uploading
– Extraverted; extraversion (E): the individual prefers to derive their energy from the outside, such as from activities, people and objects. They are directed to action and experience, and are broadly oriented.
– Introverted; introversion (I): the individual prefers to derive their energy from the inner world, including thoughts, feelings and ideas. They are shyer and more withdrawn, and prefer to concentrate on a limited number of subjects.

2 Data collection or 'observing':

Observing
– Feeling; sensing (S): the individual prefers to concentrate on information obtained by connections, patrons and meanings.
– Instinctive; intuition (N): the individual prefers to concentrate on information obtained by the five senses and practical applications.

3 Decision-making or 'deciding':

Deciding
– Rational; thinking (T): the individual prefers to make decisions based on logic and objective analysis. They are not influenced by the emotions of others.

- Sensitive; feeling (F): the individual prefers to take into consideration what is important to people. They take the wishes of others into consideration and strive to obtain harmony.

4 Styles of decision-making or 'living':
- Judge; judging (J): the individual prefers a planned, organised way of life. They have a clear purpose and are directed to it.
- Observant; perceiving (P): the individual prefers a flexible, spontaneous approach and keeps all options open. They are flexible and adapts easily.

Living

The answers a person selects to a variety of questions clarifies their position on these four scales. There are eight possible positions. If they are combined, sixteen types arise.

For example, someone may be a INFJ-type. An INFJ-type is introverted, intuitive, sensitive and judging. They are stable, scrupulous and takes pity on others. They are persevering, original and does what is necessary or wanted. They are respected because of their integrity.

This indicator can also be used to explain individual behaviour, and to benefit personal development, team building, communication improvement, and coaching.

8.5 ATTITUDE

The final individual concept to be discussed is manner, or attitude. An attitude is a person's relatively consistent response to particular circumstances. These circumstances can vary: they may be a person, a situation, an object, an organisation, and so on. Everyone has a certain attitude with respect to particular circumstances. Past experience gives rise to attitudes. This experience may have occurred during one's childhood or study, in one's groups, and, of course, in one's work-related experiences. Attitude formation takes place throughout one's entire life and can change under particular circumstances. Attitudes are therefore not innate.

Attitude

Interestingly, attitude and behaviour have much in common. If someone has a particular attitude to a certain subject, they will act accordingly. It is useful for organisations to be aware of what gives rise to a certain attitude, as well as to how that attitude affects behaviour. This information can be helpful in guiding and coaching, as well as in selecting employees. Unwanted behaviour can be analysed and, by offering a person an insight into the origins of their attitudes, possibly corrected.

A person's attitude may be affected by three aspects.
1 **Cognitive aspect.** The cognitive aspect concerns knowledge. A person refers to various sources (including personal experience) to obtain information about a subject.

Cognitive aspect

2 **Affective aspect.** The affective aspect has to do with feelings or emotions. Feelings exert a strong influence on people's attitudes. In fact, attitudes are primarily formed via this aspect.

Affective aspect

3 **Behavioural aspect.** Information and emotions tend to manifest themselves through particular behaviour.

Behavioural aspect

The most efficient countries, contribution to GDI in hours worked, in Euros

FIGURE **CONTRIBUTION TO GDP PER HOURS WORKED, IN EUROS**

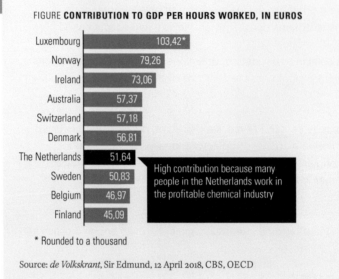

Luxembourg 103,42*
Norway 79,26
Ireland 73,06
Australia 57,37
Switzerland 57,18
Denmark 56,81
The Netherlands 51,64
Sweden 50,83
Belgium 46,97
Finland 45,09

High contribution because many people in the Netherlands work in the profitable chemical industry

* Rounded to a thousand

Source: *de Volkskrant*, Sir Edmund, 12 April 2018, CBS, OECD

8.6 MOTIVATING PEOPLE

This section discusses the issues relating to the methods that organisations and/ or managers use to motivate their employees. It deals not only with financial incentives, but also with formulating tasks and stating objectives.

8.6.1 Motivating by means of financial incentives

Financial incentives

It is an accepted fact that financial incentives increase motivation. However, research has shown that they are mainly effective in the short term, and that higher income is not the prime motive. A challenging job and personal development are usually more motivational. However, financial incentives keep people active. Financial incentives are rewards for performance: the employee receives a wage increase in proportion to the extent to which they perform in accordance with agreements. Performance reward is an example of motivation that is job extrinsic (see Section 8.3).

It is essential to strike a good balance between the intended performance and resulting rewards. This is not just a matter that concerns the organisation and the individual employee, but is increasingly becoming a social problem. Should there be a fixed level of financial incentives for executives? When can such motivational methods remain socially justified? Many organisations have developed performance rewarding criteria not only for the top level of management, but also for other employees at many other levels of the organisation. Performance rewards are usually tied to a certain basic salary, with a variable reward paid on top of a basic salary.

Financial incentives can take many forms. The most frequent are:

a **Bonuses.** A once-only payment for an agreed performance. A bonus may also be awarded if a particular contribution has been made.

b **Profit sharing.** This is payment in the form of a percentage of the net profit obtained over a certain year. The amount depends on net profit and consists of a percentage.

c **Shares-option arrangement.** This is a payment in the form of shares. The employee has the right to buy shares for a fixed price in the future.

Bonuses

Profit sharing

Shares-option arrangement

8.6.2 Motivation by means of task design

While financial incentives constitute an example of job extrinsic motivation, motivating employees via a job itself is an example of motivation that is job instrinsic. Research has shown that employees whose motives are job intrinsic receive a high degree of satisfaction from their job. Work-based motivation involves a range of duties attuned to the needs of a specific employee. As a result, the employee will view their job as a challenge to which they can gradually adapt. The tasks to be performed can be made attractive in three ways:

1 task enrichment: elements of a qualitatively higher level are added to the range of duties;

2 task enlargement: elements of a qualitatively equal level are added to the range of duties;

3 task rotation: employees rotate the tasks they perform.

Task enrichment

Task enlargement

Task rotation

One method of designing one's own function is job crafting. Job crafting is a pro-active, autonomous way for employees to adjust the tasks and limits that are part of their jobs. Employees reshape their work into a way that improves satisfaction, commitment, and dedication. Job crafting can take a number of forms.

First, there are the tasks themselves. One might adjust the limits of a job by assuming or rejecting tasks, by expending or restricting the scope of a task, or by changing the implementation of a task. Then, there are changes to the way people perceive their tasks. This is known as the cognitive aspect. And there is also the relational aspect: people can achieve much greater work satisfaction by changing the way they interact with their colleagues.

'Redesigning' is not a one-time event. It is a process that involves a large number of employees, and one that proceeds gradually. It comprises the following phases:

a Employees are motivated to design their own jobs.

b Employees invent new possibilities for their own jobs, and the form these possibilities could take.

The end-result is strongly related to the job crafter's performance. Employees can chase their passion for their work during the job crafting process. Moreover, it lets them take the initiative to change their work in such a way as to make it more interesting, and to engage in real discussions on changes to their work with their managers. Employers should afford employees enough room to influence their work, creating a work environment based on trust, and join their employees in discussing ideas for changing their work in all openness.

There are clear differences between employees in higher and employees in lower functions. Higher functions are led by their own notions about the division of their time and others'. Lower functions generally consider the description of their function and the expectations of others to be a given. As a result, each group wields a different strategy: higher functions strongly adapt their expectations and behaviours based on their perceived possibilities. They adjust their priorities and apply more of their time to tasks they have selected. Lower functions more readily adapt their expectations to create possibilities for job crafting. They apply more time to gaining the trust of their colleagues, leading to greater autonomy or power they would not otherwise be able to obtain.

There is also a substantial difference in the way senior and junior volunteers design their jobs. Senior employees tend to focus on task adjustment. Junior employees involve themselves in all aspects of job crafting: task adjustment, changing their own notions about their work, and changing their interactions with colleagues.

In today's society, it makes increasing sense for managers to call on their employees' initiative to better design their own jobs. Although the resourcefulness needed should be provided by the employees themselves, managers can still choose to go to great lengths to support and encourage employees.

The subject of task design is covered in greater detail in Chapter 11 (subsection 11.2.1).

8.6.3 Motivating by setting high objectives

A good way to motivate people is to require optimal performance of duties. To do so is to call on the best the individual has to offer. Motivation via setting high
Theory of objectives
objectives is known as the theory of objectives. The theory of objectives involves agreeing on specific objectives in order to improve performance.

Not all agreed-on high objectives lead to motivated employees. For them to do so, objectives must satisfy a number of conditions, being (Alblas & Wijsman, 2018):

a The objectives should be high but realistic
b The objectives should be specific;
c The objectives should be accepted by the employees;
d There has to be regular feedback on progress.

SMART principle
The SMART principle is an aid that can be used to formulate objectives. The SMART principle indicates what conditions should be met for a desired objective:

1 **Specific (S).** The purpose must be described as concretely as possible. The purpose should not be liable to different interpretations, and must not be formulated in terms that are too general.
2 **Measurable (M).** The purpose must be formulated quantitatively. If a purpose has been formulated quantitatively, it is verifiable. These has to be some kind of standard.
3 **Acceptable (A).** The purpose has to be accepted by the person or persons that have to realise the goals.
4 **Realistic (R).** Realisation of the goal should be possible with an acceptable amount of effort. The goal must be challenging but not impossible to reach.
5 **Time-fixed (T).** The goal must be reached within an agreed period.

An example of a SMART objective is increasing the volume of trade of product X by 5%, measured in euros, in the Netherlands, in 2008.

Advantages and disadvantages of managing and rewarding for results (SMART)

Advantages

Results in improved clarity on intended results.

Enables more explicit direction of business processes.

Is a good means of employee differentiation, based on results-dependent rewards.

Reinforces communication between supervisors and employees (explicate expectations).

Provides greater transparency with respect to the relationship between results and related variable rewards.

Encourages the desired cultural change: a more results-oriented approach.

Disadvantages

Hinders supervisors in differentiating between employees.

Is subject to a possibility for arbitrariness, as results are sometimes hard to measure objectively.

Can be hindered by employee results often being mutually dependent, and therefore hard to attribute to individual employees.

Can be counterproductive if the results-based rewards reinforce mutual competition at the cost of collaboration.

8.7 EMOTIONAL INTELLIGENCE

While a high IQ, some extra studies, or specific technical knowledge are important, these are not all that is needed. Emotional intelligence (EQ) is just as important as IQ – or even more so. Emotional intelligence is more general in nature than merely one's capacity to understand other people and deal with others appropriately. It also concerns one's own personal emotions. Dealing with one's own emotions rather than ignoring them makes it easier to assess a tense situation or gain control of an imminent conflict.

A general definition of the concept of emotional intelligence is 'a series of non-cognitive capacities, competencies and skills that influence an individual's success and their ability to meet demands and combat environmental pressure'.

Emotional intelligence

The five main EQ qualities are:

1 **Self-awareness**. People with a high EQ are conscious of their feelings.
2 **Emotional control**. People with a high EQ are positive about their own qualities and are not easily dismissed.
3 **Self-motivation**. People with a high EQ are able to deal with things in the longer term.
4 **Empathy**. People with a high EQ are good at interpreting the feelings of others.
5 **Social skills**. People with a high EQ can deal equally well with both familiar figures and strangers.

Twelve secrets of Emotional Intelligence for professionals

These days, EQ is seen as a particular factor for success where proper professional functioning is concerned. Studies show that the link between these aspects is quite strong – 90% of top-level management has a strong emotional intelligence quotient.

1 Strong emotional vocabulary
2 Natural curiosity about others
3 'Change' is a personal friend
4 Clear insight into one's personal strengths and weaknesses
5 The ability to appreciate others fairly
6 (Near) unflappability
7 Knowing when and how to say NO
8 The ability to stop dwelling on mistakes
9 Give without expecting something in return
10 Do not hold grudges
11 The ability to distantiate oneself from 'toxic' people
12 There is no 'perfect'

Source: 12 geheimen van Emotionele intelligentie voor professionals, Henk Veenhuysen, https://www. ikovertrefme.nl/communicatie/eq-fascinerende-voorspeller-van-werksucces-heb-jij-het, consulted 18 May 2018

The concept of emotional intelligence became well-known after the publication of *Emotional Intelligence* by the psychologist and Harvard instructor Daniel Goleman in 1995. His book *Working with Emotional Intelligence* (1998) served to increase familiarity with the concept.

Emotional intelligence is an ability that lets one exert a major influence on every aspect of their functioning, and therefore on personal and social success (see Table 8.2).

TABLE 8.2 **FIVE COMPONENTS OF EMOTIONAL INTELLIGENCE**

Component	Definition	Characteristic
Self-awareness	• The capacity to recognise and understand one's moods, feelings and motives as well as their effects on others.	• Self-confidence. • Realistic self-assessment. • Sense of humour and relativity
Emotional control	• The ability to control destructive impulses or emotions or to redirect them.	• Reliable and honest • Can handle unclear situations • Open to change
Self-motivation	• A passionate desire to work for non-financial reasons or status. • The tendency to put a lot of energy and persistence into realising goals.	• Strongly competitive spirit. • Optimism, even when facing failure. • Strongly committed to the organisation.
Empathy	• The ability to understand what drives others on the emotional level. • The ability to treat others with sensitivity	• Experienced in encouraging and retaining talent. • Cross-cultural sensitivity. • Experienced in delivering services to clients and customers.
Social skills	• Skilled at managing relationships and to build networks. • The ability to identify common interests.	• Effective in complementing changes. • The ability to influence others. • Experienced in the development and management of teams

Source: Daniel Goleman, *Working with Emotional Intelligence*, Bantam Books, 1998

8.8 OVERLOADING, STRESS, STRESS PREVENTION, AND BURNOUT

An employee is psychologically influenced strongly by experiences and events occurring at work. Work penetrates into the private lives and leisure activities of the employee. Negative emotions have an especially significant influence on one's private life. Employees who are not happy at work will often not be happy in their private lives either, regardless of how long they spend at home or on holiday. Strikingly, while work-related emotions nearly always have an effect on one's private life, the opposite is less likely to hold true. While at work, little thought is given to family or holidays, though major private problems may influence the quality of one's work.

This section deals with the topics of overloading, stress, stress prevention, and burnout.

8.8.1 Overloading

Overloading can take four different forms, namely:

1 **Emotional overloading.** This factor has the biggest influence on one's private life. Concerns, problems, but also feelings of satisfaction and pleasure are carried into the home. The mood is determined by the positive or negative experiences of the past working day.

Emotional overloading

2 **Physical overloading.** After a busy and strenuous day, the employee comes home tired. Their only interest is in food, TV or sleep. They do not have the physical strength or time for a lively private life.

3 **Attitude and behaviour overloading.** The views and behaviour exhibited in the employee's life are strongly related to social experiences during work. An employee with a job which requires strength and offers little room for showing one's emotions will encounter difficulties in showing their feelings of attachment and tenderness at home.

Attitude and behaviour overloading

4 **Existential overloading.** People who are dissatisfied with their job encounter psychological problems more than others. A failed career may cause a deep depression which extends to all aspects of life.

Long-term tension makes employees insensitive to events in their private lives and diminishes their ability to enjoy things when they are not at work.
Emotional outlets, such as feelings of enjoyment, sorrow, rage and pleasure are suppressed. Psychological withdrawal is also typical (as the French say: *Il n'est pas disponible*).

8.8.2   Stress

Stress as a condition
Process-related stress

Stress is the main cause of overloading. A distinction can be made between stress as a condition and stress as part and parcel of a process. Stress as a condition means the psychological and physical situation that arises when a person is faced with demands they cannot satisfy. Process-related stress can be seen as the physical, psychological, and social changes that are connected to stress as a condition.

Michigan model

The so-called Michigan model sums up the consequences. This model depicts a number of stages of progressive stress (Figure 8.3), in which the influence of stress on a person's health is described as a chain of events. Job requirements and threats may lead to feelings of stress, which then cause physical and psychological reactions and eventually have a negative effect on health.

FIGURE 8.3 **THE PROCESS OF STRESS ACCORDING TO THE MICHIGAN MODEL**

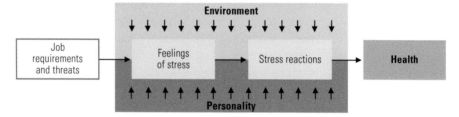

Personal and environmental factors may decrease or increase problems.
Personality factors can be subdivided into:
1 exarcerbating factors, such as excessive and aggressive fixation on one's job, and a need to alienate oneself from others;
2 calming factors, such as good social contacts, self-confidence, flexibility, and a good physical condition.

The environmental factors are:
a physical working conditions;
b ergonomic factors;
c safety risks;
d work and leisure times;
e travel times and circumstances;
f private circumstances.

There is, however, a number of factors that are highly likely to cause stress, and which are characteristic of the work situation though not connected to personality or environmental factors:

a Problems at work that have been occurding long or regularly (e.g. when a person realises that they cannot perform their task well).

b Problems at work with important consequences for the individual's performance within the organisation and from which they are unable to withdraw (e.g. not being aware of volume of trade and profit objectives for which they are responsible).

c A psychologically taxing work situation that is not easy to change (e.g. having to collaborate with a colleague with whom one has great difficulties).

d Problems at work that radiate to other functional areas, such as one's situation at home (e.g. job uncertainty, uncertainty about the future).

Burn-out affects 15% of Dutch employees

O&M IN PRACTICE

Nearly 15% of all employees in the Netherlands regularly suffer from work-related over-exhaustion. Women between 25 and 35 years old in particular are troubled by burn-out complaints, a joint study by the Dutch Central Bureau for Statistics and research institute TNO shows. Singles also tend to feel greater emotional fatigue, exhaustion, or emptiness at the end of a work day.

Generally speaking, the number of employees with fatigue-related complaints as a result of a psychological issue is largest in the category of 25 to 35-year-olds. According to the CBS, this is due to the group's longer average working week, combined with the fact that they are more often single. The fact that women are subject to burn-out more frequently than men is due to the fact that women are more often employed in healthcare or education, where working pressure is high and there possibilities of being able to determine one's own working pace are few, says CBS.

Source: *Het Financieele Dagblad*, 15 February 2018, https://fd.nl/economie-politiek/1241815/bijna-15-werknemers-heeft-last-van-burn-out, consulted 18 May 2018

But not all stress is disastrous. According to Selye, a Canadian endocrinologist who made a lifetime study of stress, complete freedom from stress equates death.

It is also important to make a distinction between positive and negative stress, where positive stress may even strengthen a manager and invigorate them. In the

literature, positive stress is also known as 'positive tension'.

Research has shown that stress at work is caused mainly by:

a time pressure;
b long working days;
c too much work;
d personal relationships;
e employee quality.

8.8.3 Stress prevention

Given the frequency with which stress occurs amongst employees, and its potential for serious consequences, it is important to look at ways of reducing or even preventing stress at work.

There are three distinct approaches to stress prevention or reduction, namely the organisational approach, the individual problem-solving approach, and handling and managing stress.

The organisational approach

The organisational approach involves making changes to the job, or more successfully attuning the employee to the job. The changes may take various forms:

- Changing the organisational structure;
- Changing the reward structure;
- Clarifying the expectations that the organisation has of the employee;
- Improving individual opportunities and changing work demands;
- Training management in human-directed leadership;
- Improving communication;
- Providing personnel facilities (child care, a social worker).

In general, organisational approaches fall within in the area of social management.

The individual-directed approach

This approach focusses on the individual and aims at increasing employees' problem-solving capacities and abilities to cope with their workload. It emphasises the organisation of training programmes directed at:

- Acting purposefully;
- Being assertive;
- Cooperating;
- Managing time;
- Solving problems;
- Dealing with conflict;
- Improving and applying social skills.

Handling and managing stress

Individual stress management is aimed at decreasing a person's susceptibility to stress, not at solving the problems that cause stress. This approach cannot be considered separate from the individual-directed approach. The two overlap and can be combine.

Stress-management techniques are based on scientific stress research. Research has shown that stress can be countered by good social support, a capacity for putting things into perspective, self-confidence, and physical relaxation. The following techniques are utilised:

1 Techniques for physical relaxation (e.g. meditation);
2 Techniques for improving physical condition (e.g. company fitness, jogging). Company fitness is caring for the physical and spiritual health of an organisation's employees. Participating in company fitness may have a favourable influence on absenteeism, work output, and business culture. Physical exertion relieves body and mind, and reduces stress. In Japan and the United States, company fitness forms part of company strategy for improving business culture.
3 Systematic desensitisation. This is a technique based on the notion that one's susceptibility to tension is decreased if tension is introduced and increased gradually.
4 Cognitive structuring. With the help of this technique, people are taught to look at requirements and possibilities realistically.
5 Techniques for increasing social support. Improved social skills make people more prepared to fall back on each other in times of need.

8.8.4   Burnout

Burnout can be seen as a specific form of stress. Burnout may occur after some time spent in an occupation where contact between people is frequent and intense. Burnout is difficult to describe because it comes in so many forms. An often-used definition is the following: a psychological issue of emotional exhaustion, depersonalisation, and a feeling of decreasing competence. As someone who suffered from burnout once described it: 'Burnout is a neglected situation of overstrain that has been going on for a long time. It manifests itself in various complaints in the physical, psychological, emotional, cognitive, and social areas'.

Burnout

The definition includes three core concepts of burnout:
1 **Emotional exhaustion.** An important characteristic of burnout is a loss of energy and a feeling that the emotional reserves have been exhausted. It is accompanied by feelings of frustration and sadness, because those suffering from burnout realise that they cannot continue to give themselves fully or accept responsibility in the same way as they did before.
2 **Depersonalisation.** Victims have a tendency to consider people as objects rather than individuals. This attitude is often accompanied by a negative and cynical attitude towards employees and the job.

Depersonalisation

3 **Feelings of decreasing competence.** There is a tendency for victims to judge themselves negatively. They have a feeling of underperforming and of being less successful in their work. They have a negative self-image.

Feelings of decreasing competence

Burnout differs from stress in that if the causes of stress are taken away, one can quickly recover and regain one's balance – while for a burnout, the symptoms remain. Burnout is the product of an accumulation of stress factors and frustrations over a long term, usually years.

What causes burnout? It is too simplistic to assume that burnout is related solely to the job itself. It has various causes. They can be divided into three groups: work-related causes, personality related causes, and organisation-related causes.

Work-related causes

The causes of work-related burnout are:

Interpersonal contact

1 **Interpersonal contact.** Burnout that occurs when the job requires direct and intense contact with other people, sometimes in emotionally loaded circumstances.

Role conflicts

2 **Role conflicts.** Burnout that occurs when there are different (and often contradictory) expectations about the division of roles between employees.

Role ambiguity

3 **Role ambiguity.** Burnout related to a lack of clarity about the employee's role and how to fill it.

Job overloading

4 **Job overloading.** Burnout that may take the form of either qualitative or quantitative job overloading. Qualitative overloading means the person often finds the work too difficult, and has the feeling of missing some of the skills required to do the job efficiently. Quantitative overloading occurs if there is too much work and the person has the feeling of not being able to complete their tasks within the time available.

Personality related causes

The following personality related characteristics may cause burnout:

Biographical

1 **Biographical.** Some people are more susceptible to burnout than others. Burnout occurs mainly in the beginning and middle stages of one's career. Singles, people without children, highly educated people, and women have a higher risk of burning out.

High expectations

2 **High expectations.** Expectations (personal and within the organisation) about position and personal suitability may contribute to burnout.

Career progression

3 **Career progression.** People who are successful in their careers are less sensitive to burnout.

Social support

4 **Social support.** There is a relationship between social support and burnout. The chance of a burnout increases as less support decreases. Help and support from colleagues and top-level management directly responsible, as well as the opportunity to develop and utilise one's skills play a big role in avoiding burnout.

Organisation-related causes

Apart from the quantity of work, the chance of burnout is much larger if there is increasing frequency and intensity of contact, especially in situations without positive feedback. Individuals need affirmation and clarity from their clients and their organisations.

Job Demand Control-model

Job Demand-Control model
Job demands Control

Lastly, there is the Job Demand-Control model by Kasarek (1979). His model relates job demands to control. Job demands are linked to the quantity and degree of difficulty of one's work. Control is about the extent to which an employee can decide how to execute their duties: for example, how quickly they carry out work activities. Other aspects that may play a role in this respect are the influence and control that an employee (or executive) has on their and others' work (Figure 8.4).

The model suggests that, in principle, job demands should cause no problems. The risk of stress and burnout increase only if major job demands are accompanied by little control. A high level of tension builds up, and in a situation where an executive carries responsibility for certain affairs but cannot actually influence or control them, the result is stress – especially if the executive's superior also exerts a lot of pressure on them to achieve results.

FIGURE 8.4 **KASAREK'S MODEL (1979)**

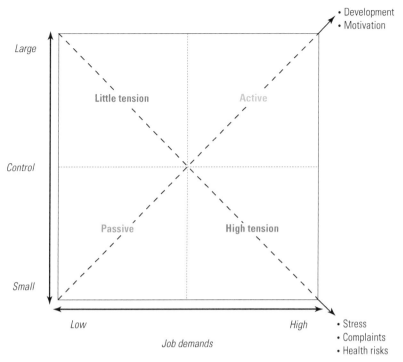

Source: Gert Alblas en Ella Wijsman, *Gedrag in organisaties*, Noordhoff Uitgevers 2018

High job demands combined with a large amount control give rise to a positive situation. Because the employee can do something about the situation that is causing stress, they experience the tension as being of a positive kind.

8.9 INTUITION AND CREATIVITY

This section deals with intuition and creativity within organisations. It also describes how creativity in organisations can be encouraged and organised.

8.9.1 Intuition

Intuition is often mentioned as a key to success. Intuition is knowledge obtained via non-logical ways of thinking. Intuition can be described as an immediate awareness of the truth of a matter – an awareness that is not based on thinking in concepts or reasoning. A characteristic of intuition is that connections are made between certain entities, leading to a conclusion or idea while skipping a number of logical steps. Intuition is often a premonition, knowing without knowing why.

Intuition appears to play an important role in scientific breakthroughs. As Albert Einstein stated, 'there are often no logical roads leading to particular laws: they are inspired only by intuition based on the instinctive insight of experiences'. Einstein called his theory of relativity the best discovery of his life.
Many executives in the business world agree that intuition plays a very important role in their style of management. It is not always possible to model decision-making processes, and inner feelings are often ultimately decisive. Moreover, intuition can play an important role in the creation of ideas, the choice of alternative strategies and the acceptance of new employees.

Intuition

Insufficiently stress-proof?

Are you insufficiently stress-proof? Here are some indicators.
- You are quick to become restless or panicked in case of unexpected, hard to assess, or undesired situations.
- You feel hounded when having to work under time pressure.
- You take your work home with you due to deadlines; you find it hard to let go of your work during off hours.
- You find it hard to retain an overview.

- You find it hard to cope with adversity, and are unable to properly roll with the punches or put matters into perspective.
- You feel restless or powerless if matters do not go as expected.
- You find it hard to recover from setbacks.
- You are quick to lose you balance when faced with difficulties.

Source: https://www.desteven.nl/training-coaching-vraagbaak/competenties/stressbestendigheid, consulted 18 May 2018

The business world's increasing interest in intuition is evident in the fact that intuition is a topic of certain training sessions for higher management.

8.9.2   Creativity

Creativity

Just like intuition, creativity within the modern organisation is indispensable. According to Picasso, the famous painter, creativity is destructive – but in a positive sense. By this, he meant that creativity demolishes old views, insights, opinions or feelings in order to create something new. Creativity can be described as a way of thinking that produces new ideas and new solutions.

Process of creativity
Figure 8.5 shows that, without creativity, innovation is impossible. In areas where figures and rationality provide insufficient information for the development of new products (such as new planes and cars) creativity is crucial for decision-making. The creative process consists of three steps:
1 generation of ideas;
2 screening;
3 implementation.

FIGURE 8.5 **THE RELATIONSHIP BETWEEN CREATIVITY AND INNOVATION**

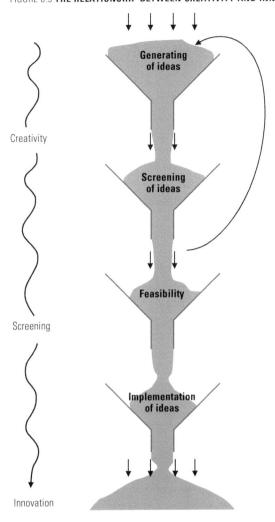

Generation of ideas

There are many ways of generating ideas: for example, brainstorming, synectics, lateral thinking, day-dreaming and the COCD technique. The first three examples are discussed in Chapter 7, which deals with decision-making.

The COCD technique has nothing to do with decision-making. This technique was developed by the Belgian Center for the Development of Creative Thinking (Centrum voor de Ontwikkeling van het Creatief Denken – COCD). According to this theory, the human mind thinks in patterns which rise to a chain reaction. Thought is a process of moving from one certainty to another certainty, rather than from one truth to another. If the basis is wrong, the emerging certainties will not be reliable, with disastrous results.

COCD technique

What the COCD theory boils down to, is that people can be encouraged to be creative by teaching them how to build onto their initial premises, and thus develop a new kind of logic.

According to Prof. R. de Bruyn of the University of Antwerp, the instruments used by COCD include:

a searching continuously for more possible alternatives;

b taking an arbitrary idea and drawing connections between this idea and the problem;

c looking for obvious ideas and eliminating them in order to develop new views;

d isolating the problem by considering the case as part of the whole;

e sketching the problem three times, eliminating one particular dimension on the fourth occasion and looking at the consequences.

Screening

Screening involves first 'filtering' ideas and then testing them for commercial feasibility. Ideas can be screened in various ways, including:

a **Clustering of ideas**. With this method, all available ideas are written on separate pieces of paper and subsequently put on a table or a wall. Then, the ideas are divided into as many categories as possible. This produces a number of manageable groups. Each group has now become a higher level idea.

b **Setting up hurdles**. This involves the use of increasingly challenging criteria which an idea must satisfy in order to pass the filter. It is important for everybody to agree on the chosen hurdles, as well as with the order in which these are placed.

c **Weighing up ideas**. Every aspect of an idea is assigned a value. This allows ideas to be compared and selected.

d **Speculating**. If information is minimal and a decision has to be made quickly, this method may be appropriate. The general knowledge and intuition of the decision-maker are important factors when using this method.

Implementation

Once the ideas have been screened, they can be implemented: innovative solutions, such as new products, services, or methods, are put into practice.

Organisation of creativity

Although everyone admits that having creative managers and employees is of vital importance to the continuity of an organisation, many major organisations seem to be unintentionally slowing down the development of their employees, and with it employee potential for innovation. While companies pay a lot of attention to increasing productivity and quality, creativity is barely promoted.

But creativity is the very factor needed to promote productivity. It can do the following:

a improve the quality of solutions to organisational problems;

b indicate how to be profitably innovative;

c motivate people;

d bring personal skills to a higher level;

e act as a catalyst to group performance.

Creative managers have means at their disposition to stimulate and enhance the innovative mentality, and with it the performance of both organisation and employees. Figure 8.6 shows how creativity can be organised.

FIGURE 8.6 **THE ORGANISATION OF CREATIVITY**

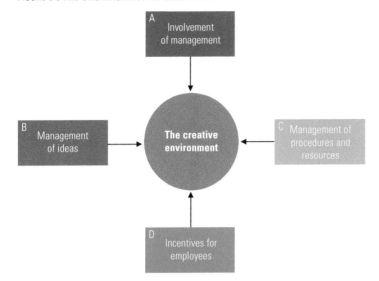

The various elements of Figure 8.6 are:

a **Involvement of top management.** The involvement and support of top management is crucial to organising creativity in the organisation as a whole. Management's commitment will become visible through the availability of budgets for organised creativity, and by showing interest in ideas via active participation and the evaluation of creativity in its concrete realisation.

b **Management of ideas.** This involves not only developing methods for stimulating the creation of ideas, but also having a positive attitude towards this development. This is expressed by establishing a creative climate, which can take such forms as using a suggestion box system, registering and evaluating ideas systematically, or raking together all sorts of 'odd' ideas. What should be avoided, is slating any brand new ideas.

c **Management of procedures and resources.** The development of administrative aids such as planning methods, follow-up methods, building expert networks, and creating idea databases is central to this.

d **Stimuli for employees.** Employees can be encouraged to be creative by:
– giving them access to information (e.g. literature, conferences, seminars);
– making budgets available;
– allowing time for developing creative ideas;
– letting them travel;
– supporting them in their research.

Twelve tips for a conductor-less orchestra, by concertmaster Candida Thompson

1 Keep up the tempo.
2 Do not over-rehearse.
3 Offer space.
4 Offer frames of reference.
5 Schedule small-circle preliminary discussion.
6 Delegate.
7 Reaffirm.
8 Use humour.

9 Dare to stop.
10 Dare to get angry (on occasion).
11 Lead by example.
12 Be open to feedback.

Source: 13 Lessen voor een dirigentloos orkest van concertmeester Candida Thompson, *Het Financieele Daglad*, https://fd.nl/morgen/1245897/sinfonietta-doet-het-zonder, consulted 18 May 2018

8.10   GROUPS AND TEAMS

Being active within an organisation means working with other employees. In any definition of an organisation, collaboration is a concept that is always mentioned: any kind of collaboration towards a common purpose. Goal-oriented, appropriate collaboration is an important aspect of successful organisations. This section of the chapter considers the phenomenon of collaboration from various perspectives.

Group
A group is formed when two or more people consciously collaborate in order to reach certain objectives. Interaction takes place as they realise that they need each other to achieve their aim. From this definition of a group, it becomes apparent that organisations are made up of many active groups, including projects, committees, brainstorming sessions, and management teams. A branching organisation may be considered a group. Groups form the binding factor within organisations.

Group scan be categorised in various ways. The most obvious division is formal groups versus informal groups, and virtual teams.

8.10.1   Formal and informal groups

Formal group
A group is defined as formal if it has a place within the structure of the organisation. A formal group can have a permanent or a temporary character. An

example of a formal permanent group in an organisation is a management team. A formal temporary group can be a study group responsible for a digitisation project. Once the project is completed, the group is dissolved. A formal temporary group is also called a taskforce.

Besides formal groups, informal groups are also present in organisations. These are groups outside the structure of the organisations. Employees may choose to form a group themselves. These groups are mostly based on friendship and/or common interests. The importance of informal groups should not be underestimated. Communication between people in informal groups can be important for the development of policies and the execution of all kinds of activities, as well as for strengthening common standards and values in an organisation.

8.10.2 Horizontal, vertical and mixed groups

If group members derive from the same hierarchical level of the organisation, it is known as a horizontal group. Horizontal groups can be active at various hierarchical levels of the organisation. An important purpose of a horizontal group is harmonising and coordinating particular activities.

Horizontal group

A group is known as vertical if the group members originate from different hierarchical levels of an organisation. The purpose of a vertical group is usually found in the domain of communication. A combination horizontal-vertical group is known as a mixed group.

Vertical group

Horizontal, vertical and mixed groups can be present as formal or as informal groups within an organisation.

Mixed group

These are traditional kinds of groups. Groups that are rather more out of the ordinary include:
a virtual groups or teams;
b autonomously operating teams.

8.10.3 Virtual teams

To an increasing extent, organisations have employees who are active in different countries. With large multinational organisations, the countries may be distributed over the entire world. With so many borders, collaboration is a special problem in this type of organisation. Modern information and communication technology mean that there are new opportunities for this type of organisation. Collaboration no longer means meeting physically: members can now 'meet' each other via the digital highway. This can take place in different ways. Conference calls, and seeing each other 'live' by means of a 'video conference'. Exchange of information and communication can take place via a digital platform. A virtual team is also known as an electronic group network.

Virtual team

Collaboration in virtual teams means that organisations can save considerably on expenses, and still reach the organisation's goals. It should be remembered that, besides the technical problems of virtual teams, other problems can also play a role in virtual teams. The very fact that virtual teams often bring together people from different continents means that the composition of the team is an important issue, too. A multiplicity of cultures might be present in a virtual team. This may hamper collaboration.

To see and experience each other physically remains important, even with new technology. Many organisations choose to arrange meetings both virtually and physically (though the latter meetings are likely to be infrequent).

8.10.4 Self-governing teams

Self-governing teams (also called autonomously working teams) have recently become much more common.

Self-governing team   Traditional teams are known as functional teams, and are composed of an executive and the employees who are responsible to the executive. In self-governing teams, a group of employees is responsible for its own activities to a certain degree. This group of employees makes the decisions necessary for carrying out activities. These decisions concern both operations and management. In traditional teams, management tasks are reserved for the executive.

A self-governing team has to satisfy the following characteristics:

a There has to be a fixed group of employees who work together and are responsible as a team for all the tangible activities needed to supply a product or service to an internal or external customer.

b The team must be able to manage itself to a certain extent and to take responsibility for the tasks to be carried out, based on a common purpose.

c In order to do so, the team must have relevant information, and necessary abilities and aids. at its disposal. The team has the authority to make independent decisions in relation to its activities.

Self-governing teams are nothing new. They were already in use in British coal mines in the 1950s, where they carried joint responsibility for the entire process of mining coal.

The difference between a functional team and a self-governing team is shown diagrammatically in Figure 8.7.

FIGURE 8.7 **THE DIFFERENCE BETWEEN FUNCTIONAL AND AUTONOMOUS TEAMS**

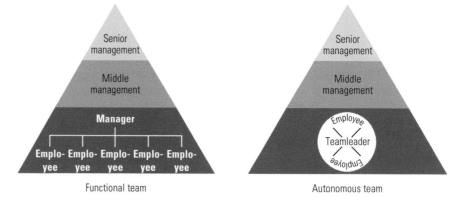

Source: John Schermerhorn, *Management*, Academic Service 2002

By using self-governing teams to organise activities, various different objectives can be reached. These objectives cover the following areas:

Management   **1 Management.** Making management more efficient and effective. Research has shown that self-governing teams can improve productivity as well as flexibility and customer service.

Quality of the work   **2 Quality of work.** This concerns the employees themselves. Teamwork requires active involvement by the team members. People become increasingly willing to view their activities in terms of the team's common purpose. Team members are not only responsible for their own tasks, but also for the results achieved by the team as a whole. Self-governing teams often rotate their tasks. This gives

People and organisations
PART B

© Noordhoff Uitgevers bv

employees the opportunity to learn how to perform each other's tasks, thereby increasing opportunities for further development.

3 **Learning organisation.** Among self-governing teams, there arises a situation where the creativity and the learning capacity of the employees are put to better use than would be the case with functional teams, where everybody is responsible for their specific task only. Creativity and the learning capacity of the employee are important elements for organisations in a strongly variable environment.

Learning organisation

Dutch community care expanding self-governing teams

For the second year running, Stichting Buurtzorg Nederland, the Dutch community care program, has been crowned the Netherlands' Best Employer. The home care organisation has not scheduled any impressive expansion: it seeks to take over 7,500 employees from loss-making home care company TSN Thuiszorg. For TSN Thuiszorg employees, this would mean an entirely new working method as part of small, self-governing teams – the concept

that led to solid success for Buurtzorg Nederland. TSN Thuiszorg has teams sort out their own planning and assess their own requirements. Teams are supported by a coordinator, but take care of most of their activities themselves.

Source: https://www.pwnet.nl/organisatie-strategie/nieuws/2016/02/buurtzorg-breidt-zelfsturende-teams-uit-101694, consulted 28 May 2018

8.11 CHARACTERISTICS OF GROUPS

This section deals with the specific characteristics of groups or teams, including stages of group development, group cohesion, and group standards. The objective is to give more insight into group processes.

8.11.1 Stages of group development

Stages of group development

Everyone has experience with working in groups. When one is first introduced to a group or assumes a position within an existing group, one can perceive vast differences in atmosphere and working style. Research has shown that groups develop through a number of stages. A well-known model is that by Caple. It deals with the stages of development of new groups working together intensively for a certain time. Their collaboration is therefore temporary in nature.

Caple observed five stages during the development of such groups:
1 **Forming.** The group members have just met. During this period, the members get to know and understand each other. There is uncertainty within the group and the group members try to become acquainted with the rules and purpose of the joint effort. During this stage, the group can be characterised as 'a collection of individuals'.

Forming

2 **Storming.** After some time, the group members start to show their true colours. Conflict situations arise. Group members operate in accordance with their own specific knowledge and insights, and try to impose these on the activities and functioning of the team. Within the group, smaller conflicting subgroups may be formed. This is known as 'clique formation'. This stage is important in the development of the group, because it eventually helps clarify

Storming

others' contributions, position, opinions, approaches, and so on. Foundations are laid for a certain degree of group cohesion. During this stage, the group can be characterised as 'a starting group'.

Norming   **3 Norming.** In order to achieve its goals, a certain amount of unity must exist within in the group. While Stage 2 focussed on differences between members, stage 3 looks for agreement within the group, and members are more willing to compromise. Their dealings are more 'adult'. During this stage, the group can be characterised as 'an advanced group'.

Performing   **4 Performing.** During this stage, everything is directed towards the joint effort needed to deliver a good performance. Effective team work is now imperative. The group is busy with organising and performing its activities in such a way as to fulfil the purpose as best as possible. Conflicts may occur, but now tend to exert a positive influence on the final result. During this stage, the group can be characterised as 'an effective group'.

Adjourning   **5 Adjourning.** The purpose of the collaboration has been achieved. Group members will feel pride in what they have achieved. The group often finds a way to mark the end of their collaboration and say goodbye. For some group members, this is an emotional time; others will look back on it as mainly an instructive and interesting experience.

It should be mentioned that the stages described represent the standard. In actual fact, some groups do not even get to Stage 3, having already been dissolved or reconstituted by that point, with some members leaving and others joining in. If Stage 3 is not passed satisfactorily, it may diminish the results achieved via the joint effort. It may also cause scepticism about working together, with this feeling bleeding over into the next project.

8.11.2   Group cohesion

Group cohesion   An important aspect of a group is its cohesion. Group cohesion is the degree of mutual relationship within the group. Group performance is strongly dependent on mutual relationships. Solidarity and team spirit are important characteristics of group cohesion. There is a relationship between cohesion and group productivity. This relationship is shown in Figure 8.8.

FIGURE 8.8 **RELATIONSHIP BETWEEN GROUP COHESION AND GROUP PRODUCTIVITY**

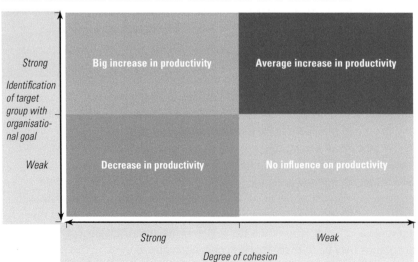

Source: Robbins, Coulter, *Management*, Pearson

'Group think' is especially characteristic of group cohesion. Group think is the tendency of groups to lose their capacity for objective judgement. This is particularly common in highly cohesive teams. Group members may become less critical toward each other, which has an adverse effect on group functioning.

Given these facts, one might whether large groups perform better then small groups. Some general findings in this respect are listed below:
a When fast results are required, small groups are more effective.
b The contribution of each member shows up better in small groups and there is tendency towards group think.
c Group members who contribute greatly to a group also have a big influence on final results.
d The input of individual group members usually remains at the same level. Those who exert a major influence continue to do so over time.

8.11.3 Group standards

How should people deal with each other? What kinds of behaviour are acceptable and what kinds are not? As a member of a group, one is confronted with these questions at home, among friends, and at work. Group standards develop according to the extent of group cohesion. The greater the cohesion within a group, the more discussion there is about group standards. Group standards can differ between groups. Group standards develop spontaneously. The following is an example of a group standard: 'We always address each other with 'Mr' and Mrs/ Ms' and always shake hands upon meeting'.
Group standards can affect many situations, including mutual relationships, loyalty, conflict handling, contact with other branches, and so on. Group standards are unwritten rules that determine group behaviour within a group. They indicate what behaviour is desired in particular situations. Groups standards are not comparable to formal rules within an organisation.

Executives can make an important contribution to the development of desired group standards. An executive may, for example:
a reward desired behaviour and punish unwanted behavior;
b provide training sessions and promote team building;
c set a good example themselves;
d select new employees on behavioural criteria;
e make standards debatable and talk about such matters with each other;
f show that the desired behaviour has advantages.

8.12 TEAM MANAGEMENT AND CHARACTERISTICS OF SUCCESSFUL TEAMS

Organisations involve substanial teamwork. An organisation's success is strongly linked with how well people in the teams work (together). Various authors have looked into the matters of optimum team composition and optimising team success.
In this context, this section addresses three approaches to team management, followed by a discussion of the characteristics of successful teams:

1 Belbin Team Roles;
2 Team member personality styles;
3 High performance teams;
4 RealDrives.

8.12.1   Belbin Team Roles

Belbin Team Roles

In the 1960s, scientist R. Meredith Belbin performed many studies into the effectiveness of management teams. In his book 'Management teams. Why they succeed or fail', he describes the theory of team roles and team conditions. People do not need to be able to do everything, but a clear role distribution in a group often leads to the best results. This is the real secret behind team management: composing groups and demarcating and distributing tasks in such a way as to achieve optimum group work results. People fulfil not only a functional and a professional role, but also a team role. The professional role is fulfilled based on a person's professional skill set, which ties in with their function. The organisational role is fulfilled based on a person's position, their place in the organisation's hierarchy. These character roles complement one another, as should the people that fulfil them. There are three supporting principles of team role management:

1 Every role is a quality;
2 Each person's nature allows them to properly fulfil two to three roles;
3 In every group, there should be a proper distribution of roles, and each person's role should correspond to their natural character as much as possible.

In short, team composition requires the following core roles: doers, thinkers, wanters, and feelers.
The following paragraphs discuss team roles, team conditions, and effective team characteristics.

Team roles

In order to optimise team results, team composition is not the only required aspect. Another important factor are the conditions to which team members and the team are subjected. How to ensure that the team roles can achieve an effective work implementation? This, it appears, is a complex matter. The work of teams and team members is influenced by a multitude of factors.

Team roles

The following eight distinct roles may be present in a team:

1 **Coordinator.** Organises and manages team activities, making the best possible use of the potential offered by the team (members).
2 **Shaper.** Helps develop and concretise team activities.
3 **Resource Investigator.** The most prominent source of team innovation and ideas.
4 **Monitor Evaluator.** Analyses ideas and proposals, and evaluates these for usability and practical applicability in relation to the team goals.
5 **Plant.** Investigates external possibilities and develops contacts that may be useful for the team.
6 **Teamworker.** Improves the overall functioning of the individual team members.
7 **Implementer.** Translates general concepts and plans into practical tasks and activities, and ensures systematic implementation.
8 **Completer Finisher.** Ensures that team efforts are perfected, and that the work is scrutinised for errors.

The eight roles are shown in Figure 8.9.

FIGURE 8.9 **EFFECTIVE TEAMWORK SHOWN DIAGRAMMATICALLY**

Each individual team role does not need one single available individual to fulfil it. Some roles can be fulfilled by one or more persons on the team, for example. Depending on a team's (main) goal, one or more of the team roles may receive particular emphasis.

Team conditions

The next steps is to focus on the team conditions required by the different roles for thei effective implementation. Some examples of team conditions are:

a clear goals to which great importance is attached;

b a results-oriented communication structure: an information system, for example, should not be the source of a surplus of cluttered data, but instead offer a minimum of constructive information needed to direct business processes;

c competent team members, both in terms of technical and team-playing skills;

d identifying with and feeling committed to the team;

e a cooperative atmosphere of collaboration;

f maintaining performance standards;

g additional support and recognition;

h vision-based leadership.

Team conditions

Effective team characteristics

This paragraph on team management pays attention to team roles and team conditions, with the issue at hand being how to optimise the results of group work. There has been a lot of practical research into effective group work, due to the fact that effective group work has a positive influence on organisational results. A practical study by Professor Hubert Rampersad (2002) shows that an effective team has the following characteristics:

– clear objectives to which all team members want to commit fully;

– cohesion and consensus;

– acceptance and recognition of other members' cultural differences, in addition to mutual understanding and respect;

– a broad basis of trust between team members;

– the ability to solve problems and internal conflicts effectively;

– the ability to learn from experience collectively;

– team members with knowledge of their own style of learning;

- interaction between, on the one hand, a number of different personalities and, on the other hand, the required skill(set)s, harmoniously distributed between all team members;
- knowledge and acceptance of a person's own team role and the team roles of others;
- a balance between individual team members' team roles and functions;
- a harmonious working climate of mutual respect, trust, attention, and useful feedback;
- open communication, providing all members with relevant information;
- continuous team member training.

8.12.2 Team personality styles

In their article 'The new science of team chemistry' (2017), Suzanne Johnson Vickberg and Kim Christfort describe how any team is a combination of four personality styles. These four personality styles are pioneers, drivers, integrators, and guardians. In principle, any person is comprised of a combination of these styles; however, one or two of these styles are usually dominant. Every style may potentially contribute to developing new ideas, solving problems, and making decisions.

The four styles are defined as follows:

Pioneers
1 **Pioneers**: people who are often the first to explore new and uncharted terrain, on the look-out for new entrepreneurial possibilities – fields that are, as yet, outside the realm of experience. Pioneers are strong at finding new paths to solving certain issues, using their innovativeness and creativity. They are used to taking risks and relying on their intuition. New ideas are broadly outlined, requiring help from others to fill in the details.

Drovers
2 **Drovers**: people whose strength is in encouraging a change or challenge. They take the task upon themselves and are expeditious in their approach, working in a task and results-oriented fashion. Drivers keep up the pace and motivate others to join in. They have a clear view of the eventual goal of a change or challenge.

Integrators
3 **Integrators**: people whose strength is in joining up people or parties. They are able to easily ignore personal interest for the sake of solidarity. They are empathic individuals who excel at listening to others and looking for the similarities between people or parties. When looking for similarities, integrators are diplomatic in their approach, and are able to put the opinions, circumstances, and points of view of others into perspective.

Guardians
4 **Guardians**: people strongly focussed on 'herding the team'. Guardians attach importance to stability, structure, rules, and order within the team. Their approach is pragmatic, and focusses on usefulness and results. Risks are avoided where possible. In contrast to pioneers, who work in broad strokes, guardians feel compelled to pay attention to detail.

A study involving thousands of groups led the researchers to conclude that teamwork can only be optimised if all four styles are present in the team. If one or more of these styles is missing, overall teamwork is less effective. It is through the combination of these styles that effective and efficient teamwork is made possible. As the four styles have the potential to come into conflict with each other, it is generally necessary for teams to be 'managed'.

'Team management', say the researchers, should focus on the following needs:

a the need for the best possible balance between opposing styles;

b the need for adequate emphasis on underrepresented styles;

c the need to ensure that sensitive and/or introverted team members are given their own 'space' in the teamwork effort.

8.12.3 High Performance Teams

High Performance Teams

In any organisation, there are teams whose performance leads to very good results, often even better than the results of other teams in the same organisation. These teams are also known as High Performance Teams. A High Performance Team may be defined as any group of people with specific roles and complementing talents and skills, aligned and connected through a common goal, showing a consistently high level of cooperation and innovation, and achieving superior results. High Performance Teams achieve results their individual team members would never have been able to.

In their book *De kracht van High Performance Teams. Zes ingrediënten voor excellent presteren in de publieke sector* (The power of High Performance Teams. Six ingredients for excellent performance in the public sector), Ben Kuipers and Sandra Groeneveld list seven components for creating a High Performance Team.

1 **Team commitment**: team members feel loyal and connected, and are passionate and energetic about fulfilling their task.

2 **Self-management**: the team is autonomous and takes the initiative to improve its performance.

3 **Goal-oriented collaboration**: the team formulates clear and ambitious goals to which it commits through a close partnership.

4 **Task-oriented collaboration**: the team uses a clever form of mutual information-sharing and knowledge valorisation to perform its task.

5 **Stakeholder-oriented collaboration**: the team actively maintains its relationships with the stakeholders, and uses stakeholder feedback to improve team performance.

6 **Leadership**: the leader places the team first, supports the collaboration, and encourages working towards team goals.

7 **Team performance**: the extent of the team's effectiveness (goals met), efficiency (goal-oriented work using available means), and legitimacy (working in accordance with their interests).

Team commitment

Self-management

Goal-oriented collaboration
Task-oriented collaboration
Stakeholder-oriented collaboration

Leadership

Team performance

A Dutch organisation that makes heavy use of High Performance Teams is Ordina. Ordina is an ICT service provider operating in the Benelux countries. Ordina uses a special method to develop High Performance Teams, which allows teams to rapidly develop towards high customer value. The method comprises three steps:

1 **Forming**: teams are composed from multiple disciplines, ensuring they have complementing skills and profiles.

2 **Facilitating**: teams are facilitated in various ways, for example through the use of (agile) coaches, automation experts, and serious gaming.

3 **Valuating**: team thinking style is always strongly focussed on maximising customer value.

Seven considerations for diverse High Performance Teams

Organisations looking to build diverse and complementing High Performance Teams are recommended to take the following 7 suggestions into consideration. This list was compiled following experience gained through working with dozens of organisations with regard to diversity and high performance teams:

1 Start out small.
2 Coach the team intensively for the first 100 days.
3 Celebrate conflict.
4 Prevent the formation of sub-groups.
5 Aim for long-term collaboration.
6 Document to learn.
7 Celebrate and sell success.

Source: https://www.leiderschapontwikkelen. nl/artikel/7-aandachtspunten-diverse-high-performance-teams/?cn-reloaded=1, consulted 28 May 2018

US company Google also relies heavily on High Performance Teams. Google itself has also conducted many studies into why some teams function better than others. Their research shows that there are five characteristics particular of High Performance Teams:

Psychological safety

1 'Psychological safety': team members should feel safe within the team. Precisely because they are required to stick their necks out and take risks, it is of the greatest importance that they are allowed to make mistakes and ask for help. For that reason, mutual trust is very important. This approach considers confrontations between people to be a productive tool. Things can only get better as a result of confrontation.

Dependability

2 'Dependability': team members are strongly aware that they rely on each other for results. This dependence ensures a strong focus on mutual communication in the team.

3 **'Structure & Clarity'**: the roles and objectives should be clear to all team members. There is a clear and accessible plan for achieving goals. Google's studies have shown that the way in which team members cooperate is more important that individual team member quality. This means that individual team members are interchangeable but that the collaboration method is not!

Structure & Clarity

4 **'Meaning'**: implementing team roles does not depend on what individual team members consider to be important; rather, attention should be paid to what is meaningful to other team members. This creates a culture of mutual encouragement and motivation, where team members help each other reach the best results.

Meaning

5 **'Impact'**: team members are aware that achieving the established goal is important not just to them, but also to the customer or the company. In other words: team results can make a difference.

Impact

8.12.4 RealDrives

A final approach to team functioning is the RealDrives methodology. RealDrives was developed by Hans Versnel and Machiel Koppenol in 2008. RealDrives incorporates both an individual-level and a team-level perspective. The most important basic concepts underlying RealDrives are:

RealDrives

a that people and their motivations are different: what do people really want, what drives them ('real drive');
b that individuals have preferred drives;
c that people adapt their drives and resulting-behaviour to their surroundings/place of work. The context or place of work is important and has consequences for peoples' actual behaviour.

The RealDrives methodology thus establishes a relationship between drive preference, work environment, and the behaviour a person displays in that environment. In a schematic form, this relationship is as follows (Figure 8.10):

FIGURE 8.10 **RELATIONSHIP BETWEEN PREFERENCE, ENVIRONMENT, AND BEHAVIOUR**

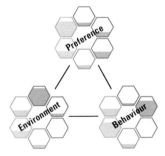

Source: http://www.realdrives.com/nl/colors/, seen on 1st of June 2018

The RealDrives methodology aims to measure both individual and team drives. It creates drive-profiles for both the individual team members and a team pattern. These insights can be used to improve team composition and management. To establish the relevant drives, the individual team members are asked to fill in a questionnaire.

Individual and team drives
Drive-profiles
Team pattern

The RealDrives methodology is based on six differently coloured drives, as shown in Figure 8.11.

FIGURE 8.11 **THE SIX REALDRIVES**

Purple	The drive for familiarity, safety, and shelter Key words: privacy, unity, stability, security
Red	The drive for a personal domain, creates speed and ferocity Key words: swift, alert, confrontational, fearless
Blue	The drive for order and certainty Key words: clarity, discipline, reliability, responsibility
Orange	The drive for results and progress Key words: ambition, status, effectiveness, flexibility
Green	The drive for the human dimension, putting mutual harmony first Key words: equality, openness, spontaneity, sharing
Yellow	The drive for knowledge and insight Key words: understanding, consistency, vision, future

Source: http://www.realdrives.com/nl/colors/, seen on 1st of June 2018

The RealDrives methodology views human behaviour as a tool for achieving particular goals. This means that people assess their environment from the perspective of their drive, and display behaviour to achieve their goals based on their assessment. As a consequence, the preferred colour is not necessarily the behavioural colour. It is important that a person is able to change their preferred colour in their quest to achieve a goal if a different colour would lead to better results.

Reasons for changing the preferred colour in a certain context (environment) are shows in Figure 8.12.

FIGURE 8.12 **REASONS FOR CHANGING THE PREFERRED COLOUR**

I apply more purple because	• I intend to protect the people around me. • I intend to shield my employees from management. • I want to engender trust. • I want a build a secluded atmosphere.
I apply more red because	• I am very angry. • I need to show my teeth. • I need to kick things up a notch. • I do not want to be seen as soft.
I apply more blue because	• I do not want to make mistakes. • things need to be organised better around here. • we need to take matters one step at a time, otherwise I will lose it; it is a madhouse in here.
I apply more orange because	• we need to see some progress. • I want to make a statement. • I want to advance my career. • there is much to be gained in terms of efficiency.
I apply more green because	• I want to be a member of this team. • I want to be likes. • we need to improve communication. • I really want to listen.
I apply more yellow because	• things are muddled. • I am looking for a part to play; what am I doing here? • we are dealing with very complex matters. • I fail to see the point.

Source: http://www.realdrives.com/nl/colors/, seen on 1st of June 2018

Visualising the colours associated with people in terms of preference and behaviour creates a situation where mutual behaviour becomes easier to understand and discuss.

In addition to insight into individual team members, the RealDrives methodology also offers an insight into a team as a whole. Figure 8.13 shows two teams, with the existing drives of the individual team members. The percentages take into account the dynamic and interaction between the persons in the teams.

FIGURE 8.13 **TEAM DESCRIPTIONS BASED ON EXISTING DRIVES**

Group 1:
- Slower
- Committed
- Inside out thinking
- Norm-based
- Stable
- Responds to threats
- Wants to help
- Seeks security
- Wants subservient leaders

Group 2:
- Faster
- Opportunistic
- Outside in thinking
- Facts-based
- Flexible
- Respons to challenges
- Wants to steer
- Seeks adventure
- Wants directing leaders

Source: http://www.realdrives.com/nl/teams, seen on 1st of June 2018

The visualisation of the drives in a team can be used to assess and quantify group characteristics. How effective would the team be in achieving a particular goal? This makes it possible to established and improve team alignment, team composition, team building, and team development.

8.13 ORGANISATIONAL CONFLICT

Within organisations, there may arise situations where the goals, interests, standards, and/or values of individual employees or groups of employees are incompatible. If this means that individual employees or groups of employees are unable to reach their own objectives, the situation can be described as one of organisational conflict.
Because organisational conflict occurs regularly, it is important for managers to be able to cope. Conflict within organisations has consequences for organisational performance and, in extreme cases, the survival of the organisation.

Organisational conflict

Dealing with conflict

**"Wish me luck. I'm going in there
and not coming out until all conflicts are resolved."**

There are five ways of dealing with conflict. These are:

1 adapt;
2 avoid;
3 fight;
4 collaborate;
5 negotiate.

The difference between these styles is in the way each deals with the two elements that make up all conflict: the contents or occasion of the conflict and one's relationship to the other party.

Importance of the issue Importance of the relationship	Low	High
Low	avoid	fight
High	adapt	collaborate /negotiate

Source: http://www.carrieretijger.nl/functioneren/samenwerken/sociale-vaardigheden/conflicten-hanteren, consulted 18 May 2018

Relationship between organisational conflicts and level of performance

The relationship between organisational conflict and level of performance is shown in the diagram in Figure 8.14.

Figure 8.14 indicates that, in the absence of conflict, performance is not necessarily optimal (situation A in the figure). This can be attributed to the employees (either as a group or individually) being insufficiently challenged to get the best out of the situation. Differences of opinion mean more discussion and hence better decisions. A certain degree of critical appreciation of others is essential for making the right decisions (situation B). If there is too much conflict and those involved are only interested in pursuing their own purposes or playing political games, then the obvious result is a negative influence on the organisation's performance (situation C).

FIGURE 8.14 **THE EFFECT OF CONFLICT ON ORGANISATIONAL PERFORMANCE**

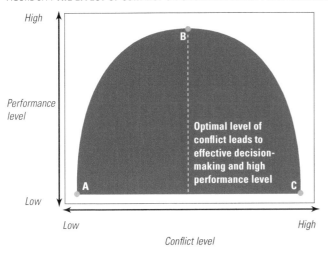

In conclusion, organisational conflict has a certain function and should therefore not be avoided for the sake of avoidance. To control conflict, it the important to have an insight into the various types and sources of conflict.

Types of organisational conflict

The following types of organisational conflict can be identified (see Figure 5.14):

1 interpersonal conflict (such as conflict between individual employees);
2 conflict within groups (such as that within a department);
3 conflict between groups (for example, a conflict between the marketing and production departments);
4 conflict between organisational entities, such as branches.

Types of organisational conflict

FIGURE 8.15 **DIFFERENT TYPES OF ORGANISATIONAL CONFLICTS**

Sources of organisational conflict

The following may cause conflict within organisations:

1 **Irreconcilable purposes and time frames**. Conflict may arise if employees from organisational entities (such as different departments, committees or branches) have different purposes and different time frames.
2 **Overlapping responsibilities**. Conflict may arise if various employees or organisational entities feel that they are entitled to claim responsibility for the same activities or tasks.
3 **Task dependence**. Conflict may arise if employees or organisational entities become involved in activities for which they have joint responsibility.

Sources of organisational conflict

4 **Different assessment and reward systems**. Conflict may occur if employees or organisational entities are assessed and/or rewarded differently.
5 **Scarce resources**. Employees or organisational entities having to compete for scarce resources such as financial means and staff may create conflict.
6 **Different status**. Difference in status between employees or organisational entities may become a source of conflict.

Figure 5.15 shows this in the form of a diagram.

FIGURE 8.16 **SOURCES OF ORGANISATIONAL CONFLICT**

A successful end to conflict

Successful end to conflict

Managers have a duty to address and rectify organisational conflict between employees or organisational unities. A successful end to conflict is only possible if employees or organisational unities are willing to compromise in order to be able to work together. Managers are able to give direction to this process by using conflict management techniques. Conflicts are easier to resolve if the various parties have insight into whatever it was that motivated the other party's point of view. Conflict will then become an occasion for discussion. Other possible techniques include task rotation, allotting temporary tasks to enable greater insight into the problems, transferring employees, or, if the matter is no longer under control and no other solution can be found, dissolving the team.

Summary

- The motivation of employees in an organisation plays an important role. Motivation is a person's internal willingness to perform certain actions.

- Job-intrinsic motivation relates to the job itself, and is supported by the need for self-development and recognition. It is a long-term stimulus.

- Job-extrinsic motivation is a short-term stimulus dealing with work-related payment.

- Motivational theories: Alderfer proposes the ERG-theory: existential, rational, and growth needs. He also introduces the frustration-regression hypothesis. McClelland assumes that a needs-profile is acquired during a person's first years of life. Vroom attempts to explain the motivational process. He distinguishes between the variables of expectation, instrumentality, and value.

- Organisations benefit greatly from the right connection between an individual's personality and the organisation – a click. Examples of models that qualify personality are:
  – The enneagram, based on nine personality types. Every person falls into one basic type from which they can develop further.
  – The Myers-Briggs Type Indicator, which supposes that people have different preferences that largely determine their behaviour. There are four scales: social interaction, data gathering, decision-making process, and decision-making style.

- To a large extent, individual behaviour is determined by attitude: a person's relatively stable stance with regard to a particular subject. Attitudes develop through past experience, and have a cognitive, an affective, and a behaviour aspect.

- Employee motivational tools:
  – financial stimuli: improves short-term motivation;
  – task-design: work-intrinsic motivation;
  – setting high, specific targets that are agreed upon in advance.

- Aside from IQ, another important factor for organisations is emotional intelligence (EQ). Five important EQ characteristics: self-knowledge, optimism, capacity for suffering, empathy, and social skills.

- The recognised four types of overloading:
  – emotional;
  – physical;
  – attitudinal and behavioural;
  – existential.
  Stress is the most important cause behind the occurrence of overloading.

- According to Michigan, whether or not stress is aggravated depends on personality and environmental factors.

- Attempts to prevent or reduce stress benefit from an organisational approach and/or an individual problem-solving approach.

- Burn-out is a specific form of stress. It is a psychological issue of emotional exhaustion, depersonalisation, and a sense of decreasing competence.

- Intuitive knowledge is knowledge obtained without logical thought. Intuition is important for managers.

- The process of innovation comprises three steps: creativity, screening, and innovation.

- To obtain an insight into employee strengths and weaknesses, various tests may be used. Examples are Core Quadrants, Learning Styles test, and Belbin Team Roles.

- Organisations rely heavily on groups or teams. There are different types of groups:
  – formal and informal groups;
  – horizontal, vertical, and mixed (diagonal) groups;
  – virtual teams;
  – self-governing teams.

- Caple designed a model for mapping the various phases of group development: forming, storming, norming, performing, and adjourning.

- A specific characteristic of groups is group member cohesion. Group cohesion can lead to 'group thinking', with the leader's judgement becoming impaired. The stronger group cohesion, the likelier the existence of group norms.

- Team results are often improved by a good role division: resource investigator, teamworker, coordinator, plant, motivator evaluator, shaper, implementer, completer finisher. One person can fulfil more than one role. Team working conditions also deserve attention.

- Suzanne Johnson Vickberg and Kim Christfort described how a team is a combination of four personality styles. These styles are pioneers, drivers, integrators, and guardians. A team that works well together includes all four of these personality styles.

- A High Performance Team can be defined as a group of people with specific roles and complementing talents and skills, aligned and connected to a common goal, displaying consistently high levels of cooperation and innovation, and achieving superior results.

- The six ingredients for high-performance teams are: team commitment, self-management, target-oriented cooperation, stakeholder-oriented cooperation, leadership, and team performance.

- RealDrives also looks at team functioning. The most important basic concepts behind RealDrives are:
  that there are differences between individuals and their drives, that individuals prefer certain drives to others, that individuals adjust their drives and drive-based behaviours to their (work) environment.

- The RealDrives methodology aims to measure both individual AND team drives. This creates a drive-profile both for team members and for individual teams. This insight can help improve team composition and management. The concept of RealDrives is based on six different (coloured) drives.

- Organisational conflict is the result of individual employees or groups of employees being unable to achieve their objectives because their goals, interests, norms, or values are irreconcilable. This type of conflict can endanger an organisation's existence.

9
LEADERSHIP AND MANAGEMENT

Contents

After studying this chapter

- you will be up to date on the most important management concepts;
- you will be familiar with the most important management tasks;
- you will have gained insight into general organisational decision-making problems;
- you will be able to distinguish between various types of decision-making processes;
- you will have gained insight into the problems surrounding the phases of the rational decision-making process;
- you will have gained insight into and an understanding of the various aspects that influence decision-making;
- you will have gained insight into the tools and techniques used in the decision-making process;
- you will be able to distinguish between various styles of leadership;
- you will have gained insight into the way managers direct an organisation;
- you will be familiar with insights and leadership practices from positive psychology;
- you will be familiar with a number of aspects of managers as individuals;
- you will be familiar with the relationship between management and information.

Homerr: pick-up and returns network

Every day, 200,000 parcels across the Netherlands go undelivered because there is nobody at home to receive them. Start-up company Homerr wants to address that problem using a network of private and professional service points.

Homerr is a pick-up and returns network for parcel deliveries. Parcels can currently be dropped off at 700 private NeighbourhoodSpots and professional ServiceSpots, including bakeries and coffee shops. Consumers can have their online purchases sent directly to a nearby Homerr location, and pick it up at their convenience. Delivery points remain open after 6pm, making it easier to pick up a parcel after working hours. But if that also proves impossible, parcels can even be picked up the next day. Using this principle, Homerr wants to drastically reduce the number of movements needed for parcel transport in the Netherlands. Currently, there is no recipient for parcels in 30% of cases. Undelivered parcels remain in the care of the delivery service and are resubmitted the next day – often to no avail, as the recipient will not be home the next day either. According to the founders of Homerr, this leads both to increasing consumer frustration, as well as to increased costs and environmental stress.

Juriaan Matthijssen (33) is the inventor and founder of Homerr. He began his career with Dutch communications company KPN. Right after marketing the Homerr concept, Matthijssen was joined by Mark-Jan Pieterse (35) as co-founder. Pieterse worked for Dutch mail and parcel delivery service PostNL for years, and understands exactly what goes on in the parcel delivery industry. The founders of Homerr believe that the current parcel delivery system will prove not to be future-proof. They expect deliveries at pickup points will become the standard, and that consumers will be charged an additional fee for at-home delivery.

The founders of Homerr want to keep things as simple as possible in terms of both the service itself and their business model. The company receives a standard commission fee for parcels delivered using its network, independent of parcel size. The pick-up points also stand to earn a modest amount for each parcel, namely 40 Eurocents. That does not seem like very much, but the entrepreneurs claim it is more than the market price. Moreover, it helps retailers to draw in a bigger crowd, potentially leading to additional customers. In 2018, Homerr landed a 1 million Euro investment from a group of private investors – capital that will be spent on a significant boost to the company's growth and the creation of a network of national coverage, with 5,000 pick-up points being the goal for 2019.

Source: www.sprout.nl, www.homerr.com, www. logistiek.nl

9.1 INTRODUCTION

Whether as employee or buyer of products and services, everyone deals with managers or leaders in some way. The news frequently highlights the connection between a manager's behaviour and the ensuing organisational success or failure. Job sites abound with financially and professionally appealing jobs, with titles like Management Team Member, Managing Director, Commercial Manager, HR Director, etc.

A manager can be defined as a person who can stimulate and direct the behaviour of other people within an organisation. A manager is usually responsible for the (financial) results of a division or department through the direction they provide to groups of employees.

Manager

While the definition may suggest otherwise, the function is not a cushy job, that depends less on the hours one puts in than on one's ability to delegate. In reality, many Dutch managers are workaholics, working more than fifty hours per week on average, not including travel times.

Studies have shown that managers invest even more of their energy on their work – even when not working or emailing, they are still occupied with their job, for example mentally reviewing activities or problems to be resolved.

Leadership is defined as the specific ability to make others follow (Meyer and Meijers, 2018). It has less to do with one's acquired position, even though the chance that people will follow a person officially named manager is, of course, higher than average. In his book *Agile Leiderschap* (Agile Leadership), professor Ron Meyer argues that the formal position of manager in no way guarantees that one will be accepted as a leader. A person who wants to lead others has to earn this right by, for example, fulfilling a position based on the influence that follows from expertise, charisma, experience, drive, empathic ability, etc.

The terms 'manager' and 'leader' are often used interchangeably, but mean different things, as indicated. To some, the word 'manager' refers to 20th century managerial practice, associated with terms like: boss, egocentric, limited expertise, putting organisational interest before employee interest, untrustworthiness, etc. The following table offers a differentiation between managers and leaders.

TABLE 9.1 **MANAGERS VERSUS LEADERS**

	The manager's world	The leader's world
What do you do?	I have a JOB with rights and responsibilities.	A perform a ROLE with or without a formal function.
How did you get this position?	I am ASSIGNED by higher management	I am ACCEPTED by others who want to follow.
What are your available resources?	I have FORMAL AUTHORITIES to assign work, spend budgets, assess, and correct.	I have INFORMAL AUTHORITY based on trust, skill, inspiration, and power of conviction.
What is your approach?	I enforce OBEDIENCE through reward and punishment.	I earn COMMITMENT by capturing people's hearts and minds.
How do others respond?	Our relationships are CALCULATING ('how do I benefit?').	Our relationships are RECIPROCAL ('what is our common goal?').
What is the best outcome?	ACCEPTABLE performance, based on extrinsic motivation.	EXCELLENT performance, based on intrinsic motivation.
Conclusion?	MANAGE THINGS. Make them HAVE TO.	LEAD PEOPLE. Make them WANT TO.

Source: Ron Meyer and Ronald Meijers, *Agile Leiderschap*, 2018

It is essential that the terms 'manager' and 'leader' are kept separate, because appointed 'managers' must realise that the formal power they obtain from their appointment is no guarantee that they will be(come) a successful leader.

9.2 MANAGEMENT

Management/
organisational
managers

Management is often given to mean the collective organisational managers tasked with directing an organisation. Since the group performing this task often consists of various individuals, another frequently encountered term is the 'management team'.

Management team

Within such a team, there are often specialists representing the various functional departments of an organisation, such as Purchasing and Sales, Finance, Production, Personnel and Auditing. In the business world, divisional managers or managers of business units are frequently also members of a management team. Within government organisations, heads of departments may participate as team members. There is an obvious interest in management courses and training institutions, varying from one-day seminars to complete studies that might last many years.

A management function is often the gateway to a promising career perspective, at both the local and the international levels.
This section reviews the tasks and roles of managers, and addresses differences between various types of managers, specifically top-level managers, middle management, government managers, and female managers.

9.2.1 Managerial activities

Looking at management in organisations, it is possible to distinguish between various managerial levels and activities.

Management levels

Management levels

Within a growing organisation a need may arise to separate operational control from leadership. This situation will give rise to the development of a number of levels at which managers are required to coach their employees. The number of levels of (hierarchical) control depends heavily on the size of the organisation, the degree of specialisation, and the type of organisational policy.

Top-level management
Middle management
First line management

There are three main management levels within an organisation's hierarchy: top-level management, middle management and first line management. It is the responsibility of the senior level to provide leadership to the organisation; middle management directs the activities of the operational levels, including the first line management level (especially within large enterprises). First line includes heads of departments or group managers, who are located between the operational levels and the middle management level. Within a modern, flat organisation, there is far less need for multiple tiers of management, as less distinction is made between the lower and middle levels of management.

These management levels have different managerial tasks, specifically: policy formulating tasks and executive tasks.

Policy formulating (constituent) tasks are tasks in the fields of diagnosis, prediction, planning and organising activities. The executive (directive) tasks involve mainly the delegating of activities and the supervising and motivating of employees.

As shown in Figure 9.1, top-level management should mainly be concerned with policy formulating tasks. Middle management is involved with policy formulation and execution. The policy formulated by the top layer should be translated into operational division or department policy by the middle layer. Any lower managerial branch is then tasked with the execution or implementation of the policy set by middle management.

Policy formulating tasks
Executive tasks

FIGURE 9.1 **MANAGEMENT LEVEL ACTIVITIES**

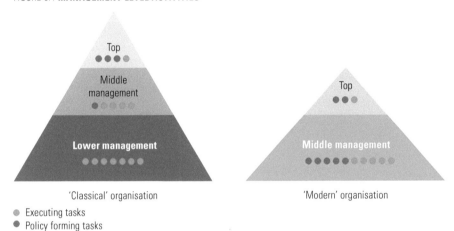

'Classical' organisation   'Modern' organisation

- Executing tasks
- Policy forming tasks

Functional and general managers

There is a general distinction to be made between the two main management groups of functional managers and general managers.

The responsibilities of a functional manager relate to the management and performance of a single main activity within an organisation. Employees are coached by this manager to focus on one task only. Purchasing managers and marketing managers are two examples of functional managers.

Functional manager

A general manager, on the other hand, may be responsible for all the activities within a certain part of the organisation, including production, marketing, and finance. The business unit manager and the divisional manager are two examples of managers with general managerial duties.

General manager

Within the activities performed by management, a number of trends has become visible:

1 Organisational structures are becoming increasingly flat through the assimilation of lower and middle management levels. Consequently, the number of management levels and the number of managers has also declined.

Flattening

2 The task of the manager is increasingly changing from the classical, directive leadership style to a style that is more oriented towards coaching and guiding employees.

3 There has been a shift away from the recruitment of functional managers to the development of more general managers in the workplace. This has been caused by the subdivision of organisations into more autonomous business units, charged with, for example, all activities aimed at a certain product-market combination.

Business units

As a result, more and more policy formulating tasks are assigned to middle management, with top-level management being responsible for creating the required conditions.

One reason for this is that it is particularly the level of the business unit or division where one may find the knowledge relating to the environment of the organisational unit. This makes adjustments to changes in that environment easier and quicker to implement.

O&M IN PRACTICE

Moderate industrial management

Dutch industry is not maximising its returns from its management. A study by the University of Groningen and Rabosearch (among 450 Dutch companies, each with around 200 employees) shows that Dutch companies, if they were to organise their affairs with the same efficiency and effectiveness as their Swedish and Germany counterparts, they could increase their turnover by 4% and their profit margin by 7%.

There is room for improvement particularly in HR management and objectives, including non-financial rewards for well-performing employees and timely dismissal of underperforming employees. According to Barbara Baarsma, Rabobank's director of knowledge development, productivity will be the main source of economic growth in coming years. Managers are often subject to overconfidence, and Dutch companies also perform poorly with respect to setting objectives – not only in financial terms, but also in customer satisfaction and risk management.

With regard to HR management, the study shows that good employees are often insufficiently appreciated; appreciation should be shown not only by awarding high salaries or bonuses, but also by offering career opportunities and general pats on the back. Companies should be more quick to proceed to relocation and dismissal for poorly performing employees. Baarsma: 'We do not like the confrontational approach. The Netherlands is a country of compromise.'

Source: *Het Financieele Dagblad*, 4 September 2018

9.2.2   Managerial roles

The main function of the manager is to direct employees and manage the resources in an organisation.

Managers spend their time performing three important roles which originate from this function (Figure 9.2). A role is defined as an expected behavioural pattern, or an organised collection of behaviours that are identified as belonging to a particular position.

The three types of managerial roles are:

1 the interpersonal roles;
2 the informational roles;
3 the decision-making roles.

FIGURE 9.2 **THE ROLES OF A MANAGER**

Source: Mintzberg, *Mintzberg over management, de wereld van onze organisaties*, Business Contact, 1991

The interpersonal roles. The manager directs employees and is responsible for the progress and results of processes within their competence. By maintaining relationships, the manager needs to govern processes and promote group interests as best as possible, both at higher organisational levels and externally. Constructing and maintaining formal and informal informational networks is part of this activity.

Interpersonal roles

The main aspects of a manager's interpersonal role are as:

a figurehead;
b leader;
c liaison officer.

The latter role includes establishing contacts outside one's own organisational unit. These contacts constitute a distinct externally-directed information system and are used during the daily activities of the unit.

The informational roles. A manager needs to be informed of any changes within the organisation that will affect the operational results of the division. The manager shares this information with both the organisation's members and other interested parties outside the organisation. The ability to react quickly within a changing environment requires accurate information, and thus information becomes increasingly important.

Informational roles

The main aspects of a manager's informational role are as:

a observer;
b disseminator;
c spokesperson.

The decision-making roles. As the person in charge of a business unit, a manager is responsible for implementing policy. Using gathered information and personal contacts, the manager translates the organisation(al unit)'s opportunities, threats, strengths, and weaknesses into decisions.

Decision-making roles

A manager needs to continually evaluate situations in order to achieve the required objectives. Managers need to make optimal use of the staff and resources available. In order to make the right decisions in such a complex situation, managers must be able to rely on their staff.

The main aspects of a manager's decision-making role are as:

a entrepreneur;
b trouble-shooter;
c resource allocator;
d negotiator.

Section 9.3 pays more in-depth attention to decision-making in an organisation. The activities described show that managers spend the majority of their time on
Communication   communication with organisational members and people outside the organisation.

As the activities of the manager are varied, managers need to be skilled and competent in many areas. Figure 9.3 illustrates a manager's main tasks. For each individual function, the time that each task consumes also differs. The span of a manager's control can be limited to a smaller number of management task requirements.

FIGURE 9.3 **MANAGERIAL ACTIVITIES**

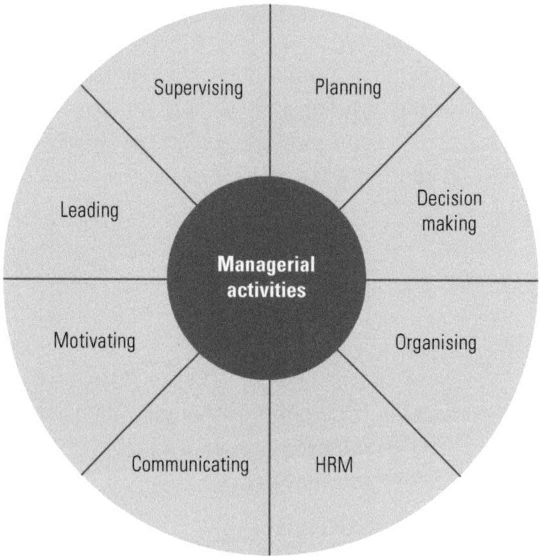

9.2.3   Top-level managers

Director   It was not too long ago that the most senior manager was known as the director; later on, they came to prefer to be known as manager, but an increase in the number of line and staff managers has caused this term to lose some of its value. Nowadays, chairpersons of the board or directors would prefer to be known as top-level executives or entrepreneurs.

Top-level manager   Despite considerable decentralisation of competencies, a top-level manager in an organisation is the main motivator and initiator of the enterprise in its current,
Symbolic function   modern form. Moreover, top-level managers often serve a symbolic function. They are held responsible and accountable for the future successes or failures of the organisations they lead. As such, the role of top-level manager requires specialist qualities.

A top-level manager needs to be a great communicator, able to inspire their employees. Other characteristics are their creativity, enthusiasm, and open-mindedness. Aside from that, top-level managers need to be ethically uncompromised; and last, but not least, they must be able to take a political approach toward all parties the organisation deals with, both internal and external.

Great communicator

9.2.4 Middle management

The largest group of managers, the middle management level, is the level immediately below the top management level.

Middle management basically consists of all managers below top-level, including divisional managers, assistant directors, heads of department, store managers, and chiefs. Middle management is important as it is tasked with implementing general policy and, often, with providing direct leadership to the executive branch.

Middle management

The most important middle management tasks are:
a managing and directing general activities;
b making operational decisions;
c passing along information top-down and bottom-up;
d planning;
e organising work activities;
f motivating employees;
g maintaining internal and external contacts;
h reporting;
i generating business.

As discussed, the nature of middle management is both one of policy formulating and executing tasks. Depending on its position, middle management's tasks lean either towards formulation or implementation. Given the trend towards decentralisation of top-level management authorities, the policy formulating tasks are shifting towards middle management, thus causing the function to increase in importance.

Policy formulating tasks

The position of middle management in organisations is of particular importance where the implementation of change is concerned. After all: top-level management may create wonderful new plans and strategies, but it is middle management that needs to motivate employees into giving life to these concepts. It is a characteristic of the position of the middle manager to be caught between a rock and a hard place: top-level management on the one hand, and employees on the other.

It stands to reason that, given the broad task package and increase in responsibilities, middle management must be subjected to high demands. A development that middle management will need to face now and in future is the phenomenon of organisational flattening: a decrease in the number of organisational layers. Many (major) organisations are getting rid of superfluous bureaucracy and hierarchy, and middle management is taking the hit. There are economic factors at the basis of this development: organisations need to present themselves are more competitive and incisive.

Organisational flattening

Moreover, a strong sense of individualism and restricted appreciation for power could mean a flat organisation would be effective in Dutch culture. This flattening of organisational structures will, of course, have further consequences for changes in management style, budgeting policies, and personnel management.

Restricted promotion from middle to higher management has also been seen as one consequence of flatter organisational structures. In order to give people new challenges and promote further business effectiveness, the notion of staff horizontally transferring between various business positions will become more widespread.

Horizontal transfer

In the future, it seems likely that the demise of more traditional business activities, such as planning and control, will lead to these roles eventually being phased out, and the workload taken over by computers. As a consequence, some middle management roles will become less important or disappear entirely, imposing ever-increasing demands on a reduced middle management staff. The educational levels of employees will continue to rise to meet the higher standards required and, as a consequence, current management leadership styles will be challenged. Demands made by an organisation's top management for a continually improving performance by its middle management level will result in middle management staff becoming indistinguishable from the category of entrepreneurial staff.

9.2.5 Managers in government

Administrative and political factors

Managers in governments require different skills from managers in the business world. In governmental management functions, the administrative and political factors are of greater significance.

Managing board
Top-level management

Management positions in governments fall roughly into positions associated with the managing board and positions in top-level management. In general, the managing board is responsible for making new policy decisions, and top management is responsible for putting the policies into practice. This is changing, however, as responsibilities and competencies are increasingly being delegated to top management. This mainly affects internal policy, with top management having to inspire and motivate staff to ensure implementation of those policies.

Top-level ministerial official

As well as their job requirements, the managerial problems faced by top-level ministerial officials and central government bodies differ from those of managers of decentralised or (semi) governmental bodies, or even the market sector. There are several reasons for these differences:

a The government is not part of a market-oriented organisation. Activities are not determined directly by a buyer of a service, but by the decisions of parliament, regional government, or city councils.

b Services provided by governments and the costs of delivering those services have an unstable character, as they are produced within a political and administrative decision-making process that is constantly changing.

c Within government, the influence of financial results on management is less clear than within the market sector, since the financial position of a business is more transparent.

d Additionally, a government has certain requirements and duties not found in the market sector: for example, the principle of good governance, the acceptance and prioritising of certain duties of care to special groups, and transparency of administration.

As such, top-level government managers require additional skills in order to effectively carry out their main duties:

1 Managers must have an understanding of the social and administrative ramifications of the democratic process;

2 Managers must be able to deal appropriately in areas of conflicting interests;

3 Managers should have a very thorough knowledge of their area of business.

Top-down organisational direction is becoming a thing of the past

Pieter Saman (40) helms successful outdoor-goods chain Bever. Bever is doing well: its number of stores has grown to 40; the chain employs 900 people. Online retail is also on the rise, with Bever managing to closely interweave in-store and online sales. Thus, the company has managed to create a customer experience that has led to international recognition.

Saman: 'Leadership has a directive ring to it, but that is not how we do things at Bever. There is a more organic process of collaboration. Many employees are outdoor enthusiasts with a common goal, namely to get as many people as possible to enjoy as much time as they can out of doors. A passion for sports is a strong motivator. Of course, it remains important to ensure there is a balance between the interests of the shareholders and our idealism. But it many ways, the two are extensions of one another. Our way of working is more informal, not self-directing. Things that need sorting out often benefit from ad hoc coalitions, and this autonomous method of collaboration is supported and facilitated by management. And management shares a lot of market information, such as customer detail, in weekly kick-off meetings. There are also town-hall meetings and quarterly meetings; workshops in tepee tents and around campfires, where nothing should be left unsaid. Directing an organisation from the top is slowly becoming a thing of the past. You will continue to see forms of governance similar to what we use, with a common goal, core values, and customers being the decisive factors, and management allowing employees the chance to play around within the confines of those factors. Each organisation will need to find its own way of managing.'

Source: www.mt.nl, 28-06-2018

The management profiles of semi-governmental organisations such as municipalities, health care, social work, and education are becoming increasingly similar to those in the business world, tending to be more independent in terms of both policy and financial decision-making. There is a much stronger similarity to the business world's supplier-customer model.

Additionally, managerial functions in (semi-)governmental institutions are increasingly filled by people with a specific managerial education instead of specialists in a particular field. In the health care industry, for example, there is a call for managers with a background in business, administration, or economics.

9.3   DECISION-MAKING

As discussed, problem-solving and decision-making is one of management's most important tasks.

In organisations, there is a continuous need for attention to issues or problems that need resolving. These can range from the everyday to those that can have enormous ramifications for the continued existence of an organisation. Some problems can be solved quickly and easily, but others require a more thorough analysis. It is the latter problems in particular that tend to be complex in terms of structure, and their associated decision-making must be seen in terms of multiple factors. Consider the problems caused by changing the organisational direction for the coming years, changing an organisation's intended market segments of operation, the best way of implementing internationalisation strategy. In such cases, a well-founded decision-making process is of key importance.

Selection process   An important aspect of decision-making is that it often involves a selection process. In most situations, there are different alternatives; the task is in selecting the best possible option. Naturally, the availability of sufficient and relevant information to weigh the possible options is of paramount importance in this respect. Therefore, the decision-making process is closely linked to the processes of data gathering and data processing. There is an additional problem: a large number of decisions are made in situations that involve a certain degree of uncertainty and a partial (or complete) lack of relevant information.

FIGURE 9.4 **THE FACTORS THAT COMPLICATE DESICION-MAKING**

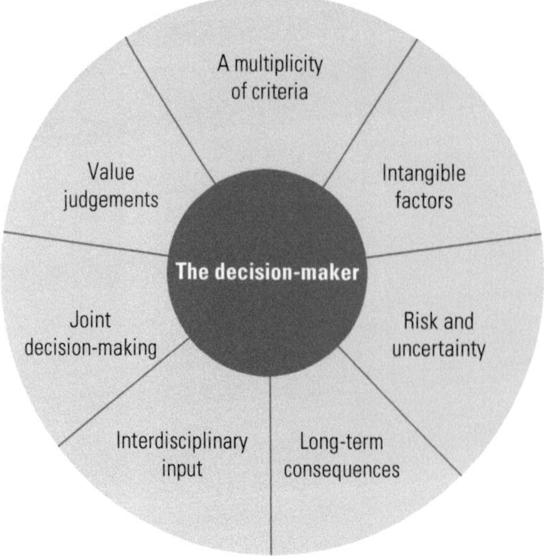

People and organisations
PART B

© Noordhoff Uitgevers bv

Decision-making is mainly a human activity where mutual collaboration and creativity play an important role. In order to ensure effective decision-making, various tools and techniques can be employed.

The context of decision-making is becoming increasingly complex (see Figure 9.4). This increase in complexity is caused by a number of factors:

1   **Multiplicity of criteria.** Decisions are made by various parties who often have conflicting interests and use different criteria for the same problem, thereby increasing the complexity of the problem.
2   **Interdisciplinary input.** Increasingly, companies are involving specialists in the decision-making process. Specialists may include those with an in-depth knowledge of technology, law, taxation, and/ot marketing. Their various skills must all play a part in reaching the final decision.
3   **Joint decision-making.** It is essential that decisions are made by a number of people representing the various organisational functions, particularly for decisions that are crucial to the future of the organisation. External expertise is sometimes called for, and even governmental bodies may want their say.
4   **Risk and uncertainty.** Markets are changing so quickly and global economic developments are so unpredictable that competition can come from unexpected angles. When making decisions, it can be very hard to gauge what future events and changes are just around the corner.
5   **Long-term consequences.** Decisions made from a short-term view (controlling expenses, for example) may have indirect long-term consequences (for example, on the competitive position of the enterprise). Cost management decisions rely on short-term results; otherwise, they are ineffective. But how about their long-term consequences?
6   **Value judgements.** Decisions are often made by people from various backgrounds, and on the basis of different perceptions, aspirations, norms and values. The recent growth of sustainable entrepreneurship and ethical awareness has not made this any easier.
7   **Intangible factors.** Decisions are often made in a context of monetary value. This allows for an objective assessment of potential options or solutions. Organisations, however, are increasingly expected to take into account issues related to their corporate social responsibility, such as the environment and consumer morale.

9.3.1   Decision-making in organisations

Decisions in organisations are about issues or problems that are of a varied nature, that derive from a variety of situations, and that need to be worked on by various people or groups. If there is a significant discrepancy between what *should be* and actually *is*, there is a problem.

The nature of a problem lies in whether the issue at hand is a routine problem or a specific problem (Figure 9.5). Routine problems, such as handling complaints, required pre-programmed decision-making (a procedure), whereas a specific problem, such as price setting, benefits from a less structured solution.

FIGURE 9.5 **PROBLEMS AND DECISION-MAKING**

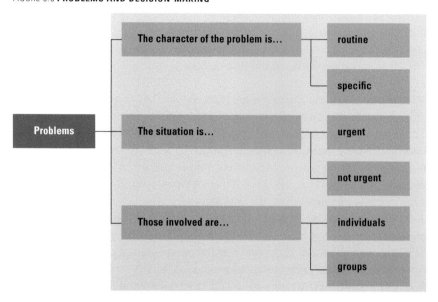

Sometimes, a quick decision is needed (if, for example, a competitor lowers their prices, prompting other businesses to decide whether to follow suit); while in other cases, more time is available, and a careful assessment can be made (if, for example, a new office location is needed). Both individuals and groups may be involved in the decision-making process.

An important characteristic of decision-making is that a choice has to be made between a number of alternatives. Often these alternatives are linked to unpredictable future events: for example, economic growth in South East Asia, a competitor's reaction when a new product is introduced, future wage costs, etc.

Predictability
The extent to which future events can be predicted plays a major role in decision-making. The degree of predictability varies along a scale that distinguishes between the following scenarios (see Figure 9.6):

Absolute certainty
1 **Absolute certainty.** Where the exact objectives and outcomes of all alternatives are known: for example, when selecting a printing company for this textbook, the publisher knows the precise number of copies required, the required quality and the deadline. The publisher can then invite tenders from a number of printing companies, and compare offers.

Partial certainty
2 **Partial certainty.** Where the objectives are clear but the exact outcome of the alternatives is unknown though, to a certain extent, predictable. In the example, if sale figures from the past are available, a prediction can be made about the number of books likely to be sold.

Partial uncertainty
3 **Partial uncertainty.** Where the various outcomes are virtually unpredictable though the objectives are clear. In the example of the publisher, it may not be known whether competing publishers are also bringing out new books. Another uncertainty could be the overall increase or decrease in the number of class hours scheduled for the subject 'Organisation and Management' next year.

Absolute uncertainty
4 **Absolute uncertainty.** Where there is absolutely no way of making predictions and the objectives are unclear. The director of the publishing company may choose not to go ahead with printing this book at all. Complete uncertainty is often caused by a rapidly changing and turbulent environment.

382

People and organisations
PART B

© Noordhoff Uitgevers bv

FIGURE 9.6 **DECISION-MAKING AND PREDICTABILITY**

In addition to the extent of predictability, an organisation may be faced with two different types of problems:

a well-structured (incidental) problems, and;

b poorly-structured (unique) problems. These different types of problems require their own approach with regard to decision-making.

Well-structured problems. An incidental problem is a simple, common and easily defined problem. How to deal with employees who report in sick for work is an example of such a problem. The message is dealt with by a member of staff who follows a clear-cut procedure. This is known as a pre-programmed decision. The staff member can deal with a problem of this kind in a routine manner, as the organisation has down procedures, rules and guidelines:

1 **Procedure**. A series of mutually coherent and successive steps for responding to a problem.

2 **Rule**. An explicit agreement regarding what should or should not be done.

3 **Guideline/policy**. Provides general direction for decision-making.

The bulk of the workload associated with resolving this type of problem lies at lower organisational levels.

Poorly-structured problems. Problems of this sort are problems new to the organisation, and they occur less frequently. Typically, the information available is incomplete and unclear. An example of such a problem is how to develop a new product in the absence of pre-programmed processes. A 'one-off' decision is needed. This type of problem (and its solutions) is unique.

The bulk of the workload associated with resolving this type of problem lies at higher organisational levels.

Well-structured
problems

Pre-programmed
decision

Poorly-structured
problems

'One off' decision

9.3.2   Rational decision-making process

The various ways in which people make decisions in organisations are known as decision-making processes. Rational decision-making is one such process. The process starts with defining the problem and ends with choosing a solution. A number of phases are worked through in a systematic manner. Solutions to problematic situations can be found using the framework of this approach. Information is collected over the course of the process, and analysed. It is then used both as input and output in the decision-making process.

Rational decision-
making process

In order to have an effect on the process, information should meet a number of requirements:

a It should be relevant to the decision.
b It should be reliable.
c It should be available on time.
d Its costs should be in proportion to its value.

Informational demands e It should be subject to informational demands in terms of present, including lay-out, scope, distinction between the important and the incidental, and detail.

Sources of information The many possible sources of information include one's own data resources, specially commissioned and executed market research, literature studies, external databases, and consultation with suppliers and customers. Without information, therefore, a thorough decision-making process is impossible.

The rational decision-making process distinguishes between the following phases (see Figure 9.7):

1 defining the problem;
2 developing alternatives;
3 evaluating alternatives;
4 selecting an alternative;
5 implementing and monitoring the selected alternative.

FIGURE 9.7 **PHASES OF THE RATIONAL DECISION-MAKING PROCESS**

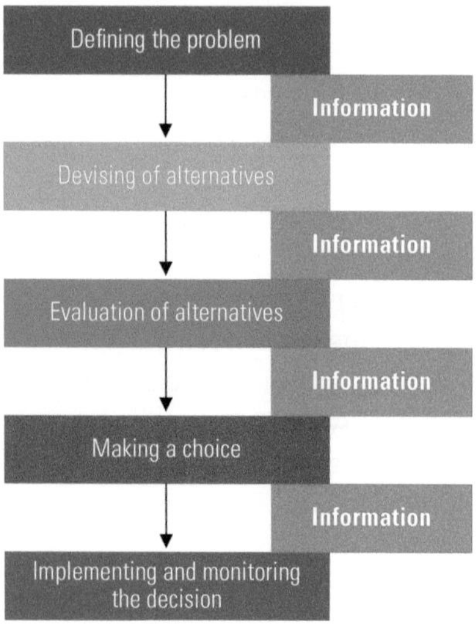

Defining the problem

Problem identification
Problem definition

There are two aspects to defining a problem: identification and analysis. Problem identification is the detection and determination of a problem. A problem arises if a desired situation (the norm) deviates from the actual situation in either a positive or a negative sense (see Figure 9.8).

Problems arise in various ways. They may be caused by external circumstances (for example, a delay in the delivery of an order), or form a logical consequence of a management decision (for example, sales of a particular product needing to be increased by 10% within three years).

FIGURE 9.8 **PROBLEM DETECTION BY DETERMINING DEVIATIONS FROM THE NORM**

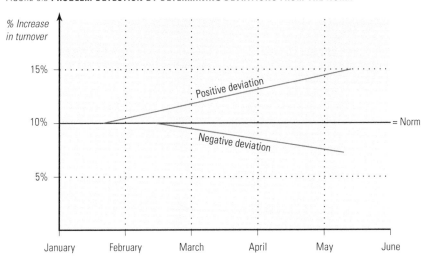

If a problem is detected, it is important to ascertain its exact character. 'A well-formulated problem is halfway to being resolved', as the saying goes. It is important to realise that not everybody is interested in identifying problems. Some people are susceptible to problem denial and evasive behaviour. A lack of clear objectives and norms in certain fields is common in many organisations, and makes problems difficult to recognise.

Once a problem has been recognised, it has to be analysed. This involves searching for the real causes and consequences of the problem. Facts corroborating the existence of the problem have to be found. Since these are often based on subjective ideas about certain developments, extreme care should be taken at this stage.

Problem analysis

During this phase of the process, the following questions should be asked:
1 Is the problem structural or incidental?
2 What is the level of urgency of the problem?
3 What is the scope of the problem?
4 How does the problem relate to other areas divisions within and outside the organisation?
5 Is the nature of the problem relational or organisational?

Developing alternatives

During this phase, viable alternatives for resolving the problem as identified during the previous phase have to be developed. Sometimes, the solution is already evident from the way the problem has been described and analysed. Sometimes, the solution is not as evident.

Developing alternatives

How alternatives are devised partly depends on the organisation's familiarity with the problem. If the problem is a well-known one, a solution used in the past may be suitable. New problems need as many potential alternative solutions as possible and it is important not to simply take the first option devised.

Finding as many alternatives as possible imposes major demands on the creativity of an organisation's members.

Creativity

Alternative: Education

You feel ready for something new. Education seems a logical step: there is a howling shortage of teachers. The higher educated in particular have begun making a career switch in recent years, as shown in figures by Dutch Central Statistics Agency CBS. Of all working residents in the Netherlands between 25 and 45, 13 percent changed their profession last year; lateral entrants are welcomed with open arms. The motivation to make a switch specifically takes the form of serving societal interests: education is very relevant, it lets you help children develop themselves, and the results are immediately visible. The extended vacation time and the possibility for part-time work are also appealing, making it attractive to combine a career in education with a family with young kids. On the other hand, a professional may be faced with a wage drop, hard work, peacekeeping, a lot of meetings, etc. One-third of teachers drops out before they are thirty years old, and many lateral entrants also bid their farewell to education after a while: coping with difficult pupils and demanding parents regularly leads to emotional exhaustion.

The fact that people are still willing to take the step is largely down to their phase in life. At around 40 years old, many people are fed up with commercial targets: they want to have a direct impact on others.

'Transferring to a different line of work is good for the soul', says psychologist Marc Schabracq. 'But it is not always easy. It means saying good-bye to a former way of life, which is a painful process. Our lives are the result of a crazy amount of order. Removing a chunk of that order causes stress-levels to increase. But if you feel the freedom that comes from change and if you manage to make yourself at home in a new environment, then the transition can be very healthy.'

Source: *Het Financieele Dagblad*, magazine, no. 40, 06 October 2018

Evaluating alternatives

Selecting the right alternative

Now that all the options have been identified, the aim of this phase is to select the right alternative. Two aspects play an important role: establishing criteria, and assessing the likely consequences of each alternative.

Making a wise decision involves weighing up all the criteria. The complexity and specific nature of some problems means that criteria are difficult to formulate and are not universally applicable. However, it is fair to say that the criteria should meet a number of requirements:

1 **Criteria must be measurable where possible**. Criteria must be quantifiable; else, testing alternatives against criteria becomes ambiguous and differences in interpretation may arise.

2 **Criteria must be feasible**. A selected option must be possible to implement, and the people responsible for the implementation must be convinced of this possibility.

3 **Criteria must fit the problem**. There must be a plausible link between the criterion and the problem. If the terms are too general, the wrong choice could be made.

4 **Criteria must complement one another where possible**. If the criteria are in contradiction with each other, a situation arises where no final choice can be made. A compromise may need to be reached, or certain criteria may need to be prioritised or weighted over others.

5 **The criteria must relate to all aspects of the alternative**. A limited number of criteria might result in certain consequences not being tested or taken into consideration. This may lead to unpleasant surprises during implementation. Whether a solution stands or fails depends on how extensively each aspect of the option is tested.

When studying the options, the most important consideration should be that the alternative that best resolves the problem is the one that should be selected. This requires all consequences of all alternatives to be known, meaning it is necessary to chart the expected effects resulting from the intended alternatives as best as possible. Each potential option has its own positive or negative consequences mapping these out in full is of great importance to the selection process. Studying the consequences may mean that certain alternatives are discarded outright, due to major problems with respect to their acceptance or costs.

Positive and negative consequences

Selecting an alternative

Following the evaluation, it is time to begin selecting an alternative by exposing the various possibilities to the established criteria. Testing the various alternatives using these criteria may result in one of several outcomes:

Selecting an alternative

a If one of the alternatives fulfils the criteria and best resolves the problem, then it is selected.

b If none of the alternatives fulfils the criteria, the result is a situation where either new alternatives are defined or the criteria are adjusted.

c If one or more alternatives produce the same results, an additional examination of these alternatives is required. A possible solution in such a situation is not only to look at the ultimate consequences of choosing a particular alternative, but also at considerations such as timing, resources and risks associated with each alternative.

A factor that may influence the choice is the degree of uncertainty. As discusses, not all of the required information may be available, and predictions may only be possible to a limited extent.

Uncertainty

Implementing and monitoring the selected alternative.

Once a particular alternative has been selected, the decision has to be translated into plans and actions. It is important that the decision is supported by the organisation. Decisions that lead to organisational change may encounter heavy resistance. This may be due to a number of reasons:

Implementing and monitoring the selected alternative

a **Perceptual**. An inability to imagine a new situation.

b **Emotional**. Fear and/or uncertainty of the unknown.

c **Cultural**. A desire to maintain existing norms, values, and convictions.

d **Environmental**. Anxiety about management's commitment to providing information and support.

If these aspects are not taken sufficiently into account, the resulting selected option may turn out not to have been correct. Finally, it should be made clear how progress is to be monitored and reported for the sake of the success of the project.

9.3.3 Non-rational decision-making processes

Ideal model

The rational decision-making process discussed should be seen as an ideal model. It supposes that decisions are based on a clear problem definition with an option being chosen after careful assessment of the alternatives. In reality, the decision-making process may be very different for the following reasons:
a insufficient available information;
b an overly lengthy rational decision-making process;
c limited financial resources for acquiring additional information;
d limited decision-maker capabilities;
e conflicting decision-maker interests;
f occasional intolerance to deviating opinions.

In practice, there are four distinct types of decision-making processes (see Figure 9.9), namely: neo-rational, bureaucratic, political, and open-ended. This classification is based on the degree of centralisation (the top-down influence of decisions), and the degree of formality (the issuing of rules).

Degree of centralisation
Degree of formalisation

FIGURE 9.9 **IRRATIONAL DECISION-MAKING**

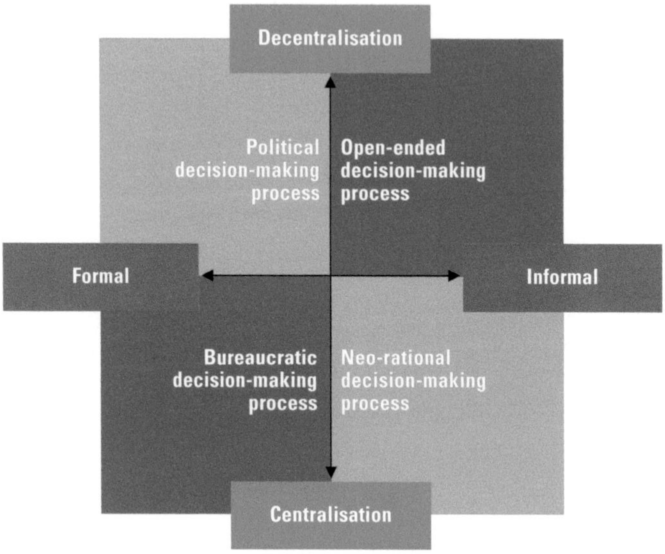

In practice, the various decision-making forms are hardly ever encountered in their purest possible form. Often, there is a situationally determined decision-making process, which can have the character of a neo-rational decision-making process one moment, and an open-ended decision-making process the next. Employees, however, depend on knowing which decisions their organisation makes, because it allows them to take up their own position in the decision-making process.

Situationally determined decision-making processes

Neo-rational decision-making

This process resembles the rational type previously discussed. It is informal and centralised and, in most cases, only one person makes the decisions. There is no extensive prior research and the decision-maker is not impeded by many rules. It is known as the 'neo'-rational process because emotional and intuitive aspects also play a role. The advantage of this decision-making process is that it is directed by one point of view and has clear targets that are acceptable to all. A disadvantage is that not many people are involved: there is little room for the opinion of anyone other than the central decision-maker.

Informal and centralised decision-making

Neo-rational decision-making process

Intuition has a place in the boardroom

According to Swedish politician, entrepreneur, and writer Per Schlingmann, companies preparing for the future should learn to better listen to their instincts. Schlingmann: 'In an age where data and AI (Artificial Intelligence) are playing an increasing role in decision-making, it is important to consider how we, as human beings, can distinguish ourselves. Data and AI are based on the recognition of past patterns, and making predictions based on that recognition. But the major shifts in business actually came from angles where

no corporations were to be found; for example, the rise of Airbnb.

Intuitive decision-making does not mean making decisions based on nothing; it means listening closely to how you feel, and testing those feelings using all available technology. It is of paramount importance to create a culture that respects different opinions and that allows people to speak their mind. And the path to such a culture is through greater managerial diversity.'

Source: www.mt.nl, 01 Oct 2018

O&M IN PRACTICE

Bureaucratic decision-making

This type is characterised by decisions based on fixed rules instead of consciously made choices as is the case in the neo-rational decision-making process. Extensive use of rules, planning and control mean that this type of process is very formal and centralised. The rules may be internal (e.g. corporate guidelines for the lay-out of

Bureaucratic decision-making process

advertisements) as well as external (e.g. legislation). There is a central governance of strongly formalised decision-making processes. Its strong point is that experience from the past is taken into consideration, and that the rules are known by all – so there is no ambiguity. The downside of the bureaucratic decision-making process is, however, that innovation is stifled.

Political decision-making

Political decision-making process

This process has a formal and a decentralised character. The latter results from the involvement of many different parties with divergent interests. Decisions result from negotiations and interactions between groups. The advantage of this process is that everybody has a good opportunity to influence decision-making. However, the process carries the potential for a lot of energy to be spent on internal political

Internal political gamess

games, and the final result might be a stalemate or even a severely damaged organisation.

Open-ended decision-making process

Open-ended decision-making process

The open-ended decision-making process has both a decentralised and an informal character. It is characterised by its lack of clear starting and finishing

Lack of clear starting and finishing points

points. Decision-making is erratic and unpredictable. There are no clear objectives, and decisions have an ad hoc character, with chance playing a large role. The turbulence creates new situations to which one has to adapt constantly. Step-by-step (incremental) decisions are advisable, with follow-up decisions based on new developments and information. The process is flexible and allows for corrections. There is always room for new ideas and creativity is stimulated. However, the down side is that the decisions made may not be very effective.

9.3.4 Aspects of decision-making

Running an organisation means ongoing decision-making. To react to changes in the environment and to safeguard the continuity of the organisation, these decisions must be as flexible, efficient, and effective as possible in an attempt to address the changes confronting the organisation in the best possible way. Thus, this section addresses the following aspects of decision-making:

a creativity;
b participation;
c meetings;
d negotiations;
e power (see Section 9.5.1);
f decision-making styles.

Creativity

Creativity

Whatever the current phase of the decision-making process, creativity can increase an organisation's competitive advantage. Therefore, employee creativity should be utilised to the fullest at all times. A broad range of tools is available to free up and encourage creativity.

Brainstorming

One widely used tool is brainstorming, a method that can be used to generate a lot of new ideas quickly. The focus is on generating these new ideas rather than evaluating them or making a selection.

During a brainstorming session, criticism of new ideas is discouraged as it would put off others from adding new suggestions of their own, thereby defeating the whole purpose of the exercise. It is important to create the sort of atmosphere in which individuals feel empowered to be creative. During a brainstorming session, initial suggestions should be used as a springboard for ideas to be developed further by others and for creating new perspectives.

Brainstorming sessions often take place at a location that is quite different from the normal working environment, and the participants are often a specific group in so-called off-site sessions. For example, office workers might meet at a rural location, a potentially stimulating change. Brainstorming works best in small groups of 10 to 15 people. Involving people from various backgrounds enhances the results since they introduce new perspectives on the problem.

Off-site sessions

It must be clear to participants what the key problem is. Experience shows that brainstorming is at its most effective when:
1 Subjects or problems are simple in nature. The greater the complexity, the more specialists are needed, which this is detrimental to the particular nature of brainstorming sessions.
2 Sufficient knowledge of the problems is available.
3 Problems or subject matter are clearly defined.
4 Participants are keen to suggest solutions to the problem.
5 Sessions do not last longer than an hour.

Participation

Many employees find a challenging job essential. It increases their motivation, and motivated staff will take on all sorts of tasks and feel more involved in helping the organisation reach its goals. One aspect of a challenging job is the opportunity for the job holder to be included in general and work-related decisions.

Employee participation combines the rights and authorities of staff to influence the establishment, execution, and control of company policy, and the decisions that lead thereto. Participation may be indirect (workers councils where elected staff members discuss issues) or direct (staff representatives meeting department heads to ratify employment conditions). In both cases, workers are able to influence decision-making in their own department, increasing their commitment to their work. Within Europe, employee participation in multinational organisations occurs via a European Works Council.

Participation

Works councils

The 1950 Dutch *Works Council Act* mainly referred to communicative function, which was aimed at ensuring a works council was set up as a body for discussion between employers and employees. The authorities of the works council were significantly expanded upon in 1979. Employee position in management and policy matters was greatly reinforced. In 1982 and 1984, the Act was adjusted with respect to its impact on small organisations and the provision of financial information to works councils.

Works Council Act

Major amendements to the Act date from 1998. In addition to expanding on the right to advise and consent, the new Act distinguished between three organisational categories:
1 **Companies with fifty or more employees**. A works council is required.
2 **Companies with ten to fifty employees**. Three possible options:
   a Business owners may voluntarily create a so-called staff representative committee (src) of at least three individuals.
   b The collective agreement can dictate whether an src is obligatory. The src's authorities are limited. The right to consent relates to labour condition,

absenteeism, and working hours arrangements. The right to advise only applies to plan that may lead to loss of labour or to important changes in the work (or labour conditions) for at least a quarter of employees.

 c If no src is established, company management must schedule and complete a staff meeting twice every year.

3 Companies with fewer than ten employees. A business owner may create an src voluntarily. The authorities of this body are restricted to the right to consent to working hours.

Enterprise
: In a legal sense, an enterprise is any independently operating organised unit in which labour is performed (virtually) exclusively under the terms of a labour agreement. Whether or not the organised unit works for profit is irrelevant in this respect. The Works Council Act also applies to government institutions at the levels of, for example, province, municipality, ministery, water board, or municipal social service.

Works council
: When composing a works council, representatives must be selected to represent a cross section of the company as a whole. This means there is a demand for representativeness in both breadth and depth of functions.

According to the Works Council Act, works councils are awarded rights in three areas, namely:
1 a right to information and discussion;
2 a right to advise;
3 a right to consent.

Right to information and discussion
: **1 Right to information and discussion**: The principle is that the business owner must provide all information the works council deems necessary. The business owner is required to provide the information requested in so far as this information is required for the works council to fulfil its function.
A meeting and discussion between the works council and management must take place six times per year.

Right to advise
: **2 Right to advise**: Organisational management is required by the Works Council Act to request written advice from the works council before making decisions in various fields, including:
 a transfer of authority;
 b organisational activity cessation;
 c major downsizing or changes in activities;
 d major organisational changes;
 e major investments;
 f applying for an important line of credit;
 g appointment or dismissal of a managerial member;
 h implementation of or adjustment to a major technological provision;
 i measures related to the organisation's environmental duties;
 j relocation of the organisation.

Right to consent
: **3 Right to consent**: In addition to the right to information and discussion, the works council has a right to consent (joint-decision-making authority) in the case of decisions in various fields, including:
 a reward or job valuation systems;
 b arrangements for working hours or vacation time;
 c pension insurance;
 d policies of appointment, dismissal, or promotion;

e staff training;
f work meetings arrangements;
g privacy;
h performance monitoring systems;
i complaints management systems.

If a business owner fails to live up to their obligations to the works council, then compliance must be enforced. Specifically, by the Company Audit Committee. A company audit committee consist of at least six employer representatives and at least six employee representatives from similar enterprises. The committee is appointed and assigned by the Social Economic Council.
The most important task of the company audit committee is to mediate in case of differences between the works council and the company. The works council is obligated to consult the company audit committee before seeking legal proceedings.

Company audit committee

Work meetings and other forms of participation

In addition to the previous forms of participation, every organisation is subject to work meetings: regular, direct discussions between group management and executives that cover work and working conditions at a department. This way, employees can influence the decision-making in their own department. This makes the work meeting a form of discussion that increases employee commitment to their work.
In conclusion, it can be said that, in addition to indirect participation (works councils) and direct participation (work meetings), participation is also subject to other arrangements in the Netherlands, including legislation on annual accounts, health and safety legislation, and legislation with reference to boards of supervisory directors).

Work meetings

European Works Councils

A decision of the European Commission made in 1994 ('The Establishment of a European Works Council'), obligated European multinational enterprises to establish European Works Council. The enterprises affected are those with at least 1,000 employees spread throughout the European Union, with a minimum of 150 employees in two member countries.

In 2009, a new European directive was implemented, determining that every country in the European Union must have formulated its legislation with regard to participation at the European level. The directive applies to all EU countries, as well as those that are members of the European Economic Area but are not members of the EU: Norway, Iceland, and Liechtenstein.

An European Works Council is a body that informs and advises employees on international issues.
The procedure to appoint and implement a European Works Council can be triggered by both the central management or by a group of at least 100 employees (or its representatives). These 100 employees must be from at least two different member states. A special negotiations group, consisting of employee representatives, is created to discuss various topics with central management. These topics range from the work area of the European Works Council, its composition, its authorities, and its duration of tenure.

European Works Council

The special negotiations group should represent each member country in the organisation through at least one individual. An addition, based on the numbers of employees in the various member states, additional special negotiations members can be appointed. Member states that are home to a quarter, half, or three quarters of employees are entitled to additional representatives: one for a quarter, two for half, and three for three quarters.

For example: multinational company X employs 10,000 people distributed across eight EU member states. The members of the special negotiations division are distributed as follows (Table 9.2):

TABLE 9.2 **MEMBERS OF SPECIAL NEGOTIATIONS DIVISION**

	Number of employees	Number of representatives
• Germany	5,000	3
• Spain	2,500	2
• Italy	900	1
• Sweden	600	1
• The Netherlands	550	1
• Iceland	350	1
• Portugal	80	1
• Denmark	20	1

Source: www.fnvbondgenoten.nl

This example illustrates that the number of representatives in the special negotiations group does not depend on the number of employees, but on the distribution of employees across member states.

Most member states have implemented the directive, and there are around 650 European Works Councils in existence. The Dutch (Central) Works Council has its usual rights of participation in a foreign concern with a facility in the Netherlands. The Dutch (Central) Works Council, however, cannot influence the decisions of a foreign concern's top-level management made abroad; hence the implementation of a European Works Council.

Meetings **Meeting skills**

Decisions are generally made during meetings. Nowadays, with participation considered important, meetings are essential. Quite a few organisational members complain that they spend too much time in meetings. Meetings have a number of different functions:

1 **Being together.** Meetings serve a social function, making members feel that they belong to the same group.
2 **Being informed together.** A group has more available knowledge than an individual. Meetings allow accumulated knowledge to be used to generate greater insights.
3 **Working together.** A group has a greater capacity for creativity than an individual. By sharing ideas, better and more efficient solutions to problems become possible.
4 **Implementing together.** One is often more committed to carrying out a task if one was involved in its decision-making.

Fish-net model of meetings   For a meeting to be as effective as possible, it should be structured as shown in Figure 9.10, the so-called 'fish-net model'.

People and organisations
PART B

The fish-net model consists of the following steps:

1 **Opening.** A word of welcome, recording of attendees and absentees, verifying that everybody has received the minutes, questions and comments about the minutes, confirming finishing time of the meeting.
2 **Initialisation.** Choice of subject to be discussed.
3 **Contextualising.** Inventory subject aspects, use of visual media (such as flip-over sheets), but no discussion.
4 **Organising.** Summarising and ordering subject aspects, reaffirming objectives and criteria, initiating discussion, encoring problem-solving.
5 **Opinion forming.** Intermediate summarising, ensuring relevance of discussion keeping time, working purposefully, handling critiques and differences of opinion professionally.
6 **Decision-making.** The process of preparing a decision.
7 **Concluding.** Making and recording a decision.
8 **Closing.** Establishing a brief summary of decisions and agreements made, discussing final questions, setting next meeting date.

FIGURE 9.10 **THE 'FISH-NET MODEL' OF MEETINGS**

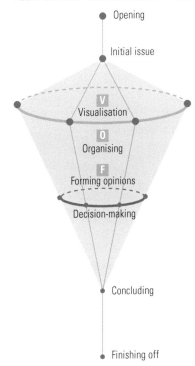

An important feature of a meeting is the way in which decisions are ratified. Decisions can be ratified in various ways:

1 **Democratic decisions**. The proposal is decided by vote, with half those present plus one being the required number.
2 **Majority rule**. As above, but with two-thirds of those present being the required number.
3 **Unanimous decisions**. Proposals must be fully accepted or rejected by all voters.
4 **Consensus principle**. Only proposals without principal objections from any members present are accepted.
5 **Vetoed decisions**. A single vote against means a proposal is rejected.

Democratic decisions

Majority rule

Unanimous decisions

Consensus principle

Vetoed decisions

6 Delegations. The decision-making is delegated to one particular person or group.

7 Authorities. Decisions are made by one person. The meeting serves as an advisory body to an autocratic manager.

When choosing a decision-making method, its effects on the speed and organisation-wide should be considered, with the influence of decision-making on speed schematically demonstrated in Figure 9.11, and its influence on acceptance in Figure 9.12.

FIGURE 9.11 **THE RELATIONSHIP BETWEEN THE DIFFERENT WAYS OF DECISION-MAKING AND THE SPEED OF DECISION-MAKING**

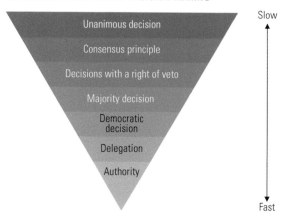

FIGURE 9.12 **THE RELATIONSHIP BETWEEN THE DIFFERENT WAYS OF DECISION-MAKING AND ACCEPTANCE OF THE DECISION**

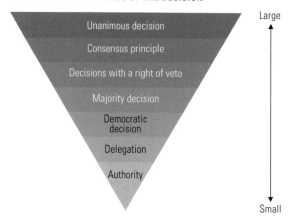

Negotiating

Like attending meetings, negotiating is a common activity that takes place whenever parties pursue different goals. The purpose of negotiation is to find a compromise that is acceptable to all parties. It differs from collaboration, where the various parties have similar interests. During negotiations, the parties are mutually dependent – yet at the same time, they have different interests. Negotiations demonstrate two characteristics: the parties involved are mutually dependent on each other, and the parties involved have differing (or conflicting) interests.

Negotiations distinguish the subject of negotiation from the method of negotiation. In practice, it is the latter of these that causes issues: what position should one take, and how is the opposition likely to respond?

People and organisations
PART B

Recently, participants of the Harvard Negotiation project have developed a method of negotiation that has been successfully applied in many countries: principle negotiation.

Principled negotiation

This method abandons the notion of a hard of soft position, and replaces it with a method based on the principle that points of disagreements are judged on their merits.

The Prisoner's dilemma: to cooperate, or not to cooperate?

O&M IN PRACTICE

The Prisoner's Dilemma is a situation often found in decision-making processes. It focusses on the question of whether or not to cooperate. For example: you and a buddy have been caught robbing a store. You are both confined separately, and interrogated. Your interrogator informs you that, should you confess to the robbery, you will get a milder, one-year jail sentence; your buddy, on the other hand, will be given a more severe, ten-year sentence. Should you both confess, you will each get eight years in prison. But if neither of you confesses, you will both be sentenced to a less severe, two-year stint in prison.

Your decision now is whether or not to confess. Confessing may earn you the lowest possible (one-year) sentence. But if your buddy confesses as well, you both get eight years. This means that, in order for both parties to benefit equally, neither should confess: both will be jailed for only two years. But can either of you trust the other enough to keep their mouth shut? The moral of the story is that organisational studies show that parties generally fare better if they cooperate, instead of only chasing after their own interests.

FIGURE **PRISONER'S DILEMMA**

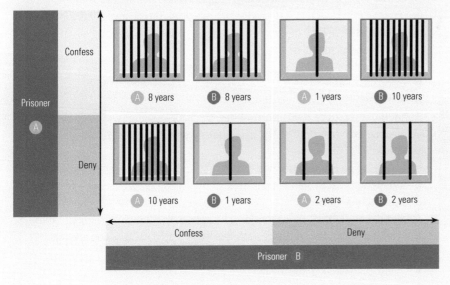

Principled negotiation is based on four aspects of negotiation, which can be used to formulate advice that can be applied to any situation:

1 **People.** Separate the people from the problem. It is important to avoid a situation where participants take up subjective positions and end up being too attached to an issue.

2 **Interests.** Concentrate on the interests, not on positions. All too often, parties concentrate on the starting positions instead of the issues that are fundamental to those positions.

3 **Choices.** Create all sorts of possibilities before making a decision. All too often, the creativity needed to come up with alternatives is suppressed by time pressure and the presence of opposition. In such situations, it is advisable to take more time to formulate alternatives that promote common interests and reconcile conflicting ones.

4 **Criteria.** The result has to be based on objective norms. These norms should be disconnected from the personal sphere as much as possible, and drawn up independently of any of the parties. Norms that are generally accepted are preferred: market values and legal precedents, for example.

Decision-making styles

Way of thinking
Tolerance

Each person makes a decision in their own way. Looking at this more closely makes it possible to identify different styles, depending on the way people think and the extent to which they tolerate ambiguity. Thinking can be rational or intuitive. A rationally thinking person follows a structured way of reaching decisions. An intuitively thinking person follows a less structured but more creative way. One person might be able to make decisions in a highly obscure context and not find it difficult to deal with a great deal of information at the same time. Another person may prefer to deal with a multitude of information in a logical way, through planning.

Four styles of decision-making
Directive style

Relating a person's way of thinking (rational intuitive) to their tolerance of ambiguity (low high) gives rise to four styles of decision-making (see Figure 9.13), namely:

1 **Directive style of decision-making.** People who make decisions in this way are rational and have a low tolerance of ambiguity. The characteristics of this style are that decisions are made:
   a quickly and efficiently;
   b with short-term focus;
   c using little information;
   d after assessing few alternatives.

Behavioural style

2 **Behavioural style of decision-making.** Decision-makers with a behavioural style work well with others. The characteristics of this style are that decisions are made:
   a focussing on others and their input;
   b focussing on acceptance by others;
   c avoiding conflicts.

Analytical style

3 **Analytical style of decision-making.** In contrast to the directive style, there is a high tolerance of ambiguity with this style. Its characteristics are that decisions are made:
   a using information extensively;
   b after assessing more alternatives;
   c taking calculated risks;
   d coping with irregular situations using adaptability.

4 Conceptual style of decision-making. Individuals using this style combine an Conceptual style intuitive manner of thinking with a high degree of tolerance of ambiguity. This style's characteristics are that decisions are made:

a from a long-term focus;
b through a broad perspective on the problem;
c after assessing many alternatives;
d with a strength of creativity shown in the solutions.

FIGURE 9.13 **STYLES OF DECISION-MAKING**

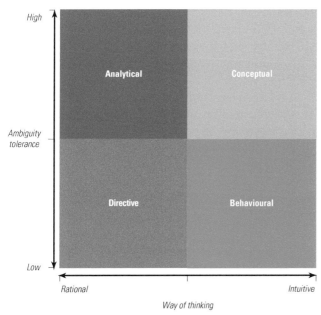

Source: S.P. Robbins en D.A. De Cenzo, *Supervision Today,* Upper Saddle River: Prentice Hall, 1998, p. 166

In closing, it should be noted that very few people always adhere to a single style, but that a person's approach consists of a combination of aspects of the different styles. There is, however, generally a difference between a person's dominant and subordinate styles. In reality, people also adjust their decision-making style based on their situation.

9.3.5 Decision-making tools and techniques

Decision-making is one of the fundamental tasks of a manager, but it is not always Fundamental task a simple one, as the information needed is not always available. If decision-making were based exclusively on facts, one would simply enter all data into a computer and wait for the decision to appear. The manager would be superfluous. However, decision-making is also about uncertainties, which is where entrepreneurship comes in!

Decision-making techniques and decision-supporting systems can be used to simplify or accelerate the process of finding the right solutions to a number of problems. The following decision-making techniques are discussed: the balanced scorecard, the decision matrix, and the decision tree. Expert systems and simulation models are two examples of decision-supporting systems.

Balanced scorecard

Many top and mid-level managers are often dissatisfied with their management reports. Reports are often too one-sided, and neither directed towards the future nor related to strategic targets. Management reports as the exist today are almost completely based on financial information, information from annual accounts or interim figures. By definition, these elements can only provide retrospective information. However, organisations need a future perspective. Another major drawback is that present financial-performance indicators hardly give any information about the extent to which strategic targets have been reached. The *Balanced scorecard* balanced scorecard refers not only to financial but also to non-financial indicators, which can give management a more complete and balanced picture of the results achieved. In fact, the balanced scorecard combines financial performance with underlying driving factors. It is a regulation and measurement system aimed at translating a strategy into concrete action. It is a compass of sorts, an instrument to help a manager reach their desired objectives.

Aside from being a system used to translate strategy to concrete actions (Management Compass), the balanced scorecard is also:
a a support tool for formulating or reformulation of strategy (ongoing improvement);
b a tool for future-orientated management (insurance of continuity);
c an internal means of communication;
d a way of integrating vision, strategy and objective.

The idea behind the balanced scorecard is simple (Figure 9.14). The organisation's performance is looked at from four different perspectives:
1 The financial perspective: how can the organisation represent the interests of the shareholders?
2 The internal perspective: what abilities are needed by the organisation?
3 The perspective of the customer: how is the organisation assessed by its customers?
4 The innovation perspective: how can the organisation improve?

FIGURE 9.14 **BALANCED SCORECARD**

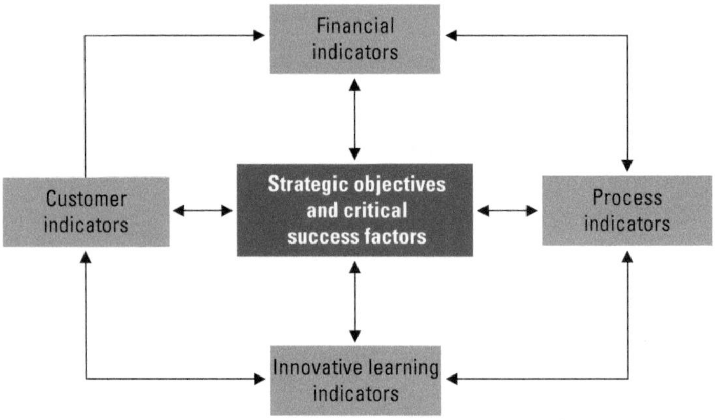

Critical success factor Strategic objectives are translated into concrete measurements by establishing of critical success factors. A critical success factor is a business variable that is crucial either to reaching a strategic goal or to carrying out a key business activity. As a qualitative description of a part of the business or its strategy, it indicates those areas in which the organisation must excel if it is to be successful. Success can be seen as the extent to which an organisation reaches its strategic goals, or how well it carries out its core activities.

The critical success factors are measured using units called performance indicators or, to put it another way, performance indicators are used to measure critical success factors. These indicators are quantitative and expressed in numerical or percentage form (see Figure 9.15).

Performance indicators

Successful implementation of a balanced scorecard requires an integrated approach. It should fit in smoothly with the entire managerial process. Although it is important to involve line management closely, what often happens is that the balanced scorecard is approached abstractly, as a tool for staff. It is, of course, essential that each organisation's balanced scorecard is custom-made.

FIGURE 9.15 **EXAMPLES OF CRITICAL SUCCESS FACTORS AND PERFORMANCE INDICATORS**

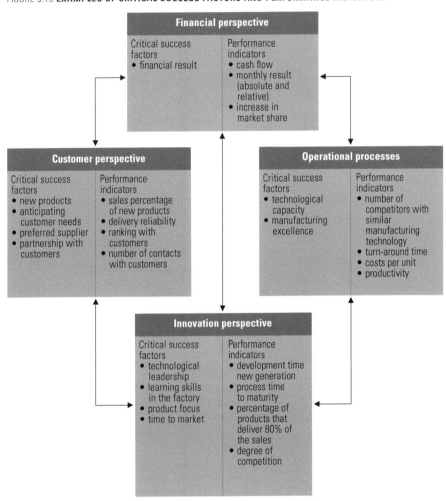

Source: *Management Accounting en Control*, prof. dr E.G.J. Vosselman, Lemma, 2001

In cases where the implementation of the balanced scorecard is problematic, the following factors are often involved:

1 There is an absence of a clear strategy: goals are not specific and not measurable.
2 Authority and responsibility within the organisation are poorly defined.
3 There is a lack of continuity in the way that process-control activities are organised

4 Internal culture and management style have not been geared towards the use of the balanced scorecard.

5 The expenses profits relationship has not been a matter for consideration.

Another steering instrument has recently been developed under the name of 'value-based management' (VBM). This is a management approach used for increasing the value of the enterprise and creating shareholder value. VBM came about due to the increasing pressure exerted by shareholders and financial markets on organisations to maximise the economic value of enterprises. An increasing number of organisations has adopted this concept. VBM requires the value-creating capacity of strategies and investments to be judged in advance. Managers have to be aware of the long-term effects of their actions. Value-based management can be supplemented by integrating it with the balanced scorecard. The result is a value-oriented directing and measuring system known as the value-based scorecard (VBS).

Decision matrix

A decision matrix is a method for comparing solutions (=alternatives) by means of assigning scores to weighted criteria.

The procedure is as follows:

1 Identify a number of alternatives.

2 Select evaluation criteria.

3 Assign a weighting factor to each criterion.

4 Allocate values to each criterion in each alternative.

5 Multiply these figures by the weighting factor and calculate the totals for each alternative.

6 Decide.

For example: A personnel manager has to select a candidate for a commercial position in the company. After a number of interviews two candidates remain. The manager enters the data into a decision matrix (Figure 9.16).

FIGURE 9.16 **DECISION MATRIX**

Evaluation criteria	Candidates							
	C. Jansma				A. Bergsma			
	WF	×	**VA**	=	**TOT**	**WF**	×	**VA**	=	**TOT**
• academic education	5		2		10	5		3		15
• communication skills	3		1		3	3		2		6
• job experience	2		3		6	2		1		2
• commercial skills	4		2		8	4		2		8
• salary wishes	2		1		2	2		3		6
• fit in with the team	5		3		15	5		1		5
• induction time	1		2		2	1		2		2
total					46					44

Decision matrices can also be used to choose a location for a branch or head office, to determine the sales price of a product, to identify market segments, and to select an organisational structure.

The advantage of this method is that alternatives can be quantitatively compared both easily and quickly. A drawback is the difficulty of objectively determining the weighted factors, the criteria, and their values.

Value based management

Value-creating capacity

Decision matrix

Decision tree

A decision tree is a graphic illustration of the alternatives and consequences associated with a particular problem. The style of illustration often has a significant influence on the final choice of solution. A decision tree is created by answering a series of questions. A 'yes' or 'no' to each question is, ultimately, the best option. For example, an enterprise wants to increase profits by expanding trade volume and visualises the alternatives by means of a decision tree (see Figure 9.17). The decision-tree method is very suitable in situations where one wants to compare the consequences of alternative decisions in a structured way. The method is also used by medical physicians for diagnosing an illness and technical experts for locating a car defect.

Decision tree

FIGURE 9.17 **A DECISION TREE**

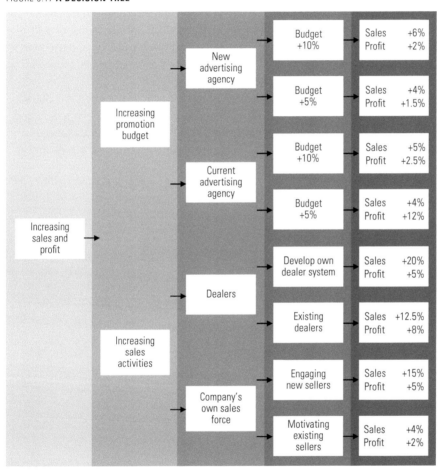

Decision-supporting systems

It should go without saying that the rapid developments in the field of computers and software are having an effect on decision-making within organisations. A great deal more information is now more readily and accessibly available. To a certain extent, computers can even be utilised as a support tool in the decision-making process. A decision-supporting system is defined as a computer-based system that helps decision-makers solve problems of a non-routine nature by means of direct interaction with raw data.
Expert systems and simulation models are two examples of decision-supporting systems.

Decision-supporting system

Expert systems

Expert system/
knowledge system

Expert or knowledge systems are automated systems that have been devised to solve problems using stored specialised knowledge (expertise) in a dialogue with the user. An expert system consists of three components:

1 the knowledge and experience bank (knowledge and experience of the expert);
2 the concluding system (reasoning mechanism that uses imported data for analysis and diagnosis);
3 the operating system (link between reasoning mechanism and user).

Expert systems contain knowledge and expert experience. The knowledge includes generally accepted facts and published information. Experience is based more on the personal opinion of the expert, so consists of rules of thumb, estimates, and judgements. If a system contains only generally accepted published information, it is known as a knowledge system.

Artificial intelligence

Expert and knowledge systems are basic applications of artificial intelligence. Their advantages are in the fact that non-experts can use the knowledge and experience of an expert for decision-making, and transferring and distributing the knowledge and experiences is much faster and much simpler.

It is the expert's responsibility to ensure that the required information is included in the knowledge and experience bank. They also give advice on the structure and features within the reasoning and concluding system. The user inputs questions into the expert system and, in return, gets an answer in the form of advice and an explanation of the basis for the advice (Figure 9.18).

FIGURE 9.18 **BASIC STRUCTURE OF AN EXPERT SYSTEM**

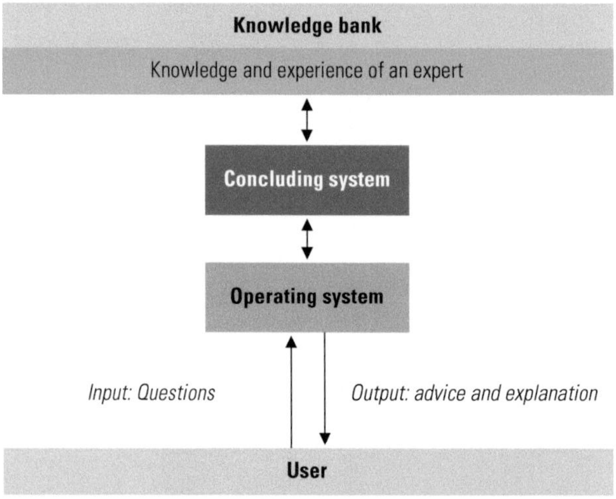

It is estimated that, in future, expert systems will increasingly be used for a range of decision-making areas, including medical diagnoses, investment protection, purchasing stocks and shares, legal planning based on precedents, mortgage advice, credit acceptances, and the development of industrial products.

The large-scale introduction of expert systems will, however, have an influence on the position of experts both within as well as outside the organisation (e.g. consultants and managers). After all, in current society, knowledge goes hand-in-hand with power. What are the consequences likely to be if, for example, the knowledge possessed by a lawyer or an accountant is transferred into a knowledge system? Will there be a need for these people in future?

As things are now, much of the knowledge and experience possessed by experts cannot be replaced by expert systems, although in future, the demand for the services of experts may significantly decrease. In addition, compared to computers, humans are creative and capable of combining new knowledge and experience with existing knowledge.

Moreover, humans can apply their acquired experiences to any problem and switch quickly between different contexts.

Simulation models

The simulation model is another type of decision-support system. Simulation techniques have been used for as long as people have made plans and made decisions. Strategist Alexander the Great, Emperor Charles V, and automobile pioneer Henry Ford all used the technique. Simulation is nothing more than translating as yet unknown quantities to a given situation and considering the resulting consequences. With the help of computers, simulation has become a generally applicable management instrument. The computer simulations most commonly used in this field are known as business simulation models.

Simulation model

A business simulation model is a software model that simulates the economic situation of a particular sector or enterprise. This is done by inputting data of various sorts into the model, including:

Business simulation model

a market and industry data;
b data relating to competitors;
c macro-economic data;
d company data (turnover, profit, expenses, number of staff members, products, budgets, etc).

This information is combined with a number of hypothical situations constructed using variable parameters, such as price and market variations, industrial relations indices, changes to oil and gold prices, exchange rate fluctuations, effectiveness of advertising and growth in Gross National Product (GNP).

Simulation models can also be used as an aid for decision-making and policy development. Simulation models allow various policy scenarios to be developed and tested for their feasibility. Shrinkage or growth in the market, the consequences of reorganisations, product positioning in particular market segments and the consequences of a takeover are some such scenarios. The use of simulation models can help to reduce uncertainty when important investment decisions have to be made.

9.4 THE MANAGER'S INFORMATIONAL ROLES

As mentioned at the beginning of this chapter, most of a manager's time is taken up by interpersonal, informational and decision-making activities. According to Mintzberg, a manager spends 40% of their time on information exchange. There are four distinct informational roles for managers (Figure 9.19).

Informational roles

The 'Antenna' role entails the manager collecting as much information as possible from external sources (personal and business contacts and experts) and internal environmental sources (employees and other managers) in order to obtain a description of the organisation's activities that is as complete as possible. For the most part, this information comes from informal personal contacts; to a lesser degree, it is comes from formal channels such as memos, written reports, executive pronouncements and the company's magazine.

Antenna role

FIGURE 9.19 **THE INFORMATION ROLES OF THE MANAGER**

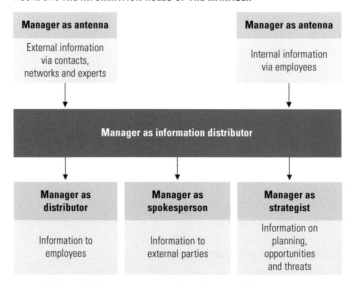

Source: R.T.M Bots & W. Jansen, *Organisatie en informatie,* Noordhoff Uitgevers

It should be noted that information is not synonymous with data. Data represents facts. When those facts are transformed in such a way as to become useful to the receiver, they become information. Data is therefore the raw material required to provide information. A manager analyses and interprets the information received before distributing it in a particular quantity and form to other members of the organisation. As such, the manager performs the role of information distributor.

Information distributor

The manager also provides information to external stakeholders such as clients, suppliers, and the press (serving the role of mouthpiece).

Moutpiece

Lastly, a manager also plays an important role in determining organisational strategy because they are equipped with a full overview of the organisation (role of strategist). To be able to provide leadership to the organisation and make the most appropriate decisions, a manager must have relevant, fast, and future-directed information.

Strategist

In general, it is possible to identify three types of information:

Strategic information

1 **Strategic information**. This information relates to the organisation's position within the environment and often provides the basis for medium-range decisions. Information about competitors, the market and politics are some examples of such information

Tactical and organisational information

2 **Tactical and organisational information**. This is information that relates to the internal management of the organisation and includes decisions on how to go about strategic decision-making.

Operational information

3 **Operational information**. This information concerns the primary processes in the organisation, such as production, transport, administration and sales. Decisions on how to implement tactical decisions are based operational information. Production figures, cancellation and waste percentages, figures on absenteeism, amount of overtime per employee, and so on, fall under this category.

Informational need

The degree of informational need is dependent on management level and decisions made at that level. In general, the executive management level is the first to create strategic information. Lower management levels within the organisation contribute to that information, generating information which flows to the executive levels in summary form, where it is then combined with other information, resulting in an overall view.

Figure 9.20 should not be taken to imply that top-level managers never feel a need for tactical/organisational or operational information. The same is true of lower managerial echelons.

FIGURE 9.20 **THE RELATIONSHIP BETWEEN VARIOUS TYPES OF INFORMATION AND THE NEEDS OF MANAGEMENT**

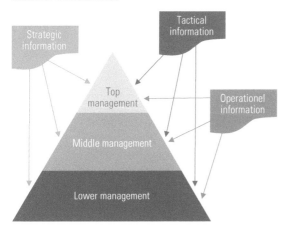

Since the tasks of middle management are continually shifting towards policy formulation, there is a definite need for strategic information.
It should also be noted that a manager's informational need is determined by their specific management function (e.g. the sales manager needs sales figures and a production manager needs figures on manpower in relation to production lines), management level (top, middle, lower), and individual management style.

It is often felt that management information should be:
- **recent**: information is often provided too late;
- **reliable**: managers must be able to trust information blindly;
- **global**: condensed, without detail but in summary format many people who think they are presenting information are actually merely providing data;
- **accessible**: layout; managers are all too often confronted with muddled piles of print-outs;
- **predictive**: information is needed for decisions that relate to the future.

Management information

For a manager, completeness of information is often of less importance than the information criteria mentioned above. Less information on time is often better than extensive information that arrives too late. A flexible information system can help managers fulfil their informational needs.

An information system consists of people, machines, and activities that transform data into information that satisfies the needs of both organisational and non-organisational members. As this definition implies, virtually everyone and everything within an organisation is part of the information system or acts on its behalf (e.g. telephoning people, filing, producing and distributing lists). With increasing organisational automation, the informational needs of managers are changing, too. Technological advancement means better information is available faster – and a need for information that increases correspondingly. Supplying information, however, should not be a goal in itself. It must relate to the goals of the organisation as a whole (see Figure 9.21).

Information system

Many organisations still have information systems that were once relevant but are now redundant: for example, overviews on paper that are now available electronically. Organisations need to reflect on the requirements that an information system needs to meet. To maintain control over their operational processes, managers need to define what information they actually require.

It is essential that top-level management is involved in determining the information supply. Top-level management has the following important tasks in relation to the supply of information:

Information strategy

1 To help determine information strategy. Such a strategy should be derived from a general organisational strategy. An information strategy should show how the information supply can contribute to the goals of the organisation. It should also specify how to go about implementing and supervising the supply of information.

Organisational functions

2 To indicate the relationships between the various organisational functions and departments (purchasing, sales, production, personnel, finance and other information) and their operating conditions.

3 To indicate the degree of integration between the various information systems both within and outside the organisation. Since information systems are concerned with communication, they run the risk of becoming fragmented, causing coordination problems. Many organisations, for example, have computerised administrative, production and office systems. It is up to management to decide to what extent these information systems should be integrated.

4 To indicate informational needs, particularly focussing on the various levels of management.

An informational advantage over others may be used as a tool for exerting an influence on decisions. One's own store of specialised information may be used to obtain a position of power over others. Competitive relationships between mangers or departments, each trying to secure their own interests by managing the supply of information in a 'creative' way, are typical of organisations. However, personal or departmental interests are not necessarily contrary to the interests of the organisation: rivalry may lead to increased effort and alertness on the part of the organisation's staff members.

Information can be used improperly, as in the following:

a supplying too little information in order to paint a false picture;

b presenting information in such a way that it looks more positive than is justified (e.g. by adapting the scale division within a diagram);

c spreading information to certain departments in order to provoke certain emotions;

d withholding information in order to influence the decision-making process in either a negative or positive way;

e supplying too much information in order to delay decision-making or to cause confusion.

Thus far, this chapter has discussed that the task of the manager to direct others. Henri Fayol (see the Introduction chapter) distinguished between a number of managerial leadership tasks, being:

a anticipating;

b organising;

c commanding;

d coordinating;

e auditing.

A narcissist CEO spells trouble for your company

O&M IN PRACTICE

Companies with a narcissist CEO often end up finding themselves in protracted legal battles, research has shown.

Narcissism is rampant at the top of the industrial ladder. There is evidence to suggest narcissist individuals look for positions that let them show their awesomeness to others. But those are also the positions where they often slip up: they become involved in tax evasion, manipulate accounts, spend too much of the company's money, and help themselves to outrageous rewards. Narcissist CEOs also often expose their companies to legal consequences: they do not tend to be objective about risks and ignore the advice given by others.

Narcissists are not very sensitive to negative consequences; they tend to favour the view that they will emerge victorious. The higher the risk, the greater their potential for demonstrating their heroics. Moreover, narcissists are often very skilled at manipulating and reading others, and have little trouble telling lies. Unfortunately, narcissist CEOs often walk away unscathed from the companies they have placed in harm's way, frequently dodging any consequences to their person. They leave others to pick up the pieces.

Source: www.mt.nl, 29-08-2018

9.5.1   Managers and power

The aim of leadership is to help direct an organisation in realising its goals. Power – the ability to influence the behaviour of employees – is an import feature of leadership. In this context, there are two important aspects of power that should be considered: sources of power, and power relationships.

Sources of power

Authority

A manager's authority depends on the way they manage the power they have been given. The extent of one's authority depends on the level of acceptance and legitimacy of that power experienced by others. Organisations recognise that employees are entitled to exercise the power that is linked to their position.

Sources of power

Apart from position, a manager has various other sources from which they can tap to exercise power. French and Raven identified five sources of power that can be used either positively or negatively. These sources of power are:

Reward power

1 **Reward power**. This is the capacity to influence someone's behaviour through rewards. The reward is thus an instrument for encouraging particular behaviour.

Coerced power

2 **Coerced power**. This is the ability to influence somebody's behaviour by punishment: the opposite of reward power. Here, the options are to prevent or to combat specific behaviour. In essence, this means obtaining a minimum level of achievement by force.

Legitimate power

3 **Legitimate power**. The employee accepts it as a given that, within certain limits, the manager is entitled to exert an influence on behaviour.

Expertise power

4 **Expert power**. This is the capacity to influence someone's behaviour using specific and relevant knowledge. The power is based on the manager's expertise.

Referent power

5 **Referent power**. This is the capacity to influence someone's behaviour based on prestige or on admiration for the manager. In the eyes of the employees, the manager possesses a certain charisma.

These five sources of power are either linked to the position or to the personality of the manager.

Position-related means of power

Position-related means of power

An organisation assigns managers certain tasks. To carry out these tasks, a manager has power linked to their position at their disposal. A manager can use these means of power to stimulate or discourage certain types of behaviour, including:

Physcial means

1 **Physical means**. These concern indirect resources: for example, the design of offices and facilities for employees.

Economic means

2 **Economic means**. These concern all kinds of financial arrangements.

Informational means

3 **Informational means**. The maxim 'Knowledge is Power' is a familiar one. Access or denial of access to certain sources of information can influence the preconceptions or the opinions of the employees.

Person-related means of power

Person-related means of power

These means of power are strongly linked to a manager's personality, and consist of two distinct aspects:

Knowledge or expertise

1 **Knowledge or expertise**. This kind of power was discussed earlier in this section.

Relational means

2 **Relational means**. This concerns the way a manager handles employees, and thus strongly depends on character and modus operandi.

If applied positively, power can lead to success in management. The limits within which a manager is permitted to make decisions are fixed. Decision-making power is necessary for an organisation to reach its targets. Two models are relevant in this connection: the harmony model and the faction model.

The harmony model supposes that the members and/or divisions of an organisation have the same interests. There is a balance of power and, consequently, the manager does not have to do much to coordinate their staff.

Harmony model

In the faction model however, such harmony is presumed absent. Employees or divisions may have conflicting interests, and managers have to resort to power to achieve the organisation's goals. The faction model comes closer to reality, and makes the need for power in organisations far more obvious. However, in practice, the power at a manager's disposal falls somewhere between the two models. The nature of a manager's power depends on the way it is exercised and on how employees react.

Faction model

Power relationships

A relationship between two people is always one of power, whether at work or in a private setting. One person is considered by the other to be either less or more powerful. These power relationships both guide behaviour and determine the level of one person's dependence on another. Power relationships can have one of three basic formats:

Power relationships

1 equal versus equal;
2 high versus low;
3 high versus middle versus low.

These basic power relationships influence the various behaviours of the people concerned. One should be aware of their presence within organisations and try to neutralise their inherent disadvantages by highlighting one aspect or reducing others.

The basic forms are shown schematically in Figure 9.22.

FIGURE 9.22 **THREE BASIC FORMS OF A POWER RELATIONSHIP**

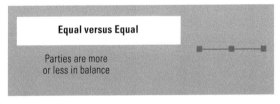

Equal versus Equal

Parties are more or less in balance

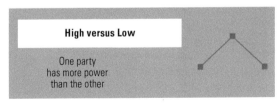

High versus Low

One party has more power than the other

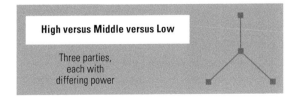

High versus Middle versus Low

Three parties, each with differing power

1 Equal versus equal.

Here, a balance of power is the basis. Such power relationships appear in a situation where there is a tendency to compete. In extreme cases, the contacts remain at a formal level. In a situation where an employee concentrates on their own work and pays little attention to the organisation as a whole, this can lead to an imbalance between the functions of the organisation. To avoid such a problem, it is necessary that:
- parties are better aligned with each other;
- parties are trained in negotiating skills, emphasising issues over personalities;
- emphasis is placed on common organisational interest and on group-feeling ('we'). This strengthens mutual dependence and encourages cooperation rather than competition;
- the dividing line between everyone's work are clearly defined with respect to tasks and responsibilities, as well as to competences.

2 **High versus low.** In this form of power relationship, there is a hierarchical relationship between the various parties. This may lead to a situation where the higher-ranking person wishes to increase their power over a subordinate, but the subordinate wants to maintain or even increase their own autonomy. The two parties can use various mechanisms to help increase their power. To avoid a lack of motivation and resistance to change, a manager may adopt various methods of control:
- adapting a leadership style, emphasising mutual interdependence in the power relationship, and taking on the role of coach;
- enhanced participation in the decision-making process. The power relationship is then viewed as normalised and legitimate;
- avoiding personal displays of power. Increased use of procedures and various other methods such as 'management by objectives';
- delegating responsibility and accompanying competences, thus stimulating motivation. The employee becomes more independent, thereby increasing their sense of responsibility.

3 **High versus middle versus low.** And lastly, a few notes on the high versus middle versus low power relationship. In this situation, the position occupied by middle management is a relevant factor. Such a relationship may lead to a conflict of loyalties, to uncertainty about where the responsibility lies and to stress, as there may be situations of conflict with both the upper and the lower levels. Any recommendations with regards to functioning in the context of this relationships boil down to two possible options in practice: either leave it in place as it is and combat the disadvantages where possible, or discard it and implement another type of power relationship.

To keep the relationships in equilibrium depends on an improvement in communication (especially in terms of the quality of information exchanged) and better delineation of functions. The position of middle management should be clearly defined in terms of expectations, goals and priorities: what is middle management expected to do, what are its objectives, and what should it focus on first?

Adjusting the power relationship may be done by flattening the organisational structure. This reduces the number of 'intermediate functions' and is less likely to lead to the disadvantages indicated. Another option is to expand the tasks of the remaining organisational levels, thus making them more appealing.

9.5.2   Leadership

Leadership was already touched upon briefly at the beginning of this chapter.
In order to achieve the goals of the organisation, a leader should possess a number
of specialist qualities. Aptitude and training are important, but life experience also
appears to have a great influence on the quality of leadership.

Qualities

Reality shows that a leadership role cannot be enforced; a manager can only wield
a leadership role as long as they can demonstrate that others will follow.

Paul de Blot (94): 'Leadership from the heart'

O&M IN PRACTICE

Paul enthusiastically presents us with his new book: *Duurzaam zakendoen door liefde voor de natuur* (2018) (Sustainable business through love for nature). His next work, on gratefulness as the foundation of sustainability, will hit stores soon: Paul is a life-long-learner and a writer through and through. A turbulent life, a passionate man. We meet with Paul at Nyenrode Business Universiteit where he has been professor of Business Spirituality since 2007.

Paul: 'In principle, human beings are free to make their own individual decisions. This freedom creates confusion. People look for coherence and meaning in their existence, which can be found in a connection to nature. This helps one reach "Omega", spirituality. Spiritual forces, including love and inspiration, are what makes it meaningful to be human, to follow one's heart'. Therefore, he argues in favour of management from the heart. According to Paul, there are two kinds of business economics: from the heart, and from the mind.
Paul: 'Here, nature is out mentor; nature is an ecological stronghold that seamlessly integrates all of its components. There is virtually no leadership, but there is small-scale existence and adaptation to one's immediate environment. Nature also has immense internal strength. For a company, the lesson might be to strive for cooperative cores which link together like a chain. A large company should be comprised of cohesive links. Friendship is a prerequisite for that cohesion; companies

should be seen as network organisations. This way, entrepreneurs discover that, by being more human, both externally and to their colleagues, they can improve their results, run their operation, and take greater pleasure in life.

Humanity's strongest drive is its desire to be more humane, more human to others and with others, more 'Gemeinschaft'. A company, after all, is only as strong as its weakest link, and this also applies to society in general. Education should be focussed on the whole of human-ness, not just through knowledge but also through character building and physical education.'
When asked what wisdoms we should use as our life's compass, he answers: 'The history of your life should be a learning experience. People have a large amount of freedom – freedom in terms of the choices available: people can choose between life or death. Animals cannot, they choose life. Always.' And: 'Take the time to contemplate your life, your trials and errors; you are your own best teacher. Be at peace with yourself.'

Among other things, leadership means a leader uses their position to determine organisational developments through their collaboration with other employees. In doing so, a true leader will avoid being steered by coincidence. True leaders have certain qualities that distinguish them from others. Some of these are innate, while others can be learned.

Leadership

A study dealing with charismatic leaders showed that the relationship between the leader and his employees had these following qualities:

a A leader is considered by employees (followers) to be superhuman in some ways.

b Employees do not question the opinion of the leader.

c Employees follow their leader unconditionally.

d Employees give a leader their complete emotional support.

According to Charles de Gaulle, leadership is characterised by 'the eagerness to undertake big things and the determination to bring them to a good end'. He added that 'the effective leader has to be well informed about the details of specific circumstances, they should not think in abstract or vague general theories, and should have more self-confidence than their rivals'. Other historical examples of great leaders are Napoleon, Winston Churchill and Eisenhower. The task of the leader becomes simpler after being accepted and valued by employees. Real loyalty has to be won. If a manager bases the daily activities on the rules mentioned above, a good foundation for successful cooperation will have been laid.

 Professors Ron Meyer and Ronald Meijers (2018) distinguish five dimensions of leadership and required roles for leaders. Leadership domains are varied fields susceptible to a person's leadership. These five fields are:

1 leadership and the self: how does one relate to one's environment and the challenges it presents;

2 interpersonal leadership: one-on-one influence on others;

3 organisational leadership: influencing groups with the aim of effective collaboration;

4 strategic leadership: concentrates on the issue of how to get groups of people to successfully chart and follow a certain course;

5 leadership and mission: the leader's role in making a group of people embrace a certain raison d'etre.

In addition, there are five leadership roles that are each in line with one of the leadership domains. These roles come with specific leadership tasks (see Figure 9.23).

FIGURE 9.23 **FIVE DIMENSIONS AND ROLES OF LEADERSHIP**

Source: Ron Meyer en Ronald Meijers, *Agile Leiderschap*, 2018

9.5.3   Leadership styles

A leadership style is shaped by its methods and attitudes towards leadership. Each style has certain features. Existing theories deals with various aspects of leadership and take their own approach to the phenomenon. Moreover, every theory studies certain facets of management with regard to leadership styles, thus precluding the existence of a fully integrated theory of leadership.

The Scientific Management-theory, for example, emphasises task-directed leadership; the Human Relations-movement, on the other hand, focusses on the human-directed style of leadership.
In this section, the following theories with regard to leadership styles are discussed:

1 classifying leadership according to employee participation and ability to make decisions;
2 X-Y theory;
3 leadership diagram;
4 the 3-dimensional leadership model;
5 situational leadership;
6 situation-dependent leadership;
7 transformational leadership;
8 self-leadership;
9 agile leadership

1 Classifying leadership according to employee participation and ability to make decisions

This approach distinguishes three styles of leadership, based mainly on the potential for employee participation and the actual extent of employee participation.
The leadership styles are:

A authoritarian leadership;
B democratic leadership;
C participatory leadership.

A Authoritarian leadership. A leader gives orders to employees concerning their work and their behaviour. Power is used to establish authority. There is a strict hierarchy between the leader and subordinates. There is no room for participation or discussion. All decisions are made by the leader themself, who has access to all the required competencies. There may be person-to-person control and the leader is strongly focussed on results.

B Democratic leadership. In contrast to an authoritarian style of leadership, group participation is the normal procedure here, and leadership therefore becomes a function of the group. Members of the organisation are thus involved in the management of the organisation or department. The leader coordinates the group decision-making process. A drawback of this type of leadership is that it might also give rise to indecision and ineffectiveness.

C Participatory leadership. This type of leadership is situated between the authoritarian and democratic styles. The leader retains responsibility for the manner in which the tasks of their department are carried out. Members of the organisation are asked to participate in discussions, and to inform and advise their leader. The final decisions are made by the leader after the consultation process with employees has concluded. The relationship between power and these three leadership styles is shown diagrammatically in Figure 9.24 .

Leadership style

Authoritarian leadership

Democratic leadership

Participatory leadership

FIGURE 9.24 **THE RELATIONSHIP BETWEEN POWER AND LEADERSHIP STYLES**

	Power influence		
	Authoritarian	*Participating*	*Democratic*
Goal	Submission	Co-responsibility	Co-determination
Via	Sanctions	Effort and insight	Group experience
Relationship	X-theory	Y-theory	Y-theory

Source: *De middle manager in confrontatie met de praktijk, de middle manager en zijn organisatie*, Marcel Pieterman, Uitgeverij H. Nelissen 1994

Naturally, it is important to consider which leadership style is most suitable. Studies into the influence of the various leadership styles show that:

a in the short term, authoritarian leadership may lead to the best performance from employees;

b with an authoritarian leadership style, employees become more dependent on the leader;

c with participating and democratic leadership styles, employees are better motivated and show greater initiative; employees work more independently; there is less aggression within the group, and team work improves.

Although the advantages of democratic and participating leadership are clear, one should not assume that these styles are always preferable to an authoritarian leadership style. In times of crisis, authoritarian leadership can be more effective, with many decisions being made more quickly.

2   X and Y theory

X theory

In his book *The Human Side of Enterprise*, (revisionist) Douglas McGregor relates leadership style to the leader's views of subordinates and their motivations. Under the name 'X and Y theory' McGregor identifies two opposite viewpoints within the human mentality. The X theory assumes that a human being:

a is lazy and dislikes work;

b cannot and does not want to think;

c has to be forced to perform tasks and is interested only in money;

d does not want to accept responsibility and prefers to be led.

Y theory

The Y theory, on the other hand, assumes that a human being:

a is eager to work and considers it a natural process;

b is inventive, creative and has imagination;

c achieves more when development is made possible and when rewarded in an immaterial way – money is not the only incentive;

d is prepared to accept responsibility.

The leadership style resulting from the X theory is characterised by submission, compulsion, control, punishment, and lack of feedback. It is an authoritarian leadership style. If the leader bases their actions on the assumptions of X theory, they run the risk of never making any progress. Employees working with an authoritarian type leader will eventually demonstrate the very behaviour

People and organisations
PART B

© Noordhoff Uitgevers bv

described by X theory. By contrast, the leadership style resulting from Y theory shows features such as participation, discussion, opportunities for employee development, encouragement, and reward. This is a form known as participatory or democratic leadership.

Nowadays, with greater emphasis being placed on achieving organisational goals, it is important to have a leadership style based on the assumptions behind Y theory. Neglecting the needs of employees can lead to a situation where organisational members try to satisfy those needs outside the organisation. For example, they may actively participate in boards or clubs, or put their other talents to use in their hobbies. In time, these employees lose interest in the organisation and function only at a minimum level. They will not want to accept responsibility and will resist change. This may result in an unnecessary loss of talent and ultimately prove harmful to the organisation. But it should be noted that not all members of an organisation want (or are able) to accept responsibility to any great extent.

Leadership models: Leaders and their stories

Insead associate professor Gianpiero Petriglieri, trained psychiatrist, is mainly concerned with new leadership models. Petriglieri: 'We must return to a broader notion of leadership. Leaders must be connectors, story tellers.

Good leaders are by definition good story tellers, but what is it that makes them excel? They have followers who derive meaning from the story; they are the story. There is a healthy level of tension in a leader looking to distinguish themselves while simultaneously being aware of existing limitations. A person who is indecisive has a hard time being a successful leader. A person who never experiences self-doubt also has a hard time remaining successful. Organisations try too hard to make people either part of the story or part of the audience. If all you do

is follow the lines others expect you to, you are not a leader. Many companies, in truth, do not want differently-minded people; they want good followers who they call leaders to make those followers feel better. At the core of leadership is courage: the courage to act, to contemplate, to do nothing, and to wonder why it is what you do, and what it all means. Thus, it is important to know which people you should surround yourself with. They should challenge you with their questions, but not obliterate you. They can help you experience self-doubt, but should not lose confidence in you. As a leader, make a space for yourself. That is why so many leaders meditate; they are carving out their own space.'

Source: *Management Team*, April 2017

3 Leadership diagram

In their book *The Leadership Grid*, Robert Blake and Jane Mouton (two revisionists, see Introduction Chapter) developed a grid which shows a large number of different leadership style (see Figure 9.25).

Leadership grid

FIGURE 9.25 **THE BLAKE AND MOUTON LEADERSHIP GRID**

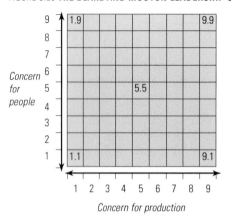

Production orientation
Human orientation
Task orientation

This model is based on their assumption that a leadership style has two dimensions: concern for production (task orientation), and concern for people (relationship orientation). The diagram shows the degree to which a manager focusses on these dimensions. Blake and Mouton used their model to develop five different leadership styles:

Impoverished management

1 Style 1.1 (Impoverished management): This style is characterised by low concern for production and low concern for people;

Task-oriented/ authority-compliance management

2 Style 9.1 (Authority-compliance management): This is a very directive style which focusses on production rather than people;

Country club management

3 Style 1.9 (Country club management): This 'social club' style is characterised by a high concern for the welfare of the employee and little attention to production;

Middle-of-the-road management

4 Style 5.5 (Middle-of-the-road management): Concern for production and people is balanced.

Team-oriented/ democratic management

5 Style 9.9 (Team-oriented/democratic management): Team leadership, which uses good group atmosphere and collaboration to strive for high efficiency.

In practice, style 9.9 seems to provide the best results with the fewest undesirable side effects.

Figure 9.26 compares these different leadership styles from five perspectives. The value of the leadership grid is that it projects the different styles that a manager can adopt. Most managers employ different styles, one of which is prominent. Depending on the situation, a manager will change consciously or unconsciously to another style.

FIGURE 9.26 **COMPARISON OF DIFFERENT LEADERSHIP STYLES**

Perspective	Leadership styles				
	1.1	*9.1*	*1.9*	*5.5*	*9.9*
Productivity	Small	High	Small	Moderate	High
Communication	Superficial	One-Way	Intense	Considerate	Open
Attitude towards employees	Hardly involved	Directing	Positive	Listening	Pleasant
Motivation	Little	By punishment and fear	Strong	Moderate	Very strong
Reaction towards mistakes	Indifference	Ignoring	None	Solving	Removing causes

People and organisations
PART B

4 Three-dimensional model of leadership

William Reddin added a third dimension to Blake and Mouton's leadership grid, namely effectiveness.

Effectiveness

The three dimensions of Reddin's model are:

1 attention to people;
2 attention to production or task;
3 effectiveness.

Based on the two-dimensional model of Blake and Mouton, Reddin developed four basic leadership styles (see Figure 9.27).

FIGURE 9.27 **THE FOUR LEADERSHIP STYLES OF REDDIN**

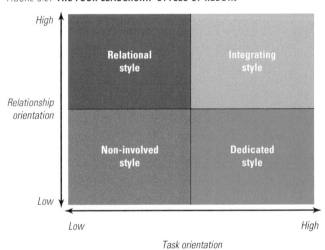

Source: *The best of Bill Reddin*

The characteristics of these style are:

1 **The relational style**. This style is applied by managers who communicate with their employees regularly and at length. Such a manager is receptive to all that goes on with their employees and possesses good social skills.

Relational style

2 **The integrating style**. The manager gears their activities to other managers, making less use of power but more use of various other kinds of motivational techniques.

Integrating style

3 **The non-involved style**. The manager attaches value to procedures, guidelines, methods and systems. These mainly concern routine affairs that need to be assigned and executed according to specific instructions.

Non-involved style

4 **The dedicated style**. The manager is often a specialist who directs subordinates that have to do a large amount of work within a short time frame. This style often has the features of autocracy and absolute power.

Dedicated

Reddin argues that position 9.9, as indicated by Blake and Mouton, which Reddin terms the integration style, is not always the most effective style, as the degree of effectiveness depends on the situation of both leader and employees. According to Reddin, managers need to possess certain qualities in order to be effective in various situations:

1 **Style awareness**. A manager is aware of different styles and is able to evaluate them.

2 **Situational sensitivity**. A manager is able to assess and evaluate situations.

3 **Style flexibility**. A manager is able to adapt their leadership style to (changing) situations.

4 **Talent for change**. A manager has the capacity for change in any given situation, in such a way as to be able to manage the situation more effectively.

An analysis of a situation can indicate which leadership style is likely to be the most effective. Figure 9.28 shows how these different types of managers evolve as they apply leadership styles with varying degrees of effectiveness. The essence of this model is that it suggests the manager should match leadership style to situational demand.

FIGURE 9.28 **THE FOUR LEADERSHIP STYLES OF REDDIN, RELATED TO THE EFFECTIVENESS OF THE STYLE**

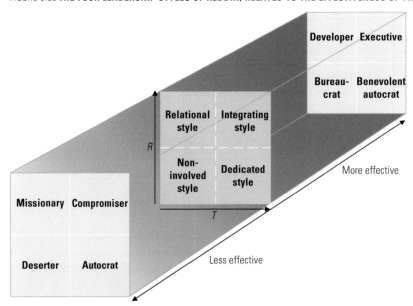

5 Situational leadership

Effective leadership depends on many factors. Practice has shown that effective managers possess various qualities, and that, to obtain optimal results, different situations require different leadership styles. This leads to the conclusion that no single effective leadership style exists. This is why further research is particularly focussed on isolating factors that influence the effectiveness of a style in specific situations. This approach is also known as the 'contingency approach'. The factors that influence effective leadership styles are shown in Figure 9.29.

Like Reddin and Fiedler, Hersey and Blanchard are proponents of this approach.

Paul Hersey and Kenneth Blanchard's approach is known as situational leadership. Successful implementation of this leadership style depends on various factors, including the level of expertise the employee possesses with respect to carry

out the required business tasks – their 'task maturity', defined as the ability to carry out a certain task and the willingness to take on that task together with its corresponding level responsibility. The extent to which an employee demonstrates task maturity is thus determined by two main criteria:

1 the capability of the employee (training, experience etc.);
2 the willingness of the employee to accept responsibility (curiosity, self-confidence etc.).

FIGURE 9.29 **FACTORS THAT INFLUENCE EFFECTIVE LEADERSHIP STYLE**

Employees can be scored and assessed according to their individual acceptance level in performing a task. Hersey and Blanchard identify four levels of task maturity:

1 unable and unwilling insecure (M1);
2 unable and willing motivated (M2);
3 able and unwilling insecure (M3);
4 able and willing motivated (M4).

Here, a specific leadership style is linked to each of the four levels of task maturity. Using this method, two main features relating to direction (task orientation) and support (relational orientation) can be analysed.

Task orientation entails the manager giving certain directions to an employee in relation to the execution of various tasks, based on the ability of the employee to perform those tasks. Relational orientation concerns the level of support the manager needs to provide. This implies that attention is paid other aspects, such as an achievement orientation and responsibility (see Figure 9.30).

Task orientation

Relational orientation

FIGURE 9.30 **HERSEY AND BLANCHARD LEADERSHIP STYLES**

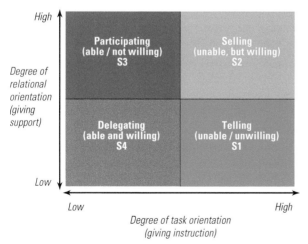

The main concepts used in Figure 9.30 are:

Participating **a** **Participating**. This leadership style is characterised by a strong relational orientation but a weak task orientation. The employee receivea little direction from the manager, but a lot of support. Decision-making occura jointly, with the manager encouraging the employee in the completion of the required activities.

Selling **b** **Selling**. This style is characterised by a strong emphasis on both the directional and support dimensions. Employees are given a lot of direction as well as a lot of support in the execution of their tasks.

Delegating **c** **Delegating**. This style scores low in both dimensions, with the manager giving little direction and support to the employee with respect to completing a certain task, and delegating the accompanying responsibility to that employee. The employee is therefore acting autonomously in the execution of those tasks.

Telling **d** **Telling**. Employees are given a lot of instruction, but little in the way of support. This leadership style scores high on task orientation, but low on relational orientation.

The essence of Hersey and Blanchard's approach is that it treats leadership style in relation to the employee's level of task maturity. Hersey and Blanchard therefore call their model a development model, as employees pass through a number of phases (see Figure 9.31).

FIGURE 9.31 **EMPLOYEE TASK MATURITY**

It is the manager's task to stimulate the employee's task maturity. As such, managers need to be aware of the maturity of their employees, and be able to encourage employee development. It is also important that a manager is able to adapt their behaviour to various new situations, instead of being restricted to a preference or style.

If a leadership style fails to fit the level of task maturity required of an employee, the employee may start developing their skills in the wrong direction. The result may be the activation of various defence mechanisms on the part of the employee as they may feel singled out for unfair criticism. Once the employee's level of task maturity has increased to a more acceptable level, the manager should adapt the management style to this new behaviour. The manager should also be very mindful of differences in task maturity between employees. The manager is ultimately the one who delegates certain tasks to employees, which in turn allows the manager to take on additional tasks. This development is shown in the model (see Figure 9.32).

FIGURE 9.32 **MATCHING LEADERSHIP STYLE WITH TASK MATURITY**

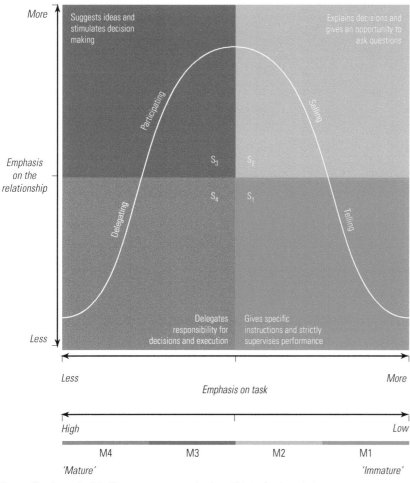

Source: Keuning en Eppink, *Management en organisatie*, p. 439, 4e, herziene druk

The leadership styles described by Hersey and Blanchard (situational leadership) have also been used to develop a model of leadership reception styles.

Leadership reception style

The style of leadership reception depends on the following three factors:
1 situation;
2 receiver's capabilities;
3 receiver's willingness.

The four leadership reception styles are:
1 The **inquisitive receiver** – wants to develop both knowledge and skills. This person is self-motivated in approach and inquisitive, wanting to know everything about the task as quickly as possible.

Inquisitive

2 The **drop-out receiver** – needs both instructions and support, lacks the required ability, and is not yet willing to execute tasks.

Drop-out

3 The **misunderstood receiver** – does not need many instructions, but requires a large amount of acknowledgement. This receiver is reasonably capable and has a lot of ideas about how things could be performed better.

Misunderstood

4 The **independent receiver** – is very capable and has a lot of self-confidence. This acquirer likes to be given high levels of responsibility.

Independent

FIGURE 9.33 **THE LEADERSHIP RECEIVER**

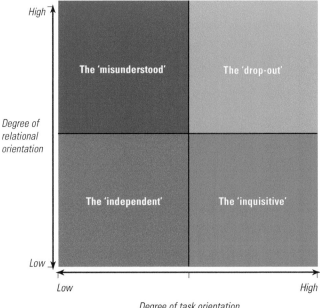

A manager should coach employees who fall under the drop-out and misunderstood categories so that they can develop into the preferred category of independent receiver. The drop-out should also be coached to develop assertiveness skills. The misunderstood receiver in particular should also be coached to develop both communication and attitude skills.

6 Contingency leadership

Contingency leadership

Fiedler has made an important contribution to the theory of leadership. Fiedler stated that it is difficult for managers to change their leadership style, especially when the situation is itself unfavourable. His model links the decisiveness of a manager to the work situation of the team. A manager's decisiveness is influenced by personal qualities and the favourability of the situation in the eyes of the leader. A team can only perform well if the manager is attuned to the situation, and vice versa. Fiedler measures effectiveness in quite a simple way: the extent to which one is positively or negatively assessed by their co-workers, which can be determined by using the LPC (LeastPreferred Co-Worker) Scale.

Leadership situation

Fiedler also identifies three aspects of the leadership situation which affect a leader's success in implementing a certain leadership style:
1 leader-member relationship and leader-group relationship (to what extent is the relationship based on mutual trust?);
2 task structure: both the size and nature of the task given to the group (what are the objectives? Is it a routine job? Could unexpected problems arise?);
3 the manager's position of power (how far does the manager's power extend?)
Based on these three aspects, Fiedler constructed eight situations and indicated matching effective styles, summarised in Figure 9.34.

FIGURE 9.34 **EIGHT SITUATIONS AND EFFECTIVE LEADERSHIP**

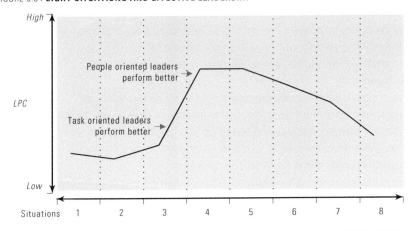

Leader-group relationship	Good	Good	Good	Good	Bad	Bad	Bad	Bad
Task structure	Structured		Unstructured		Structured		Unstructured	
Position of power of the manager	Strong	Weak	Strong	Weak	Strong	Weak	Strong	Weak

This model emphasises that managers should adjust their management style to the various situation types.

Two examples of situations that require an adjusted leadership style are:

A an organisation that employs professionals;

B an organisation at a certain phase of its development.

A An organisation that employs professionals. Increasingly, managers are having to deal with professionals whose educational level is higher than that of the organisation's employees. Professionals can be described as people who use their intelligence, know-how, expertise, experience and problem-solving skills in a creative and relatively independent way in order to realise the goals of the organisation, and by implementing efficient management skills. A professional of this kind can be compared to a person whose abilities have been shaped by advanced academic training and who belongs to the higher vocational professions: the architect, consultant, lawyer, economist, sociologist, physicist, and so on. Knowledge is also an important weapon in the competitive business arena. Product life cycles are increasing becoming short, while investments in R&D, production facilities, and marketing are growing, thereby also increasing the importance of knowledge skills and, consequently, the work of professionals. Some regard professionals as difficult to manage. Their loyalty is more often to their specialist occupation than to the organisation that employs them. Professionals are regarded by many as being perfectionists in the application of their specialist skills but as seeing office work as more of a hobby. Professionals like to work in isolation from the organisation, since they have an aversion to management methods. As such, managing professionals requires a certain culture and management style.

Professionals

According to Mintzberg, the difficulty involved in managing this group lies in the fact that they cannot be controlled by imposing rules and procedures. Professionals experience and expect a natural freedom in relation to their work. This freedom is fed by a number of views and opinions that professionals hold. According to research, the opinions held by professionals are based on seven points of view:

1 The professional desired the right to be exempted from management decisions if they do not comply with their own norms and values.
2 The professional desires a management style that is an absence of being managed.
3 The professional must be able to critically appraise the manager.
4 The professional must be able to work in isolation from management practices.
5 The professional's conclusions based on their professional skill should be given priority over management's own conclusions.
6 The professional owns the work they produce.
7 The professional must be provided with information that is clear, consistent and true.

Based on research and experience, M. Weggeman, a consultant at Twijnstra Gudde, a Dutch consultancy firm, formulated six propositions. These aim to describe the specific style a leader should adapt when working with professionals.

O&M IN PRACTICE

Mo Gawdat (Google) on leadership

Google's former chief business officer Mo Gawdat believes that the end of the age of the top-level director is nigh. He feels that power will increasingly shift in the direction of organising 'crowds'. The establishment or established order will no longer dictate proceedings.

As he explains it, Gawdat was never a manager, but a leader; albeit a *reasonably okay leader'* who was part of a team, listened to its members, and was available when needed. People who do not follow those principles are no leaders, merely managers. And, according to Gawdat, there is a big difference. A leader is a visionary who enables others to realise this vision in their own way. There is a huge shortage of leaders, and there is a shortage of managers. Too few directors are asking themselves the crucial question of whether their business is functioning correctly.

In his time for Google, Gawdat opened new offices all over the world. The first 17 employees are critical, in his experience. He selected them based on their passion for the organisation's mission. Those mainly interested in a pay check were shown the door. Candidates had to believe that their work could mean a significant improvement for people's lives. What can employees contribute to the community or to a nation? How will that improve people's lives? Therefore, Gawdat argues in favour of spending time and energy on matters you can actually influence.

Source: *Management Team*, February 2018

People and organisations
PART B

The propositions for leading professionals are:

1 The manager should translate the organisational goals into group goals in consultation with the group. An agreement should be reached between these group goals and personal goals.

2 The success of the group leader is mainly determined by their capacity to select professionals with the required level of skills to work in existing teams, and to create productive positions for professionals with particular potential.

3 The manager should not use rules, procedures and data systems to lead professionals, but should pay particular attention to clearly defining the desired results.

4 Professionals that aspire to management positions because they consider these positions more attractive or 'higher' than their own are probably not functioning at the optimum desired level. This reduces their chance of acceptance into a future management position and also increases their tendency to become averse to rules and procedures.

5 Managers of professionals should be given more freedom to delegate interesting, challenging and difficult problems to their employees. If the most interesting tasks are completed by a manager rather than employees, not much should be expected in the way of *esprit de corps*.

6 A manager should find a balance between flexibility and efficiency within the department. Plans and activities should be carefully arranged in consultation with the group.

B An organisation in a certain phase of its development. Organisational theory describes the various phases of organisational development, the first being the pioneer phase, and the last the maturity phase. A manager should tailor their leadership style to organisation's current phase. It may be possible to typify this phase of development in terms of the nature or direction of strategy chosen by the organisation. Certain types of managers match certain phases of development (see Table 9.1).

Phases of organisational development

TABLE 9.1 **DEVELOPMENTAL PHASE AND TYPE OF MANAGER**

	Strategic direction	Type of manager
1	explosive growth	pioneer
2	expansion	strategist
3	continued growth	steady stayer
4	consolidation	administrator
5	anti-skidding strategy	frugal manager
6	cutting back	persevering diplomat

Managers can be typified using a certain number of behavioural characteristics (as demonstrated in Figure 9.35).

7 Transformational leadership

Organisations having to contend with big changes over a short period require a special kind of leader, namely a transformational leader. Interest in this specific type of leadership style has increased strongly during recent years.

The notion of transformation in the business world is seen as emanating from the so-called New Age movement. This movement was based on the premise

New Age movement

that business life is on the eve of a major revolution that will ultimately bring about an entirely new culture. The key to this culture is a new way of thinking and perceiving. Some key words relating to transformational leaders are awareness, insight, creativity, harmony, spirituality, and intuition. Moving towards the new age, individual transformation takes a more prominent place. Only a person with a 'new' awareness will be able to meaningfully contribute to the new era.

Circa 1982, a number of business people became inspired by New Age notions. This gave rise to conferences built around the notion of the transformational process of management within organisations, with participants encouraged to exchange their experiences. Over the years, organisational transformation – an accompanying process that grew out of individual changes in management – has led to radical changes within organisations.

Organisational transformation

FIGURE 9.35 **THE RELATIONSHIP BETWEEN DEVELOPMENT PHASE AND MANAGEMENT STYLE**

Development phase organisation	Type of manager	Behavioural characteristics				
		Conformity	Sociability	Activity	Competitive spirit	Way of thinking
Explosive growth	**Pioneer**	Very flexible, very creative, divergent	Very extroverted, a lot of flair and glamour, but driven by circumstances, solitary and suspicious	Hyperactive, agitated, anticipating, uncontrolled	Stormy, daredevil, looking for challenges, motivated by uniqueness	Intuitive, irrational, fragmentary, original, divergent
Expansion	**Strategist**	Adapting non-conformist, creative, structured towards the new	Selective extroversion, forms groups of favourites	Energetic, responds to weak signals, nervous, some degree of self control	Increasing sphere of influence, calculated risks	Cross-border vision, generalist, rational
Continuous growth	**Steady stayer**	Strictly structured according to time-table, security	Aimable, team-worker, keeping the grip, keeping it nice	Goal-oriented, stable, by agreement	Balanced growth, getting satisfaction by controlling the situation	Thorough, systematic, depth, specialist
Consolidation	**Administrator**	Reproductive, routine, obedient	Introverted, coaching	Stable-static, via procedures, expectant, 'yes, but'	Maintaining status quo, defending territory	Thorough and conformist vision, linked to previous situations
Anti-slip-strategy	**Frugal manager**	Bureaucratic, dogmatic, rigid	Directive, procedural	Laissez-faire, doing what needs to be done, little initiative	Reactive behaviour, external incentives	Legalistic, conservative
Cutting back, slimming down	**Persevering diplomat**	Maximal flexibility within accepted limitations	Attentive, human, considerate, decisive, inspiring, trust, responding to emotions	Steady, persevering but flexible	Strategically more oriented in the long term, goal-oriented in the short term but also well balanced efforts	Thorough, systematic, depth, specialist

Several characteristics of organisational transformation are that:

1 its onset is sudden: a particular event, such as a merger, new management, or organisational restructuring;
2 the old structure disappears completely, and a new one takes its place. The transitional process is not gradual. For example, a new production process which completely replaces the old one is introduced;
3 there is a complete change of awareness on the part of the organisational members. For example, a governmental organisation might change their centralised control system with employees being given individual responsibility for the quality of their work in the new system.

Transformations within organisations can take place at two levels: at the individual or at the collective level. These levels also apply to the structural and cultural dimensions. Figure 9.36 shows that the transformational process always starts with an individual and ends with a change in the organisational structure. If one wishes to change an organisation, one should always start with the people in that organisation.

The branch of management engaged in organisational transformation is called transformation management. Its purpose can be defined as 'enhancing the ability to function well in a situation of turbulent social transition, characterised by a high degree of complexity and an enormous speed of change'. The form and consequences of transformation management within organisations depends strongly on the individuals involved.

Individual collective level

Structural cultural dimension

Transformation management

FIGURE 9.36 **TRANSFORMATION PHASES**

		Individual level	Collective level
		Individuals	**Organisations, groups, societies**
Structural dimension	**Change of form**	Opinions, way of thinking (paradigms)	Organisational structure, basic policy, strategy
Cultural dimension	**Change of awareness**	Attitudes	Organisational culture

Source: E. van Praag, Management zonder Controle, *Intermediair*, 1988

According to transformation theory, a leader must possess a number of specific qualities, specifically:

1 the ability to anticipate change: in a continuously changing environment, a leader must have a visionary outlook;
2 vision: a leader must be able to direct organisational members to new goals and challenges, generated either individually or as a team;
3 the ability to take a broader scale of factors into account, including economic, spiritual, aesthetic and psychological factors. Moreover, a leader should turn these into collective goals.
4 the capability to shares power with their employees.
5 a large degree of self-knowledge and awareness of their own goals and motives, as well as those of employees.

8 Self-leadership

Coach

In many ways, this approach is similar to the approach whereby the manager becomes the coach. In this viewpoint, a manager is not considered superior to their employees, but as being on the same level. The main tasks of a manager are to stimulate employees and make it possible for them to function optimally. The current trend within organisations to limit the number of management levels was discussed earlier. This development is also accompanied by adding levels of competency to lower organisational levels, taking over responsibility for the formation and results of business units. This requires a new management style,

Horizontale management style

characterised as a horizontal management style. Within this process, planning, organising, checking and coordinating are mainly done by autonomous units. With employees becoming better trained and more mature in the performance of their tasks, a manager must be able to create an atmosphere that encourages change by developing, training, delegating and creating the necessary facilities. This is a strongly interactive role and requires managers to prove their leadership skills in order to promote better levels of communication with staff members.

Research has shown that organisations today are demanding a high level of capability from their staff. In assessing employee performance, managers use criteria such as responsibility, commitment, and creativity. Employees are expected to complete their work and to be both loyal and disciplined in all their dealings (see Figure 9.37).

FIGURE 9.37 **PYRAMID OF NEEDS FOR LEADER AND EMPLOYEE**

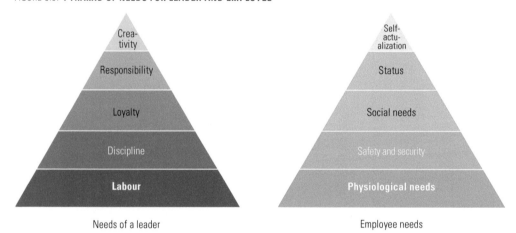

Source: A.W. de Korte en J.F. Bolweg, *Een verkenning naar veranderingen in werknemerswensen en de managementconsequenties daarvan*, Van Gorcum/Stichting Management Studie, 1993

Comparing the changing needs of a manager to the needs of employees, highlights an emphasis on appreciation, respect, and self-realisation. Physiological and social needs are not as crucial. The 'higher' needs as described by Maslow in his pyramid may sometimes be the same for managers and employees. They share a mutual interest in such things as equality, respect, and attention, and it is in these areas where one should look for a basis for cooperation.
Communicative skills are also of crucial importance to a manager. Employees must be given all due attention. Outcomes relating to new leadership styles are shown in Figure 9.38, and explained below.

People and organisations
PART B

FIGURE 9.38 **THE MANAGER AS COACH: MANAGEMENT ASPECTS**

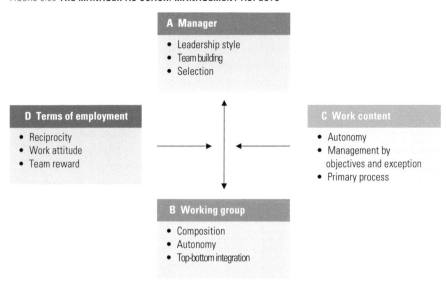

Source: A.W. de Korte en J.F. Bolweg, *Een verkenning naar veranderingen in werknemerswensen en de managementconsequenties daarvan*, Van Gorcum/Stichting Management Studie, 1993

1 **Managers**. The manager should have an open style of communication and be attentive to employees, stimulating their motivation and commitment. This can have far-reaching consequences for the autonomy and the delegation of responsibility within organisations.
A lot of emphasis should be placed on teambuilding, with managers selected according to their capacity to cultivate a sense of belonging.

2 **Work groups**. Great emphasis is placed on the functioning of the group and its composition. A group that functions well is said to have strong mutual bonds. Such a group will have a large degree of autonomy, with the manager providing support in areas such as facilities and training. Employees are integrated within the organisation via the work group, which equates to integration of the top and bottom levels of the organisation.

3 **Work content**. There is a strive towards autonomy in executing activities, and this strive is aligned with management support. 'Management by objectives' is a management technique that encourages this approach, as is 'management by exception'. With the former, individual or departmental objectives are predetermined; with the latter, only predetermined deviations from targets are raised with the manager. All of the activities are related to the primary processes of an organisation, and any changes in these primary activities mean the formulation of new work content.

4 **Terms of employment**. Employees' personal lifestyle is at least as important to them as their job. To adapt to a changing culture, organisations need to provide greater flexibility for their work force. This includes adapting the terms and conditions of employment to an individual's needs and requirements (part-time working hours and career-based criteria). Seen in terms of its ability to attract high-quality staff, this is one of an organisation's most important areas. The various types of rewards need to be linked to performance.

9 Agile leadership

Which type of leadership should be expected to be declared the winning strategy for now and for the future? More and more companies are realising that top-down direction has become inadequate; they are slowly beginning to reorganise their directive approach. The focus of companies has also shifted towards adding value for customers; customer-orientation is becoming more of a focal point. This calls for a new definition of the leader's task description. A relatively new term used in this context is that of 'agile leadership'.

Implementing agile work methods and an agile work environment through transformative measures, such as autonomous and self-directing teams, has an impact on the working methods of managers and boards. Employees are assigned greater responsibility, and can largely decide what needs to happen, and how it needs to happen, themselves. Leadership is still required, for example in drafting a bigger picture and communicating that picture to the employees. Moreover, team activities have to fit into the company's strategy. It is the agile leader's task to ensure that everyone has the same goal in mind, that teams work from their strength, allowing them to freely advance organisational success.

The current era is one of change and disruption, which calls for a change in mind-set. Previously, a sense of control was maintained through multi-annual strategic plans in a hierarchical organisation that held on firmly to its patterns of activity. But keeping a business on its feet and making it excel in a time of change calls for different and new managerial skills. The art is to forego the formal power of a leader, but to make people follow on the merit of one's vision, conviction, and behaviour.

Agile leadership is mainly founded on trust. It offers greater room for individual employers and teams; room to experiment. Agile leaders encourage their employees to grow and be all that they can be. Improving intrinsic employee motivation is of great importance in this respect.

Agile leaders have a clear vision. They do not command, but inspire and motivate. They create a work environment which does justice to all employees and lets them work unhindered. Agile leaders are not locked in a certain leadership style; they wield multiple styles. This makes them more flexible.

The most prominent properties of an agile leader are that they:

a have good communicative and empathic skills;
b inspire and motivate teams and employees;
c are able to delegate and retain an overview;
d steer and coach instead of control;
e continue to develop themselves and encourage employees to do the same;
f are patient and persistent;
g tolerate and even encourage experimentation, even if it leads to error.

Overview of leadership styles

Lastly, the various theories of leadership styles are shown in Figure 9.39.

FIGURE 9.39 **CLASSIFICATION CRITERIA AND LEADERSHIP STYLES**

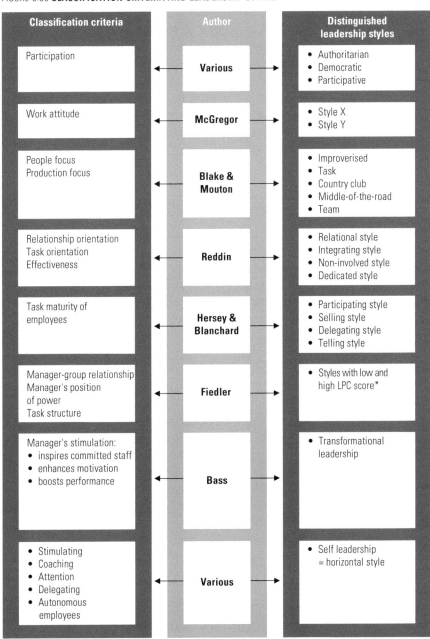

Classification criteria	Author	Distinguished leadership styles
Participation	Various	• Authoritarian • Democratic • Participative
Work attitude	McGregor	• Style X • Style Y
People focus Production focus	Blake & Mouton	• Improverised • Task • Country club • Middle-of-the-road • Team
Relationship orientation Task orientation Effectiveness	Reddin	• Relational style • Integrating style • Non-involved style • Dedicated style
Task maturity of employees	Hersey & Blanchard	• Participating style • Selling style • Delegating style • Telling style
Manager-group relationship Manager's position of power Task structure	Fiedler	• Styles with low and high LPC score*
Manager's stimulation: • inspires committed staff • enhances motivation • boosts performance	Bass	• Transformational leadership
• Stimulating • Coaching • Attention • Delegating • Autonomous employees	Various	• Self leadership = horizontal style

* LPC is 'least preferred co-worker score'. A high score indicates that the leader focuses on humans.
A low score indicates that the leader focuses on the task.

In practice, the selected leadership style depends on various factors, including:

a organisational culture (is the culture based on a formal or an informal style?);

b size of organisation (within small businesses, the employees know one another and are more aware to what is happening in and around the enterprise);

c the nature of the work (routine or varied, simple or complex);

d the level of education of employees compared to management (lower versus higher education);

e societal trends (advanced democratisation?);

f labour market scarcity concerning a particular skill (if an employee does not like the leadership style, they might look for work elsewhere).

9.5.4 The international manager

Mergers and joint business ventures mean that organisations are confronted with various different leadership styles. Unsuccessful mergers and joint ventures are evidence that these differences can cause great problems within the workplace. Internationalisation is expected to lead to greater alignment of management styles. The offer of internationally oriented studies will be one factor that is going to improve the capabilities of emerging managers in foreign management cultures. This section first addresses the differences in leadership styles from one European country to the next, and then looks at ways of achieving success and resolving difficulties in intercultural management.

Leadership styles per country

The EU research paper *Culture and Management* presented the following findings:

The Netherlands: In general, Dutch organisations are fairly flat, and flexible in their hierarchies. The Dutch leadership model is reflected in business cultures. The boss is often considered to be 'one of us'. When setting personal targets, job security, independence and a sense of duty are important considerations for managers. Managers are expected to be experts in their area of responsibility. They are also expected to take risks. Managers are inclined to short-term decision-making and their decisions are made reactively and intuitively.

France: In France, managers are strict and authoritarian in style. Their subordinates are used to being led. Respect is based mainly on the leader's competence level. The French attach great importance to a person's expertise and experience level. For French managers, their self-development, competence, wealth and acceptance by work colleagues are important personal targets. The decisions they eventually make are often intuitive and in response to specific short-term issues.

Germany: Germans look for strong and convincing leaders. High positions in management are viewed with respect and awe. Managers often have a somewhat detached relationship with their subordinates. Managers expect obedience from their subordinates, and they, in turn, require clear instructions from their leaders. Achievement and realising one's ambitions are important, with self-development, prosperity and independence also scoring high on the list of priorities.

Spain: The Spanish manager is a kind autocrat, steadfast in their approach; clarity and courage are the most important qualities. Rules, procedures, and a formal hierarchy are all subordinate to loyalty. The most important characteristic of the Spanish leadership style is its devotion to commitment. Decisions are often made intuitively by the manager and any decision-making by the group constitutes an adverse reflection on management style. Being supportive of others, pursuing self-development, prestige and a sense of duty are important managerial attributes.

Great Britain: Honesty in relationships is very important. This is demonstrated in particular in communication and decision-making, with both being participatory and open in style. People trust in the capacity of others. The well-known reserved British approach to personal contact results in a more detached relationship style.

This is also why British managers and their subordinates often appeal to rules and procedures, thus avoiding unnecessary risk-taking. Important personal targets are job security, and the pursuit of pleasure and wealth.

What makes a successful manager in an international context? There is no simple answer to this question. Depending on culture, people have different ideas on leadership style and responsibility. Fons Trompenaars, an author who has researched intercultural management, argues there is no such thing as the 'Ten Commandments' of the successful international manager, as cultural differences vary too greatly.
However, his research did reveal rules for success and potential issues ('communication jammers'), with intercultural communication playing an important role.

Rules for success
According to Fons Trompenaars, the rules for success are:

Rules for success
Intercultural
communication

1 **Knowing oneself**. Everybody communicates with others on the basis of a particular attitude, prejudice, or opinion. In order to be able to communicate successfully in an international context, it is very important to be aware of one's style of communication.
2 **Taking the physical and human setting into account**. Each culture has its local customs, and it is very important to be able to adapt to these customs. Knowledge of these things can mean the difference between success and failure.
3 **Trying to understand different communication systems**. It is important to find some common ground (such as language) when doing business. Language is strongly related to culture. There are advantages to being able to speak the local language, since culture is entrenched in language.
4 **Developing empathy**. Be receptive to other cultures. An interest in other cultures and what motivates people can be of crucial significance.

Communication jammers
Communication plays an important role in an international context. While it is important to be aware of the factors that can contribute to success, being aware of the factors likely to detract from success – 'communication jammers' – also contributes to a manager's effectiveness. Communication jamming is usually the result of ignorance. Working in and around other cultures causes uncertainty, and this might make one act in a way detrimental to a successful outcome, even to the extent of causing a nuisance. How can one decrease that uncertainty, and the threat of being a nuisance? One important measure is to be properly prepared when taking on an international job, reading up on the new culture, and talking to people who have been, or worked as, part of that community. Learning to speak the language is also important. Try to take in as much of the culture as possible, always asking for extra information. Managers tend to act fast – but in a different cultural context, this can mean a wrong decision if it is based on the incorrect assessment of a situation, culture, and so on. Take the time to adapt and learn how things are done and how one should handle situations. In doing so, focus not only on differences, but also on similarities.

Communication
jammers

Leave the office, hit a ball around, and score

'The ultimate art is in avoiding or breaking down the barriers between you and your clients. Consultancy should reach a point where the client sort of forgets you are, in fact, their advisor.' Thus says a senior consultant at a Big Four office in London. What is the secret of customer retention? Consultants in various countries all have their own methods for making themselves indispensable. The following list documents cultural differences and pitfalls.

Sweden
Bring either a hunting rifle or a towel. The Swedes do not think much of a shared meal as the icebreaker for informal contact. They would rather go hunting for elk or hop in a sauna. Incidentally, Swedes attach little value to personal relationships in business dealings, because of their potentially disruptive effect to impartiality. But if one is taking part in a business lunch, it is fine to talk shop. Just do not expect alcohol to be plentiful.

France
Business deals in France are conducted across lunch or dinner tables. The idea, however, is to refrain from discussing business (wine is a better topic). Foreigners have found that the French codes of conduct in this regard are inscrutable. The Dutch and the Germans, for example, feel that the French strictly separate business from pleasure, never inviting clients to their own home. The French themselves, however, feel their integration of private and professional is impeccable.

Germany
Nowhere is it more difficult to engage in informal contact than in Germany. Both Germans and foreign visitors alike feel Germans are formal and reserved, and not inclined to risk wasting time. Germans continue address others with 'Sie' long before others would have resorted to more informal modes of address. Do not make the mistake of entering into topics like religion or politics in informal conversations, because these avenues of conversation are not appreciated.

United Kingdom
The British are masters at maintaining informal contact. The central hub is the pub. But keep track of the class system: it is fine for a high-level manager to get all chummy with a senior consultant, but a junior should know their place. British politeness may be another source of confusion, as no Brit is likely to say exactly what they mean outright. Knowledge of social codes is essential for understanding what is being implied.

Italy

Italians may prefer to talk about wines and traditional foods, but they definitely do talk. No other country places greater value on personal contact. A consultant does not provide a physical product, but a text. And the written word is not held in the highest esteem in Italy. If one wants to earn one's client's trust, one will need to be in their inner circle. Moreover, the South of Italy is even more focussed on relationships than the North, where content is more important.

The Netherlands

Direct, pragmatic, preferring a quick sandwich at one's desk to a copious meal at a restaurant: Dutch consultants have little sense of decorum or displays. They prefer formal environments when engaging with clients. And Friday nights are a private matter – setting appointments on a Friday after business hours is a no-go.

9.6   THE MANAGER AS AN INDIVIDUAL

In recent years, increasing attention has been paid to the personal qualities of the manager. As a leader in an organisation, the manager is at the hub of things. Just like during the Human Relations movement of the 1930s, there is a strong interest in the human factor associated with management. Human Resource Management is also one of the core tasks of management. Whether a manager succeeds depends upon their personal character and the interaction between their professional activities and private life.

Personal qualities

The manager has an exemplary function. They need to develop a vision that takes account of norms and values. This section looks at the manager's norms and values in some depth and draw connections between relationship matters in private and professional life.

Examplary function

Lastly, this section discusses the notion of 'entrepreneurship', an additional personal quality of management.

With a working week of over fifty hours, a manager has less time for other activities, especially those related to family. In the book *Is the price of success too high?*, the authors relate private and work circumstances after a study of 532 managers from more than 20 nationalities, 95% of whom were European. The answer given by the authors corroborates the frequently encountered suggestion that the modern manager is a professional in business life, but an amateur at home.

9.6.1   Career

Career This section discusses three different career paths, namely that of a manager, that of a partner and that of a parent. Managers are also scrutinised according to age category (see Figure 6.21):

a the junior manager (between 27 and 34);
b the middle-aged manager (between 35 and 41);
c the senior manager (between 42 and 67).

Figure 9.40 shows the relationships between the age category of the manager and the importance attached to the various career stages.

FIGURE 9.40 **CAREER STAGES OF A MANAGER**

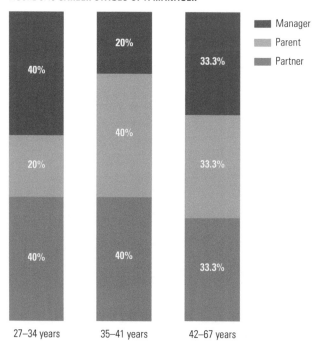

Clarification: According to the researchers, role patterns for female managers are comparable to those of their male colleagues. The dilemmas and conflicts faced by women trying to manage both a private and professional life are even harder than those faced by men.

In order to demonstrate the relationships between possible career decisions, the manager types in their various age categories are discussed in greater detail.

Junior manager (27 to 34)
A manager who falls in this category has launched their career at an early age and succeeded in obtaining a managerial function. To have reached that point, the manager will have displayed considerable ambition and have invested large amounts of time and energy in their work.
The career of the junior manager is characterised by many uncertainties and challenges. If the work is not going well and the manager feels that the chosen career path is in danger, the standard response is to work even harder. However, if the work is going well, the manager reduces their effort spent on personal and private situations even further, though these also require a great deal of constant maintenance.

Five tips for your next career move

We are often reluctant to work explicitly on our careers. Won't we be noticed by just doing our work well enough? In practice, not really. When discussing possible participants for promotion, other issues become important: one's network, one's accomplishments in recent projects. What can you do to advance your own career?

1 **Take matters into your own hands**. Organisations often use career ladders, where employees progress according to a logical pattern. But that does not necessarily have to tie in with your profile. Find your own drives and energisers. This will let you take a more focussed look around for work that suits.

2 **Find a mentor**. A mentor or coach can be a huge help, particularly if they are found in your own organisation. Good mentors will offer not just valuable career advice, but are not afraid to hold up a mirror, or ask the hard questions either, for example: how could you be better?

3 **Get educated**. Training is often the first step to promotions or new jobs. Not only will you find new knowledge and insights, you will also expand your network. Moreover, a long, work-related education is shown to lead to increased chances of promotion.

4 **Find the organisation's sore points**. Leaders often appreciate some sense of initiative, but your efforts may go unappreciated. If, however, your initiative ties in with management's sore points, you can make a solid contribution.

5 **Help others**. Display informal leadership. Help colleagues, lend a hand, coach! The law of reciprocity takes effect: people higher up in an organisation tend to be 'givers'.

Source: www.mt.nl, 10-10-2018

It is difficult to maintain different activities at the same level. Since the career of a manager is probably given priority, the job of parent and partner normally takes either second or third place. Even though this might cause a great deal of conflict, managers are likely to prioritise their career and have a correspondingly apparent lack of sensitivity to what is happening within the marriage or other relationships. The mañana syndrome, implying that 'things will look different in the morning', is a well-known phenomenon. Investments in family life will just have to wait; even if their marriage is on the rocks, this does not necessarily lead to changes in the way that managers spend their time or divide their attention.

Mañana syndrome

Middle-aged managers (35 to 41)

The midlife crisis looms. During this middle period, the successful manager spends 70% to 80% of their energy at work, and start to worry about the consequences

Midlife crisis

for family life. After a period of reflection, they will probably choose to create a more harmonious balance between their professional and private lives. In addition to paying greater attention to their partner and children, managers should also develop greater interest in leisure activities such as sports, hobbies, and intellectual interests.

It is only during a crisis that the career should be given special attention.

According to Evans and Bartolomé, the threat of midlife crisis becomes real if something goes fundamentally wrong either in the job or in the relationship with one's partner, children, or friends.

Senior manager (42 to 67)

In this age category, managers start to break away from their career paths. Work remains important in this phase, but the career itself is no longer paramount. After all, most managers will have already reached the summit of their career by this point. There is now likely to be more of an equal distribution of attention over the three different career paths, with family life and children now becoming the most important area. A private evaluation of one's career now becomes important, with approximately 60% of managers in this age category more concerned with their lifestyles. Time is spent on reassessing and doubting one's own values, accomplishments, and lifestyle. The integration of professional work and private life has either become more entrenched or more fragmented. In case of the latter, a manager is unlikely to go looking for new challenges; in case of the former, thae manager will continue to find new possibilities for personal development, either job internally or job externally.

Retirement?

A study by consultancy firm Twijnstra Gudde shows that only 30% of managers reach their pensionable age in good health. Of the remaining group, 40% end up claiming for a work related disability, either through private insurance or a government scheme, and 30% do not make it to a pensionable age. This is why older managers should be given the opportunity to step down or to one side of their career ladder. Obviously, this depends on personal circumstances and choice. Moreover, it is claimed that a manager functions at their best between the ages of forty and fifty. Thereafter, managerial qualities are likely to decrease (perhaps even quickly).

In many scenarios, it may be better to relinquish some managerial control rather than to keep going and endanger the stability of an organisation. This does not mean that an older person should be forced to leave the organisation: expertise can still be utilised in other ways, and older employees can still continue on, even with a more relaxed lifestyle. Besides permanent employment, there are other options available, including part-time employment or consultancy work.

9.6.2   Leisure activities

Leisure activities

Naturally, decisions about leisure activities are needed, as time is often a scarce resource for managers. One would expect managers to become very critical of how to spend their time, and to manage it efficiently. However, interviews show that 77% of managers say that they often just 'potter about the home a bit'. Four different sorts of leisure activities can be identified:

1 **Leisure activities as a means of recovery**. These are the abovementioned activities of 'just messing around'. A manager does this in solitude and, in general, conversation is not appreciated.

2 **Leisure activities in order to release tension**. These are sports and other serious hobbies. Tennis, golf, swimming, skiing, and sailing are popular among Dutch managers. These activities provide a good outlet for pent up inner aggression and tension.

3 **Leisure activities as an investment in private and family life**. These may be individual, parallel or joint leisure activities. Some examples of parallel activities include painting the house, going to the movies, or gardening. The presence of a partner is not essential for these activities, though other parallel activities, such as having dinner together, going on holiday, and playing games are helped by a partner. It is a well-known fact that these joint activities contribute positively to 'relationship happiness'.

4 **Leisure activities for personal development**. These concern hobbies and occupations of a semi-professional character, often leading to alternative careers. They may include a study course, political involvement, music, art, and writing or translating books

Better coping with stress through learning new skills

O&M IN PRACTICE

One would not think that those overwhelmed by work-related stress would be energised or willing to learn new things. Nevertheless, it has been shown that learning new things can help people better process the effects of stress.

People's strategies for coping with stress can be roughly divided into two categories. The first is one of 'steady on'; do not complain, and put your back into it: the *perseverance* strategy. The other is by withdrawing into oneself, by temporarily vacating the stressful environment: the *flight* strategy. The latter has resulted in an increase in meditation areas, fitness rooms, and table tennis tables at work. But both options come with their drawbacks, because, as many studies show, they do not address or remove the cause of stress.

Researchers Zhang (Tsinhua University), Myers (John Hopkins), and Mayer (University of Michigan) studied a third coping mechanism: *focussing on learning*. By learning new skills, gathering new information, or seeking out meaningful challenges, people can reduce the effects of negative emotions, and reduce unethical behaviour and lower the chances of a burnout. Moreover, learning new things improves our self-image; we are making headway instead of being stuck. This effects makes us more stress-resilient. Learning is not something you should only do when faced with overwhelming stress. A continued career of learning can help you develop coping mechanisms that will let you deal better with the pressures of working life.

Source: www.mt.nl, 09 Oct 2018

Figure 9.41 shows a reflection of the relationship between work and private life, and the selected concepts of leisure activity.

FIGURE 9.41 **LEISURE ACTIVITIES AND PROFESSIONAL LIFE**

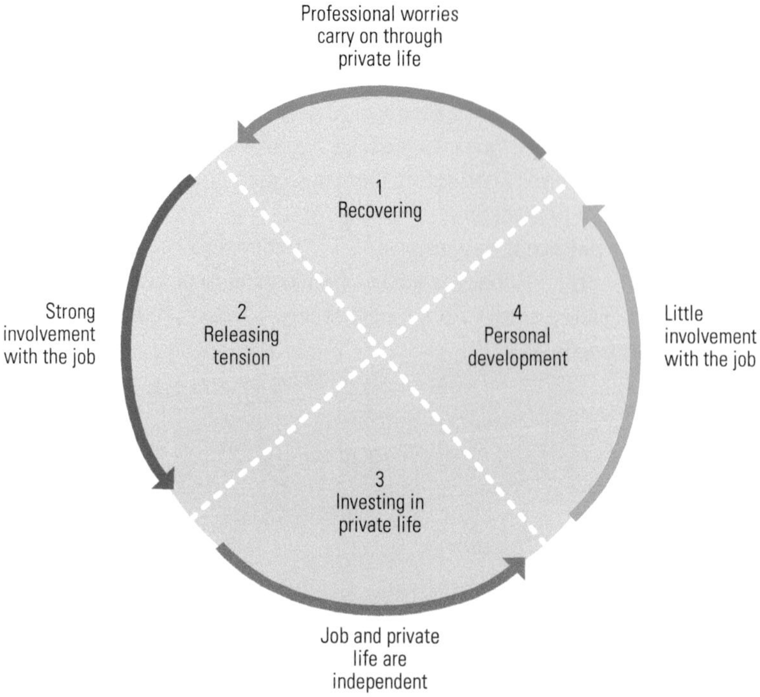

Professional worries
carry on through
private life

Strong
involvement
with the job

1
Recovering

2
Releasing
tension

4
Personal
development

Little
involvement
with the job

3
Investing in
private life

Job and private
life are
independent

Source: B. Evans en F. Bartolomé, *Wordt succes duur betaald?*, Samsom/Intermediair, 1981

Concept of leisure activities

For a manager, the concept of leisure activities constitutes an important choice. However, the choice is largely determined by the degree of career success. If a manager still needs to spend a large portion of their time and energy at work and has little time left, this will also have an effect on their ability to pursue leisure activities.

9.6.3   Entrepreneurship

Entrepreneurship

Entrepreneurship could very well be the manager's most important personal quality. If the environment is very turbulent, many organisations need entrepreneurial management capable of tuning in to trends and developments earlier than their marketplace competitors, and then transforming these hunches into new plans. Entrepreneurship is a function of having a particular vision and a feeling for a market. It also involves some risk-taking behaviour.

Entrepreneurial management

Some characteristics of people to whom entrepreneurship, or entrepreneurial management, applies, are that:
1   they have highly energetic personalities, they are fast decision-makers, and they are driven by challenges;
2   their activities are highly pioneering and inspiring. They make new plans all the time and the changes they make have a motivational effect on employees;
3   they possess the ability to control and check their plans and activities;
4   they are good listeners and are able to detect employee problems or frustrations quickly;
5   they must have a healthy dose of common sense!

All entrepreneurial managers need to possess some of these characteristics. Managers who understand their own limitations and take these into account when selecting new employees become the most accomplished managers. Managers who fail to develop such entrepreneurial qualities are more likely to opt for an unchanged policy, as this is considered to be the 'safe' option. Paradoxically, in the long term, this option becomes the riskier one.

9.7   POSITIVE LEADERSHIP IN THE 21ST CENTURY

Positive leadership is an umbrella term for various insights and practices developed in (positive) psychology and business economics in recent decades. These insights and practices have been proven to have a positive impact on the wellbeing of people in organisations and, essentially, on their performance. Positive leadership focusses on elevating individuals and organisations. In doing so, a positive leader focusses on what is going well, on what is special, on what is inspirational. Positive leadership also means: building good relationships at work; taking an interest in the lives of one's colleagues; helping each other; sincerely listening to colleagues and taking them seriously. These practices serve to create a positive business culture, a culture that energises people.

Despite increasingly well-educated leaders, and advances in the literature on the wellbeing of people in organisations, there are still many organisations that could improve their 'health' in terms of how they treat employees and leaders. Study after study shows that, for example, most employees experience their managers to be demotivational. The direct supervisor has a large, perhaps the biggest, impact on a team in terms of productivity, job satisfaction, and commitment. A recent international study by Hay Group indicates that 55% of employees feel their superior creates a demotivational work atmosphere. In the Netherlands, this figure was as high as 68% (see Figure 9.42).

FIGURE 9.42 **THE INCONVENIENT TRUTH ABOUT LEADERSHIP PRACTICES**

Work is not fun
'Only **13**% of employees are committed to their work.'
- Gallup, 2016

Leaders care little about people
'The most important reason for people to resign is their poor relationship with their superior.'
- Harvard Business Review, 2016

Lack of trust
'Only **27**% of employees in the Netherlands claim to feel their CEO is trustworthy or highly trustworthy.'
- Edelman 2017

People are not happy in their work
'87% of people are unhappy and unmotivated at work.'
- Gallup, 2016

Limited personal development
'**2/3** of Dutch employees claim to learn nothing or next to nothing by doing their work.'
- CPB, 2016

People experience high stress
'**1 in 5** people experience work-related stress.'
- WHO, 2018

When studying organisation and their leadership, one can chart the most and the least prosperous organisations and leaders, and distribute them along a normal distribution curve (see Figure 9.43).

FIGURE 9.43 **A NORMAL DISTRIBUTION CURVE OF PROSPERING LEADERS AND ORGANISATIONS**

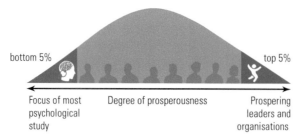

bottom 5%   top 5%

Focus of most   Degree of prosperousness   Prospering
psychological   leaders and
study   organisations

Clinical and organisational psychology mainly focusses on studying leaders and organisations that are the least prosperous, in an attempt to make them 'healthier' or 'better'.
Positive psychology is a relatively new psychological branch, and is mainly concerned with the most prosperous forms of leaderships and the most prosperous organisations. It aims to apply the successful practices it uncovers to the remaining population, thus helping it to improve its prosperity.

Positive psychology was developed as a counterpart to regular psychology, which mainly focussed on hurdles and impossibilities. Positive psychology can be seen as a logical continuation of humanist psychology. Developed in the 1950s, humanist psychology was itself a reactionary movement to behaviourism and psychoanalysis. Humanist psychologists such as Rogers and Maslow (1908-1970) wanted to increase the attention to psychological growth and meaningfulness in psychology. Their perspective on human nature is a positive one: they assume that people have an innate drive to self-actualisation; people want to develop themselves and make the best of their abilities.

This philosophy was continued along a more scientific approach towards the late 1990s. Now referred to as positive psychology, its founders Martin Seligman (1942) and Mihaly Csikszentmihalyi indicated that it was a concept that focussed on humanity's strengths. It is a scientific and social psychological philosophy centred on wellbeing and optimum functioning (individually, relationally, organisationally, and societally). Happiness, for example, is not the result of good genetics or happenstance, but of being able to identify and apply one's given strengths. According to Seligman and Csikszentmihalyi, positive psychology focusses on three issues:
1 positive experiences, such as happiness, hope, and love;
2 positive characteristics, such as vitality, perseverance, and wisdom;
3 positive institutions, or ways in which institutions can make a positive difference in society.

Subsequently, scientists such as Cameron (positive leadership), Ben-Shahar (happiness), Frederickson (positive emotions), and McKee (happiness at work) identified, studied, and charted individual areas of positive psychology. The subject of positive psychology has since become the most popular elective course at Harvard and Yale.

People and organisations
PART B

Positive Psychology

Abraham Maslow	Martin Seligman	Eileen Rogers - Nick van Dam	Tal Ben Shahar	Kim Cameron	Annie McKee	Barbara Fredrickson

Positive work and leadership practices

Leadership characteristics are the skills, tools, abilities, and behaviours required to successfully motivate and direct others. Yet there is more to leadership. The ability to help people grow through the use of their skills and competences. The most successful leaders, therefore, are those who encourage successfulness in others. Leadership has a major influence on employee commitment and motivation. Superiors can create either a motivational or a demotivational atmosphere. People who voluntarily resign frequently do so because of their 'boss'. Supervisors who cannot function hinder the progress of teams, organisations, and individual employee development.

In order to become a true leader, one should realise that it is personal skills in particular that are essential. The most successful leaders are people who, in addition to being experts in their field, are also equipped with excellent soft skills. They increase their influence through their professional social skills. They have less difficulty achieving faster and more effective results at work thanks to their excellent communication and collaboration with colleagues, customers, superiors, and other stakeholders.

FIGURE 9.44 **EXAMPLES OF POSITIVE WORK AND LEADERSHIP PRACTICES**

Positive relationships	Positive communication	Positive meaning	Reframing	Positive emotions	Growth mindset	Development of strengths

Lifetime of learning	Optimism and positivity	Mindfulness	Appreciative inquiry	Commitment & flow	Developing trust	Emotional intelligence

Inspiring	Empathic listening	Authentic self-confidence	Appreciation	Caring for others	Gratefulness	Living in the moment

Some example of positive work and leadership practices are listed below; several are discussed in this chapter.

9.7.1 Optimism and positivity

Shortly before his death in 2008, computer science professor Randy Pausch hosted a lecture which gained great renown, and whose title provided the name for a book on his life: *The Last Lecture*. In his speech, Pausch told the story of his illness: cancer (*The Last Lecture* had long been a tradition at the University of Carnegie Mellon in the US; every year, a different professor pretended to host the last lecture of their life). There was a bitter irony in the fact that Pausch had already been selected to host The Last Lecture when he found out about his terminal case of pancreatic cancer. Even though his tale could easily have taken a turn for the bleak or morbid, Pausch's speech proved hopeful and full of humour. Pausch spoke of the positive sides to his illness and mortality, and inspired others to fulfil their childhood dreams. He said that everyone should strive to possibility, whatever happens. From a basis of optimism and strength, Pausch said: 'We cannot change the cards we are dealt, just how we play the hand.'
It is not easy to see the positive side to something as final as death. Many people have difficulty staying positive in much less difficult times. All change is a challenge, either negative or positive, personal or professional, elected or imposed. The familiar must be abandoned in favour of the unknown. According to pessimists, there is no possible good side to change; optimists, on the other hand, actively seek the advantages of change, and know that there are upsides to every downside.

The word optimism derives from the Latin *optimum*, meaning 'best', or 'superlative'. In point of fact, it deals with the notion of tending to trust in the future. It is a philosophy or conception of the world which vies situations and circumstances in a positive light, focussing mainly on chance and opportunity. Optimists expect the best possible results, even where those are unlikely. Optimism inspires, energises performance, and helps people, teams, and organisations to excel. Optimists have a hidden competitive advantage in both their professional careers and private lives.

According to Martin Seligman, professor and co-founder of positive psychology and Pennsylvania University, around fifty percent of personal characteristics can be attributed to genetics. To a certain point, one's degree of optimism or pessimism is locked in one's DNA. But what about the remaining fifty percent? Fortunately, research conducted over the past twenty years shows that optimism can be learned. The mind can convert despair, negative contemplation, and angry presentiments to positive, hopeful, and happy thoughts, which is highly useful in times of change. Seligman had good reason for focussing on optimism. He noted that optimists tend to live longer, earn more, be healthier, have more lasting relationships, are more successful at work and at school, and more often win at sports. Optimism is an essential characteristic of great leaders, and of entrepreneurs in particular. Optimists are more resilient, and persevere where others would throw in the towel. They ban negative thoughts from their minds, and do not want to contemplate failure, loss, or problems. Instead, they shift their focus quickly towards the positive aspects and possibilities afforded by their circumstances.

Research shows that there are more advantages to optimism than to pessimism. Optimists are less worried in difficult times, are more resilient to adversity, develop more effective strategies for perseverance, and display behaviours that improve physical and mental health. Their lives, relationships, and careers are more satisfying.

Happiness as the measure of success

O&M IN PRACTICE

Bob Chapman is the CEO of Barry Wehmiller, a global company that manufactures machines for various industries, such as the packaging industry. He introduced the company to the principles of Truly Human Leadership, which focusses on employee happiness. Bob Chapman: 'In early 2000, we began creating a company culture inspired by the principle of Truly Human Leadership: the idea that you can judge success on the degree to which you touch other people's lives. Our most important role is involving people in the company, enabling them to develop their skills and competences, and allowing them to lead meaningful lives. To do that, we build machines for companies all over the world, and provide consultation. At the core of leadership is giving people the feeling that what they do is meaningful – that is the way to improve happiness. As an employee, you are part of an organisation where you come in every day, are told what to do, and are never asked how you feel. You do ten things right, and nobody says a word. You make one mistake, and that is all you hear about. Consider the message an employee like that takes home: their self-image is shot, their attitude towards others is likely to turn unpleasant, particularly towards their partner. As an employer, you have to recognise your influence on the families of your staff. If I send 11,000 people home satisfied, I will have impacted a multitude of lives. Listening is the way to this kind of change. Our business university offers a course on empathic listening: we are sending all the time – really listening is much harder than we think.

It is all very well to talk about a business like it is a charity, but it is not. Sometimes, you need to make a fist; if people cannot properly function in a company, we ask them to leave. It is not a matter of either/or: you care for your people *and* you lead your company well.'

Source: *Management Team*, March 2018 Spotlight

9.7.2 Emotional and social intelligence

Rapid technological development and change have also meant adjustments to management styles. Instead of the previous approach of command and control, a style developed that centred on team spirit and commitment, and that focussed on coaching teams and individuals. This new style required strong emotional and social skills. Emotional intelligence has become an increasingly important competence for people's functioning.

Emotional intelligence concerns the way one handles emotions, both one's own and others'. More specifically, Daniel Goleman, the founder of the notion of emotional intelligence, distinguished five aspects:

1 Knowledge of one's own emotions (self-knowledg); having to a large extent self-knowledge in order to assess one's own philosophies, possibilities, and impossibilities, and to draw relevant conclusions;
2 Regulating one's emotions (self-control); the ability to consider one's capabilities from a positive perspective, and avoid being discouraged;
3 Self-motivation (enthusiasm/optimism); people with high emotional intelligence can endure to work on their long-term goals;
4 Recognising others' emotions (empathy); the ability to transport oneself into another's feelings;
5 Coping with relationships (interpersonal); the ability to get along with both friends and strangers.

As the level of emotional intelligence increase, one's judgement improves, one's productivity increases, one's professional relationships and client connections improve, individuals are prepared for 21st century leadership, teams become more effective, and competitive advantages becomes possible. Emotional intelligence can help in controlling negative emotions, and improve mastering of the self. By recognising and managing one's own emotions, it becomes possible to recognise and manage the emotions of others in order to reinforce new and existing relationships.

FIGURE 9.45 **SOCIAL INTELLIGENCE**

	SELF	OTHERS
RECOGNISING	**SELF-AWARENESS** *Emotional awareness, self-criticism, self-confidence*	**SOCIAL CONSCIOUSNESS** *Empathy, organisational awareness, service provision*
MANAGING	**SELF-MANAGEMENT** *Emotional self-control, transparency, adaptability, performance-awareness, initiative, optimism*	**RELATIONSHIP MANAGEMENT** *Developing others, inspirational leadership, influence, implementing change, conflict management, collaboration*

Source: Daniel Goleman, *Social Intelligence, The New Science of Human Relationships* 2009.

9.7.3 Developing trust

The concept of trust is complex, broad, and elusive. There is hardly a unified definition of trust, because it depends on the situation and on various other independent forces, such as culture. Simply put, trust is the result of a positive relationship between two parties. There is trust if both parties are convinced that the other will not attack them in a moment of vulnerability. Stephen Covey, author of *The Speed of Trust,* considers trust to be the deciding factor in organisational success. Developed and reinforced trust has the ability to create unique organisational success and prosperity, indeed for any of life's dimensions. And yet, it is the least understood, most frequently ignored, and most underestimated opportunity of the modern age. Nothing is as quick as trust. Covey establishes a very clear link between trust, speed, and cost: trust increases speed and reduces cost. Business is made faster and cheaper – that is the dividend of trust. Moreover, trust creates a very favourable climate for innovation. Trust is not only a socially desirable quality; it should be thought of as being an economic motivator as well. Trust, and the ability to earn trust, is the most important quality a leader can have. If one is able to inspire trust in others, this reinforces and accelerates other developments. If, on the other hands, trust is lacking, organisations pay the price in the form of assessments, delayed decision-making, and a loss of time and money.

Trusting and trustfulness are qualities that can be learned and developed. They are not given personal characteristics; they are competences that can be improved and nourished. In his book *Smart Trust*, Covey describe the five keys to trust. First: the choice to believe in trust and trustworthiness, and that trust is a better foundation of leadership. Better than auditing and micromanaging. The second key is: start with oneself, be a reliable spokesperson for one's own philosophy. The third key: be forthright about one's intentions, clearly tell others what it is one wants to do, and why. Be transparent. The fourth key is: practice what one preaches, or one will never move past the rhetoric. And the fifth is: spread trust around, that is what makes a good manager a great leader. Leadership is engendering and spreading trust.

9.7.4 Mindfulness

One morning, at a Washington metro station, a man was playing the violin. Sonatas by Bach, for 45 minutes. Out of the 1,097 people who moved past him on their way to work, only seven stopped to listen. Twenty others slipped him some money, but did not stop to hear his music. In total, the man earned a total of 32.17 dollars. When he was done playing, there was silence. Nobody noticed, nobody applauded. There was no response whatsoever. What none of the passers-by had known, is that they had been listening to Joshua Bell, one of the world's leading violinists, play one of the most complicated pieces of music ever written, using a violin constructed in 1713 and worth 3.4 million dollars. Two days prior, Bell had played the Boston concert hall, where people had paid an average of 100 dollars per ticket to hear him play the same music. This is the true story of a real event organised by the Washington Post. Joshua Bell anonymously played music at a metro station as part of a social experiment involving perception, taste, and priority.
The research question was: 'Can people perceive beauty at unexpected times and places? And, if they can, do they stop to enjoy it? Do people recognise talent in an unlikely location?' The commuters that day showed that they do not. If people will not stop to listen to one of the world's finest musicians playing wonderful music on one of the greatest instruments ever made, how many other things are they letting slip through their fingers while mindlessly hurtling through their existence?

What is mindfulness? The most relevant definition comes from one of the founders of the practice of mindfulness in our age, Jon Kabat-Zinn (1944): 'Paying attention in a certain way: consciously, in the moment, without judgement. Mindfulness is about awakening and being aware of the fullness of every moment in life.' It is a practice that helps one navigate life's continuous change and stress – a life that is becoming ever faster, more complex, and more disruptive in a time of globalisation and rapid technological development. Kabat-Zinn has spent a great deal of time researching the application of mindfulness in healthcare. He studied the interaction between body and mind, and the clinical application of attention training for people with chronic pain or stress-related complaints. He also trains (former) inmates, business people, and healthcare professionals.

Practicing mindfulness focusses one on the **here and now** as the only real moment in time, since the past has already passed, and the future is not yet here. Mindfulness helps one to accept life as a process of change, and to develop an active, curious, flexible, and open mind-set. What started as a meditative technique is now increasingly being applied by business professionals in order to improve work performance. In order to lead change effectively, the development and maintenance of a calm and open mind are essential.

Managers practicing mindfulness cultivate the ability to improve their focus and concentration, reduce their stress, increase their self-awareness and empathy, improve their listening skills, trust their instincts, and adjust to change more quickly. They create a culture of affiliation, openness, and balance. The influence of mindfulness meditation on stress management and mental focussing has frequently been researched by various institutions, and results have been impressive every time, in terms of advantages to general health, wellbeing, and productivity.

A short meditative exercise is enough to gain several interesting insights:
- finding out how little control one has on one's conscious mind;
- discovering that one's senses become sharper as one ceases one's activities and becomes still;
- the fact that some people feel drowsy following meditation illustrates how exhausting it is to continually be in contact with one's conscious mind;
- the idea is to continually refocus one's attention to the here and now.

Practicing mindfulness meditation helps one calm the mind and increase awareness of emotions and thoughts. One gains ownership of oneself. Exercising one's mental muscles reinforces one's attention and focus. One becomes more receptive and enthusiastic, and take greater joy in the present.

9.7.5   Commitment and Flow

Commitment
Commitment means the individual rallies behind the mission, the vision, and values of the organisation, relates themself to the organisation emotionally and intellectually, and is willing to put in an independent effort in order to maximise results. Committed employees are often more willing to go beyond their job description in order to attain a state of flow or optimised experience.

Commitment reduces stress, low-spiritedness, dissatisfaction, absenteeism, staff turnover, and cynicism, while increasing effort, sense of responsibility, happiness, satisfaction, and fulfilment. Employee commitment has many clear advantages: companies with a culture of commitment enjoy higher profit margins, higher productivity, and lower staff turnover.

An organisation is responsible for its culture, content, and framework for full commitment. A culture of commitment is obtained through the following measures:

a by providing employees with challenging work;
b by ensuring variation in work;
c by encouraging employees to develop various skills;
d by affording employees a large degree of responsibility;
e by offering positive feedback: 80% positive and focussing on strengths, and 20% focussing on development;
f by giving employees the feeling they can make an important contribution.

When employees feel they are striving for an important and meaningful goal, and doing work that is personally relevant, it has a positive influence on health, staff turnover, and absenteeism. Commitment also helps to improve effort, happiness, and satisfaction.

Flow

According to psychologist and professor Mihaly Csikszentmihalyi, co-founder of positive psychology, flow is the considered energetical focus on a pleasant activity that is so fascinating as to render external reality, such as temporal progress and physical discomfort, seemingly irrelevant. In short, flow means the best way to experience a given moment. Flow means being positively and intensively occupied with something that affords a degree of happiness. Following many studies, Csikszentmihalyi concluded that people feel happiest when totally absorbed by an activity.

Csikszentmihalyi encourages organisations to increase and support work place flow, and lists three requirements to establish flow:

1 adequate balance between task and challenge;
2 clear objectives, particularly with regard to the way the task fits into the general organisational plan, and the way in which success can be achieved, creating a feeling of effectiveness and meaning;
3 immediate and manifold feedback in order to improve motivation and reinforce effectiveness.

An adequate balance means work should be divided into 65-70% flow, 5-15% low effort and low concentration activities, and around 20% demanding tasks and objectives. While organisations have a major responsibility to satisfy this goal, individual employees can make a huge contribution to both commitment and work place flow by creating a calling for themselves. Aside from one's job (financial reward) and career (personal growth), a calling (the work itself, working for a greater good than one's personal betterment) is very important.

Employees are most strongly committed if they feel they are appreciated and have a vested interest. As research shows that the commitment of employees is strongly correlated to positive business results, organisations that try to actively improve commitment, consciously introduce a performance-boosting culture to an environment, and a context that lets people realise their highest potential.

For this reason, many businesses employ the concept of job sculpting. The inventors of the concept, Timothy Butler and James Waldroop, designed the Business Career Interest Inventory (BCII), which employees can use as a key to unlocking their interest. The Business Career Interest Inventory is based on the notion that a career should be based on interest instead of on skill.

Since employees are not always aware of their own values and strengths, it is important to help them uncover those aspects. Tools that can be used to obtain this insight are StrengthsFinder, Realise2 and Values in Action.

9.7.6 Learning from one's strengths

"Are you able to do what it is that energises you the most every day?" Buckingham and Clifton, both employed by research agency Gallup, found that many people have to answer this question with a 'no'. Following extensive studies with successful people across the world, they concluded that the extent to which one can apply one's talents to one's work determines success and satisfaction. Based on that information, they developed a method that helps one discover one's talents and a way to apply these to one's work more consciously. Their name for this method is the Strengths finder. What is a strength? Positive psychology defines a strength as something one takes pleasure in doing and can do almost perfectly. The method begins with a digital test: a combination of questions and statements that results in a description of one's five most decisive talents. Next, one investigates how to further develop these talents into one's specific Strengths, and how these can be used in one's everyday work. This process of testing can be a very encouraging factor in a process of change. People, teams, and organisations switching to a mind-set based on personal strengths demonstrate a measurable effect on motivation, as well as a reduction in staff turnover. Business results and productivity are improved. Regardless the nature of the strengths that are applied, the ability to apply them is very important for job satisfaction, enjoyment, and meaning. Working on improving weaknesses can be relevant if these weaknesses are an impediment to general performance, but these types of repairs can never result in excellence – which an only be brought about by investing in the reinforcement of strengths.

FIGURE 9.46 **STRENGTHS**

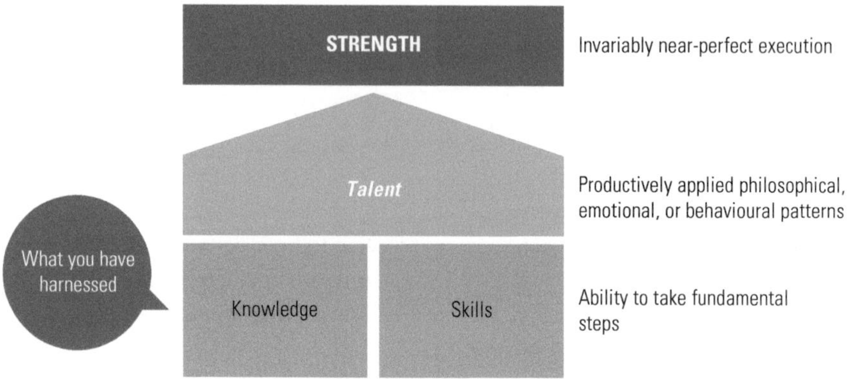

Source: Nick van Dam, *De verandering begint bij jou*, 2015.

9.7.7 Using Appreciative Inquiry

'Appreciative Inquiry is the art and ability to pose questions about an organisation's potential with the intention of helping it reach its full potential,' says David Cooperrider, founder of the AI philosophy.

Appreciative Inquiry is based on a principle of positivity. It offers a comprehensive insight, with a strengths-based approach to learning, discovering, and innovating.

Using AI, the first order of business is to discover what is good about an organisation and its people. The basis is that an organisation is a social system to which all of its members contribute, and that change can therefore only be implemented if all parties involved collaborate in the direction of a common and meaningful goal.

How is Appreciative Inquiry applied?

FIGURE 9.47 **STEPS OF APPRECIATIVE INQUIRY**

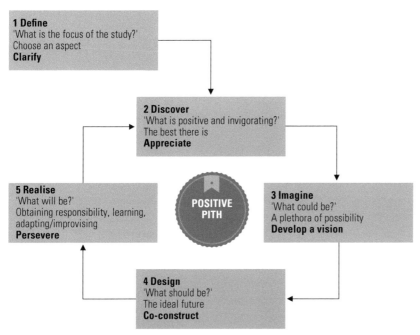

Source: Nick van Dam, *De verandering begint bij jou,* 2015.

Explanation of terms used:
Defining: defining is done by people in the organisation and stakeholders. The process of defining is preceded by preliminary discussion. Moreover, it demands people to reformulate negative issues in a positive manner.
Discovering: focussing on what is best and appreciate what is good given current circumstances. Discovering means asking series of questions with the intention of letting people visualise recent concerns, positive images, and a better future.
Imagining: trying to picture 'what might be'. Build on the results and on the positive core themes revealed during the discovery phase lets people visualise a future by putting their ideals into words.
Designing: looking at 'what ought to be'. This step names and defines the (possible roads to) opportunities, and prioritises accordingly, for example developing a new organisational design structured around a positive core.
Actualising: creating a future based on 'what will be'. Here, the future is brought to life: new approaches, processes, systems, organisational designs are implemented.
The process can be used for individual coaching, to prepare teams and departments for challenges, and to implement large-scale organisational changes.

Summary

- Management is the organisational body tasked with directing an organisation.
  Manager: the person who triggers and directs the behaviour of other people in an organisation.

- Management levels:
  - top-level management: policy formulating tasks;
  - middle management: policy formulating and executive tasks;
  - first line management: executive tasks.

- Two types of managers:
  - functional managers: responsible for one activity;
  - general managers: responsible for all activities in an organisational unit.

- Managerial roles:
  - interpersonal roles: figurehead, leader, liaison-officer;
  - informational roles: observer, disseminator, mouthpiece;
  - decision-making roles: entrepreneur, trouble-shooter, allocator, negotiator.

- Top-level managers: function as inspirers and initiators, with a symbolic function.
  Middle managers: responsible for implementing the policy set by the top-level. 'Caught between a rock and a hard place'.

- In governmental managerial functions, the governmental-political factor is of major importance. Managerial functions in government can be divided roughly into those held by management and the official top-level.

- A well-formulated decision-making process is important for organisations looking to solve complex questions. An important aspect of decision-making is the selection process.

- When address issues, it is important to establish whether:
  - the problem is structural or unique;
  - the situation is urgent;
  - the parties involved are individuals or groups.

- The extent of predictability of future events is 'absolute certainty', 'partial certainty', 'partial uncertainty', or 'absolute uncertainty'.

- Well-structure problems (e.g. calling in sick) or poorly-structured problems (e.g. developing a new product) call for different types of approach.

- Five phases of rational decision-making processes:
  - defining the problem;
  - developing alternatives;
  - evaluating alternatives;
  - selecting an alternative;
  - implementing and monitoring the selected alternative.

- In reality, the decision-making process often differs from the rational decision-making process, for example due to incomplete information or insufficient time or means.

- In practice, a distinction is made between:
  - neo-rational decision-making: informal and centralised;
  - bureaucratic decision-making: formal and centralised;
  - political decision-making: formal and centralised;
  - open-ended decision-making: informal and decentralised.

- The decision-making process should make the best possible use of people's creativity. A frequently applied method is that of brainstorming.

- ▶ Participation is translated into indirect participation in works councils and direct participation in work meetings.

- ▶ The Works Council Act states that a company with fifty or more employees is required to have a works council. The council has:
  - a right to advise;
  - a right to consent;
  - a right to information and discussion.
  Multinational organisations in Europe with at least 1,000 employees across European Union member states and with at least 150 employees in at least two member states are required to create a European Works Council. In a so-called special negotiations group, each member country in the organisation must be represented by at least one representative. Based on the number of employees in the various countries, additional representatives may be appointed.

- ▶ Work meetings are the regular and direct meetings between group management and the executive employees, where work and working conditions are discussed.

- ▶ The four functions of meetings are: being together, knowing together, working together, and doing together.

- ▶ Decisions can be established in various ways:
  - democratic;
  - consensus;
  - majority rule;
  - unanimity;
  - vetoed;
  - delegation;
  - authority.
  When choosing a method of decision-making, the speed and acceptance of the decision-making process are the deciding factors.

- ▶ The Harvard method known as principled negotiation has four principles related to people, interests, choices, and criteria.

- ▶ People apply different decision-making strategies:
  - prescriptive;
  - behavioural;
  - analytical;
  - conceptual.

- ▶ The balanced scorecard is an alternative to managerial reports. It is based virtually solely on financial information. The balanced scorecard method uses strategic goals to compile critical success factors, which are then quantified using performance indicators.

- ▶ Value-based management (VBM) is a management tool that focusses on increasing organisational value for shareholders. It involves a prior assessment of the value-creating ability strategic and investment decisions.

- ▶ To simplify or accelerate the decision-making process, a manager can use:
  - a decision matrix: compares various alternatives;
  - a decision tree: visually illustrates the alternatives;
  - an expert system: automated system that hold specific knowledge can be used to solve problems in its field through user dialogue;
  - a simulation model: software model which emulates the business situation of a certain industry or organisation.

- ▶ A manager has four distinct informational roles:
  - antenna role;
  - information disseminator;
  - mouthpiece;
  - strategist.
  Information can be divided into strategic, tactical, and operational information.

- ▶ A manager's informational need is determined by
  - function type;
  - management level;
  - personal management style.

- ▶ The provision of information in an organisation is not a goal in and of itself, but instead derives from organisational goals.

It is the joint-task of top-level management to determine organisational strategy.

- A manager utilises power; there are five distinct sources of power, as well as positional and personal means of power.

- Two theories on power:
  - harmony model: employees in an organisation have the same interests;
  - party model: conflicting interests between employees.

- Three basic forms of power relationships: equal versus equal, high versus low, and high versus middle versus low. Each form has its own disadvantages, and the trick is in making sure these are avoided.

- Differences between managerial styles:
  - by employee participation (authoritarian, participative, and democratic leadership);
  - by the manager's notions about the employees (McGregor, X and Y theory).

- Blake and Mouton distinguish five basic styles along the degree of production and person-orientedness of a manager. Reddin adds a third dimension: effectiveness.

- Hersey and Blanchard (contingency approach): the effectiveness of a leadership style depends on the level of task maturity of the employees. Each of these four levels is linked to a leadership style.

- Fiedler also argues that leadership style should be adjusted according to situation. He distinguishes three aspects that influence leadership success: the leader-group relationship, the task structure, and the leader's power position.

- An organisation that employs professionals calls for an adjusted leadership style.

- An organisation's phase of development calls for a particular leadership style.

- Transformation management is a particular requirement for organisations dealing with major changes that have to be implemented rapidly.

- A flat organisation demands a horizontal management style. The manager's task is mainly to coach, develop, train, delegate, and facilitate.

- There are major differences between leadership styles in various European countries. A manager working in an international context must rely on intercultural communication.

- A manager's personal functioning is strongly determined by the interplay between their work and private lives:
  - There seems to be a relationship between a manager's age, and the extent to which they attach importance to their various career roles.
  - The choice of how to spend leisure time is largely determined by the extent to which the manager is successful in their work.

- Positive leadership is an umbrella term for various insights and practices developed in (positive) psychology and business economics in recent decades.
  A number of important practices covered in this book are: optimism and positivity, emotional and social intelligence, trust, mindfulness, commitment and flow, learning from one's strengths, and using appreciation inquiry.

Sections A and B of this book dealt with the influence of the environment and of people on organisations respectively. This last section discusses the ways in which organisations are managed, how they are structured, and how they adjust to changes within their environment.

PART C
STRUCTURE AND ORGANISATION

INTERVIEW WITH CHIEF CHOCOLATE OFFICER HENK JAN BELTMAN FOR TONY'S CHOCOLONELY

The minds behind Tony's Chocolonely are journalist Teun van der Keuken and Chief Chocolate Officer Henk Jan Beltman.

'Tony', derived from Teun van der Keuken, the journalist whose Dutch TV programme 'De Keuringsdienst van Waarde' (*The Inspection Service of Value*) ran investigations into slavery in the chocolate industry from 2002 through 2007. He found that, even then, there were still (child) slaves at work on West African cacao plantations; he engaged various chocolate confectionery manufacturers about the issue. Their lack of response made Teun decide to manufacture his own chocolate bars, driven by the notion that if you cannot beat them, you should join them. The solitude he experienced in his war on slavery resulted in the second half of the brand's name, 'Chocolonely'. The wrappers of the bars they sell are colourful and uplifting; they jump out at you from the supermarket shelves.

Van der Keuken (1971), the son of Dutch filmmaker Johan van der Keuken, is a journalist and TV and radio producer. Following his shocking discovery that so much of the chocolate available in supermarkets is produced using slave labour, he began his slavery-free range of Tony's Chocolonely chocolate bars in 2006. It was the first step on the road towards '100 percent slavery-free' production, using no forced or child labour on African cacao plantations – initially, the notion of fully slavery-free products proved untenable, thus the 'on the road towards' caveat. As Van der Keuken is essentially a journalist and not an entrepreneur, Henk Jan Beltman assumed a majority interest in the company in 2010. Van der Keuken has not been involved in the brand for some years now. But he keeps a careful and critical eye on chocolate bar developments from the side-lines.

Henk Jan Beltman (1974) is the current Chief Chocolate Officer for Tony's Chocolonely. Previously, he worked for sustainable brand Innocent. The socially responsible organisation, located in the Westergasfabriek in Amsterdam, has a small branch in Portland, USA, a turnover of 45 million Euros (2017) and a 16.7% market share in the Netherlands. His mission is to make the production of Tony's Chocolonely 100 percent slavery-free by 2025.

What is your definition of corporate social responsibility?
Henk Jan: 'I think the most important aspect, and one that we had not been taught before, is that money should be a means – not an end. To many companies, money is sacred. You work all day to make money so that you can spend it on your hobbies in the evenings and weekends. I feel that this is the issue with the economic system. We need to take the time to consider

who we are, what we want, what we value. Once we manage to do so, money becomes a means; a means you should use to take part in the race, but not one that should be the reward for that race.'

Why did you choose to go with Fairtrade chocolate?

Henk Jan: 'When Tony's was founded, Max Havelaar (Fairtrade in the Netherlands) was the only existing system working to improve trade and living conditions for farmers. Their products are required to meet a number of minimum criteria with regard to social and environmental circumstances. Fairtrade is also the closest to our mission with regard to its focus on organising farmers and establishing fixed premiums. But certification is only a jumping-off point and a model on the path to an honest chain.'

100 % slavery-free, is that feasible?

Henk Jan: 'Tony's Chocolonely buys cocoa directly from farmer cooperatives in Ghana and Ivory Coast with whom we have a long-term relationship. We pay 25% on top of the regular cocoa prices normally offered to farmers, to help them improve their income past the poverty threshold. We are also able to offer traceably processed cocoa butter – an important step towards 100% slavery-free chocolate. The world is not a fair place. That is a topic we must not be afraid to discuss in public. Our chocolate bars aim to offer a visual, tangible reminder that gains in the cocoa industry are unevenly distributed: some bits are smaller or bigger than others. Once people realise that, we will have made our point.'

How about environmental awareness, is that part of your agenda?

Henk Jan: 'Most certainly! To us, it makes sense to have farmers treat the environment responsibly. We encourage environmentally friendly cocoa production among the farmers from whom we purchase our cocoa beans. 'Environmentally friendly' means using as little pesticides as possible, and using fertiliser as professionally and economically as possible. Deforestation is right out. We offer training and education to the cooperatives we work with. Moreover, the wrappers of our bars have been adjusted to use FSC-recycled paper (Forest Stewardship Council), which means the wrapper is not coated with porcelain or chalk. The resources for our wrappers come from responsibly managed forests.'

How about the competition?

There is one on the market now: Chocolatemakers, also from Amsterdam. The companies know each other well. Chocolatemakers are the genuine Willy Wonka. They retrieve their cocoa beans from South America by sailing boat, which is a stroke of genius. The approach used by Tony's Chocolonely and Chocolatemakers is the future, Henk Jan is convinced. 'Fewer and fewer people are comfortable with major corporations. Guys like Enver and Rodney of Chocolatemakers handle cocoa beans day in, day out. Managers for Milka, Verkade, or Mars are too far

together we make chocolate
100% slave free

this is what you ♥ can do!

share our chocolate
chop chop, to our chocoshop!

become serious friends
support our mission and join us

find us here
check our store locator

removed from the production process. There is a return to passion for products – you can taste and see it everywhere. Social enterprise is the future. There is more to life than making money. And success and idealism combine very well. And you need that idealism, or you will not get any recognition.'

What are your goals for Tony's Chocolonely?

Henk Jan: 'Teun van der Keuken, the founder, made tremendous efforts to ensure the global recognition of the problem in the cocoa chain. With that recognition established, the next step is to achieve success. We want to show the world that a company can be serious about a problem on the one hand, and still be commercially successful on the other. Therein lies my added value. Over the past few years, we were rated the best employer in the Netherlands, the strongest brand in the Netherlands according to NIMA, and one of the fastest growing companies in the Netherlands. Our end goal is to leave a lasting impression on the beginning of the cocoa chain

– which requires us to be a source of inspiration for our competitors. We collaborate with 2,000 farmers, but there are 2 million of them out there. Our efforts are a drop in the ocean, and we have to apply our strengths and our 'success' to inspire others to become more responsible for their decisions. Companies like Mars, Nestlé, Mondelez, all of them major chocolate companies who, like we have, must take a serious look at the value chain for cocoa. If we

can manage that, we can move closer towards our vision of 'moving towards 100% slavery-free chocolate together'. Of those three steps, my added value is clearly found in step two; therefore, over the coming period, we will focus on committing our competitors to taking their responsibility.'

Source: MT.nl, *Het Financieele Dagblad*, 26 September 2017, rug.nl September 2015, www. tonyschocolonely.com

10
PROCESS AND CONTROL

Contents

After studying this chapter:

- you will have learned about organisational control-related issues;
- you will have learned the difference between various types of business processes;
- you will have gained an insight into both the way in which business processes are controlled, and the relationship between business processes and added value and quality;
- you will have learned how to distinguish between different management levels and their most important tasks;
- you will have gained knowledge of and insight into the Six Sigma, Lean Management and Lean Six Sigma methods;
- you will have gained knowledge of general methods used to run an organisation.

Pastbook: photobook specialist

Amsterdam company PastBook has created an app which can be used to convert Facebook or Instagram pictures into a printed book. Late 2015, the new My Year functionality was launched, which lets users print out a full year of Facebook or Instagram pictures. The app is currently only available for iOS. Photobooks range in price from 29 to 120 US dollars (depending on their size).

Paradoxically, there has never been a generation more trigger-happy with their cameras yet less inclined to properly store their photos. Our pictures are drifting along the currents of cyberspace. It may seem fine to use Instagram or Facebook as the standard depositories for your images right now, but how about in ten or twenty years? Where will your holiday snapshots be found then? Internet start-up company Pastbook has capitalised on this issue and created an online environment where you can gather all of your images in just a few clicks. You can compile digital picture books using the photos found in various of your social accounts. You can save these books online, share them through networks, or print them and store them in a cupboard.

Pastbook is the initiative of two Italian entrepreneurs who joined Rockstart Accelerator in Amsterdam. For 100 days, Rockstart grooms a start-up for Demo Day, when the ideas are presented to a group of over 250 investors. Pastbook intends to take the world by storm from Amsterdam, by giving people back control over their social media pictures. PastBook accepted a two-million-dollar investment for additional international expansion. The Amsterdam start-up claims to have increased its turnover tenfold over the past three years.

Source: www.dutchcowboys.nl, www.sprout.nl, www.pastbook.com, www.emerce.nl

10.1 INTRODUCTION

Organisational processes

Business processes

This chapter discusses the management of organisational processes. This should be understood as: leading the organisation towards the goals that have been set. These goals can only be achieved if a number of business processes (i.e. human activities) is carried out effectively. A business process is a set of organised human activities relating to the production of goods and/or services. These processes can apply to both profit as well as non-profit organisations.

Some examples of business processes are acquisition, production, administration, marketing, and sales. Each business process can be subdivided into sub-processes. In order to be sure that businesses processes reach their objectives, they need to be supervised by management. This activity is known as process control. Process control is defined as the effective management of business processes through planning, coordinating, and adjusting.

This chapter consecutively pays attention to various types of business processes, business process control, quality and quality methods, and the various levels of organisational management and their specific tasks.

10.2 BUSINESS PROCESSES

Every organisation acquires raw materials and resources (input) and transforms these into products and/or services (output). This transformation process consists of a number of business processes. The first of these to be discussed are input and output, followed by the transformation process (see Figure 10.1).

10.2.1 Transformationprocess

When transforming production factors, there is always input and output (see Figure 10.1).

FIGURE 10.1 **THE PROCESS OF INPUT, TRANSFORMATION AND OUTPUT**

Input consists of four factors. These are:

1 **labour**: people;
2 **natural resources**: raw materials, semi-manufactured products, energy etc.;
3 **capital**: money, plants, and machinery;
4 **information**: about competition, demographic data etc.

These production factors must be brought in by organisations from specialised markets, such as the labour market, the energy market, and the information market (e.g. market research firms). Following the transformation, the resulting products and/or services are sold to the customers and other interested parties. These are also found on various markets. Figure 10.2 shows several examples.

FIGURE 10.2 **THE RELATIONSHIP BETWEEN INPUT, TRANSFORMATION AND OUTPUT**

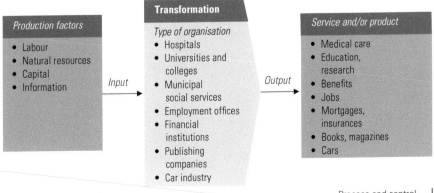

Organisations are not only judged by their products and/or services, but also by the quality of other outputs:

a **labour**: employees leaving the work force (through dismissal, retirement, long-term disability);

b **natural resources**: waste, heat loss, noise, pollution, smell;

c **capital**: profit, depreciation of machinery etc.;

d **information**: annual reports, public relations, advertising.

Organisations can only survive if the production process is continuous – which depends, among other things, on the organisation's relationship with society and the demand for its products.

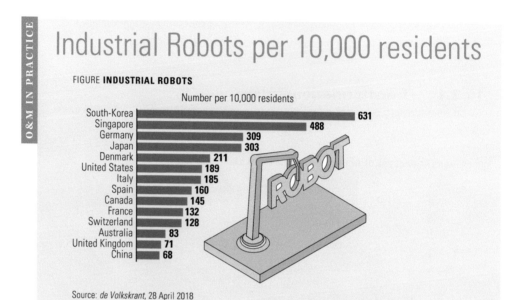

Industrial Robots per 10,000 residents

FIGURE **INDUSTRIAL ROBOTS**

Number per 10,000 residents

South-Korea	631
Singapore	488
Germany	309
Japan	303
Denmark	211
United States	189
Italy	185
Spain	160
Canada	145
France	132
Switzerland	128
Australia	83
United Kingdom	71
China	68

Source: *de Volkskrant*, 28 April 2018

10.2.2 Types of business processes

Three types of business processes can be identified:

1 primary processes;

2 secondary or supporting processes;

3 administrative processes.

Primary processes

Secondary processes

Administrative processes

Primary processes are the activities that contribute directly to making a product or service (purchasing, producing, selling, and furnishing), and to the overall goal of the organisation. Secondary processes include all activities that support the primary processes, such as the management of personnel, finances, and data systems. Administrative processes are the activities that direct the primary and secondary processes, and help the organisation reach its goals.

A summary of the relationships between the primary, secondary, and administrative processes is given in Figure 10.3.

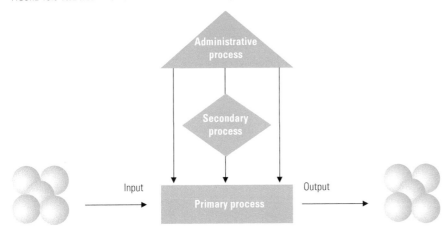

The tasks of the administrative processes are:

a **Strategy selection**. During this process, a vision of the future is established, and a strategy is selected. Strategies need some flexibility and should anticipate fluctuations in demand for products and services to avoid market saturation.

b **Planning**. To reach the goals set by the organisation, primary and secondary processes need to be coordinated. Planning the tasks carried out by staff members, the means of production and scheduling time are used to increase control over the processes (see Section 8.5).

c **Structuring**. This means setting up a system within an organisation that enables people and resources to be utilised (see Chapter 9).

d **Process control**. Processes can be executed in an appropriate and purposeful way by planning, measuring, comparing, and adapting the business.

The relationship between the various business processes and administrative tasks is shown in Figure 10.4.

FIGURE 10.4 **DIFFERENT PROCESSES AND THE RELATIONSHIP BETWEEN THEM AND ADMINISTRATIVE TASKS**

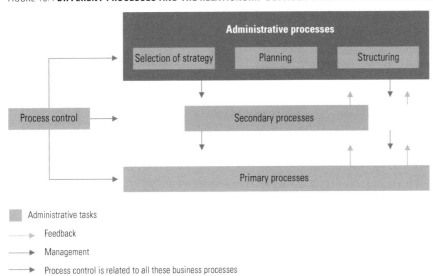

10.2.3 Business process management

It is in the interests of the organisation that the business processes are managed in such a way as to reach predetermined targets. This requires that three conditions are met:

1 The targets should be unambiguously and, ideally, quantitatively formulated (e.g., the development of a particular product under defined quality standards, produced within a certain time span and at a fixed price).
2 The targets should be feasible (e.g., sufficient manpower and means must be available).
3 It should be possible to influence the business processes (e.g., to accelerate development by putting in extra manpower and resources).

Control activities Business processes can only be efficient if they are properly controlled. In this respect, companies often choose a structural and cyclical approach. A well-known such approach is the PDCA-cycle. The initial foundations for this cycle were laid by physicist Walter A. Shewhart ('The Shewart Cycle') in the early 20th century. Around 1950, William E. Deming rebranded it the PDCA-cycle; as a tool, it is now frequently used as part of the later Six Sigma (Section 10.3.1) and Lean Management (Section 10.3.2) methods. PDCA is short for: Plan – Schedule; Do – Measure; Check – Compare; Act – Steer.

a **Planning**. There must be a plan for managing the processes. This plan should be based on production norms and work standards. Production norms include such things as the avaible number of employee and machine hours, and budget. Work standards include particular development or production methods.
b **Measuring and comparing**. This pertains to measuring the business process and comparing measurements to the plan's norms and standards.
c **Adjustment**. This pertains to steps that need to be taken if certain benchmarks are exceeded.

Figures 10.5 and 10.6 show management activities and the relationship between adjusting and managing tasks.

FIGURE 10.5 **THE MANAGEMENT ACTIVITIES OF A BUSINESS PROCESS**

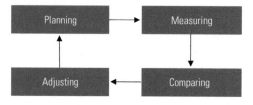

If there is some deviation from the planned standard, intervention is necessary. The following aspects may need to be adjusted:

1 **Objectives**. Have the objectives been well chosen?
2 **Strategy**. Have the right strategic choices been made?
3 **Plans**. Is there an effective and efficient balance between people, resources, and time?
4 **Structure**. Has the right organisational form been chosen?
5 **Primary process**. Has the process been efficient?
6 **Secondary process**. Has the available information been interpreted correctly?

FIGURE 10.6 **THE RELATIONSHIP BETWEEN ADJUSTING AND MANAGING TASKS**

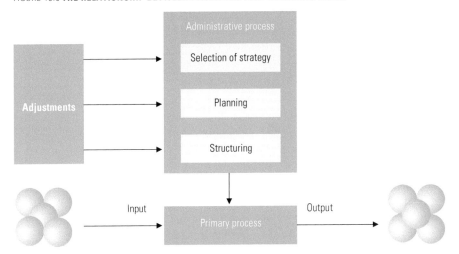

A growing number of organisations have come to the conclusion that process control is important for obtaining a competitive advantage. Michael Hammer, an American professor of computer science, devised an approach known as business re-engineering – or business processes re-engineering. In this approach, the organisational process is not seen as a system of separately organised activities, but as a collection of related core business processes.
A core business process consists of a number of linked activities that add value for a buyer. This added value can be measured using a combination of four criteria: quality, service, expenses and cycle time. These criteria enable buyers to compare products and/or services supplied by different organisations, and then decide between them. Within each organisation, some five to eight different core business processes can be identified, and put to use to obtain a competitive advantage.
The core business processes should be developed from the buyer's perspective.

Business re-engineering
Business processes re-engineering
Core business process
Extra value

Buyer's perspective

The business re-engineering approach is an approach which centres on business processes. It aims at eliminating the divisions that have arisen within an organisation following a splitting up of functions and divisions.
Traditionally, processes such as product development and order handling were split up into small parts. These parts were distributed across the various divisions of an organisation. A slow and inflexible system was the consequence. When markets are stable, such subdivisions do not constitute a risk. However, this is not the case in strongly changing markets, where flexibility, quality and service are necessary. The overall results of the process, rather than of the constituent parts, are therefore at stake.
The aim of business re-engineering is to offer additional added value for the buyer through process orientation.

Overall results of the process

Process orientation

Business re-engineering is not new. In the 1960s, the Japanese successfully organised their production processes according to this approach. At the end of the 1970s, a number of Western enterprises adopted the approach, giving it such names as Just in Time (JIT) and total quality management (TQM) (see Section 10.2.5). By implementing process orientation, the results for businesses improved considerably. This result is measured in terms of the added value that products offer a buyer.

Just in Time
Total quality management

Business re-engineering influences the style of leadership used. Employees are given broader tasks as well as responsibility for the end result. They are judged on their contribution to the increase in added value, and not simply on the way they perform certain tasks. In this context, coaching, motivating, and stimulating become important tasks for managers. The main task of a manager boils down to creating an environment in which staff can function effectively.

Result

Coaching

There are five basic principles that organisations need to uphold when implementing the business re-engineering process within an organisation:

1 **The customer is the centre of attention**. Everything begins and ends with the customer. The customer is the key to the entire business process, from the first contact to any after-care.
2 **Business re-engineering can be applied to all business processes**. All activities are focussed on increasing added value for the customer.
3 **The improving of processes is a domestic affair**. Responsibility for process improvement should not be shifted to the suppliers, although they must be involved: business re-engineering does not stop at the gate.
4 **Business re-engineering must yield clear market results**.
5 **Business re-engineering is a phased process**.

O&M IN PRACTICE

Internet of Everything: cleverly connecting the world!

Not too long ago, the internet was mainly a worldwide network linking up PCs and servers. Social media brought the second revolution, connecting individuals instead. But all of that is child's play compared to the next leap forward: The Internet of Everything (IoE). This will link up basically anything you can think of: billions of gadgets, but also machines, people, cameras, refrigerators, and thermostats. Smart devices communicating cleverly to enable countless innovative applications.

Companies that fail to embrace the Internet of Everything will not survive the near future. Traditional organisations will need to reinvent themselves or be left behind. But getting on board is not enough: the only path to success is a clever application of this new technology.

Source: https://www.managementsite.nl/internet-of-everything-hele-wereld-slim-elkaar-geknoopt, consulted 8 May 2018.

The first step is defining the core business processes and targets. Then, a plan should be formulated to adapt the chosen core processes in order to reach the intended goals. The last phase is the implementation phase. Employees must be very mindful of the role they play in the entire operation and the responsibilities associated with this role.

10.2.4 Business processes and added value

A business process adds value to raw materials or semi-manufactured articles. This added value fundamentally increases an organisation's competitive power, according to Michael Porter. He states that a competitive advantage is obtained by lowering the costs of production or by creating added value for products for which customers will pay extra.

Added value
Competitive power

Porter's theory is based on the so-called 'value chain' which comprising all activities needed to present a product to the market. In other words, the value chain indicates the amount of added value produced by the various components of an organisation. These different components are coordinated by what Porter calls 'linkages'. By carefully structuring and coordinating the business processes, a competitive advantage over other suppliers arises.

Value chain

Linkages

The value chain provides a framework for the analysis of the various activities within an organisation. Within business processes, the added value comes from a combination of the costs (such as for raw materials and work) and the profit that the organisation is willing to incur. The value chain diagram is shown in Figure 10.7.

FIGURE 10.7 **PORTER'S VALUE CHAIN**

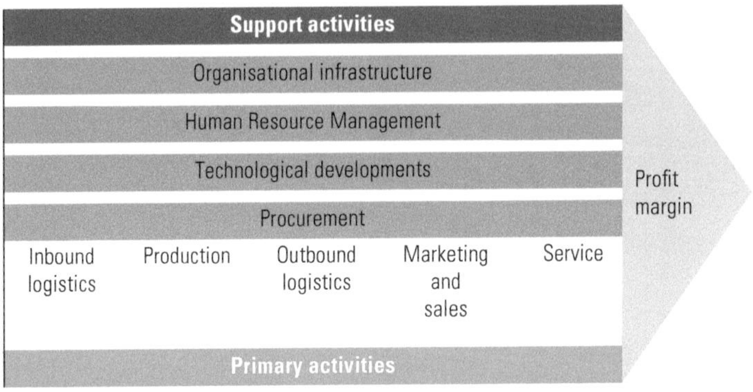

The value chain distinguishes between primary and support activities. Primary activities are activities that add value directly to products; support activities have supporting roles. They create the conditions needed by the primary processes, thus contributing indirectly to the value of the products.

Primary activities

Some examples of primary activities are:
a **Inbound logistics**. Purchasing and storing materials needed for production.
b **Operations (production)**. Transforming purchased materials into products (packaging included).
c **Outbound logistics**. Distributing products to buyers (drafting orders, transporting, and storing).
d **Marketing and sales**. Stimulating the demand for a product (promotional campaigns, advertisements, and sales representatives).
e **Service**. Maintaining or increasing product value through customer service (installing, repairing, and training buyers).

Support activities Some examples of support activities are:
  a **Procurement**. Purchasing the materials needed for the entire value chain.
  b **Technological development**. Researching and developing products or processes.
  c **Human Resources**. Recruiting, rewarding, training and motivating the organisation's employees.
  d **Administrative infrastructure management**. Performing managerial and supporting activities, such as finance and quality control.

Information provision According to Porter, the provision of information in an organisation does not belong to the primary or support activities, but occupies a central position. Like a spider in a web, it connects the separate primary and support activities. Information is a definite factor in increasing competitive advantage.

Organisations can obtain a competitive advantage by structuring and coordinating the business processes in the value chain in a particular way. The invention of a new production process (a supporting activity) can add more efficiency to production (a primary activity), considerably lowering the costs of a product (Figure 10.8).

FIGURE 10.8 **COMPETITIVE ADVANTAGE VIA IMPROVED INTERNAL ORGANISATION**

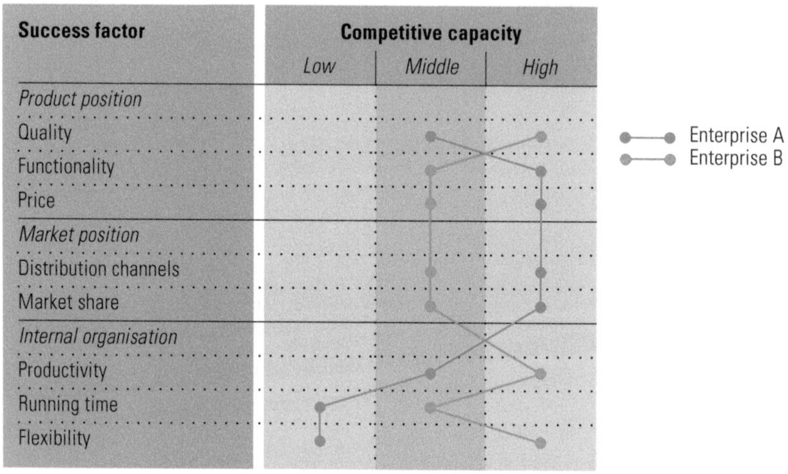

According to Porter, competitive advantage can be obtained in three ways.

Lowest costs
  1 The first strategy is to run operations against the lowest costs. This depends on knowing the effects of particular activities or factors. The so-called 'cost-drivers' must be traced and analysed. A change in structure or coordination can lead to considerable cost savings.

Differentiation
  2 The second strategy is based on product differentiation. The product is given unique characteristics compared to competing products. The consumer is willing to pay extra for these new features. For the organisation, it is important to structure and to coordinate the value chain in such a way that this competitive advantage can be used to gain a favourable ratio of price to quality.

  3 Both low cost and differentiation strategy can be combined with a segmentation strategy (Porter's focus strategy). The organisation can choose to **Focus strategy** address anywhere from one to a number of segments in the market.

Porter's strategies are covered in Chapter 2 (Section 2.2.2).

10.2.5　Business processes and quality

Many enterprises pay attention to quality management in the area of business processes. Quality management is the aspect of management that falls under quality strategy, and is implemented by management as a whole.

This section takes a closer look at quality management, the ISO-certification of quality programmes and a specific quality system, Six Sigma. The last section addresses the INK-management model quality monitoring system.

Quality management

Quality Management

While quality is a frequently used term, it can be defined in different ways. Traditionally, it is associated with the technical specifications of a product, with degree of quality determined by a number of scores representing measurements of technical specifications. A high score is indicative of a high-quality product. This definition of quality is referred to as technological quality.

Technological quality

Hybrid solution goods-to-goods

There are major changes afoot for warehouses used in e-commerce. These changes come with both opportunities and threats, including for the implementation of robotics systems, such as Kiva (Amazon) and Carrypick (Swisslog). While these systems are relatively simple in terms of hardware, their software uses highly advanced algorithms for process control. These smart algorithms help to determine which pod (transportable shelving module) to use for which ideal combination of products. What is the best position to park a pod? Which

pod should be picked from first? For a large share of the assortment, a hybrid solution seems the most obvious choice. In practice, this would lead to a 'goods-to-goods' solution, with robots using outstanding orders to construct one or more picking streets (either parallel or sequential). The added value of robots is the highly dynamic potential for the adjustment of the picking street to accommodate whichever products need picking within a short space of time.

Source: *Logistiek*, 21 May 2015

The so-called relative quality is quality directed to the needs of the buyer and the competitive position (Gale & Buzell, 1989). Here, quality is judged from the perspective of the market (a marketing approach), and the product is assessed

Relative quality

in terms of a number of individual qualities, differing in value according to customer needs and product uses. Quality is defined as the degree of satisfaction experienced by the target group. In addition to technical aspects, a number of other aspects plays a role, including delivery time, after-sales service, and design. Implementing relative quality requires a different organisational approach to that used for technological quality, and is known as total quality management. This is a system aimed at achieving the desired level of quality at minimal expenses. Total quality management integrates and performs all quality-related activities and makes decisions that influence quality, irrespective of position within the organisation (see Figure 10.9).

Total quality management

FIGURE 10.9 **LINKS IN THE PROCESS OF TOTAL QUALITY MANAGEMENT**

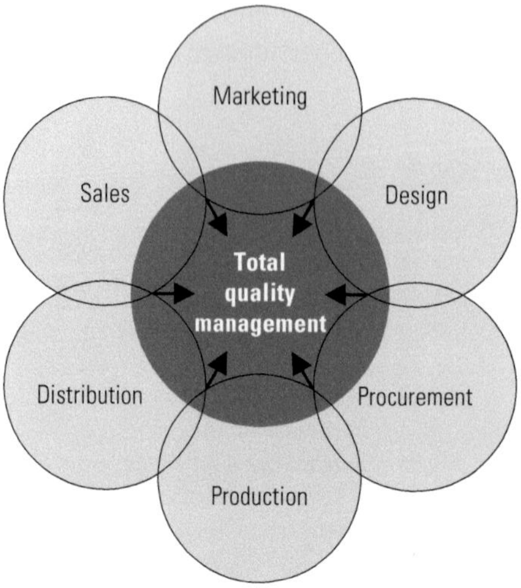

Total quality management should therefore:
a form part of the general policy of an enterprise;
b include all phases of the production process, from market analysis to delivery and after-sales service;
c be adopted by all levels of the organisation, from top-level management down to the work floor.

Total quality management is often abbreviated to TQM.
Four important reasons for quality control are:
1 **Increasing competition**. Many enterprises have witnessed decreased growth in their traditional consumer markets, while competition from outside has gradually increased. The increasing globalisation of the market has only added to the overall effect. Success depends mainly on selling products with a very favourable price to quality ratio.
2 **Increasing buyer awareness of quality**. Buyers are increasingly better informed about the characteristics of products, and are therefore demanding higher quality.
3 **Costs of quality**. The costs associated with making high quality products constitute an important part of the cost price. These expenses can be broken down into costs associated with the prevention of errors during the production process, such as control expenses and non-quality costs and repairs. Non-quality expenses can make up 20% of the cost price of products. The problem is that, in many businesses, these quality costs are insufficiently taken into account in price calculations. The costs associated with the prevention of poor quality are initially high, but decrease over time.

4 **Changes in legislation**. Organisations are increasingly being held legally
   responsible for the delivery of inferior products, with financial penalties also
   rising.

While quality programmes should always focus on the customer, in reality, such   Quality programmes
programmes often only focus on improvements to business processes. However,
it is the customer who ultimately determines quality, as market success is a
consequence of customer decisions. As such, quality programmes should be
aligned with customer needs.
To achieve this alignment, customer needs must be identified and integrated with
the production processes. Figure 10.10 shows how this can increase market share.
The figure also demonstrates that quality has both active and passive effects. For
example, through word-of-mouth, new customers are attracted to an organisation,
while existing customers remain faithful.

FIGURE 10.10 **QUALITY LEADS TO A BIGGER MARKET SHARE**

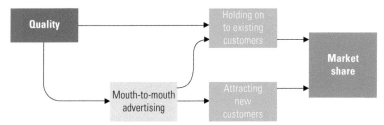

ISO-certification of quality programmes
A quality programme forms the basis for quality care, and includes organisational
structure, responsibilities, procedures and supply. If a quality programme meets
the standards and requirements of an external authority, it is awarded a certificate.   Certificate

Gaining quality certification is important for an organisation for a number of
reasons:
a In a market where quality demands are increasing, the buyer gains a feeling of
    security and trust from products whose quality is certified.
b European unification has led to an increase in competition on certain markets.
    An internationally recognised quality certificate can improve an enterprise's
    market position.
c New international and national legislation has been introduced in relation to
    product liability. Manufacturers can be held responsible for damages caused
    by their products. The possession of a quality certificate may limit the size
    of any claims for damages, and insurance companies sometimes have input
    concerning demands in this respect.

In 1987, the European Commission decided to introduce international quality
standards that originated from the International Organisation for Standardisation   International
(ISO). The Dutch version of the standard is known as NEN-ISO, while the Flemish   Organisation for
version is BIN-ISO.   Standardisation ISO
Some requirements for this standard are:
a Management must set up the quality system together with a description of
    objectives.
b Competencies and responsibilities should be determined with quality principles
    in mind.

c Educated staff should be attracted and given training in relation to quality systems and processes.

d Quality should be measured during all phases of the production process.

e The monitoring process should be organised so as to correct mistakes and prevent them from reoccurring in the future.

European and international standards

NEN not only develops and manages Dutch national standards; it is also the gateway to European and global ones. The most common international agreements:

European norm (EN)
A European EN-norm is a valid qualification in all European member states. Normalisation-institutes are required to implement these standards at the national level (implementation requirement). For the Dutch market, for example, European norms are coded NEN-EN; for Germany, DIN-EN.

International norm (ISO or IEC)
International norms are developed by international ISO or IEC collaborations. Global norms do not necessarily need to be implemented by other countries. Any documents accepted at a national level, for example in The Netherlands, are coded to represent this information – in this case: NEN-ISO or NEN-IEC.
Some international norms are also accepted at the European level, resulting in an NEN-EN-ISO format.

Technical specifications (CEN/TS or ISO/TS)
The Technical Specification (TS) is created with a temporary application in mind, in case the technical state of affairs or consensus is insufficient for the application of a norm. The Technical Specification can also be used for rapid interim publication of the results of a norm-development program.

Technical report (CEN/TR of ISO/TR)
A Technical Report (TR) is informative in nature. TRs are issued if publishing certain information, such as technical data or an inventory of legal norms and requirements per country, proves desirable.

Workshop agreement (CWA or IWA)
A CWA or IWA is developed during a CEN (European) or an ISO (international) workshop. These workshops are open to all interested participants. CWAs and IWAs are often drafted as the forerunners to EN- or ISO-norms.

Source: www.nen.nl

In general, ISO standards put more emphasis on processes than on results. The ISO certificate is a minimum requirement for many organisations and indicates a basic level, just as a driving licence indicates the basic ability to drive. In time, the quality system (or driver's ability) develops further.

Quality manual   A description of the quality system has to be made if an organisation decides to apply for ISO certification. This description should include a quality manual, thus making it possible to check the quality system against the ISO standards. (Figure 10.11).

FIGURE 10.11 **PHASES IN THE DEVELOPMENT OF A QUALITY SYSTEM**

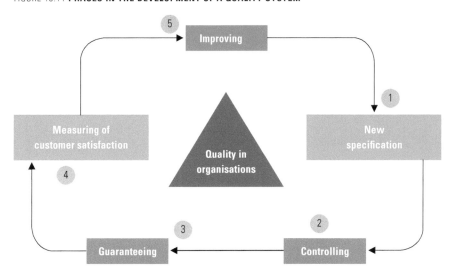

As shown in this figure, a quality system develops in phases. The example of a commercial training is used to offer a detailed illustration of how these phases work. To obtain an ISO certificate, the quality system described should be established and documented. Next, a certification institution is asked to carry out an audit. An audit is an examination intended to assess if all ISO standard requirements have been satisfied. The quality system is examined first, and if it meets the requirements, the organisation's processes are observed to see if they match what has been written down.

Audit

10.3 LEAN SIX SIGMA

This section discusses a method used by many organisations to help them work better and smarter on one hand (using Six Sigma), and faster and more efficiently on the other (using Lean Management) (George e.a., 2015).
In order to fully come to grips with this method, its separate components Six Sigma and Lean Management are discussed first. After that, the two are combined into Lean Six Sigma.

Lean Six Sigma

10.3.1 Six Sigma

Six Sigma is a quality system used by many organisations to improve and speed-up processes. At the core of Six Sigma is that it improves the quality and results of processes. The application of Six Sigma eventually improves profitability as a result of cost savings.
Originally from the US, Six Sigma was invented in 1986. Motorola, the company responsible for the development of this quality improvement program, had intended to create a program that had a strong quantitative (statistic) orientation. Following its highly successful implementation, other US multinationals began using Six Sigma: American Express, Ford, Citibank and General Electric. More and more companies (including some Dutch ones, such as Philips) are applying Six Sigma, and the program is currently being used by many organisations the world over. It is a quality system that can be used both in a production environment and in a service environment. Six Sigma is not only usable by large organisations; SMEs can also apply Six Sigma with good results.

Six Sigma

Robots taking fewer jobs

Robots are less of a threat to the job market than had been assumed. And the Netherlands is among the eight most robot-proof countries in the industrial world, a new OECD study shows. This is due to the fact that many jobs are comprised of component activities, none of which are easy to automate.

Source: *de Volkskrant*, Thursday 5 April 2018

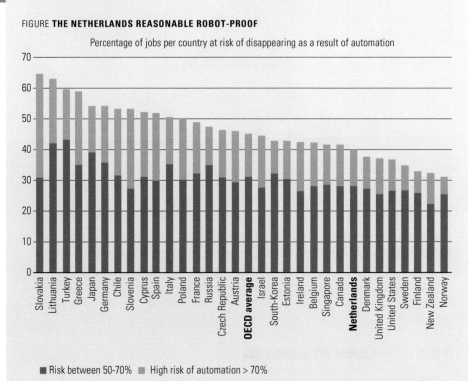

FIGURE **THE NETHERLANDS REASONABLE ROBOT-PROOF**

Percentage of jobs per country at risk of disappearing as a result of automation

■ Risk between 50-70%   ■ High risk of automation > 70%

Six Sigma is best described as a comprehensive and flexible system which allows an organisation to achieve maximum and sustainable success. This success is realised by:
a closely monitoring customer needs;
b limiting oneself to the use of facts, data, and statistical analyses;
c paying extensive attention to the management, improvement, and innovation of business processes.

Standard deviation

Standard deviation

Sigma is the ancient Greek letter σ – a symbol used in statistics to indicate standard deviation. Standard deviation indicates discrepancy. When manufacturing a certain line of products, there is always some discrepancy with regard to individual product quality. Many business processes operate at 3σ-level. This means there is a deviation or discrepancy of 6.7%. Companies that use Six Sigma are highly ambitious with regard to the 'quality' of their production – they strive for 6σ-level (six sigma). The goal of the system is to ensure that there are no more than 3.4 failures or deviations per one million units. The Six Sigma-quality system aims to keep the variance (deviation) in any process as low as possible.

Minimised variance

This minimised variance (deviation) is achieved through various factors, such as eliminating causes of errors, combatting waste, optimising resources, optimising machine calibration, and increasing process speeds.

An important aspect of the Six Sigma method comes in the form of customer opinions, expectations, and needs; the consumer is the jumping-off point for all change. Six Sigma labels this concept the 'Voice of the Customer' as the 'Critical-to-Quality' (CTQ). This is the expectation or demand that customers have when experiencing a process. CTQ can be based on various perspectives, for example quality, speed, safety, reliability, costs, or hours.

Voice of the Customer
Critical-to-Quality

Customers expect products they have ordered to be delivered within 5 days (CTQ). Looking at the actual delivery times in a certain period shows the following:

FIGURE 10.12 **FREQUENCY TABLE OF PRODUCT DELIVERY DATES**

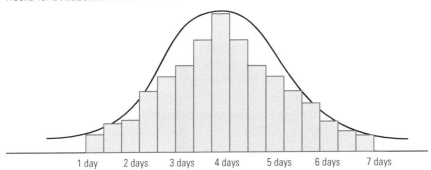

Source: Morgan, J. & Brenig-Jones, M., *De kleine Lean Six Sigma voor dummies*, Amersfoort, BBNC Uitgevers, 2017

This table demonstrates that many deliveries take place within the CTQ (no more than 5 days), but that some do not. These deliveries take longer than the CTQ. Including the standard deviation in the figure shows the following:

FIGURE 10.13 **STANDARD DEVIATIONS**

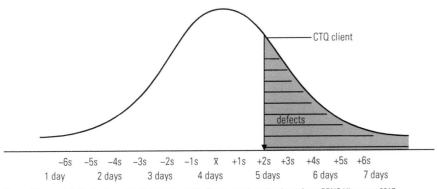

Source: Morgan, J. & Brenig-Jones, M., *De kleine Lean Six Sigma voor dummies*, Amersfoort, BBNC Uitgevers, 2017

All deliveries that take longer than 5 days are known as 'defects' in Six Sigma terms. Within the realm of this example, the sigma value is at the 2 σ –level. The next step is to analyse, improve, and accelerate the processes in order to reduce the possibility of 'defects' as much as possible.

To achieve these process improvements, Six Sigma is used as a basis for improvement projects, which cover five phases (DMAIC):

1 Define (defining the problem). The definition phase is when project goals are formulated. It is also when the focus and boundaries of the project

DMAIC
Define

are established. Establishing the goals is more than just defining quality characteristics and demands; it also depends on defining the aspects that are of influence on the desired quality.

Measure

2 Measure (measuring the data required). The measurement phase is mainly one of information-gathering, specifically on the current status of process quality. The process is charted schematically, for example through flowcharts or diagrams. The Six Sigma-quality system attaches great importance to measurements. How many defects and failures occur? What is the percentage of process implementations that succeeds on the first attempt? What are the risks involved in the process? All of this information is documented statistically. This phase is about establishing reliable information. That includes a careful look at what measurement instruments to use, and how to apply them.

Analyse

3 Analyse (analysing the problem). The analysis phase is about obtaining profound knowledge of and insight into the process. This knowledge and insight are required in order to achieve cost savings and/or quality improvements. Knowledge is gained through the application of statistical techniques on the information gathered. Consider variance analysis, cross tables, regression or correlation analysis. This phase also makes use of techniques from other fields, such as systems development and project management.

Improve

4 Improve (implementing the improvement). The improvement phase aims to optimise the working method. The goal is to use simulations and experiments to create the best possible design of the activities in the process, based on knowledge and insights gathered.

Control

5 Control (verify, manage, and safeguard the improved process). Merely establishing the best possible working method is not enough – the results should also be verified. The control phase focusses on evaluating and safeguarding the results from the Improve phase. A lack of control can easily lead to old behaviours and conduct being resumed, and that the lessons that have been learned fail to continue to be applied.

Belts

The proper application of Six Sigma requires a specific project organisation, known as 'Belts' in Six Sigma terminology. 'Belts' are employees of a specific level of Sig Sigma training. The term refers to the belts used in various martial arts to indicate the wearer's level of skill. Six Sigma recognises the following 'Belts', or project leader roles:

Champions

Champions

Champions are the highest-ranking employees with regard to Six Sigma. Champions carry the final responsibility with regard to all Six Sigma activities in the organisation. Champions are managers who report directly to top-level or division management. It is their job to ensure that all Six Sigma activities support the organisation's goals. Champions lead the Black Belts.

Black Belts

Black Belts

Six Sigma-projects must be completed by employees who are (frequently) involved with those projects in their day to day activities. These employees are referred to as Black Belts. Black Belts need to be experts in two fields. Black Belts are trained in statistical problem-solving techniques. Their position also requires them to have an insight into project handling and leadership. Black Belts have had a minimum of four to five weeks of training. In major organisations, Black Belts are involved in Six Sigma projects fulltime. Black Belts employees responsible for Six Sigma projects, and lead Six Sigma project groups.

Yellow and Green Belts

Black Belts are supported by Yellow Belts and Green Belts, who offer input from the workplace. Yellow belts are employees with a basic level of training in the most commonly used Six Sigma tools, such as process analysis and process measurement. Green Belts are similar, but additionally lead simple projects and have also had more training.

The following is an example of the application of Six Sigma:

Decreasing the number of rejected batches at a production company

Objective

A production company in the medical sector frequently was experiencing issues: the production process was unable to produce units within the required specifications. To correct this problem, a Six Sigma project was implemented.

Primary objective: reduce the number (1.75) of rejected batches per week (2.3% or 3.5 sigma) by a factor ten (4.3 sigma) or better. Secondary objective: Introduce Six Sigma DMAIC team approach.

Project approach

Three improvement teams were founded, and an internal black-belt trainee was assigned. The teams consisted of the machines' operators, supplemented with employees from the following departments: TD, Manufacturing Engineering, and R&D.
TEAM 1: Equipment optimisation
TEAM 2: Working Methods and Procedures optimisation
TEAM 3: Tooling and Materials optimisation.

Project duration

2 months to chart the problem areas and found improvement teams.

7 months to use DMAIC to solve the component problems.

Themes

1   Careful climate conditioning of the working space
2   Preventing product contamination
3   Creating detailed working procedures
4   Improving maintenance equipment and tools
5   Optimisation of tooling equipment design
6   Training operators and exchanging Best Practices

Results

The objective was met in 27 weeks: the problem of the rejected product batches no longer occurred from week 7 onwards. The final 20 weeks were used for results-safeguarding and imbedding the working method in the organisation. Eventually, the issue of rejected batches was reduced from 3.5 sigma to better than 4.7 sigma.

Source: www.aimingbetter.nl

FIGURE **REJECTED BATCHES**

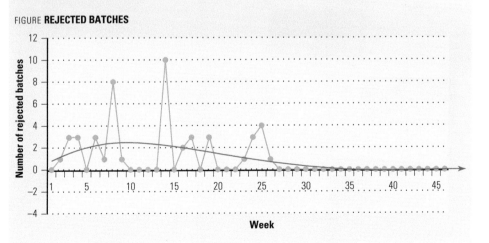

10.3.2 Lean Management

The principles of Lean Production were first applied in Japanese industry. The term 'Lean' was coined by John Krafcik in 1988, who used it in his article *Triumph of the Lean Production System* in which he discussed his study into quality care in the NUMMI enterprise, a joint-venture between Toyota and GM. Based on this study, Toyota developed the Toyota Production System (TPS), based on three MU's: Muri, Muda, and Mura.

Muri
1 **Muri**: represents overloading, the result of a machine or an individual being taxed beyond capacity.

Muda
2 **Muda**: this a component part of an activity of a process that does not add value for a customer – wastage. Wastage is the essential focus of lean production; to only perform those activities that add value for customers. Other activities only lead to wastage and should be eliminated or removed. Wastage can have various causes, including these frequently found examples:
   - over-processing: adding more to the product or service than the customer needs;
   - transporting: shifting intermediate and final products and employees = around;
   - waiting: employees or customers having to halt production or service until a colleague or supplier has performed their task;
   - correcting: a product or service requiring additional handling because a mistake was made the first time around.

Mura
3 **Mura**: this focusses on inequalities in a process. Mura is best compared to the phrase 'stop-and-go': undesirable differences in pace.

Lean Management
Muda is a core concept in Lean Management, with each process designed to maximise customer value and minimise wastage. By shifting the focus to the customer, added process value at minimal effort becomes the most important factor. This approach also lowers costs and increases profit.

In 1996, James. P. Womack and Daniel Jones used their book *Lean Thinking: Banish Waste and Create Wealth in Your Corporation* to introduce five phases needed to arrive at a lean organisation.
These five phases are shown in the figure below (Figure 10.14):

FIGURE 10.14 **THE FIVE PHASES OF A LEAN ORGANISATION**

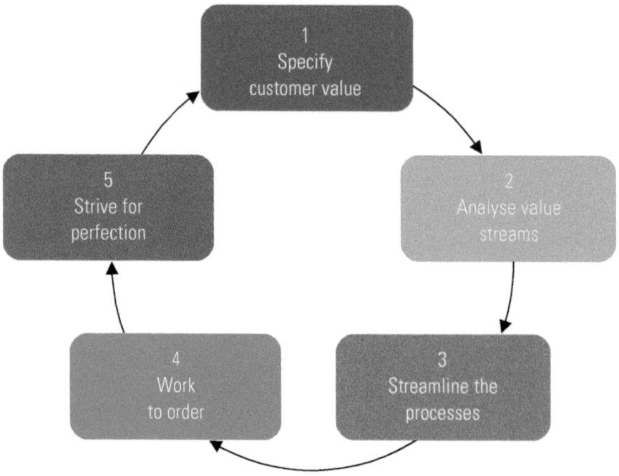

1
Specify
customer value

2
Analyse value
streams

3
Streamline the
processes

4
Work
to order

5
Strive for
perfection

Source: www.sigmaonline.nl

1 Specify customer value. This phase pays attention to the questions: "what is it the customer really wants? What do they expect?" The objective is to form an accurate image of the customer's demands, and of how they define value. What is it that the customer wants to pay for?

It is important to realise that customer demand is not the same as customer value. Customers (frequently) do not realise exactly what their needs and desires are. Customer value can partly consist of elements a customer does not (or cannot) mention or indicate.

2 Analyse value streams. Phase 1 was used to create an accurate impression of customer value. This value is linked to organisational processes in phase 2. The relevant question is: "which processes do or do not add value for the customer?" If a process or partial process fails to add value for a customer, it is known as 'wastage' in Lean Management. A useful tool for establishing wastage is 'Value Stream Mapping': a technique used to analyse the flow of goods and information. It deals with describing or drawing the flow of goods and services through the production process (In 't Veld, 2013)

Figure 10.15 is an example of a Value Stream Map:

FIGURE 10.15 **VALUE STREAM MAPPING**

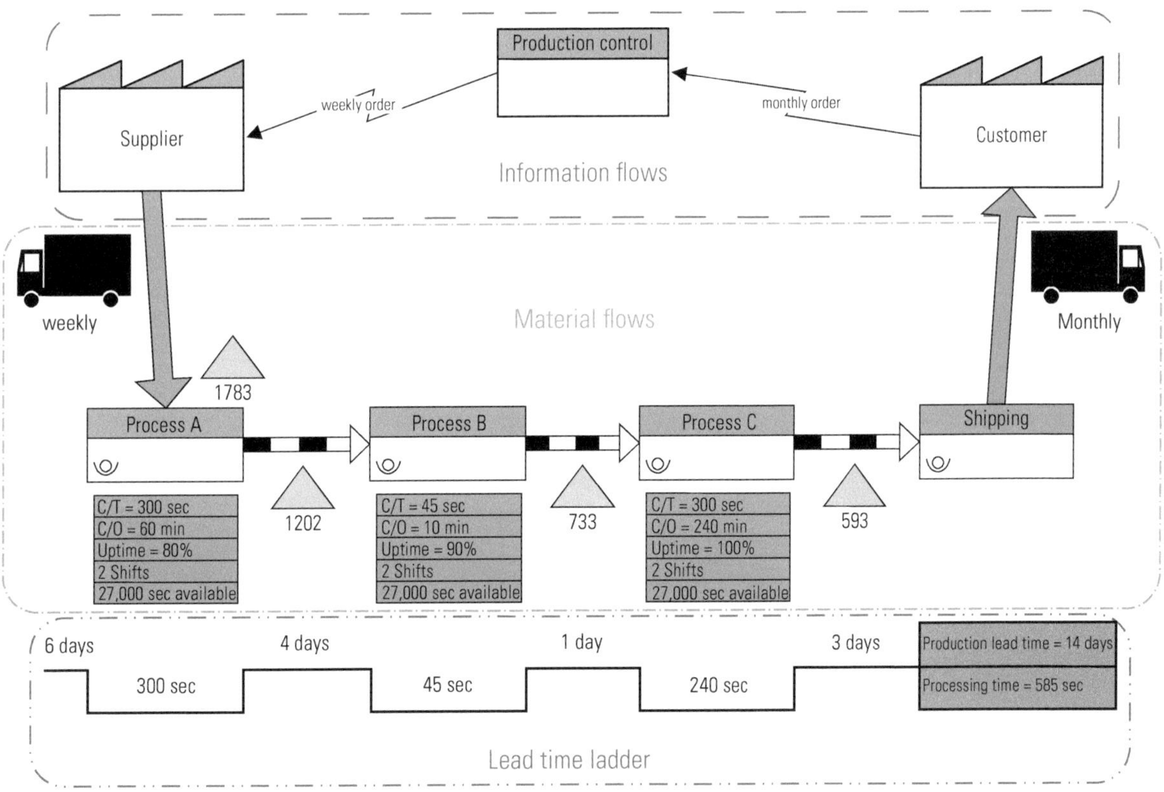

Source: https://nl.wikipedia.org/wiki/Value_stream_mapping

3 Streamline processes. The previous phases resulted in a map of all (partial) processes, including insight into which of those (partial) processes do or do not add value for customers. Phase 3 is the removal or minimisation of the non-value-adding (partial) processes. The 'Muda' paragraph discussed the various different causes of wastage. The removal or minimisation of wastage usually requires that (partial) processes are redesigned. The intended result of this phase is that the remaining (partial) processes are streamlined in such a way that the product flows through the entire process to the customer without loss of time or quality.

4 Work to order. Where phase 3 streamlined the processes, phase 4 considers when these processes should be initiated. Here, the basis is that the customer is king: it is the customer who determines how many products or services are to be supplied. By specifically catering to order, unnecessary inventory can be avoided – even though some inventory may be necessary in order to be able to meet with sudden peaks in demand.

5 Strive for perfection. Perfection cannot be attained, but it can be pursued! The final phase is about creating a work process that continually looks for ways to improve the (partial) processes. Process improvement should be everyone's responsibility and should be a normal part of everyday work. The objective is to become a learning organisation.

O&M IN PRACTICE

Lean distinguishes eight forms of wastage

1 Overproducing: doing more than is needed.
2 Waiting: periods of inactivity for both customers and employees.
3 Transporting: unnecessary movement of equipment, people, or materials.
4 Over-processing: taking more process steps than is needed.
5 Inventory: keeping more inventory than is needed.

6 Movement: travelling distances within a single process step.
7 Correcting defects: performing additional activities because of first-time failures.
8 Making inadequate use of employee knowledge to improve the production process

Source: https://www.managementsite.nl/echte-leanmanager, consulted 8 May 2018

10.3.3　Lean Six Sigma

Where Section 10.3.1 paid attention to Six Sigma and Section 10.3.2 to Lean Management, both methods are usually applied in combination in practice both in production and in service environments.

As indicated, Six Sigma mainly aims to quantifying the quality of (partial) processes. Lean management focusses mainly on the elimination of wastage and the improvement of (partial) process streamlining in order to create value for customers. Quantifying quality (Six Sigma) can reinforce the use of Lean Management. Six Sigma involves one aspect of the process, namely quality. Lean Management involves processes as a whole, but has less of a quantitative basis. It is through the application of Six Sigma to Lean Management that a quantitative basis is added. Basically, the joint application of Six Sigma and Lean Management creates a situation where a company works on improving both quality and process efficiency design. In other words: a perfectly slimmed down organisation of processes.

The power of the combined application of Six Sigma and Lean Management into Lean Six Sigma is found in the following areas:

Lean Six Sigma

1 **Quality improvement**: the application of Six Sigma creates a strong focus on a quality improvement that has broad organisational support due to its specific approach (improvement projects using the DMAIC-method);
2 **Lead time improvement**: the application of Lean Management creates a strong focus on avoiding wastage, increasing speeds, and improving the efficiency in (partial) process design. The application of Lean results in a strong focus on customer value creation;
3 **Learning organisations**: the application of Six Sigma and Lean Management creates a situation of continuous quality and process improvement: an organisation that is always learning and improving, while keeping a central focus on customer value;
4 **Improving business results**: both Six Sigma and Lean management offer a positive contribution to the improvement of business results.

A schematic impression of Lean Six Sigma serves as the summary and conclusion to this section (Figure 10.16).

FIGURE 10.16 **SCHEMATIC IMPRESSION OF LEAN SIX SIGMA OVERVIEW**

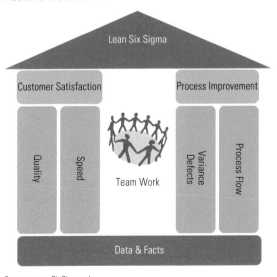

Source: www.SixSigma.nl

10.4 MANAGEMENT LEVELS AND SPECIFIC TASKS

Organisation An organisation is defined as 'any group of people cooperating to achieve a common purpose'. The managing body of an organisation is tasked with realising the established organisational goals. These goals can be reached if the business processes in an organisation are implemented efficiently and effectively. In most organisations, it is not possible for one person to do all of the work. Therefore, the activities need to be distributed. This distribution of tasks across various individuals creates a division between leadership and implementation. This division results in the creation of an organisational hierarchy.

The larger the organisation, the greater its number of hierarchical layers. These organisational hierarchic layers are expressed in terms of various managerial or executive levels. Each management level is tasked with a specific assignment related to the realisation of the established organisational goals (see Figure 10.17).

Management level

FIGURE 10.17 **MANAGEMENT LEVELS WITHIN AN ORGANISATION**

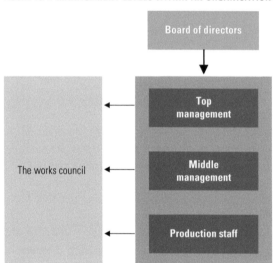

Top-level management is mainly concerned with strategic decision-making, whereas the executive branch deals mainly with operational decisions with regard to business processes. Middle management performs the function of a hub that translates strategic decisions into operational decisions. From the perspective of top-level management, middle management has an executive function; from the perspective of the executive branch, it has a managerial function.

Section 9.2 also pays attention to top level management and middle management

Top-level management

There are various names for the highest level of organisational management: top-level, supervisory board, or directorate. The tasks of this level of management are mostly in the realm of policy development. Looking at organisational management, there are various types of governance whose composition, task-division, and decision-making differ from one to the next. The most important manifestations are:

a General Manager;
b Board of Directors;
c entente structure;
d collegial board.

Structure and organisation
PART C

Management that consists of a single General Manager places all authority in terms of decision-making with a single person. This may be the case in a situation where there is a single director, or where a board of directors has a chairperson who has final decision-making authority.

The advantage of this form of governance is that it makes rapid decision-making a possibility. A potential disadvantage is the risk that important questions are only assessed by a single person, that business continuity may be threatened in case of long-term illness, and that there is a greater risk over overloading the entire board (who is only one person).

General Manager

A Board of Directors uses a division of tasks, such as one General Manager for general affairs, a Financial Manager for financial affairs, and a Commercial Manager for commercial affairs. The advantages of this form of governance are that managers may supplement and correct each other, that the risk of overloading the entire board is smaller, that there is less chance to interrupt continuity, and that there is more knowledge and experience available. A disadvantage is the potential for delayed decision-making, and the possible emergence of insurmountable differences of opinion between the board members.

Board of Directors

With regard to decision-making, a board may make use of either the collegial board structure or the entente structure.

Collegial board governance means governance through consensus. An agreement between all of the various board members is required. This means that collegial board governance operates on the basis of equal decision-making authority. The board members are collectively responsible for the success of the entire operation – not merely for their own organisational component.

The entente structure means that board members have both individual and collective decision-making authority. This structure is mainly applied in organisations that rely on the board having major expertise in a particular field. In addition to their individual authority in a specific field, the board members have a common authority in more general fields.

Collegial board structure
Entente structure

Figure 10.18 offers a schematic overview of individual and collective decision-making authorities.

FIGURE 10.18 **INDIVIDUAL AND COLLECTIVE DECISION-MAKING POWERS**

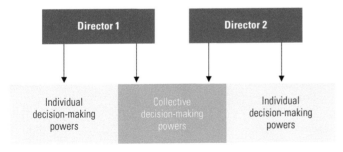

Lastly, there is the example of entente structure in legal practice. Using individual decision-making authority:

a *director 1* International law;
b *director 2* Entrepreneurial law;
c *director 3* Criminal law.

Using collective decision-making authority:

a Financial affairs;
b Promotional activities;
c Investments.

Middle management

Middle management

The task of middle management is to implement the board's general policy. In addition, it performs a managerial function to executive employees. Based on the board's policy, middle management establishes divisional policy, translates this policy into departmental plans, assesses and steers the implementation of these plans, and reports the results to the board. In addition to its managerial tasks, middle managers also have executive tasks. The job content of middle management is experiencing major changes, with their added value shifting towards the entrepreneurial.

Due to organisational flattening and restructuring along the lines of business units or operating companies, middle management is being given new tasks. Middle management, in charge of these business units and operating companies, is increasingly being tasked with establishing the strategy of the organisational unit in additional to its organisational task.

O&M IN PRACTICE

Digital leadership: a must-have!

Many people fail to realise the speed at which technology is currently developing. This is true for consumers and organisations alike. In 10 years' time, the world will look completely different. The speed at which biotech, robotisation, and artificial intelligence are developing is turning our lives upside-down: our jobs, our health care, our transportation, the entirety of our daily lives will change. This process has already begun and will not be slowed down – let alone stopped. World 4.0, with all of the opportunities and threats that the digital revolution is promising, can no longer be ignored!

Digital transformation calls for more than simply investing in IT. Digital transformation calls for leadership! No organisation should be satisfied with some ready-made playbook; doing nothing means a disadvantage before you have even started!

Source: https://itexecutive.nl/partner/partner-whitepaper/digital-leadership-een-must, consulted 8 May 2018

Executive employees

The executive employees perform the actual transformation process that turns input (nature, labour, capital, and information) into output (products or services). At this level, there are primary processes that directly contribute to the creation of goods or services. The secondary processes ensure that the primary processes proceed correctly and uninterruptedly. Governance processes help steer the primary and secondary processes.

At the level of the executive employee, most of the tasks performed are policy-implementing or policy-directing. Governance mainly takes the form of taking operational decisions, such as the verification and steering of activities.

Executive employees

Works council

The works council essentially exists parallel to the regular levels of organisational governance. It is comprised of members who have been elected directly by individuals working in the organisation. The works council has an influence on the decision-making in an organisation (see Chapter 9 for more information).

10.4.1 Board of Commissioners

The Dutch 1971 *Structuurwet* (Structure Law) dictates that certain Dutch *NV* and *BV* companies (comparable to LLCs and PLCs) are required to establish a *Raad van Commissarissen* (Board of Commissioners). The companies that are subject to this requirement are those that fulfil the following criteria:

1 The issued capital and the reserves amount to at least 16 million.
2 The partnership is legally obligated to establish a works council (see Chapter 9 for more information).
3 The partnership employs more than 100 employees in the Netherlands.

Board of Commissioners

Such partnerships are known as *structuurvennootschappen* (structure partnerships). They are required to establish a Board of Commissioners of at least three individuals. A member of such a Board is known as a *commissaris* (commissioner). These boards are headed by a *president–commissaris* (president-commissioner). In addition to the *Raad van Commissarissen* (Board of Commissioners), there is also the *Raad van Toezicht* (Supervisory Board). This supervisory body plays a role in foundations and societies, and in cases where supervision on behalf of the government is required. A member of the Supervisory Board is known as a supervisor.

Smaller Dutch LLCs and PLCs, as well as other legal entities (such as one-man businesses and general partnerships), are not legally obligated to establish these types of boards.

The following paragraphs address the roles of the Board of Commissioners in the Netherlands, and the concepts of independent supervision and appointment.

Structure partnerships

Tasks of the Board of Commissioners

The main task of the Board of Commissioners is to monitor management's policy and general organisational affairs. To fulfil this task, the BoC requires expertise in various fields. As a result, the composition of a BoC is usually heterogenous. Various areas of expertise, such as finance, legislation, and marketing, may be represented in the BoC.

The BoC should aim to uphold the interests of the entire organisation, and not merely those of stakeholders inside or outside of the organisation (employees or capital providers).

Monitor management's policy

The BoC is not involved in actual business management, since that is the task of (top-level) management. A commissioner does not operate in the service of the organisation, but receives some form of remuneration for services rendered.

Over the past years, there have been changes to BoC activities. The role of commissioner is slowly changing into that of joint-decision-maker: someone actively involved in proceedings. A commissioner who wants to deliver a good performance must put more effort into their commissariat, while their heightened responsibility also comes with greater demands.

As a result, there seems to be an impending shortage of candidates who can bring to the table not only a wealth of experience and a network of useful business contacts, but who are also able to free up enough time to fulfil their commissariat-related duties.

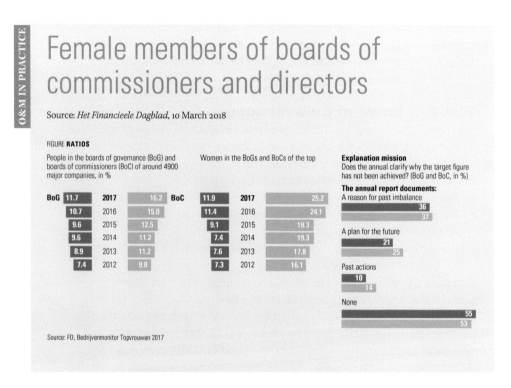

O&M IN PRACTICE

Female members of boards of commissioners and directors

Source: *Het Financieele Dagblad*, 10 March 2018

FIGURE **RATIOS**

People in the boards of governance (BoG) and boards of commissioners (BoC) of around 4900 major companies, in %

BoG			BoC
11.7	2017	16.2	
10.7	2016	15.0	
9.6	2015	12.5	
9.6	2014	11.2	
8.9	2013	11.2	
7.4	2012	9.8	

Women in the BoGs and BoCs of the top

11.9	2017	25.2
11.4	2016	24.1
9.1	2015	19.3
7.4	2014	19.3
7.6	2013	17.8
7.3	2012	16.1

Explanation mission
Does the annual clarify why the target figure has not been achieved? (BoG and BoC, in %)

The annual report documents:
A reason for past imbalance
36
37

A plan for the future
21
25

Past actions
10
14

None
55
53

Source: FD, Bedrijvenmonitor Topvrouwen 2017

In addition to its supervisory tasks, the BoC has additional authorities in structure partnerships. These authorities are in the following areas:

a The BoC is the only body with the authority to appoint or dismiss a director. If the BoC wants to appoint a manager, the general shareholder meeting is notified. In addition, the BoC is required to ask the works council for their advice regarding the intended appointment. The BoC's authority to appoint managers cannot be limited by any binding recommendation. The BoC may only dismiss a director after it has heard the general shareholder meeting.

b The annual account (balance sheet and income statement) is established by the BoC. The BoC submits the annual account for approval by the general shareholder meeting. The annual account must also be submitted for review by the works council.

c Crucial decisions, such as mergers, issuance of new shares, major investments, and the dismissal of large numbers of employees, must be submitted for approval by the BoC.

Independent supervisions and appointment of the Board of Commissioners

The Dutch Structure Law operates on the basis of a two-tier system: a system that demands a strict separation between an organisation's management and its supervision. This is also known as the Rhineland model, a model that assumes that the BoC is required to weigh up the interests of various stakeholders. From this perspective, companies exist for more than mere profit – they also have a societal impact. This model is also in use in Germany.

Besides the Rhineland model, which separates management and supervision, there is the Anglo-Saxon model, a one-tier system. The one-tier system is not based on a strict separation of management and supervision. UK and US companies use a mixed top-level body (board of directors) which includes both executives and non-executives. The Anglo-Saxon model is based on the dominant position of capital providers.

In recent years, the growing trend towards internationalisation has raised the question of whether a one-tier board should not also be possible for Dutch organisations. The facts are clear: the one-tier board is the most frequently found model the world over. To that end, the Cabinet of the Netherlands set out to arrange the possibility for Dutch companies to choose between a one-tier and a two-tier board. An important motivation for a one-tier board is that it engages supervisors more actively and directly with management's decision-making processes. In addition, the supervisors hold the same information as management. The two-tier board operates on the basis of an assumed knowledge deficit between the boards of commissioners and directors. A final note is that increasing numbers of members of BoCs in the Netherlands no longer have the Dutch nationality.

On 1 January 2013, the right to choose between one-tier or two-tier was legally established (for BVs and NVs alike). Since 1 January 2013, BVs and NVs are allowed to opt for a one-tier board, including companies subject to the Dutch Structure Law. Major multinational companies whose headquarters are in the Netherlands but whose workforce majority works abroad do not fall under the Structure Law.

A one-tier board essentially means that the supervisors are part of management. In a one-tier board, the executive managers (formerly the board of directors) are at the same table as the non-executive managers (formerly the board of commissioners). Only the non-executive managers can appoint, supervise, and define the rewards of executive managers.

In the Netherlands, it had long been the case that the members of the board of commissioners were appointed using the so-called co-optation system. This meant that members of a board of commissioners appointed their own successors. In recent years, the co-optation system has come under enormous pressure. It is an outdated system which, in practice, is usually based on an old boys' network. Per the end of 2004, legislation with regard to structure partnerships was updated through the *Wet Wijziging Structuurregeling* (the Structural Regulations Adjustment Act). This new legislation meant that the co-optation system was abolished. Under this new legislation, commissioners were no longer appointed by the board of commissioners, but by the general shareholder meeting – who still based their decision on individuals submitted by the board of commissioners. Both the general shareholder meeting and the works council can submit individuals to the board of

Two-tier system

Rhineland model

Anglo-Saxon model

One-tier board

Executive managers
Non-executive managers

Co-optation system

commissioners. The works council has a right of nomination for one-third of the total number of members.

Other important changes resulting from the *Wet Wijziging Structuurregeling* are that:
1 the general shareholder meeting determines the broad outlines of the remuneration policy for company management;
2 the general shareholder meeting is entitled to veto any management decisions that have a drastic impact the identity or character of the organisation;
3 individual shareholders are given more opportunities to submit agenda items for general shareholder meetings;
4 the general shareholder meeting can dismiss the entire board of commissioners through a motion of no confidence;
5 a structure partnership places the responsibility for appointing managers with the board of commissioners. The general shareholder meeting is free to offer their suggestions for review. The board of commissioners is entitled to disregard these suggestions.

10.4.2 Logistics management

Controlling an organisation's business processes involves quite a number of logistical issues, including supply volume optimisation, delivery time optimisation, and customer order optimisation. Logistics is about the flow of goods and/or services within the business chain. Logistical management deals with planning and controlling these flows, plus the corresponding information stream.

Logistical management

Logistics management is also of increasing importance in general service and health care. Dutch insurance company Centraal Beheer is a good example. In this company, insurance can be ordered by telephone or by internet, without having to go through an agent. 'Patient logistics' is increasingly common in the health care sector.
Since the foundation of the European Union, it has become possible for a factory in one member country to quickly supply a product to a customer in another member country without having to go through a wholesale trader's warehouse. In the near future, all organisations are likely to improve their logistics management with the aim of lowering costs and improving services, and thereby increasing their overall performance. Logistics management (business logistics) has two focal points:
1 material management;
2 physical distribution management.

Material management
Physical distribution management

Material management includes all logistical activities from the supply of raw material to the final product. Physical distribution management includes all logistical activities from the completion of the product to delivering it to the buyer. Figure 10.19 shows the relationship between these activities.

FIGURE 10.19 **LOGISTICS MANAGEMENT SHOWN DIAGRAMMATICALLY**

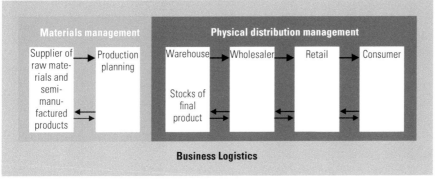

→ Product flow

⇐ Information flow

Source: C.G. Bakker, A.R. van Goor en J.W.M. van Houten, *Logistiek/Goederenstroombesturing,* Stenfert Kroese, 1988

As any organisation fulfils certain tasks in the business chain, it has to deal with various logistical problems, depending on its place in this process. In relation to material management, organisations need to make decisions with particular regard to the following:

1 planning and control of the production process;
2 inventory management of raw materials and semi-manufactured products;
3 transport and storage of raw materials and semi-manufactured products. In physical distribution, it is important that the goods are made available at the right place and time.

Decision-making in this area is mainly concerned with:

1 inventory control of the end product;
2 warehouse management;
3 transport control and distribution planning.

Well-executed logistics management may increase competitive advantage by, for example, reducing purchase prices, making production capacity flexible, more effective using machines, and reducing delivery times.
Research has shown that a customer's choice of supplier depends not only on price but, to a large extent, on delivery time and reliability, service, and personal contacts. When considering these advantages, the relationship between logistics, marketing, financing, and the development of products and processes should also be kept in mind.

In order to maximise the advantages of logistics management, it is crucial to coordinate the different activities. Theoretically, four strategies are possible:

1 **Incorporating margins**. Lowering the performance level creates surplus capacity. Accurate coordination of activities will no longer be necessary, though there will be a drawback in the form of costs increases and products potentially becoming hard to market.
2 **Creating autonomous units**. This makes the divisions of the organisation less dependent of each other, but decreases the advantages of economies of scale.
3 **Investing in vertical data information systems**. Coordination is enhanced through better availability of information.
4 **Introducing a lateral structure**. This lets decisions be made at lower levels, where the relevant information is available.

The flow of goods and data plays an important role in logistics management. A

Radio Frequency Identification

well-known method is the use of the barcode or its improved successor, the Radio Frequency Identification (RFID) – which has many advantages compared to the barcode. RFID uses radio signals for longer distance transmission. It is based on a system consisting of two parts, a 'tag' and a write/read unit. The tag has a chip and an antenna. The components can be miniaturised by current technological developments. Technological developments have also brought down the price of RFID, which has allowed significantly broader application of the system. RFID has many applications, such as:

a tracking & tracing;
b product protection (e.g. against theft);
c identification in unfavourable surroundings (heat, liquid and noise);
d logistical activities within the distribution chain;
e quality control.

In summary, RIFD can be applied more widely than barcodes, and will be used widely in the future. It makes better control of logistical activities possible, and can reduce costs.

10.5 ORGANISATIONAL MANAGEMENT METHODS

The management of organisations sometimes involves the use of methods for process clarification and comprehension, thus making it possible to make the coordination, supervision and directing of processes within the organisation more efficient and effective. A method can be defined as a well thought-out plan used to accomplish a desired goal.

This section deals with the various methods under the following headings:

1 methods directed towards individual employees: management by objectives and management by exception;
2 methods directed towards the organisation as a whole: risk management and unit management;
3 process-oriented methods: project planning and network planning.

However, these divisions are only of limited value, as the various methods cannot be viewed in complete isolation from each other.

10.5.1 Methods directed towards individual employees

A common feature of the three methods directed towards the individual is

Individual's performance

the optimisation of the individual's performance within a specific area of the organisation.

Management by objectives

Management by objectives

Management by objectives (MBO) is a method by which a manager and their subordinates determine the objectives and the results for the coming period by mutual agreement. MBO is based on the assumption that people perform better and more happily if they:

a know what is expected of them;
b are involved in setting these expectations and accept them as being realistic;

c have the opportunity to determine how they can fulfil these expectations in the sense that they can plan their activities themselves;

d are kept well informed about their performance, and are therefore able to learn from their own experiences.

Deciding on the objectives jointly is more profitable than merely giving orders. The objectives of the organisation and the objectives of the employees need to be geared towards one another. Doing so increases motivation, and will result in employees executing their tasks more purposefully. Since objectives and results are determined at every level of the organisation, the result is improved coordination between the hierarchical levels. This is why MBO sees an organisation as a hierarchy of objectives, with the lower-order objectives directed towards the next objective in the chain.

Hierarchy of objectives

Practical objectives should conform to the following criteria:

Practical objectives

a they should be quantitatively measurable.

b they should be specific.

c they should be results-orientated.

d they should be realistic and attainable.

e they should be have a clear and limited time frame.

MBO essentially means determining objectives along with the necessary competencies and responsibilities needed to reach those objectives. The process can be broken down into eight steps (Figure 10.20):

Step 1 Defining responsibilities and competencies

Step 2 Determining priorities

Step 3 Selecting measurement criteria

Step 4 Jointly deciding objectives

Step 5 Establishing plans of action

Step 6 Jointly agreeing on goals and tasks

Step 7 Checking progress

Step 8 Reviewing results

FIGURE 10.20 **FROM BUSINESS STRATEGY TO MANAGERIAL OBJECTIVES**

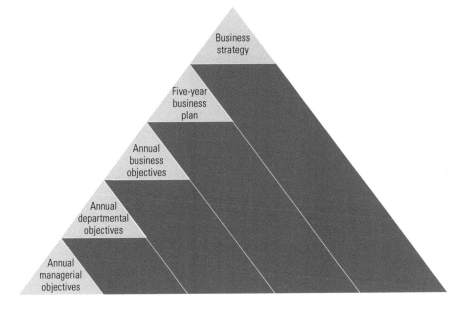

In deciding the objectives, two important matters should be taken into account. Only those areas that the subordinate can influence and that contribute towards effectiveness in terms of completing the task should be selected. The objectives should also be as measurable as possible – so that, at the end of the period, the performance of the employee can be appraised.

Norm   Appraising someone's performance requires a norm. Formulating the objectives and norms quantitatively allows for the measurement and appraisal to become more objective. Following the appraisal, the process of setting objectives and results recommences (see Figure 10.21)

FIGURE 10.21 **MANAGEMENT BY OBJECTIVES SHOWN DIAGRAMMATICALLY**

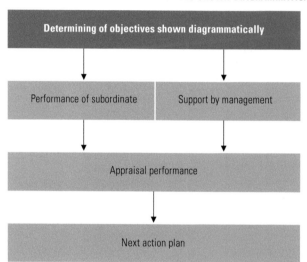

After the objectives and the result have been decided, the real work starts. Both the manager and the employee have specific tasks. The employee tries to accomplish the established objectives by executing specific actions. It is the manager's task to support the employee during this process. Obstacles that block the employee should be removed where possible. Wherever possible, factors outside their influence should not be permitted to interrupt the employee.

MBO is a method used in many organisations. The manager, the subordinate, and the organisation are all able to gain advantages from MBO.

The advantages of MBO for managers are as follows:
1 It motivates subordinates.
2 It strengthens relationships between managers and subordinates.
3 It provides a framework for coaching and support.
4 It forms a basis for the appraisal of employees.

The advantages of MBO for subordinates are:
1 Subordinates know what is expected of them.
2 Subordinates can measure their own performance.
3 Authority and responsibilities are clearly described and defined.

The advantages of MBO for the organisation are:

1 It gauges the effectiveness of managers.
2 It focusses the activities of a manager on what they should accomplish.
3 It simplifies the coordination of activities.
4 It offers objective criteria for reward.
5 It keeps track of the need for management development, thus providing opportunities for well-directed training and education.

However, MBO also has a number of drawbacks. These impede the attainability of positive results:

1 **The 'paper tiger'**. Too many changes and additions may result in a mass of paperwork, hampering real work.
2 **The 'activity trap'**. Everybody enthusiastically formulates the most desirable objectives they can think of. The eventual result is overloading, and the risk that even the smallest result might not be obtained.
3 **The order mistake**. If too much energy is put into conforming to objectives, proper coordination may be neglected, with adverse consequences.
4 **Mutual harmony**. In this situation, employees fail to bring errors to each other's attention. It is important to maintain a critical attitude in relation to each other.
5 **Timing problems**. There is a danger of results being expected in too short a time span. Essential changes can only be produced gradually.
6 **Leadership problems**. MBO and the existing leadership style may be incompatible. MBO requires a working style with an emphasis on task performance and cooperation.

Management by exception

As indicated (in the paragraph on management by objectives), task division (a feature of every organisation) involves defining the objectives to be carried out by each unit, division, or person. Checks to assess results should be carried out at regular intervals, and if any deviation from the agreed tasks is detected, this should be corrected. In practice, this is often necessary. If assessment were solely a managerial responsibility, there would be a risk of overloading. To avoid such a situation, a method known as 'management by exception' is frequently used.

Deviation

Management by exception

To secure good results, those responsible for the delegation of tasks (including inherent responsibilities and authority) should retain control (see Section 11.2.3). But delegation as such means that the delegator is freed from routine tasks and has time to concentrate on other tasks more appropriate to management. A middle manager may then take over tasks from their superior. Within certain limits, the middle manager is entitled to define and use specific means needed to make corrections. If these limits are exceeded, this is seen as exceeding the limits of their authority. Their superior is informed, and necessary actions are taken. But such appeals to the top manager should be avoided where possible.

Limits

10.5.2 Methods directed towards the organisation as a whole

For improved organisational functioning, organisation-directed methods such as risk and unit management can be used.

Organisation-directed methods

Risk management

Entrepreneurship is not free from risk. Buildings or premises may be susceptible to fire, the computer system could fail, and the sales of a certain product might be very disappointing. Risks can be divided into two categories: dynamic risks and static risks.

Dynamic risk

Dynamic (speculative or entrepreneurial) risks can result in either profit or loss (e.g. the introduction of a new product or investment in a new enterprise). Static risks (pure risks) have only negative consequences (e.g. fire, flood or criminal damage). This handbook deals only with static risks.

Static risks

To a certain extent, static risks can be avoided by the systematic and periodic evaluation of the risks threatening people, goods, activities, and interests, followed by the development of procedures to address these risks (risk management) (Claes & Meerman, 1991).

Risk management

Initially, risk management involves categorising and analysing risks. Then, a risk management plan is implemented for the biggest risks. Risk management is a common activity in most organisations. It demands that all members adopt an attitude of responsibility towards risk minimisation. The activities that form part of risk minimisation must, of course, be managed – and the necessary expertise should be delegated to specialists or a dedicated department. To that extent, risk management resembles the marketing activities that an organisation undertakes.

The goal of risk management is to avoid disturbances from identifiable risks, and to ensure that the objectives of the enterprise remain attainable. As discussed, the primary processes contribute to reaching these objectives. Managing these processes includes managing inherent risks. Risk management is shown in the diagram in Figure 10.22.

FIGURE 10.22 **RISK MANAGEMENT**

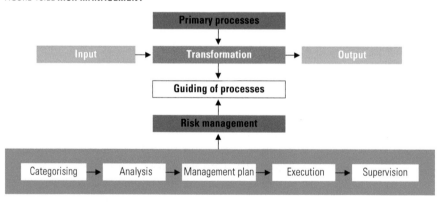

As a general rule, managing risks safeguards continuity. Figure 10.23 shows an inventarisation of the different kinds of risks. Risk management has to be planned, and Figure 10.24 shows that it is important for an organisation to know what kind of risks and associated coping methods exist.

Risks that are a characteristic of the type of organisation cannot be removed. To deal with these, options for special financing or services should be considered.

FIGURE 10.23 **AN INVENTORY OF DIFFERENT TYPES OF RISKS**

FIGURE 10.24 **A SYSTEMATIC APPROACH TO RISK MANAGEMENT**

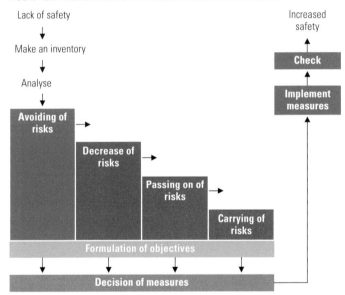

Several measures can be taken to help avoid risks and their associated damages:

1 **Preventive measures**. The purpose here is complete risk avoidance (e.g. safeguarding of equipment).
2 **Protective measures**. For instance, by wearing special clothing.
3 **Reduction measures**. The purpose here is to minimise damages (e.g. setting up a first aid centre).
4 **Repair measures**. The purpose here is to limit damage repercussions.
5 **Staff training and instruction**.
6 **Maintenance activity planning**.

The measures that need to be taken each require a particular investment, which can vary according to the degree of complexity of the measure in question.
Risks may vary in their potential for damage. The following list defines damages according to their severity:

1 **Trivial damage**. Very minor damage that can be repaired within the existing budget.
2 **Small damage**. Damage that occurs relatively frequently.
3 **Medium-sized damage**. Damage low in frequency, but whose impact is relatively great – though not posing a threat to the survival of the organisation.
4 **Large-scale damage**. Damage that occurs rarely, but whose consequences are severe. It poses a severe threat to the continuity of the enterprise, potentially even forcing it to close down.

Knowledge of the frequency and amount of damage is necessary when trying to decide which risks should be handled first, and what measures should be taken to avoid or reduce its effects. Only then will it be possible to set up a management plan, and rank the risks according to their importance.
The relationship between the frequency and the extent of the damage is illustrated in Figure 10.25.

FIGURE 10.25 **MATRIX OF DAMAGE FREQUENCY AND EXTENT CATEGORIES**

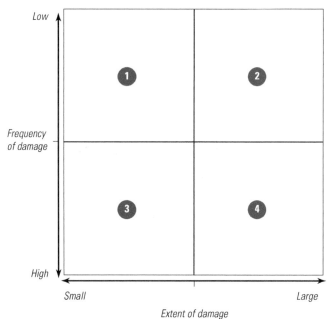

Some examples are:
Category 1: broken windows
Category 2: storm damage
Category 3: theft from stores
Category 4: fire

Category 1 damages can generally be dealt with by the organisation itself. Damages that fall under categories 2 and 4 are usually covered by insurance, and therefore not paid for by the organisation. The amount of insurance cover bought is a question of weighing up profits against expenses. Any remaining uninsured risk is then born by the organisation. Damages that fall under category 3 attract a lot of attention and are dealt with using special measures. This sort of damage has to be dealt with by the enterprise itself.

Unit management

Markets are rarely static, especially with respect to consumer behaviour and technology. As a consequence, organisations may need to change their strategy and structure often. Structural changes may include increasing the autonomy of certain units to some extent, thus enabling them to adapt to the changing environment while still benefiting from the facilities of the organisation as a whole. The goal here is to improve competitive position by reacting quickly.
An organisational form that is currently enjoying some interest is unit management. This is a management method directed towards a policy of decentralisation within the organisation.

Adapt to the changing environment

Unit management

The conditions for successful unit management are:
a short reporting lines (fewer levels between top management and unit management);
b each unit having its own goals to fulfil;
c units having a high degree of autonomy in respect of the primary functions (purchasing, sales, production, etc);
d a well-set-up management data system;
e exclusive support services or the freedom to use certain external staff services;
f personal definitions of jobs a matter for team discussion;
g the power to make major decisions;
h a common code of behaviour (or culture) for the entire organisation (Wissema, 1987).

By setting a clear risk appetite and embedding a strong risk culture throughout one's businesses, it becomes possible to identify, measure and control risk exposures, and respond effectively to shocks.
Units can be described as semi-independent if they behave in similar ways to independent enterprises. These have been dealt with already in the section on the portfolio model of the Boston Consulting Group, where they units were referred to as business units or product-market combinations.
Since the unit remains part of the organisation, it shares the advantages of the larger organisation. Such advantages may include shared sales teams, the use of common grounds and buildings, the exchange of experience, and so on.
Unit management thus combines the advantages of small-unit autonomy and the advantages of a larger organisation (see Figure 10.26).

Semi-independent units

FIGURE 10.26 **ADVANTAGES OF UNIT MANAGEMENT**

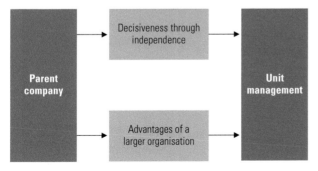

Unit management is characterised by both a large degree of autonomy and a mutual dependence. As these units have been established to have more autonomy, they could conceivably compete with each other – to a certain extent.

Autonomy mutual dependence

To avoid this from happening, a strong corporate culture with the organisation as a whole is required. There will also be situations where the units need to cooperate with each other. The unit culture should consequently be in line with the organisational culture.

The organisation as a whole must remain governable. This imposes particular demands on both unit management and on top-level management. The unit manager should have general skills rather than specialist ones. They are responsible for the unit as a whole. Just like any other head of a commercial concern, they have to make decisions and must be able motivate their team to ensure proper performance.

The top management level must be completely willing to grant autonomy. The advantages of unit management can only be fully enjoyed if responsibilities and authorities are truly delegated. If delegation remains a partial affair, the result is ambiguity, causing conflict and discouragement. For top-level management, decentralisation carries the advantage of allowing it concentrate on responsibilities of a more general and strategic nature.

The disadvantages of unit management are as follows:
1 There may be diminished efficiency as tasks are duplicated in every unit.
2 Coherence between the units may lessen as each unit may consider itself to be an independent enterprise.
3 Short-term interests may prevail over the long-term view.
4 The image of a single coherent organisation may become blurred.

10.5.3   Process-oriented methods

Process-oriented methods focus on the control of specific organisational processes and projects. First, this section looks at project planning: a method is used for processes in which employees from various departments work together on a temporary basis in order to find solutions for particular problems. Network planning is a technique that can be used within project planning. It shows the relationships between the various project activities.

Process-oriented methods
Project planning
Network planning

Project planning

If an organisation wants to develop new activities, such as the development of a new IT system or a new product, a project-oriented approach is, in general, the preferred option. The distinguishing feature of this kind of activity is that solutions cannot come from a single department or specialist. The problem needs to be addressed from various angles.

For the sake of coordination, a specific project group responsible for a particular problem is set up within the existing organisational structure. The members of this group represent all departments and/or areas of expertise needed for the project, and may be recruited from various levels of the organisation. The cultural differences between these levels could lead to problems within the group: the members may speak a different language, so to speak, or be unfamiliar with the approaches used. In the context of the project, they will be required to work together as equals – while in other situations, they might encounter each other on a different footing. Group members must be able to accept this inconsistency.

A project-oriented approach is often used in situations where:
a involvement of various functional areas is required;
b a one-off goal needs to be accomplished.

Part of the nature of a project is that it is temporary. Upon completion, the project's findings must be incorporated into the main organisation. A project is characterised by various phases (see Figure 10.27):

FIGURE 10.27 **PHASES OF A PROJECT**

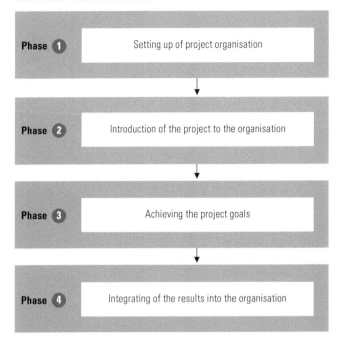

Phase 1: During this phase, the project is set up, and the necessary conditions and authorities are established. Decisions about the employees needed to participate in the project are also made.

Phase 2: The project and its members are introduced to the organisation. This phase should not be underestimated. Underlining the importance of the project and the creation of broad support are important conditions for reaching a good final result. This is why management should support and encourage all aspects of the project.

Phase 3: The group works towards achieving the project's goals.

Phase 4: The project results are incorporated into the organisation, and become a permanent feature of that organisation. Former project members might be made responsible for this process. Section 11.3.8 discusses the organisational aspects of project planning further.

Network planning

Network planning is used to control large, one-off activities such as assembling an aeroplane, building a house, or developing a new payment system. Over time, various techniques for network planning have been developed, each with their own characteristics. In general, each technique operates from the same basis. This section focusses on the Critical Path Method (CPM).

Network planning can be used for any project of a temporary nature, and combines a number of tasks. It provides an overview of the project as a whole and details the occasionally complex relationships between the various activities that constitute the project. Network planning aims to obtain an understanding of the project's running time. This leads to improved control of the project (see Figures 10.28 and 10.29).

Network planning

Critical Path Method

Aim of network planning

FIGURE 10.28 **EXAMPLE OF A NETWORK PLAN**

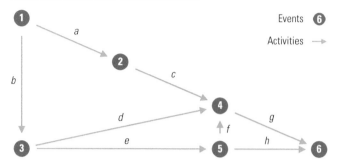

FIGURE 10.29 **EXAMPLE OF A NETWORK PLAN INCLUDING TIME FACTORS**

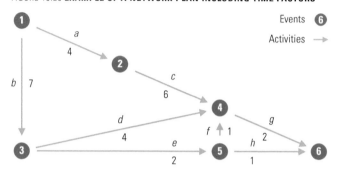

In order to set up a network plan, several steps need to be taken:

Step 1: **structural analysis**. What tasks or activities need to be carried out? What relationships between tasks need to be determined? The logical sequence of the project stages needs to be determined.

Step 2: **chronological analysis**. The duration of the various elements needs to be estimated.

As soon as the structural and chronological aspects of the project have been determined, the time needed for each individual element are added and the project's run-time is estimated. Figure 10.30 shows the longest possible run-time.

Running time

FIGURE 10.30 **PATH WITH THE LONGEST RUNNING TIME**

From (1) to (3) via b	7 units of time
From (3) to (4) via d	4 units of time
From (4) to (6) via g	2 units of time

Running time	13 units of time

The other run-times are shorter, as demonstrated by the calculations. The run-time that gives the earliest possible moment for the project to be finished is known as the critical path. This path shows the minimum time needed to complete a project. Any delay to the activities on this path delays the project as a whole.

Critical path

Network planning can improve project control if:
a there is insight into what activities determine project run-time;
b resources can be assigned to each activity;
c it is possible to check whether the project is going according to plan, and the consequences any occurring delays are also clearly visible;

d the roles of the various activities within the project are clear. This allows for better coordination.

What are the consequences of delay to a particular activity? Assuming that, during the project, activity E is delayed by 4 days, the total duration of E is now 6 days (see Figure 10.31).

FIGURE 10.31 **THE CONSEQUENCES OF A DELAY TO ACTIVITY**

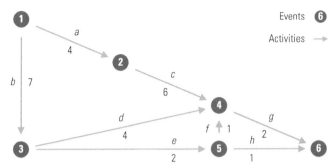

The adjusted critical run-time is shown in Figure 10.32.

FIGURE 10.32 **REVISED CRITICAL RUNNING TIME**

From (1) to (3) via b	**7 units of time**
From (3) to (5) via e	**6 units of time**
From (5) to (4) via f	**1 units of time**
From (4) to (6) via g	**2 units of time**
Running time	**16 units of time**

The total run-time is extended and the critical path has changed. If this problem is spotted early on, the project managers might decide to assign additional resources to activity E so that the projects completion may still be achieved in the original run-time. The costs and benefits of assigning additional resources need to be carefully considered.

The next chapter discusses organisational design.

10.5.4   The EFQM Excellence Model

In today's globally competitive business world, organisations need to review their management systems to remain successful. The EFQM Excellence Model is a practical management model which can be used to identify an organisation's excellence, possible gaps, and potential areas of quality improvement. The model, which was first applied in 1992, is used by around 30,000 European organisations today, and is regularly updated to remain aligned with international developments. The European Foundation for Quality Management was set up in 1989 with the support of the European Union (then the EEC) and a number of large companies such as Philips, Fiat, Nestlé, Bosch, BT and Renault. The EFQM Excellence Model can be used to map out and assess different aspects of the management, quality, and maturity of a business, and to highlight desired improvements.

EFQM Excellence Model

European foundation for quality management

The EFQM Excellence Model is based on nine criteria (see Figure 10.33). Five of these focus on what an organisation does and how it does it; these are called 'enablers'. The other four criteria focus on what the organisation has achieved; these are called 'results'.

Enablers

Results

FIGURE 10.33 **THE NINE CRITERIA OF THE EFQM EXCELLENCE MODEL SHOWING CAUSE AND EFFECT BETWEEN ENABLERS AND RESULTS**

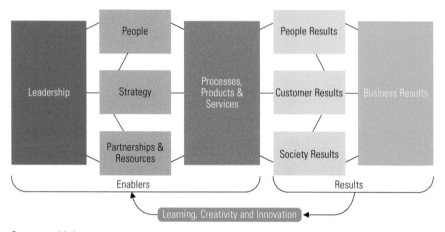

Source: www.ink.nl

Within the results, a distinction is made between an organisation's four stakeholder groups, being employees, customers and partners, society, and key business stakeholders (government and finance providers). The model's strength is inthe fact that all criteria are looked at holistically rather than merely in isolation. The five enablers can be managed internally and are influenced by the organisation's own policies. A strong performance by one or more of the enablers has a visibly positive effect on one or more of the result areas. At its core, the EFQM philosophy includes a number of concepts that combine the five enablers in such a way as to reach sustainably excellent results. The fundamental characteristics of the enablers are inspirational leadership, trust and integrity, cooperation and empowerment, performance orientation, and continuous improvement and innovation.
The nine criteria are explained below in greater detail.

Holistically

The five organisational criteria:
1 **Leadership**. Leadership shapes the future of the organisation in a way that satisfies the stakeholders. Anticipating future developments requires clear vision, which inspires all levels of management to constantly grow and move the organisation forwards.
2 **People**. Employees are supported to achieve personal and organisational goals so that their skills and knowledge are fully developed and utilised. The organisation cares for, recognises, motivates and communicates with its staff.
3 **Strategy**. This involves the translation of policies into plans and budgets. The related aspects of internal and external communication with staff and other stakeholders play an important role.
4 **Partnerships and resources**. Excellent organisations manage external partnerships with suppliers, members of the supply chain and others in such a way as to generate added value. They have the ability to ensure sufficient future resources, including means of production, knowledge, and technology, to allow for future goals to be achieved efficiently and effectively.

5 **Processes**, **products and services**. This refers to the way in which the organisation designs, manages and improves primary, secondary and administrative processes, so that its products and services meet or exceed the expectations of internal and external customers.

The four 'results' criteria:
1 **People**. This concerns the organisation's added value for its employees, and the nature of this added value.
2 **Customers**. This concerns the appreciation of customers, partners and suppliers for the organisation's products, services and collaborative efforts. This also includes the availability of knowledge about what the different groups do, or do not, want.
3 **Society**. It is not just about what the organisation provides in terms of products and services. Society looks at all of the organisation's output. It also reviews the organisation's partial responsibility for areas such as the environment and quality of life. Which elements of CSR has the organisation adopted in order to contribute towards society's development, for example?
4 **Business**. At the end of the day, the issue at hand is the organisation's continuity. This includes its ability to achieve strategic objectives, secure its market position, and maximise its returns on invested capital.
Organisations need to be creative and innovative in applying the model's nine criteria. An organisation's capacity for learning needs to be at its peak if it is to remain adaptable.

Summary

▶ Organisational control: leading an organisation to reach its established goals under the condition that business processes are implemented effectively and efficiently.

▶ Process management, the efficient functioning of business processes, is the task of an organisation's management.

▶ Every organisation acquires production factors and transforms these into products. This process comprises input, transformation, and output.

▶ Three types of business processes:
  – primary processes: contribute directly to products/services;
  – secondary processes: ensure that the primary processes function properly;
  – administrative processes: steer processes through strategic policy-making, planning, structuring, and process management.

▶ Management activities: planning, measuring and comparing, and steering.

▶ Business re-engineering (Hammer): the company process as a collection of interwoven core business processes. The objective: to attain competitive advantage.

▶ 'Value chain' (Porter): the relationship between the added value of organisational components and competitive strength. Competitive advantage through low cost price, differentiation, and focus strategy.

▶ Quality care: designs and implements quality policy.
  The concept can be applied to two distinct aspects: technological and relative.

▶ The application of the relative quality concept requires integral quality care: a system whose goal is to control the organisational processes influencing product quality in such a way as to ensure that the product has the desired quality at minimum costs.

▶ The implementation of (integral) quality care needs to be based on a quality system: an organisational structure, responsibilities, procedures, and provisions.

▶ An organisation whose quality system meets the standards and demands of an external agency may apply for certification. Frequently used standards are those established by ISO.

▶ The PDCA-cycle is frequently applied in the Six Sigma and Lean Management methods. PDCA is short for: Plan, Do, Check and Act

▶ The phases of the development of a quality system are: new specifications, control, safeguard, measure customer satisfaction, and improve.

▶ Six Sigma is a quality system used by many organisations to improve and expedite processes. At the core of Six Sigma is that its intended result is to improve process quality and process results.

▶ Six Sigma can be described as a comprehensive and flexible system which allows an organisation to achieve maximum and sustainable success. This success is realised by closely monitoring customer needs; limiting oneself to the use of facts, data, and statistical analyses; paying extensive attention to the management, improvement, and innovation of business processes.

▶ Six Sigma places great emphasis on the opinions, expectations, and needs of customers. The customer is the basic point of reference, a concept known in Six Sigma as the 'Voice of the Customer' (VOC).

▶ Six Sigma: five-phase quality system: define, measure, analyse, improve, and control.

- To properly implement Six Sigma, a specific way of organising projects is required.

- The lean-principles are based on the Toyota Production System (TPS). TPS is based on the three MU's: Muri, Muda and Mura.

- Muda is a core concept in Lean management. Lean Management means designing processes in such a way as to maximise customer value while simultaneously minimising wastage.

- The five phases of lean organisation: specify customer value, analyse the value flows, streamline the processes, work to order, and strive for perfection.

- Essentially, the combined application of Six Sigma and Lean Management (Lean Six Sigma) creates a situation where an organisation works simultaneously on both quality improvement and process efficiency – in other words: a perfectly lean organisation of processes.

- The strength of the combination of Six Sigma and Lean Management into Lean Six Sigma comes from the following four areas: quality improvement, lead time improvement, learning organisations, and improvement of business results.

- In most organisations, there is a division between the managerial and executive branches. This division creates organisational hierarchy, leading to the following levels of management:
    - Board of commissioners
    - Direction or top-level management
    - Middle management
    - Executive employees

- The most important managerial forms are the General Manager and the Board of Directors (entente structure and collegial board).

- The Dutch 1971 *Structuurwet* (Structure Law) dictates that certain Dutch *NV* and *BV* companies (comparable to LLCs and PLCs) are required to establish a *Raad van Commissarissen* (Board of Commissioners). The companies that are subject to this requirement are those that fulfil the following criteria: the issued capital and the reserves amount to at least 16 million euros, the partnership is legally obligated to establish a works council, and the partnership employs more than 100 employees in the Netherlands.

- The BoC's main task is to supervise management policy and general organisational affairs.

- The BoC is not involved in actual management, since that is the task of the direction or top-level management. A commissioner does not work in the service of an organisation, but receives some form of remuneration for services rendered.

- In the Netherlands, it had long been the tradition that members of a Board of Commissioners are appointed via a so-called co-optation system. Since the end of 2004, members of the Board of Commissioners are appointed by the general shareholder meeting.

- In addition to the Rhineland-model (two-tier system) which separates management and supervision, there is the Anglo-Saxon model, a one-tier system which does not enforce a strict separation of management and supervision.

- The Netherlands uses a two-tier board. The continuing growth of internationalisation has led to the decision to allow Dutch organisations to choose between a two-tier board or one-tier board.

11
STRUCTURING

Contents

After studying this chapter:

- you will have gained insight into the relationship between the management of business processes and issues of structuring;
- you will have gained knowledge of and insight into the division and coordination of labour in an organisation;
- you will have gained knowledge of and insight into the various organisational systems and into division organisation;
- you will have gained knowledge of and insight into new forms of organisational structure;
- you will have gained knowledge of and insight into the agility of organisational design;
- you will have gained knowledge of communication and discussion structures.

Etergo: the AppScooter with a 240 kilometre radius

Etergo is building an 'AppScooter' with a 240 kilometre radius. The vehicle comes equipped with a 7-inch touchscreen and internet connectivity. Using the AppScooter's buttons, drivers can operate their phone via Bluetooth, take calls, stream music, and set their sat nav.

The Amsterdam start-up was founded by Bart Jacobsz Rosier and Marijn Flipse in 2015. Both are giving it their all to make their electric scooter a reality, and investors have rewarded their efforts with 17 million Euros in investments. The entrepreneurs' faith in their mission is solid.

'The reason we set up this company is to accelerate the transition to sustainable transport and energy', says Marijn Flipse, describing a mission that is virtually the same as Tesla's. 'It is one of the largest problems of our time. We feel that, as entrepreneurs, we can use our skill set to make a significant contribution to solving this issue. That is our drive. And, in all honesty, it is also just a really cool product.'

The growth of the market for (electric) scooters is still very large, says Flipse. 'The reason for that is that people are becoming more aware of the issues associated with fossil-fuel vehicles, such as particulates, noise, and smell. They see that electric vehicles provide a solution to this problem, with the additional extras of increased acceleration speeds and no more trips to the petrol pump.' Governments are also boosting companies like Etergo; Amsterdam, for example, put a ban on scooters from before 2011 this year.

The scooter start-up also wants to capitalise on the hype around shareable scooters, a concept that has put Felyx on the map in the Netherlands. 'Our scooters are shareable *out of the box* – they are unlocked using a telephone, the locks are electronic, removing the need for a physical key. The scooters are also connected to the internet and GPS. The fact that there is storage for two helmets under the seat is also helpful.'

'In 2015, Bart and I felt we could do things much more quickly,' Flipse agrees. 'But when you involve a more experienced crew, you soon find out there is more to it than you had originally thought. The optimistic entrepreneur is faced with reality – and that is something you have to deal with.'

'We are doing everything we can to make our AppScooter available to our customers, but we want to make sure we are offering a good product. A vehicle should definitely be a safe and quality product. And if that should take a few extra months, then, unfortunately, so be it.'

Source: www.sprout.nl, December 2018

11.1 INTRODUCTION

The management of company processes was examined in Chapter 10, which first looked at the various company processes in an organisational context, followed by the way in which company processes are monitored. The conclusion was a discussion of some of methods for giving direction, to see if they could be applied to the management processes.

This chapter continues this line of exploration. After establishing an insight into the various company processes within the organisation and into the management of those processes, it is important to consider how these activities can best be organised. Implementing and managing company processes requires a high level of efficiency and goal awareness. On the one hand, external factors that affect the organisation should be taken into account and any necessary adjustments should be implemented, depending on the choice of strategic management process (discussed in Chapter 2). By setting strategic objectives, the organisation plots the general direction of the route towards achieving the desired goals. On the other hand, internal factors involving individual staff members, machines, and other equipment must be taken into account, with day-to-day operations being given all due attention. Internal factors need to be utilised in such a way as to support each other. Of particular importance are the start-up processes and the managing of daily operations.

The internal and external factors that influence the organisation of activities are illustrated in Figure 11.1.

External factors

Internal factors

FIGURE 11.1 **DUAL INFLUENCES ON THE ORGANISING OF ACTIVITIES**

Because organising is situation-bound, it is safe to say that there is no one best way of going about it. In any set of circumstances, one must look for a solution that matches the situation. Structuring involves creating an organisational structure in which people and resources are utilised optimally in order to reach the organisation's objectives. Finding the ideal arrangement requires adjustments on both the external and internal levels. An organisational structure defines tasks, competencies, and responsibilities, and establishes the patterns of relationships between positions. When designing an organisational structure, both the organic form and the staff structure should be considered.

Structuring

Organisational structure

The organic structure

Wherever people work together towards particular goals, their tasks need to be divided between the various departments of the organisation. This means having to form groups to carry out certain functions: the organic structure.

Then, a coordination mechanism must be added to ensure that all the divided tasks and roles are in alignment. Consequently, designing a framework in which people are optimally occupied is just as much an issue of task division as it is of coordination.

Organic structure

Personnel structure

After the functions have been allocated to departments, the personnel structure needs to be determined. The personnel structure is the human dimension of the organisation's structure. In creating this structure, attention needs to be paid to:

Personnel structure

a **Hierarchical relationships**. Who issues the instructions?
b **Authority**. Who makes which decisions?
c **Position identification**. Which employees should be allocated to which departments and what jobs will they perform?
d **Communication**. Who informs others of what, and how?

11.2 TASK DIVISION AND COORDINATION

Task division

An organisation's business processes generate activities that have to be allocated to various workers. Task division means splitting up activities into separate tasks that are then either assigned to individuals or to other units such as departments. This division and allocation process becomes more significant the greater the number of people working in the organisation. There are many reasons why task division in organisations attracts so much attention. One reason is the desire for increased

Productivity

productivity (= number of accomplishments in a given time). Within production departments, task division has a special and significant influence on productivity. Effective task division has a considerable effect on the costs associated with production. Effective task division also makes it easier to mechanise processes. There is some potential at this level for the use of robots and other advanced forms of automation, although this is still in its infancy.
Comparing the way the various organisations allocate their tasks indicates that there is still a demand for custom-made solutions.

While the nature of the task division process is a general one, task allocation is more dependent on specific situations. This process has vertical and horizontal dimensions. By interpreting a number of aspects of the division of labour, the result is a detailed insight into not only individual employees' job contents, but also into the allocated area of operation and responsibility. There exists, therefore, a close relationship between task, authority, and responsibility. Job contents come with certain authorities needed to perform an associated task. The implementation of the task then becomes the responsibility of the person concerned.
Delegation and scope of control are also important; that is to say, the number of people (possibly) managed by an individual. Lastly, this section discusses the organisational chart which documents task division schematically.

11.2.1 Vertical task division

Task

The many different tasks carried out in an organisation each have their own unique characteristics. A task is the 'technical' content of a function and indicates precisely what a person does: meet, consult, manage, make calls, administrate, monitor proceedings, and so on. Differences between tasks are based particularly on required expertise, experience, and skills. Tasks fall into various different levels. For instance, a manager's tasks do not include typing up minutes and letters. The manager is too expensive for that. Cost considerations mean that these activities

Vertical differentiation

are passed down to a lower hierarchical level. This process is called vertical differentiation. Different tasks of the same level are brought together within an organisation. Where tasks are grouped according to level, it is important to ensure that the resulting collection of duties constitutes a complete and worthwhile day's work. The latter consideration is sometimes ignored when tasks are divided up. Extreme specialisation can lead to a lot of monotonous work and, consequently, under-stimulation and decreased job motivation. One should always take the social aspects of a job into consideration when dividing up tasks.

As a consequence of vertical differentiation, the various activities within an organisation become hierarchical in nature. If certain activities are delegated to a lower level, the higher level will want to retain control over them. The higher level needs to provide guidelines governing the performance of lower-level activities. The issue here is the managerial aspects of task division. Effective leadership means ensuring that tasks are performed consistently and according to established guidelines. Supervision is required.

Finally, it should be noted that social aspects also play a role when an organisation allocates tasks. Society places demands on some aspects of task composition: for example, legislation in relation to working conditions (Health and Safety legislation etc).

In summary, there are four factors that influence the division of tasks:
1 **Cost factors**. Tasks must be arranged in such a way that efficient functioning and production is possible.
2 **Managerial factors**. The way in which tasks are structured and divided must lend itself to management of the organisation. Supervision of the various tasks and how they are executed is required.
3 **Individual factors**. Jobs must have a certain amount of appeal for individuals. Variety, responsibility and decision-making power all come into play.
4 **Societal motives**. Society makes enforceable demands with regards to the structure of tasks: health and safety precautions, for example.

The conscious consideration of technical, economic, and social aspects of working in an organisation or a division is known as work structuring. Work structuring is closely linked to the relationship that exists between staff needs and organisational targets. Work structuring has attracted the attention of researchers for a long time, and its central themes have developed in line with changes in society and attitude.

Work structuring has gone through the following phases:
a Initially, attention was paid to extrinsic job factors and changes in the working environment: external matters such as noise, temperature, light, music at work, humidity, and the layout and furnishing of working spaces. The working environment was improved by adapting the factors that were extrinsic to the job.
b Then, the structure of the job itself came under scrutiny, with special attention being paid to factors intrinsic to the job. Interest during this phase focussed on:
Job enrichment: the addition of elements of a more meaningful and challenging nature to an individual's tasks.
Job enlargement: increasing the range of duties by addition of tasks of a similar level.
Job rotation: staff movement from one job to another, with mutual exchange of jobs with colleagues.

What these three forms of intrinsic work factors have in common, is that they can increase work satisfaction and generate better cooperation between the various organisational layers.

Today, greater attention is being paid to the structure of departmental units. Although intrinsic work factors are still involved, it is at the level of the unit rather

Social aspects

Managerial aspects

Social aspects

Cost factors

Managerial factors

Individual factors

Societal motives

Work structuring

Extrinsic job factors

Intrinsic job factors

Job enlargement

Job rotation

than that of the individual. Departments are increasingly being regarded as individual units with specific assigned tasks, authorities, and responsibilities. A department may, for example, be divided into semi-autonomous work units, each performing an individual set of tasks and togehter performing the department's tasks.

11.2.2 Horizontal task division

Task division

The purpose of task division is not only to identify tasks of the same level. It is also to seek coherence between the various tasks. The various components of the task must have some connection with each other. When tasks are allocated,

Coordination

it is important to pay attention to how they are to be coordinated. If this is not adequately taken into consideration, the result will be a failure to reach a high level of efficiency or achieve targets.

Bringing together certain tasks results in the creation of functions. A function unites the common objective of the tasks that have to be performed, as well as the accompanying responsibilities and authorities. Functions relate not only to individuals, but also to organisational groups, such as teams or units.

Related tasks are initially grouped together according to an individual's position

Functionalism
Department formation

(functionalism). Then, the individual positions are regrouped to form departments (department formation).

The two main forms of horizontal task division are:

1 Internal differentiation;
2 Internal specialisation.

Internal differentiation

Internal differentiation

Internal differentiation involves searching for tasks that have something in common. For example, a manufacturing company that makes furniture. Various different people are responsible for performing the tasks, which include designing furniture, purchasing materials, cutting wood, assembling furniture, and selling it. In this example, task division is based on the various steps of the manufacturing process, rather than on the product itself. This type of task division is known as a

Functional division

functional division. The company's positions departments is based on the various manufacturing processes (see Figure 11.2).

FIGURE 11.2 **INTERNAL DIFFERENTIATION**

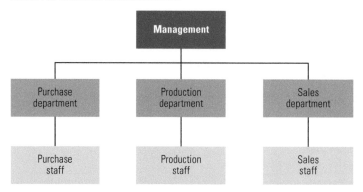

In many organisations, divisions placed directly under the executive level of management are split up into sub-divisions (see Figure 11.3).

FIGURE 11.3 **INTERNAL DIFFERENTIATION SHOWING INTERNAL DIVISIONS**

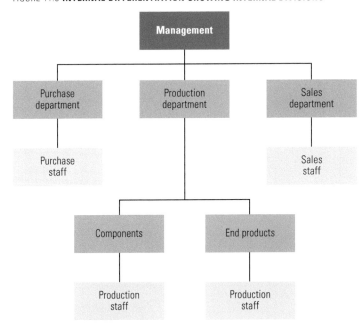

One of the dangers of internal differentiation is its potential to neglect the inner coherence between the various work processes. As such, it is essential to establish extra coordination mechanisms, such as consultation structures and planning activities, that involve the various manufacturing phases.

Internal specialisation

Internal specialisation involves grouping the activities carried out by a unit on the basis of the end result. In the example of the furniture manufacturer, certain employees focus solely on the task of making chairs, including designing chairs, purchasing materials, cutting wood, assembling chairs, and then selling them. All activities relating to chairs are brought together, and the natural cohesion of the activities to be performed remains intact. The same grouping is used for tables and cupboards.

Internal specialisation

Internal specialisation activities revolve not only around products; they may also be concerned with markets or buyers and geographical areas, the so-called Product, Market, and Geographical division of tasks (see Figure 11.4).
With a division of tasks according to any of these three criteria, the highest organisational level (under the board of directors) is:
– *A product division* (e.g. different product units A, B, and C);
– *A market division* (e.g. retail and wholesale);
– *A geographical division* (e.g. Europe, Asia, and America).

Product, market, and geographical division

Differences between internal differentiation and internal specialisation

The choice between internal differentiation and internal specialisation depends on an organisation's given situation. Small organisations almost always chose internal differentiation. As soon as a company has reached a certain size and manufactures and sells different products, there is some basis for internal specialisation. In general, differentiation and specialisation carry the following advantages and disadvantages.

FIGURE 11.4 **INTERNAL SPECIALISATIONS**

1 P(roduct)-**division**

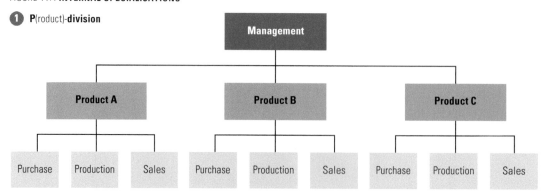

2 M(arket)-**division**

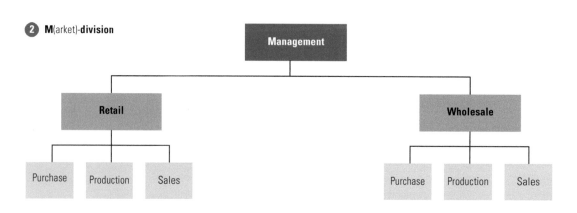

3 G(eographical)-**division**

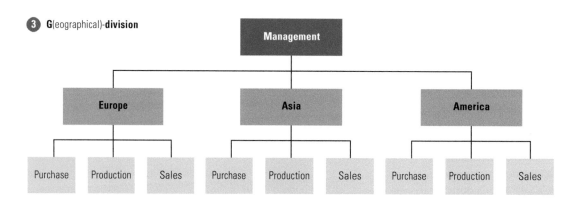

The advantages of internal differentiation:
a efficient use of available manpower, because it can be put to use in a greater number of activities, creating greater capacity;
b higher skill levels and more efficient routines;
c greater opportunities for automation.

The disadvantages of internal differentiation:
a coordination problems due to splitting up work processes;
b repetition and monotony;
c little flexibility for individuals, since they each perform a limited number of processes.

The advantages of internal specialisation:

a greater guarantee of efficient coordination between the various steps of the work process;
b shorter communication lines and faster problem-solving;
c less monotonous work.

The disadvantages of internal specialisation:

a less efficient use of resources as a consequence of inevitable duplication;
b reduction in expertise in relation to technical know-how;
c fragmentation of skills due to the broader range of work processes undertaken by each person.

In larger organisations, various internal specialisations may be grouped under a particular section of the organisation (see Figure 11.5). The first level under top management level has a product-based structure. Activities below this level are split up based on geographical regions. This organisational form is suitable if consumers in different continents are prepared to buy the same (combinations of) products or minor variations on those products. Production can be carried out efficiently (even though the production activities will, of course, take place at different locations). After the production phase, the products are exported to those countries that have a market. Each continent has its own sales organisation.

FIGURE 11.5 **EXAMPLE: VARIOUS SPECIALISATIONS IN ONE ORGANISATIONAL STRUCTURE**

Both methods, internal differentiation and internal specialisation, aim at converting tasks to functions. Once the functions have been compiled, job descriptions containing the following elements are created:

Job descriptions

a task content;
b authority;
c responsibilities;
d level within the organisation;
e relationships with other organisational members;
f nature of the position.

11.2.3 Horizontal task division

By distributing tasks between individuals and departments, jobs are formed. A job consists of a combination of tasks, authority, and responsibilities.

Authority

Authority is the right to make the decisions necessary to perform a task.
Responsibility Responsibility is both the moral obligation to perform a task to the best of one's ability as well as the duty to report back on the progress of that task.

Dividing work horizontally By dividing work horizontally, the tasks, authorities, and responsibilities are split up across the hierarchical level of that organisation. When work is divided **Dividing work vertically** vertically, the tasks, authorities, and responsibilities are divided across the various hierarchical levels. When tasks alone are transferred without any accompanying authority or responsibility, the individuals at the lower level simply become operators, with all decisions made at the higher level.

In such a situation, staff in the lower level can never be held completely responsible for the execution of their tasks, because all powers of decision are held elsewhere. Lower level staff can only be held responsible for carrying out their tasks if they are given some involvement in decision-making. If tasks, and their associated **Delegation** authorities and responsibilities, are handed over, this is known as task delegation Delegation is rarely complete; however, a complete absence of delegation is equally rare. Yet delegation does exist in degrees, as shown in Figure 11.6:

a Obtain the facts and report back.
b Obtain information and make recommendations in relation to some activities.
c Investigate and make recommendations in relation to all planned activities.
d Analyse the situation, develop and take a course of action, and report back on the results.
e Obtain the facts and take action.

FIGURE 11.6 **THE DELEGATION CONTINUUM**

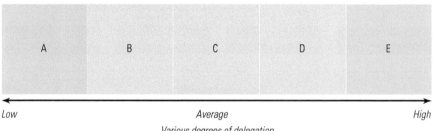

Low   *Average*   *High*
Various degrees of delegation

Delegation of tasks does not always involve responsibilities and authorities being transferred from a higher to a lower level. What is important is that tasks, authority and responsibility remain in balance when delegating. If a manager delegates, they remain responsible for the task even though they do not perform the activity themselves. A subordinate carries out the duties and the manager remains responsible for the choice of both delegate and manner of delegation. The manager therefore retains control of the activities carried out by the subordinate.

The extent to which tasks are delegated within an organisation differs. The level at which decisions are made may also differ. Such factors give an indication as to where the power in the organisation lies. If the power to make decisions is **Centralisation** concentrated in one place (usually at the top), this suggests centralisation. In such a situation, a significant proportion of important decisions is made high up in the organisation. There is little delegation. In contrast, with decentralisation, **Decentralisation** the decision-making powers re distributed over a greater number of positions, including those lower down the organisational structure. In such a situation, significant decisions are also made at lower levels in the organisation. There is a lot of delegation (see Table 11.1).

How to delegate in ten steps

Although delegation is one of the most important managerial skills, it is also one of the most complicated. Delegation is the transferral of a task to a suitable employee, as well as assigning them the appropriate means and authorities, while retaining final responsibility

Follow this ten-step-plan as a practical method to becoming proficient in the art of delegation:

1 Determine why you want to delegate and what is preventing you from doing so.
2 Determine which tasks you can delegate.
3 Decide to shed certain tasks.
4 Link these tasks to a team member.
5 Prepare a delegation meeting.
6 Set clear agreements in a delegation meeting.
7 Relinquish control, and verify at agreed-upon moments.
8 Evaluate the end results.
9 Reassume the task (where necessary).
10 Evaluate and improve.

Source: www.leren.nl

TABLE 11.1 **CENTRALISATION AND DECENTRALISATION CONTINUUM**

	A strongly centralised organisation	**A strongly decentralised organisation**
How many decisions are being made at the lower levels of the organisation?	No decisions or just a few	All or almost all decisions
How important are the decisions being made at lower organisational levels?	Not very important	Very important
How many different functions (e.g. marketing, human resources, finance) count on decisions being made at lower organisational levels?	None or just a few	All or almost all functions
Does senior management check whether decisions are being made at lower levels and does it take action when needs be?	Yes, almost always	No, or virtually not

The first large-scale attempt at decentralisation took place in the 1950s in the United States, and was followed a decade later in Europe. The focus was on assigning at least partial independence to other organisational bodies, such as divisions, subsidiaries, and departments. In order to promote cooperation and coordination between autonomous bodies, coordinating organisations were set up with extensive support services. Soon after, there was a second wave of decentralisation, in which the structure of some units became completely product or market-oriented. Under this structure, the relatively independent units operated in clearly separated product or market segments.

Intrapreneurs

Staff in such units thinks and acts independently in a professional sense, and is highly entrepreneurial (so-called 'intrapreneurs'). The parent company looks after the control and allocation of financial and human resources.

11.2.4 Span of control

Delegation involves handing over tasks and their associated responsibilities and authorities to lower levels. The person who delegates a task retains ultimate responsibility for that task. To make sure that the delegated tasks are carried out as required, those who have been given the tasks must be managed. The issue here is: how many subordinates can a manager effectively manage? This is known as the manager's span of control. If a manager tries to direct too many subordinates, the resulting situation is one where there is insufficient time to effectively direct all activities. It also becomes difficult to take a break or look at the quality of the completed tasks. One solution to this is to appoint extra managers. This gives rise to a new hierarchical layer in the organisation, making the organisational structure taller. A large span of control for managers causes a flatter organisational structure to develop. A smaller span of control generates a steeper organisational structure. Figure 11.7 and 11.8 give an overview of a large and small spans of control.

Flatter organisational structure
Steeper organisational structure

FIGURE 11.7 **LARGE SPAN OF CONTROL: FLATTER ORGANISATIONAL STRUCTURE**

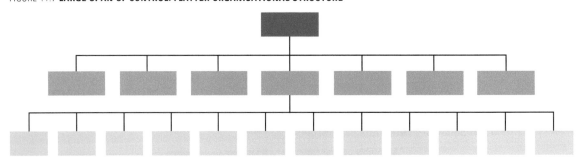

FIGURE 11.8 **SMALL-SPAN OF CONTROL: STEEPER ORGANISATIONAL STRUCTURE**

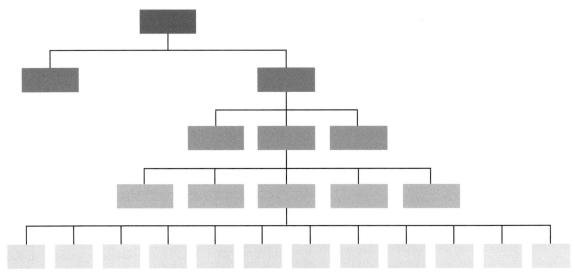

Structure and organisation
PART C

Span of control has two dimensions.

1 **The horizontal dimension**. This is the number of direct subordinates a manager supervises. It is known as the span width or span breadth.
2 **The vertical dimension**. This is the number of levels affected directly or indirectly by a manager. What matters here is the degree of influence that a manager exercises over the lowest levels in the organisation (also called the 'depth of control').

Depth of control

Span breadth is mainly determined by the following factors:

Span breadth

a **The manager's qualities**, dependent on the personality characteristics and the expertise of the manager as well as the time available.
b **The qualities of the employees**, dependent on staff personality characteristics and the expertise.
c **The nature of the organisation**, dependent on degree of delegation, lines of communication, attitude towards planning, task divisions, corporate culture, and decision-making procedures in the organisation.
d **The nature of the work**, dependent on the variety, complexity, routine, and uniformity of the activities to be accomplished.
e **The character of the job**, dependent on the extent to which the work involves either leadership or simple execution of tasks.

Considering these factors, it can be concluded that span of control depends on the situation. If a situation arises where a manager is supervising too many subordinates, a solution can be sought on the basis of:

1 Greater delegation of tasks to a lower level, together with the accompanying responsibility and authority. The manager must retain the capacity to delegate further and to adjust the delegated tasks as necessary.
2 Appointing an assistant manager hierarchically below the manager, but with complete authority over subordinates in respect of general or supervisory tasks (see Figure 11.9).

Assistant manager

FIGURE 11.9 **ADDING AN ASSISTANT MANAGER**

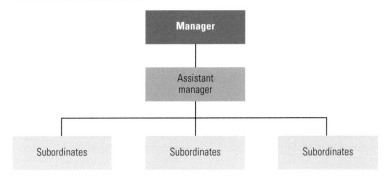

3 Appointing a personal assistant (such as a secretary) to the manager to take over some routine activities. The assistant does not have any supervisory authority over the manager's subordinates (see Figure 11.10).

Personal assistant

4 Involving other bodies in the organisation, such as support staff (see 9.3). This may result in some of the 'brain-work' being transferred to another unit within the organisation on the one hand, leaving the manager more time for managerial activities. But on the other hand, as a result, some managerial activities can be transferred from the manager to another section in the organisation, allowing more attention to be spent on policy work.

FIGURE 11.10 **HET TOEVOEGEN VAN EEN PERSOONLIJKE ASSISTENT**

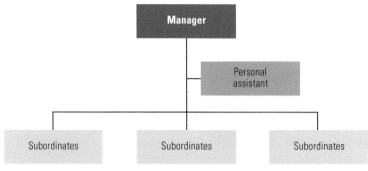

Source: www.asml.com

ASML Organisational Structure

ASML is a Dutch high-tech enterprise, and an important supplier of machines for the semi-conductor industry. These machines are used in the production of computer chips. ASML's clients are usually computer chip manufacturers. ASML's main offices and plants are in Veldhoven, the Netherlands. ASML is the result of a joint venture between ASM International and Philips.

Source: www.asml.com

FIGURE **ASML**

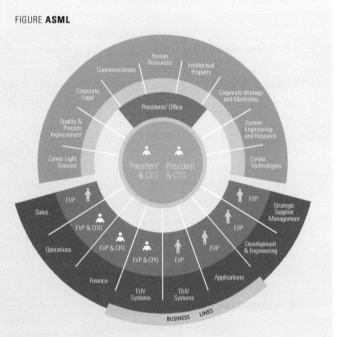

11.2.5 Organisational diagram

Organisational diagram

An organisational diagram (also called an organisation chart) is a simplified chart of the way in which tasks are formally divided between individuals and/or departments. It also shows the hierarchical relationships between individuals and divisions. One could therefore say that such a diagram is a simplified reproduction of the formal organisational structure. It is 'formal' in the sense that the task divisions, job descriptions, manuals and procedures are all written down and have an official nature. The formal organisation is the organic structure plus the staff structure.

Formal organisations

Other contacts, relationships and divisions of tasks do occur within the organisation, but do not fall under the formal organisation. In practice, the formal organisation is always in a state of flux, and therefore additional guidelines are necessary to support desired organisational behaviour. For example, some rules may not fit in with the current situation, while others are undesirable from the customer's point of view.

All activities and relationships that do not fall under the formal organisation can be included in the informal organisation. Informal organisational behaviour can influence an organisation in a positive or a negative way. If negative informal organisational behaviour occurs, the undesirable activities need to be corrected or addressed by imposing additional rules. An organisational diagram enables one to obtain an overall insight into the organisational structure and the functioning of the organisation. Tasks and function descriptions, planning, and procedures also represent part of an organisation's functioning.

An organisational chart may take many different forms. It should provide answers to the following questions:
1 When was the diagram drawn up?
2 Has the organisational chart changed since then?
 – If so: what was the date and the nature of the changes, and why did they occur?
 – If not: has the organisation really remained stable?
3 How many hierarchical levels does the organisation consist of?
4 Is there a further division in:
 – main units, such as departments, product units, or principal divisions?
 – main unit departments?
 – groups within departments?
 – consultation units between groups and departments?
5 According to what criteria has the organisation been structured (F, P, G, or M structure)?

11.3 TRADITIONAL ORGANISATIONAL SYSTEMS

An organisation can be described based on a number of characteristics, including organisational structure, division of tasks, authority, responsibility, power and decision-making style. Based on these characteristics, two very different organisational systems, known as mechanistic and organic, can be identified. In the following sections, the main organisational systems are reviewed. They display features that illustrate characteristics that are at least to some extent either mechanistic or organic.

11.3.1 Mechanistic and organic organisational systems

The main characteristics of mechanistic and organic organisational systems are listed below.

Mechanistic organisational system

To a large extent, a mechanistic organisational system resembles a machine in its structure and functioning. Key features are technical and financial efficiency. The organisation has been set up on rational and practical grounds. It presupposes a stable business environment. With this system, changes in the business environment rarely lead to organisational change. As such, they are primarily effective in stable environments.

A mechanistic organisational system has the following characteristics:
1 **Organisational structure**. Hierarchical in nature.
2 **Division of tasks**. Every member of staff has their own tasks. Individual achievement is a priority.
3 **Authority and responsibilities**. Clearly stated and to be respected.
4 **Respect**. Determined by the position an individual occupies within the hierarchical structure.
5 **Decision-making**. Decision-making is a matter for the top levels of the organisation, and there is only a minimum of consultation with, or involvement, of subordinates.
6 **Cooperation and communication**. Employees work together according to formal hierarchical lines. Communication is one-way, namely from the top down. It is also highly formal and its contents are concerned strictly with the matter in question.
7 **Operating method**. Standardised and limited to established procedures.
8 **Adaptability to change**. There is a preference for tested and reliable management principles, whatever the company's circumstances.

Organic organisational system

Organic organisational
system

Dynamic environment

An organic organisational system closely resembles a living organism in the way it is structured and operates. In such a system, the actions of those within the organisation are crucial. The organisation serves their social needs. An organic organisational system is appropriate in a dynamic environment. The organisation is flexible in nature and capable of dealing with change. These types of organisations are only effective in environments that are subject to change.

An organic organisational structure has the following characteristics:
1 **Organisational structure**. Rather than having a traditional hierarchical structure, it has horizontal working units (that is, it has a flat organisational structure).
2 **Division of tasks**. Individuals have specialist tasks but execute them as a team. The focus is on team achievements.
3 **Authority and responsibilities**. Authorities are broadly defined and responsibility lies with the team as well as the individual.
4 **Respect**. Derives from the knowledge and skills of the individual.
5 **Decision-making**. Decentralised decision-making, shared by various members of the organisation, with participation and group consensus playing an important role.
6 **Cooperation and communication**. The various teams and departments work together intensively. Communication takes place bottom-up as well as top-down. Communication channels are open so that everybody has access to relevant information.
7 **Operating method**. Deviation from the norm is permitted whenever necessary.
8 **Adaptability to change**. The organisation adapts itself to changing circumstances without question.

Wolters Kluwer Global Organisational Structure

Wolters Kluwer, founded 1836, is a Dutch leading global provider of information, software, and services. Professionals in the legal, business, fiscal, accounting, accounting, auditing, risk management, and compliance sector, and even the health care industry; they all rely on high-quality information, software, and services offered by Wolters Kluwer. Their solutions help professionals work more efficiently, offer results to their customers, and be successful in an increasingly dynamic world. Wolters Kluwer, its head office in Alphen aan den Rijn, the Netherlands, operates in over 180 countries in Europe, North America, Asia, and Latin America, and employs around 19,000 people worldwide.

Source: www.wolterskluwer.nl and www. wolterskluwer.com

FIGURE **WOLTERS-KLUWER**

11.3.2   Line organisation

Line organisation is the most traditional organisational structure, and the form from which most other structures are derived. The main characteristic of line organisation is that orders travel exclusively along a simple line, with strict hierarchical relationships maintained between manager and subordinates.
The fundamental principle of unity of command means that everyone in the organisation reports to just one manager. This manager is the only person with the authority to assign employees their tasks. Within line organisation, a manager needs to have broadly-based knowledge. Line organisation arises through tasks being passed down to lower levels as a consequence of growth or overloading higher up.
Line organisation can be represented very simply (see Figure 11.11). The relationships between individuals and departments are very clear.

Line organisation

Unity of command

FIGURE 11.11 **LINE ORGANISATION**

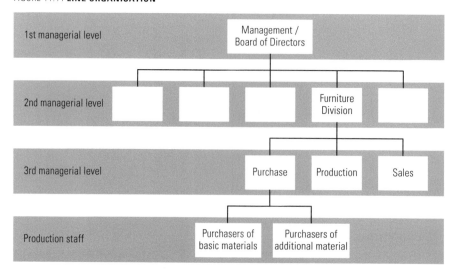

The advantages of line organisation are that:
a the organisational structure is simple and clear;
b the power relationships between individuals in the organisation are clear (every employee knows who their superior is);
c the tasks, authorities, and responsibilities can be clearly defined and allocated;
d good supervision and control of company processes can be achieved;
e quick decision-making is possible;
f management and organisation costs are relatively low.

The disadvantages of line organisation are that:
a all communication has to go via a single line; as a result, bottlenecks may arise, leading to delays in decision-making;
b management's expertise is not always sufficient for making the right decisions in all situations;
c coordination between departments can only take place via a senior manager, who is responsible for both;
d line structure can lead to many organisational levels, as managers can only supervise a limited number of people.

Line organisation structure is often adopted by small and medium-sized businesses. Previous iterations of international armed forces and the Catholic Church are good examples of the line organisation in its purest form.

11.3.3 Line and staff organisation

Line and staff organisation

Advise/inform

Where staff with specialist knowledge and expertise (so-called support staff) assist managers in line organisation, this is described as line and staff organisation. Support staff are often located in staff departments.
The tasks of staff departments are to advise and inform line management in their area of expertise. They do not have direct authority over other employees or departments (see Figure 11.12).

Structure and organisation
PART C

FIGURE 11.12 **LINE-STAFF ORGANISATION**

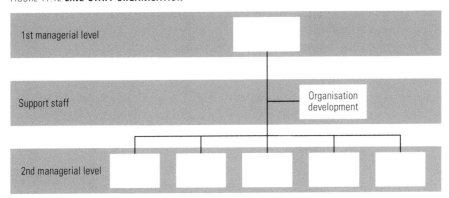

Overall responsibility remains with the line manager, who is also in charge of decision-making. The staff department, on the other hand, is responsible for the quality of the advice or information that is supplied to the line manager.
The advantages of line and staff organisation are that:

a greater expertise is available to the line manager; therefore, better decisions can be made.

b involving support staff can save time and increase efficiency. The span of control of line managers can therefore be extended.

c the principle of unity of command is maintained.

The disadvantages of line and staff organisation are that:

a staff departments may only have a theoretical understanding of operations; therefore, they may not be aware of the practical elements of a situation.

b there is a greater chance of slip-ups occurring within the department, as the support staff are not responsible for the decisions being made.

c staff departments are inclined to expand, which increases overhead costs. Additionally, it is not always easy to objectively determine whether the contribution made by support staff has lead to better decisions being made.

d there is a chance of the line manager becoming too dependent on the staff function.

Almost every large organisation has staff departments such as Human Resources (HR), Marketing Research, and Research and Development (R&D).

11.3.4 Functional and line staff organisation

If the advice of the support staff becomes so specialised that the line official can no longer assess it, the advice will take the form of an instruction or task (such as legal advice) that has to be followed. The staff relationship will therefore develop a 'functional' character.

Functional responsibility can be assigned to individuals and departments. In the event of the latter, it is termed functional staff division. The main characteristic of a functional staff division is that part of the actual task is also executed.

Because of its specialist responsibility, functional staff division uses its position to give instructions to other departments or managers on the policy (such as the subcontracting of certain activities), operational method (e.g. an administrative method) or procedures (such as the selection of staff) to be followed.

Functional and line staff organisation

Functional staff division
Specialist responsibility

Line managers are often compelled to consult functional staff division before making decisions that require its expertise, such as advice concerning legal, automation, or construction issues.

If an organisation is striving for uniformity and consistency, it is wise to give certain departments functional responsibility, for example setting up an hourly work monitoring system, designing forms, leaflets or brochures, purchasing computer equipment, or analysing a production processes. The expertise required for these sorts of activities is often either absent or difficult to coordinate from the line structure.

In the following organisational chart, the functional relationships are indicated by a dotted line (see Figure 11.13).

FIGURE 11.13 **FUNCTIONAL LINE AND STAFF ORGANISATION**

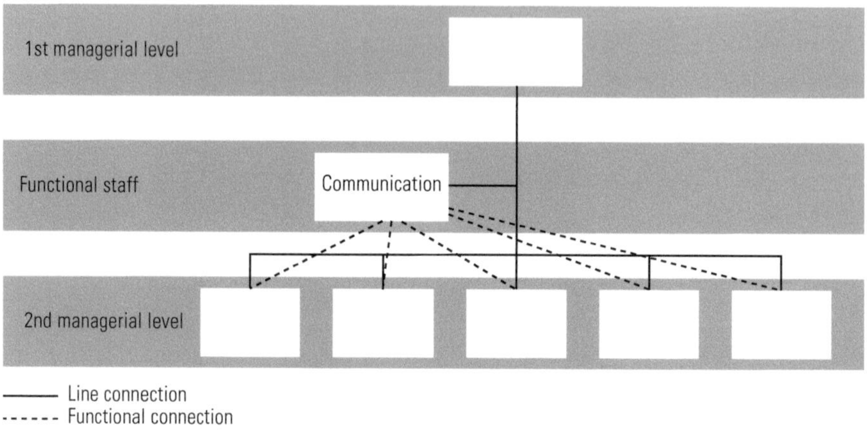

The advantages of functional staff division are that:
a there is greater input of expertise in company processes;
b there is involvement of members of the functional staff department in the end result;
c policy, guidelines, and procedures are uniform and consistent.

The disadvantages of functional staff divisions are that:
a employees have to deal with different managers. The principle of unity of command is abandoned, and that can lead to confusion;
b it may become more difficult to retain control over the way the tasks are executed.

Functional staff divisions include the following: Administration, Human Resources, Finances, Secretarial support, Maintenance, Automation, Legal Matters, and Communications. Obviously, the more frequently line managers are caught up in functional relationships with other departments, the less time they can put expend on their own area of activity.

11.3.5   Line-staff-committee organisation

Line-staff-committee organisation

In the previously mentioned organisational formats, all communication needs to go along 'the line'. Theoretically, this means no consultation between employees of the various departments other than that between the departmental heads. However, it is often necessary to involve other departments and their staff in business activities. Establishing committees or consulting bodies can boost cooperation between employees and departments, as well as assist in the coordination of activities. Such committees are set up for purely consultative purposes and have no authority to make decisions. The advice of a committee has to be approved by management. The committee structure represents a variant on the line or the line-staff (functional or otherwise) organisation.

Committees or consulting bodies

The line-staff committee is often found in large organisations, especially those in the service industry. Figure 11.14 shows a line-staff-committee organisation. The committees are indicated separately.

FIGURE 11.14 **LINE-STAFF-COMMITTEE ORGANISATION**

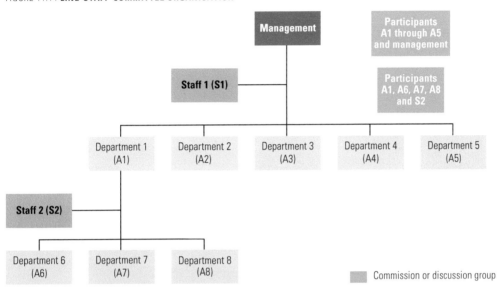

The advantages of a line-staff-committee organisation are that:
a there is input of know-how from different experts;
b there is greater acceptance of decisions that involve a group of people;
c there is improvement of coordination and cooperation between line and staff officials.

The disadvantages of a line-staff-committee organisation are that:
a officials can hide behind a group decision, resulting in a potential decline in individual (feelings of) responsibility;
b group decisions can be time-consuming, and can slow down the decision-making process.

11.3.6 The matrix organisation

A matrix organisation is an organisational form in which professional specialists from various departments are temporarily transferred for a specific project for a limited time. Some issues or problems (for example, office computerisation, the development of a new product, the construction and furnishing of a new building) may not be able to be resolved by one department only, requiring the involvement of a project group. Part of the project members' working time is spent on the project; the rest of their hours are assigned to their regular tasks. Once the project has ended, the project team members return to their own departments.

Matrix organisation

This organisational form is based on line or line-staff organisation. Project managers responsible for completing the project are appointed, meaning that many of the employees need to deal with two managers: department heads and project managers. Those responsible for the project report to a project manager. This format is called a 'matrix organisation' because of the way in which the lines of authority can be drawn (within a matrix – a diagram with two axes). A matrix organisation is characterised by joint authority. There needs to be a balance in the division of authority linking the interests of the project on the one hand, and the requirements of the department on the other (see Figure 11.15).

Project managers

Joint authority

FIGURE 11.15 **THE MATRIX ORGANISATION**

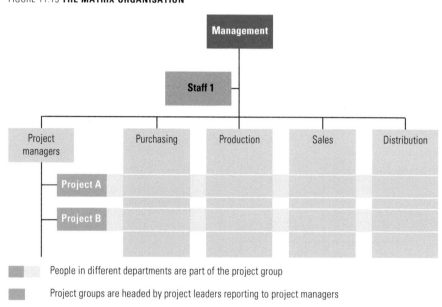

■ People in different departments are part of the project group

■ Project groups are headed by project leaders reporting to project managers

The advantages of a matrix organisation are that:
a the establishment of project groups means that cross-departmental tasks can be tackled.
b the existing line organisational structure can be maintained, and organisational leadership's requirements are also met.

The disadvantages of a matrix organisation are that:
a tensions and conflicts between project managers and department heads may occur because of conflicting interests (line managers are not always pleased to relinquish their staff to new project teams).
b project members may take advantage of their dual roles: within the department, and as project team members.
c individuals who have been busy in a project team for a long time, potentially suffer detrimental effects on their awareness of departmental colleagues and activities.

BAM Organisational Structure

FIGURE **BAM**

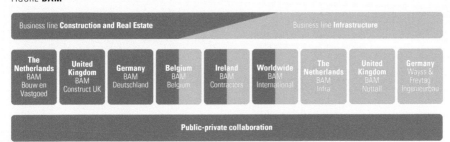

Koninklijke BAM Groep nv is a Dutch construction business group with ten operating companies in five European domestic markets and in specific markets worldwide. The BAM operating companies are active in the business lines of Construction, Real Estate, and Infrastructure, as well as in Public-private collaborations.

BAM's domestic European markets are the Netherlands, Belgium, the United Kingdom, Ireland, and Germany. In addition, the group is helping to realise projects in Denmark, Luxembourg, and Switzerland. BAM employs approximately 19,500 people, and its shares are listed with Euronext Amsterdam.

Source: www.bam.nl

11.3.7 Project-Based Organisation (PBO)

Section 11.3.6 mentioned that, in a matrix organisation, part of the line managers' authorities and responsibilities are assigned to the project managers. If project management has full control and all necessary authority to run the projects, the organisation can be termed a project-based organisation. Here, the authority of the project manager is equal to that of the head of a department in line organisation. Figure 11.16 compares the matrix organisation and the project-based organisation. Whether an organisation can best be described as a matrix organisation or a project-based organisation depends on the extent of the influence exerted by the line organisation and the project organisation.

Project-based organisation

FIGURE 11.16 **MATRIX ORGANISATION AND CLASSIC PROJECT ORGANISATION**

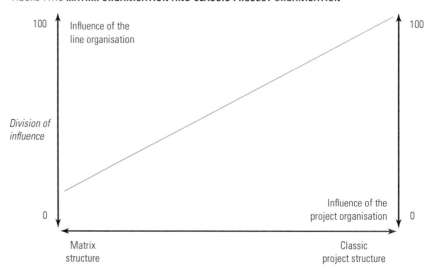

Another characteristic is that a project-based organisation is split up into different
Pools divisions, or 'pools' (see Figure 11.17).

FIGURE 11.17 **CLASSIC PROJECT ORGANISATION**

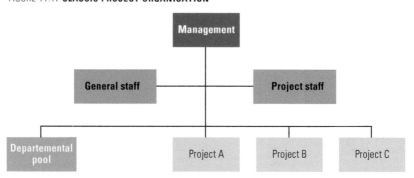

Staff from various departments are allocated to various projects. They focus 100%
percent of their time and energy on these projects. After finishing a project,
these staff members return to the departmental pool, after which they may be
re-allocated to another project.
Job agencies specialising in the IT sector often have a project form of organisation,
with staff from a pool being outsourced to various different projects.
The advantage of project-based organisation is that it has a single manager,
ensuring optimal functioning of those involved in the project. Its drawback is
the constant shifting of its employees from one project to another, with full
employment depending on new projects being created.

11.3.8 Internal project organisation

Internal project The last topic that addressed here is that of internal project organisation. This
organisation section discusses three possible variants. In practice, these three are used in
combination with each other. They are:
1 the steering committee working group model;
2 the programme model;
3 the phase model.

The steering committee working group model

This model of internal project organisation consists of a steering committee, a project manager, and one or more working groups. The steering committee occupies the highest level in the hierarchy and is appointed by the organisation's top management.

Policy considerations with regard to certain projects have to be approved by the steering committee. The members of a steering committee participate a basis of equality.

The steering committee is usually composed of heads of functional departments, selected on the basis of their expertise.

It is the task of the project manager to direct all aspects of a project, including the coordination, motivation, control, and monitoring of the activities of the project working groups. The project manager answers to the steering committee. The working groups are staffed by specialists and experts who take on the actual work and report to the project manager. The working groups are required to study specific problem areas, and to give advice.

This model is mainly applied to organisations that sometimes carry out extensive, complex or advanced projects (see Figure 11.18).

Steering committee/
working group model
Steering committee

Project manager

Working groups

FIGURE 11.18 **STEERING COMMITTEE / WORKING GROUP MODEL**

The programme model

If project-based work is frequent and extensive, and complex or advanced projects are common, the programme model is another option – particularly if some parts of the projects have a close mutual connection and common features.

Such a model requires a programme manager, a location manager, and a project manager (see Figure 11.19).

Programme model

FIGURE 11.19 **PROGRAMME MODEL**

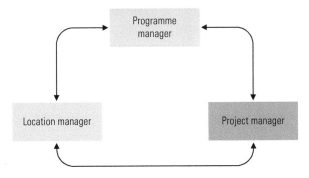

Programme manager

The programme manager is responsible for policy coordination between the various aspects of the projects that fall within one programme and are carried out at different locations (for example, an urban renewal project).

The project manager is responsible for achieving the required project result according to agreed preconditions (for example, building a new suburb within the existing urban limits). The project manager is also jointly responsible for the operational coordination between projects that fall within a single programme.

Location manager

The location manager is responsible for the operational coordination between projects within one location or establishment (e.g. the electrical installations in a house). Their responsibility is directed towards efficient deployment of people and resources in one location.

The phase model

Phase model

This model is usually applied when relatively standardised projects are regularly carried out on behalf of a certain client. Such projects are characterised by a few short-term activity phases: for example, a definition phase, a designing phase, a preparation phase, and a completion phase. At the start of each new phase, the project is handed over to another team (see Figure 11.20).

This model has the advantage that each phase is cared for by specialists, and that there is no risk of a clash of authority. However, there is the risk of the various managers responsible for the project each having divergent opinions, and thus the potential for disagreement with the client.

FIGURE 11.20 **PHASE MODEL**

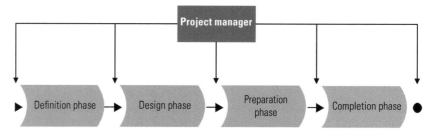

11.4   DIVISIONAL ORGANISATION

Divisional organisation

In a divisional organisation, the activities and processes within a company are grouped around a number of related products or markets, and located within divisions. This organisational form is found in big, often multinational, enterprises that produce a variety of products for various markets, and are often located in a number of different locations (see Figure 11.21).

FIGURE 11.21 **DIVISION STRUCTURE**

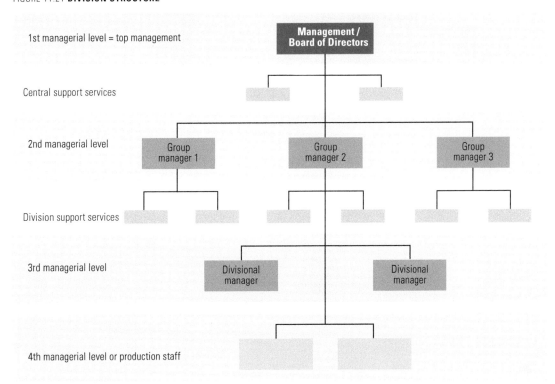

1st managerial level = top management	Management / Board of Directors
Central support services	
2nd managerial level	Group manager 1 / Group manager 2 / Group manager 3
Division support services	
3rd managerial level	Divisional manager / Divisional manager
4th managerial level or production staff	

The head of the division is the divisional director or manager. Theoretically, they are responsible for the strategy within that division, the way in which the division is structured, and the way in which tasks are carried out in the division.

Divisional director

The so-called 'group management' level is the level between the board of directors and divisional management, responsible for general strategic planning, overall control, and reaching the goals of the divisions. To do so, group management uses the services of specialist staff departments, known as group services. The divisions can also consult these services. Divisions with a large degree of independence and scope often have their own support services.

Group management
Group services

Since the divisions are completely responsible for their own achievements, management has to allow the division the necessary room to manoeuvre. The extent to which a division can remain independent of management depends on future decisions that need to be made by the division. Their powers of decision-making in the following areas are often limited:

a strategic management;
b reorganisations and mergers;
c financial planning methods and procedures;
d large capital investments;
e human resources policy in relation to payment structures, selection procedures, and training.

Holland Casino Organisational Schedule

FIGURE **HOLLAND CASINO**

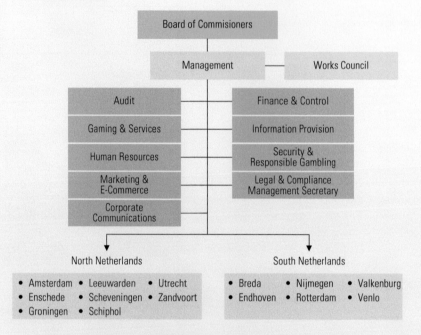

Holland Casino has fourteen casinos right across the Netherlands. Our casinos are welcoming entertainment venues with a varied range of games and food and beverage options. Guests play games for money safely and responsibly. Our employees are ready to give our guests a warm welcome 364 days a year. Our guests are guaranteed honest games and the highest pay-out percentages in the Netherlands. The range of games provides a choice for every visitor aged 18 and above.

But even guests who do not play casino games can also count on quality service.

Holland Casino's games are under the strict supervision of Dutch Measurement Institute *NMi* and Dutch Gambling Authority *Kansspelautoriteit*. The machines at Holland Casino offer an average pay-out rate of approximately 92% (the legal norm being 80%); this ratio can be as high as 98.6% for table games like roulette.

Source: www.hollandcasino.nl

Although divisions are held responsible for generating profit, they rarely have any influence over where that generated profit goes. Management can decide to transfer any profits to divisions that are underperforming. Such a division might well become a future cash cow for the organisation (see Chapter 3).
The advantage of a divisional organisation is that the assets of a small unit can be combined with those of a big unit. The division can be regarded as a relatively small unit within a relatively big group.

Other advantages of a divisional organisation are that:
a a division can anticipate the wants of the customer quicker, better, and more decisively.
b a division can make use of the know-how of those group support units that are too expensive for the division alone to set up.

c a division can bid for resources (such as financial resources and research results) and people (management) within the group.

d profitability within a division can be used as a ready standard for measurement and evaluation of achievements.

The disadvantages of a divisional organisation include that:

a (sometimes short-term) self-interest in a division with a high level of responsibility for profit can take precedence over the group's long-term interests.

b the costs of extra management and overheads resulting from setting up divisional staff support units can have a negative effect on the overall results.

c the independence of the divisions may result in the the knowledge and experience present in the other divisions not being used to everyone's full advantage.

Decentralisation helps a growing company to be more flexible and more decisive. But the parent company has to keep a grip on its divisions, running them in such a way as to maximise their return. But what is the best way of doing so? The answer depends on external and internal factors. Theoretically, there are three possible ways for a parent company to direct its divisions:

Parent company

1 **The strategic planning model**. This is appropriate when the parent company focuses primarily on strategy development and places little emphasis on controlling its subsidiaries.

Strategic planning

2 **The strategic management model**. This is appropriate when the parent company is mainly interested in testing and adapting strategies for its subsidiaries.

Strategic management

3 **Financial management**. This is appropriate when the parent company has set itself up as an institutional investor of sorts, and needs to check whether its subsidiaries meet the output requirements laid down.

Financial management

Compared to financial management, strategic planning can be considered the opposing end of the spectrum; strategic management should be seen as an intermediate form.

The main internal and external circumstances that determine which method best suits a decentralised company can be divided into two groups.

1 **The degree of solidarity between the subsidiary companies**
– **The portfolio.** If the portfolio is one-sided, then strategic planning is ideal. If the portfolio is diverse, financial management is more appropriate.
– **The organisational structure.** If the subsidiaries are relatively close, strategic planning is necessary. If the units are independent, financial management is the proper way to direct them.
– **Synergy.** If the subsidiaries are relatively close, strategic planning is necessary to generate synergy.

2 **The extent of intervention by the parent company**
– **The preferred method of planning.** If the goal of the main company is mainly to obtain long-term results, then strategic planning is best. If short-term results are required, financial management is more suitable.
– **The level of risk of decisions.** If decisions are high risk, strategic planning is the obvious choice. With less risky decisions, financial management should be used.

- **Stability of the business sector.** In a stable business environment, financial management is ideal; in a dynamic environment, strategic planning is better.
- **The maturity of the organisation.** For organisations that are rapidly developing, strategic planning is desirable.
- **The performance.** If company performance is uncertain, the parent organisation becomes more involved in directing, so strategic planning is necessary. When performance shows a high degree of certainty, financial management is ideal.

Figure 11.22 illustrates the choice of directive method in a diagram.

FIGURE 11.22 **THREE WAYS TO MANAGE A DECENTRALISED COMPANY**

	Strategic planning	Strategic management	Financial management
	Degree of connection		
• Portfolio	Limited	←——————→	Wide
• Organisational structure	Related	←——————→	Independent
• Synergy	Large	←——————→	Limited

	Degree of intervention		
• Planning orientation	Long-term	←——————→	Short-term
• Importance and risk of decisions	Large	←——————→	Small
• Sector status	Variable	←——————→	Stable
• Maturity of the organisation	In development	←——————→	Stable
• Performance	Vulnerable	←——————→	Reliable

11.5 MINTZBERG AND ORGANISATIONAL STRUCTURES

Henry Mintzberg

As mentioned briefly in the Introduction Chapter, Henry Mintzberg's book *The structuring of organisations* (1979) attempted to compile the main theories concerning the structuring of organisations. In one of his later works, *Mintzberg on Management* (1991), he expands on, and refines, his theories.

11.5.1 Organisational properties

According to Mintzberg, the most appropriate organisational structure becomes apparent by linking a number of the organisation's properties. Instead of organisational structures, Mintzberg refers to organisational configurations.

Configurations

Figure 11.23 shows the properties that determine an organisational structure. They are:

a the organisational parts;

b coordination mechanisms;

c design parameters;

d contingency factors (situational factors).

These organisational characteristics need to be integrated in such a way as to create cohesion. The process of 'integrating organisational characteristics' is known as the configuration approach.

FIGURE 11.23 **PROPERTIES THAT DETERMINE THE ORGANISATIONAL STRUCTURE**

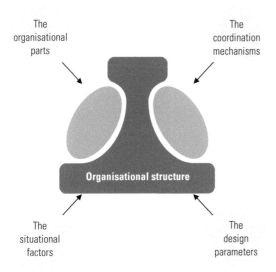

The organisational parts

The coordination mechanisms

Organisational structure

The situational factors

The design parameters

The organisational properties previously mentioned (the organisation's parts, coordination mechanisms, design parameters and situational factors) must match each other in such a way as to create coherence. The configuration approach can be described as the 'mutual adjustment of the organisation's properties'.

The organisational part

The so-called primary processes – work that is directly related to the production of goods and services – form the basis of the organisation. Mintzberg calls these the operational core.

Every organisation needs to have at least one manager who is able to supervise all processes and manage the organisation. This individual is located within the strategic apex. In larger organisations, the Board of Directors and the Council of Commissioners form the strategic apex.

If an organisation increases in size, there is a need for more managers. These do not necessarily have to be managers who direct staff, but may include managers who direct other managers. An intermediate or middle line thus arises. This layer of management was referred to in Chapter 6 as middle management.

The more complex the organisation becomes, the greater its need for a staff that is able to analyse and support the primary processes. This staff makes plans and manages the work. This section of the organisation is known as the technical staff area. Supervisors, planners, and planning engineers fall into this category.

Many organisations have support staff who supply services of one kind or another to the various departments. Salary administrators, public relations officers, and Research & Development staff fall into the category of support staff.

Figure 11.24 shows that the narrow strategic apex is connected to a broad operational core. This is a hierarchical structure. The support staff divisions fall outside the hierarchy and can only indirectly exercise influence over the operational core and strategic apex.

Organisational part

Operational core

Strategic apex

Middle line

Technical staff

Support staff

FIGURE 11.24 **ORGANISATIONAL PARTS**

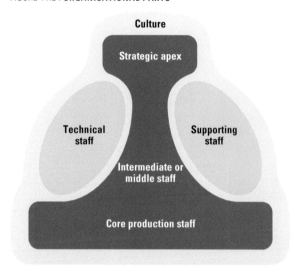

Coordination mechanisms

Coordination mechanisms

A characteristic feature of organisations is that the current work must be divided amongst employees (task division), and that these activities have to be coordinated. This is done primarily to ensure that activities are performed efficiently and effectively. Mintzberg identifies mechanisms that can be used to coordinate activities (see Figure 11.25).

FIGURE 11.25 **SIX COORDINATION MECHANISMS**

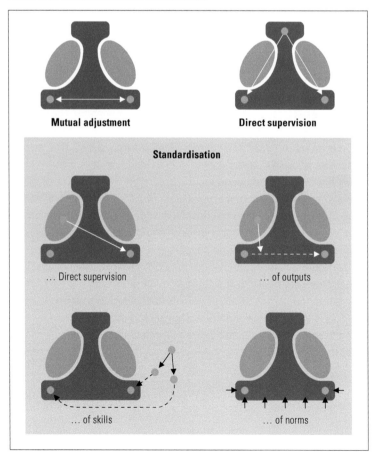

These activity coordination mechanisms are:

1 **Mutual adjustment**. This method is characterised by significant formal and informal communication between employees. Regular consultation, evaluation sessions, speech and communication techniques, internships, meeting facilities, and informal contact are some examples of the forms that this communication may take.

Mutual adjustment

2 **Direct supervision**. Managers issue assignments and instructions to staff with respect to the tasks that need to be performed. This can happen during progress reviews or as part of a performance evaluation interview. The manager makes use of various techniques and skills, as well as their own experience and knowledge.

Direct supervision

3 **Standardisation of work processes**. In this method, tasks are specified and standardised (usually by technical staff). This is done on the basis of established procedures, manuals, and instructions. Mechanisation and automation are essential aspects of this process (the production of standardised letters for making offers, for memos, etc).

Standardisation of work processes

4 **Standardisation of outputs**. In this method, a specification of results is drafted. It may be related to financial targets for each company unit, to the content of contracts, to customer satisfaction norms, to quality criteria for the products to be developed, and so on.

Standardisation of outputs

5 **Standardisation of skills**. The activities to be performed are coordinated on the basis of the training and experience of the individuals. For example, a surgeon and an anaesthetist are able to anticipate each other's standardised procedures virtually automatically.

Standardisation of skills

6 **Standardisation of norms**. In this method, the staff in an organisation behaves similarly as they share a similar set of opinions (a religious order, for example). Norms can also develop from a point of view shared by those in an organisation.

Standardisation of norms

Research has shown that coordination mechanisms have a certain natural order. As the work becomes more complicated, the coordination mechanisms shift from mutual adjustment to direct supervision. They then shift to standardisation of work processes, output, skills, or norms then back to mutual adjustment. This coordination mechanism also adapts well to complex processes.
All organisations make use of each of the different coordination mechanisms. However, they normally have a preference for a particular one.
Coordination mechanisms are arguably the most essential elements of an organisational structure.

Natural order

Design parameters
Design parameters are parameters that determine the way tasks are divided in an organisation. The main design parameter variables are:

Design parameters

a **Specialisation of tasks**. This refers to the number of tasks per function and the way that responsibilities and authorities are assigned.

b **Size of departments or groups**. This is connected to the number of employees per unit or group.

c **Centralisation or decentralisation**. This is the degree to which decision-making authorities are assigned to staff lower down the hierarchy.

d **Formalisation of behaviour**. The extent to which rules, procedures, job descriptions, and similar, standardise employee duties.

Contingency factors (situational factors)
During the 1960s, a number of experts on organisational theory suggested that there was no single best organisational structure. Instead, it was claimed that the

most appropriate form of organisational structure depended on the situation the organisation faced at a particular time. This approach is called the contingency approach.

Contingency factors Contingency, or situational, factors influence organisational unit set-up, coordination mechanisms used, and the most appropriate design parameters. Each of these aspects also has an effect on situational factors.

According to Mintzberg, the organisational structure is dependent on the following situational factors:

1 **The technical system of an organisation**. The level of automation used by the operational core (e.g. machines, automation). Organisations with complex technical systems generally have extensive professional support departments.
2 **The environmental characteristics of the organisation (dynamic, complex)**. Organisations with a dynamic environment have an organic organisational structure. With a complex environment, an organisation opts for decentralisation of responsibilities and authorities.
3 **The age and size of the organisation**. As an organisation ages or grows in size, it also becomes more formal in nature.

Tata Steel Nederland retains autonomy following agreement with Indian shareholder

Tata Steel Nederland (TSN) has reached an agreement with Tata Steel Limited, the Bombay-based Indian shareholder. The agreement paves the way for the intended joint-venture between Tata Steel European steel industry and German company ThyssenKrupp.
The Indian mother enterprise TSN was willing to accede to four important demands set by the central works council and the unions. These demands are that the IJmuiden location is to continue to exist as an integrated industrial complex, that TSN retains its financial authority and can apply its free cash flows for future investments, and that the company's current managerial model continues to exist, with its own board of commissioners and board of management.

Source: Het Financiële Dagblad, 22 February 2018 https://fd.nl/ondernemen/1242953/tata-steel-nederland-bereikt-akkoord-met-indiase-aandeelhouder, consulted 7 May 2018

11.5.2 Organisational forms

During his research involving hundreds of companies, Mintzberg isolated the following seven different organisational configurations:

1 the entrepreneurial organisation;
2 the machine bureaucracy;
3 the professional organisation;
4 the diversified organisation;
5 the innovative organisation;
6 the missionary organisation;
7 the political organisation.

Figure 11.26 looks at the most important properties of each configuration.

FIGURE 11.26 **MATRIX OF MOST IMPORTANT ORGANISATIONAL PROPERTIES PER CONFIGURATION**

Name configuration	Characteristic organisational part	Coordination mechanism	Design parameters	Situational factors
Entrepreneurial organisation	• strategic apex	• direct supervision	• organic decentralised structure	• developed technical system • well-organised and dynamic environment • young and small organisation
Machine bureaucracy	• technical staff	• standardisation of activities	• formalised organisational behaviour • tight vertical structure • decentralisation	• rationalised oriented technical system • well-organised and stable environment • large and mature organisation
Professional organisation	• core production staff	• standardisation of knowledge and skills	• horizontal decentralisation	• simple technical system • complex but stable organisation
Diversified organisation	• middle level	• standardisation of results	• limited vertical decentralisation	• considerable market diversity • largest and most mature organisations
Innovative organisation	• support staff	• mutual adjustment	• selective decentralisation	• high-quality and most automated technical system • complex and dynamic environment • usually a young organisation
Missionary organisation	• ideology	• standardisation of norms	• decentralisation	• differs
Political organisation	• none	• none	• differs	• differs

The next section briefly explains the above-mentioned configurations.

The entrepreneurial organisation

Figure 9.27 shows that the entrepreneurial organisation has a flat organisational structure, without staff departments. There is no room for middle management either. All activities revolve around the entrepreneur or manager, who has a charismatic and/or autocratic style of leadership. The strategy is somewhat visionary in nature. The entrepreneurial organisation is flexible, spontaneous in its actions, and highly market-oriented.

Entrepreneurial organisation

Visionary in nature

FIGURE 11.27 **ENTREPRENEURIAL ORGANISATION**

This organisational form is encountered in small, new businesses. Communication is informal and the work is rarely, if ever, standardised.

The great advantage of this organisational form is that one can quickly anticipate changing market circumstances. The disadvantages of the form lie in its driving force: namely, dependence on the entrepreneur. This strategy runs the risk of becoming unbalanced or unable to be implemented.

The machine bureaucracy

Machine bureaucracy

The machine bureaucracy contains formalised communication channels and decision-making processes. Technical and support staff play an important role. The technical staff are charged with the standardisation of duties such as the development of procedures, work instructions, and plans. Figure 11.28 shows that both supporting units are separated from the 'trunk' of the organisation. These departments are independent.

FIGURE 11.28 **MACHINE BUREAUCRACY**

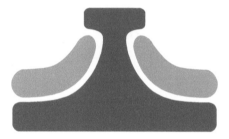

Strategic programming

The process of strategic management may look more like strategic programming and, in fact, a strategy is often formed with the help of various planning procedures.

The machine organisational structure is typical of larger organisations with a relatively stable business environment. Typical businesses include mass production manufacturers, non-profit organisations, organisations with large-scale services, and organisations that prioritise control of processes and safety. The advantage of this organisational form is that it is rational, reliable, and consistent. However, it runs the risk of 'control obsession': of management trying to organise everything neatly and according to rules and procedures, sometimes at the cost of efficiency and effectiveness. Another disadvantage is that machine organisations are not really inclined to change. If, and when, changes take place, it may therefore seem more like a revolution.

The professional organisation

Professional organisation

This structure is found frequently in organisations with highly skilled or professional staff, in which activities are carried out in a fairly routine or professional manner. Intensive training programs can be developed to master difficult tasks. Coordination of the professional organisation is based on the standardisation of knowledge and skills. Universities and colleges, hospitals, accountant offices, and social aid agencies fall under this organisational form. Figure 11.29 shows that the operational core and support staff are of great importance. Support staff are very important, because they assist the more expensive professionals at the operational core (specialists, professors etc.) to an extent that allows these professionals to concentrate on their primary tasks. Technical staff is limited, as work at the

Autonomy

operational core is influenced by the professional's autonomy.

FIGURE 11.29 **PROFESSIONAL ORGANISATION**

In a professional organisation, the strategy pursued is stable in character, although minor details change constantly. The advantages of this organisational form are the autonomy of the staff members and the democratic character of the organisation. The disadvantages are related to the existence of coordination problems between the different functions or fields, the danger of professionals abusing their autonomy, and possible resistance to innovation.

The diversified organisation

Mintzberg's diversified organisation basically corresponds to the divisional structure described in Section 11.4. Figure 11.30 demonstrates that the diversified organisation is constructed of a number of semi-independent units (divisions) connected by a central management or head office.

Diversified organisation

The divisions are active in different product or market combinations. There is only a small central technical department, because the divisions themselves manage their own support units. According to Mintzberg, the diversified form functions best with a machine organisation approach to its divisions. The head office formulates targets in terms of sales growth and output that the divisions have to reach. To a greater or lesser extent, this organisational form can be found in the biggest 500 companies in the world (the so-called Fortune 500). The head office defines the group strategy. The separate divisions develop their own company strategies.

Product or market combinations

FIGURE 11.30 **DIVERSIFIED ORGANISATION**

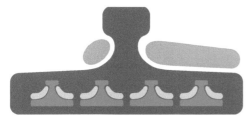

An important advantage of this organisational form is that it spreads group activity risks. In addition, the delegation of responsibility and authority to the divisions (which, after all, are closer to their market), allows for faster reactions within the market place. One of the inherent dangers of this form is its potential to be very expensive, because non-profitable divisions may be propped up using financial support from other divisions.

Spreading of risks
Delegation of responsibility

The innovative organisation

The innovative organisation (Mintzberg's ad-hocracy concept), features a highly organised structure. There is little standardisation. The organisation focusses on innovation and avoids getting fixed patterns of behaviour. This organisational form is made up of multidisciplinary teams or project groups, in which functional experts, managers or coaches, and support staff work together to bring about innovative

Innovative organisation ad-hocracy

Operational innovative
organisation

processes. Two forms of innovative organisations can be identified, namely the operational innovative organisation and the managerial innovative organisation. The former refers to the fusion of managerial and operations actions into one single activity. For example, in some projects, the design, planning, and execution are indistinguishable. Figure 11.31 shows the broad 'trunk' of the operational innovative organisation. This trunk includes the strategic axis, the middle level, the technical and support staff, and the operational core.

FIGURE 11.31 **INNOVATIVE ORGANISATION (ADHOCRACY)**

Managerial innovative
organisation

In a managerial innovative organisation, a distinction is made between managerial and operational activities. In this form, the operational core is isolated from the rest of the organisation. The dotted line in Figure 11.32 indicates the isolated operational core.

FIGURE 11.32 **MANAGERIAL INNOVATIVE ORGANISATION**

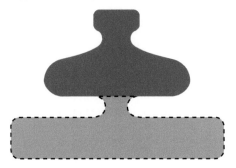

The operational core is isolated if its activities are similar to those characteristic of a machine organisation, thus preventing innovation on the part of management. This problem can be avoided in either of two ways:
- by setting up a separate company to carry out the operational activities;
- by completely discarding or contracting out the operational activities.

As indicated, innovative organisations can be found in complex and dynamic environments. Their strategy is developed from the bottom up, and tends to be shaped by management rather than assigned. The great advantage of the innovative organisation is that it is effective when innovation is required. A disadvantage is that this effectiveness may sometimes be at the expense of efficiency. Lack of clarity may also cause problems.
Despite these drawbacks, in Mintzberg's opinion, the innovative organisation was the organisational form of the second half of the 20th century. It has been widely adopted, especially in relatively young business indsutries like advertising, automation, film, aviation and space travel, and research.

The missionary organisation

A missionary organisation is based on a strong ideology and is found in organisations where an elaborate system of values and beliefs exists among employees. This sets this organisation apart from others. Values and beliefs are deeply entrenched. Leadership is charismatic and the aim of the organisation is clear and inspirational.

Missionary organisation

An ideology may be adopted by and added to any of the previously described configurations, particularly by an entrepreneurial or innovative organisation. If an ideology is the driving force behind an organisation, it gives rise to the missionary organisation.

Ideology

The missionary organisation has no distinct form (see Figure 11.33). Staff work together in small units, all aligned in the same direction. There is little difference in status between employees.

Distinct form

FIGURE 11.33 **MISSIONARY ORGANISATION**

In its purest form, individuals take it in turns to rotate their work tasks. The organisation is held together by standardisation of norms, with great importance being attached to the selection, indoctrination, and socialisation of new colleagues. Missionary organisations are often very successful. Their success can be attributed to the fact that its members are not in conflict with each other. They identify completely with the organisation, and dedicate themselves fully to it. Missionary organisations do run the risk of becoming isolated. The traditional Israeli kibbutz is an example of a missionary organisation.

The political organisation

The way an organisation functions is determined by a number of influences. These include ideology, authority, expertise, and politics. The only one of these influences not recognised as legitimate is that of politics. Politics has to do with the use (or misuse) of power.

Political organisation

Individuals often use politics for their own personal ends, with conflicts or rifts between individuals or departments as a consequence. To a lesser or greater extent, politics plays a role in practically all of these configurations. But if the extent is great enough, the organisation becomes known as a political organisation.

The arrows in Figure 11.34 show the different political influences within the organisation, all of which have an effect on its strategy and structure. Political activities in organisations are often described in terms of political games.

FIGURE 11.34 **POLITICAL ORGANISATION**

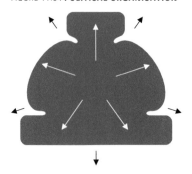

Political influences can be regarded as positive in some problematic organisational situations. If legitimate systems of influence fail to bring about necessary changes, political influences may provide a solution.
The danger of organisations under strong political influence is that most of the employees' energy is directed internally and a chain of conspiracies and conflicts may arise.

O&M IN PRACTICE

Rabobank further restricting role of local banks

Rabobank wants to further restrict the role of its local offices. Rabobank's current direction towards centralisation is to be implemented even more strongly, with additional cuts in the number of local offices.
This is part of the bank's ambition to provide its services to its customers 24 hours per day, seven days per week through all digital channels.

Basic service provision
The plans mention twelve regional 'head offices'. These are to be heavily manned with

highly knowledgeable and skilled personnel, and will continue to offer the full-service package. A total of ninety offices will remain, which will include the head offices. The activities performed by the remaining 78 smaller offers are to be scaled back to only the most basic service provision.
In order to realise its ambition of being a fully digital bank by 2020, the Rabobank still needs to make considerable investments.

Source: Het Financiele Dagblad, 23 February 2018
https://fd.nl/ondernemen/1243102/rabobank-perkt-rol-lokale-banken-nog-verder-in, consulted 7 May 2018.

11.6 DEVELOPMENTS IN ORGANISATIONAL STRUCTURING

The business environment has changed more rapidly over the past fifteen years than at any other time. Environmental events like the Internet revolution that started in the middle of the 1990s, increasing internationalisation, and the various social, political, and economical changes described in Chapter 2 have been of great significance to the commercial world, and are implicated in the creation and disappearance of many businesses, as well as in the changes they have experienced.
Organisations that cannot adapt quickly enough to new market circumstances are not likely to survive the coming years. Managers often describe traditional organisations as being too slow and bureaucratic, lacking in innovation, and inadequate focus on the needs of their customers. Their costs may be too high to be able to remain competitive. In other words, their efficiency and effectiveness may be inadequate

for long-term achievement. It is therefore important to identify the organisational characteristics able to satisfy the demands of the 21st century customer.

This paragraph describes a number of trends in organisational structure already being applied by a large number of companies, with other companies on their way to integrate them into their existing organisations. The most important trends in organisational structure are:

a agile organisation;
b horizontal organisation;
c Holacracy;
d network organisation;
e virtual organisation.

Three of these trends are addressed in detail, namely agile and horizontal organisation, and Holacracy.

Trends in organisational structure

11.6.1 Agile organisation

VUCA world

In a world of ever-accelerating change and increasing complexity, classical organisational design is no longer sufficient. This rapidly changing world is also known as a VUCA world: Volatile, Uncertain, Complex, and Ambiguous. The concept of VUCA has a military background -it is the practical term for awareness and readiness. US military personnel uses the term to describe a battlefield. These days, it has found its way to mainstream communication, as a way of describing how a continually changing market is causing the aforementioned issues of volatility, uncertainty, complexity, and ambiguity.

The world is becoming increasingly VUCA, and organisations should respond to this issue adequately. An adequate response calls for VUCA competences:

VUCA world

VUCA competences

V = Vision: the ability to steer towards a desired future;
U = Understanding: the ability to comprehend context and draw the right conclusions;
C = Clarity: the ability to provide insight and to simplify matters;
A = Agility: the ability to be adaptive and flexible.

Figure 11.35 offers a schematic overview of the VUCA world.

FIGUUR 11.35 **DE VUCA-WERELD SCHEMATISCH WEERGEGEVEN**

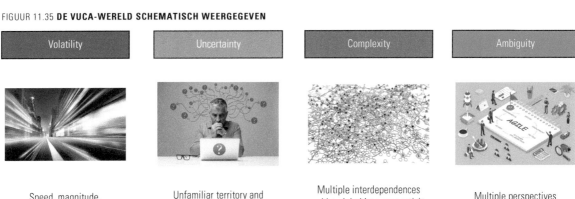

Volatility	Uncertainty	Complexity	Ambiguity
Speed, magnitude, turbulence and dynamics of change	Unfamiliar territory and unpredictable outcomes	Multiple interdependences amidst global interconnectivity	Multiple perspectives and interpretations of scenarios
Vision	Understanding	Clarity	Agility

The classical organisation

The classical organisation is characterised by a strive for stability, with a centrally formulated strategy that the organisation must implement in the most structured, effective, and efficient manner possible. Through a hierarchy in which managers instruct employees and tell them how to operate, the strategy is implemented and executed. Change and improvement are slow processes in the classical organisation, as the originally selected strategy is the guiding concept. Deviating from this strategy is only possible following a thorough analysis of, and renewed decision-making process about, changes. This is also known as unfreeze-move-freeze – and it takes time. New decisions continually lead to restructured and planned approaches which then fulfil the strategy through a linear process, step by step.

Unfreeze-move-freeze

Agile organisation

Literally speaking, agile means nimble and dexterous. An organisation that works according to agile principles is quicker and better at adapting to the circumstances of a VUCA world. In his 2016 book *De Wendbare Organisatie* (The Agile Organisation) (Deel 1; pp. 66-67), Kerklaan compared the classical organisation to the agile organisation. His list of differences can be summarised as follows:

Agile organisation

a An agile organisation is better at making use of the opportunities offered by the current age of information;

b Agile organisations are less strict in following the linear process of strategic planning. In an agile organisation, the mission and strategy are a jumping-off point for the organisation's conduct and experimentation. There is room to manoeuvre in an agile organisation: Kerklaan (2016) calls this 'agility-based strategy';

c In contrast to the classical organisation, the agile organisation is directed along broad strokes, with responsibility being placed on executive levels;

d Classical organisations steer for command & control-based performance. Agile organisations perform by anticipating and manoeuvring. Here, environmental information is the basis for the move towards improvement;

e Agile organisations place the emphasis on horizontal thought instead of on hierarchy. Decisions are delegated to the executive branch, the employees in the workplace; as a result, decision-making is faster. Departments more frequently attempt to align. Mutual collaboration is encouraged;

f Agile organisations continually strive for process optimisation, with simplification and elimination of unnecessary steps being curtailed and improved (see Chapter 10 on Process and Control for more information);

g Agile organisations involve the executive branch in strategy realisation. Together with the continual strive for process improvement, this improves the learning capabilities and processes of the executive branch, resulting in an increase in workfloor-based knowledge;

h Agile organisations see frequent experimentation. Successful experiments are implemented. Agile organisations use this dynamic in order to achieve their goals. This is contrasted with the classical organisation, whose natural drive is for stability.

TABLE 11.2 **FROM CLASSICAL TO AGILE ORGANISATIONS**

From: classical organisation	To: agile organisation
Industrial age	Information age
Detailed strategic plan	Directive intent, mission, and goals
Command and Control	Anticipate and Manoeuvre
Hierarchy	Cooperation
Months and weeks	Days and minutes
Implement and verify	Implement and learn
Unfreeze-move-freeze	Experiment and recalibrate

Source: Kerklaan, *De Wendbare Organisatie*, 2016

What is agile?

In 2001, the *Agile Manifesto* was developed by a number of experienced experts who had invented many innovative approaches to software development. In doing so, the group turned away from the traditional, process-oriented development method, also known as the waterfall method, and began to embrace working according to agile principles.

Agile principles
Waterfall method

The waterfall method is characterised by a fluent, sloping, chronologically linear process of design and development for software.

FIGURE 11.36 **WATERFALL METHOD SCHEMATIC**

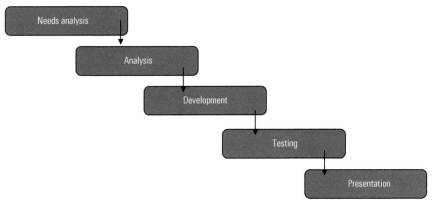

Source: https://www.consultancy.nl/nieuws/12446/aanpak-voor-het-kiezen-van-de-juiste-software-ontwikkelmethode

The waterfall method, however, did not turn out to be ubiquitously successful. Adjustments during the development process sometimes had a major impact on the outcome, duration, costs, and scope of projects. The method was often considered slow and restrictive to the creativity and effectiveness of the developer.

The Agile Manifesto emphasised the need for communal values instead of accurate adherence to a process or methodology. The manifesto comprises four values:

Agile Manifesto

1 **individuals and interactions** over processes and tools;
2 **working software** over comprehensive documentation;
3 **customer collaboration** over contract negotiation;
4 **responding to change** over following a plan.

Manifesto for Agile Software Development

We are uncovering better ways of developing
software by doing it and helping others do it.
Through this work we have come to value:

Individuals and interactions over processes and tools
Working software over comprehensive documentation
Customer collaboration over contract negotiation
Responding to change over following a plan

That is, while there is value in the items on
the right, we value the items on the left more.

Kent Beck	James Grenning	Robert C. Martin
Mike Beedle	Jim Highsmith	Steve Mellor
Arie van Bennekum	Andrew Hunt	Ken Schwaber
Alistair Cockburn	Ron Jeffries	Jeff Sutherland
Ward Cunningham	Jon Kern	Dave Thomas
Martin Fowler	Brian Marick	

The word 'over' emphasises that the notions on the left are to be preferred over those on the right. Although the agile concept originated in the world of IT, and was first used as a new approach to software development, it has since found its way to many other industries, including governments and business service providers.

Humans and interactions over processes and tools

The Agile Manifesto emphasises that the people who work in teams and the way in which they work together are the factors that determine project success. This type of interaction can take place in many different ways; Scrum, Kanban, and Lean are terms that are frequently used in this context. These methods may differ from one to the next, but they are all intended to continually optimise and improve the work process. Scrum and Kanban are discussed elsewhere in this chapter. Chapter 10 focusses on the concept of Lean.

Working software over comprehensive documentation

The traditional method of software development is characterised by the fact that it seeks to extensively document demands, costs, and tests. This process of documentation is performed by various different experts, such as analysts and designers, who all work from the perspective of their own role at a specific phase of a project. After making their contribution, they leave the project organisation. Agile suggests these people keep working with each other and with the customer, instead of consecutively. All parties together are responsible for creating an end product. Documentation is less important when working according to agile principles – it is not eliminated, but restricted to what is really necessary.

Customer collaboration over contract negotiation

The agile principles actively involve the customer in the development of the product. Customer feedback is used directly and continuously to improve product quality or implement new requirements. In the world of agile, the relationship with customers and the aspect of mutual trust is more important than an ironclad contract.

Responding to change over following a plan

Being agile means being flexible and capable of adjustment. New insights may result in a demand for a different approach. The ability to rapidly address change becomes very desirable. Working according to a clearly demarcated plan can be restrictive, since adjusting the plan takes time and money.

O&M IN PRACTICE

Agile-development methodology by SimpledCard, the new business payment method

SimpledCard – a unique, global business payment system. SimpledCard users issue their own prepaid credit or debit cards to employees or clients. The application's most important features are: a quick and easy cash distribution process; a custom, client-managed spending limit; real-time views of transaction data and reports.

Scrum in a lean approach

The application was finalised in only a few months, thanks to the application of a multidisciplinary Scrum-team. Using a clear roadmap, the first version of the system was developed in no-time, after which it was improved and enhanced based on client feedback (lean start-up approach).

Source: https://www.globalorange.nl/3-kenmerkende-voorbeelden-van-agile-ontwikkeling-binnen-bedrijven, consulted 11 May 2018

Agile project characteristics

In his 2012 book *This is Agile*, Hoogendoorn describes the characteristics of agile projects:

1 Agile projects experience short iterations, repeating processes.
2 Agile uses teams of collaborating people with different roles.
3 Jobs consists of small units over a short timespan.
4 Change is normal, and suits agile working.
5 The short iterations enable continuous measuring and short cyclical scheduling, meaning changes can be implemented easily.
6 Testing starts early on in the process and is a continuous process.
7 Small (fragments of work) products are provided from the start and often over the course of the development process.
8 Agile uses simple communication that is understood by all. An example is the task visualisation on an activity or scrum board with post-it notes indicating the work that is still to be done.
9 The team works together at one location whenever possible.

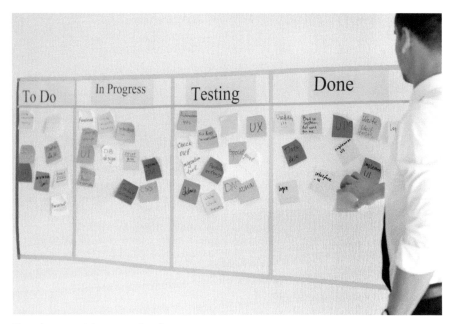

Example on an activity or scrum board

The goal of the agile approach is to optimise the workload, and to create and market products or services more often and more quickly. The characteristics listed are not objectives in their own right, but are intended to support the work process. The agile approach means working with enough room and flexibility to manoeuvre. Among other things, this means that, in case of failure of any kind, the team itself finds the best possible solution to perform the work in whatever way they feel works best.

Taking charge

As indicated, the VUCA world demands that organisations be agile. But making the transition from a classical organisation to an agile one is no easy task. It has a major impact on an organisation's processes and, therefore, on all of its employees. Working differently, collaborating without a fixed framework or structured planning; the agile approach demands that employees are adaptable. This may lead to friction and unrest in the organisation, and potentially result in dismissals. It is therefore very important that management formulates a clear vision, takes the initiative for organisational change, and leads the change process.

Agile organising

The term *agile* is used for to describe a modus operandi, and can be seen as an umbrella term encompassing Scrum and other approaches, such as Kanban, Scaled Agile Framework (SAFe), the Spotify model, PRINCE2 Agile and Lean Start-up. Both an Agile project approach and Agile line organisation require a basis of self-steering teams creating value using one of the approaches listed. Scrum and Kanban are relatively simple methods, well-suited to smaller organisations. Working from an agile approach in a larger organisation requires more fine-tuning and collaboration between more teams, and may require a Scaled Agile Framework (SAFe) or the Spotify model.

Agile organising

Scrum-based working

Scrum is based on empiricism. Empiricism assumes that knowledge is founded in experience, and that decisions are made based on what is known (Schwaber and Sutherland, 2016).

Scrum as an approach is designed to help incrementally develop a product. Incremental in this sense means that the product is developed and improved in small steps along the way. It is a value-driven approach that ensures the client and end users are presented with the most valuable product allowed under the constraints of time and budget. Scrum wants to create value for clients instead of conforming to a previously established plan. Scrum ensures that the product that is provided meet clients demands, is faster and easier to develop, and meets the required quality standards.

Schwaber and Sutherland (2016) wrote a guide to Scrum in which they explain what Scrum is, and how it can be put into practice. This paragraph describes several of the relevant aspects of working with Scrum, and discusses pillars, roles, and increment in order.

Scrum

Scrum pillars

There are three pillars that form the basis of Scrum:

1 **Transparency**. It is important to be transparent about all team activities and time spent on the project. The Scrum team should all speak the same language, understand one another, and ensure that there is a common perception of what the (final) result should be;
2 **Inspection**. The team should inspect the result. By regularly reviewing the interim products, its compliance with the established demands is safeguarded;
3 **Adaptation**. It may be necessary to adapt. Inacceptable product test results require some form of intervention takes place.

Scrum pillars

Scrum team roles

An organisation that uses the Scrum framework employs self-guiding teams, known as Scrum teams. A Scrum team includes the following roles: The Product Owner, the Scrum Master, and the Development team. The Product Owner is responsible for maximising the value of the product for the organisation and its clients. Product Owners determine 'what' is being developed. In order to retain the overview and make proper prioritisation possible, the Product Owner documents all required tasks in the Product Backlog. The Scrum Master is responsible for the process of continuous improvement, and coaches the team. The Development team is responsible for the development of the product. In Scrum terms, this is known as the 'done' increment. The Development team determines 'how' the development process should proceed.

Scrum team roles
Product Owner
Scrum Master
Development team

Scrum Events

There are five events intended to ensure that inspection and adaptation actually take place. These events are the Sprint, the Sprint planning, the Daily Scrum, the Sprint review, and the Sprint Retrospective. Each of these events has certain characteristics and a specific objective.

Sprint **The Sprint** is an established period (between 1 and 4 weeks) during which a certain amount of work is planned, implemented, and improved. During the Sprint, the Scrum team devotes all of its attention to the Sprint objective of that specific period.

Sprint Planning **The Sprint Planning** is a meeting during which the goal for the next sprint is determined. The Product Backlog (the total work overview) documents and prioritises the tasks to be completed. The work is divided into small components, which the team attempts to complete during the Sprint. The Product Owner is responsible for the prioritisation process.

Daily Scrum **The Daily Scrum**, also known as the Stand-Up, is a daily meeting during which the Scrum team discusses the work done the previous day. It is also used to assess the progress of the Sprint objective. A Daily Scrum takes no more than 15 minutes. A Scrum board is often used to visualise the work through the use of post-it notes. The post-its are moved from left to right over the course of the Sprint: from *to do* via *doing* to *done*. This helps to visually problem areas at a glance, and makes it easy to determine whether the team is still on track for reaching the Sprint objective.

Sprint Review **The Sprint Review** is a meeting between the Scrum team and other stakeholders at the end of the Sprint. The Scrum team presents the Sprint results and opens the floor for discussion, giving the stakeholders the opportunity to ask questions and offer input for upcoming sprints.

Sprint Retrospective **The Sprint Retrospective** is a meeting in which the team looks back on the work process and the quality of collaboration. The goal is to learn and come to improvement initiatives. Continuous improvement is an essential component of Scrum, and any potentially useful suggestions are immediately applied at the start of the next Sprint.

The Increment

Increment The full list of completed Backlog tasks, including the completed tasks from all previous Sprints, is known as the Increment. At all times, the Increment must meet the 'done' definition: it must meet all of the agreements set by the Scrum team. The Increment should be usable and continually advance until it reaches its final goal: a working end product.

Working according to Kanban

Kanban Kanban is less strict in terms of rules and agreements, and simpler than the Scrum framework. Kanban places particular emphasis on clearly establishing the status of the current assignment. This assignment, whether scheduled or not, is visualised just like in Scrum. Kanban does not define roles and does not work using Sprints. Therefore, Kanban is ideal for the implementation of line activities that benefit from not having too many different matters under development at the same time. It is important to remain focussed and to restrict the work in progress (Work in Process WIP Limit). The only subject of scrutiny and vigilance, in addition to visualisation and focus, is the lead time. Activities that take too long usually suffer from a bottleneck or other restricting factor.

ING fully dedicated to Agile working

O&M IN PRACTICE

ING is one of the Netherlands' leaders in the use of Agile working. Years ago, their IT department first implemented this approach, but these days a large part of the organisation is designed around the Agile principle. The first steps in this direction began with the introduction of the DevOps taskforce in the IT Internet Department. Developers (devs) and support and management (ops) are both involved in the same team, and work together actively.

DevOps introduced the concept of Scrum not too long ago: Sprints, Stand-Ups, team divisions with Scrum Masters, etcetera. Nowadays, business and IT have merged, allowing the various disciplines to work in teams according to the Spotify Model.

Source: https://www.globalorange.nl/3-kenmerkende-voorbeelden-van-agile-ontwikkeling-binnen-bedrijven, consulted 11 May 2018

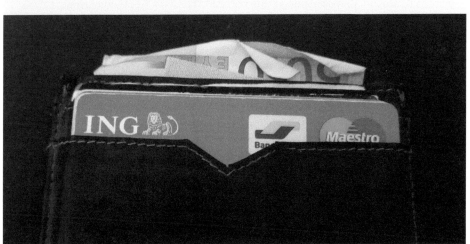

Agile work in large organisations

As stated, the Agile approach agile in larger organisations requires greater effort in terms of alignment and collaboration between more teams. The Scaled Agile Framework (SAFe) and Spotify model are methods more befitting those requirements. At their core, these methods both use Scrum or Kanban at the team level, and both methods mainly attempt to solve issues involving scalability, fine-tuning across multiple autonomous teams, and alignment with the operational organisation.

Management determines operational direction, while focussing on maximising customer value, and should approach the self-guiding teams from a facilitating perspective.

Scaled Agile Framework (Safe)

A SAFe team is autonomous where the production of software is concerned. Various teams (using either Scrum or Kanban) together create what SAFe terms a Release Train: a project or program that is a combination of elements which, when put together, have added value and lead to project results. The Release Trains should be properly integrated using various teams and, in addition, be properly aligned with the existing operational organisation.

A Release Train consists of 50-125 individuals distributed across teams. As with a real train, a Release Train operates according to a timetable. The organisation is free to set its own departure and arrival times, in the form of a mutually agreed upon

Scaled Agile Framework

recurring deadline for the release of a Program Increment, for example monthly, quarterly, or biannually.

SAFe prefers that people work on the realisation of the Project Increments fulltime and fully focussed, paying no mind to their individual role in the organisation. At the highest organisational level, the portfolio level, the focus is on value chains and the totality of Program Increments.

The Spotify organisational model

Spotify organisational model

Originally Swedish music and video streaming service Spotify saw an evolution in their use of various Agile methods into an organisational model that has come to be known as the Spotify Model. Since its foundation in 2006, Spotify has grown into a service provider catering to 140 active users per month, who have access to around 30 million songs. The company has over 1,600 employees and saw a turnover of 2.18 billion dollars in 2015. Little wonder, then, that so many organisations, including ING Bank, have copied and adopted Spotify's organisational model.

The Spotify model explained

The Spotify organisational model encompasses the following components: Squads, Tribes, Chapters and Guilds.

Squads
a **Squads** are autonomous teams (comparable to Scrum Teams) that are each responsible for small portions of the total end product. Each squad has a mission and a product owner.

Tribes
b Multiple squads working on the same product form a **Tribe** with a Tribe Leader.

Chapters
c Different **Chapters** exist within each Tribe. Chapters are discussions between employees from different Squads with the same expertise

Guilds
d **Guilds** are groups of people with different expertise from different Tribes exchanging knowledge together.

On the one hand, the strength of the Spotify model is that it groups employees with various expertise together (in Squads) to work fully autonomously and produce a product or service; on the other hand, it enables a group of employees with similar expertise (in Chapters and Guilds) to exchange knowledge and experience to further develop their expertise (see Figure 11.37).

FIGURE 11.37 **REPRESENTATION OF THE INTERACTION BETWEEN THE DIFFERENT COMPONENTS OF THE SPOTIFY MODEL (KNIBERG EN IVARSON, 2012)**

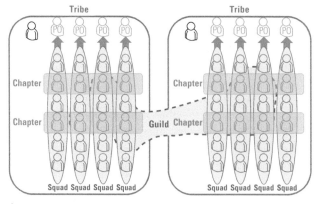

Source: https://agilescrumgroup.nl/spotify-model

Structure and organisation
PART C

© Noordhoff Uitgevers bv

11.6.2 Horizontal organisation

Economic and social developments, like globalisation, the rise of information technology, the increase in individualisation, and the failure of the financial system, have had a great deal of influence on humanity's approach to organisation. Vertical notions of organisations shifted to horizontal ones. The horizontal organisation was introduced. A horizontal organisation focusses on horizontal, or process-oriented, collaboration instead of on the more traditional vertical hierarchical working methods.

Cause

In their book *Horizontaal organiseren* (Horizontal Organisation), Bakker and Hardjono (2013) delve deeper into the cause behind this revolution. The authors describe the effects of up-scaling, the centralisation of power, concentration, synchronisations, specialisation, and standardisation, as these notions were frequently applied in the last century.

Horizontal organisation

Company up-scaling, for example through mergers or take-overs, was hardly always successful. The resulting organisation sometimes grew unwieldy due to their size, or were unable to achieve the expected growth in turnover. Despite their capability for mass production, they were not always more efficient.

The centralisation of power may have been a common occurrence in the twentieth century, but did not always lead to desired employee behaviour. It sometimes led to a stand-offish, calculating approach. Employees had little to say in matters, and differences of opinion were not much appreciated. There was hardly any attention for individuals. Using our current benchmarks, this approach would no longer cut it. Concentration, that is to say combining all aspects of one type of activity into one location, led to substantial environmental issues, as well as large-scale outbreaks of animal and plant diseases.

The current 24-hour economy no longer meshes with last century's method of synchronisation: working fixed hours at identical pace. These days, it is not uncommon to be able to work, email, send texts, or tweet at any time of day. Specialisation and standardisation are now defunct as a result of the speed with which information technology evolves. Today's specialists may have become superfluous by tomorrow. Their job may simply become outdated following the implementation of robotics. To that end, it is important that employees are agile and are able to adapt if their job changes or disappears.

Bakker and Hardjono list a number of other organisational principles that are under pressure: money, information advantage-based management, vertical organisation, and organisational right of existence.

Money is no longer the only driving force. Many other matters have become relevant, such as human attention, pollution, and sustainability. Managers no longer always have a monopoly on information, since that is now always and readily available, spreads at lightning speed, and offers transparency. Vertical organisation no longer meshes with these changes, nor with the increasingly professionalised of employees who have become emancipated, self-asserting individuals. Individualisation and increased human attention have led to a centralisation based on the employee instead of the shareholder or client. The organisation's right of existence in the previous century existed by the grace of the existing selling market. All marketing focussed on that aspect. Nowadays, organisations have become aware of employee well-being, with some organisations assigning a Chief Happiness Officer, tasked with improving employee happiness.

Chief Happiness Officer

Bakker and Hardjono define horizontal organisation as follows: The (re)designing of an organisation in such a way as to ensure that optimum design and collaboration mean that clients are swiftly provided with quality products and services using responsible resource allocation.

The scale at which organisations are implementing horizontal organisation or process-oriented collaboration is increasing.

Paradigm shift

Bakker and Hardjono (2013) argue that the change from vertical to horizontal may be called a paradigm shift. The term paradigm shift is meant to indicate the emergence of a new reality, with old theoretical notions abandoned in favour of new theories.

Thoughts about the nature of collaboration and the role and meaning of leadership have changed. Power has become influence, with influence being gained by conveying a vision, being an example, serving as a source of inspiration for meaning. This influence has to ensure that the leader becomes a facilitator with regard to obtaining resources (money, materials, information). In order to collaborate, mutual trust is essential. Table 11.3 expresses the paradigm shift in the form of buzzwords.

TABLE 11.3 **PARADIGM SHIFT EXPRESSED IN BUZZWORDS**

Vertical	Horizontal
Power, hierarchy	Added value, influence
To have	To be
Instructions from above, assignments going down	Input from the left, output to the right
Us and them	Collaboration
Order	Negotiation
Who is the boss of whom?	Who works with whom?
The boss is responsible	I am responsible
I am looked after	I participate
Inequality	Equality
A function is an organisational entity	A function is a network hub
Position	Transaction
Polarisation	Connection
Compartmentalise	Decompartmentalise
Single-stakeholder approach	Multi-stakeholder approach
Compartments, silos	Chains, flows
Boxes	Links
Rendered	Sustainable
Departments are groups of people implementing strategy	Processes are the verbs that operationalise strategy
Process management is required: process must be described, craftsmanship must be documented, and then the assignment must be completed	Process management is required: interaction between professionals must be defined to facilitate collaboration
Growth = ascend along the organisation, direct more people	Growth = ascend in professionalism
Management control = hierarchy, reporting lines, costs/returns, directives, obedience, function, control, departmental interests, budget realisation, yield	Dominant principles in management control: working process, interface, added value, collaboration, chain, audits, internal client-supplier relationship, flow, lead time, performance indications, continuous improvement

Source: Bakker en Hardjono, *Horizontaal organiseren* (2013), Chapter 2 p. 75

Building a new organisation

Changing an organisation from vertical to horizontal means changing much. The old structure has to be abandoned; a new organisation has to be established.

Establishing a horizontal organisation starts with de-verticalisation. Organisational layers disappear, and differences in power between the various layer dwindle. This has serious consequences for employees. On the one hand, it may lead to fear, de-integration, and a feeling of loss of direction. Hierarchically-sensitive employees may have difficulty finding their place in an organisation that expects more openness and places more responsibility on the individual. On the other hand, managers may fear the resulting loss of power, which may come with a sense of loss of status, salary, and possibilities for promotion. As a result, the change process may be slowed down or hindered. It is therefore that the new organisational form offers adequate security, direction, and integration.

De-verticalisation

The change from a vertical to a horizontal organisation means a cultural turning point.
To steer the organisation along this turning point, an organisation needs a vision, one that is recognisable and understandable for employees (Bakker and Hardjono, 2013). Employees must believe in the vision and have to want to contribute to the organisation. It is important to place responsibility at a lower point down the organisational ladders, since this will achieve the desired effect of offering greater employee autonomy and engendering in them a greater feeling of responsibility for their work. Decisions are made at lower levels of the organisation. Employees become less dependent on their managers.

Cultural turning point

Principles of horizontal organisation

Alkemade (2012) described the 5 principles of horizontal organisation:
1 There is a common goal to which everyone *wants* to contribute instead of *has* to contribute;
2 Employees do not depend on central management, but are buoyed by their own initiative;
3 Management and implementation of a required activity lie with the same party;
4 There is mainly horizontal collaboration, including the associated mutual alignment and discussion, instead of vertical direction;
5 Every member of the organisation contributes to the success, and restricting oneself to freeloading or criticising is not acceptable.

Principles of horizontal organisation

Advantages of process management
a **Improved effectiveness and efficiency**: every process centres on customer results. The organisation strives for an optimised implementation of people and resources, and thus for an effective and efficient approach. Employee contributions must add value for customers.
b **Improved transferability**: uniform documentation means processes are more easily transferable. Know-how can be transferred quickly and easily, for example to new employees.
c **Improved controllability**: By aiming for established standards, the organisation becomes easier to manage. Results are fixed. Employees can set to work on their own terms as long as they work and perform within the standards. This improves self-management.
d **Improved learning capacity**: By charting processes together, employees form a basis for improvement. Best practices are defined. It teaches people to

look beyond their own desk, and helps to locate bottlenecks in processes and collaborations between departments. Because processes are repeating and the measurement results continually improve or deteriorate, the organisation automatically learns more about its own actions.

The horizontal structure

Horizontal structure
Collection of processes
Collection of departments

The process-oriented approach is based on the organisation of a collection of processes instead of a collection of departments, people, or product-market combinations. The task of horizontal organisation, therefore, is to construct processes in such a way as to ensure quality operational performance (Bakker en Hordjano, 2013). Bakker and Hordjano define a process as a sequence of activities characterised by input, transformation, and output. The activities are linked and add value to the product for the sake of the client. In its most basic form, a process can be described as follows (see Figure 11.37).

FIGURE 11.38 **BASIC FORM OF A PROCESS**

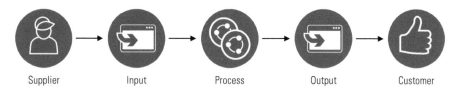

| Supplier | Input | Process | Output | Customer |

Combining horizontal and vertical structure

In practice, horizontal and vertical structure can coexist well in an organisation; indeed, the combination is a necessity. Designing organisational units, such as staff and function structure, is not covered by the processes. On the other hand, the organisational structure does not offer an integral insight into the activities, people, and means needed to achieve certain results. Both structures are required and, importantly, should be designed as a single structure (see Figure 11.39).

FIGURE 11.39 **HORIZONTAL AND VERTICAL ORGANISATION**

Vertical organisation

Vertical organisation
- 'Rake'
- Hierarchy rules
- Static
- Management layers
- Do your job
- Work within departmenal borders

Organisational structure

Supplier

Client

Process structure

Horizontal organisation

Horizontal organisation
- Process flows
- Process rules
- Dynamic
- Flat organisation
- Achieve results
- Multidisciplinary team

Source: 123management.nl/0/020_structuur; Nieuwenhuis, M.A., *The Art of Management* (the-art.nl), 2003-2010

Process thinking has a large number of advantages over traditional organisational thinking. By thinking only in terms of organisational structure, the 'Rake' and hierarchy dominate. The organisation is compartmentalised, with employees focussing only on tasks instead of end results or client interests. Work is confined to the space between the department's walls, and problems are often addressed from above, instead of directly confronting a colleague at another department. Process thinking breaks with compartmentalisation. Thinking in terms of client results leads to horizontal organisation. The client determines the desired results and the process is designed and directed on the basis of those results. The resulting structure is much more dynamic, the organisation much flatter. Supervisors become process owners who systematically direct process design and results. Departmental boundaries fade; if the process calls for it, employees are assigned to multidisciplinary teams.

Process thinking

Example of the process-oriented approach: a bakery

O&M IN PRACTICE

FIGURE **PROCESS-ORIENTED APPROACH**

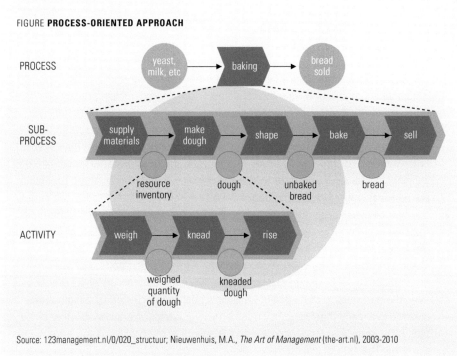

Source: 123management.nl/0/020_structuur; Nieuwenhuis, M.A., *The Art of Management* (the-art.nl), 2003-2010

11.6.3   Holacracy

Holacracy is a new organisational model, used as a way of both organising and governing. Holacracy is not based on the traditional top-down decision-making approach common to organising, but instead distributes authority (and responsibility) across all employees in the organisation. This results in a flat organisational structure in the form of teams or circles. The teams or circles are self-regulating on the one hand, but also part of a larger whole on the other, making them dependent on each other. Employees all have their own role or roles, their responsibilities are clearly delineated. Employees are the managers of the role

Holacracy

or roles they have been assigned. Holacracy leads to a new approach to division of labour, decision-making, and hierarchy in organisation. In Holacracy, decisions are made by whichever employee or employees are doing or are closely involved with the work. Employees can develop leadership within the context of their role. Holacracy makes the most and best possible use of the knowledge and creativity of employees. Unlike Lean Six Sigma, horizontal organisation, or agile organisation, is fully internally focussed. The end-user or client plays no part in Holacracy.

Holacracy was developed by Brian Robertson in 2007. He first described this system in his book 'Holacracy: The New Management System for a Rapidly Changing World'. Brian Robertson developed the system through his experiments with new (more democratic) forms of organisational governance in organisations. In 2010, Brian Robertson described the foundations of the Holacracy concept in a so-called 'Holacracy Constitution'.

Holarchy | The term Holacracy derives from holarchy: self-organised employees leading to a (collective) development of knowledge and creativity. As employees are awarded a high degree of responsibility, the resulting situation is one with a much more dynamic structure, which can rapidly respond to internal and external developments – much better than an organisation using the traditional top-down setting. In the traditional setting, decision-making simply takes more time because it involves more organisational layers.

Stakeholder-theory is reminiscent of Holacracy in many ways. Both stakeholder-theory and Holacracy are based on shared interests that need to be in balance.

Holacracy constitution | The 'Holacracy constitution' lists four principles (known as 'articles' in the terminology of the constitution) which comprise Holacracy.

Energising roles | 1 **Energising roles**: Holacracy's organisational structure is not based on tasks and/or functions, but on roles. An employee can have one or more roles in an organisation. From the perspective of their role, the employee performs various activities, for example in order to achieve certain results. A role, therefore, is not the same as a function. A function is based on a defined set of tasks and largely fixed processes. A role means the responsibility of achieving a particular result rests with the employees. The path to that result can largely be determined by the employee. In other words, there is a lot riding on employee initiative.

Circle structure | 2 **Circle structure**: In the context of Holacracy, a role is a component of self-organising circles. Each circle develops, implements, and measures its processes from the perspective of its goal(s). A circle's goal is determined by a higher-level circle. This means that Holacracy does employ a form of hierarchy. Another circle task is the organisation of change and the selection of employees to perform the roles. The task of linking the circles to each other is performed by a specially

Link | designed role, the so-called 'link'. 'Links' are part of multiple circles and, as such, ensure the common implementation of the entire organisation's established mission, vision, and objective (known as its 'purpose' in Holacracy). Visualisation of the content of the roles is often done using digital tools as well as physical 'role boards'. The largest circle is the organisation as a whole. Within this main circle, there are various sub-circles which, potentially, hold sub-sub-circles. In addition to its business activities, each circle accommodates four fixed roles. These roles are intended to ensure the organisation works as effectively and as efficiently as possible. They are:

Lead link | a **the 'lead link'**: has the authority to assign roles to other employees, or dismiss them from a role. In addition to being a circle member, a lead link is also part of a circle one level up. In traditional organisation, this would be a role assigned to a manager. In Holacracy, it is not.

b **the 'facilitator'**: an organisational role. Many discussions take place in Holacracy, and a facilitator heads these discussions according to fixed schedules and rules. On the one hand, Holacracy offers employees great freedom; on the other, there are many boundaries defining that freedom.

Facilitator

c **the 'rep link'**: a governance–process related function (discussed below). Tensions between employees are a critical part of this process, and the rep link may, where required, join the lead link in ensure that a certain issue is given attention by or is escalated to a higher-level circle.

Rep link

d **the 'secretary'**: a role tasked with documentation and registration of various discussions.

Secretary

3 **Governance process**: In order to develop its roles and policies, each circle uses a structured governance-process. This governance-process consist of carefully formulated rules, and results in integrative decision-making in each circle. Each employee is involved in this integrative decision-making and is free to submit changes or objections. Holacracy decision-making is not consensus-based, but seeks to take all relevant employee input under consideration. This is not the same as the democratic principle of decision-making, which is: one employee, one vote. Decision making in Holacracy is based on the principle that none of those present should have prevailing objections to a particular decision. Objections must be reasonably substantiated. This principle is known as the principle of consent, which is to say 'acceptance'.

Governance-process

Consent does not require consensus of decision-making. It does mean that there should be no parties 'against'. Another important phenomenon in Holacracy are the so-called 'tensions'. These are the driving force behind the adjustments to internal and external developments. There exist various collisions and conflicts between the roles and responsibilities of employees. It is particularly important, especially for a Holacracy, that any tensions that are discussed are explicated. Solutions to these tensions are developed within the circles in which they occur. Solutions may mean that roles are redefined and/or that other agreements are made. A Holacracy thrives on mutual approachability with the goal of improved collaboration. In that sense, Holacracy is comparable to Agile organisation: both systems aim to rapidly adjust activities and processes to changing circumstances, making the organisation more flexible. Two forms of discussion existing in Holacracy: the governance meeting and the tactical meeting. A central topic of both forms of discussion is the aforementioned concept of tension.

a **Governance meeting**: employee tensions resulting from the implementation of one or more roles are discussed. The idea is for all employees to be allowed to submit their feelings based on the tensions they experience. Tensions in governance meetings may involve formulated goals and strategy roles, and responsibilities.

Governance meeting

b **Tactical meeting**: this intends to offer a platform for the discussion of the substantive aspects of the work, meaning operational matters.

Tactical meeting

4 **Operational process**: In Holacracy, the necessary processes are defined and aligned within the different circles. Tasks are assigned to team members based on these definitions. The employees, in turn, are responsible for the most effective and efficient implementation of these tasks not only with regard to their own role, but also with regard to the objectives set by the circle as a whole. The differences between the traditional organisational approach and Holacracy are best illustrated using the following schematic (see Figure 11.40).

FIGURE 11.40 **HOLACRACY VERSUS HIERARCHY**

HOLACRACY VS. HIERARCHY

Holacracy takes powers traditionally reserved for executives and managers and spreads them across all employees.

In a traditional hierarchy, layers of management establish how products are approved and monitored.

SUPER-CIRCLE
One that contains Sub-circles. This could be Marketing.

CEO

UPPER MANAGEMENT

MIDDLE MANAGEMENT

SUPERVISORS

STAFF

ROLE
A task related to a function. This could be social Media producer.

SUB-CIRCLE
Each is dedicated to a function. This could be Digital Advertising.

Source: Van Linn, 6 May 2016; www.scrumcompany.nl/holacracy-wablief, consulted 14 May 2018

O&M IN PRACTICE

How to move your organisation towards Holacracy in baby-steps:

1   Restrict meetings to a platform for making announcements and establishing progress instead of for discussion.
2   Slowly create a structure in which employees are given greater responsibility to see how they cope.
3   Be open to all sorts of matters in your task as employer. Try to join the debate about other issues instead of sticking to what you know.

4   Be an accessible and transparent boss, approach your employees with social equality.
5   Look for warning signs from the perspectives of both manager and employee. In case of tensions, keep your ship adrift by acting immediately – open tensions up for discussion.

Source: Gerald Essers, *Wat is Holacracy en wat kan je ermee*, 29 April 2014, https://timemanagement.nl/wat-is-Holacracy, consulted 14 May 2018

One organisation that has been applying Holacracy in its organisation for a long time (since 2013), is online US shoes and clothing store Zappos (part of Amazon. com). Dutch examples are telecom-provider Voys and educational institute Springest. The municipality of Venlo has also embraced Holacracy. Organisations that apply Holacracy are often smaller companies. One discernible trend is that more and more organisations are applying (elements of) Holacracy in their organisation.

In conclusion, the differences between traditional top-down methods and Holacracy can be summarised as follows (see Figure 11.41).

FIGURE 11.41 **DIFFERENCE BETWEEN TRADITIONAL TOP-DOWN METHODS AND HOLACRACY**

Without Holacracy **FROM...**	With Holacracy **TO...**
Central direction	Distributed authority
Long-term predictions and plans where possible	Dynamic direction: everything is changeable at any time
Hierarchic, pyramid structure OR flat, consensus-based	Neither: everyone is 'pack leader' in their own role – and 'follower' of other roles Core objective-oriented
Interests-oriented	Core objective-oriented
Tension as a problem	Tension as fuel
Reorganisation and change management	Natural development and movement
Function descriptions	Dynamic roles
Heroic leaders, employees, and process consultants	Vital individuals fulfilling their roles
Organising people	Organising work
Instrumental use of human relations to further organisational objectives	Clear separation of people, relationships, roles, and organisation

Source: *Hoe organiseer je Holacracy? Holacracy vraagt om discipline*, Jasper Rienstra, Koen Bunders en Arjen Bos; www.managementsite.nl/hoe-organiseer-inspiratie-holacracy, consulted 18 May 2018

11.6.4   Other organisational structure trends

Network organisations

Nowadays, many organisations and/or individuals work together as part of a network. Mutual collaboration allows many different organisations and/or individuals to make use of each other's strengths, creating added value for their common client circles. A network organisation can be described as a collaborative effort between mutually interdependent, autonomous organisations and/or individuals who collaborate to realise goals that the individual organisations and/or individuals would not be able to achieve.

Characteristic of a network organisation is that its added value cannot be realised without the network. This is the reason the network members are described as being interdependent. The added value may differ per network, with some aiming for mutual product development or development of expertise. The advantage of a network organisation is that collaboration is a way of reducing individual risk.

Network organisation

The emergence of network organisation has been greatly influenced by the globalisation of the world's economy and the possibilities presented by information technology. This means that a network organisation shares some of its characteristics with the virtual organisation; the most notable exception being that a network organisation does not require virtual collaboration.

Modular organisation

A network organisation is also known as a modular organisation, particularly if the network operates in the production industry. Network organisation in the production industry is characterised by the fact that the participating organisations are each responsible for part (or a module) of the product.

A network organisation requires a party that ensures the various organisations and/or individuals collaborate along the established agreements, and that they stay focussed on the established objectives. This brings us to the second point. Whereas a classical organisation operates based on a hierarchical relationship between employees, the participating organisations in a network organisation are each other's

O&M IN PRACTICE

The Core: Nobody is smarter than everybody else

In their book *UNBOSS*, Lars Kolind and Jacob Botter takes us on a trip through time to the age of Taylor, at the height of the hierarchical organisation's effectiveness: a highly structured division of labour in an effective and stable environment. But times have changed, and our modern culture requires a fundamentally different approach. Nevertheless, many existing companies are still founded on the conventional notions from Taylor's time. The authors illustrate the entire process of the traditional classification of activities and how this

process may be changed, demonstrating that the traditional division into departments should be revisited to improve its dwindling effectiveness. But they also show use that the boundaries between client, partner, supplier, and employee are slowly starting to fade: clients can become your best salesman while simultaneously working on your R&D. These changes offer both a great deal of confusion and a great deal of new opportunity.

Source: https://www.nieuworganiseren.nu/toolbox/unboss, consulted 11 May 2018

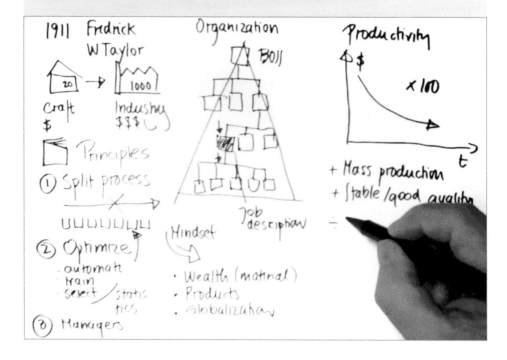

equals in a horizontal relationship. Collaboration therefore hinges on trust. This prerequisite for trust opposes the notion that the collaborating parties should view each other as competitors. To that end, a properly functioning network organisation can only exist and continue to operate if this balance of equality is maintained and closely monitored. The added value of the collaboration must, therefore, be made explicit. Network organisations are also discussed in Section 2.6.1.

Compared to the more traditional organisational forms, the advantages of network organisations are in (Pullens, 2018):
a a wider market reach resulting from access to clients via collaborating partners;
b reinforcement or innovation of the business propositions to the client via the availability of multiple products and services;
c reinforcement of the specific positions of the collaborating partners;
d retention of autonomy for the partners;
e retention of the ability to adjust to changes in circumstances;
f relatively low investments;
g accelerated innovations;
h accelerated return-on-investments;
i lower risks.

Cluster organisations with teams

Organisations are increasingly making use of employees with a broad spectrum of knowledge, skills, and experience. All organisational forms frequently place people together in teams. There are various distinct types of teams, such as project teams, quality teams, and cross-functional teams. Professional specialists can be part of more than one team. A team is dissolved as soon as its intended result is met.

An organisational form that focusses on team structure is known as the cluster organisation (see Figure 11.42). According to management thinker Peter Drucker (see the Introduction for more information) most organisations will be structured around teams in future.

Cluster organisation

FIGURE 11.42 **CLUSTER ORGANISATION**

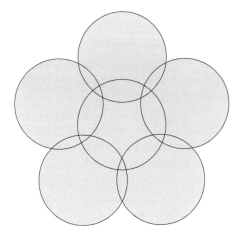

Virtual organisations

Until the Industrial Revolution, employees worked from home, in the employ of entrepreneurs. The Industrial Revolution moved work from the home to the great factories, and later to the modern office.

The rise of the internet and other technologies has enabled people to communicate, discuss, learn, and exchange information without necessarily having to be in the same physical location (e.g. an office). Examples of these enabling technologies are email, text messaging, WhatsApp, voicemail, and virtual internet meeting rooms.

As a result, companies no longer rely on a specific main location for their employees to perform the activities their jobs require. Companies can employ people from all over the world, fromy workers in a company's employ to autonomous individuals and/or companies entering into a strategic collaboration with the company to develop and/or sell new products/services together.

Virtual organisation   In this context, the most frequently encountered term is the 'virtual organisation', sometimes known as the 'borderless enterprise' (see Figure 11.43).

FIGURE 11.43 **VIRTUAL ORGANISATION**

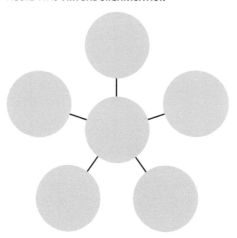

This organisational structure can result in cost reductions, as it eliminates the need to develop and maintain a complex, international organisational structure. Many people in these types of organisations do not necessarily need to be under contract, but can be connected to the virtual organisation on a project basis.

Virtual work   Looking at the past ten years of virtual work, there are three distinct wave forms of priority. Each wave form slightly readjusts the emphasis on employee and employer interests. New technological developments have also enabled new forms of communication and collaboration. The wave forms can be summarised as follows (based on Holland/ Belgium Management Review, 149/2013):

a **The first wave: virtual freelancers**. In the 1980s and early 1990s, numerous email networks were developed. This presented the public with the opportunity to work on a freelance basis. Technological developments meant employees could become independent contractors offering their services to organisations; some would even continue to work for the same employer. For a freelance agent, this was the ideal way of restoring and retaining their work/life balance. Employers were able to assign people to particular activities with greater flexibility.

b **The second wave: virtual entrepreneurial colleagues**. The first wave had its downsides. Freelance workers had little to no commitment to the organisations for which they worked, and had to sort out many administrative details themselves. Employees, on the other hand, had lost their grip on a large number of 'their' people. Both parties felt the need for improved commitment and structure. Why not remain in the service of an organisation while improving flexibility at home or at work? This development gave rise to time and location independent work.

c **The third wave**: **virtual network colleagues**. Time and location independent work developed into a huge success, and many organisations introduced this working method. However, the principle held one major disadvantage: many employees performed their work on a very individualistic basis, lacking some degree of togetherness and teamwork – a loss experienced not only by the employees themselves, but by their employers as well. The proper implementation of certain activities requires some level of teamwork. This development led to employers designing common work spaces for their employees, both at the national and the international level. This situation allows people to improve their balance between individual work and teamwork.

11.7 COMMUNICATION AND CONSULTATION STRUCTURES

The greater the complexity of an organisational structure, the greater the necessity for coordination between people, departments, divisions and locations in order to ensure that the organisation works effectively and efficiently. Managers have at their disposal six different integration tools that may contribute to the improvement of coordination and communication (see Figure 11.44).

FIGURE 11.44 **TYPES AND EXAMPLES OF INTEGRATION MECHANISMS**

Simple

Direct contact A marketing manager and a research & development manager meet to 'brainstorm' about new product development.

Liaison role A manager and a project manager identify the best product ideas to develop.

Task forces Various staff from Marketing, Research & Development and Production meet to talk about releasing a product on to the market.

Crossfunctional group A cross-functional group derived from various divisions is formed to supervise the product development process until the moment of product release.

Integration roles and divisions Senior management provides staff from cross-functional groups with important information from other groups and divisions.

Matrix structures Senior managers decide to adopt a matrix structure to ensure that a lot of new products can be developed simultaneously.

Complex

Designing a communication and consultative structure is one of the necessary aspects of creating an organisational structure. After all, company activities must be linked to each other. It is very easy for coherence to become lost during the division of tasks, as some activities may be split and transferred to employees in various different departments. Coherence can be restored by providing a good communication and consultative structure.

Communication and consultative structure

A communication and consultative structure can be thought of as a coordination facility which needs to be built into every organisation. Communication can be defined as all those activities through which information is transferred to other people: the exchange of data, facts, thoughts, and feelings. This description contains two essential aspects:

Coordination facility
Communication

1 The flow of information throughout the organisation;
2 The interaction and cooperation between people.

These two core aspects need to remain in balance. After all, if information is not flowing smoothly, this has consequences for cooperation within the organisation – and vice versa.

Communication is a process (see Figure 11.45) in which a 'sender' transmits a message to a 'receiver'. This receiver interprets the message and sends a reaction to the sender, thereby enabling the sender to check whether the message sent has been understood correctly and that there have been no misunderstandings during the transmission.

FIGURE 11.45 **THE COMMUNICATION PROCESS**

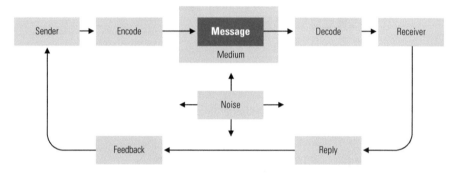

Personal communication
Impersonal communication

Within an organisation, communication can take place in two ways: via personal communication between two or more people, or via impersonal communication using communicative means like memos, e-mail and staff magazines. Personal information is, in general, the more effective, because of the possibility of obtaining direct feedback. Impersonal information has the advantage that the receiver can decide when to take in the information themself. The disadvantage is lack of certainty about the quality of reception: will the message be understood? Will it even be read?

Communication structure

A communication structure can be described in terms of the way and the direction in which the communication takes place. Communication can be either written or oral in nature, and follow one of three directions:

Horizontal communication
a **Horizontal communication**. This includes communication between divisions, departments or even individuals at the same hierarchical level of the organisation.

Vertical communication
b **Vertical communication**. In contrast, this is communication between divisions, departments, or individuals at different hierarchical levels.

Lateral communication
c **Lateral communication**. This refers to relatively open communication that takes place between all individuals within the organisation, irrespective of hierarchical level.

Communication matrix
A communication matrix is a good way of ensuring that everybody is kept sufficiently informed. Use of such a tool ensure that no group is overlooked, that the best means of communication is used, that the messages are spread out, and that timing for optimum effect is determined. Table 11.4 shows an example of such a communication matrix.

TABLE 11.4 **COMMUNICATION MATRIX**

Target groups	Means of communication	Senders	Planning
Internal 1 Department heads	1.1 Staff meeting	1.1 General manager	1.1 Initial
2 Initiative takers	2.1 Extraordinary meetings	2.1 Project manager	2.1 Same day as department heads
3 Staff	3.1 General staff meeting	3.1 General manager	3.1 Day after department heads
	3.2 Speech on notice boards	3.2 Human resources posts	3.2 Right after the meeting
	3.3 Discussion of work progress	3.3 Department heads	3.3 Within two weeks of the meeting
	3.4 Interview in staff magazine	3.4 Project manager and two executives	3.4 Within a month of the meeting
4 Works council	4.1 Extraordinary works council meeting	4.1 General manager	4.1 On the same day as department heads
External 5 Shareholders	5.1 Extraordinary shareholders meeting	5.1 General manager	5.1 The week preceding the department heads
6 Customers	6.1 Informing big clients verbally	6.1 Head of sales/account managers	6.1 Within two weeks of the staff meeting
	6.2 Informing small clients in writing	6.2 Inside service sales	6.2 Right after the staff meeting
7 Suppliers	7.1 Informing regular suppliers verbally	7.1 Buyers	7.1 Within two weeks of the staff meeting
	7.2 Informing remaining suppliers in writing	7.2 Purchase	7.2 Right after the staff meeting

Source: *Kwaliteit in bedrijf,* May 2001

Communication between staff in different departments or divisions and on different hierarchical levels of an organisation can take place via a suitable consultative body, such as a consultative group or committee. These consultative bodies can be set up within the organisation on either a temporary or a permanent basis.

Consultative body

The so-called 'linking pin' structure (Figure 11.46), developed by Rensis Likert, depicts less standard consultative situations.

'Linking pin' structure

FIGURE 11.46 **EXAMPLES OF LIKERT'S LINKING PIN-STRUCTURE**

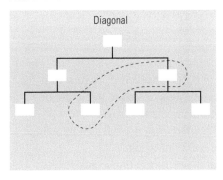
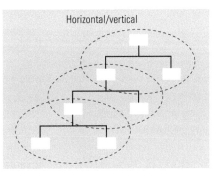

Likert described an organisational structure which features overlapping groups. The linking pin is the leader of a lower-level group. This person participates and can influence decision-making in a higher level group. The link may be horizontal, vertical, or diagonal. Likert also argued that workers would be more motivated if they participated as members of consultative groups rather than as individuals. Such a form of participation could deliver deliver better results for the organisation. Organisations are in a constant state of development. In the next chapter, this issue is reexamined.

Overlapping groups

Summary

▶ Structuring refers to the issue of designing an organisational structure that aligns people and resources to the organisation's intended objectives.

▶ Designing an organisational structure involves both organic and personal structure.

▶ Designing an organisational framework is an issue of both division and coordination of labour.

▶ Division of labour: dividing the activities into subtasks that are assigned to individual or other cooperative units in an organisation. There are a vertical and a horizontal dimension to division of labour.

▶ Vertical division of labour (vertical differentiation): tasks are grouped in terms of similarity of level. This vertical differentiation is determined by four motives (costs, managerial, societal, and social).

▶ Horizontal division of labour aligning different activities to each other. Initially, related tasks are assigned to the functions of individuals (functionalisation). Then, these individual functions are further assigned into departments (departmentalisation).

▶ With regard to functionalisation, there are two main forms:
  - internal differentiation: grouping similar activities;
  - interne specialisation: grouping activities based on product, market, or geographical layout.

▶ Distributing tasks across persons or departments creates functions.

▶ Decision-making power can be centralised (little delegation) or decentralised (much delegation).

▶ The number of subordinates under each supervising manager (scope of control) has a horizontal and a vertical dimension (span width and span depth respectively).

▶ In a situation where a supervisor has to manage too many subordinates, the solution may be found in delegating tasks; installing an assistant-manager or personal assistant, or activating other bodies.

▶ Organisational schedule (organigram): a simplified, schematic representation of the formal distribution of tasks across persons and/or departments as well as their relationships of authority.

▶ Informal organisation: any division of labour or relationships not part of the formal organisation.

▶ The following organisational systems display characteristics whose nature is either more or less mechanistic or organic:
  - line organisation;
  - line staff organisation;
  - line and functional staff organisation;
  - line staff committee organisation;
  - matrix organisation;
  - line project organisation.

▶ An internal project organisation can be designed according to the:
  - steering/working group model;
  - program model;
  - phase model.

▶ A divisional or business-unit organisation assigns the business activities related to a number of associated products/markets to a division or business unit, which may behave as autonomous entities within a larger whole.
Advantage of the divisional organisation: combining the advantages of a small organisation with those of a large one.

▶ According to Mintzberg, organisational structure is established by aligning a number of organisational characteristics, such as organisational sections, coordinating mechanisms, design parameters, and contingency (situational) factors.

- Mintzberg distinguishes the following organisational structures (configurations):
  1. entrepreneurial organisation;
  2. machine organisation;
  3. professional organisation;
  4. divisional organisation;
  5. innovative organisation;
  6. mission organisation;
  7. political organisation.

- The rapidly changing world is sometimes referred to as the VUCA world: Volatile, Uncertain, Complex, and Ambiguous. These issues need to be address by organisation through the VUCA-competences Vision, Understanding, Clarity, and Agility.

- An organisation working according to Agile, literally nimble and dextrous, principles has an easier time adjusting to the circumstances created by the VUCA world.

- The Agile Manifesto emphasises communal values over the strict adherence to a process or method. The manifest comprises four values: Individuals and Interaction over Processes and Tools, Working Software over Comprehensive Documentation, Customer Collaboration over Contract Negotiation, and Responding to Change over Following a Plan.

- Both an Agile project approach and Agile line organisation should be based on self-guiding teams that create value. Scrum and Kanban are relatively simple working methods suitable for smaller organisations. Applying the Agile method to larger organisations requires greater alignment and collaboration between more teams, which is made possible by the Scaled Agile Framework (SAFe) or the Spotify model, for example.

- Scrum is an approach for incremental product development. It is a value-driven approach that ensure both client and end-users are presented with the most valuable product that time and budget allow. Three pillars form the basis of Scrum: transparency, inspection, and adaptation.

- The Spotify organisational model encompasses the following components Squads, Tribes, Chapters, and Guilds.

- Horizontal organisation is the (re)designing of organisations to allow for an optimised design and collaboration to ensure that clients receive quality products/services in rapid time, while keeping use of materials reasonable.

- Establishing a horizontal organisation starts with de-verticalisation. Organisational layers disappear and differences in power dwindle. The change to a horizontal organisation also means a change in culture.

- Holacracy means self-organisation by employees, resulting in the development of (collective) knowledge and creativity. The high degree of responsibility assigned to employees creates a situation with a much more dynamic structure that allows for a much more rapid response to internal and external developments compared to a traditional top-down approach.

- The Holacracy Constitution lists the following principles (known as 'articles'): energising roles, circle structure, governance process, and operational process.

- Important trends in organisational structure are network organisations, cluster organisation with teams, and virtual organisations.

12
CULTURE

Contents

After studying this chapter:

- you will have been familiarised with the most important concepts related to organisational culture;
- you will have gained knowledge of and insight into various organisational culture typologies;
- you will have been informed of the various aspects that influence culture;
- you will have been informed of the purpose and mechanics of three important international cultural models.

Boatsters: Airbnb for boats

Three years ago, Boatsters started in Amsterdam as a kind of Airbnb for boats: Boatsters is an Amsterdam internet company that mediates between boat owners and boat renters. Nick Gelevert, himself from an actively boating family, set up the company with his partner Milhando in 2015; their first step was to immediately market themselves as an international undertaking.
Boatsters operates on the principle of the sharing economy, with boat owners earning money by renting out their boats to other enthusiasts. Boatsters charges a 15% commission per successful rental transaction. On average, a boat is docked 93% of the time, making it very interesting for boat owners to cover the costs of ownership by renting their craft to other boating fans. In order to sail a boat, both renter and boat have to be in compliance with sailing licence requirements.

The heart of the business is the Mediterranean area, although it is still possible to rent a boat to cruise through the canals of Amsterdam. Mallorca is the number one cast-off location for pleasure cruises in the Mediterranean. The majority of the team therefore relocated to

the island in order to more easily address the demand for deluxe yacht rentals. This places them at the heart of their target audience. Southern France, Croatia, and Greece are easily accessible from Mallorca. In addition to the Palma office, Boatsters has locations in Amsterdam (development and support) and Miami. The company also has a new Ibiza office in the works.

Boatsters is currently operational in 63 countries, managing over 12,000 boats. There is fierce competition in this market, however. The company is looking to distinguish itself by offering more than a rental platform. In addition to yacht rental, the company provides the exclusive Boatsters Black label, with personalised sailing routes and full-package trips. Deluxe yachts are also available via Boatsters Black. These yachts, ranging in length from 20 to 80 meters, often come with their own on-board crew, thus offering renters the experience of a hotel on the water. Boatsters obtained slightly under a million Euros from private investors in 2017.

Source: Telegraaf.nl, 26-04-2018, www.wikipedia.org, www.boatsters.com

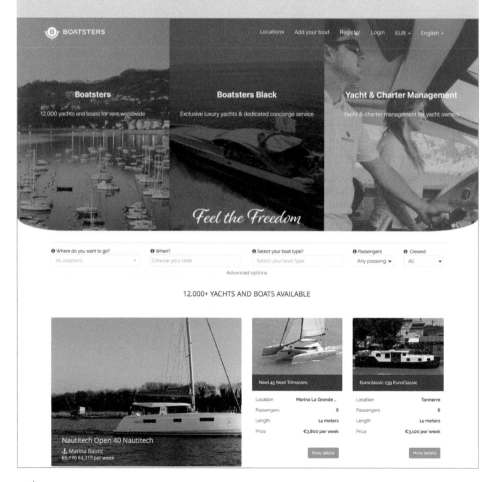

12.1 INTRODUCTION

Throughout one's life, one is faced with many different groups, including organisations. People live in a world of social connections and systems, and these groups and organisations are usually referred to in terms of cultural and behavioural elements. 'This organisation treated us very professionally' or 'They really listened to what we had to say' are both expression of the culture and behaviour that typify an organisation.

It is common knowledge that no two organisational cultures are exactly alike. Some are vastly different from others. Culture is best expressed through the behaviour employees demonstrate to the 'outside world'. To some extent, people are also influence by culture. Culture, after all, influences the way people live and think.

But what exactly is culture? The subject has been thoroughly explored in the literature.

Culture

The word culture originally derives from the word 'cultura', itself derived from 'colere'. 'Colere' means to farm, to process, to worship, and to maintain. The Romans used it in their phrase 'agri cultura': the tilling of the land. The word was only given its current connotations in the 18th century. Up until the early 1700s, it had always been used as a verb: *to give shape or purpose*; it was only towards the end of that century that the word 'culture' came into vogue as a noun: *civilisation*.

Hofstede & Hofstede's cultural onion

Various authors have covered the subject of culture. This chapter is based on the 'onion model', covered in the book 'Allemaal andersdenkenden, omgaan met cultuurverschillen' (*Different thinkers all, coping with cultural differences*) by Hofstede & Hofstede (2016). This book takes a broad approach to the concept of culture, in the sense that it is regarded from both a sociological and an anthropological perspective. Hofstede & Hofstede describe culture as 'the collective mental programming that distinguishes one group of people from another', a definition that applies to both organisations and countries alike.

Hofstede & Hofstede's cultural onion

This division is also used in the remaining chapter. Paragraphs 12.1 through to 12.3 address organisational culture, paragraph 12.4 covers international culture. The fact that Hofstede & Hofstede identify differences between groups in different organisations is due to the fact notions and ideas about work, others, the self, and the organisation differ from one organisation to the next. Much of what is understood to be culture is therefore a mental construct, making it difficult to quantify or comprehend. The result is a spectrum of notions and behaviours: a complex matter indeed.

Hofstede and Hofstede's cultural onion is similar to the regular onion in that a culture is comprised of a number of interrelated layers. Differences between culture can therefore occur in each of the layers as well as because of interaction between the layers. By defining the layers of the onion, it becomes possible to obtain a better insight into the concept of culture. The different layers are shown in Figure 12.1.

FIGURE 12.1 **THE DIFFERENT LAYERS OF CULTURE ('CULTURAL ONION')**

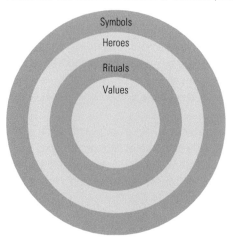

The four layers of the model are discussed below, working inwards from the outer layer.

Symbols

Symbols

The onion's outer layer is known as the layer of symbols. This is the most superficial layer of the onion model. Symbols are visible to all, in the form of gestures, logos, sense of humour, clothing, hairstyle, use of media, flags, or objects – whose underlying meaning is only understood by members of the culture.
The symbols of space, time, and language deserve particular attention.

Space

Space

Buildings speak volumes about organisational culture. The way in which space is put to use serves as an insight into the type of organisation and work processes concerned. Symbolic aspects of space include:
a a building's architecture and environment (location);
b the interior, with factors like accessibility, size, colour schemes, and office layout playing a role.

Time

Time

The way in which an organisation arranges time says much about the meaning of the function and nature of the work. Symbolic aspects of time include:
a a function's temporal boundaries (clear division between work/non-work or continuous service);
b the flexibility/rigidity of the timetable;
c the starting hours.

Sequential Perception of time

An example of temporal symbolism is the difference between a *sequential* or *synchronous perception of time*. A person's perception of time is sequential if time governs their life: Time is seen as a kind of finite resource, which should be put to the most efficient use. This perception of time prevails in many Northern and Western countries, such as the Netherlands; it emphasises the importance of meeting deadlines and arriving on time. People usually only do one job at a time.

Synchronous perception of time

A synchronous perception of time sees time as a more relative concept, 'flexible', in a sense. There are no strict or precise units of time in this perception of time.

Structure and organisation
PART C

© Noordhoff Uitgevers bv

People may be engaged in several activities at the same time, and there is no real awareness of an optimally efficient progression through time.

Examples of countries whose inhabitants view time from the synchronous perspective are the Latin American, African, and many Asian countries. This perception of time is also found in Europe, with Spain, Portugal, and Greece being examples.

Language

Language is an excellent means of communicating with others. At the same time, it is a tool used to share the meaning that is assigned to objects and concepts with others. The way people use language shows the symbolism they (attempt to) bestow and impart. Symbolic aspects of language include:

a influence, which can be exerted in many ways, ranging in directness, subtlety, conviction, or threat;

b identity, which can be expressed through language in the form of a community's distinctiveness.

Language

O&M IN PRACTICE

The Top 10 Most Spoken Languages in the World

English is a *lingua franca*: a language that will get you where you need to go wherever you are. At least, that tends to be our European perspective. Whether it is actually the most frequently spoken language is another matter altogether. This top 10 looks at the number of people whose mother tongue or second language is one of the following.

1 Mandarin Chinese – 1.026 billion speakers
2 English – 765 million speakers
3 Spanish – 466 million speakers
4 Hindustani – 380 million speakers
5 Arabic – 353 million speakers
6 Russian – 272 million speakers
7 Bengali – 250 million speakers
8 Portuguese – 217 million speakers
9 Indonesian – 163 million speakers
10 Swahili – 140 million speakers

Source: https://www.alletop10lijstjes.nl/meest-gesproken-talen-in-de-wereld, consulted 6 November 2018

Heroes

The second layer is known as the layer of heroes, usually people who are or have been in high standing in the organisation. This standing may result from leadership, charisma, effectiveness, or entrepreneurship. Examples are Steve Jobs for Apple

Heroes

and Johan Cruyff for Dutch and International football. Heroes can be living as well as deceased – or even fictional, such as TinTin. Heroes are respected and serve as important examples or behavioural role models.

Rituals

Rituals

The third layer is that of the rituals: an organisation's collective activities. Rituals are essentially superfluous but are very important to the organisation and its culture from a social perspective. Rituals are performed because they simply have to be: they are part of the usual way of life. Examples of organisational rituals are birthday celebrations, greetings, different receptions, morning work outs, and working pace.

Values

Values

The fourth layer of culture is that of values. Values are the deepest layer of a culture, and are invisible. Part of an organisation's values are its notions of right and wrong, standard and non-standard, usual and unusual. Openness or lack therefore towards others is also a part of an organisation's values. In other words: values are the notions in an organisation that lead to a particular code of conduct, one that is important to an organisation when making decisions.

One could say that the values of an organisation are invisible, and the hardest aspect to change. However, their function in a culture is the most important. If one truly wants to change cultural behaviour, paying attention to cultural values is essential. Changes to the other three layers, symbols, heroes, and rituals, while visible, have less of a direct influence on organisational culture.

Positive effects of culture

The existence of a particular culture can have positive effects for an organisation. These positive effects are related to the following four aspects Source: Weber, A. en Doelen, A. (2018), *Organiseren en managen*, Groningen Utrecht: Noordhoff Uitgevers):

a **Commitment**: a clear and powerful culture helps to create commitment among the employees in an organisation. They are part of something and are proud to be part of it. Employees exude this commitment both internally and externally.

b **Standardisation**: shared norms and values help to create a situation of improved, more efficient collaboration. Employee behaviour becomes predictable, in a sense. From this perspective, culture has the role of an 'invisible' coordinating mechanism.

c **Internal security**: since behaviour, notions, norms and values are shared and predictable, a sense of security and calmness emerges in the organisation. Employees know where they stand with each other, and know how to respond to particular issues.

d **External force**: the presence of a clear and powerful internal culture also has external advantages. Employees who are proud to be part of an organisation exude this pride to their contacts outside the organisation as well. The outside world is presented with an image of what the organisation represents and how it deals with particular issues (Weber & Doelen, 2018).

What makes a strong culture? A strong organisational structure is one whose core values enjoy intensive commitment and broad support. The characteristics of a strong culture are (Robbins & Coulter, 2015) that:

a values enjoy broad support;.

b culture expresses a consistent message regarding what is important.

c most employees can relate stories about company heroes and history.

d employees strongly identify with (the) culture.

e there is a strong relationship between shared values and behaviour.

The different levels of culture

Hofstede's onion model distinguishes a number of organisational cultural layer. The same is possible for the four different levels of culture, shown in Figure 12.2 below:

1 **National culture**: the culture of a country or region. Examples are the differences between Germany and Italy in terms of greeting others or doing business.

National culture

2 **Business or industry culture**: the culture of a certain industry or profession. Examples are the financial, education, and building industry. Each of these has its own specific notions, norms, and values.

Business or industry culture

3 **Corporate culture**: the organisational culture as described in Hofstede's cultural onion.

Corporate culture

4 **Individual behaviour**: the behaviour exhibited by a person themselves. The individual aspect is determined by education, profession, and other individual situations and experiences.

Individual behaviour

FIGURE 12.2 **THE DIFFERENT LEVELS OF CULTURE**

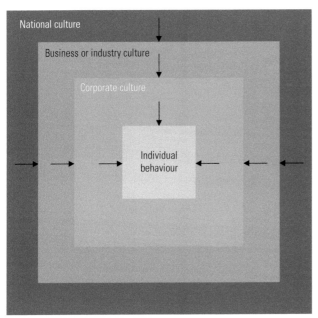

Source: Hollensen, S (2010), *Internationale marketing*, Benelux: Pearson

The various levels of culture are not separate entities, but in fact influence each other. In order to understand a person's behaviour, it helps to look at their 'context'. Where are they from, which industry do they work at, and for what company?

Unilever, our culture

Our values are part of an open culture centred on the strive for optimum performance. They guide our day-to-day decisions and actions, and are the foundation of everything we say and do.

INTEGRITY: Integrity is essential for us, because it is the cornerstone of our reputation. Therefore, we will never compromise our integrity. It determines how we behave, wherever we operate. Our guiding principle is to do the right thing for the long-term success of Unilever.

RESPECT: We promote respect because we feel people should be treated respectfully, honestly, and fairly. We celebrate human diversity and respect people for who they are and what they contribute.

RESPONSIBILITY: We aim to treat our consumers, clients, and employees with care, and to do the same for the environment and the communities where we operate. We will always honour our word.

PIONEERING: Our pioneering spirit is what made us great, and it is what drives us to this day. It inspires our passion for being the best and creating a better future. It means we are always willing to take an informed risk.

Source: https://www.unilever.nl/careers/
professionals/werken-bij-unilever/index.html,
consulted 7 May 2018

McClelland's iceberg model

McClelland's iceberg model

This section on culture concludes with a look at behaviour. Much of what is visible of an organisation's culture is expressed through the behaviour of its employees. But what determines this behaviour? American psychologist David McClelland (1917 – 1998) created his iceberg model to illustrate how behaviour (and knowledge and skills) are shaped and influenced. He chose an iceberg because only a small part of it is visible – the rest is below the surface. So it is with behaviour: most of it is unseen and even unconscious: convictions, norms and values, properties, motives. In other words: above the water it is about what a person does, below the water it is about what a person thinks and wants. In schematic form, the iceberg model looks like this (see Figure 12.3):

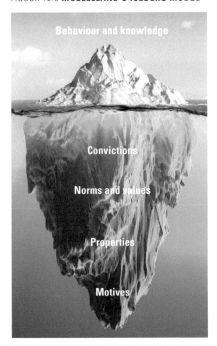

Source: communicatietraining.nl/inspiratie/ijsbergmodel-mcclelland

Convictions

Convictions can be described as people's notions about situations, developments, other people, and themselves. Convictions are the result of one's education, for example through individuals (role models), religion, and experiences. Examples of convictions are: 'You should never trust other people', 'You should try everything once', 'Bring it on, I can take anything'. Convictions strongly influence one's personality, behaviour, and presentation.

Convictions

Norms and values

Norms and values govern people's responses to question of what is 'right' and what is 'wrong'. They have a strong influence on a person's convictions and therefore on behaviour. An example of a norm or value is that a person never asks for help, even when it would be desirable for them to do so – possibly resulting from the personal norm of never wanting to bother others with one's own questions or issues.

Norms and values

Properties

Properties are a person's competences and personal characteristics. The introverted individual firsts take the measure of a person or situation they are confronted with for the first time; the extroverted individual will dive in headfirst.

Properties

Motives

Motives are the driving force behind action or inaction. Driving forces (or drives) direct human behaviour. The questions underlying motives range from 'What is it you are after in your life or at work?' and 'Where do you want to see yourself in five years' time?'. Answering life's questions helps one direct which actions (not) to take.

Motives

The value of McClelland's iceberg model is in the fact that behaviour change demands changing the elements below the water. Behavioural change requires change in convictions, norms and value, properties and/or motives. If an organisation chooses to change certain cultural aspects, this has consequences for employee behaviour. In order to change employee behaviour (for example in order to make it more positive), a company also needs to work on the components underlying that behaviour.

12.2 TYPOLOGIES OF ORGANISATIONAL CULTURE

Relevant theory describes various approaches to or typologies of (aspects of) organisational culture. In this context, the following approaches or typologies are discussed:

a group process and organisation culture approach;
b Harrison and Handy's typology;
c Sanders and Neijen's typology;
d typology according to professional culture;
e Schein's three-layer model;
f Kets de Vries and Miller's typology;
g Quinn and Rohrbaugh's typology.

12.2.1 Group process and organisational culture approach

Orientation of the group

This approach looks at the behaviour of individual group members from the orientation of the group. Each individual organisational member is part of one or more organisational groups. Individuals' actions are influenced mainly by the processes in these groups. The description of a group process is based on the following six aspects.

1 **Affectivity**. Is there a professional or an emotional connection between the organisational members?
2 **Causality**. Are people or systems capable of causing problems for organisational members?
3 **Hierarchy**. What is the behaviour of organisational members regarding position, role, power, and responsibility?
4 **Change**. Is there a uniform response from organisational members to environmental threats or opportunities?
5 **Collaboration**. Which attitude is prevalent: 'all for one' or 'everyone for themselves'?
6 **Orientation with respect to groups with other interests?** Are other groups in the organisation approached with sympathy or antipathy?

By describing these aspects, it is possible to gain an insight into the group process. A group's culture covers the direction in which people move in any given situation. Changing an individual's undesirable organisational behaviour is possible if one 'steers' the individual's group towards a different culture. If, for example, one wanted the members of a group to be more open to change, the aspects of the group process should be adjusted to encourage (instead of discourage) this openness. This approach does not preclude the fact that the actions of individual organisational members may be influenced by other factors than the group process, such as task content, regulation, etcetera.

VodafoneZiggo Culture

'Open up' is one of the company values at Dutch telecom and cable operator VodafoneZiggo. Nancy Hoogland guides corporate behavioural change in the company, and feels deeply committed to this value. In January of 2017, after months of preparation, we introduced the Culture Crew. A group of 44 colleagues from both of the former companies that now make up VodafoneZiggo, whose chief interest is the new company culture. The group is a community that represent the entire company. They organise sessions, canvas the organisation, and compile and share their findings. Their objective is to encourage a continuous dialogue between employees and the senior leadership team. Co-creation is our gateway to building our new organisation. Culture is not something that is imposed; culture is created together. It is a dynamic, ever-evolving concept that deals with the personality of the organisation itself.

Source: https://www.vodafoneziggo.nl/314/door-samenwerking-heb-ik-mezelf-opnieuw-uitgevonden, consulted 7 May 2018

12.2.2 Harrison and Handy's typology

Harrison (1972) and Handy (1979) created a typology that is widely using in order to describe organisational culture. This typology describes four ideal types' which, in reality, are never expressed in such clearly defined forms. A combination of the types is much more likely. Handy named the four ideal types after four Greek mythological gods. The typology is based on two dimensions:

1 **Degree of cooperation**. The extent to which collaboration between employees is possible and occurs;
2 **Distribution of power**. The extent to which decision-making authority is centralised or decentralised.

A high degree of cooperation means a great deal of solidarity among organisational members. A high distribution of power means a situation characterised by a high degree of delegation. Degree of cooperation and distribution of power can range from extremely high or extremely low.

Combining these two dimensions leads to the diagram depicted in Figure 12.4

Ideal types

Degree of cooperation

Distribution of power

FIGURE 12.4 **FOUR TYPES OF ORGANISATIONAL CULTURE**

		Power distribution	
		Low	High
Degree of cooperation	Low	Role culture	Person culture
	High	Power culture	Task culture

The four types of culture are the following:

Role culture

1 Role culture. An organisation based on rule and procedure offering stability and security. Organisational functions, not the people in those functions, set the tone. Role culture is demonstrated by bureaucratic organisation. Handy named this culture Apollo: the god of ordainments and law. In Mintzberg's terms (see Chapter 11), this organisation is most similar to a machine organisation.

Power culture

2 Power culture. An organisation that revolves around the top-level figure, functioning, as it were, as their extension. The top-level individual chooses a circle of loyal employees based on recognition. This cultural type uses few rules and procedures, with decisions made on an ad-hoc basis. This power structure is often found in smaller and younger organisations. Handy refers to this cultural type as Zeus, who represents 'power' as the father of the gods. In Mintzberg's terms, this is most like an entrepreneurial organisation.

Person culture

3 Person culture. Characterised by the emphasis it places on the individual, this organisation operates in the service of its people. A manager in this type of organisation is equal to any employee. Management is a necessary evil required to keep the organisation afloat. Examples of person cultures are in service provision, such as legal or accountancy firms. Handy calls it Dionysus, due to the god's individualistic nature. This cultural type is most similar to Mintzberg's professional organisation.

Task culture

4 Task culture. Characterised by task-orientation and professionalism, this organisation comprises a network of loose/fixed task units. Each unit has a higher degree of autonomy and, at the same time, carrier a specific responsibility as part of the whole. Achieving results is of paramount important. An example of a task culture is found in a matrix organisation. Handy refers to this cultural type as Athena, the goddess of wisdom. Mintzberg's approach would label this as being most like the innovative organisation.

Handy attempted to relate the various characteristics of these cultural types to their technological properties. Which cultural type is the best match for which type of technology? Handy drew the following conclusions:
a routine technology → role culture;
b valuable technology → role culture;
c mass production → role culture;
d coordination-heavy technology → role culture;
e unit production → power or task culture;
f flexibility-heavy technology → power or task culture.

Mapping subcultures

O&M IN PRACTICE

Literature on internal subcultures is rare, but there are two sources that deserve attention:

De Caluwé and Vermaak (1999) use different colours to distinguishes between schools of thought. Blueprint thinking represents a planned approach whereas yellowprint thinking represents power. A redprint thinker focuses on the quality of social relationships, while the greenprint tinker approaches the work environment mostly from the perspective of a learning situation. Lastly, the whiteprint thinker has great capacity for reflection, bestowing on them a great eye for relationships, and helps them to conserve their energy and use it selectively.

Scheltens (1998; 1999) sees a connection between environmental factors and subcultures. Different circumstances require different behaviours, which explains why effective functioning is highly situationally-dependent. Depending on external pressure, goal-orientation, and restrictedness, Scheltens sees various subcultures emerge. He describes these as teams, taskforces, societies, companies, coalitions, political arenas, clans, or clubs.

Both perspectives offer a contribution into the insight into the tension field of someone existing between two subcultures, providing them with a better understanding of why either environment responds the way it does.

Source: https://www.managementsite.nl/omgaan-cultuurverschillen-binnen-organisaties, consulted 7 May 2018

CORPORATE
HIERARCHY

12.2.3 Sanders and Neuijen's typology

In their book *Bedrijfscultuur, diagnose en beïnvloeding* (1999) (Business culture, diagnosis and influence), G. Sanders and B. Neuijen distinguish between six dimensions of company culture. Companies position themselves at a point along each of these dimensions, which represent a 'scale'. Analysing and defining the six dimensions for an organisation leads to a cultural diagnosis of the organisation. Sanders and Neuijen's six dimensions deal with the behaviour experienced by an organisation's employees and exist independently of each other.
Figure 12.5 offers a concise summary of these dimensions.

Dimensions of
company culture

FIGURE 12.5 **SUMMARY OF SANDERS & NEUIJEN DIMENSIONS OF COMPANY CULTURE**

Process-oriented

Avoiding risks
As little exertion as possible
Every day about the same

Result-oriented

At ease in risky situations
Do their utmost
Every day represents a new challenge

People-oriented

Take personal problems into consideration
Take responsibility for well-being of employees
Groups make decisions

Work-oriented

Exert strong pressure to complete work
Interested exclusively in the work that one delivers
Individuals make the decisions

Organisation-bound

Employees identify with their organisation
Attract staff from the right families,
social class and educational background
Work norms also apply at home
Do not think very far ahead

Professional

Employees identify with their profession
Attract those staff who are most suitable for the job
Private life is one's own business
Think years ahead

Open

Openness towards newcomers and outsiders
Nearly everyone fits into the organisation
New staff members quickly feel at home

Closed

Closed and secretive, even towards own staff members
You have to be unusual in some way to fit into the
organisation
New staff members do not feel at home instantly

Tight control

Awareness of costs
Adhere strictly to meeting times
Talk seriously about company and work

Loose control

Lack of awareness of costs
More or less adhere to meeting times
Joke about the company and work

Pragmatic

The customer's wishes must be met
Results are more important than procedures
Pragmatic attitude towards ethics
Minimal contribution to societal goals

Normative

Procedures are adhered to
Procedures are more important than results
High ethical norms
Useful contribution to society

12.2.4 Typology according to professional culture

The typology according to professional culture describes four professional cultures using (central) metaphors or myths. These metaphors emerge as the result of the different professional groups striving for specific ideals. These ideals have consequences for the cultural type that are best suited to the organisational members in terms of functioning. In reality, there are few, if any, organisations that are entirely constructed according to these central metaphors or myths, but some subcultures in organisations may fit the bill.

The following distinct cultural types exist:

Bureaucratic culture **1 Bureaucratic culture.** A culture based on rationality, allowing organisational members to be goal-oriented about their work. Established organisational goals are most easily realised using this goal-orientation. In their day-to-day activities, organisational members are bound by a multitude of rules and processes. Tasks are carefully demarcated. Each organisational member is a small link in the larger chain. As long as the organisational members work in accordance with the bureaucratic setup, the goals are automatically (if eventually) reached. Bureaucratic cultures are found not only in government institutions, but also in other organisations. The bureaucratic culture is reminiscent of Handy's role culture, also found in Max Weber's theory of bureaucracy (circa 1920), in the Introduction Chapter of this book.

2 Official culture. In addition to bureaucratic characteristics, organisations also have specific characteristics related to their social function. This social function involves ordering and directing the desired social developments and processes. Exercising the social function leads to an official culture that is strongly internally oriented. This culture has its own mythology, which includes:

a the myth of societal manageability;
b the myth of the superiority of the self over society;
c the myth of government rules as tools for legal certainty and equality;
d the myth of the impartial official, free of notions, values, and desires.

Official culture

3 Professional culture. The professional culture focusses on individual organisational members, who wield power. The organisation is, in a sense, a collaborative partnership between professionals who are also in charge of the organisation. As a result, there is no contrast between the executive and managerial branches, as both are comprised of professionals. This culture is founded on the myths of superiority of knowledge and autonomy. As a result, the professional is an individual, and their relationship to a team is of subordinate interest. Professional culture is reminiscent of Handy's person culture, and in fact has its roots in the medieval concept of the guild, whose craftsmen established communal leadership in the Middle Ages.

Professional culture

KLM Culture

Passion, energy, decisiveness, and brainpower

These are the characteristics typical of many KLM-members. And it shows in the company's culture. KLM has a wide variety of business units, activities, cultural backgrounds, levels of education, and specialisms. Passenger transport, freight transport, and technical maintenance are KLM's core activities. Overall, KLM-members are proud of their company and their work. Every KLM-member matters:

from the platform to the baggage area, from the tech department to the freight crew, at the office or in the air.

Working with KLM means being part of our big, blue family. KLM-members rely on each other's enthusiasm, flexibility, and clout – because together, they make the difference. Every individual effort helps KLM remain the leader in international aviation.

Source: https://www.klm.com/jobs/nl/over_klm/klm/klm_cultuur/index.html, consulted 7 May 2018

O&M IN PRACTICE

4 Commercial culture. This culture revolves around the client and/or the market. It is founded on the myths that everything is for sale and that the organisational members can achieve whatever they want if they work hard enough. There is great mutual competition and 'the man' is the focal point.

12.2.5 Schein's three-layer model

Edgar Schein developed his three-layer model in 1980. In a 1996 publication, Schein described culture as 'the fundamental, unspoken suppositions about how the world is and ought to be, shared by a group of people and determining their perceptions, thoughts, feelings, and outward behaviours'.

His model attempts to define two aspects of culture: how is organisational culture constructed, and how can an organisation achieve cultural change? The model includes mechanisms that act directly and mechanisms that act indirectly. The direct-acting mechanisms can influence organisational culture directly. Examples include organisational notions and role behaviour. Indirect-acting mechanisms do no influence culture directly, and include house style and organisational mission and vision.

The three-layer model is often represented as an onion diagram. Each layer represents a level of organisational culture; the more layers are peeled away, the harder it gets to change or adjust the culture. Figure 12.6 indicates the three levels of organisational culture.

FIGURE 12.6 **EDGAR SCHEIN'S THREE-LAYER MODEL**

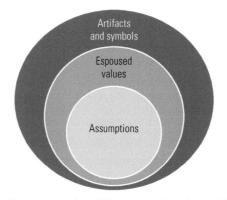

Source: www.toolshero.nl/leiderschap/organisatiecultuur-model

1 Artefacts and symbols: These are found along the outside of the onion diagram. The easiest cultural level to adapt and change, artefacts and symbols are the visible elements, like organisational structure and processes as well as clothing and logos. Other visible elements can include use of language, modes of address, and building design and layout. Artefacts and symbols are obviously visible not only to employee, but also to external parties. Artefacts and symbols influence organisational culture indirectly.

2 Espoused values: Espoused values form the organisation's established strategies, objectives, and managerial theories, as well as norms, values, and codes of conduct. The espoused values are conveyed throughout the organisation and are well-known to all. The espoused values also influence organisational culture indirectly.

3 Assumptions: At the heart of the cultural onion are the assumptions: (basic) notions consisting of conscious and unconscious ideas, perceptions, thoughts, and feelings. These (basic) notions are shared by all organisational members,

and form the 'heart' of the culture. They are similar to codes (of conduct) applied by employees inside and outside of the organisation. "How do we treat each other, and how do we treat our clients?" To a large extent, these types of rules and basic assumptions determine manners and etiquette inside and outside of the organisation. The assumptions eventually become mostly subconscious processes, but are still considered to be self-evident.
These basic suppositions influence organisational culture directly, but are very hard to change or adjust.

In order to truly change organisation culture, the basic assumptions must be changed or adjusted. Changing or adjusting artefacts, symbols, and espoused values is insufficient, as their influence on organisational culture is only indirect. Implementing cultural change is only possibly if the basic assumptions are clearly defined; something that requires a lot of investigative work among employees in many situations. As the assumptions are deeply rooted, cultural change necessarily always involves a transformational process, often accompanied by intervention. The process must also be integral, and include the artefacts, symbols, and espoused values.

12.2.6 Kets de Vries and Miller's typology

A typology that takes an entirely different approach to culture is that by Manfred Kets de Vries and Danny Miller (1984). Their typology looks at the personality traits of the organisation's leading figures (usually top-level management). It is these leading figures whose exemplary behaviour is the determining factor for culture across the entire organisation. Kets de Vries and Miller focussed their typology on the negative effects on the personality traits of leading figures, who often have neurotic tendencies leading to ineffective employee behaviour, often leading to sub-optimal effects across the organisation. For example, employee growth may be restricted, with various unfortunate consequences for the organisation as a whole. In order to clarify this exact issue, Kets de Vries and Miller distinguish between five sub-optimally performing cultures described from a psychoanalytical framework; Manfred Kets de Vries is a psychotherapist by trade.

The five cultures are the following:
1 **The depressive culture**: depression is a mood disorder characterised by a loss of zest for life, or by gloominess. Projecting these traits onto an organisation describes an organisation lacking in confidence, possibly even exhibiting behaviour that approaches everything from a negative perspective: 'We have not succeeded and we never will'. There is little initiative in these organisations, and everyone is essentially only interested in covering their own hide, due to an uncharismatic leading figure who (probably) does not have all of the answers either.

Depressive culture

2 **The compulsive culture**: a compulsion is characterised by order, persistence, and inflexibility. Perfectionism and inflexibility are key personality traits for organisations that are mainly concerned with managing and controlling. Management and control are achieved by implementing highly detailed systems that are documented and prescribed to a fault. Leading figures in these cultures are rather arrogant and overly focussed on details and trivialities.

Compulsive culture

3 **The dramatic or theatrical culture**: a theatrical personality is characterised by (excessively) emotional displays, a need for attention, affirmation and/or affection. This organisation focusses on the leader; all organisational aspects

Dramatic or theatrical culture

are about the leader. The organisational direction is largely based on subjectivity instead of objectivity – feeling and instinct over figures and analyses. Much of the information in the organisation does not get past the leading figure, preventing other employees from performing to the best of their ability, and giving them no choice but to be swept along by the leading individual's strong 'ego'. The leading individual in this type of culture displays narcissist behaviour.

Paranoid culture **4** **The paranoid culture**: paranoid behaviour is characterised by (excessively) high degrees of suspicion and mistrust towards others. These types of individuals regularly perceive others' behaviour as malicious, threatening, or misleading. Suspicion and mistrust are the leading figure's guiding principles, and such leaders should be treated with kid gloves. The leading figure tends to take a negative view of many issues, resulting in many organisational opportunities to go unused.

Schizoid culture **5** **The schizoid culture**: schizoid behaviour is characterised by a high degree of detachment and by little involvement in terms of social contact. The leading figure has little need for (close) relationships and seems indifferent, and there is little engagement between them and organisational employees. The leading figure does not, in fact, lead the organisation – causing people to go their own way. As a consequence, employees begin to make their own arrangements, leading to the formation of organisational 'islands'. This, in turn, results in conflicts/arguments occurring in the organisation every so often, which may lead to power struggles.

12.2.7 Quinn and Rohrbaugh's typology

With their *Competing Values Framework*, Quinn and Rohrbaugh (1983) developed a typology based on the following two dimensions:

1 Is there a high degree of flexibility or a low degree of flexibility in the organisation?

2 Is the organisation internally oriented or externally oriented?

Quinn and Rohrbaugh's typology

Combining these two dimensions leads to four distinct organisational structures, schematically represented in Figure 12.7.

FIGURE 12.8 **FOUR ORGANISATIONAL CULTURES BASED ON THE DIMENSIONS OF FLEXIBILITY AND ORIENTATION**

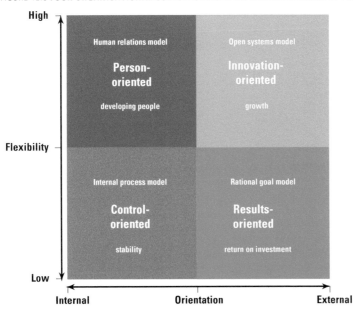

Source: www.123management.nl/0/030_cultuur/a300_cultuur_02_typering

1 **Control-oriented organisational culture**: A control-oriented organisational culture combines a low degree of flexibility with an internal orientation. Rules and procedures are key in this organisation. There is a strong focus on enabling processes to progress as good and as stable as possible. It is therefore known as the 'Internal Process Model'. In these kinds of organisations, there is a clear hierarchy and a great deal of discussion and alignment.

Control-oriented organisational culture

2 **Results-oriented organisational culture**: A results-oriented organisational culture combines a low degree of flexibility with a high degree of external orientation. As its name indicates, this type of culture focusses on end results: achieving profit or targets is key. This is known as the 'Rational Goal Model'. Organisations with a results-oriented organisational culture often offer variable rewards (results-dependent) and have a strong focus on quality and/or speed.

Results-oriented organisational culture

3 **Innovation-oriented organisational culture**: An innovation-oriented organisational culture combines a high degree of flexibility with a strong external orientation, and has a strong focus on the development of new products and/ or services. Growth is key. This type of organisation is also known as the 'Open Systems Model', and pays a great deal of attention to developing the creativity

Innovation-oriented organisational culture

and speed needed for developing ideas into successful, marketable products or services.

Person-oriented
organisational culture

4 **Person-oriented organisational culture**: A person-oriented organisational culture combines a high degree of flexibility with an internal orientation. Personal development is key in this organisation, earning it the name of 'Human Relations Model'. This type of organisation offers its employees excellent possibilities for development and care.

Comparing this typology to that of Harrison and Handy shows many similarities, as shown in table 12.1 below:

TABLE 12.1 **SIMILARITIES BETWEEN THE MODELS BY HARRISON/HANDY AND QUINN/ROHRBAUGH**

Harrison and Handy's typology	Quinn and Rohrbaugh's typology
Power-oriented culture	
Role-oriented culture	Control-oriented organisational culture
Task-oriented culture	Results and innovation-oriented organisational cultures
Person-oriented culture	Person-oriented organisational culture

12.3   CULTURAL CHANGE

An organisation's culture should correspond to its target effectiveness. On the one hand, it should be noted that there is no single optimal cultural type that meets this demand (see Paragraph 12.2). Looking at any organisation usually shows a combination of cultural types. The marketing department's culture is different than that of the production department. This means there are internal differences in organisations in terms of orientation, objective, and power. If an organisation has a powerful department or group of people, this may result in a dominant culture. On the other hand, there may be changes to an organisation's environment, which may result in the organisational culture becoming misaligned with this new environment. This (potentially) requires change on the part of the organisation. Organisational culture is (strongly) related to organisational results. Therefore, management will want to influence organisational culture. To that end, they are equipped with a number of options that can be used to direct and/or influence organisational culture (see Figure 12.8).

FIGURE 12.9 **POSSIBILITIES FOR GUIDING / INFLUENCING ORGANISATIONAL CULTURE**

Structure and organisation
PART C

The organisation can influence its culture through the following aspects:

a **The organisation's 'figurehead'**. In practice, appointing a new top-level manager results in a breath of fresh air that inspires new organisational norms and values in the organisation. The new standard bearer will gather around them a group of people whose task it is to exemplify this new approach throughout the organisation.

Organisation's 'figurehead'

b **Ceremonies and rituals**. Establishing ceremonies and rituals formally emphasises and visualises the norms and values. Suitable times are during the recruitment process, periodically at festivities, or during special occasions like presentations or annual awards ceremonies.

Ceremonies and rituals

c **Stories and language**. Anecdotes, use of language, stories about (heroes of) the past reveal much about an organisation's culture. They show employees what types of behaviour are (un)desirable, and how certain issues should (not) be approached.

Stories and language

d **Socialisation**. Working with incumbent employees teaches new recruits the cultural expressions of the organisation. It shows them how to address work issues effectively and efficiently within the 'cultural rules' of the organisation. Many organisations also offer their new employees courses intended to convey and teach the organisation's norms and values.

Socialisation

Another aspect of cultural change is the path towards it. Cultural change has much to do with organisational change, a topic thoroughly discussed in Chapter 13. From this perspective, one could say that cultural change is, in fact, similar to behavioural change. Linking this to Edgar Schein's three-layer model (see Paragraph 12.2.5) leads to the conclusion that cultural change deals with the inner layer of the onion, the (basic) assumptions. The artefacts and symbols and the espoused values influence culture indirectly. The hardest, but most direct and effective, path to realising cultural change is through changing the basic assumptions (the underlying norms and values). This is a hard path to follow, and requires an intensive approach which must certainly include the following activities (Alblas & Wijsman, 2018):

a Creating awareness of the need for change;

b (Top-level) management developing a clear vision to establish the extent and direction of the cultural change (related to the elected strategy);

c Top-level management needing to show a great deal of involvement and inspiration for the change program;

d Ensuring a supporting consensus throughout the organisation. Organising this type of support is done through specific events and activities;

e Providing courses or training sessions may lead to the intended cultural change;

f Visualising the results of cultural change.

Cultural change? Great!
Eight rules of thumb

1 **Combine thought with action**: The most fruitful approach is one of 'thinction' – thinking and action going hand in hand. Learn by doing.

2 **Focus on the positives**: look for, facilitate, support, and celebrate good examples.

3 **Organise idea-pollination**: create new clouds of meaning by establishing connections between colleagues that normally would not cross paths, by inviting speakers from outside to tell their story, etcetera.

4 **View culture as behaviour**: where cultural change is concerned, why not address the behaviour directly? See something, say something. Cultural change starts with you.

5 **Change starts at home**: if you want to see changes, modif-I. You can only change yourself (or rather, display a change in behaviour), and that is hard enough as it is.

6 **Do not think on others' behalf**: let people make their own plans. Nearly every organisation is made up of people with ideas and teams doing wonderful things, all meshing with the desired culture. Give them space and support them.

7 **Break the cycle**: when things get tense, we often subconsciously start doing lots of things that interrupt the change process. This leads to vicious cycles. Instead, break these cycles before they emerge by naming that-which-must-not-be-named. "Here is what I see is happening, what is my part in it?"

8 **Do what you did, get what you had**: if we take new initiatives using our old way of thinking, nothing changes. As Einstein put it: 'Problems cannot be solved by the level of awareness that created them.'

Source: https://www.managementsite.nl/cultuurverandering-leuk

12.4 INTERNATIONAL CULTURAL MODELS

Many organisations work in an international context, leading to cultural differences between countries becoming a factor. Insight into these cultural differences is required if a collaboration between countries with difference cultures is to be successful. The phenomenon of cultural differences between countries is the subject of a great many studies, with three major ones being:

1 Hofstede's cultural model (section 12.5.1);

2 the GLOBE cultural model (section 12.5.2);

3 Trompenaars's cultural model (section 12.5.3).

Structure and organisation
PART C

12.4.1 Hofstede's cultural model

One of the most accessible and frequently used models for cultural classification and the interpretation of cultural differences is that by Dutch social psychologist Geert Hofstede, internationally renowned for his intercultural studies. In his book *Cultures and Organizations: Software of the Mind* (Hofstede, 2010), Hofstede offers great insight into the phenomenon of culture, based on scientific studies into the subject. Hofstede's own study with IBM (in the 1960s) is the basis for a model that describes four dimensions of national culture. These four dimensions are particularly useful in an organisational environment in which intercultural communication, business, and negotiations are of the utmost importance. The model offers an insight into the cultural differences between countries, which can be used to bridge those very differences. Collaborations between organisations from various parts of the world can benefit from the combination of their strong cultural characteristics. Two additional dimensions were added to the model at a later point, and all six dimensions are described below.

Hofstede's cultural model

Power Distance Index, PDI

Inequality between people is everywhere: one individual has more status than another and enjoys greater respect. However, countries differ in the way in which they cope with and accept these inequalities. In countries with a higher PDI, the less powerful accept the fact that power, expressed as respect and wealth, is distributed unevenly. Countries with a smaller PDI use the equality of all individuals as a basic principle, and are less quick to accept an uneven distribution of power. Countries with a high PDI attach great importance to status and education because it is often only the upper classes who have access to education and therefore well-paid functions and jobs, with differences in the distribution of wealth only increasing over time. Power distance correlates negatively to a country's wealth: the lower the PDI (like in Western-European countries), the wealthier the country. Inversely, in countries with a high PDI, many people exist below the poverty line. See Figure 12.10.

Power Distance

FIGURE 12.10 **POWER DISTANCES (PDI) IN SEVERAL COUNTRIES**

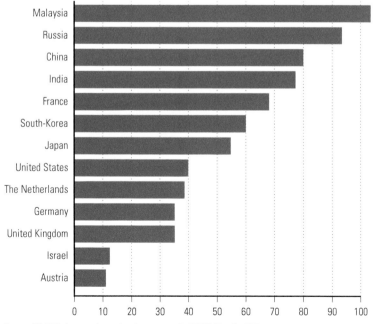

Source: P.T.H.M. Janssen, *Interculturele competenties* (2018), Noordhoff Uitgevers

In countries with a high Power Distance Index, superiors and subordinates are principally unequal. Power in companies in countries with a high PDI is concentrated at the top, with those companies espousing a hierarchy in which higher-ups control and instruct the lower-downs. Things are substantially different in countries like the Netherlands, where the Power Distance Index is low: bosses and subjects see each other as equals. Any formal hierarchy, which is limited vertically, is only a useful tool that offers structure and clarity.

Individualism vs. collectivism (group orientation), IDV

Group orientation

All human beings are individuals. But individuals in collectivist countries feel a very strong connection to a group (family, company, tribe, society) from which they derive their identity. The group's interests outweigh the individual's. People are loyal to their groups, and groups offer protection. In individualist countries, individual interest triumphs over collective interest: the bonds between individuals are looser and everyone takes care of themselves. A person's way of life in terms of loose mutual connections or strongly delineated groups is known as group orientation, indicated by Hofstede with the terms 'individualism' (IDV) and 'collectivism'. The least group-oriented (most individualist) countries are the Anglo-Saxon and Scandinavian ones; the Central and South American countries are the most collectivist, followed by all of the Asian and most of the African countries. See Figure 12.11.

FIGURE 12.11 **DEGREE OF INDIVIDUALISM (IND) IN SEVERAL COUNTRIES**

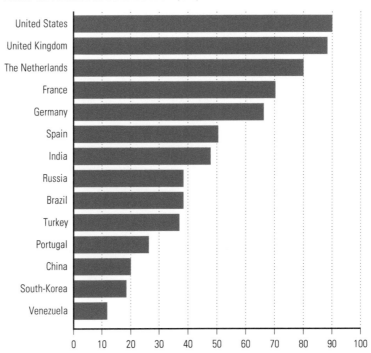

Source: Janssen, P. (2018), *Interculturele competenties*, Groningen / Utrecht: Noordhoff Uitgevers

A country's level of wealth shows a strong correlation with its degree of individualism. Poor countries are more oriented towards groups, whereas residents of rich countries are more self-interested and focussed on personal gain. Hofstede argues that collectivism may be seen as an adaptation to cope with poverty and scarcity, whereas individualism is more of an adjustment to wealth and prosperity. Japan is an exception to the rule: it has high wealth and a relatively strong group orientation.

Structure and organisation
PART C

There is a positive correlation between PDI and IDV: the strong group-dependence characteristic of collectivist cultures generally goes hand in hand with large differences between people and greater dependence on those in whom power is concentrated most strongly.

Masculinity vs. femininity, MAS

Men and women across the world are either tough and focussed on material gain, or take a more modest and caring role. The behaviour attributed to either sex varies per society. There are countries where gender-roles (being: toughness, assertiveness, and a drive for material gain for men, and a gentleness, modesty, and a focus on quality of life for women) are clearly distinct; there are also countries where traditional gender-roles actually overlap. The first category is known as 'masculine', the second one as 'feminine'. The result is that, in masculine countries, concepts like income and promotion are important; whereas in feminine countries, more importance is attached to working relationships with supervisors or quality of collaboration with others. See Figure 12.12.

Masculinity vs. femininity

FIGURE 12.12 **MASCULINITY (MAS) IN SEVERAL COUNTRIES**

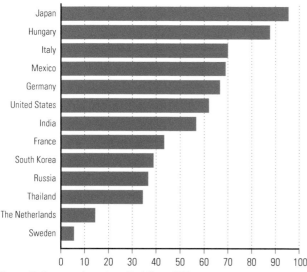

Source: *Werken met andere culturen*, Frank Garten 2001

The Netherlands holds an unusual position; like the Scandinavian countries, it is very feminine. Virtually all parts of the world have their own extremes in the MAS scale, in contrast to the earlier cultural dimensions discussed. In Asia, Japan, for example, is highly masculine, whereas South Korea and Thailand are more feminine.

Uncertainty Avoidance, UAI

Uncertainty avoidance here refers to the extent to which people try to stay away from risky situations. The question is: how does a society cope with the given fact that the future is uncertain? Does it try to control the future or does it let the dice fall as they may? A low score on the UAI indicates that a society has no difficulty coping with lack of structure, clarity, or certainty. Countries with high uncertainty avoidance require rules and formality. Latin America, Latin Europe, Eastern Europe, and the Mediterranean countries score high on uncertainly avoidance. Denmark, Jamaica, and Singapore score the lowest. The Netherlands is an average scorer. See Figure 12.13

Uncertainty Avoidance

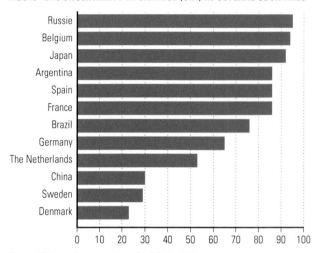

FIGURE 12.13 **UNCERTAINTY AVOIDANCE (UIA) IN SEVERAL COUNTRIES**

Source: *Werken met andere culturen*, Frank Garten 2001

Long-Term Orientation (temporal dimension), LTO

Long-Term Orientation

A fifth, temporal dimension (Long-Term Orientation) was added to the model in 1991. Countries oriented on the short-term are normative in their approach, show great respect for tradition, and are focussed on rapid results. Money that is earned is quickly spent in these countries. The focus is not on saving money; it is on putting money to use. Long-term oriented countries are able to adjust their traditions to changing circumstances, and are persistent in their drive for results in the long-term. These countries are more focussed on the future. The focus is on living frugally and economically. See Figure 12.14.

FIGURE 12.14 **LONG-TERM ORIENTATION IN SEVERAL COUNTRIES**

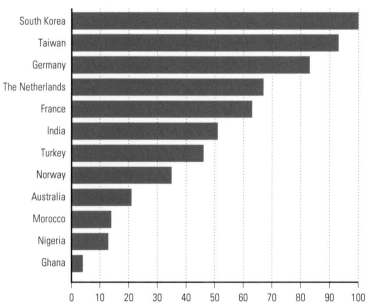

Source: Janssen, P. (2018), *Interculturele competenties*, Groningen / Utrecht: Noordhoff Uitgevers

Indulgence vs. Restraint, IND

Indulgence vs. Restraint

The sixth dimension, Indulgence vs. Restraint (or hedonism vs. sobriety), was added in 2010. This dimension is mainly concerned with the three themes of happiness, control over one's personal life, and the importance of free time.

Indulgence represents countries that are fairly relaxed about allowing people to fulfil their natural human needs and drives, and advocate the enjoyment of life. They are countries where people feel happy and are optimistic about the future. People have a large degree of control over their own lives, and feel free time is important. The restrained countries tend to repress needs and regulate them using strict social etiquette. These are countries with a clear division of roles between men and women, countries that do not hold human rights and democracy in the highest regard. People have little control over their own lives, and free time is not considered to be important. A final note is that there is a link between hedonism and wealth. The more hedonistic a country is, the higher its level of national wealth seems to be. Countries that tend towards sobriety are also usually the poorer countries. See Figure 12.15.

FIGURE 12.15 **INDULGENCE INDEX (IND) IN SEVERAL COUNTRIES**

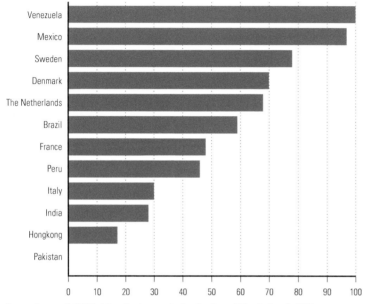

Source: Janssen, P. (2018), *Interculturele competenties*, Groningen / Utrecht: Noordhoff Uitgevers

O&M IN PRACTICE

They do things differently in Germany

German workplace etiquette is different than in the Netherlands. You need to know about these cultural differences if you want to enjoy your time across the border. The Dutch sometimes have difficulty conforming to the German hierarchic company structure. In the Netherlands, relationships are less complicated. You have greater responsibility and feel committed to your company.

There are downsides to the resulting loyalty. Your employer will not hesitate to call on you to put in an extra effort, which can cause you to lose track of time and work more overtime.

Source: *De Twentsche Courant Tubantia*, 6 December 2017 Wednesday, Enschede Edition

12.4.2   The GLOBE-cultural model

GLOBE-cultural model

Another model comparable to Hofstede's cultural model is the model created by the GLOBE-project. GLOBE is an acronym for Global Leadership and Organizational Behavior Effectiveness. The GLOBE-project was first completed in 1991 and uses Hofstede's model as its basis. Developed by Robert J. House (University of Pennsylvania), the GLOBE-project is a global study among 17,000 middle managers in clusters of countries, 62 in total. It is a study that indicates cultural differences between countries or clusters of countries. As with Hostede's model, the cultural differences between countries are represented using different dimensions; the GLOBE-model uses nine such dimension. Six are formulated in the same way as in Hofstede's model. The nine dimensions are:

Uncertainty Avoidance

1   **Uncertainty Avoidance**: formulated in the same way as in Hofstede's model, Uncertainty Avoidance also refers to the extent to which people steer clear of risks.

Assertiveness

2   **Assertiveness**: this dimension corresponds to the Masculinity dimensions in Hofstede's model. Men and women are either tough and focussed on material gain, or take a more modest and caring role.

Future Orientation

3   **Future Orientation**: this dimension also has many parallels with one of Hofstede's. Future Orientation is all about a country's attitude towards time: a country is either long-term or short-term oriented to a certain degree.

Power Distance

4   **Power Distance**: comparable to Hofstede's dimension of the same name. The difference between the extent to which countries cope with an accept inequality.

Individualism/
Collectivism

5   **Individualism/Collectivism**: corresponds to the group-orientation dimension in Hofstede's model. Does the government or any other social agency encourage either individualism or some form of group solidarity?

Humane Orientation

6   **Humane Orientation**: corresponds to the concept of the Feminine in Hofstede's model. Does a society encourage a caring and selflessness approach?

In-Group Collectivism

7   **In-Group Collectivism**: a dimension that is new to this model. It does not focus on the perspectives of a government or social institution, but on those of people themselves. Are people proud to be part of the groups they belong to, such as family or work organisation?

Gender Egalitarianism

8   **Gender Egalitarianism**: another dimension that is new to this model. How does a society cope with gender differences when it comes to decision-making and status?

Performance
Orientation

9   **Performance Orientation**: the final dimension is also new to this model. Does society attach great value to performance-drive and performance-orientation? Is this type of behaviour encouraged by society?

Country clusters are scored either low, average, or high on each of these nine dimensions. Example scores are shown in the table below:

TABLE 12.2 **OVERVIEW OF COUNTRY SCORES ON THE NINE DIMENSIONS OF THE GLOBE-CULTURAL MODEL**

Dimensions score	High	Average	Low
Uncertainty Avoidance	Germany	US	Russia
Assertiveness	Spain	Ireland	Switzerland
Future Orientation	Denmark	Egypt	Poland
Power Distance	Thailand	France	The Netherlands
Individualism/Collectivism	Hungary	US	Japan
In-Group Collectivism	China	Israel	Sweden
Gender Egalitarianism	Morocco	Italy	Denmark

Dimensions score	High	Average	Low
Human Orientation	Indonesia	Taiwan	France
Performance Orientation	US	Sweden	Greece

In conclusion, in can be stated that the GLOBE-cultural model is an intensification of Hostede's cultural model.

United Airlines to exchange loyalty-system for lottery

O&M IN PRACTICE

The top executive at United Airlines calls it 'a new, exciting reward policy'. But the plan to exchange employees' quarterly bonus payments with a lottery (cars, holidays, and a 100,000-dollar grand prize) has caused the aviation company a different kind of commotion than they had been hoping for. Up until now, employees were given a bonus of up to 125 dollars per month if the company was able to meet certain targets. It is part of a larger initiative that has been

christened Core4. Its goal: to establish a cultural change in the company. Criticism of management's lottery idea is sizeable: "I cannot really picture myself driving into a parking spot in a Mercedes while everybody else, who worked as hard as or even harder than me, gets nothing," says one stewardess.

Source: *de Volkskrant*, 6 March 2018 Tuesday

12.4.3 Trompenaars's cultural model

As indicated, Hofstede's model uses six dimensions to describe culture; the GLOBE model uses nine dimensions to do the same. The final cultural differentiation model discussed is that by Fons Trompenaars, whose model is based on seven dimensions. Trompenaars's model is also based on a study among a large number of managers (nearly 8,000), across a variety of countries (43 in total). Together with Charles Hampden-Turner, Trompenaars published the book 'Riding the Waves of Culture: Understanding Diversity in Global Business' in 1997. This book first described the cultural model, the structure of which differs from the other two in many ways. The dimensions used are different, and are more directly linked to doing business in countries with different cultures. How can one come to understand business etiquette in different countries, and how does one adjust one's role to match? How can one achieve success in a different culture? Trompenaars's cultural model focusses more on gaining insight into the habits and rituals of another society by scoring them across seven dimensions with the eventual goal of facilitating business.

Trompenaars's cultural model

The seven dimensions of Trompenaars's cultural model are:

1 **Universalism versus Particularism**: universalism is when a society clearly agrees on what is right and what is wrong. Norms and values apply to all and are always applicable; they are, in a way, universal. Particularism centres on individuals, and has a greater eye for circumstance which is used as the basis for moral decision.

Universalism versus particularism

2 **Individualism versus Communitarianism**: this dimension is also found in the Hofstede and GLOBE models, namely: does the society centre on individuals or groups?

Individualism versus communitarianism

Neutral versus
Emotional

3 **Neutral versus Emotional**: this dimension deals with emotion, such as public displays of laughter or anger. A neutral culture tends to restrict public displays of emotion (either positively or negatively). In a neutral culture, the norm is not to show how one feels. In an emotional culture, things are the other way around: one is expected to show one's emotional state, whether it be positive or negative.

Specific versus Diffuse

4 **Specific versus Diffuse**: to what extent does a society emphasise the development of personal relationships, at home and at work? A specific culture clearly distinguishes between work and private life. Manners and customs are restricted characteristics of whichever group one belongs to (or functions in). This distinction does not exist in a diffuse culture. Personal life and professional life are intertwined. Manners and customs are much more individual aspects of the person one is dealing with.

Achievement versus
Ascription

5 **Achievement versus Ascription**: a dimension that focusses on status. What is the basis for status? A culture of achievement awards status based on someone's performance and accomplishments. Any activity performed results in a certain level of (loss of) status. A culture of ascription focusses less on performance than on origin, age, gender, or class. Here, status is something that is attributed regardless of achievement.

Sequential versus
Synchronous

6 **Sequential versus Synchronous (Time)**: this dimension focusses on how a society experiences the concept of 'time'. Does a culture favour a timely arrival, or is 'being on time' a relative notion? A sequential culture emphasises adherence to schedule; people are expected to structure and plan their affairs neatly. A culture that takes a less restrictive approach, and tolerates or even appreciates a less structured approach, is known as a synchronous culture. In a synchronous culture, time is a more abstract notion.

Internal Direction
versus External
Direction

7 **Internal Direction versus External Direction**: how does a culture define the concept of 'environment'? How is one's environment experienced? In an internally directed country, people tend towards a harmonious coexistence with their environment. Life is a matter of give and take, and one cannot stay in control of everything that happens. Sometimes, one has to bend to certain societal/ environmental developments. An externally directed culture is more interested in controlling the environment or society.

TABLE 12.3 **COUNTRIES SCORED ALONG THE SEVEN DIMENSIONS OF TROMPENAARS'S CULTURAL MODEL**

Dimension	Example country	Dimension	Example country
Universalism:	Germany	Particularism:	Russia
Individualism	US	Communitarianism	India
Neutral:	The Netherlands	Emotional	Italy
Specific	The Netherlands	Diffuse	Asia
Achievement	The Netherlands	Ascription	Japan
Sequential	Germany	Synchronous	South America
Internal Direction	Asia	External Direction	US

Structure and organisation
PART C

Cultural dilemma

Trompenaars uses an example of a cultural dilemma, one he discussed earlier in The Social Conference. Hypothetically: You are a passenger in your friend's car. He is driving at 50 mph in a 30-mph zone, and hits a pedestrian. You are asked to testify in court, knowing that you are the only witness. Would you tell a lie on your friend's behalf? The answers vary per culture: protestant cultures (US, Switzerland) tend towards telling the truth, Asians are more likely to stick up for their friend. In many cases, the answer depended on circumstance: the French were more likely to base their answer on the pedestrian's condition, and one Italian asked about the state of the car...

Source: https://www.marketingfacts.nl/berichten/fons-trompenaars-culturele-verschillen-beter-beeld-van-de-werkelijkheid

12.5   DOING BUSINESS IN OTHER CULTURES

Businesses are continually increasing their international or intercultural collaborations. Many people experience this as a real enrichment to their work, even though it does come with its fair share of challenges. This applies to people from all countries, whether or not they are even passingly familiar with other business cultures. The following paragraphs briefly address the cultures of different countries, in terms of a nation's characteristics, business mentality, cultural orientation, and business practices.

12.5.1   The Netherlands

A prosperous nation, the Netherlands has an open economy which is heavily dependent on foreign trade. The economy is typified by stable relationships, moderate inflation, and a healthy financial policy due to its important role as Europe's transportation hub. Food processing, chemicals, oil refining, and the manufacture of electrical appliances are the most important industrial activities. The Netherlands has 17 million inhabitants (2018).

Business mentality

The Netherlands is a nation of trade, with Dutch professionals being highly experienced and sophisticated. The Dutch are known for their professionalism, 'let's get to business'-mentality, and culture of 'no-nonsense'. Honesty and fairness are highly valued, and people are not afraid to get to the point in terms of doing business. A promise made is a promise kept. Words, invitations, and promises are often taken literally. The Dutch clearly separate their business life and their private life. There is a significant aversion to a strict hierarchical structure in businesses and society.

Cultural orientation

Planning, regulating, and organising dominate Dutch culture. The average resident of the Netherlands is creative and rather individualistic but, when making decisions, people prefer involving teams of multiple people and multiple perspectives. This results in a relatively slow decision-making process. Decisions are final once made. Subjective and emotional arguments are not accepted, and emotions are not put on display. Moderation is a key concept of Dutch culture.

Business practices

Punctuality is very important in the Netherlands. Not managing to arrive or deliver on time is interpreted as a lack of reliability or competence. Spontaneity is not appreciated. Practicing openness is the standard, with all employees generally being able to access important information. Efficiency and directness are characteristics considered normal in Dutch business life. Decision are often made according to the consensus principle, the notion of the widely supported decision, often referred to as the Polder Model, associated with harmonisation: the opinions of all employees are equally important and worthy of consideration. There is no room for superiority in an egalitarian society.

12.5.2   Germany

Unlike the Netherlands, Germany is a not a unitary state but a federal republic. This means that countless areas of policy are not governed by a central government but by the province. The Federal Republic of Germany is relatively poor in resources. Its economy is based mainly on industry and service provision. Agriculture is responsible for a modest contribution. Export is the lifeblood of the German economy. The best-known Germany export product is its cars, but machines, chemical products, foodstuffs, textiles, and metals are also significant. Germany is the most important trade partner of the Netherlands, and has over 80 million inhabitants (2018).

Business mentality

Germans are analytical, with a conceptual orientation. Order, industriousness, discipline, professionalism, and sobriety are highly appreciated. Argumentation based on the thorough consideration of facts and examples is very normal. Promises are made to be kept. Business encounters are based on reason and logic, and well-prepared. Nothing is left to chance. People are very loyal to their companies, and Germans often spend their entire careers in the employ of a single business. This is changing with the younger generation. Competition based on price alone is unheard of; quality is what counts.

Cultural orientation

Historically speaking, Germany was a solitary community, with little information shared with other countries. This is slowly changing. The German thought-process is very thorough, and every aspect of a project is scrutinised, generally making it a time-consuming affair. German business life knows a strong hierarchy, with its origins in the feudal-hierarchic and Lutheran influences of Germany's past. This is exemplified by the use of the business title in corporate life. A person's position in a business clearly demarcates their responsibilities.

Business practices

Punctuality is sacred in Germany, with timeliness considered essential in both the professional and social arenas. Great respect for order is another characteristic. Decisions are made with society's best interests at heart, followed by those of the company, and only then those of the family. Germans avoid risk, look for stability, and are often oriented on the short-term. As a result, German business relations are very reliable trade partners: tight schedules and clear rules are typical.

12.5.3   India

With 1.35 billion inhabitants (2018), India is the world's largest democracy. Its political and judicial systems are the same as those of the UK, and corporate India is oriented on the West, with many highly-trained employees. The Indian economy is among the top ten largest in the world, and is also one of the world's fastest growing.

Over 60% of the population is in the agricultural industry. India also has a high potential for mining, with the industry expanding steadily, supported by the low wages. The service and IT industries are strong growth industries. India's economy has been deregulated since the 1990s.

Business mentality

Over the past decades, work environments and, as a result, mentality in India has experienced drastic change. Decisions are made more readily, but traditional, ancient business customs are still honoured. Networks, personal meetings, and building on client relationships are highly valued concepts. Visiting Indian businesspeople at home is part of those ideals. Negotiating and haggling are culturally ingrained. Indians are very reliable business partners.

Cultural orientation

Religion and the caste system are deeply ingrained in Indian culture. This hierarchic social structure classifies people according to their inherited social status. This makes Indian culture a collectivistic one; individual decisions must be in harmony with one's family or group/social structure. There is great cultural inequality: male dominance in business culture, no equal rights or privileges for women. Levels of commitment and loyalty among employees are very high, and there is great confidence in management, the organisation, and its future.

Business practices

IST, the abbreviation of 'Indian Standard Time', is often the subject of the jocular colloquial interpretation of 'Indian Stretchable Time'. 'Yes Sir' is frequently the last phrase spoken in a conversation, but does not always mean your conversation partner agrees with you. It is not customary to disagree with someone; saying 'no' is considered the height of rudeness. Not everyone in India is accustomed to taking responsibility. Initiative is infrequent, and Indians will frequently ask for confirmation. Non-verbally, however, there are many signals to indicate whether a message has come across: the more vigorous the 'bobble' of the head, the clearer the message.

12.5.4 France

As one of Europe's largest countries, France has, historically, often taken a nationalist approach. The French market is highly protectionist, strongly self-oriented, and much less Europe-minded. The French have a large domestic market and do not feel a very strong need to move abroad. Agriculture plays a larger role than in the economies of most other industrialised countries. Important industries are machinery, chemical products, cars, metals, aircraft, and foodstuffs. France invests heavily in its infrastructure, environmental technology, sustainable energy, and innovation. France is the third-largest economy in Europe, after Germany and the United Kingdom. France has 67 million residents (2018).

Business mentality

Many French companies are characterised by a strict hierarchic structure. From an early age, French children are taught to obey their teachers and to not show any assertiveness. This results in an obedient, compliant worker. People are comfortable with rules and regulations. Status, power, and strong leadership are ubiquitously respected. The French appreciate clarity when it comes to decision-making authorities in their potential business partners. To the French, knowing the right people is important in terms of networking.

Cultural orientation

Since the French Revolution of 1789, the state has had an important function: to regulate, intervene, distribute, and rule: *La France, c'est nous*. The French state embedded standards of linguistics, ethics, and propriety in the French identity. The French centralist visions works well because it operates on three basic and unquestioned principles: assimilation, general interest, and equality. French culture is fairly reticent; social groups are important to the French. Grandeur and eloquence are highly valued and socially accepted in France.

Business practices

The French do not care for a ready-made presentation that concisely summarises what can be achieved at what cost. They want to start by building up a personal relationship. One must demonstrate erudition, sophistication. This indirect approach is the result of the highly valued notion of honour. Decisions are taken either before or after, but certainly never during, a meeting. Meetings are meant to voice one's ideas and to allow everyone the opportunity to develop their thought processes. Other, more literal cultures, like the Dutch, consider this approach one of endless, pointless debate, where real problems are swept under the rug.

12.5.5   The United Kingdom

There are approximately 66 million residents in the UK (2018) and its surface area is around five times that of the Netherlands. Its economy is one of the largest and most open, and it is strongly geared towards services (banking and insurance). Strong emerging industries are the tourist, communication, and IT industries. London, an important financial and business centre, is the absolute metropolitan heart of the country, and home to 7 million residents. Even though the UK is a member of the European Union (for the moment), the country decided not to introduce the Euro, and has not entered the EMU (European Monetary Union).

Business mentality

British businesspeople are generally conservative and reserved, seemingly unconvinced by (rapid) change. Building a business relationship is a rather lengthy and important process, and one for which the British like to take their time. British organisations know a stronger hierarchic division than the Dutch. The labour market is flexible, thus improving labour mobility. People resign more readily, but can be dismissed more easily as well. This is often seen as an advantage. As a result, British workers' morale is rather flexible.

Cultural orientation

The United Kingdom does not consider itself to be a European constituent, even though its residents recognise the importance of the EU. The class system still has a major impact on the British way of life and business, and is demonstrated in corporate life by the ease with which people accept the existence of 'layers'. The top-level of a company decides what needs to happen; rather autocratically and directively, and not always very diplomatically. Where negotiations are concerned, it is recommended to send in one's most senior executives as a way of enforcing respect.

Business practices

Punctuality is incredibly important. Timely arrival is a must. Meetings tend to proceed in a highly structured and formal manner. The British are not very quick to make a decision, and the more important choices are generally made by directors/ managers. It is recommended that one find out who the decision-maker is as soon as possible. Strong leadership is a prerequisite for company leadership. The British go to extreme lengths to avoid insulting (or rather: embarrassing) their clients; this also applies to their desire to show hospitality. However, they have a tendency to communicate through double layers and understatements. This mastery of the understatement can make it complicated to glean a conversation partner's exact intentions and meaning. Being told that something is "rather interesting" may, in fact, be a polite way for the speaker to indicate their utter and complete disinterest. One should make sure to ask for additional and adequate confirmation to make sure one is on the right track.

12.5.6   United States of America

The US economy dominates the globe; the United States are the world's largest industrial nation. The country, with its 327 million residents (2018), is rich in minerals and fossil fuels (including coals, oil, and gas), and its vast surface area and favourable climate have always favoured the importance of agriculture. Even though its output has declined, the US is still the global leader in the production of raw iron, steel, motor vehicles, and synthetic rubber. Its economy is largely based on the principles of free market and private enterprise, with government influence restricted to a minimum.

Business mentality

Do not underestimate the speed of business dealings in the US; the country has a 24-hour economy. It is not unusual for Americans to reach a deal during a first meeting. Nothing is impossible. Phrases like "losing is not an option" or "get the job done" are accurate representations of the mentality of both the country and its people. Moreover, US culture is competition-oriented, making it a typical

masculine culture. The mentality and drive of American employees tends to be highly ambitious.

Cultural orientation

The lack of a notion of a previously established class awareness means Americans are not subject to the same values as the 'old world'. They care more about opportunity than equality, however. The social mobility of the American is virtually limitless, and class is not inherited but acquired. In the US, one is what one wants to be. Yet class does exist; it is usually based on profession and position (and wages). Money is the measure of success. Patriotism, nationalism have a religious quality in the US. This is evident from the flag being the national symbol. Loyalty to the nation (symbolised by the flag) is deeply ingrained in society. Americans are very confident in themselves and their future. Nothing is impossible, their competitive spirit is the deciding factor. Moreover, it is still the nation of invention and innovation, born from a positive spirit towards improvement and progress.

Business practices

US business culture is direct, and addressing others, even business partners, on a first name basis is common practice. The business culture is very focussed on the short term, on results, and on individuals. It is also quite normal to be offered a percentage of one's income based on performance, thus allowing an employer to place the risks with their employees. A tendency towards hard work and a huge drive to advance one's career are represented in the phrase 'live to work'. The US follows a political philosophy of 'acquire and discard', with a very flexible labour market. There is a can-do mentality, and decisions are made rapidly.

12.5.7   China

An economic powerhouse, China is sometimes referred to as the dual-system nation: capitalism and communism. There is a strive for economic development through the creation of special economic zones, which offer free trade capitalism. This policy of economic liberalisation has led to vast economic growth over the past two decades. China's population numbers some 1.4 billion people (2018). Agriculture is far and away the most important industry: over half of Chinese residents works in this industry. Nevertheless, it represents only 20% of the country's gross domestic product. China is one of the most important countries in the world in terms of mineral production; it is the world's largest producer of coal. Important export products are machinery, transportation equipment, chemical products, and manufactured products.

Business mentality

Chinese (business) culture is relationship-based. A good relationship is a prerequisite for doing business, more so than efficiency or timeliness. Negotiation and relationship management with the Chinese takes great patience and tact. Chinese people are loyal, tough negotiatiors who excel at playing out their competitors against one another. Establishing a good personal relationship is essential. Another prevailing principle is that of reciprocity: quid pro quo. Chinese culture is indirect, with no direct questions asked. Respect, dignity, and reputation are more important than honesty. Conversational partners should never be made to feel as though they have been offended either in terms of their person or their reputation. As a result, no Chinese person is every likely to respond 'No' directly.

Cultural orientation

Confucianism still plays an important role in Chinese society. It emphasises duty, honesty, loyalty, respect for seniority. Maintaining harmonious relationships between individuals results in an overall harmonious society. The Chinese hold the collective in high esteem, and people attempt to avoid conflict: no arguments in public. Personal feelings and interests are seen as subordinate to those of the group. Hierarchy plays an important rale; this is certainly also true in business. An important part of establishing business dealings is the creation of a relational circle. Relationships are more important than knowledge.

Business practices

Doing business with the Chinese demands infinite patience and an iron constitution. Never lose patience and always show respect. Punctuality is very important in China. Assume that many Chinese people will not speak English, making a professional interpreter an important asset. Moreover, having the right connections is of very high importance. Once mutual trust and understanding have been reached, then 'my business is your business and your business is my business.'

12.5.8 Brazil

Brazil is the largest country in Southern America, and the fifth largest country in the world (surpassed only by Russia, Canada, the US, and China). With nearly 211 million inhabitants (2018), Brazil ranks seventh in the list of the world's largest economies, with its emerging agriculture, mining, heavy, and service industries. Roughly a third of the workforce is involved in agriculture, with coffee being the most important commercial crop (Brazil is the world's largest manufacturer and exporter). Sugar cane, citrus fruits, cocoa, cotton, and tobacco are other important crops. The country has vast mineral wealth, including iron one, diamonds, tin, bauxite, and crude oil. Its most important industries are textiles, chemical products, steel, machinery, and shipping. The majority of its electricity is hydro-plant based; Brazil has exceptional, largely untapped hydro-electric potential.

Business mentality

Brazil is essentially fully self-sufficient, which is expressed in the Brazilian mentality: English is spoken only very infrequently, and the closed economy means limited basic global development for the average Brazilian. Moreover, Brazilians are short-term oriented. Brazil's many periods of high inflation are one source of a tendency to spend money straight away. Brazilians are opportunistic, and tend not to think in the long-term.

Cultural orientation

Class and status are largely economic factors, with major differences between the wealthy and the poor. Moreover, Brazil is a 'macho' society; women are frequently subordinate to men. In addition, the 'extended family', or **parentela**, plays a large role. This social structure affords Brazilians their stability. Family is more important in Brazil than in other Latin American countries. There is also a strong interrelationship between Brazilian culture and Catholicism.

Business practices

Doing business in Brazil takes time (people are not punctual), a great deal of chit-chat, patience, and trust, and a good relationship. Establishing or having contacts before doing business is essential. Social communication is of the utmost importance. Brazilians do not do business with companies or organisations, but with people. Decisions are made by people more than they are based made on profit margins. The style of conversation is cordial and intense: Brazilians enjoy physical contact, with distance potentially interpreted as refusal. To establish a good relationship, it is often essential for a newcomer to contract the services of a 'despachante': a person who can ensures one approaches the right people, establishes contacts, and handles the required paperwork in a bureaucratic nation. Speaking Portuguese is a bonus. Lobbying is very normal. Having friends, particularly in high places, is very important, more so than in Europe.

12.5.9 Russia

The world's largest country, Russia has around 144 million inhabitants (2018), and was a communist country within the Soviet Union until 1990. After that, the country rapidly westernised into a 'capitalist' nation, mainly to the benefit of the new elite and the business world. Russia has seen strong economic growth since 1999, owing in particular to the devaluation of the Rouble and the high oil prices. Future challenges are in the area of the development of small and medium enterprises. The economic climate is currently dominated by oligarchs, and an inadequate banking system. Crude oil, natural gas, electricity, coal, ore, wood, and wood products are Russia's most important exports. Moscow fulfils the roles of both the country's capital and its economic centre.

Business mentality

Negotiating styles have seen drastic changes since the great shift. Formerly rather a spirited, dramatic affair with the omnipresent threat of the sudden cessation of business, it now an efficient, effective process, particularly among the younger generation. There is one aspect that has remained: Russian patience is legendary. Business meetings in Russia are rather formal, frequently attended with full delegations. The clear relationship between age, wisdom, and position is a relic of the Soviet era. It is natural for a senior partner to know more than a junior one, which also makes them more important. It is therefore required that one show respect to one's seniors.

Cultural orientation

From a historical perspective, team building was always considered a cultural tradition of the Russian collectivist lifestyle. Now, it is seen as an innovative, prized aspect. Russians tend to engage in very strong alliances fairly easily. There is a high degree of communal responsibility. In times past, the communist party dictated company lines; now, with the party's presence removed from the board tables, there is still the mentality of needing and accepting a strong boss. Being offered feedback by one's employees remains a sore spot. Stability and safety used to be guaranteed by the communist system; now, people turn to religion, social groups, and family for the same.

Business practices

Doing business in Russia is a complex affair. Proper preparations and a reliable partner or representative are essential for finding one's way in Russia. One should also take into account that business proceedings are a middle-to-long-term effort. There is no easy path to a quick deal in Russia. Corruption and a web of rules, regulations, decrees, and laws complicate business dealings. Moreover, Russia's constitutional state is a weakened one, and the judicial branch often lacks political autonomy. The domestic market has experienced rapid growth over the past ten years. Business activities must be aligned to the Russian market specifically.

12.5.10 Japan

Japan is one of the world's largest economies. Japan has 127 million residents (2018), with 30 million housed in the Greater Tokyo Area, making it the largest metropolitan city in the world. Japan is poor in terms of resources; it is a true nation of trade that depends on export. Following a time of a currency that remained strong throughout years, the country is now experiencing a massive decline in its exports. The only role of significance in the primary industry in Japan is played by the fishing industry. Following World War Two, Japan claimed its place on the global market in the shipbuilding, plastics, and steel and automobile industries. These industries are mainly based on foreign technologies. The US is Japan's most important trade partner; Japan also exports a large amount of capital.

Business mentality

Personal relationships are paramount, and people prefer to do business with someone introduced by a friend or partner. Matters like punctuality and good correspondence are valued highly. Status and age are important factors to the Japanese. The senior person in a group is always treated with respect. This is partly related to etiquette. Greetings, for example, should always address the person with the highest status (generally one of the elders present). The Japanese

preference for harmony has led to a great emphasis on non-verbal, more indirect communication. Even though most Japanese companies adhere to a strict hierarchic business structure, employees are expected to contribute a high degree of initiative and problem-solving skill.

Cultural orientation

Respect and loyalty are important aspects of Japanese life. Every effort is made to prevent loss of face. Moreover, Japanese culture focusses on harmony and trust, as does Japanese business life. The Japanese are raised for a life of cooperation and collaboration, not one of independence from one another. This mentality permeates Japanese life in general. Decisions are often taken in groups (bottom-up process). Politeness, responsibility, and collaboration in the service of the greater good are the most important values – not individuality. To the Japanese, harmony leads to improved production. Combined with an appreciation for hard work (over 40 hours per week), this has led to Japanese expansion following and during a period of reconstruction.

Business practices

It should be noted that the Japanese will never say 'No' outright. Rather, phrases used indicate that 'one is on top of it', or that 'certain things are being taken under consideration'. There are no open criticisms or insults. A bow by way of greeting is preferred, though foreigners are permitted their tendency to shake hands. The depth of the bow depends on the other person's position. Talking softly, rather slowly, and politely, without being intrusive is also recommended.

Summary

- Hofstede describes culture as 'the collective mental programming that distinguishes one group of people from another'.

- Hofstede & Hofstede's onion model comprises four layers: symbols (space, time, language), heroes, rituals, and values.

- Positive effects of culture are: commitment, standardisation, internal security, and external force.

- The four levels of culture are: national culture, business or industry culture, company culture, and individual behaviour.

- David McClelland's iceberg model describes how behaviour (and knowledge and skills) are shaped and influenced. Behaviour is determined by the following four layers: convictions, norms and values, properties, and motives.

- Examples of typologies of organisational culture are:
  - Group process and organisational culture approach: the group process is described using six aspects: affectivity, causality, hierarchy, change, collaboration, and orientation with regard to groups with other interests.
  - Harrison and Handy's typology: based on two dimensions, degree of cooperation and division of power, there are distinct cultural types: role, power, person, and task cultures.
  - Sanders and Neuijen's typology: there are six distinct dimensions, namely: process or result-oriented, people or work-oriented, organisation-bound or professional, open or closed, tight or loose control, pragmatic or normative.
  - Typology according to professional culture: this typology distinguishes between the four types of bureaucratic, official, professional, and commercial culture.
  - Schein's three-layer model. Schein describes culture as 'the fundamental, unspoken suppositions about how the world is and ought to be, shared by a group of people and determining their perceptions, thoughts, feelings, and outward behaviours'. The model's three layers are: artefacts and symbols, espoused values, and (basic) assumptions.
  - Kets de Vries and Miller's typology: a typology that focusses on the negative effects of the personal characteristics of leading figures. There are four distinct types of cultures: depressive, compulsives, dramatic or theatrical, paranoid, and schizoid culture.
  - Quinn and Rohrbaugh's typology: based on two dimensions, degree of flexibility (high/low) and orientation (internal/external), this typology distinguishes between four cultural types: control-oriented, results-oriented, innovation-oriented, person-oriented.

- Management has several options when it comes to directing or influencing organisational culture. A change in organisational culture can be achieved by adjusting the organisation's figurehead, ceremonies and rituals, stories and language, and socialisation.

- Three examples of international cultural models are: Hofstede's cultural model, the GLOBE-cultural model, and Trompenaars's cultural model.

- Hofstede's cultural model distinguishes six dimensions: power distance, individualism, masculinity, uncertainty avoidance, long-term orientation, and indulgence.

- The GLOBE (Global Leadership and Organizational Behavior Effectiveness)-cultural model distinguishes nine dimensions: uncertainty avoidance, assertiveness, future orientation, power distance, institutional collectivism, humane orientation, in-group collectivism, gender egalitarianism, and performance orientation.

► Trompenaars's cultural model distinguishes seven dimensions: universalism versus particularism, individualism versus communitarianism, neutral versus emotional, specific versus diffuse, achievement versus ascription, sequential time versus synchronous time, and internal direction versus external direction.

13
ORGANISATIONAL CHANGE AND DEVELOPMENT

Contents

After studying this chapter:

- you will have gained knowledge of and insight into the strive for organisational effectiveness and aspects of organisational culture, and working in teams;
- you will have gained knowledge of and insight into organisational growth models, reorganisations, and aspects of learning organisations;
- you will have gained knowledge of and insight into organisational consultancy;
- you will have a global insight into organisational studies.

Lilium flying cars

The flying car has long been at the top of the tech-enthusiast's wishlist, but now, things seem to moving much closer in the right direction – with German Lilium. Around six months into 2018, Lilium successfully concluded its first test flight. The company has now obtained a 90-million-dollar investment, with the majority of the amount contributed by Tencent, a Chinese company with a hand in many different industrial pies: online, gaming, medical technology, and even aeronautics.

The VTOL (Vertical Takeoff and Landing) two-seater Lilium, known as Eagle, is a prototype miniature jet aircraft. As part of its test flight, it ascended vertically and proceeded successfully in a forward direction by rotating its engines. Lilium's design is unusual, though; it has 36 engines distributed across twelve wing-flaps that can all be directed manually. The onboard computer takes care of lift-off, and switches to manual once the VTOL is ready for forward movement. Once in the air, pilots can enjoy a 1-hour flight on a single battery cycle, which translates to around 300 kilometres travelled.

Lilium has been designed to maximise passenger safety: each of the 36 engines operates on its own redundancy system, meaning that a failure in one engine will not result in failures in the others. The same goes for the batteries, which are individually connected, meaning that, at worst, losing one results in a shortened trip – which certainly beats plummeting to the ground. Even the piloting system is fool-proof: the internal system ignores any manoeuvres it identifies as unsafe.

Source: www.dutchcowboys.nl

FIGURE **LILIUM**

2013 IDEA IN GLASGOW
CEO and co-founder Daniel Wiegand has the initial idea behind the aircraft concept.

2015 FLIGHT OF THE FALCON
Lilium is founded by 4 co-founders. The first 1:2 scaled prototype takes flight.

2019 FIRST MANNED FLIGHT
The first fully functional jet will take off.

2010   2015   2020   2025

2017 TEST FLIGHT IN ORIGINAL SIZE
The first full scale prototype takes off.

2025 YOU CAN BOOK A LILIUM JET
On-demand air transport is becoming a reality.

Structure and organisation
PART C

13.1   INTRODUCTION

Because organisational environments are continually subject to change, organisations have to change along with them. As indicated, an organisation must be and remain aligned with its environment. Organisational adjustments to match one's environment come in many forms, such as manufacturing different products, implementing an updated organisational structure, reward system, or information system, or refocussing efforts towards other markets. Change can be a continuous process, such as the continued search for new products to attain or retain competitive advantage; or change can be abrupt, as in the case of a far-reaching reorganisation.

In order to survive, organisations continually remain 'in motion'. Since the 1950s, increased turbulence and decreased stability around and within organisations has meant increased attention to organisational change and ways of managing change processes. However, until around the end of the previous century, organisations looking to 'adapt' to their environment had at least some certainty of what was going to be happening in the near future. In recent, years, this degree of predictability has dropped dramatically. The current world is a VUCA world – a frequently encountered term to describe a decline in predictability. VUCA is short for Volatile, Uncertain, Complex, and Ambiguous. Originally used by US armed forces, the term was adopted to apply to a new global context following the Cold War. Ever since the 1990s, it has been a frequent feature of the literature on strategic leadership. Combined with growing interdependence and collaboration betwee businesses, governments, and the midfield, these changes influence how people deal with strategic developments in and around organisations. The following section address the concrete global trends that result from today's VUCA world.

VUCA world

13.2   NINE GLOBAL TRENDS OF ORGANISATIONAL INFLUENCE

A study by McKinsey (2017) defines three encompassing themes describing nine global trends that influence the organisational playing field of the modern age. At the core of these themes is the idea that the 'interaction' between trends creates greater disruption – unpredictability is key. Opportunities and threats are two sides of the same coin. The world, and the notion of change management, are raised to an entirely new level through these developments. The three themes and accompanying nine trends are described below.

Growth shifts
The first theme is that of growth shifts on a global scale. These days, national growth no longer behaves like it used to; the 2008-2009 financial crisis marked a turning point. Any predictability has gone completely out the window, and opportunities for growth have shifted to developing countries, now more than ever. The challenge facing organisations is to understand how to make use of this shifting playing field, as well as to ensure it is approached correctly. This umbrella theme contains three different trends:

1 The world has moved past 'traditional' globalisation. One the one hand, there are growing sentiments favouring a tendency towards nationalisation and anti-globalisation (e.g. Brexit), with traditional trade and capital flows stagnating or declining. On the other, there is a huge growth of international products and services, and people are more mobile than every before, both in terms of living across borders as well as the vast increases in virtual connections, social networks, and international online purchases. Organisations are attempting to capitalise on these paradoxical developments by combining the power of internationalisation and globalisation with a retained sense of local character or focus. In other words: there is a continual increase in competing on an international scale with local precision.

2 From BRIC to ICASA, the power of the enormous market. For a long time, the focus of growth has been on 'BRIC' countries: Brazil, Russia, India, and China. Now, the focus has shifted to 'ICASA' as the countries with the greatest potential for growth: India, China, Africa, Southeast Asia. Over the coming ten years, over half of the world's growth is expected to come from these countries. For many internationally operating businesses, this (potentially) means a much-needed reorientation in terms of their intended markets.

3 Resources what is the limit? The positive growth in technology as a solution to difficult challenges has, unintentionally, also resulted in negative side-effects (e.g. environmental consequences). These negative side-effects in turn trigger greater creativity in finding new solutions, thus boosting innovation. However, they can also be of a more 'unexpected' variety, presenting opportunities for new resources which can cause huge industrial shifts and result in changes.

Increasing disruption

The second theme addresses increasing industrial disruption. Disruption here refers to the fact that many industries are experiencing shifts leading to changes that result in a complete overhaul. Example are the shift in the balance of power between buyers and sells, the shift in the economic basis and basis of power, changes in the type of competition, and shifts in industrial limits. This presents both opportunities and threats. The three trends that are part of this theme are described below.

1 The synergetic effects of technologies are explosive. Whether or not it is a coincidence, there is an increasing number of examples of how the effective merging and combining of technological and digital innovations in turn leads to an explosion of new technological innovations. As discussed in Chapters 3 and 6, examples are blockchain, machine learning, 3D-printing, the mobile internet, the internet of things, etc. These effects are not yet entirely identifiable, though it is clear that there are potentially huge upcoming shifts within industries, with some possibly industries becoming entirely superfluous in future.

2 The consumer is king. Increased digitisation has meant that consumers have become a deciding factor in purchasing. Possibilities abound, as does choice, and even customisation. Consumers can, for example, sometimes fully calibrate their products to their own individual demands. The question is: for how long will consumers remain willing to purchase this level of customisation at a premium?

There is an interesting combination of 'open source' market, where everything is possible at little cost, and a market where consumers are still paying for new films and books. It is not just the consumer that decides – organisations also have the possibility of establishing their business models to re-empower their position in the balance of buyers and sellers.

3 Ecosystem revolution. From a more traditional model of value creation, the lineary value chain, the shift has been towards organisations using different 'value models'. Companies whose value is constructed entirely around platforms (e.g. Microsoft, Google, Amazon) have made a huge contribution to value shifts. An example is the so-called 'any-to-any' business model as used by Alibaba, Uber and Airbnb, none of whom own any assets. The boundaries between these three categories are shifting, thus influencing the business models of tomorrow's organisations.

New social contract
The third theme addresses the new social contract or new social agreement. Companies, governments, and the midfield are no longer working in isolation. This has long been the case, but the need to increase collaboration and create new opportunies is greater than ever. Otherwise, important emerging issues cannot be resolved. There are three trends in this category.

1 The dark side of progress. The enormous progess made in recents decades as the result of digitisation and technological advance has had its dark side. The Cyberthreat is ubiquitous, making it a real risk for any organisation. Reinforcing one's 'digital resistance' should be given major attention, and can also be accomplished by companies working together.

2 A changing middle class. Globalisation and automation have resulted in an increasingly polarising job market. The middle class in India and China is growing. There are rapidly changing requirements in terms of skills, as well as a shift in labour towards offshoring resulting in a decline in trust in the government, and a stronger tendency towards increased income polarisation.

3 Macro-economic policy and experimentation. The traditional policy measures for market regulation are seemingly less effective in current market environments. There are ongoing experiments to encourage growth and cope with demographic changes and income inequalities in the market, etc. The resulting impact on organisations is both direct and indirect due to its effects on future pensions and healthcare. Companies trying to contribute positively to social issues are rewarded for their efforts because they are better at recruiting and retaining better motivated employees.
At first glance, these trends would seem far removed from the day-to-day changes in organisations. However, nothing could be further from the truth. Either directly or indirectly, these trends influence what is happening or is going to happen in organisation; the enormously disruptive character of these trends means this applies to organisations both big and small.

The influence of UN Sustainable Development Goals on organisations

The Sustainable Development Goals (SDGs) established by the United Nations are meant to end poverty, inequality, and climate change by 2030. But these goals are also offering businesses a framework for accessing new markets and developing new business models, products, and services. Companies can use the SDGs to make use of growth opportunities, and to offer attractive products and services in a way that offers societal advantages without exerting detrimental pressure on the environment. In short: creating value for the global community. There have been fundamental changes to the playing field of organisations. There are five trends forcing companies to find new ways to grow and increase shareholder value:

1 **Global demand landslides**. The world's balance of power has shifted from developed countries to emerging economies, such as China, India, and Brazil. This shift is partly due to the emergence of new markets causing a wave of urbanisation, thus leading to more prosperity and increased consumer demands.

2 **Demographic changes**. In 2050, nearly a fifth of the world's population will be over 60 years old. Moreover, the average age in emerging countries is considerably lower in Europe (21 years old compared to 42 years old). By focussing on younger or older target groups, new commercial opportunities are created.

3 **The unrestrictedly informed consumer**. In addition, consumers have gained access to virtually all digital technologies. This comes with an increase in consumer expectations and information.

4 **Digital responsibility**. There is a growth in the amount of consumer data as a result of the exponential growth in digital possibilities. This data needs to be handled carefully to ensure it is treated ethically.

5 **The scarcity of natural resources and the limitations of our planet**. At its current rate, consumption will drain the earth. Scarcity will have an enormous impact on the price of resources, and there will also be high environmental costs. Economic growth will need to be detached from the consumption of resources.

Companies looking to grow will need to change, whatever their intentions. The SGDs offer guidelines to go from corporate social responsibility to corporate social opportunity.

Source: www.managementscope.nl, 21 Dec 2017

SUSTAINABLE DEVELOPMENT GOALS

13.3 EFFECTIVENESS AND SUCCESSFUL ORGANISATIONS

Organisations are collaborations whose goal is to realise certain objectives. An organisation's activities are all related to achieving these objectives. The extent to which the objectives are reached is known as the organisation's effectiveness. There are four distinct varieties of effectiveness and accompanying criteria:

1 **Technical and economic effectiveness**. This is the extent to which an organisation's means are used efficiently. Efficient use of means equals using as few production factors (as little input) as possible to achieve a certain output. The organisation's activities are purposeful.

2 **Psychosocial effectiveness**. This is the extent to which the interests of the organisation's employees are realised, and therefore concerns the satisfaction employees experience when performing their tasks.

3 **Societal effectiveness**. This is the extent to which the needs of the various parties in the external environment are met. Associated questions are: is it possible to pay out sufficient dividends; does the organisation produce according to demand; do emission levels meet environmental requirements? An organisation only has a right to exist if the needs of external parties, such as consumers and finances, are met.

4 **Administrative effeeveness**. The extent to which an organisation can react to changing circumstances. Organisations must be able to address change quickly. In order to develop sufficient speed, the provision of information and decision-making in the organisation must meet certain requirements: there has to be flexibility and decisiveness.
   Flexibility is defined as an organisation's ability to change and adapt. Decisive organisations have the ability to act quickly and effectively.

Organisations generally emphasise reaching a high level of effectiveness in both the economic and technical sense. These organisations are characterised by their internal focus, being the maximum improvement of organisation's business operations. However, organisations can only be successful if they score adequately in all four varieties. The term used in this respect is organisational equilibrium. Organisational equilibrium means that both internal and external participants are rewarded in such a way as to ensure their continued motivation as part of in the organisation.

These days, if an organisation is confronted with changes in its environment, it will be inclined to look for ways of achieving a new organisational equilibrium. This is complicated by the fact that the various varieties of effectiveness cannot be seen as separate aspects – in fact, they are strongly interrelated.

It may be that an organisation is very efficient in implementing its manpower. However, if staff derive little satisfaction from their work, the likely outcome is a situation of increased absenteeism as well as costs.

Studies of successful organisations show that there is a relationship between success and an organisation's cultural characteristics. These cultural characteristics include quality assurance, customer focus, flexibility, internal entrepreneurship, innovative strength, teamwork, leadership style, and common norms and values of organisational members.

Collaborations

Effectiveness

Technical and economic effectiveness

Psychosocial effectiveness

Societal effectiveness

Administrative effectiveness

Organisational equilibrium

Successful organisations

Triodos Bank: an example of an effective social enterprise

Triodos Bank N.V. is a Dutch bank with subsidiaries in the United Kingdom, Spain, and Germany. The bank was founded in 1980. The name *Triodos* derives from the Greek for a three-fold approach, here used to refer to 'people, planet, profit'. An important question the founders had to ask was: who are the bank's real owners? Does it belong to people who have entrusted their savings, to shareholders, to itself, or to society? According to co-founder and owner Peter Blom, Triodos chose the latter option: society.

The bank's goal is to offer a sustainable, ethical, and transparent way of banking. To Triodos, sustainable banking means investing in companies that add value, either socially, culturally, and environmentally. Triodos offers its clients the possibility to invest in sustainable sectors in Europe using integrated loan and investment products, thus using banking as a means of contributing to a sustainable society focussed on human dignity and improving quality of life. For example, Triodos invests in bio-organic nutrition and agriculture, energy and climate projects, corporate social responsibility, micro credits, and art and culture.

Lending funds means a bank needs a financial buffer. Triodos Bank has a capital buffer that consists not of regular shares, but of share certificates. Certificate holders are involved intensively in the bank's affairs, thereby also safeguarding the bank's independent structure and embedding its mission.

At the moment, Triodos Bank has around 40,000 certificate holders. Over 80% of its capital exists in the form of certificates of shares, and is held by private individuals. In principle, anyone can be a certificate holder. In addition to private individuals, there is a number of organisations holding share certificates. The maximum number of share certificates held by a single person or organisation is 10% of the total capital. An essential requirement for the bank is to remain independent; spreading ownership across multiple certificate holders contributes to the bank's independent position.

Source: www.triodos.nl, www.socialenterprise.nl; www.bankenvergelijking.nl

Triodos ⊛ Bank

Money has the power to change

Any action, no matter how small, puts something into motion. Together, we can turn small into the new big.

13.4 ORGANISATIONAL DEVELOPMENT

Organisations are continually having to adapt to changes in their environments. This means that they are, in a sense, living organisms looking for organisational equilibrium. Adaptation comes with change, both for the organisation and for its employees. Organisational development, therefore, is a process of change that involves growth for the organisation's employees and the organisation itself, thus improving the functioning of both. The process of organisational development increases the quality of an organisation and its employees. The improvement of the quality results in an improvement to the organisation's ability to resolve problems related to responding to changing circumstances in its environment.
Successful organisations are able to address and (to some extent) plan the developments they need to deal with constructively. In most situations, this process of development has a continuous character. In addition, there are situations characterised by abrupt developments. This refers to reorganisation. This section first addresses the continuous change processes, followed by a separate discussion of reorganisations.

Organisational development

The characteristics of a succesful organisation are:
a clients in various countries;
b many alliances and cooperative forms;
c focus on core activities;
d growth through merger and takeover;
e quality technology supporting business processes;
f divison of concerns into small, flexible, and market-oriented units;
g expenditure of important portions of professional staff functions; limited number of staff functions at the level of both holding and operating company;
h flexible and flat organisational structure;
i employee empowerment;
j virtually full authority in the operating company level; only financing, cash flow, and acquisition position are centralised;
k managers act as entrepreneurs; a substantial part of their wages is variable in nature and depends on business results.

An organisation's development process can be described in various ways:
1 **Growth models**. These focus in particular on the various phases which organisations experience during their development. (13.5)
2 **Change leadership**. This mainly deals with the change processes needed to develop an organisation. (13.6)

13.5 ORGANISATIONAL GROWTH MODELS

There is more than one growth model. The models developed by Scott and by Greiner are discussed below.

13.5.1 Scott's growth model
Scott distinguishes three phases of organisational growth, each with its own characteristics.

Scott's growth model

Phase 1: The small organisation

Small organisation

The first phase is that of the small organisation. This organisation has only a limited number of functions which, in most situations, are fulfilled by the owner. As the organisation grows, the functions are subdivided further. A number of employees is then recruited.

The characteristics of a small organisation are:

a **structure**: functional division with little internal differentiation;
b **personnel assessment**: uses non-formalised criteria;
c **management system**: personal management;
d **strategising**: depends on the owner's personality.

Phase 2: The fully departmentalised organisation

Fully departmentalised organisation

The second phase is known as the fully departmentalised organisation. Functional divison in these organisations is fully developed. The size of this type of organisation allows it to attract specialism in various functional fields. Specialism is assigned to the organisation through a staff or auxiliary service.

The organisation's growth is often realised through increasing its market share and expanding its product and market development.

The characteristics of a fully departmentalised organisation are:

a **structure**: centralised functional division with high levels of internal differentiation;
b **personnel assessment**: based on technical and economical criteria (e.g. function classification);
c **management system**: increasingly based on delegation in the operational field;
d **strategising**: personal decision-making;
e **research**: occurs systematically, emphasising product improvemen and development, and process innovation.

Phase 3: The multidivisional organisation

Multidivisual organisation

The final phase is known as the multidivisual organisation. Directly managed by the top-level, there is a split according to product-maker combinations. Another possibility is geographic division. Growth in these organisations is mainly the result of diversification, resulting in the creation of business units. In addition to independent organisational divisions, the top-level of the organisation houses so-called concern services, applied to, for example, concern strategy, and legal and personnel matters.

Characteristics of a multi-divisional organisation are:

a **structure**: decentralised divisional form with internal specialisation;
b **personnel assessment**: heavy emphasis on profit and other financial criteria;
c **management system**: strategic and operational decision-making that is decentralised with regard to product-market combinations;
d **strategising**: highly procedural. Top-level is mainly focussed on distributing the concern's resources, and entering and exiting business industries.

13.5.2 Greiner's growth model

Greiner argues that there are five phases to the growth process of organisations.

Greiner

Compared to Keuning's model, Greiner adds two phases (6 and 7) that result from far-reaching developments. Each phase is itself characterised by gradual development (evolution). These gradual phases are characterised by a certain

Management style

management style, typical of the organisation's phase.

Once a phase is near its end, the organisation is confronted with a crisis situation (revolution). The organisation is faced with a problem that can no longer be resolved through gradual development. Therefore, the organiaiton will also experience a breach in managerial trends.

Crisis situation

Greiner argues that the development process of organisations depends rather on conquering internal crisis situations than on surviving changes to the external environment.

Internal crisis situatins

Figure 13.1 offers a schematic overview of the phases of an organisation's development.

FIGURE 13.1 **THE GROWTH PHASE AND ORGANISATIONAL CRISES**

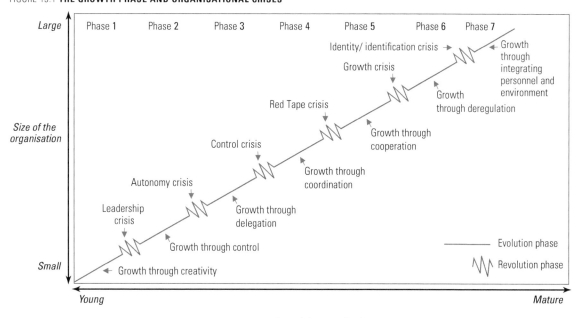

The seven phases of organisational development are:

Phase 1: Growth through creativity
The organisation's starting or pioneering phase, where creativity is the main factor. The emphasis on developing products and markets. In this phase, there is barely any formal organisation. The organisation is characterised by informal communication. Strong organisational growth results in a crisis of leadership, necessitating increased organisation and control of activities. The time has clearly come for (a form of) new management to take the helm

Crisis of leadership

Phase 2: Growth through direction
New management will emphasis strong governance, or concern itself with directing the organisation to realise its expansion.

Directing

Organisational employees are restricted in their independent functioning. If this is allowed to continue, the result is a situation where organisational employees or departments come to require increased responsibility. The result is a crisis of autonomy.

Crisis of autonomy

Phase 3: Growth through delegation
Implementing greater autonomy in an organisation results in a greater sense of responsibility across the organisation. This implementation of autonomy is

Delegation

realised through delegation: assigning responsibilities and authorities to lower organisational levels. The advantage is that the motivation of the organisational employees is improved. Top-level management feels as though they have let the reigns slip. The result is a crisis of control.

Phase 4: Growth through coordination

Coordination

In order to regain lost ground, additional coordination mechanisms are required. The likely result is an increase in communication and information – which must be bound by rules and procedures. This makes the organisation's character inflexible.

Crisis of bureaucracy

A crisis of bureaucracy looms.

Phase 5: Growth through collaboration

Collaboration

To improve efficiency and flexibility, an organisation should implement all sorts of collaborative forms between departments, committees, and work groups. The goal is to increase work effectiveness. The most time-consuming aspect in this regard is aligning the various forms of deliberation in an organisation. Should these issues

Crisis of deliberation

result in a culture of deliberation, a crisis of deliberation is the result.

Phase 6: Growth through commercialisation and deregulation

Commercialisation and deregulation

Phase 5 emphasises deliberation as the way to improved alignment between activities. This results in a blurring of results-orientation. In order to reemphasise the basic organisational orientation, the first step is that various superfluous procedures, deliberation structures, etcetera, start to disappear. Deregulation is to be expected.

Secondly, the emphasis on internal entrepreneurship is reinforced. The organisation is likely to implement business units with a potential for a high degree of independence. A cool-down, a strive for a higher degree of efficiency, and cuts in organisational components become the leading factors. Internally, the company

Crisis of social identity
Crisis of legitimacy

gives rise to a situation that may be called a crisis of social identity. Externally, the company becomes subject to a crisis of legitimacy.

People and environment policy
Public affairs

Phase 7: Growth through integrated people and environment policy

In this phase, management emphasises 'public affairs'. A great deal of attention is paid to environmental issues, effective organisational culture, organisational image and identity, and the relationship between employee satisfaction and organisational quality, efficiency, and productivity.

13.6 CHANGE MANAGAMENT

The acceleration, impact, and complexity of change are becoming ever greater. The number of approaches to and methods for change management have increased along with that change, and both have adapted over the years. There are nearly as many approaches to change as there are change books on change management. The following subparagraphs discuss a number of influential approaches, being:
a Lewin's change model;
b Ezerman's change strategies;
c James Belasco's empowerment model;
d Kotter's model;
e Reitsma and Van Empel's change model;
f De Caluwé's colour model;
g the McKinsey Influence Model for behavioural change in organisations.

13.6.1 Lewin's change model

Lewin's change model

The initial response to the increased turbulence and decreased stability inside and outside of organisations since 1950 led to a sharp increase in the attention to internal organisational change and the methods for managing such processes. One of the first theoretical founders of the study, comprehension, and explanation of change in organisations was Lewin (1951), who imagined two forces at work in every organisation: status quo and change. If the processes related to change have too much of a disruptive effect on status quo, the result is resistance in the organisation. He distinguished three phases of change in line with his vision (see Figure 13.2).

FIGURE 13.2 **THE THREE PHASES OF LEWIN'S MODEL OF CHANGE**

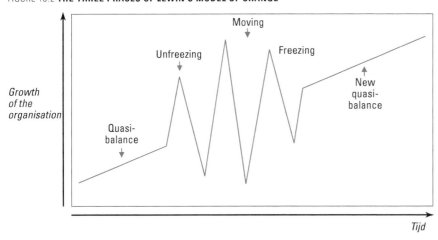

Phase 1: Unfreezing

This phase prepares employees to imminent changes. The consequences of those changes are clarified. Employees need to unfreeze from their past and current working methods. This phase is very important because many people feel resistance to change, a resistance that is a normal consequence of the uncertainties accompanying change. In addition, employees must be motivated to work under their new circumstances. The acceptance of change is influenced positively if the people facing that change are involved in the process from early on.

Unfreezing

Phase 2: Moving

Once employees accept the changes, they can be put into effect. Changes to, for example, communicational and informational flows are implemented. Employees are given the opportunity to prepare for the new situation through training and education.

Moving

Phase 3: Freezing

Once the changes have been put into effect, they are locked into place. The changes have become the organisation's new norm. It is not unusual to see employees relapse into old habits during this phase, but it is an issue that requires extra attention.

Freezing

Lewin proposes that a planned approach to implementing change, one that involves designing the change as far in advance as possible, and having top-level management lead the implementation in the form of an operation or project. Despite Lewin's highly linear approach to organisational change and this rather simplistic representation of the process as a congealing or freezing entity, his work served as an example to many change advisors and organisational scientists.

Change management: Start small and leave the big stuff till last

One of the favourite maxims of Peter de Prins, professor at Gent's Vlerick Business School, is: 'People don't change because they see the light, people change because they feel the heat.'

Aoccording to De Prins, drastic organisational change means using the existing organisation as a foundation. Not with the focus on the intended organisation. And yet, that is what many companies do.

De Prins: 'A risk-avoidant organisation looking to become an agile entrepreneurial one use self-directing teams needs to take the risk-avoidant aspect into account. Employees' entrenched values must be taken into account: these are the necessary conditions that dictate people's intention to stay or go. It is of the greatest importance to work from the employee's perspective – not just from the organisational one of a market position that is in danger, or results that are disappointing. Look for the real reasons people joined and remain part of the organisation. Entrenched values are disruptive: each of us wants to retain and defend them. People's resistance is often the result of pressure placed on their entrenched values. Let people find out for themselves how these values are endangered if they fail to change with the organisation.'

Source: www.mt.nl, 20 Sept 2018

13.6.2 Ezerman's change strategies

Change strategy

The goal of change strategy is to improve the acceptance of change by the employees involved. This involves implementing a real, instead of an apparent, process of acceptance. The following strategies all aim to maximise cooperation, and are usually applied in tandem. Exerman distinguishes seven change strategies:

Ezerman

1 **Avoid.** People can only become motivated if they understand the necessity for change. Sometimes, the first step is to effect a break down in order to clearly demonstrate the need for change.

2 **Facilitate.** This creates conditions or facilities allowing for change to come into effect. One way is through the tangible, such as installing a personal computer in a domestic situation, or through the intangible, such as implementing a communal coffee break to improve informal contact.

3 **Inform.** Employees involved can be informed of the imminent changes, allowing them to prepare for and/or get used to the idea.

4. **Educate.** The strategy is used to train, educate, coach, and supervise people with regard to the change process. The emphasis is either on transferring information, teaching skills, or changing attitudes.

5. **Negotiate.** If people are unlikely to go along with the changes without offering resistance, negitiations are a possibility. In most situations, the outcome is a compromise.

6. **Convince.** This strategy attempts to use reasoned arguments and logic to make people change their minds. It often involves a representation that maximises the advantages and minimises the disadvantages.

7. **Overpower, enforce, and pressurise.** The final strategy is simply enforcing the change. The emphasis is on penalty versus reward following the change implementation.

13.6.3 James Belasco's empowerment model

Empowerment is a current trend in organisation and management theory. The foremost guru in the field is James Belasco. His book *Teaching the Elephant to Dance: Empowering Change in Your Organisation* is considered a manual for change processes that managers should apply to their organisations, particularly large ones – organisations are comparable to elephants, according to Belasco: a habit, once acquired, can be hard to shake. Organisational behaviour is conditioned, and transferred from one generation of employees to the next. Organisations are, as it were, the victims of their own behaviours. This is especially evident in successful organisations, which have trouble letting go of their past. In his book, Belasco tries to formulate an answer to the question: 'How does one teach an elephant how to dance?' According to Belasco, the critical factor in change processes is organisational culture. As such, he indicates the tools that can be used to change acquired habits into desired behaviours.

He views organisational change not as a one-time procedure, but more as a process that should be approached from a basis of systematic modelling. Figure 13.3 shows a schematic model of this process.

Empowerment

Behaviour

FIGURE 13.3 **STEPS IN BELASCO'S MODEL FOR CHANGE**

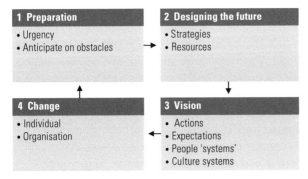

Step 1: Preparing

When preparing for change processes, it is important to consider two important aspects: urgency and potential obstables. The urgency of change should become entrenched in the DNA of the employees, with all their energy focussed on this urgency. There is an important role for top-level management in accomplishing this aspect.

Obstacles are found in the behavioural aspect, with examples being outlandish expectations, laxity, and mistakes.

Urgency

Obstacles

Step 2: Shaping the future

The (behaviour of the) organisation must be in a state of continual change if it wants to remain aligned to its organisation and survive. The entire organisation is continually shaping its future. There are two tools for shaping this future, namely strategy and available resources.

Important aspects of strategy are:

a a change that is based on organisational strenghts;

b focussing on core activities;

c avoiding a focus on a stretched time horizon.

Resources come mainly in the form of manpower and money. According to Belasco, appointing key organisational positions is crucial if the organisation wants to truly implement change.

Step 3: Envisioning

This step translates the general strategy into a vision that should offer insight into the organisation's conduct. The vision is the difference between quick short-term success and extremely long-term change. On the one hand, a clearly described vision empowers employees to change; on the other, it empowers the company to ensure years of employee service and operationality. The vision is what eventually gets the conditioned elephant to dance. Here, top-level management's task and exemplary function is very important.

Stap 4: Changing

During the actual change process, the commitment of all employees is essential. Without this commitment, the organisation runs the risk of getting stuck part way through the process. Tools for implementing and maintaining the actual change are the appointment of change agents to lower organisational key positions,

Performance culture

and the implementation of a measurable performance culture. The vision of the change agents and the vision of top-level management should not only be firmly intertwined, but should be established as a unified and outspoken vision of 'what we are doing and how we are doing it', fully aimed at daily employee activities and their day-to-day realities. Implementing a performance culture links the various organisational activities and makes them quantifiable. Performance must be customer-oriented, in relation to both internal and external customers.

In practice, empowerment places responsibilities, authorities, and decision-making at the lowest possible rungs of the organisational ladder. This enables a high

Self-directing teams

degree of change affiliation, because employees work in self-directing teams and are responsible for their own results. Employees show high levels of commitment to their results and are prepared to work in a more customer-oriented manner. Belasco feels this approach has become a necessity due to organisational environments: intense competition and rapidly changing markets. This type of environment requires organisational units to take a flexible and highly agile stance.

Self-management

Other terms used in place of empowerment are self-management, self-steering, or entrepreneurship. In practice, the application of the concept of empowerment has shown to improve the profitability of self-directing teams over those of traditional organisational forms.

13.6.4　Kotter's change model

Harvard professor John Kotter has performed extensive studies into organisational change processes. He has defined eight errors related to the efforts made in implementing organisational change processes.

FIGURE 13.4 **MISTAKES MADE DURING THE PROCESS OF CHANGE**

Common mistakes	Consequences
• Allowing a feeling of self-satisfaction • Failure to form a powerful coalition of leaders to guide the process of change • Underestimating the power of vision • Insufficiently communicating the vision • Allowing all kinds of obstacles to block that vision • Failure to achieve short-term results • Insufficient anchoring of changes in the company culture	• Insufficient implementation of new strategies • Takeovers do not deliver the expected results • The re-engineering process takes too long and is too expensive • Downsizing does not deliver the expected cost advantages • Quality improvement programmes do not deliver the expected results

Source: J. Kotter, *Leading Chance,* Harvard Business School Press, 1997

Making one or more of the aforementioned errors can be extraordinarily costly for the organisation committing them, for example preventing them from marketing their new products or services at competitive prices and/or quality in a timely manner. This may lead to budget shrinkage, dismissals, and high insecurity and stress for the remaining employees. Many of these errors can actually be avoided.

Kotter defined eight phases for the successful implementation of major changes.

1　Clarify the urgency of the situation

If there is sense of 'five minutes to midnight', it is harder to mobilise management at the right level to commit to allocating sufficient time and energy to a change process.

2　Compile a coalition of leaders

It is essential to compile a team of leaders with the power to lead change processes. This coalition of leaders must work closely together. There is no organisation in which a general manager can be the only one to lead a change process and succeed.

3　Develop a vision and strategy

Make sure to develop a vision that directs the change process. There is also a need for visions aimed at implementing this vision.

4　Communicate the 'change vision'

It is critical that the vision is continually communicated as widely as possible, and that the coalition of leaders shows exemplary behaviour in this respect.

5　Ensure broad empowered-action

It is important to take risks and allow enough room for inconventional ideas, activities, and actions. In addition, structures and systems that risk undermining the change vision must be adjusted.

6　Generate short-term results

Visible organisational improvements following the change must be planned and realised. The people that contribute to these results must be recognised and rewarded.

7　Consolidate the efforts and generate even more change

It is essential to retain improved results and to reinforce the change process using new projects, themes, and persons to lead the change. Make sure to hire, develop, and promote the staff able to implement the change vision.

8 Make sure changes become culturally entrenched

Improved results are achieved through client and productivity-oriented behaviours, as well as more and improved leadership and management effectiveness.
The relationship between new behaviours and organisational success must be espoused internally by the organisation.

In his book XLR8 (2014) *Accelerate: Building Strategic Agility for a Faster-Moving World* (XLR8 here used to abbreviate 'Accelerate'), Kotter emphasises a more novel approach to change – one that fits today's organisations: a more agile approach, as indicated earlier in this chapter. Kotter explains that, in larger organisations, there are two sides of progress management that must be able to work together. On the one hand, there is the emphasis on continued business operations within the more traditional hierarchy that ensures stability and continuity. On the other, there is the need for a rapid acceleration of innovation and renewal through collaborations with a flexible network of innovation and test teams. The traditional organisation meets the new modern organisation under the same roof.

Kotter clarifies five principles and eight accelerators that should form the foundation of this dually operating system (hierarchy and network). These principles and accelerators are a better fit in the current organisational climate with its focus on the Agile approach:

The five principles are:
1 a change process in which many different people are important from many organisational perspectives – not just the people assigned to manage the change;
2 a mindset of 'will', not a mindset of 'must';
3 actions driven by hearts and minds, not just minds alone;
4 a great deal more leadership, not just more management;
5 an inviolable partnership of hierarchy and network, not just an expanded hierarchy.

The eight accelerators are:
1 to create a sense of urgency around a major opportunity.
2 to build and develop a coaching coalition.
3 to form a change vision and strategic initiatives.
4 to set up a network of volunteers.
5 to faciliate actions by breaking down barriers.
6 to generate (and celebrate) short-term success.
7 to ensure sustainable acceleration.
8 to institutionalise change.

Change at Ikea: from 'mass consumption' to 'mass circularity'

Every measure IKEA takes has a huge impact. Take, for example, the retail company's focus on a more sustainable use of raw materials, and their efforts to recycle their own waste flows. But IKEA also experiments with new business models, such as renting instead of purchasing furnishings, a transitional direction into the circulary economy. This possibilty already exists in Japan; apartment furniture is rented for a duration, and then returned once that period expires. Customers play an essential part in this new direction; they are the ones asking for sustainability. IKEA makes this demand affordable and appealing for a large target audience. All over the world, customers are encouraged to engage in circularity. In Spain, IKEA focusses on repairing and refurbishing, and offers tips and tricks for improving the lifespan of their furniture. In the Netherlands, mattresses (and now sofas) can be returned for recycling. Customers feel that the company is shouldering part of their burden, and are willing to pay extra in return.

Thus, the circle is complete: when IKEA was established 75 years ago, founder Ingvar Kamprad argued that wastage was a mortal sin, and indicated his desire to minimise waste flow.

Source: *Het Financieele Dagblad*, Duurzaam Bedrijfsleven, nr. 14 2018

13.6.5   Reitsma and Van Empel's change model

In their 2004 book *Wegen naar verandering* (Paths to change), Reitsma and Van Empel list four types of approaches to change, namely:

1 **Direct approach**. This establishes the content of the change in advance, with strong control based on the exercise of power. The emphasis is on planning and monitoring progress.
2 **Tell & sell approach**. This deals with making the change more appealing, and selling the change based on that appeal. Suggestions are appreciated but not always processed. The informal circuit should be used to established whether the change is being taken up.
3 **Negotiating approach**. This looks for the most appropriate changes within established frameworks. Key figures are actively involved. The content of the change is not established in advance.
4 **Developing approach**. This deals with directing the process in favour of directing its concents. The change comes from within. This approach focusses on reinforcing competences (skills, knowledge, and attitudes).

Reitsma and Van Empel's change model

Direct approach

Tell & sell approach

Negotiating approach

Developing approach

The success of these approaches strongly depends on the intended goal and the context of the change. In addition, the selection of any particular approach strongly depends on the organisational culture, and the personal preferences and competences of the change facilitators.

The authors developed a so-called route map for change processes. This route map offers the change facilitators footing for the change process.

The route map starts with recognising a problem or task statement, for example: the integration of two organisations following a merger. It is essential that the problem or task statement is formulated in such a way as to lead to a certain objective. If the problem is difficult to formulate, the recommendation is to perform a so-called problem analysis.

FIGURE 13.5 **KEY MAP FOR CHANGE PROCESSES**

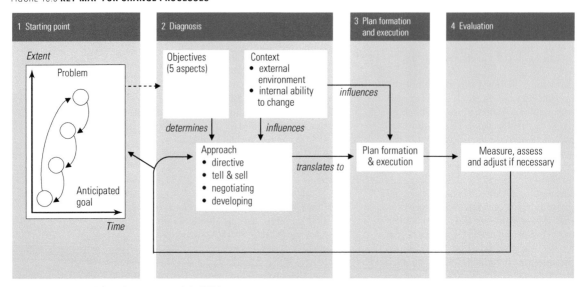

Source: Reitsma and Van Empel, *Wegen naar verandering* (2004)

The situation at the start of a change process can be described thoroughly, to include the vision, mission, and core values of the organisation.

The second phase is the diagnosis, which consists of the objective, context, and approach. There is a relationship between these three aspects, for example the objective and context, which have a major influence on the intended approach.

The third place is drafting a plan of approach focussed both on systems and structures (hard factors) and on people and culture (soft factors). Implementation is part of this phase, and utilises instruments (tools) and intervention tools.

The final phase is the evaluation phase, which assesses whether the objective hase been reached, and whether there are issues to be reviewed and revised. This may lead to a need to select an entirely new approach to reach the objective, even going through the entire process again.

13.6.6   De Caluwé's colours model

De Caluwé's colours model

Another perspective on dealing with change in organisations is Leon de Caluwé's colours approach, developed in tandem with Hans Vermaak. The approach explains five 'types' of change, which have each been assigned a different 'colour' to help explain their particulars. Figure 13.6 offers a brief explanation of each colour.

The idea behind the model is that each interpretation of change can be different from the next, and depends on the organisation or situation. The ability to identify the types of change (and, in the parlance of de Caluwé and Vermaak: assign a colour) makes it easier to develop a fitting change strategy. The colours put the types of change in plain language for change managers (Caluwé, 2006). The underlying idea is that people or things in a certain system can change as long as they adhere to the 'rules' of that system (or colour). In other words: the type of change programme must align with the philosophy of change in the organisation, group, or team as much as possible. Determining the 'colour' of a person (or team) can be done by completing a questionnaire.

FIGURE 13.6 **CHANGES EXPRESSED IN COLOURS BY CALUWÉ AND VERMAAK (2006)**

	Yellow-print	Blue-print	Red-print	Green-print	White-print
Change happens if you …	combining interests	think first and act (according to a plan)	stimulate people correctly	place people in learning situations	make room for spontaneous evolution
in …	power play	rational process	a trade exercise	a learning process	a dynamising process
into …	a manageable solution, win-win situaiton	the best solution, an achievable world	a motivational solution, the best 'fit'	a solution people must find together	a solution that frees up energy
interventions like…	coalition-formation, top-level structuring	project-based working, strategic analysis	assessment and re-ward, social gatherings	gaming and coaching, open systems planning	open space meetings, self-directing teams
through …	a process manager who applies their power	a substantive expert, a project leader	HRM-expert, a coaching manager	a coaching process manager	a self-sacrificing pattern-signifier
aimed at …	positions and context	knowledge and results	procedures, inspiration, and atmosphere	setting and communication	complexity and meaning
Results are …	unknown and shifting	described and guaranteed	imagined, not guaranteed	outlined, not guaranteed	unpredictable
Safeguarded through …	policy documents and balance of power, loyalt	measure to manage, adjust	HRM-systems, good relationships, communication	learning organisation	self-management, quality of dialogue
Potential failure through …	dry-running, lose-lose situation	ignoring external or irrational aspects	oppressive systems, poor long-term results	including everyone, lack of action	superficial comprehension, laissez-faire attitude

The approach explains that, in a scheduled 'yellow' change, organisations can change as long as the existing interests are brought together by, for example, creating win-win situations and convincing relevant parties using the insights into each party's position. 'Blues' feel it is more important to take a highly procedural approach, with each step clearly explained and followed by proper progress-monitoring. Complexity is reduced wherever possible. The 'red' scheduled change places importance on the idea of motivating people, and showing them that their situation is one of give and take. The 'green' situation depends on people being involved in the process, and making them understand why certain changes are necessary. There is a strong assumption that people are willing to learn, and will realise what is required once it is explained to them. The 'white' approach is based on the ability to self-govern, the acceptance of complexity, and the desire to explain and direct of the people involved.

This philosophy of change is very compatible with other approaches; for example with the way one interprets the various aspects of change processes using a practical tool like the Influence Model by McKinsey & Company. The next section discusses this change tool in greater detail.

13.6.7 The McKinsey Influence Model for behavioural change in organisations

The McKinsey & Company transformation process, described by Keller & Price (2011), emphasises the importance of both performance and health during change processes. Health refers mainly to organisational culture and behaviour, which can often be predictive of future performance. The researchers explain their ideas in the five-phase-model of sustainable change, briefly discussed below.

McKinsey Influence Model

1 **Aspire** – "what do we want to achieve?"
2 **Assess** – "how prepared are we to reach our aspirations?"
3 **Architect** – "what do we need to do to reach our aspirations?"
4 **Act** – "how will we manage this process?"
5 **Advance** – "how can we continue to make progress and keep eveloping?"

Many studies show that 70% of all transformations result in failure (Gleeson, 2017) – in around 70% of these failures, the lack of success is the result of incorrect mindsets and related behaviour: the 'health' side of sustainable change. This appears the hardest factor to realise. Failure is largely due to the fact that employees do not agree with the changes, or that there is a lack of exemplary behaviour and support from management and leadership, either consciously or subconsciously. Therefore, it is important to use the third phase of sustainable change (Architect) to consider which interventions should be developed and implemented in order to effect and maintain the intended transformation. To that end, McKinsey & Company introduced a simple but very powerful tool, based on years of research and scientific insight: the Influence Model (see Figure 13.7)

Influence Model

FIGURE 13.7 **THE INFLUENCE MODEL (MCKINSEY QUARTERLY, 2016)**

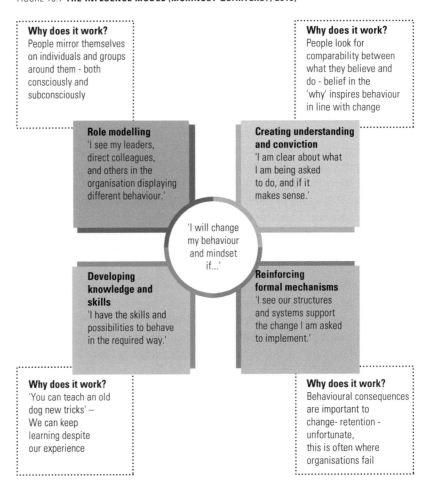

The Influence Model was designed around a core statement: 'I will change my behaviour and mindset if…'. This core statement is completed using a response from one of four categories or elements that constitute points of attention:

1. I have been given a credible assignment that I can understand (*A compelling story*).
2. I see that our structures, processes, and systems support the changes I have been asked to implement (*Reinforcement mechanisms*).
3. I have the skills and opportunities to conduct myself in the required manner (*Skills required for change*).
4. I see a change in the behaviour of my managers, leaders, and colleagues (*Role modeling*).

These four categories are displayed in the model's visualisation in Figure 13.7. Studies have shown that each element of this influence model provides a powerful contribution to the success of the transformation. If the organisation displayed proper exemplary behaviour, for example, transformations had a chance of succeeding that was 4.1 times greater than normal. Having a compelling story resulted in the likelihood of success being 3.7 times greater. The right reinforcement mechanisms raised chances of success by a factor of 4.2. Lastly, developing the right skills to cope with change meant chances of success became 2.4 times as likely.

Compelling Story

People look for congruence between what they believe and what they do. Changing people's behaviour is easier if their hearts have been captured. Chances of people acting in line with the change visions are improved if they believe there is a good reason for the change. In practice, this is easier said than done. It often turns out that the leaders managing the transformation feel that the reason for the change should be self-evident. *They* are clear on the issue, but that does not mean that all of their colleagues, looking at the same story from a different angle, have the same perspective on the change. Studies show that people often overestimate others' knowledge and perceptions. For that reason, it is very important to be clear on the 'why' behind a change. McKinsey, for example, offers the CEO 'change story': If the leader of an organisation is able to offer a clear story explaining where the organisation is coming from, what the context for the change is, and what inspiring vision awaits, stakeholders have less difficulty comprehending and explaining the change. Stories are very powerful, and easily remembered. Having a compelling story, or a 'reason to believe', is the most important basis for ensuring this category is successfully addressed. Next, it is important to consider the communicative means or channels to be used in disseminating the core messages behind the change throughout the organisation. Examples are weekly 'townhall' meetings, the company intranet, personal leader-stakeholder meetings, viral marketing, leaflets, posters, etc.

Reinforcement Mechanisms

Even once a compelling story has been told, any convincing argument to change one's behaviour will quickly be undone if the organisation's infrastructure does not support the change. Infrastructure is here used as an umbrella term for policy and processes, such as performance management and rewards, as well as (work) systems like IT and methodology. If, for example, a sharper focus on quality is desired, and the desired behavioural change is for employees to involve multiple functional disciplines in developing a product, but teams are simultaneously held accountable for efficiency and speed of delivery, then there is a basis for conflict. The performance indicators, used to hold people accountable, need to be updated to stay in line with the desired behaviour.

Another example is of a company looking to support flexible working fom home. The desired behavioural change is for employees not to focus on employee presence but on the the quality of the results they provide, which do not need to suffer from flexible working. However, if the reality of the situation is that persistent on-site presence is valued as more important, or that important decisions are often made in face-to-face office meetings, flexible working is unlikely to become successful. Instead, clear agreements on important meetings are needed, for example when these are to be scheduled or whether telephone conferencing is possible.

Other examples in the same category are 360-degree feedback mechanisms, communication plans, the official appointment of team challengers, daily work routines like check-ins, etc.

Skills Required for Change

Behavioural change is a combination of both the will and the skill: with the right will but without the right skill to work differently, no transformation can become a success. But it is a matter of more than merely developing a new skill; it also involves understanding what, exactly, is expected. What is the new definition of 'good' in the organisation's intended 'new' world? This category, therefore, is a blend of creating awareness in tandem with developing new skills. Interventions that are part of this category include integration in existing training programmes, developing new training programmes, and on-the-job coaching using actionable feedback.

Role Modeling

From a person's earliest moments, their learning process includes copying the behaviours of others: parents, siblings, class mates, teachers, etc. Part of this is conscious, but an even larger part is subconscious. Very often, exemplary behaviour is offered as a key factor in organisational change something to be espoused by senior management, those with the highest visibility, possibly directly in line with the change. One of the driving factors behind this notion is that senior management are the ones who influence employee assessments. This influence cannot be denied, but there is much more that influences employee conduct: exemplary behaviour by colleagues, both direct and and indirect, borne by organisational culture, is also influential. Brassey (2011) illustrates, for example, that leadership, whether physically close or distant, has a huge influence on employee behaviour. This influence is shaped through various processes, verbally, non-verbally, and/or borne out through the organisation's environment, for example through word-of-mouth descriptions of what has been observed. There are other role models who also have a potentially high degree of influence; they are not found in hierarchic leadership, but constitute informal leaders, such as leaders of opinion who have a great deal of influence by way of disseminating their opinions or merely changing their behaviours. Interventions that are part of this category include: leadership givig the right examples; interventions to achieve a strong, aligned team; visualising top-level team actions (which may overlap with the other four aspects); celebrating success; actively using collegial support networks to reinforce the change; personal monitoring; sponsoring, etc.

Change capacity: evolving towards a new balance

The capacity of organisations for change is severely threatened by the emergence of new disruptions, while the after-effects of previous ones are still tangible. How can a CEO withstand the onslaught of digitisation and disruptive innovation?

Professor Peter de Prins of the Vlerick Business School wrote *Six Batteries of Change*; a book he uses to present a simple model for organisational change in change processes. His analysis led him to consider successful change from the perspective of energy management. The model comprises six 'batteries': a metaphor for energy sources which need to be fully charged in order to effect the desired change.

There are three rational batteries: *clear strategy, powerful management infrastructure, and solid implementation*. These are complemented by three emotional batteries: *an ambitious team at the top level, a healthy culture, and committed employees*. Companies whose batteries were charged the fullest were also demonstrated to be the most successful in realising change. Following frequent studies among managers, the batteries for management infrastructure and implementation demonstrated the lowest energy levels.

Each battery must be fully charged to effect optimum change. If you want to make sure people feel committed to the change, the smart thing to do is to start with the most depleted battery, and then ensure that all batteries are fully energised. We are in a transitional phase of highly invasive changes: rapidly evolving technology and increasing societal complexity are making it increasingly difficult to make and implement broadly-supported and clear decisions. This requires a strong top-level team that shows visible passion: a voice, a message. Only then can the evolution towards a new balance become a success.

Source: www. Managementscope.nl, 15-02-2018

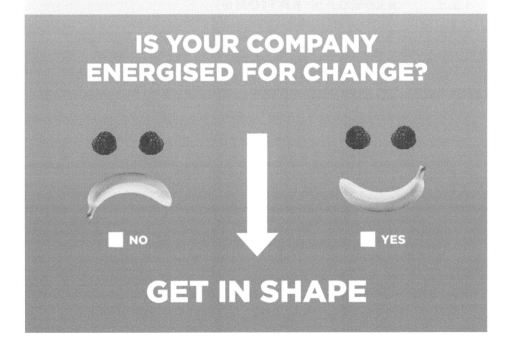

13.7 ORGANISATIONAL CHANGE VERSUS ORGANISATIONAL DEVELOPMENT

In the past, there has been much debate about the distinction between organisational change and organisational development. It has been said that, in the grand scheme of change, organisational development represented a more 'incremental', less rigorous transformation. Organisational change, on the other hand, was thought to address the more urgent need for organisational change, with a demand for a thorough course adjustment that needed to happen quickly; it involved intensive work on both structural and behavioural change. In recent years, 'change' has become an inherent part of organisational life. There is no 'stability' and malleability has become part and parcel of modern organisations. This ties in with a concept previously discussed: the agile organisation. Despite the fact that change is often an inherent part of organising, it is a process that often triggers a demand for outside 'help', serving to illustrate, among other things, that change is not an easy matter; and that, as previously indicated, a broader, outside perspective – often made easier by contacting an external agency – is necessary for a successful transition. Some criticism in this respect comes from Professor Steven ten Have, a Dutch expert in the field of organisational change. In one of his most recent publications, 'Reconsidering Change Management' (Ten Have, 2016), he offers a critical reflection on the change management industry and the need to approach organisational change from a more evidence-based, scientific perspective.

13.8 REORGANISATIONS

Reorganisation

Organisational change or development often opens the door to reorganisation. Reorganisation is an incidental and generally dramatic adjustment to the decision-making powers and division of labour in an organisation. A reorganisation is a one-time event, and frequently results in drastic changes. The reasons for a reorganisation can be manifold: worsening results, changes in the external environment – such as technological developments – and changes in consumer behaviour, changes in managerial convictions, and (excessively) swift organisational growth without regular adjustments to organisational structure. In practice, many organisations will show certain signs if a reorganisation is pending: increased staff turnover, distribution of dividends, applications for government aid, a bleak future perspective, implementing a recruitment stop, threats of merger or take-over, etcetera.

Objectives of reorganisation

The objectives of reorganisation are to avert impending discontinuity and promoting organisational recovery. Reorganisation is intended to ensure the reinforcement of the organisation's strategic position, to optimise internal organisation, and to improve the organisation's financial position and profitability. In order to achieve its goal, a reorganisation may demand changes to various organisational areas:

a discontinuing or shutting down loss-incurring organisational units;
b increasing efficiency and improving decision-making;
c reducing taxation and organisational management workload;
d reducing overheads (downsizing);
e improving coordination;
f improving distribution of responsibility;
g updating organisational culture.

Structure and organisation
PART C

Implementing a reorganisation depends on a number of preconditions, which can be found in various operational aspects, including the technical (production), the economic (costs), the staff-related (resistance) and the legal (collective agreement and works council).

The success of a reorganisation depends on many factors. In his book *Turnaround Management, het saneren van ondernemingen in moeilijkheden (*Turnaround Management, reorganising troubled enterprises), J.M.M. Sopers describes a model that includes a number of recommendations for successfully completing a reorganisation. The model formulates three levels of reorganisational objectives (see Figure 13.8):

a **level 1**: the end-goal of the reorganisation;
b **level 2**: the objectives related to substantive and procedural aspects;
c **level 3**: the objectives aimed at fulfilling the preconditions for a substantiated plan on the one hand, and establishing the change process on the other.

Levels of reorganizational objectives

FIGURE 13.8 **THREE LEVELS OF OBJECTIVE DURING ORGANISATIONAL RESTRUCTURING**

Source: J.M.M. Sopers, *Turnaround Management, het saneren van ondernemingen in moeilijkheden,* Stenfert Kroese, 1992

It is usually recommended that top-level management is replaced due to its (potential) contribution to the current situation, as a way to send out a clear signal to the organisation's stakeholders, and to seriously address the problems. Restoring stakeholder faith in the organisation (both internally and externally) during reorganisation is crucial. A high degree of stakeholder commitment is often a requirement for reorganisational success; it calls for a strong staffing of top-level management, as well as a well-constructed reorganisation plan. It is also recommended that important parties are contacted and involved in the discussion surrounding the reorganisation well in advance.

Stakeholders

A separate issue that is part of reorganisations is creating a social plan. Usually, a reorganisation means a reduction in staff. A social plan is the employer's way of describing how to deal with staff in times of reorganisation. The parties involved in drafting a social plan are the board, the employees, and the union.

Social plan

The social plan replaces the collective agreement from which employees derive individual rights. It deals not only with settlements, but also with the procedures to be followed.

In principle, with regard to staff, there are four possibilities following reorganisation:

1 **Relocation within the organisation**. An important element here is that relocation takes place at the same level.
2 **Relocation to a new employer**. The function offered should, in principle, involve comparable employment conditions.
3 **Voluntary termination of employment**. The objective here is natural attrition. This option can take many different forms, ranging from repatriation aid to start-up aid.
4 **Involunary termination of employment**. Here, the employer may also make use of a one-time payment to buy their way out of their obligations.

In addition to the aforementioned options, employers can also make use of tools like outplacement and job banks.

13.9 ORGANISATIONAL CONSULTANCY

Organisational consultancy

Change processes are often supervised by an organisational consultant. The organisation concerned (the client) askes for specialist aid (the consultant) with regard to certain organisational aspects. Organisational consultancy means providing independent, expert advice with regard to establishing and resolving organisational problems and, where necessary, assisting in the implementation of the suggested solutions. The goal of consultancy is to improve the efficiency and/ or effectiveness of the organisation.

OOA

ROA

In the Netherlands, the majority of consultants are a member of the OOA, or the *Orde van Organisatiedeskundigen en -Adviseurs* (Order of Organisational Experts and Consultants), or the ROA, or *Raad van Organisatieadviesbureaus* (Council of Organisational Consultancy Firms).

The most important objective of the OOA is to promote the expert and societally useful practice of professional organisational behaviour. This objective includes the monitoring of professional ethics and the quality of professionaly performance. The objective of the ROA is two-fold:

1 to promote the (collective) interests of member firms;
2 to promote optimum conditions for the completion of consultancy assignments. This includes educating clients, applying entrance standards, and supervision compliance with codes of conduct.

Complaint handling
Performance Review
Commission
Board of Appeal

With regard to complaint handling, the OOA and ROA use a single system: First, cases are handled by a Performance Review Commission. If no concensus in the commission is reached, there is the possibility of appeal with a Board of Appeal.

Areas of organisational consultancy are:

a general management issues;
b strategy and policy formation;
c organisational structure;
d organisational culture;
e leadership styles;
f public relations.

Organisational consultancy: Using your (digital) wits

O&M IN PRACTICE

Consider the cinema, the trusted travel agent's, the corner store. They are a long way away from yielding to their digital competitors. In fact, they are reinventing themselves.

TUI, a Germany travel agency whose growth is based on reselling hotel accomodations and offering trips to all-inclusive holiday destinations, is employing a strategy that is radically different to that of several years ago. The company is making huge investments in its own resorts and cruise ships, and even aviation companies. The answer to its problems seems to have been vertical integration: the company wants to be able to offer all travel-related services from its own storefront. From the inspiration for a holiday to advice to booking a flight, hotel, or on-site excursion.

In a battle to capture the audience's interests, cinemas are pulling out all the stops to stay ahead of on-demand services like Netflix. Moving chairs and sprinkler systems create a social experience that cannot be trumped by any VR-supported home theatre experience. New theatres with more leg room, even better projection and sound systems and, recently, 4D-support, which offers viewers both the regular visual 3D experience combined with physical effects. Cinemas have a long tradition of coping with disruptive agents, from TVs to video rental stores to digital streaming services. Their response has always been to heavily invest in new and existing multiplexes, improved services, better movie selections, and additional options for booking.

Source: *Het Financieele Dagblad*, Transformers, 22-06-2018

13.9.1 Organisational consultancy models

There are many different models and approaches to organisational consultancy. The following two models are discussed below:

1 doctor-patient model;
2 process model.

This section also addresses the potential roles a consultant can fulfil, depending on circumstance.

Doctor-patient model

The doctor-patient model involves clients (the organisations looking for assistance) themselves indicating the problem to be resolved by consultants (see Figure 13.9).

FIGURE 13.9 **SCHEMATIC DOCTOR-PATIENT MODEL**

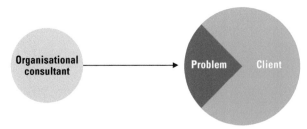

Source: J. Kotter, *Leading Change*, Harvard Business School Press

The problem presented is, as it were, obtained from and isolated by, the existing organisation. Next, this problem is studied by the consultant. The resulting product is a report drafted by the consultant, which includes their suggestion(s) for resolving the problem. During their activities, the consultant is generally in touch mostly with their direct client (usually the board); the organisational employees are involved in the process only to a limited degree.

With respect to this model, the following issues and questions should be noted:
- Has the client properly defined the problem? Is the problem not actually found in one or more different areas?
- Can the problem actually be separated from the rest of the organisation?
- Since employee involvement is minimal, the acceptance of suggested solutions may be hampered.

Process model

Process model

The process model is based on the fact that a problem should not be seen as an isolated incident, but as part of a coherent whole (see Figure 13.10). In addition, the employees involved in the problem should be made part of the process of consultancy. In this model, the client approaches the consultant with a 'vague' problem. The consultant, in tandem with employees concerned, identifies the organisation's problem, and the parties work on a solution to problem. This means that, in this model of consultancy, the problem is much less structured. The consultant's role is more that of a supervisor or coach who teaches the organisation to increase its problem-solving abilities.

FIGURE 13.10 **SCHEMATIC PROCESS MODEL**

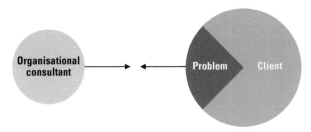

Consultant roles

The factors influencing the choice for either of these models are found in the areas of:
a top-level management prestige;
b the organisation's style of leadership;
c the problem's urgency;
d the size and scope of the change;
e the control systems in the organisation.

Based on the description of the two models, it should be noted that the role of the consultant differs from one process to the next. In some situations, the consultant is limited mainly to a substantive contribution. In others, the emphasis is on supervising and coaching the change process.

Consultant

In practice, this results in the following three consultancy roles:
1 **The expert role**. The emphasis is on the consultant's substantive contribution. The consultant mainly applies their knowledge and expertise in a certain area as part of their activities.

Expert role

2 **The social-emotionally-oriented role**. The consultant is mainly concerned with the human aspect of the change processes. For example, the consultant may teach employees to revise their views on organisational problems, thus increasing their ability to solve problems themselves. The consultant performs the role of change process-coach.

Social-emotionally-oriented role

3 **The procedurally-oriented role**. The consultant emphasises the development of guidelines and procedures to improve the efficiency and effectiveness of certain changes.

Procedurally-oriented role

13.9.2   Characterisation of consultancy relationships

There are different forms of consultancy relationships. The previous subsections discussed two of these: the doctor-patient model and the process model. How should this relationship be structured? When entering into a consultancy relationship, there are two important factors. These factors are an important part of determining the recommended type of consultancy relationship: the client's expert, and the nature of the issue. The client's expertise ranges from small to large, and the nature of the issue from instrumental to strategic. Using these factors as the axes of a graph results in a model for the characterisation of consultancy relationships (Figure 13.11).

Consultancy relationship

FIGURE 13.11 **CHARACTERISING ADVISORY RELATIONSHIPS**

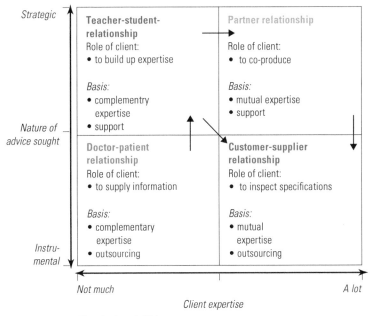

Source: *Management Magazine*, issue 1, 2001

Lastly, it should be noted that the lifecycle of a single consultancy assignment may pass through all phases of the consultancy relationship, for example from doctor-patient to teacher-student to a partner relationship to end up as a customer-supplier relationship.

13.10 ORGANISATIONAL STUDIES

Organisational studies

Organisations are always changing. As stated, organisations are living systems in a changing environment. In order to assess whether an organisation needs to change, organisational studies are needed. Organisational studies are the systematic review and assessment of (part of) an organisation. This process of study is not a one-time affair, but should be performed periodically. An organisation's alignment to its internal and external environment is, after all, a process of continuous development.

Preventative studies
Curative studies
Partial studies
Integral studies

Organisational studies vary in their objectives and subjects. Goals can be aimed at preventing future problems (preventative studies) on the one hand, and at resolving existing problems (curative studies) on the other.
The subject can be an organisational unit (partial study) or the entire organisation (integral study). If a study only looks at part of the organisation, it is important to ensure that its relationships with other organisational units are not overlooked.

Next, relating the various objectives to the various subjects of organisational studies results in an overview of all types of organisational studies, as depicted in Figure 13.12.

FIGURE 13.12 **DIFFERENT KINDS OF ORGANISATION RESEARCH**

		Research object	
		Partial	Integral
Goal	Preventative	*Example* • Management Audit • Social Audit • Marketing Audit	*Example* Company diagnoses
	Curative	*Example* Most organisational research is based on problem situations such as: • Work atmosphere investigation • Conflict resolution • Information requests	*Example* A few common types of organisational research such as: • Survival probability research • Integral investigation

Dutch consultancy firms use various research methods for organisational studies. These methods are distinct in terms of the number and types of indicators and the (mathematical and statistical) techniques they use.
Often, a combination of checklists (either automated or non-automated), analytical schedules, planning schedules, and interviews is used.

Summary

- Organisations must be and remain in alignment with their environments. The success of this alignment relies on the organisation's effectiveness in reaching its objectives.

- There are nine global trends that influence organisations: The world is past traditional globalisation, From BRIC to ICASA, Resources: what is the limit, The synergetic effects of technologies are explosive, The consumer is king, Ecosystem revolution, The downside of progress, A changing middle class and Macro-economic policy and experiments.

- Four aspects of effectiveness:
  - technical and economic;
  - social;
  - societal;
  - managerial.

- Organisations are more successful as they score (more) adequately on all aspects of effectiveness (organisational equilibrium).

- Organisational development is a change process, with both organisational employees and the organisation itself experiencing growth that helps improve their functioning.

- Three types of organisations in Scott's growth model:
  - small organisation;
  - fully departmentalised organisation;
  - multidivisional organisation.

- There are seven phases to Greiner's growth model. Each is characterised by a gradual development linked to a certain management style. Once a phase comes to its end, the organisation is confronted with a crisis situation that demands a change process.

- Lewin distinguishes three phases in each change process: unfreezing, moving, and freezing.

- Ezerman distinguishes seven change strategies: avoid, facilitate, inform, educate, negotiate, convince, and overpower, enforce, and pressurise.

- According to Belasco, acquired habits are hard to unlearn. Belasco sees change as a process that should be dealt with procedurally.

- John Kotter defines eight phases for the successful implementation of major changes, as well as eight accelerators.

- Reitsma and Van Empel list four types of approach, being the direct, tell & sell, negotiating, and developing approaches.

- De Caluwé illustrates change using colours.

- McKinsey developed the Influence Model to support change.

- Reorganisation: a one-time change process of drastic alterations. Objectives of reorganisations: averting impending discontinuity and promoting organisational recovery.

- Sopers's model formulates three levels of reorganisational objectives.

- Reorganising means paying separate attention to restoring stakeholder trust, drafting a social plan, and selecting a method of staff downsizing.

- Change processes are often supervised/coached by organisational consultants. The majority of Dutch consultants is a member of the OOA or ROA.

- Two models of consultancy relationships are discussed:
  - the doctor-patient model;
  - the process model.

- Structuring relies on characterising the consultancy relationship. Depending on the nature of a change process, the consultant's role can be: an expert role, a social-emotionally-oriented role, or a procedurally-oriented role.

- Organisational studies: a systematic review and assessment of (part of) the organisation. Organisational studies can vary in terms of their objectives and subjects.

Sources and literature

Ad Introduction Chapter:

Wilde, F.H.P. de (2008), *Stoeien met organisaties*. Eburon Uitgeverij, Delft.

Ad Chapter 1:

Evers C.W.A., Mantz-Thijssen, E.L., & K.F. van der Woerd (1991), *Milieumanagement in stappen*. Kluwer Bedrijfswetenschappen, Deventer.

Gratton, L. & A. Scott (2016), *The 100 Year Life: Living and working in the age of longevity*. Bloomsbury, London

Hutchinson, Colin, 'Corporate Strategy and the Environment', in: *Long Range Planning*, augustus 1992.

Raworth, Kate (2017), *Donuteconomie, In zeven stappen naar een economie voor de 21e eeuw*. Nieuw Amsterdam.

www.fd.nl-klimaatakkoord-gaat-iedereen-in-nederland-raken

www.klimaatplein.com

www.nos.nl-het-klimaatakkoord-nadert-je-voordeur

www.rijksoverheid.nl/klimaatverandering/klimaatbeleid

Ad Chapter 2:

Assen, van M. & G. van den Berg (2012), *Strategische conversatie, aanpak en instrumenten voor strategische conversatie in organisaties, ketens en clusters*. Vakmedianet, Deventer.

Badaracco, J.L. (1991), *The Knowlegde Link, how Firms compete through strategic alliances*. Harvard Business School Press, Boston.

Boekema, F.W.M. & D.J.F. Kamann (1989), *Sociaal-economische netwerken*. Noordhoff Uitgevers, Groningen/Utrecht.

Chan Kim W. & R. Mauborgne (2005), *Blue Ocean Strategy, How to create Uncontested Market Space and Make the Competition Irrelevant*. Harvard Business Review Press.

Collis, D. & M.G. Rukstad (2008), *Can You Say What Your Strategy Is?* Harvard Business Review Press.

Collis, D., 'Strategievorming als lean proces', *HMR,* 166, March/April 2016.

Crijns, Hans, *De durf om te ondernemen anno 2001*, www.ktnobrief.be.

Dobbs, R., Manyika, J. & J. Woetzel (2015), *No Ordinary Disruption: The Four Global Forces Breaking All the Trends*. McKinsey&Company, McKinsey Global Institute, Public Affairs Books.

Faas, drs. F.A.M.J., 'Breng uw stafdiensten op de markt', *FEM*, January 1990.

Golsorkhi, D., Rouleau, L., Seidl, D. & E. Vaara (2010), *Cambridge Handbook of Strategy as Practice*. Cambridge University Press, United Kingdom.

Gray, D.H., 'Gebruik en misbruik van strategische planning', *Harvard Holland Review*, Autumn 1986.

Hamel, C., Dos, Y.L. & Prahalad, C.H., 'Profiteren van samenwerking met de concurrent', *Harvard Holland Review*, Winter 1990.

Hamel, G. & C. Prahalad (1996), *Competing for the future*. Harvard Business Review Press.

Hamel, G. & C. Prahalad (2010), *Strategic Intent*. Harvard Business Review Press.

Hartog, prof. dr., (e.a.) (1973), *Encyclopedie van de economie*. Elsevier, Amsterdam.

Hillesum, P. (2015), *De kern van Lean Startup*. 22 February 2015

Keuning, D. & D.J. Eppink (2011), *Management & Organisatie, Theorie en Praktijk*. Noordhoff
    Uitgevers, Groningen/Utrecht.

Kouwenhoven, drs. V., 'Publieke Private samenwerking stoelt op wederzijds vertrouwen',
    Binnenlands Bestuur Management, no. 2, 1989.

Lorange, P., Roos, J. & P.S. Bronn, 'Long Range Planning', *PEM-select*, no. 2, 1993.

Mulders, M. (2018), *Business- en Managementmodellen*. Noordhoff Uitgevers, Groningen/
    Utrecht.

Reich, R.B. & E.D. Mankin, 'Joint Ventures with Japan Give Away our Future', *Harvard Business
    Review*, March/April 1986.

Robbins, S.P. & M. Coulter (1997), *Management*. Zevende druk, Pearson, Benelux.

Roos, J. de, 'De fusiegolf: Europa staat pas aan het begin', *ELAN*, March 1990.

Schoot, drs. ir. E.J. van der, 'Postfusiefase meestal zwaar onderschat', *Het Financieele Dagblad*,
    18 October 1988.

Ster, W. van de & P. van Wissen (1983), *Marketing in de Detailhandel*. Noordhoff Uitgevers,
    Groningen/Utrecht.

Thuis, P. (2017), *Toegepaste organisatiekunde*. Noordhoff Uitgevers, Groningen/Utrecht.

Whittington, R., Cailluet, L. & B. Yakis/Douglas (2011), 'Opening Strategy: Evolution of a
    Precarious Profession', *Britisch Journal of Management*, Volume 22, Issue 3.

Ad Chapter 3:

Weegen, J. van, 'Businessmodellen in een tijd van digitalisering en disruptie',
    Managementscope, 21 June 2017.

Westermann, G., Bonnet, D. & A. McAfee (2014), *Leading Digital*. Harvard Business Press,
    Boston.

Ad Chapter 4:

Chetty, S & C. Hunt (2004), 'A Strategic Approach to Internationalization: A Traditional Versus a
    'Born-Global' Approach', *Journal of International Marketing*, Spring 2004, Vol. 12, No. 1, pp.
    57-81.

Ebbers, H. (2016), *Internationale bedrijfskunde en globalisering*. Noordhoff Uitgevers, Groningen/
    Utrecht.

Hessels, S., Overweel, M. & Y. Prince (2005), *Internationalisering van het Nederlands MKB*. EIM-
    onderzoek voor bedrijf & beleid, Zoetermeer.

Hollensen, S. (2010), *Internationale Marketing*. Pearson Benelux BV.

Jethu-Ramsoedh, R & M. Hendrickx (2015), *Internationaal ondernemen*. Noordhoff Uitgevers,
    Groningen/Utrecht.

Ad Chapter 5:

Bossink, B. & E. Masurel (2017), *Maatschappelijk Verantwoord Ondernemen*. Noordhoff
    Uitgevers, Groningen/Utrecht.

Dalen, van, W (2017), *Ethiek de basis*. Noordhoff Uitgevers, Groningen/Utrecht.

Hupkes, S (2010), *Maatschappelijk verantwoord, Hoe? Zo!, Morele oordeelvorming en
    normbesef in de praktijk*. Noordhoff Uitgevers, Groningen/Utrecht.

Kaptein, M., Klumer, H. & A. Wieringa (2003), *De bedrijfscode, aanleiding, inhoud, invoering en
    affectiviteit*. Stichting NCW, Ethicon en Stichting Beroepsmoraal en misdaadpreventie.

Leeuw, de, J. & J. Kannekens (2013), *Bedrijfsethiek en MVO*. Uitgeverij Damon, Budel.

Luit, F. van (2017), *Corporate governance*. Noordhoff Uitgevers, Groningen/Utrecht.

McDonough, W. & M. Braungart (2002), *Cradle to Cradle Remaking the Way We Make Things*.
    Rodaler Press, Ney York.

Robbins, S. & M. Coulter (2015), *Management*. Pearson, Benelux.

Roorda, N. (2015), *Basisboek Duurzame Ontwikkeling*. Noordhoff Uitgevers, Groningen/Utrecht.

World Commission on Environment and Development (1987), *Our Common Future*, the
    'Brundtland Report' explained.

Ad Chapter 6:

Arntz, M., T. Gregory & U. Zierahn (2016), *The Risk of Automation for Jobs in OECD Countries: A Comparative Analysis*. OECD Social, Employment and Migration Working Papers, No. 189, OECD Publishing, Paris.

Benson-Armer, R., Gast, A. & N.H.M. van Dam (2016), *Learning at the Speed of Business*. McKinsey Quarterly, New York.

Bowles, J. (2014). *The computerization of European jobs who will win and who will lose from the impact of new technology onto old areas of employment?* Bruegel blog, 17 July 2014.

Brassey, J. & N.H.M. van Dam (2017), *Staying Relevant in the Workplace: Develop Lifelong Learning Mindsets*. Bookboon (ebook), Copenhagen.

Brynjolfsson, E. & A. McAfee (2014), *The Second Machine Age*. W.W. Norton & Company, New York NY.

Bughin, J., Staun, J., Andersen, J.R., Schulz-Nielsen, M., Aagaard, P. & T. Enggaard (2017), *Shaping the future of work in Europe's digital front runners*. McKinsey Global Institute, New York.

Chui, M, Manyika, J, & M. Miremadi (2015), *Four fundamentals of workplace automation*. McKinsey Quarterly, New York.

Chui, M, Manyika, J, & M. Miremadi (2016), *Where machines could replace humans– and where they can't (yet)*. McKinsey Quarterly, New York.

Dam, N.H.M. van (2016), *Learn or Lose*. Nyenrode Business Universiteit, Breukelen.

Dam, N.H.M. van (2017), *21st Century Corporate Learning & Development, Trends and Best Practics*. Boonboon (ebook), Copenhagen.

Dam, N.H.M. van (2017), *The 4th Industrial Revolution and the Future of Jobs*. Boonboon (ebook), Copenhagen.

EU, (2014), *A Common European and Digital Competence Framework for Citizens*, www.ecvet-info.de/_media/ DIGCOMP_brochure_2014_.pdf.

EU (2015), *DESI indicator on digital skills*. Eurostat data: Http://digital agendadata.eu/datasets/desi/indicators.

Forster, R. & S. Kaplan (2001), *Creative Destruction: Why Companies That Are Built to Last Underperform the Market and How To Successfully Transform Them*. Double Day, New York.

Frey, C.B. & M.A. Osborn (2013), *The Future of Employment: How susceptible are jobs to computerisation*. Oxford Press, London.

Garten, D., Grimbergen, J.A.P.M., Sherman, P. & N.H.M. van Dam (2017), *Ga doen wat je echt belangrijk vindt! Positieve Psychologie in de Praktijk*. Vakmedianet, Deventer.

Gratton, L. & A. Scott (2016), *The 100 Year Life: Living and working in the age of longevity*. Bloomsbury, London.

Hartgers, M. & A. Pleyers (2016), *Een leven lang leren in Nederland: een overzicht*. CBS, Den Haag.

Kegan, R. & L.L. Lahey (2017), *Een cultuur voor iedereen*. Haarzuilens: Het Eerste Huis, Utrecht.

MacAfee, A. & E. Brynjolfsson (2012), *Race Against The Machine: How The Digital Revolution is Accelerating Innovation, Driving Productivity, and Irreversibly Transforming Employment and the Economy*. MIT Sloan School of Management, Boston, MA.

Manyika, J. (2017), *Technology, Jobs and The Future of Work*. New York: McKinsey Global Institute, New York.

McKinsey Global Institute (2017), *Jobs lost, jobs gained: workforce transition in a time of automation*.

McKinsey Global Institute (2017), *Digitally-enabled automation and artificial intelligence: Shaping the future of work in Europe's digital front-runners*.

McKinsey Global Institute (2013), *Disruptive technologies: Advances that will transform life, business, and the global economy*.

Miralles, F. & H. Garcia (2016), *Ikigai. Het Japanse geheim voor een lang en gelukkig leven*. Meulenhoff, Amsterdam.

Moran, G. (2016), *These Will Be the Top Jobs in 2025 (And The Skills You'll Need To Get Them. Fast Company.* March.

Rademakers, M.F., editor (2014), *Corporate Universities: Drivers of the learning organization.* Routledge, London.

Schwab, K. (2016), *The Fourth Industrial Revolution.* World Economic Forum, Geneva.

SER-rapport SER Advies (2017*), Leren en ontwikkelen tijdens de loopbaan een richtinggevend advies.* Advies 17/4.

Werkverkenners: 'Een leven lang leren en werken', *Het Financieele Dagblad,* 24 November 2015.

Willyerd, K. & B. Mistick (2016), *Stretch.* John Wiley & Sons, Hoboken, NJ.

World Economic Forum (2015), *Deep Shift –Technology Tipping Points and Societal Impact.*

World Economic Forum (2016), *The Future of Jobs: employment, Skills, and Workforce Strategy or the Fourth Industrial Revolution.*

Ad Chapter 7:

Benson-Armer et a.l, 2016

Capelli, P. & A. Tavis, 'HR wordt agile', *Holland Management Review* 178, March/April 2018

Lombardo & Echinger, 2000

Noe, Hollenback, Gerhart & Wright, 1997

Paffen, P. (2013), *Loopbaanmanagement.* Vakmedianet, Deventer.

Raet (2015), PW. 8 December 2015.

Smet, de et al., 2014

Van der Sluis, 2008

Weidema, N., 'Onboarding, wat betekent het?' *PWnet,* 20-7-2017

www.loonwijzer.nl

Ad Chapter 8:

Alblas, G. & E. Wijsman (2018), *Gedrag in Organisaties.* Noordhoff Uitgevers, Groningen/Utrecht.

Caluwe, L. de & H. Vermaak (2002), *Leren Veranderen.* Wolters Kluwer, Deventer.

Gids voor Personeelsmanagement, jaargang 83, no. 3, 2004.

Jansen prof. dr. P.G.W (1996), *Organisatie en Mensen, Inleiding in de bedrijfspsychologie voor economen en bedrijfskundigen.* Nelissen, Baarn.

Rampersad, prof.dr.ir. Hubert, 'Effectief Teamwork', gebaseerd op *Total Performance Scorecard*, Sciptum Management, October 2002.

Robbins, S. & M. Coulter (2015), *Management.* Pearson, Benelux.

Tjepkema, S. (2003), *Werken, leren en leven met groepen.*

www.burnin.nl

www.dsz.service.rug.nl

www.goodfeeling.nl

www.intermediair.nl

Ad Chapter 9:

Alblas, G. & E. Wijsman (2018), *Gedrag in Organisaties.* Noordhoff Uitgevers, Groningen/Utrecht.

Boertien & Partners, *Syllabus Vergadertechniek, theorie en praktijk,* 1980.

Bono, E. de (1985), *Six Thinking Hats.* Mica, 1e druk.

Bots, R.T.M. & W. Jansen, W. (2001), *Organisatie en Informatie.* Noordhoff Uitgevers, Groningen/ Utrecht.

Butler, T. & J. Waldroop (1999), *Job sculpting: The art of retaining your best people.* Harvard Business School Working Knowledge.

Chen, G. (2000), *Subject-object meaningfulness in knowledge work.* Thesis, University of Michigan.

Covey, S.M.R. (1989/2004), *The 7 Habits of Highly Effective People.* Simon & Schuster.

Covey, S.M.R. (2008), *De snelheid van vertrouwen (oorspronkelijke titel: The Speed of Trust)*

Covey, S.M.R. (2011). *Smart Trust.*

Csikszentmihalyi, M. (1990), *Flow: The Psychology of Optimal Experience.* Harper Perennial.

Effting/Kint & Partners, *Personal change & growth.*

Evans, P. & F. Bartolomé (1981), *Wordt succes duur betaald?* Samsom/Intermediair, Alphen aan den Rijn.

Fisher, R. & W. Ury (1981), *Succesvol onderhandelen, de Harvard-aanpak.* Veen, Utrecht.

Goleman, D. (1995), *Emotional Intelligence: Why it can matter more than IQ.* Bantam Books.

Kabat-Zinn, J. (1994), *Wherever You Go, There You Are: Mindfulness Meditation in Everyday Life.* Hyperion.

Keuning, D. & D.J. Eppink (2011), *Management & Organisatie, Theorie en Praktijk.* Noordhoff Uitgevers, Groningen/Utrecht.

Korte, A.W. de & J.F. Bolweg (1993), *Een verkenning naar veranderingen in werknemerswensen en de managementconsequenties daarvan.* Van Gorcum, Stichting Management Studies, Assen.

Mintzberg, H. (1973), *The nature of Managerial Work.* Prentice-Hall, Englewood Cliffs.

Mintzberg, H. (1991), *Mintzberg over Management, de wereld van onze organisaties.* Veen, Utrecht.

Muir, R., 'The Importance of Emotional Intelligence in Law Firm Partners', *Law Practice Magazine*, 2007.

Pausch, R. (2008), *The Last Lecture.*

Pol, van de, Messer en Wissema, in: *Holland Harvard Review*, Spring 1989, no. 18.

Praag, E. van (1988), *Management zonder controle.* Intermediair.

Robbins, Stephen P. & M. Coulter (2003), *Management.* Practice Hall, New England, 7th edition.

Seligman, M.P. (2002), *Authentic Happiness.* Free Press.

Siereveld, E., 'Leiderschapskwaliteiten, wat zijn dat?' *P&B Improvement*, 2013.

Stoner, J.A.F. (1994), *Management.* Academic Service, Schoonhoven.

Washington Post (2007), *Joshua Bell and the Washington Post Subway Experiment*

Ad Chapter 10:

Bakker, C.G., Goor, A.R. van & J.W.M. van Houten (1989), *Logistiek/Goederenstroombesturing.* Stenfert Kroese, Leiden.

Bakker, R. & T. Hardjono (2014), *Horizontaal organiseren, horizontaal en procesgericht denken, construeren, besturen, samenwerken.* Vakmedianet, Deventer.

Bij, J.D. de, 'Certificering en de structuur van kwaliteitssystemen', in: *Bedrijfskunde*, 2, 1990.

Claes, P.F. & H.J.J.M. Meerman (1991), *Riskmanagement, inleiding tot het risicobeheersproces.* Stenfert Kroese, Leiden.

Empel, M. van & H.A. Ritsema (1988), *Met recht een onderneming, inleiding in de juridische aspecten.* Noordhoff Uitgevers, Groningen/Utrecht.

Gale, B.T. & R.D. Buzell, in: *Planning Review*, March/April 1989.

George, M., Rowlands, D. & B. Kastle (2015), *Wat is Lean Six Sigma, Sneller en slimmer werken met beter resultaat.* Uitgeverij Thema Van Schouten & Nelissen, Zaltbommel.

Groot, B., in: *Harvard Holland Review*, no. 14, Spring 1988.

Heijnsdijk, J. (1988), *Besturen van het bedrijf.* Noordhoff Uitgevers, Groningen/Utrecht.

Hupkes, S. (2010), *Maatschappelijk verantwoord. Hoe? Zo!* Noordhoff Uitgevers, Groningen.

Johansson, H., McHugh, P., Pendlebury, A.J. e.a., 'Business Proces Re-engineering. Breakpoint Strategies for Market Dominance', *Management Selectuur*, no. 5, October 1993.

Lap, drs. H.H.M., 'Resultaatgericht management', *Human Resources Management*, 1988.

Maes, J. & V. Wiegel (2017), *Succesvol Lean.* Copyright 2017 John Maes, Vincent Wiegel

Mittelmeijer, M. & R. van Stratum (2014), *Kijk op bedrijfsprocessen.* 3e druk, Noordhoff Uitgevers, Groningen/Utrecht.

Morgan, J. & M. Brenig-Jones (2017), *De kleine Lean Six Sigma voor dummies.* BBNC Uitgevers, Amersfoort.

Niezink, D., Diepenmaat, M., Tiel, P. van P. & E. Ruijters (2017), *Lean: van hype naar verbetercultuur, bouwstenen voor een lean transformatie in de publieke sector.* Vakmedianet, Deventer.

Reddin, W.J. (1977), *Effectief MBO.* Samsom/NIVE, Alphen aan den Rijn.

Schieman, C.J. & RA en J.H. Huyen (1981), *Bedrijfsbestuur en -organisatie.* Stenfert Kroese, Leiden.

Schieman, C.J. (e.a.) (1997), *Management Beheersing van bedrijfsprocessen.* EPN, Houten.

Stuive, R. (2019), *Basisboek Procesmanagement.* Noordhoff Uitgevers, Groningen/Utrecht.

Tideman, ir. B. (1993), *Prestatieverbetering door Business Process Design.* Lansa Publishing BV.

Veld, Cees in 't (2013), *Focus op verbeteren, Continue leren en verbeteren.* Position paper (www.focusopverbeteren.nl).

Wissema, J.G. (1987), *Unit-management, het decentraliseren van ondernemerschap.* Van Gorcum/Stichting Management Studies, Assen.

www.aim-ned.nl

www.emerce.nl

www.logicaomg.com,

www.modifiedcontent.com

www.mvonederland.nl

www.mvoplatform.nl

www.or-online.nl

Ad Chapter 11:

Bakker, R. & T. Hardjono (2014), *Horizontaal organiseren, horizontaal en procesgericht denken, construeren, besturen, samenwerken.* Vakmedianet, Deventer.

Heijnsdijk, J. (1988), *Besturen van het bedrijf.* Noordhoff Uitgevers, Groningen.

Hoogendoorn, S. (2012), *Dit is Agile, Van introductie tot implementatie.* Pearson, Benelux.

Jaarverslag Coopers & Lybrand, 1997.

Holland/ Belgium Management Review, 149/2013.

Kerklaan, L. (2016), *De wendbare organisatie, Agility based strategy in de praktijk.* Vakmedianet, Deventer.

Keuning, D. & D.J. Eppink (2011), *Management & Organisatie, Theorie en Praktijk.* Noordhoff Uitgevers, Groningen/Utrecht.

Keuning, D. (1996), *Organiseren en leidinggeven.* Stenfert Kroese, Houten.

Lalaoux, F. (2015), *Reinventing organizations.* Het Eerste Huis, Utrecht.

Nieuwenhuis, M.A., *The Art of Management* (the-art.nl)

Robertson, B. (2015), *Holacracy, De nieuwe manier van werken in een snel veranderde wereld.* Uitgeverij Business Contact, Amsterdam.

Solingen, R. van & E. Rustenburg (2016), *De kracht van Scrum, Een inspirerend verhaal over een revolutionaire projectmanagementmethode.* Pearson, Benelux.

Wijk, J. van (1989), *Bedrijfsorganisatie.* Thieme, Zutphen.

123management.nl

academy.capgemini.nl/blog/hoe-kan-scaled-agile-framework-safe-je-helpen-agility-te-verspreiden-je-organisatie

agilescrumgroup.nl/spotify-model/

www.commant.nl/blog/proces-ontwerpen-keuze-is-reuze/

www.ctrl-improve.nl

www.ctrl-improve.nl

www.globalorange.nl/3-kenmerkende-voorbeelden-van-agile-ontwikkeling-binnen-bedrijven

www.improvement-services.nl

www.innovatieforganiseren.nl

www.scrumguides.org/scrum-guide.html

zakelijk.infonu.nl/management/96666-organisatiestructuren-horizontaal-ofverticaal-inrichten.html

Ad Chapter 12:

Alblas, G. & E. Wijsman (2018), *Gedrag in organisaties*. Groningen/Utrecht: Noordhoff Uitgevers.

Hofstede, G, Hofstede, G. & M. Minkov (2016), *Allemaal andersdenkenden, omgaan met cultuurverschillen*. Business Contact, Amsterdam.

Hofstede, G. & M. Minkov (2010), *Cultures and Organizations: Software of the Mind*. Athenaeum Uitgeverij, Amsterdam.

Hofstede, G., Hofstede, G. & M. Minkov (2010), *Cultures and Organizations: Software of the Mind*. McGraw Hill Professional, New York.

Janssen, P. (2018), *Interculturele competenties*. Noordhoff Uitgevers, Groningen/Utrecht.

Robbins, S. & M. Coulter (2015), *Management*. Pearson, Benelux.

Sanders, G. & B. Neuijen (1999), *Bedrijfscultuur: diagnose en beïnvloeding*. Koninklijke Van Gorcum, Assen.

Schein, E. (2006), *De bedrijfscultuur als ziel van de onderneming, zin en onzin over cultuurverandering*. Scriptum, Schiedam.

Trompenaars, F. & C. Hampden-Turner (1997), *Riding the Waves of Culture: Understanding Diversity in Global Business*. McGraw-Hill Education, Europe.

Vries, M. de & E. Engellau (2003), *Het leiderschap van Alexander de Grote*, Uitgeverij Nieuwezijds, Amsterdam.

Weber, A. & A. Doelen (2018), *Organiseren & managen, Het &s-model toegepast*. Noordhoff Uitgevers, Groningen/Utrecht.

Ad Chapter 13:

Grumbkow, J. von (red.) (1991), *Cultuur in organisaties*. Van Gorcum, Assen/Maastricht en Open Universiteit, Heerlen.

Kempen, P.M. (1980), *Bedrijfsdiagnose alias Management Audit*. Samsom, Alphen aan den Rijn.

Keuning, D. & D.J. Eppink (2011), *Management & Organisatie, Theorie en Praktijk*. Noordhoff Uitgevers, Groningen/Utrecht.

Managementconsultants Magazine, no. 1, 2001.

Nathans, J.M.C., 'Invoeren van veranderingen', in: *Personeelsbeleid* 23, no. 10, 1987.

Orde van Organisatiedeskundigen en -Adviseurs, jaarboek 1988–1989, *VUGA*, 's-Gravenhage.

Ruijter, H. de & J.H.D. Wiersema, 'Typering van adviesprocessen', in: J.J.J. van Dijck en J.A.P. van Hoof (1976), *Organisaties in ontwikkeling*. NIVE-UPR, 's-Gravenhage.

Sanders, G. & B. Neuijen (1999), *Bedrijfscultuur: diagnose en beïnvloeding*. Koninklijke Van Gorcum, Assen.

Sopers, J.M.M. (1992), *Turnaround Management, het saneren van ondernemingen in moeilijkheden*. Stenfert Kroese, Leiden.

Swieringa, J, & A.F.M. Wierdsma (2001), *Op weg naar een lerende organisatie*. Noordhoff Uitgevers, Groningen/Utrecht.

Twijnstra, A. & D. Keuning (1988), *Organisatie Advieswerk*. Stenfert Kroese, Leiden.

Wijk, J. van (1989), *Bedrijfsorganisatie*. Thieme, Zutphen.

Index

Illustration acknowledgements

p. 11t Alamy / Image Select, Wassenaar

p. 11m iStockphoto / Getty Images, Londen

p. 11b iStockphoto / Getty Images, Londen

p. 12t Shutterstock

p. 12b Shutterstock

p. 13t Shutterstock

p. 13b Shutterstock

p. 14t Shutterstock

p. 14b Shutterstock

p. 15t Shutterstock

p. 15m Shutterstock

p. 15b Shutterstock

p. 16 Shutterstock

p. 17 Shutterstock

p. 18t Shutterstock

p. 18b Shutterstock

p. 19 Shutterstock

p. 22 Shutterstock

p. 24 Polette, Amsterdam

p. 27 Shutterstock

p. 30 Alamy / Image Select, Wassenaar

p. 31 Alamy / Image Select, Wassenaar

p. 32 Gamma Keystone / Getty Images, Londen

p. 33 Corbis / Getty Images, Londen

p. 34 Art Media / Print Collector / Getty Images, Londen

p. 35 Alamy / Image Select, Wassenaar

p. 36 Alamy / Image Select, Wassenaar

p. 37 University of Michigan, Michigan

p. 38 Alamy / Image Select, Wassenaar

p. 39 Antioch University Midwest, Yellow Spring

p. 40 Aligning the stars / Bain, Boston

p. 41 Mintzberg.org

p. 42 Tom Peters, Brentwood, Essex

p. 43 Jeff McNeill / Flickr, San Francisco

p. 44 Institute for Strategy & Competitiveness Harvard Business School, Boston

p. 45 AFP / ANP, Den Haag

p. 46 Hammer and Company, Newton

p. 47t Times Magazine, Californië

p. 47b Harper Collins-Justin Stephens, Glascow

p. 48t GAGA / Johan Hellstrom / Speakersnet, Stockholm

p. 48b Speakersnet AB, Stockholm

p. 49 Neilson Barnard / Getty Images, Londen

p. 50 Hans van den Boogaard / Hollandse Hoogte, Den Haag

p. 51t Ana Grillo, West Palm Beach

p. 51b Bloomberg / Getty Images, Londen

p. 52 Danpink.com

p. 53 World Economic Forum from Cologny, Zwitserland

p. 54 Utah Valley University, Utah

p. 55t J. Countess / Getty Images, Londen

p. 55b University of Michigan, Michigan

p. 58 / 59 Alamy / Image Select, Wassenaar

p. 60 Herman van Heusden / Hollandse Hoogte, Den Haag

p. 61t Arenda Oomen / Hollandse Hoogte, Den Haag

p. 61b Arenda Oomen / Hollandse Hoogte, Den Haag

p. 62t Shutterstock

p. 62b Shutterstock

p. 63 Shutterstock

p. 64 Shutterstock

p. 66 Shutterstock

p. 69t Duurzaam Bedrijfsleven, Amsterdam

p. 69b Duurzaam Bedrijfsleven, Amsterdam

p. 72 Duurzaam Bedrijfsleven, Amsterdam

p. 73 Ministerie EZK, 2018 / Klimaatakkoord, Den Haag

p. 76 Researchers at Harvard and MIT, Massachusetts

p. 82 Shutterstock

p. 90 Shutterstock

p. 96 Shutterstock

p. 98 Swapfiets, Amsterdam

p. 104 Shutterstock / FrameStockFootages

p. 112 Testla Benelux, Amsterdam

p. 117 Alamy / Image Select, Wassenaar

p. 120 Shutterstock

p. 126 Shutterstock

p. 129 Shutterstock

p. 134 Shutterstock

p. 149 Signify / Philips, Eindhoven

p. 151 Shutterstock

p. 154 Jock Fistick / Photoshelter, New York

p. 161 Shutterstock

p. 163 Shutterstock

p. 170 Shutterstock

p. 172 DeskBRookers, Amsterdam

p. 173 Shutterstock

p. 177 Shutterstock

p. 180 Shutterstock

p. 183 Shutterstock
p. 184t ABN AMRO Group N.V., Amsterdam
p. 184t Koninklijke KPN, Rotterdam
p. 184m Koninklijke Vopak, Rotterdam
p. 184b Wolters Kluwer, Alphen a / d Rijn
p. 184b Gransvision, Schiphol
p. 186 Shutterstock
p. 187 Orikami Data Science for Healthcare & Lifesciences, Personalized Healthcare, Nijmegen
p. 188 Shutterstock
p. 190 Tim Fishboone / Marketoon
p. 192 Vlerick Business School, Gent
p. 194 Shutterstock
p. 196 Tunga Tech, Amsterdam
p. 217 Shutterstock
p. 220 Shutterstock
p. 222 Swink / Fotograaf Yvette Wolterinck & Designer Peter van Driel, Amsterdam
p. 225 Snapcar, Utrecht
p. 226 Ahold Delhaize, Zaandam & Robeco, Rotterdam
p. 231 Apple / Dan Winters, Californië
p. 247 Transparency.org
p. 250 Bloomberg / Getty Images, Londen
p. 253 Shutterstock
p. 256 / 257 Getty Images
p. 258 Lex van Lieshout / ANP, Den Haag
p. 259t Shutterstock
p. 259b Shutterstock
p. 260 VrBlvd Photofilm / Hollandse Hoogte, Den Haag
p. 261t Michael Kooren / Hollandse Hoogte, Den Haag
p. 261b Peter Hilz / Hollandse Hoogte, Den Haag
p. 262 Shutterstock
p. 264 Psylaris, Maastricht
p. 266 Shutterstock
p. 275 IP Soft, New York
p. 280 Shutterstock
p. 282 Kijk op je Loopbaan, Groningen
p. 286 Shutterstock
p. 288 Talmundo B.V, Den Haag
p. 292 Rabobank, Utrecht
p. 294 Shutterstock
p. 296 Shutterstock
p. 297 Shutterstock
p. 301 McKinsey & Company, New York
p. 303 Shutterstock
p. 309 Shutterstock
p. 311 Shutterstock
p. 315 Shutterstock
p. 318 Shutterstock
p. 320 Magoni, Amsterdam
p. 325 Shutterstock

p. 336 Shutterstock
p. 339 CartoonStock Ltd, Luxemburg
p. 344 Shutterstock
p. 348 Sinfonietta / Anna Kooij Fotografie, Utrecht
p. 351 Shutterstock
p. 358 Shutterstock
p. 362 Shutterstock
p. 368 Shutterstock
p. 370 Homerr, Amsterdam
p. 374 Shutterstock
p. 379 Daliz, Den Haag
p. 386 Shutterstock
p. 389 Shutterstock
p. 409 Shutterstock
p. 413 Paul de Blot
p. 417 Gianpiero Petriglieri, Fontainebleau
p. 426 Shutterstock
p. 436 Shutterstock
p. 437 Shutterstock
p. 439 Shutterstock
p. 441 Shutterstock
p. 447 Barry Wehmiller, Missouri
p. 458 / 459 iStockphoto / Getty Images, Londen
p. 460 Shutterstock
p. 461t VARA / ANP, Den Haag
p. 461b Bram Belloni / Hollandse Hoogte, Den Haag
p. 462 Tony Chocolonelly, Amsterdam
p. 463t Tony Chocolonelly, Amsterdam
p. 463b Shutterstock
p. 464 Shutterstock
p. 466 PastBook, Amsterdam
p. 472 Shutterstock
p. 475 Swisslog Holding, Buchs
p. 478 Herman Zonderland / Wikipedia
p. 486 Shutterstock
p. 490 Shutterstock
p. 512 Shutterstock
p. 514 Etergo, Amsterdam
p. 523 Shutterstock
p. 535 Shutterstock
p. 546 Shutterstock
p. 552 Shutterstock
p. 553l Shutterstock
p. 553 Shutterstock
p. 553 Shutterstock
p. 553r Shutterstock
p. 557 SimpledCard, Amsterdam
p. 558 Shutterstock
p. 561 Shutterstock
p. 570 Shutterstock
p. 572 Lars Kolind, Lyngby

p. 580 Shutterstock

p. 582 Boatsters, Amsterdam

p. 585 Shutterstock

p. 588 Shutterstock

p. 589 Shutterstock

p. 591 iStockphoto / Getty Images, Londen

p. 593 Shutterstock

p. 595 Shutterstock

p. 598 Shutterstock

p. 602 iStockphoto / Getty Images, Londen

p. 607 Shutterstock

p. 609 Shutterstock

p. 611 Shutterstock

p. 612 Shutterstock

p. 613 Shutterstock

p. 614 Shutterstock

p. 615 Shutterstock

p. 616 Shutterstock

p. 618 Shutterstock

p. 619 Shutterstock

p. 620 Shutterstock

p. 621 Shutterstock

p. 623 Shutterstock

p. 626 Shutterstock

p. 628 Lilium, Munich

p. 632 Verenigde Naties, New York

p. 634 Bas Berkhout / Triodos Bank, Zeist

p. 640 Shutterstock

p. 645 Shutterstock

p. 651 Vlerick Business School, Gent

p. 655 Shutterstock